CADOGAN

Peter Neville-Hadley

W9-CBE-736

Beijing

Cadogan Guides
West End House, 11 Hills Place,
London W1R 1AG, UK
becky.kendall@morrispub.co.uk

The Globe Pequot Press
246 Goose Lane, PO Box 480, Guilford,
Connecticut 06437–0480

Copyright © Peter Neville-Hadley 2000

Book and cover design by Animage
Cover photographs by Travel Ink/Colin Marshall (front)
and Travel Ink/Abbie Enock (back)
Chapter title illustrations from photographs by Peter Neville-Hadley
Maps © Cadogan Guides, drawn by Map Creation Ltd

Editorial Director: Vicki Ingle
Series Editor: Linda McQueen
Editor: Dominique Shead
Proof-reading: Catherine Bradley
Indexing: Dorothy Frame
Production: Book Production Services

A catalogue record for this book is available from the British Library
ISBN 1-86011-933-6

The author and publishers have made every effort to ensure the accuracy of the information in this book at the time of going to press. However, they cannot accept any responsibility for any loss, injury or inconvenience resulting from the use of information contained in this guide.

Printed by Legoprint, Italy

Please help us keep this guide up to date

As China continues its headlong rush to modernisation, nothing stays the same for very long, and the more detailed a guide, the more rapidly it will seem to go out of date. We've done our best to make sure that information is accurate, monitoring changes and making last-minute updates right up to press time, but we would be delighted to hear from travellers about further changes or suggested improvements to the guide. Those making the most helpful contributions will receive a copy of the Cadogan Guide of their choice. Please write to Cadogan Books at the address opposite.

About the Author

Peter Neville-Hadley first visited China in 1986, returning repeatedly to visit new areas while improving his Mandarin. He contributed to the second edition of Cadogan's *Central Asia* guide, before spending two years crossing and re-crossing the country and writing *China, The Silk Routes* for Cadogan. He writes regularly on China and other Asian destinations for periodicals in the UK, Canada, Hong Kong, China and Japan. This new Běijīng guide is the product of three extended periods of residence in the capital over a period of 18 months, and a fourth during final corrections as the book went to press. Originally British, he now calls Vancouver home, and even occasionally spends some time there.

Acknowledgements

Thanks to many current and former Běijīng residents for their assistance, advice, hospitality and good company, and in particular to the immensely generous Guy Feest, who also roped his staff into double-checking details, and Ann Féng, who shrewdly guided me to all her favourite restaurants and helped me to see Běijīng through her eyes. Pascoe Trott suggested several out-of-town trips and played the role of chauffeur, Craig Lipman took me pogo-ing and drinking in disreputable bars around the universities, and Celeste Huò, Daniella Tonetto, Anne Stevenson-Yang, Izuno Mayumi and Blair Burns were occasional companions in search of restaurants and other entertainments.

Dr Mike Gent kindly gave up time to suggest improvements to the medical information, and much of the Chinese and *pīnyīn* was checked by Ann Féng, but any remaining errors are mine not theirs. Completion of the first draft of the manuscript took place over a three month period on Hong Kong's Lamma Island, which was made much easier by the kindness of many Hong Kong residents, including in particular Nigel Kat, Kevin Bishop, Miles Spink, Lucy Huws, Peter Fredenburg, Sasha Atepolikhin and Jennifer Friedenrich.

Thanks to Diane for putting up with the long absences, physical and mental, needed to produce this book, and without whose support it could never have been completed. It was written, designed, illustrated, and published entirely on Apple Macintosh computers. For transport between the UK, Hong Kong and Canada, thanks to Japan Airlines and Cathay Pacific.

A Note on Names

Chinese place names are spelt in the PRC official Romanisation system called *pīnyīn*. You will not find Peking in this book, but Běijīng. Every Mandarin word is marked with the tones necessary to make your meaning clear, and to help you communicate your needs to ticket sellers and others. An explanation of tones and of how to pronounce the letters and sounds is given in **Language**, p.391. Those doing background reading of histories and memoirs can expect to find a startling range of alternative spellings, and these have been left intact where other authors have been quoted.

The easiest way to communicate is just to point to the Chinese characters given throughout the book.

Contents

Maps

Whoever has paid a visit to the Lung Fu Ssu fair will remember the narrow lanes branching eastward from the main thoroughfare as one approaches from the south the Four Arches at the junction of the Hata Men, the Chao Yang Men and Pig Streets, and the prolongation of the boulevard that leads north to the Tartar City wall. The small lanes look so alike to a stranger that it is difficult for him to distinguish one from the other. Peking is a strange city and will remain strange in spite of the proposed plan for the reorganization of the city.

H.Y. Lowe, *The Adventures of Wu*, 1940

Strange it is, and reorganization on a scale beyond anything of which Lowe could have conceived more than 60 years ago has only made it stranger. Běijīng offers curly-eaved China as the West wants to find it, alongside ugly utilitarian buildings indistinguishable from those in Russia or Eastern Europe, and the latest extravagant efforts of fashionable international architects.

Introduction

The capital of a civilization whose social institutions and physical infrastructure have been in decay for centuries, Běijīng is now on the operating table as the government performs cosmetic surgery in order to hide its identity and make it identical to the major cities of more developed countries—pride of race, nation and political system demand this. Of course, what the wrecking ball and bull-dozer have left behind is often what gives other capitals their charm, character and identity, but the government cannot permit it to be seen that 50 years of communist rule and 'socialist' progress have failed to provide standards of glossiness to match those of other systems (although even the briefest trip into the countryside will tell another story).

So Běijīng sometimes disappoints in not living up to the many expectations of its visitors. Wispy-bearded old gentlemen do not throng streets of ornate mansions, their hands thrust deep into long sleeves, muttering inscrutable quotations from Confucius.

The city is neither a museum for the entertainment of foreigners, nor a Charlie Chan movie. The Chinese are abandoning their bicycles for cars when they can, their Běijīng opera for pirated Hollywood videos, and their blue cotton jackets for polyester blouses and suits. If this disappoints it is the visitor who is to blame, not the visited.

But even as mechanical assistance terminally accelerates the long-drawn-out crumbling of traditional courtyard houses to make space for the construction of some modern monstrosity, ancient temples, theatres and mansions, which have been biding their time as warehouses, workshops and police stations, are being reopened, and on every return visit to Běijīng there's more to see.

An ever more relaxed economy has permitted the growth of colourful street markets, and the opening of nearly as many restaurants as there are people. Competition has started to create hotels and other services with something more than *méi yǒu* ('not have') in their vocabularies, and even had an effect on the museum sector, where private establishments offer detailed English explanations of their well-lit and displayed contents, with at least some idea of pleasing the customer.

The newly constructed long-distance road system does double duty in conveying the city's growing middle class to the surrounding countryside, where township governments are rapidly rescuing overgrown pagodas and sprucing up temples so as to divert some of this new disposable income their own way. Běijīng really only represents Běijīng, not the reality of a China in which around 70 per cent of the population still lives in the countryside. A day trip out of the city, or a longer journey to Chéngdé or Shānhǎiguān, should be regarded as essential, not only for relatively quiet leafiness, the architecture of a rural temple, or the atmosphere of an overgrown tomb site, but for the sight of horse-drawn ploughs, the splash of yellow corn cobs spread out to dry on low roofs, and brilliant persimmons being cut from trees with broomstick-mounted knives.

The Běijīng of 15 years ago was glum, grey, and mostly shut. The Běijīng of today seethes and swarms with people in search of a little amusement, choosing between video arcades and mah-jong (*májiàng*), between newly opened sections of imperial palaces and newly opened funfairs, and between traditional hotpot restaurants and McDonald's.

Strange Běijīng is indeed, but it's never dull.

Travel

Getting to China

By Air
from or via Europe

Air China (now allied with China Southern and Northwest Airlines) often has the cheapest direct flights, and flies to Běijīng from London (three times a week), Paris, Frankfurt, Zürich, Copenhagen, Milan, Vienna, Stockholm and Rome. London ℂ (020) 7630 0919, Frankfurt ℂ (069) 233038, Berlin ℂ (030) 242 3460, Paris ℂ (01) 4266 1658, <*http://www.airchina.com/*>. **China Eastern Airlines** (allied with American Airlines) flies to Paris and Munich. **China Southern Airlines** (allied with Air China and Delta Airlines) flies from Amsterdam. Most **major European airlines** fly to Běijīng and/or Hong Kong, China's two main gateways.

Aeroflot flies five times a week from Moscow, with feeders from most European capitals, and is one of the cheapest carriers from Europe, although reliability and sometimes ancient equipment are a problem. London ℂ (020) 7491 1764, Paris (01) 4225 4381, Berlin ℂ (030) 226 9810, Frankfurt ℂ (069) 273 0060.

Air France flies from Paris. London ℂ (020) 8742 6600, Paris (01) 44 08 22 22, USA toll-free ℂ 1-800 237 2747, Canada toll-free ℂ 1-800 667 2747.

Air Ukraine flies to Kyiv (Kyev) from Budapest, Bucharest, Warsaw, Moscow, Prague, Sofia and Istanbul, and from Berlin, Brussels, Vienna, Hamburg, Dusseldorf, Copenhagen, London, Milan, Munich, Paris, Rome, Stockholm and Frankfurt, and Zürich, via Sofia, Budapest, or Warsaw, by a complicated series of codeshares, and on to Běijīng. Lengthy, and with possible visa complications, but interesting and cheap. Sofia ℂ (2) 980 7880, Prague ℂ (2) 2424 8828, Budapest ℂ (1) 318 3709, Warsaw ℂ (2) 622 0350, Bucharest (1) 311 1408.

British Airways has direct flights from London. UK ℂ 0345 222111, USA and Canada ℂ 1-800 247 9297, <*http://www.british-airways.com/*> and <*http://www.oneworldalliance.com/*>.

Cathay Pacific flies to Hong Kong from London, Glasgow, Manchester, Paris, Amsterdam, Frankfurt, Zürich and Rome, with connections to Běijīng on Dragonair. London ℂ (020) 7747 8888, <*http://www.cathaypacific-air.com/*> and <*http://www.oneworldalliance.com/*>.

Finnair often offers good fares for those prepared to go via Helsinki. London ℂ (020) 7408 1222, USA and Canada ℂ toll-free 1-800 950 5000.

KLM flies from Amsterdam to Běijīng on Wednesdays and Saturdays, also with an extensive network of European connections and smooth interchanges at Amsterdam's Schipol airport. UK ℂ (0990) 750900, USA ℂ toll-free 1-800 447 4747, Canada ℂ toll-free 1-800 361 1887, Australia ℂ toll-free 008 222 747, <*http://www.klm.nl/*>.

Kyrgyzstan Airlines flies via Bishkek from Birmingham (UK) and as a codeshare with British Airways from London. It also has flights from Hannover and Frankfurt. Hannover ℂ (0511) 726 1959, Frankfurt ℂ (069) 496 0224.

Lufthansa flies from Frankfurt to Běijīng daily with worldwide connections. UK ℂ 0345 737747, USA ℂ toll-free 1-800 645 3880, Canada ℂ toll-free 1-800 563 5954, <*http://www.lufthansa.com/*>.

MIAT Mongolian Airlines flies from Berlin and Moscow (as well as Seoul and Osaka) to Ulaan Baatar with connections to Běijīng (or there are two trains a week, *see* 'By Train', *below*).

SAS flies four times weekly from Copenhagen, *<http://www.sas.se/>*.

Tarom Romanian Air Transport flies from the main European capitals via Bucharest. London ✆ (020) 7224 3693.

Turkish Airlines has connections from all over Europe to Istanbul and on to Běijīng twice a week. London ✆ (020) 7766 9300, *<turkishairlines.uk@btinternet.com>*, Paris ✆ (1) 4266 4740, MINITEL: 6315 Turkish, Berlin ✆ (030) 262 4034, *<ber.tk@t.online.de>*, *<http://www.thy.com/>*.

The following airlines also have feeders from European capitals and onwards: **Alitalia** flies twice weekly from Milan, **Austrian Airlines** has twice weekly flights from Vienna and **Malev Hungarian Airlines** flies weekly from Budapest at cheap rates.

Budget travel. Some of the major European airlines have made it big business to use their home airports as hubs, offering travellers willing to change planes a substantial discount over those taking direct flights with their national airlines. However, for the biggest discounts travellers need to look at eastern Europe (Malev, Tarom) and beyond, preferably to countries with relatively weak economies or those well out of the way. Malaysian Airlines via Kuala Lumpur, Aeroflot via Moscow, Uzbekistan Airways via Tashkent, and PIA via Karachi or Islamabad all offer cheaper routes to Běijīng than the majors. Further east, consider Thai Airways via Bangkok, Garuda Indonesia via Jakarta, and Philippines Airlines via Manila. You might even look at Ethiopia Airlines and Iran Air. The cheapest fares on the major airlines and on alternative routes are usually obtained from discounters, consolidators, and 'bucket shops' with good reputations, such as Flight Centre or STA Travel, and others to be found in the pages of *Time Out, Village Voice, The Georgia Straight* or equivalent local listings magazines and in the travel sections of Sunday newspapers.

east from North America

Air Ukraine flies to Kyiv (Kyev) from Toronto on Saturdays and from New York on Tuesdays, Saturdays and Sundays, with connections to Běijīng. Toronto ✆ (416) 234 1170, New York ✆ (212) 599 0775, toll-free in North America 1-800 857 2463.

Tarom Romanian Air Transport flies from Chicago, New York and Montreal via Bucharest. USA ✆ (212) 687 6013.

Turkish Airlines flies from New York, Chicago and Miami via Istanbul. New York ✆ (212) 339 9650, ✆ 1-800 874 8875, Chicago (312) 943 7858, *<http://www.thy.com/>*.

west from North America

Cheaper routes involve stop-overs in Seoul or Tokyo, the Philippines or Indonesia.

Air China is usually one of the cheaper airlines, although not by much, and flies to Běijīng from Vancouver, Seattle, San Francisco, Los Angeles, Chicago and New York. Toronto ✆ (416) 581 8833, Vancouver ✆ (604) 685 0921, New York ✆ (212) 371 9898, San Francisco ✆ (415) 392 2612, *<http://www.airchina.com/>*.

Asiana flies from eight US cities via Seoul (some codeshares with American Airlines). There's also a feeder to Seattle from Vancouver, ✆ (604) 683 7824. USA toll-free ✆ 1-800 227 4262, website *http://www.asiana.co.kr/*. **Korean Airlines** also flies via Seoul. USA ✆ toll-free 1-800 438-5000, Vancouver ✆ (604) 689 2000.

Japan Airlines has flights via Tokyo. USA and Canada ✆ toll-free 1-800 525 3663, <*http://www.jal.co.jp/*>. **ANA** also flies via Tokyo and Kansai, codesharing with United Airlines. USA and Canada ✆ toll-free 1-800 235 9262, <*http://www.ana.co.jp/*>.

Canadian Airlines flies from Vancouver four times weekly, but during the life of this guide the routes will possibly be taken over by Air Canada. Canada ✆ toll-free 1-800 665 1177, USA ✆ toll-free 1-800 426 7000, <*http://www.cdnair.ca/*>, <*http://www.oneworldalliance.com/*>.

Cathay Pacific flies to Hong Kong from Toronto, Vancouver, New York and Los Angeles. Connections to Běijīng are with Dragonair. USA ✆ toll-free 1-800 233 2742, Canada ✆ toll-free 1-800 268 6868, <*http://www.cathaypacific-air.com/*>, <*http://www.onewordalliance.com/*>.

Northwest Airlines flies non-stop from Detroit, and also via Tokyo. USA and Canada ✆ toll-free 1-800 225 2525, <*http://www.nwa.com/*>.

United Airlines flies from major US cities via Tokyo. USA and Canada ✆ toll-free 1-800 241 6522, < *http://www.ual.com/*>.

from Australasia

Air China flies from Sydney, ✆ (02) 232-7277, and Melbourne, ✆ (03) 642-1555.

Air New Zealand flies to Hong Kong from Auckland, with organized connections to Běijīng. Auckland ✆ (09) 357-3000, Australia ✆ 13-2476, ✆ HK (852) 2524 8606, <*http://www.airnz.co.nz/*>.

Cathay Pacific flies to Hong Kong from Auckland, Cairns, Brisbane, Sydney, Melbourne, Adelaide and Perth. Australia ✆ toll-free 131747, Auckland (9) 379 0861, <*http://www.cathaypacific-air.com/*> and <*http://www.oneworldalliance.com/*>.

Qantas flies three times a week to Shànghǎi from Sydney with an onwards connection to Běijīng provided by China Eastern, <*http://www.qantas.com.au/*> and <*http://www.oneworldalliance.com/*>.

Other carriers with reasonable connections via a variety of Asian cities include **Singapore Airlines, ANA, JAL, Asiana** and **Korean**.

By Train

For those with enough time, travelling by train is the best way to get a feeling for the immense distances across Europe and Asia while retaining a high level of comfort.

From **Hong Kong** an express train K98 runs on alternate days directly from Kowloon to Běijīng, leaving at 15.00 and arriving at Běijīng West Station (Xī Zhàn) at 18.58 the next day. Hard sleeper (six couchettes) is around HK$600 ($74), lower berths being more expensive than higher ones (*see* p.10). Soft sleeper (four beds) is around HK$1000 ($123), and *gāojí ruǎn wò* (high class soft sleeper), two beds in a compartment with upmarket decor and upholstery, HK$1191 ($146). There is no need (and indeed it will be considerably more expensive) to buy these tickets from abroad, and even the discount travel agents in Hong Kong usually beloved of backpackers overcharge. Go straight to Hung Hom station or to CTS in Kowloon or Central, Hong Kong (*see* 'CTS and CITS offices overseas', *below*).

Beginning with the Eurostar London to Paris services it's now possible to go all the way to Běijīng by rail changing at **Moscow** for routes via **Ulaan Baatar** or Harbin, or changing at

Almaty in Kazakhstan and Ürümqi in China's northwest for the route across the width of China called the 'Euro-Asia Continental Bridge' (up to 1,200km shorter than Trans-Siberian routes). For the truly adventurous, a line linking Iran with Turkmenistan might provide an alternative route via southern Europe and Turkey. Some have succeeded in travelling from Turkey via Tblisi in Georgia and Baku in Azerbaijan across the Caspian Sea to Turkmenistan and on via Almaty and Ürümqi.

Trans-Manchurian no.20 leaves **Moscow** every Friday at 20.25 Moscow time and arrives at Běijīng Zhàn via Harbin seven days later at 05.30.

Trans-Mongolian no.4 leaves **Moscow** every Tuesday at 21.03 Moscow time and arrives at Běijīng Zhàn via Ulaan Baatar at 05.30 on Mondays. There's also train no.24 which starts from **Ulaan Baatar** every Thursday at 08.50 Ulaan Baatar time, arriving at Běijīng Zhàn the following afternoon at 15.33.

Direct train K6 leaves **Hanoi** in Vietnam on Tuesdays and Fridays at 14.00 Hanoi time, arriving at Běijīng Xī Zhàn on Thursdays and Sundays at 17.18.

By Road

For the highly adventurous it's possible to drive as far as China's borders with Kyrgyzstan, Kazakhstan or Mongolia, but proceeding further is difficult and expensive. While a few tours are now being offered in which rented vehicles may be driven along specific routes within China, self-drive car hire is new even to Běijīng. Importing your own vehicle is strictly for the resident foreigner with sound financial backing, or for the charity fund-raiser with a year or two's advance planning and all the right connections, or for someone prepared to spend a long time negotiating a route and a price with CITS or a similar government-approved agency, which will include taking along a compulsory guide (who will be unlikely to know anything at all about the places you go).

There are buses from Ulaan Baatar to the Chinese border, but not across it, and the twice weekly train is a more reliable and more comfortable choice. This is the only road crossing remotely near to Běijīng.

By Sea

There are sailings from Japan and South Korea to ports on China's east coast. For details of sailings between Tiānjīn and Inchon in South Korea, *see* p.350.

Entry Formalities

> *In Lanchow the authorities, when they gave us back our papers, had assured us that they were in order for Chinghai. But they were not; before sending us on to Sining, Lanchow should have provided us with a special passport. By failing to do so Lanchow had neatly delegated the responsibility for stopping us to her neighbours, while at the same time increasing both the likelihood and the legality of such action on their part; it was a beautifully Chinese gambit, in the best tradition of passive resistance. It looked as if we were done for.*
>
> Peter Fleming, *News from Tartary*, 1936

Under ordinary circumstances you can easily obtain a L visa at an embassy in any capital, or from a consulate if you live near it. These are tourist visas and are usually valid for one month, but two or three months may be given if requested, beginning within 60 days of the date of issue. Double entry tourist visas are also available, but these cannot be extended.

Other visa types include the F, a visitor's visa valid for periods of up to 6 months and allowing multiple entry, intended for people on temporary work assignments rather then permanent positions. It cannot be extended, and can only be obtained overseas with supporting paperwork, while in Hong Kong it's as easily obtained as a tourist visa from a variety of agents, or directly from the representative office of the Běijīng government.

The Z visa is for people working in China for periods up to one year, and is only available to those who have already arranged employment. A residence permit must also be acquired.

The X visa is for students who can supply written evidence of the offer of a place at an official education institution in China.

At times of political unrest, or if a politically sensitive event is taking place, new regulations may temporarily be introduced without notice. These may include requiring visas to be obtained only in your country of residence, requiring sight of a return air ticket or of bank statements demonstrating the possession of a certain sum of money. The authorities do not care if this disrupts your plans or causes you to lose money on services already booked and paid for.

Visas usually take five days to obtain, except in Hong Kong where same day service is commonplace, but the process can be speeded up by the payment of extra fees. In fact the visas are almost always ready the next day, and applicants who return early can often see their passports sitting in a pile on the desk, but unobtainable before five days are up unless an extra fee is paid. Visa fees vary according to your country of origin, but are typically around US$30.

When completing the application form, be sure only to list anodyne cities such as Běijīng, Shànghǎi and Xī'ān as your destinations. The visa is valid for the whole of China whatever you write, but you may be turned down if you mention Xīnjiāng or Tibet.

'L' visas can usually be extended without difficulty within China. Each extension is for 30 days and up to three are allowed, although the third one is sometimes given with reluctance, depending on the time of year, the political situation, your nationality, and the office chosen. Extensions are usually given by the Aliens Entry-Exit Department of the local Public Security Bureau (police) in larger cities, up to four days before your current visa or extension expires. In some towns this is a swift, polite and efficient process, run by fluent English speakers. In others the relevant officer may be off doing something else, and no-one else will take responsibility. *These offices are closed on Saturday and Sunday, and do not always keep to their published opening hours. Never leave it until the last moment to apply for an extension. If you overrun, the PSB will delight in inventing a fine for you to pay—as much as ¥500 ($62) per day.* Extensions are less than half the price of original visas, but vary according to the latest state of each country's relations with China. Nothing in China is ever consistent (except inconsistency), so expect whatever prices your hear about to have changed. Double and multiple entry L and F visas cannot be extended. You must leave China and start again.

The easiest place of all to acquire a visa is Hong Kong. *See* the names of agencies and the addresses of embassies and consulates worldwide on pp.26–7.

Chinese customs make little fuss over tourists. The customs declaration form is still sometimes handed out, but (read the rubric carefully) is only for people who are importing goods or large amounts of currency and not re-exporting them. In theory, currency amounting to more than $5,000 must be declared, and it might be awkward if you were caught leaving China with more than that and no copy of your entry declaration, so play safe and ask if in doubt.

Antique items on sale at mainstream tourist shops often carry a red seal which indicates that the relevant authorities have cleared the item for export, but may simply mean that a fake seal has been attached to give authenticity to a modern copy. In theory antiques should be cleared for export before you leave the country. In practice the offices for this purpose are hard to find, rarely open, and the searching of bags is also very rare.

You may export (or import) Chinese cash up to ¥6,000RMB, which might make sense if you are arriving from Hong Kong where RMB is fairly cheap, but elsewhere the numbers of foreign exchange offices accepting RMB are few, so it's best to reconvert before you leave. If you have kept receipts proving that you have exchanged more than you want to reconvert, then any excess can be converted to hard currency (usually US$) at the Bank of China before you leave. There is a nominal rule that your receipts must be less than three months old, and that the sum you wish to reconvert must be less than half the value of your receipts, but this is rarely enforced. You are also prohibited from exporting Chinese medicine worth more than ¥300, but it's highly unlikely this would be checked.

Travelling Within China

Ascertain the date of Chinese New Year, usually early February, and occasionally late January. Do not attempt to travel in China for a week or so either side unless you are on an organized tour. If you are in China at that time, plan to reach a destination worth spending a week to ten days in well before the holiday season begins. Each year hundreds of millions of journeys are made—an estimated 1.6 *billion* in 2000 and rising annually, swamping even the tens of thousands of extra bus and train services provided.

By Air

The safety record of China domestic flying, carried out by a total of more than 30 airlines, is poor by international standards, although certainly far fewer people die in plane crashes than on China's roads. Reports of domestic airline crashes often appear abroad while being suppressed in the domestic press, although crashes of foreign airliners in China are always reported. However, twelve airlines are now IATA registered, suggesting internationally recognized standards of maintenance, and a fleet of nearly 500 airliners is principally made up of Boeings and Airbuses, although some argue that the ageing Soviet planes still on some routes are easier to maintain, and thus safer. There's a lack of modern electronic navigation equipment at many airports. Pilots are rumoured to be mostly ex-military, and to need special training not to throw their civilian planes around the sky as if in combat. If this story is true, it is not always clear that the training has been effective.

Air China has a 100% safety record and has won international awards both for safety and for cabin service. Those who find this surprising are thinking of China Airlines, which is based in Táiwān. Discounts are available on feeder airlines (such as British Midland into Heathrow), and on domestic flights if booked at the same time as an international one. In a recent survey of 15,000 domestic passengers, China Southern was found to be the most popular airline, with an annual passenger volume of more than 6 million.

Losses by all but four of China's airlines after a vicious price-cutting war in 1998 (losses of the biggest three alone came to $150 million that year) led to the reintroduction of government controls over ticket prices, and a cut back of services on some routes of up to 30%, which, the government claimed, reduced losses to $30 million. Airlines retaliated with illegal under-the-counter offers of a free night's accommodation at domestic destinations and other promotions, which were squashed when discovered. For the moment, whichever airline you choose for domestic flying, your ticket price will be the same. There are no PEX, APEX, or other discount strategies common in the West, and except at Chinese New Year most air tickets are only bought a few days in advance. For now, prices are directly related to the distance travelled, but the government is considering allowing prices to be more relevant to demand—the first sign of this being their increase at Chinese New Year 2000 (although some flights were reported to be largely empty, while trains were packed solid).

Airline offices and local travel agents with terminals on the system should sell you a ticket commission-free, others charging between ¥30 and ¥50 to make your booking and collect the ticket. They may also have the *guānxi* (connections) to get you a ticket when the airline staff tell you the planes are full, but this is rare to and from Běijīng. Getting bumped off by government officials, whether you have a reconfirmed ticket or not, can also happen.

Watch out for departure taxes (CAAC Airport Management and Construction Fee): ¥50 ($6) for domestic flights, ¥90 ($11) for international ones, although there are signs these may be absorbed into ticket prices.

By Train

This is by far the best way to tackle the vast distances across China. Buses may now sometimes be faster, but the trains give you more space, the chance to move around, meet Chinese and attempt conversation, and to concentrate on the scenery rather than the driver's near misses. Trains are usually both reliable and punctual, and are gradually speeding up. The signalling system is modern and accidents are rare.

Railway tickets are the same price for foreigners and Chinese and, at 5.861 *fēn* per kilometre ($0.007), represent one of China's best bargains. Even supplements for sleeping accommodation and speed leave the trains absurdly good value. Price increases seem to be less related to inflation than to increases in disposable income. When unreserved hard seat carriages are at several times their capacity, the government raises the prices, which reduces the pressure. Following a rise at the end of 1995, passenger traffic dropped off by 12.5%t in 1996, but still amounted to *942 million* passenger-journeys, and volumes are considerably higher now.

Everything in Chinese railways is done on a grand scale. During a burst of reform in 1996 1,500 stations were closed to passenger traffic as being uneconomic, while more than 10,000km of new track was laid during the five-year plan which ended in the year 2000. The railways employ 3,370,000 workers, although numbers have been falling, as in the other

Railway Ticket

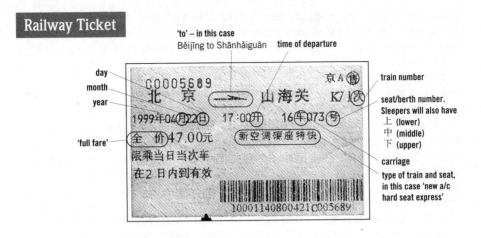

'to' – in this case Běijīng to Shānhǎiguān — time of departure

day
month
year

'full fare'

train number

seat/berth number. Sleepers will also have
上 (lower)
中 (middle)
下 (upper)

carriage

type of train and seat, in this case 'new a/c hard seat express'

state-owned industries, and in 1999 a limited degree of privatization began, although the government made it clear it planned to retain lines of strategic importance. New air-conditioned rolling stock has begun appearing on the lines mentioned in the book; in southern China trains are running as fast as 200kph, more rapid lines are planned, and the number of cross-border services has also increased.

Ordinary trains are not fast, but the best of them run at an adequate 106kph. Timetables in Chinese are on sale at stations and elsewhere if you feel like tackling them using the train numbers given and comparing place name characters. Note, however, that the authorities will frequently change the train times and not reprint tables until the current ones have expired, leaving the inaccurate ones on sale. Like the times quoted in this book, they should only be regarded as a general guide. Most will certainly have altered.

The problem with Chinese trains is **buying the tickets**. At Běijīng Zhàn, Běijīng Xī Zhàn and Tiānjīn you'll find special windows dealing with foreigners, but nowhere else in this book. Elsewhere you fight it out with everybody else, or use a travel agent to do the fighting for you. In some towns there is a separate window for sleeping accommodation, or it may be sold along with ordinary seats at the window dealing with each destination. Identify the right window using this book and the characters given for each place name, and you may be able to walk straight up and buy your ticket. Sometimes you will just be one member of a long queue, and you may seem to get further away from your window rather than nearer it as people push in or bribe those nearer the front to buy their tickets for them. However, in eastern China the increasing frequency of trains and the growth of competing bus services has made this less common outside peak periods.

While some stations are well-regulated with officials keeping the lines in order, if you see people sitting up on the counter next to the ticket window, leering vulture-like down at the queue, you are probably at a station where large numbers of tickets have been sold through the back door and where demand exceeds supply. These people are touts (scalpers) and you should not believe anything they tell you about ticket availability and still try for yourself. Buying tickets from these sources is an extreme measure, and should only be considered if you have someone to hand who can read them or you may pay soft sleeper prices for a hard seat (*see* the characters given in the Language section). Even then, there are fake tickets in abundance. When you reach the ticket window, and have physically removed those who tried to thrust in front of you at the last moment, be prepared with several different options, and not just with a request for tickets for one designated train. Tickets go on sale no earlier than four days in advance, including the day of purchase and the day of travel, and often later than that, depending on local policy. Telephone bookings can now be made earlier, and out of Běijīng Internet bookings earlier still, but for both of these options you need Mandarin.

The majority of the tickets for a train are sold in the town where it starts, and to increase your chances of getting a ticket you should always look first for trains which start from where you are. Small intermediate stations have tiny allocations for trains that stop there, or none at all. Your only hope is to buy an unreserved hard class seat, and to **upgrade** on the train. Your chances of actually sitting down with an unreserved ticket are slim, and are subject to the ends and beginnings of university terms, migrations of seasonal labourers and Communist Party official junkets, as well as the Spring Festival (Chinese New Year) and, to a lesser extent, the autumn travel season. The effect of the foreigner 'tourist season' is negligible. Even at peak times, foreign tourists are mere droplets in an ocean of Chinese. Your chances of upgrading also depend upon the attitude of the staff on board. Some go out of their way to help a lost-looking foreigner, and others will reserve any places that come free for Chinese prepared to bribe them. The on-board office will usually be at the end of one of the hard seat carriages in the middle of the train, often nos.11 or 12. In some cases soft sleeper upgrades are handled by the staff in those carriages, so if a soft sleeper is what you are after, it may be best to ask there first. Note that the train is usually so packed with humanity that walking up and down it with luggage is either very trying or impossible. Try to get on the train at the door nearest to the office.

Seating comes in four **classes**: hard seat, soft seat, hard sleeper and soft sleeper.

Hard seat (*yìng zuò*) is usually wooden benches, and a mixture of reserved and unreserved tickets, except on air-conditioned trains where all seats are reservable and no-one else is allowed on board. At its worst it is ankle deep in peanut shells, fruit peel, sunflower seed husks and mucus, dimly perceivable through choking clouds of cigarette smoke, but conditions are improving. People with unreserved seats will be asleep on the tables and, unbelievably, on the floor. In the better trains the attendants regularly empty the bins and mop the floors, stridently admonishing those not putting rubbish where it belongs. Since most like to smoke themselves, the no-smoking rule is rarely enforced.

Soft seat (*ruǎn zuò*) is relatively rare, and usually on short daylight trips such as that between Běijīng and Chéngdé or Tiānjīn. It features comfortable seats, all reservable.

Hard sleeper (*yìng wò*) has firm couchettes in piles of three, separated by partitions into groups of six altogether, with a passageway along the side of the carriage. There is no privacy or screening of any kind. The price for hard sleeper tickets decreases the further away you get from the ground, but the differences are minimal. The upper berth is often favoured by foreigners as it gets them up and away from the mêlée, and can spare them from excessive curiosity (the only kind available). Everyone sits on the bottom berths during the day, so there's little sense of control over your environment if that's the berth you have. Speakers set in the ceiling play saccharine music and broadcast announcements, including the dining car menu and extremely rosy descriptions of the next town and its happy inhabitants. In the top berth you may find one over your head. It cannot be turned off, and nor can the lights, which come on early in the morning and go off altogether at night. Each group of six berths has two thermoses of boiled water, but often someone has to volunteer to trek down to wherever the boiler is in order to refill them. It's worth trying to avoid the berths at either end of the carriage from the point of view of both noise and smell.

Soft sleeper (*ruǎn wò*), has four comfortable beds in a compartment with a lockable door. It may have plastic flowers on the table, carpeting, twin thermoses of boiled water which the attendants usually top up for you, and a volume control for the speaker. Windows, both in the compartment and the corridor, have net curtains. Soft sleepers are the haunt of the party official, the self-made entrepreneur and the employee of the multinational. Sleeper buses and trains are the only time you will sleep in the same room as Chinese. Upper and lower berths usually cost the same price, but again the upper berth offers a little more control over when you can go to sleep at night or take an afternoon nap.

If you end up with a compartment all to yourself, you may get moved in with other people so as to give the attendants less cleaning to do, or leave them space to spend the night drinking, smoking and gambling. Bed linen is provided and usually clean, although it may be collected well before you arrive at your destination if it pleases the attendant to do so. In all classes of train, the small, garishly coloured towel provided is to function as a pillow-slip. Standards of cleanliness vary from crisp and spotless on the newest trains, to rotting and dingy on older ones.

Rail **ticket prices** are calculated according to the number of kilometres travelled, with supplements added according to the speed of the train, the class of berth, whether it's upper (cheaper), middle or lower, and whether there's air conditioning. All tickets are one way, except for Chinese students travelling between 40 designated cities. Children under 1m height travel free, and under 1.3m pay 25%. There are marks on the wall near the ticket windows by which children are measured. Ticket offices are almost always entered by a different door than the one that leads to the platforms, and may be in a separate building altogether. Important exceptions in this book are Běijīng Zhàn (the main railway station) and the new Běijīng Xī Zhàn (Běijīng West Station), which have special foreigners' ticket windows inside the main station building. Your ticket is checked on the way to the platform. When you board the train for a sleeper, your ticket is taken away and you are given a plastic or metal token with the number of your berth on it. *Do not lose this.* When it is nearly time to get off (any time between five and 30mins beforehand) the attendant will come and return your ticket and retrieve the token. The ticket is checked again as you leave the station, so keep it ready.

Note that at major railway stations all baggage is **X-rayed** upon entering the station. Despite the fact that the main occupation of people on trains is staring at other people on trains, **theft** is increasing, including opportunistic snatching of valuables through train windows. Even some Chinese now tie their luggage to the racks, and it's important to have your compartment locked if it will be unattended while you visit the dining car or go for a walk on the platform.

Dining cars on trains serve poor but usually tolerable food, with a choice of six or eight dishes at slightly higher prices than you would find for a better meal in an ordinary restaurant. It's mostly soft-sleeper Chinese who use the dining car, and it's not usually full. Find the attendant at one end with a pile of coloured tickets and a handwritten menu with prices. Opportunists may occasionally attempt to charge the foreigner more than the prices written there, but they have no right to do so. Beer is always available, and sometimes soft drinks, but rarely chilled.

Breakfast is normally steamed bread. Attendants usually bring round trolleys laden with snacks and some prepared meals in styrofoam boxes. Most Chinese bring their own food and buy from vendors on platforms when the train stops. Bring some snacks of your own, as the train food is increasingly poor, and bring some extra to share as the Chinese in your compartment or carriage will almost certainly offer you something of theirs.

Be prepared for revolting lavatories, no running hot water for washing, even no cold water, and floods in the washroom, probably all at the same time. Take toilet paper, handwipes if you wish (available in China) and a mug for making tea and for cooling down boiled water to use for brushing your teeth.

By Bus

Cart transport is the most practical way of conveying a traveller and his goods over the main trade-routes of the Gobi, but unfortunately it necessitates the use of a carter and, as the Chinese proverb has it, 'As to carters, there's ne'er a good one.'

Mildred Cable with Francesca French, *The Gobi Desert*, 1942

The role of the carter is now taken by the modern-day bus driver, minibus driver, taxi driver and rickshaw cyclist. All like foreigners, but for the wrong reasons.

According to government figures 83,529 people were killed on the roads in 1999, and 286,000 were injured. It was probably worse, although these figures represented a significant increase over several previous years, when the figures had stayed suspiciously level. Even these show that with about 50 million, or 2% of the world's cars, China produces about 15% of the world's road casualties. Whenever the government reports accident figures it immediately, and rather chillingly, goes on to report the resulting 'economic losses', in that year about $250 million, 10% more than the previous year.

Most buses in China are robust to cope with the rigours of Chinese roads rather than comfortable, and most still have wooden seats with little or no padding, not designed for foreign width or thigh length. However, they are very cheap. On most routes out of Běijīng and between sights discussed in this book there are also comfortable alternatives for those willing to pay a little bit more, particularly Iveco minibuses, Volvo coaches and a variety of Chinese copies, all with more comfortable seats, air conditioning and often (less welcome) with video screens. There's now a network of highways spreading out from Běijīng which has sometimes made travelling by bus quicker than by train.

On ordinary buses luggage is usually piled high on the roof and not accessible until you arrive at your destination. It's up to you to put it there yourself, although the conductor will usually make sure that everything is secure under rope netting. Smaller items can sometimes be piled on the cowling covering the engine next to the driver. In all but the very newest buses, big or small, access to the engine is gained from the interior of the bus by lifting this cowling. In the oldest buses a pipe fed by the exhaust gases runs from here along the centre of the bus to provide primitive heating. Do not rest your feet on this or your soles will melt. In remoter areas breakdowns, and in particular punctures, are frequent, but there is an admirable can-do mentality which gets even the most major problem dealt with by the roadside. Important gasket blown? A temporary replacement is quickly cut from a cigarette sleeve.

On older buses, sit as near the front of the bus as possible, not only to get a better view, but also because sitting at the back over an unyielding suspension is something your spine will long remember if your route takes you on back roads, introducing moments of air travel to your terrestrial progress. At the front you may have to cope with frequent use of piercing air horns and deafening engine noise. Latecomers are placed on wooden stools down the aisle, produced from under the main seating, and after those are taken people stand in whatever space remains. The 'maximum capacity' of a Chinese bus is a purely theoretical quantity. Sometimes windows pop out and have to be replaced. Occasionally they are just missing, and in all cases they rattle and the latches don't work so that they must continually be reshut. Sturdy rubber bands are a useful solution, especially in sleeper buses or during storms. The newer buses deteriorate from the moment they enter service, but most avoid these problems.

Only those travelling beyond the area covered by this book will need sleeper buses. Bunks on two levels run in three rows down the centre of the bus, and can be adjusted between a near horizontal and a more upright reclining position. They are narrow and short. For the minimal disturbance and a maximum control over your environment, try to get an upper berth next to a window. All the men smoke, at least one person is sick, piles of food remains grow on the floor, where babies are also allowed to urinate. Sleeper buses are swift, but pungent. Some have two rows of double-bed size sleeping areas, and you may occasionally encounter resistance to selling you a ticket if you are travelling by yourself and will thus share such a space with a Chinese.

Ticket offices in bus stations are open all day. Prices are the same for foreigners and Chinese in all the areas covered in this book, although if you don't buy your ticket from the bus station staff it's very likely that individual initiative will be employed to cheat you. With the exception of certain special services, such as those to airports and railway stations, ticket prices are calculated according to the distance to be travelled. The price per km varies slightly from region to region, but is usually less than one US cent, although the government may allow price hikes at peak travel times, first seen with an increase of 30% around Chinese New Year in 2000. Sleeper buses cost more, and have slightly different pricing according to berth chosen. Advance booking rules vary greatly, but in general tickets can be bought the day before travel, and are not difficult to obtain. There are no charges for ordinary quantities of baggage.

On many routes you can just board the bus and buy there, but you may end up at the back of the bus. Ticket numbering is designed to be as confusing as possible. Sometimes the use of numbers is observed, sometimes not, and when the bus is part full a debate will break out between those at the front who insist that ticket numbers don't matter, and those who have low ticket numbers but who find themselves at the rear and so insist that they do. To confuse matters further, there is disagreement as to whether the number of the seat is written on its back, or the back of the one in front. On older buses numbers may be written in chalk, and partly or completely erased, and sometimes they are randomly distributed about the bus, so separated families and friends may start long negotiations for seat exchanges. Add to this that it may be a pre-dawn winter morning with no lights on the bus so no-one can see the numbers properly, and that if a conductor enforces the seat numbering *everybody tries to move at once*, and you have a bus of Babel.

Bus station staff often board to check tickets and sell to those that don't have them before the bus leaves, but some stations are now computerized—if on your way to the bus you see a *fúwùyuán* with a bar-code scanning gun you need to let her scan the ticket. Often gaggles of peasants wait on out-of-town routes, flag down the bus and haggle with the driver and conductor to get cheaper prices. You'll notice that sometimes the money is pocketed without tickets being issued. Always insist on getting yours to avoid later arguments, surcharges and attempts to charge you for the tolls payable on almost all long-distance roads, which are none of your business.

The buses usually leave the station more or less on time, but diversions for the driver's own purposes, searches for further passengers, stops to pick up those who flag it down (who usually have heavy items to load on the roof), and a pause for accountancy on the outskirts of town, may make the real departure time considerably later. Allowing for dithering, food breaks, road-works and breakdowns, the average speed of a long-distance bus on back roads is 43km per hour, nearer 65kph in Iveco buses and similar using new highways.

By Car, Motorbike or Bicycle

Foreign residents in China who obtain a Chinese driving licence and go through a large amount of paperwork can drive cars in China, and with a bit more paperwork can rent them. At the time of writing there was one company offering car rental to visitors arriving by plane, at high cost and with many restrictions. *See* 'self-drive', p.111, and accompanying cautions on the difficulties of driving in China.

Taking your own vehicle is also an option, but takes a long time to arrange and is highly expensive. Your route must be agreed in advance, with all your accommodation booked, and you will be required to carry a guide with you. If you are on a motorbike then one will follow you in a car with a driver, and you'll have to pay for all of that. Begin by contacting your nearest branch of the China National Tourism Organisation, the China International Travel Service, or similar. *See* addresses on p.17.

The fanatics of the Běijīng Airheads motorcycle club may be able to help more, including on the topic of buying a classic Chinese motorcycle and sidecar: contact Jim Bryant, ✆ 139 0132 0922, <*pmc@public.bta.net.cn*>, who also offers tours of Inner Mongolia beginning from Běijīng, with motorcycle and everything else provided.

A pushbike is the fastest form of truly independent self-drive travel easily available to visitors. Travelling across China by bicycle is now fairly common. Travellers come across relatively few problems and often get to stay in very out-of-the-way places never seen by those on buses, encountering highly invasive levels of curiosity combined with a friendliness and hospitality rarely found in destinations more popular with tourists.

A large assortment of different types of bike, almost all Chinese-made, can now be bought (*see* 'Shopping', p.52), but reliability is highly variable (although roadside bike menders with a can-do approach to even the most severe problem are everywhere). There are numerous stories of frames being welded back together and other apparently terminal problems being solved, but equally tales of the impossibility of finding replacement parts for high-tech, or even relatively low-tech, foreign bikes. Serious cyclists should take everything they need.

The Chinese also make a rather nifty electric bicycle for a little over ¥3,000 ($375), which can be charged up in six to eight hours and needs no special paperwork.

There are public buses or various kinds of organized transport (a seat in a trailer behind a tractor, for instance) to even the remotest corners of China. If a travel agent tells you that his company's vehicles are the only way that you can visit a place, that is almost a guarantee that there's some alternative. Hitching, however, isn't usually it. If you do end up hitching because you simply can't find any other form of transport, be sure that you'll have to pay, and negotiate the price first. There is still very limited casual private motoring of long distances in China (and still precious little in cities compared to their populations). Imported limousines and off-road vehicles contain officials or belong to travel companies, so if you do succeed in hitching you'll be in a truck, usually perched amongst the goods it's carrying.

City Transport

There were officially 1.3 million vehicles on Běijīng's streets in October 1998, and you can add an estimated 10,000 new vehicles per month to arrive at the current figure—Běijīng's traffic spends a great deal of time coagulated. Further disruption occurs whenever anyone of any importance is going to and from the airport, for instance, when all traffic can be cleared from the route for up to 20mins, reducing the rest of Běijīng from a crawl to a complete halt. The average speed of traffic during rush hours (which the Chinese call *gāo fēng*—high wind) on the second and third ring roads is less than 40kph, although still three times as fast as London. The driving motto is 'no scrape too narrow, no shave too close'.

Nine million people in Běijīng still own bicycles, and at the other end of the scale 30 own Ferraris. On 21 October 1998 Běijīng took a firm step backwards with a decision to ban bicycles from one of its streets (Xī Sì Dōng Dàjiē) between 7am and 8pm, although residents are allowed to wheel their bikes. More than 6,000 bicycles per hour were pouring through the street, slowing vehicular traffic. This anti-environmental move at a time when the city was stressing (as it still is) the need for environmental measures is just one example of the conflict between different agendas. According to the Chinese press, several different government departments cover the car industry and each pursues its own policies, some of which are contradictory— high taxes to curb automobile purchase and prevent pollution, but also measures to encourage car purchase in order to make the industry grow and increase employment.

City **buses and trolleybuses** often resemble overgrown '60s enamel bread bins, and travel about as quickly. Allowed to stall at every stop, some of them find they can't start again. That's when Chinese public-spiritedness comes to the fore, as perhaps only a third of the passengers get off and three-quarters of those only do so to enjoy the spectacle of the few others pushing the bus. The fleet is being modernized and numbers of relatively green LPG-powered buses introduced.

Boarding buses can be a full contact sport. Either join in or choose an alternative form of transport. Most buses have conductors at the front and rear, and sometimes at the middle if this is a concertina-style vehicle with a middle door. Distorted announcements sometimes consist of little more than 'Hurry up hurry up hurry up' at every stop addressed to those fighting to get off against the stream of those fighting to get on. In between stops it's 'Buy a ticket buy a ticket buy a ticket.' Most buses have a basic fare that covers most journeys, with additions for longer distances. If you hold out money worth more than the price of one ticket you will be asked '*Jǐ ge?*, 'How many', and '*Dào năr*', 'Where to?', so either show some fingers or say the number (plus '*ge*') and your destination. Details of the local fares are given in the 'getting around' sections, but be prepared for changes (ask the English speaker in your hotel).

A few buses have a flat fare slot as you board—at the front where there are two doors, at the front or back where there are three. No change is given. In many towns smaller private minibuses (*miànbāochē*) follow the same routes, sometimes for the same fare, sometimes for double.

City bus routes in many towns have a sign with black number which is the route number, and a red number which is the *stop* number. Don't get them confused.

Taxis in China are now fairly well-regulated in most cities, most of them running meters (although speeds may not always be consistent). In most cities the cheapest taxis are the minivans (*miàndī*—but these have been banned from Běijīng), followed by small red cars (*Xiàlì*). Flagfall varies from city to city, but the basic rate per kilometre is written clearly on the side windows. In particular *see* p.109 for a detailed description of how the meters work in Běijīng. Taxi ranks are no more havens of honesty than they are anywhere else in the world, and the foreigner should go armed with a map and preferably the destination written down in characters. Never take a taxi from outside a hotel frequented by foreigners, major tourist sites or railway stations, especially if the driver is showing a particular keenness to take foreigners. Be prepared for problems ('broken' meters, poor navigation and so on) with those from airports. Taxi drivers never have change, except that the glove compartment is usually stuffed with it. Pay the exact meter fare and not a *fēn* more. Do not tip.

However, while some drivers are sharks, most in Běijīng are perfectly reasonable people, grimly coming to terms with a society which no longer guarantees them job security. They may have worked from age 15 in a now closed factory, suddenly finding themselves willy-nilly and in middle age *xià hăi*, 'jumped into the sea' of the marketplace—although in their case they were pushed—and for them it may be no more than paying a monthly rental to a taxi firm and driving 12 to 14 hours a day, seven days a week, to make ends meet. Not all of them use this as an excuse for thievery.

There are also increasing numbers of meter-less motorized three-wheelers. Agree the fare first. Below official taxi level there are motorcyclists who will offer to take you pillion (definitely not recommended) and motorbikes with side cars (safer, but uncomfortable).

For more details on city transport, *see* the 'Getting Around' sections under each city.

Specialist Tour Operators

This book aims to make it easy for you to make all your own arrangements for travel in and around Běijīng by public transport. However, here is a list of some foreign tour operators with good reputations and a variety of specialist tours reaching well beyond Běijīng.

Abercrombie and Kent (maximum comfort and convenience), 1520 Kensington Road, Oak Brook, Illinois 60523-2141, ✆ (800) 323 7308, for brochures, ✆ (800) 757 5884, *<info@ abercrombiekent.com/>*, *<http://www.aandktours.com/html/index.html>*.

Exodus Expeditions (trekking, cycling and travel by specially built vehicle), 9 Weir Road, London SW12 0LT, ✆ (020) 8675 5550, *<sales@exodustravels.co.uk>*. Canada and the

USA: G.A.P. Adventures, 266 Dupont St, Toronto, Ont. M5R 1V7, ✆ toll-free 1-800 465 5600, <*adventure@gap.ca*>. Australia: Top Deck Adventure, 8th Floor, 350 Kent St, Sydney NSW 2000, ✆ (02) 9299 8844, <*topdeck@s054.aone.net.au*>. New Zealand: Eurolynx Tours Ltd., 3rd Floor, 20 Fort St, Auckland 1, ✆ (09) 379 9716, <*a11nz236@ gncomtect.com*>, <*http://www.exodustravels.co.uk/*>.

Explore Worldwide (overland by coach), 1 Frederick Street, Aldershot, Hampshire GU11 1LQ, ✆ (01252) 319448, <*info@explore.co.uk*>. USA: Adventure Centre, ✆ 1-800 227 8747, <*ex@adventure-center.com*>. Canada: WestCan Treks, ✆ toll-free 1-800 690 4859, <*westcan@huey.cadvision.com*>, <*http://www.explore.co.uk/*>.

Geographic Expeditions (a variety of more luxurious tours across China), 2627 Lombard St, San Francisco, CA 94123, ✆ (415) 922 0448, ✉ (415) 346 5535, <*info@geoex.com*>.

Hinterland Travel (economical overland trips across China), 2 Ivy Mill Lane, Godstone, Surrey RH9 8NH, ✆ (01883) 743584, ✉ (01883) 743912.

Mountain Travel Sobek, 6420 Fairmount Ave, El Cerrito, CA 94530, ✆ toll-free 1-800 227 2384, ✉ (510) 525 7710, <*info@MTSobek.com*>, <*http://www.MTSobek.com/*>.

Regent Holidays (tailor-made holidays throughout China), 15 John Street, Bristol BS1 2HR, ✆ (0117) 921 1711, ✉ (0117) 925 4866.

Steppes East (the last word in high quality tailor-made and specialist travel—just tell them your interests and they'll draw up a tour for you), Castle Eaton, Swindon, Wiltshire SN6 6JU, ✆ (01285) 810267, ✉ (01285) 810693, <*sales@steppeseast.co.uk*>, <*http://www.steppeseast.co.uk/*>.

Voyages Jules Verne (upmarket and comfortable), 21 Dorset Square, London NW1 6QG, ✆ (020) 7616 1000, <*sales@vjv.co.uk*>, <*http://www.vjv.co.uk/*>.

USA east coast

China Int'l Travel Service (CITS), New York Office, ✆ (718) 261 7329, ✉ (718) 261 7329, <*reservation@citsusa.com*>, <*http://www.citsusa.com/*>.

China Professional Tours, ✆ (800) 252 4462, (770) 849-0300, ✉ 770 849 0301, <*cptt@america.net*>.

Club ABC Tours, ✆ (973) 338 1122, ✉ (973) 338 1663.

Collecte Tours, ✆ (800) 832 4656, ✉ (401) 727 4745, <*http://www.collectetours.com/*>.

Orient Flexi-Pax Tours, ✆ (800) 545 5540, ✉ (212) 661 1618.

Pacific Bestour Inc., ✆ (800) 688 3288, (201) 664 8788, ✉ (201) 664 1497, <*pbi@ bestour.com*>, <*http://www.bestour.com/*>.

Pacific Delight Tours Inc., ✆ (800) 212 7179, (212) 818 1781, ✉ (212) 818 1780, <*pdt@pacificdelighttours.com*>, <*http://www.pacificdelighttours.com/*>.

Ram-Pax International, ✆ (800) 701 8687, ✉ (212) 986 1783, <*China@rim-pax.com*>, <*http://www.rim-pax.com/*>.

Regal China Cruises, ✆ (800) 808 3388 / (212) 768 3388, ✉ (212) 768 4939, <*recny@ aol.com*>, <*http://www.regalchinacruises.com/*>.

Smartour, ✆ (212) 297 0955, ✉ (212) 297 0965.

Sunshine Travel, ✆ (800) 850 2958 , ✉ (212) 268-6688, <*info@sunshinetravelusa.com*>, <*http://www.sunshinetravelusa.com/*>.

Victoria Cruises Inc., ☎ (800) 348 8084, (212) 818 1680, ✉ (212) 818 9889, <contact@victoriacruises.com>, <http://www.victoriacruises.com/>.

Visits Plus, ☎ (800) 321 3235, ✉ (212) 735 9171, <http://www.visitsplus.com/>.

USA west coast

Aberdeen Tours, ☎ (800) 282 8321, ✉ (213) 939 9769, <abdntours@aol.com>.

Asian Pacific Adventures, ☎ (800) 365 9989, (213) 935 3156, <travelasia@earthlink.net>.

China International Travel Service, GD, Inc., ☎ (800) 362 3839, ✉ (415) 989 3838, <http://www.citstours.com/>.

China International Travel Service (USA), ☎ (626) 568 8993, ✉ (626) 568 9207, <citslax@aol.com>, <http://www.citsusa.com/>.

China Travel Service (USA), Inc., ☎ (800) 899 8618, ✉ (415) 352 0399 <info@chinatravelservice.com>, <http://www.chinatravelservice.com/>.

China Voyages, ☎ (800) 914 9133, ✉ (415) 399 0827, <info@chinavoyages.com>, <http://www.chinavoyages.com/>.

Globus and Cosmos, ☎ (800) 338 7092, <http://www.globusandcosmos.com/>.

Grand American Travel Inc., ☎ (800) 868 8138, ✉ (888) 868 0593, <gatatt@worldnet.att.net>, <http://www.grand-travel.com/>.

Japan & Orient, Inc., ☎ (800) 377 1080, <http://www.jot.com/>.

Ritz Tours, ☎ (800) 900 2446, <http://www.ritztours.com/>.

Travcoa World Tours, ☎ (800) 992 2003, <requests@travcoa.com>, <http://www.travcoa.com/>.

CTS and CITS overseas offices

CTS claims to be China's oldest travel agency, as old as the People's Republic itself (although it can't have had very much to do for the first few decades of its existence), and its biggest. Originally CTS dealt with ethnic Chinese visitors to China, while CITS dealt with everybody else. A recognition of the benefits of market forces (while still calling it anything but, to save face) rather than accusations of racism, has now put these two companies into direct competition with each other, and they have the largest overseas networks and the biggest infrastructure in China.

They still handle matters on the ground for the majority of foreign companies, and charge them the same price they charge you. Ergo, contacting them in China, especially if you are there to haggle over the counter and reduce prices further, is the best idea (see 'Tour operators in Běijīng', below). But booking through a foreign company means that complaints about non-performance or sub-standard service (both quite likely) will be dealt with promptly and fairly and a refund obtained. This is by no means guaranteed if you book with CTS or CITS directly, although if you book through overseas offices you should be able to bring your country's trade laws to bear. Branches in different countries also charge different amounts for the land portions of the same tours—the Hong Kong branches being noticeably cheaper than the others.

For USA information, see above.

CITS main site: <http://www.cits.net/>.

CITS Australia Pty Ltd, 99 King Street, Melbourne 3000, ☎ (3) 9621 2198, ✉ (3) 9621-2919, <citsaust@travman.com.au>, <http//:www.travman.com.au/>.

CITS Denmark A/S, Ved Vesterport 4, DK-1612, Copenhagen V, ℗ 3391 0400, ✉ 3312 3688, <cits@cits.dk>, <http//:www.cits.dk/>.

CITS France S.A., 30 Rue de Gramont 75002, Paris, ℗ (331) 4286 8866, ✉ (331) 4286 8861, <china.international@wanadoo.fr/>.

CITS Hong Kong, 12-13 F, Tower A, New Mandarin Plaza, 14 Science Museum Rd, TST. Kowloon, ℗ 2732 5888, ✉ 2721 7154, <marketing@cits.com.hk>, <http//:www.cits. com.hk/>.

CITS Japan Ltd., 24-2 Shu Building, 6F, Shibuya 1-Chome, Shibuya-Ku, Tokyo 150, ℗ (03) 3499 1245, ✉ (03) 3499 1243, <cits-tky@magical3.egg.or.jp>, <http//:www.citsjapan.co. jp/>.

CITS Sweden, Gotgatan, 41, 1tr, 11621 Stockholm, ℗ (08) 702 2280, ✉ (08) 702 2330, <ianxz@swipnet.se>.

CTS main site: <http://www.ctsho.com/>.

CTS (Aust) Pty, 757-759 George St, Sydney NSW 2000, ℗ (02) 9211 2633, ✉ (02) 9211 3595.

China Travel Service (Canada) Inc., 556 West Broadway, Vancouver, B.C., V5Z 1E9, ℗ (604) 872 8787, ✉ (604) 873 2823; 438 University Avenue, Suite 306, Box 28 Toronto, Ont. M5G 2K8, ℗ (416) 979 8993 (416) 979 8220.

China Travel Service (France) S.A.R.L., 32, Rue Vignon, 75009 Paris, ℗ (1) 4451 5566, ✉ (1) 4451 5560.

China Travel & Trading (Deutschland) GmbH, Düsseldorfer Strasse 14, D-60329 Frankfurt/Main, ℗ (69) 238522, ✉ (69) 232324; Beusselstrasse 5, D-10553 Berlin, ℗ (30) 393 4068, ✉ (30) 391 8085.

CTS Hong Kong, Central Branch, G/F, China Travel Bldg, 77 Queen's Road Central , H.K., ℗ 2522 0450, Tsim Sha Tsui Branch, 1/F., Alpha House, 27-33 Nathan Road, Tsimshatsui Kowloon, ℗ 2315 7188, <http://www.hkcts.com/cts/english/index.html>.

China Travel Service (Japan) Co Ltd, T 103 Buyoo Building, 3-8-16, Nihombashi, Chuo-ku, Tokyo, ℗ (3) 3273 5512, ✉ (3) 3273 2667.

Singa China Travel Service Pte. Ltd, I Park Road # 03-49 to 52, People's Park Rd Complex, Singapore 059108, ℗ (65) 532 9988, ✉ (65) 535 4912.

China Travel Service (UK) Ltd, CTS House, 7 Upper St Martins Lane, London WC2H 9DL, ℗ (020) 7836 9911, ✉ (020) 7836 3121.

Tour Operators in Běijīng

This is a partial list of tour operators with licences to deal with inbound foreign tourists. You can call them to make arrangements for you, or to compare their prices with those offered by your hotel (which, however primitive, will certainly be offering *something*). Just as all kinds of ministries and industries have been opening hotels, so everybody is trying to get in on the act and milk tourism for all it's worth, as will be obvious from the names of some of the companies below. Even the innocuous 'Golden Bridge' was partly owned by the People's Liberation Army until the PLA was told to divest itself of all its businesses in 1999. At the beginning of that year the government also decided to permit Sino-foreign joint-ventures to operate in the travel sector, but only the Japanese giant JTB seemed in any hurry to set anything up. When there are more of these they will probably prove to be far more reliable than the existing operations.

The longest-established agencies (which doesn't necessarily recommend them, but they generally have the best English-speaking guides and still do most of the ground operations for inbound foreign groups) are:

China International Travel Service (CITS), ✆ 6601 1122, ✉ 6605 9512.
China Travel Service, (CTS), ✆ 6462 2288, ✉ 6461 2556.
China Youth Travel Service (CYTS), ✆ 6524 3388, ✉ 6524 9809.

Of the 300 or so agencies in Běijīng, others with licences to look after foreigners include:

China Civil International Tourist Inc., ✆ 6594 1188, ✉ 6592 6717.
China Cultural Tours Inc., ✆ 6615 0005, ✉ 6615 0004.
China Golden Bridge Travel Service, ✆ 6616 0543, ✉ 6201 8939.
China International Sports Travel, ✆ 6711 7364, ✉ 6711 7370.
China Nationality Travel Service, ✆ 6607 2737, ✉ 6602 3301.
China Posts & Telecom Tours, ✆ 6509 8010, ✉ 6509 8001.
China Supreme Harmony Travel Service, ✆ 6506 8833, ✉ 6508 5796.
China Swan International Tours, ✆ 6508 1166, ✉ 6508 1380.
China Women's Travel Service, ✆ 6513 0142, ✉ 6512 9021.
CITIC Travel Inc., ✆ 6466 1663, ✉ 6466 1598.
North International Travel Service, ✆ 6355 6932, ✉ 6354 7387.

Ignore the names—they'll all do anything for money, and can all arrange transport around Běijīng and on to other destinations in China.

NB: It is highly unwise to book with any Chinese travel agent or tour company directly from abroad, especially one discovered over the Internet. It will cost you much more than if you book in person, and many of those advertising (usually in places where they shouldn't) do not have the necessary licence to deal with foreigners or accept foreign currency, or have any real experience of the travel industry. You may lose every penny.

Practical A–Z

Books and Maps

For art books, antiquarian books and out-of-print accounts of Běijīng by travellers and former residents try Han-Shan Tang Books, Unit 3 Ashburton Centre, 276 Corbis Rd, **London** SW15 3AY, ℗ 0208 788 4464, @ 0208 780 1565, <hst@hanshan.com>, <http://www.hanshan.com/>. Their site has an efficiently updated searchable partial catalogue of their stock, which includes books in a wide variety of languages.

In the USA try Asian Rare Books, 175 W. 93rd Street (Suite 16-D), **New York** NY 10025, ℗ (212) 316 5334, @ (212) 316 3408, <arbs@erols.com>, <http://www.erols.com/arbs/>. Also try Paragon Books in **Chicago**, 1507 South Michigan Avenue, Chicago, IL 60605, ℗ 1 (800) 552 6657, (312) 663 5155, @ (312) 663 5177, <paragon@paragonbook.com>, <http://www.paragonbook.com/>. Useful non-specialist Internet-based databases of the stocks of several antiquarian booksellers include **Advanced Book Exchange** at <http://www.abe.com/> and **Bibliofind**, <http://www.bibliofind.com/>.

Various **guide books** on individual towns and provinces are published in English in China. Older ones detail the revolutionary credentials of the resident masses, and more recent ones the number of tonnes of concrete in the city's first overpass. The most recent of all have sketchy and inaccurate information which reflects what the Chinese wish to believe about themselves, but can also be wildly wrong for no particular reason at all. There's often little evidence that the places discussed have even been visited.

The Chinese were amongst the earliest known map-makers; by the 2nd century CE **maps** of most major settlements had been produced using principles set down four centuries earlier. Nineteen hundred years later this process seems to have run out of steam, and there is little attention paid to accuracy. Most cities that have maps (and not all do) only have them in Chinese characters, although Běijīng has bilingual maps and some other towns have 'tourist maps' (which only feature major roads and often can't even be bothered to get their names right). Whatever's available will be thrust at you on your way out of any railway station. Prices are always printed on the maps, and range from ¥2 to ¥5. Pocket-size and larger format **road atlases** are available in Xīnhuá Shūdiàn (the state-run bookshop with at least one branch in every city). The best place to look is Běijīng Book City, right outside the north exit of Ⓜ Xī Dān in Běijīng—a source for the reasonably detailed street atlas of Běijīng called the *Běijīng Shēnghuó Dìtúcè*, a similar volume on Tiānjīn, plus atlases and road maps covering individual provinces and some other cities. The books have no English, however, beyond at most the table of contents and the title of each map. Nevertheless, with a little patience you can compare the characters given in this book with those on the maps, which have far larger scales and much more detail than can be squeezed into a guide book. City maps also carry **bus routes** in detail, and those taking buses or planning to gull taxi drivers into believing that they know where they are should buy one for each city visited.

See also **Further Reading**, p.409.

Climate and When to Go

April and May are pleasant in Běijīng and surrounding areas, with winds from the Gobi clearing the skies. Until a few years ago these same winds would often bear large quantities of scouring sand, and rain would glue it to the streets and make them yellow, but massive forestation projects to the northwest have reduced this problem greatly. Visitors are still relatively few at this time, which helps to keep prices down too.

Běijīng's June can be flaming, sometimes producing successive 37–40°C days, and in July and August the humidity increases to uncomfortable levels, it rains quite frequently, and the city's electricity grid strains to cope with the ever-increasing numbers of air-conditioners. Sea breezes make it noticeably cooler in Tiānjīn and Shānhǎiguān, and this is also a good time to do as the emperors did and visit the mountain resort at Chéngdé.

China Daily may helpfully inform you that 'Persistent sunshine has also caused the temperature to rise'. Once, workers were allowed off work when the temperature reached certain heights. Desperate to finish preparations for the 1 October mega-rally in 1999, and faced with an extended heat wave, the newspapers consistently reported the temperature to be lower than it was.

September and October are Běijīng's most pleasant months, with warm, dry days and comfortable nights, starting to get a little chilly as November approaches. Breezes from the west may keep the skies blue for several days at a time. The trees change colour prettily, particularly in the green areas to the west of the city, and this gives added attraction to Xiāng Shān, Bā Dà Chù and western hillside temples such as Tánzhè Sì, as well as to the various wooded Great Wall sites. Peasants from areas near Běijīng descend on the capital to sell apples, persimmons, walnuts and satsumas from the back of truck, tricycle and horse cart, the fruit giving a splash of colour to the grey streets. Accommodation and transport can become a little more scarce in this period as the urban Chinese, who prefer to remain immobile in the summer heat, are taking to spending some of their disposable income on leisure travel, and do so when the temperature begins to drop.

On 15 November public buildings and apartment blocks in and around Běijīng are allowed to start up their heating systems, and the pollution worsens dramatically. Snow is possible from late November onwards. In January exterior temperatures can drop to –5°C at night, but even the meanest hotel is so overheated that you may feel the need to open the windows. In the daytime, although the temperatures aren't usually too far below zero, bitter winds require you to wrap up very warmly, especially for walks on the Great Wall and other unsheltered areas.

Spring Festival, or Chinese New Year, a lunar festival occurring in late-January or early February, should be avoided, as it's become the centre of a month-long orgy of domestic travel. In 2000 an unimaginable 1.6 *billion* trips were made during the Spring Festival period. Unless you are on a tour you will find it difficult to get either tickets or accommodation for around two weeks either side of this date. In 2000 transport operators were allowed to add 30% to ticket prices over the holiday period, and this differential may increase in future years. Expect prices for everything else associated with tourism to be higher, too.

Contraception

Condoms are widely available in Běijīng and other major Chinese cities, and familiar imported brands can often be found. These are likely to be considerably more reliable than local products: note too that popular prejudice is based on fact, and sizes made for Asian markets are smaller than those for the West. However, this presumably means that they are less likely to come off.

You will find more choice of imported brands in Běijīng then elsewhere in northern China. Branches of Hong Kong supermarkets have them, such as Park 'n' Shop, Watson's and Wellcome, mostly located in the basements of larger malls such as those along Cháng'ān Jiē, in Wángfǔjǐng and Cháoyáng Mén Wài Dàjiē. Also look in larger pharmacies, marked with a green cross.

All extra-marital sex is officially frowned upon in China, but is on the increase, as are sexually transmitted diseases (about which there is almost total ignorance), and prostitution. One city charges a 'sin tax' on unmarried couples who live together. Another fines women ¥200–¥2000 ($24–$240) if they prove not to be virgins during a required pre-marital check-up. In 1998–9 there were widespread protests at a proposal to make extra-marital affairs illegal.

Doctors involved in family planning in the countryside tell stories which are simultaneously horrifying and funny, in which women given condoms imagined they were some kind of medicine, deep-fried them and ate them, while others, following the demonstration given by the doctor, rolled them onto their husbands' fingers before sex. Oral contraceptives are sometimes taken vaginally since peasants can't work out how something taken 'up here' could affect something happening 'down there'. All of which proves that the best form of contraception is education, but the government spends less per head on that than almost any other country in the world, and while in 1999 one department produced a public information announcement for television promoting condom use to prevent the spread of infectious diseases, another promptly banned it on the grounds that sex-related products may not be advertised on television. This must have been particularly galling for the production team, which auditioned 50 actors, all of whom turned down the job when told they had to play HIV-positive people. The department concerned eventually had to pay five times the going rate to get anyone to participate, such is the prejudice against carriers of the disease and actors' concern for their personal image.

If a Chinese women sleeps with a foreigner she may get herself into serious trouble if caught, but this is less likely if the foreigner is of Chinese descent. It's also less likely to cause problems if a foreign woman sleeps with a Chinese man. Students coming to China often have to sit through lectures on this and related topics from the local police. These tend to fall on deaf ears, not least because they are in Mandarin, a language that most have yet to master. Homosexuality is scarcely recognized as existing and certainly not tolerated, although several nightclubs and bars in Běijīng, and at least one public park, are recognized gay hang-outs.

See also **Health**, p.33.

Crime

Although the police seem to be everywhere, they are never around when you need them. The policeman who is an onlooker to a fight in the street will tell you that he belongs to the 'economic police' and will show his shoulder flash to prove that it's not his business to get involved.

Other than overcharging, there is very little for foreign visitors to China to fear. Crimes of violence against foreigners tend to get wide publicity and be talked about in expat communities for months, but this merely emphasizes how unusual they are, although crimes of all kinds are on the rise. The government's response is a 'Strike Hard' policy, which leads to the execution of thousands every year, some for minor offences. Your main concern should be stealthy theft, but if you do catch a thief in the act, think twice before handing him over to the authorities, since you might not agree that the punishment, from being given a life-threatening beating through three years' hard labour without trial to execution, fits the crime.

Wearing a money belt *beneath* your clothes is advisable, containing all important documents and money that you are unlikely to need during the day. Particular care against pickpockets should be taken in crowded bus and railway stations, when bording or alighting from buses, and on the buses themselves. Despite the vast numbers of observers, theft on trains is on the increase. Ask the *fúwùyuán* (attendant) to lock your soft sleeper compartment if you are going for a platform stroll during a long stop or to the dining car and the compartment is otherwise going to be empty. Keep valuables away from the windows of the train, if they can be opened, as snatching from platforms is not unknown. Some travellers have taken to chaining their bags to the racks, although the razoring of bags is on the increase. Hotels are generally safe and staff trustworthy. Greater caution is obviously needed when staying in a dormitory.

Keep your perception of other risks in perspective. There are a few stories of visitors disappearing in some remote parts of China, but not those dealt with in this book. Occasional bomb blasts, earthquakes and rioting are considerably less likely to injure you than crossing the street (or even crossing the street in your home town). Nevertheless the British Foreign Office often advises British independent travellers to register with them (in Běijīng ✆ 6532 1961/5, ✉ 6532 1030, <*britvisa@public.bta.net.cn*>), as does the US State Department (in Běijīng ✆ 6532 3431/3831, after-hours 65321910; ✉ 6532 4153/3178, <*http://www. usembassy-china.org.cn/*>), which frequently issues warnings against venturing into certain parts of Běijīng, and in particular the Sānlǐtún Bar Street, which does tend to be the location for problems when the government has been whipping up anti-foreign feeling, never far below the surface.

Foreign governments always err on the side of caution when issuing travel advice, but you may wish to check with the relevant department before leaving home. For the UK view: ✆ (020) 7238 4503/4, <*http://www.fco.gov.uk/travel/*>, BBC TV CEEFAX p.470. For the USA <*http://travel.state.gov/china.html*>.

Electricity

220 volts, 50 cycles AC. Most sockets will take both the North American style two flat pins and the European two round pin type. In all but the very oldest buildings there is more than one alternative socket at each point, and this often also includes a three flat-pin arrangement familiar to Australians. Better hotels in Běijīng are often constructed to Hong Kong specifications and have the chunky three-pins familiar to the British, but at this level housekeeping will provide you with the adaptor or transformer of your choice.

If you get stuck, adaptors can easily be bought in department stores. Shaver sockets will only be found in the more modern and expensive hotels. Bring a battery powered shaver or use more traditional techniques. There can be problems with power surges, and those with laptops would be wise to ensure that their voltage converters are robust.

China has embassies in major capitals the world over and many consulates in larger regional cities, especially if these also have substantial Chinese expatriate populations. In general, unless you live in a city with a consulate, always apply to the embassy in your capital. It is better, whenever possible, to get your visa before leaving home unless your route into mainland China takes you through Hong Kong, where various types of visas are easily obtained either through agents or directly from the Chinese government.

The web page <*http://www.cnto.org/visaform.htm*> has a downloadable visa application form and accompanying notes. You'll need the Adobe Acrobat reader (a free, cross-platform document-reading utility you can download via the same site, if you don't have it).

in Australia

Embassy of the People's Republic of China: 15 Coronation Drive, Yarralumla, Canberra ACT 2600, ☎ (02) 6273 4783.

Chinese consulates: 539 Elizabeth Street, Surry Hills, Sydney, NSW 2010, ☎ (02) 9699 2216; 75–77 Irving Road, Toorak, Melbourne, VIC 3142, ☎ (03) 9822 0606; Level 3, Australia Place, 15–17 William Street, Perth, WA 6000, ☎ (08) 9481 3278.

in Canada

Embassy of the People's Republic of China: 511 St Patrick Street, Ottawa, K1N 5H3, ☎ (613) 234 2706, 789 9608.

Chinese consulates: 3380 Granville Street, Vancouver BC, V6H 3K3, ☎ (604) 736 3910; 240 St George St, Toronto, ON M5R 2P4, ☎ (416) 324 6455.

in Germany

Consular services will also shortly be available to Berlin.

Embassy of the People's Republic of China: Kurfürstenallee 12, 53177 Bonn, ☎ (228) 361095.

Chinese consulates: Heinrich-Mann-Strasse 9, 13156 Berlin; Elbchaussee 268, 22605 Hamburg; Romanstrasse 107, 80639 München.

in Holland

Embassy of the People's Republic of China: Adriaan Goekooplaan 7, The Hague, ☎ (70) 3551515.

in Hong Kong

In Hong Kong it's better to use an agency, but be careful to choose the right one. Hung Shing Travel Service, Room 711, 7/F New East Ocean Centre, 9 Science Museum Road, Tsim Sha Tsui East, ☎ 2369 3188, obtains L or F visas the same day and more cheaply than the better known backpacker agents around Nathan Road; six-month multiple-entry F visa HK$450. China International Travel Service charges up to HK$980 for the same service.

in New Zealand

Embassy of the People's Republic of China: 2–6 Glenmore St, Wellington, ☎ (4) 472-13823.

in the UK

Embassy of the People's Republic of China: 49 Portland Place, London W1N 3AH, ℡ (020) 7636 8845. Consular/Visa Section: 31 Portland Place W1N 3AG, ℡ (020) 7636 1835, 631 1430. 24-hour visa information (premium rate call), ℡ (0891) 880808, <*http:// www.chinese-embassy.org.uk/*>

Chinese consulate: Denison House, Denison Road, Victoria Park, Manchester M14 5RX, ℡ (0161) 224 7443.

in the USA

Embassy of the People's Republic of China: 2300 Connecticut Avenue NW, Washington, DC 20008, ℡ (202) 328 2517.

Chinese consulates: 520 12th Avenue, New York 10036, ℡ (212) 279 4275, 330 7409 (for residents of New York, Pennsylvania, Massachusetts, Connecticut, Vermont, New Hampshire, Rhode Island, Maine, New Jersey and Ohio); 104 Sth Michigan Ave, Suite 900, Chicago 60603, ℡ (312) 803 0095 (for Illinois, Indiana, Michigan, Minnesota, Wisconsin, Iowa, Missouri, Kansas and Colorado); 3417 Montrose Blvd, Houston, Texas 77006, ℡ (713) 526-4311 (for Texas, Louisiana, Mississippi, Alabama, Georgia, Florida, Arkansas and Oklahoma); 1450 Laguna St, San Francisco 94115, ℡ (415) 928 6931 (for Northern California, Oregon, Nevada, Washington or Alaska); 502 Shatto Place, Suite 300, Los Angeles 90020, ℡ (213) 380 2506 (for Southern California, Arizona, New Mexico and Hawaii). Residents of all other states should apply to the Washington embassy.

Entertainment

In China karaoke is king, in some cases spilling out of bars and restaurants onto the pavements, and not just the sound, but the equipment and the 'singers' too. There are increasing numbers of nightclubs which alternate karaoke and dancing through the evening. In all these places drink prices tend to be high, sometimes astronomical. If male, beware the pretty girl who comes over to talk to you. Conversing with her may be adding ¥200 ($25) or more to the bill, even if you don't speak Mandarin. It may even nudge it into four figures. Large gentlemen will insist you pay. Běijīng has a number of fairly conventional disco nightclubs without these probems, but they are not likely to impress serious clubbers from developed nations.

Běijīng also has areas of wannabe foreign bars catering to the kind of expat who wants to forget that he or she is in China and is willing to pay five or six times the going rate for a beer in order to suspend disbelief for a while. These bars also attract Chinese with a little money who want to stare at the foreigners living a foreign lifestyle, and those who have a genuine interest in foreigners, usually the employees of Sino-foreign joint venture companies or girls looking for foreign boyfriends, whose apparent affection may or may not be less genuine.

Traditional Chinese entertainments such as Chinese opera and acrobatics are available in bigger cities or wherever visitors gather in sufficient numbers. However, these are usually in edited-for-tourists versions where there will be few Chinese in the audience, although those that are will talk, eat and drink their way through the performance, leaving behind mounds of sunflower seed husks and peanut shells. Nevertheless, there are some beautifully restored old theatres in Běijīng and Běijīng opera should be tried at least once, as should a performance of traditional music (*see* 'Entertainment, Culture and Nightlife' p.271).

Younger people are at home with the VCD player watching pirated copies of Western and Hong Kong films. Although (until trade agreements bring changes) only 10 or so foreign films are picked for release in China each year, most are out in VCD within a week of opening in their country of origin. Those shown on the big screen are dubbed, and although you can take the opportunity to see the latest Zhāng Yìmóu or Chén Kǎigē epic before they win something at Cannes or Venice, there will be no subtitles unless you are fortunate enough to get a print made for Hong Kong.

Festivals and Public Holidays

Chinese public holidays: 1 Jan, Chinese New Year (Spring Festival), a lunar holiday around the beginning of February, 1, 2 and 3 May (Labour Day), 1, 2 and 3 Oct (National Day—founding of the PRC). Offices and businesses will be closed on these days. Chinese New Year officially lasts for three days, but its impact is much greater as all public transport is booked for days either side by everybody heading home for family reunions and feasting. Unless you're on an organized tour, being in China at that time means staying put in one place. Watch out for the government's newly developed habit of making long public holidays at short notice, particularly around 1 May and 1 October. Travel then can also be difficult.

Other holidays which receive observance by parts of society include 8 March (International Women's Day), 4 May (Youth Day), 1 June (Children's Day), 1 July (Anniversary of the founding of the Chinese Communist Party) and 1 Aug (Anniversary of the Founding of the PLA).

Important traditional festivals with no official day off, all lunar, include the Lantern Festival sometime between mid-February and mid-March (lantern hanging and riddle posing), the early April Tomb Sweeping Day (visiting and tidying grave sites, paying respect to ancestors), the Dragon Boat Festival in mid-June (boat races, special snacks), and the Mid-Autumn Festival in late September or early October (moon watching and 'moon cakes').

Observance of festival traditions has been undergoing a slight and cautious revival, and tends to focus on those from which money can be made, such as the revival of temple fairs, rather than those which require effort such as tomb sweeping (although cremation is anyway now the norm in China). Going to one of Běijīng's parks to drink and look at the autumnal full moon is increasingly popular, but catching a glimpse of it through the pollution increasingly difficult.

Lamaist/Buddhist festivals: These are all lunar and seem to vary from temple to temple, often attracting large numbers of serious-minded Tibetans and Mongolians and crowds of gawping onlookers. If you can establish when these dates are by the solar calendar you are likely to see 'sunning the Buddha', elaborate religious dances and mass chanting, accompanied by colourful fairs. In Běijīng the Lama Temple has a long-standing tradition of religious dances ('devil dances') at Tibetan New Year, also lunar and slightly later than Chinese New Year.

Food and Drink

'Last week, in class, he cursed the whole Chinese race. He said we lived only for our bellies, that we have combed earth and sky and sea for anything remotely edible, and that we should long ago have become cannibals if human flesh happened to be more delicious than pork!'

John Blofeld, *City of Lingering Splendour,* 1961

The Chinese eat all sorts of things that much of the rest of the world would shy from, but for those who prefer to stick to recognizable parts of the animal and vegetable kingdoms, there's no need to fear. The names of staple dishes, and the characters for a range of meats and vegetables are given in **Language**, p.403, and the characters for local specialities described in the text are given alongside it. If your impression of your own country is that most Chinese people work in restaurants, you may leave China with the view that the same is true there, too. Since private businesses once again became permissible there has been an explosion of growth in food operations of all kinds, from pavement noodle stalls to marble-floored mirror-balled karaoke dinner and dance parlours. Unless you live in a city with a large Chinatown and only eat in the places Chinese eat, the Chinese food in China is often *better* than anything you'll have had before, which will have been adapted for the Western palate.

Waitresses stand over you from the moment that they give you the menu. Minority and speciality restaurants aside, it rarely contains surprises, usually consisting of a greatest hits list of the main Chinese cooking schools. The Chinese discuss amongst themselves what they want to eat and then look in the menu to see how much it is. They discuss with the waitress what's good, where the cook comes from, whether he makes such-and-such a dish particularly salty, and give instructions as to the adjustment of seasonings. As your waitress is waiting to have this kind of conversation, she may either become impatient or good-naturedly start making recommendations, always of the higher priced dishes. In heavily touristed areas, letting the waitress decide for you will seriously damage your wallet. In mainstream Hàn restaurants if you don't see what you like on the menu, don't worry—just ask and it can always be made, as long as it's Chinese. While a few dishes have poetic names that don't give much idea of their contents, most simply include a cooking verb and the ingredients. Despite the simplicity of many of the dishes, no two restaurants produce them tasting exactly the same. Take with you to China a photocopy of a local restaurant's bilingual menu, and try ordering with that. Note that the characters used will be full form, rather than the simpler modern style, and so won't correspond exactly to what you see in China, but should be understood by the staff nevertheless.

Roadside noodle stalls and hole-in-the-wall restaurants don't have much of a menu, and it's often written up in chalk on the wall. Only restaurants that are used to tourists have an English menu, and this can often be a bad sign. Outside the joint-venture and top flight hotels it will frequently have higher prices than the Chinese language one for the same dishes. If this turns out to be the case, leave.

If there are credit card signs on the door, then prices will be higher but only the surroundings will improve (and usually only Chinese credit cards will be acceptable). If your chopsticks are sealed in sellophane or printed paper sleeves, if there's a small packet of tissues next to your plate, or if the tea cup is a small lidded bowl containing a mixture of tea, herbs and dried berries looking like a handful of builders' rubble, expect a cover charge of ¥5–10 per person. (The tea, known as 'Eight Treasures Tea', also contains a lump of rock sugar and has a very refreshing fruitiness.) There will usually be no cutlery, only chopsticks, so practise using these at your local Chinese restaurant before you leave home. If there *is* cutlery, you are probably eating in a restaurant inside a Běijīng international standard hotel, and your surroundings will be rather more pleasant than your bill.

Always avoid restaurants near major tourist attractions. Food will be poor, portions half-size, prices mysteriously in the hundreds rather than tens of *yuán* range, whatever the menu said, and there may be considerable unpleasantness if you refuse to succumb to this extortion. Chinese tourists suffer similar humiliations at these places, if not on quite the same scale.

Also avoid restaurants around Wángfǔjǐng and near other areas with four- and five-star hotels which clearly have Chinese and not foreign food, and which advertise in English that they have English menus. This almost always means that you are going to be fleeced. The Tian Run Pulses Flower Restaurant at Wángfǔjǐng's Dēngshìkǒu Dōng Jiē 100, for instance, advertises an English menu which turns out to have double the prices, but whose existence will be denied altogether should you subsequently go in with a Chinese. The food is excellent, but the experience leaves a sour taste all the same. The Banpo Primitive Hotpot Beer Hut, an imitation cave in a basement opposite the Wángfǔjǐng Grand Hotel in Wángfǔjǐng Dàjiē, is worth mentioning not so much for its bizarre menu, which includes scorpions, locusts, cicadas, ants, worms, poplar, willow and prickly ash, but as another example of what drives visitors away from China. An advertising leaflet offers a 10% discount which never appears, and the English language menu has prices double those of the Chinese language one, which mysteriously disappears when you ask to see it as if no one who speaks Chinese ever eats there.

In all restaurants point to the prices of dishes as you order, and keep a total so that the waitress knows that you know. Shenanigans with the bill are commonplace. Don't allow staff to shepherd you into a private room, as prices will immediately begin to rise, and exorbitant demands can be made from you while you are safely out of sight of other customers. There is no tipping, no service charge, and no charge for chopsticks or tea (except as mentioned above). Never let yourself run low on small change, so that where there are attempts to overcharge you can leave exactly the right money on the table and walk out.

Breakfast is perhaps the most difficult and unsatisfactory meal for the Western palate, since plain thin rice gruel, plain steamed bread rolls and pickles are all most Chinese restaurants can manage outside the five-star hotels. The arrival in Běijīng of Starbucks coffee shops from the USA has broadened the options, however, and in most cities there are branches of well-known US fast food chains. At street stalls there will be oily deep-fried dough sticks (*yóutiáo*), and small pots of yoghurt in most areas. You may want to skip straight to dishes that would equally do for lunch, such as noodle soups, relatives of ravioli (*jiǎozi*), fried variants (*guōtiē*) or *bāozi* (steamed, stuffed buns). Single bowl noodle dishes come in a variety of forms. There are noodles in soup (*tāngmián*) and fried ones (*chǎomián*).

In China people rarely eat alone, and restaurant dining is based around the proposition that a group will order several dishes and share them. Rice is a filler, not a constituent part of the meal, and the habit of bringing it with the main dishes at Chinese restaurants in the West indicates the origin of most of them in Guǎngdōng (Canton), where this is the norm. But in northern China if you want the rice for eating *with* your main dishes rather than after them you'll have to ask for it (*Qǐng nǐ xiànzài lái mǐfàn*). Where there are two columns of prices, the lower one is for slightly smaller portions—usually the smaller dishes are still 70–80% of the original and you'll save perhaps ¥2–5 on a ¥18 dish. Note that minimum order charges are illegal in Běijīng.

Chinese cooking tends to leave the bone in the chopped meat, and you separate bone from meat in your mouth and put the rejected bones on the table in a pile at the side of your plate. To avoid this, select dishes with the key characters *sī* (shreds), *piàn* (slices), or *dīng* (boneless pieces)—*see* **Language**, p.403. Fish and seafood should generally be avoided, certainly outside of Běijīng and the further you go west. Fish on sale is often farmed and tasteless, as well as bony, and there is no guarantee that frozen seafood has been properly kept. **Vegetarians** will have no problems in China, except occasionally in making themselves understood. Useful phrases are given in the language section, p.406. In addition to vegetables stir-fried in a variety of ways, there are various *dòufu* (tofu) dishes, noodle soups without meat and other standards such as egg fried with tomato. If in doubt, go to the kitchen (easily achievable with a little mime) and simply point to the vegetables you want cooked together. Occasionally you may meet with incomprehensible protests based on the supposed incompatibility of certain 'sour' with certain 'sweet' vegetables, but in the end what the crazy *lǎo wài* wants will be produced. Běijīng now has several vegetarian restaurants, some specializing in reproducing Chinese meat and seafood dishes using only vegetable protein and others catering for the expat market serving more conventional vegetarian food. In Běijīng, too, Italian, Indian and other foreign cuisines add to the available options. Vegans, however, may have difficulties, and should come well supplied with supplements.

Pork is the main meat of the Chinese (often called *dà ròu* 'great meat'), but beef and lamb are also widely eaten in Běijīng, appearing as kebabs (*kǎoròuchuànr*), in noodle dishes and a wide variety of other forms.

One considerable annoyance when eating out in China is a centuries-old game played wherever groups of men are dining together. Two players each simultaneously thrust out one hand with a number of fingers showing and bellow a number which they guess will be equal to the total number of fingers displayed (so between zero and ten). This is rhythmically repeated until someone gets the answer right, when his opponent is required to 'drink a cup'. As the game proceeds and the drunkenness increases, the volume becomes ever louder, and since several games may be progressing at different tables, staying in the restaurant may become intolerable. What puzzles visitors most is that, while shop assistants are universally incapable of adding together two numbers without using an abacus or calculator, these men can simultaneously shout one number, show another, and add two numbers together, all while drunk.

Drinking

The best drink, and usually the safest, is **tea**—*chá* . Tea automatically comes with your meal in China, and is free. If you want to add milk or sugar to Chinese tea you'll need to carry it with you, as most restaurants will (quite rightly) find this incomprehensible. There are thermoses of boiled water in all hotel rooms in China, however primitive, and thermoses or boilers on trains, so carry tea with you. Good **coffee** is now easily available in Běijīng, but still hard to find in provincial towns—that in foreign fast food outlets, if they exist, being the nearest you'll find to the real thing. Instant coffee sachets from Western manufacturers are available in supermarkets, and in versions where the coffee has already been mixed with some powdered milk and a little sugar.

Locally produced **mineral water** is widely available, as are imported brands, mostly from France, for about five times the price. Do not drink unboiled tap water or even brush your teeth with it (use mineral water or boiled water that's been left to cool instead).

There is no escape from the **soft drink** multinationals. Coca-Cola already has 17 plants in China and sells more than six billion cans and bottles a year, about three times as much as Pepsi, also present. Local competitors tend to be rather ersatz with the exception of the orange and honey flavoured sports drink, Jiànlìbǎo ('build strength treasure'), now in decline. Bottled and canned fruit juices are available at glitzier groceries.

Alcohol is most commonly consumed in China in the form of beer (*píjiǔ*), made in a lager style inherited from a turn-of-the-century German brewery still in production in Qīngdǎo on the east coast. China is now the world's second largest beer producer and there are dozens of brands on offer, although most of them only have localized distribution. There has recently been expansion into producing other varieties, such as a disgusting 'black beer' and a very good wheat beer. Hangovers are the least of your worries. The greatest danger from beer in recent times has been from the companies' overuse of the same bottles, and the use of bottles for vinegar and other products lacking sufficient strength for pressurised liquids. Several people have been killed by exploding bottles.

Chinese wine-making (*pútaojiǔ*) has been making good progress with French assistance, and the widely available *Dragon Seal* is a good table wine in both red and white. 'Wine' is commonly used in translation for all kinds of other alcoholic drinks which have nothing to do with grapes, including *bái jiǔ* ('white spirits') made from rice or sorghum, some of which are pleasant and tame to the palate but can unexpectedly bite you if you over-indulge.

With the exception of the odd uninforced local regulation, there is no legal drinking age, and anyone call sell or buy liquor of any kind.

Food on the Move

Several foreign manufactures are now producing biscuits (cookies), chocolate and other familiar snacks which make the best accompaniments to bus travel. On trains you can take advantage of the boiled water (*kāi shuǐ*) from thermos or boiler to make the instant noodles available in shops, or at bus and railway station kiosks. Carrying a mug is essential. A wide range of fruits in syrup (*tángshuǐ*) are sold, such as *tángshuǐmìjú* (mandarin orange segments in syrup), which can make a refreshing change in hot weather. The jars these fruits come in you will already have seen being used by office workers, bus drivers and just about everyone else to carry eternally topped-up brews of swamp-bottom tea. Chinese attempts at Western bread tend to be very white, dry and sweet, although bakeries in Běijīng provide the real thing. Easily portable, safe and easy-to-eat fruits include bananas and mandarin oranges (satsumas) in season. Apples and pears *must* be peeled, and with care (*see* 'Health', below).

Guides

Guides in China are usually employees of either one of China's rapacious travel agents or of sites. Some know their material quite well, but few can produce more than a prepared script, or have any idea of an alternative to the government-approved view. Those employed at sites tend to be better than those belonging to agencies. Only the most major sites have guides who can speak English, and very few indeed who can speak any other language. Be particularly careful if your tour guide takes you shopping. The choice of shop is almost certainly not fortuitous, and the guide, however pleasant, is not an independent and trustworthy advisor, but someone who will later be picking up commission from the shop.

In Běijīng you may occasionally be approached by students or young professionals wishing to improve their English, and who offer to show you around. This is a *quid pro quo*, not a paid arrangement, although you should offer to cover entrance fees and transport costs, and it's an excellent opportunity to get a first-hand account of daily life in China. Don't expect detailed historical or cultural information from your 'guide'.

Be aware that in some cases these pleasant young people intend to attract you into some scam or other. The long-standing 'I am an art student' game from Xī'ān has made its appearance in the capital, particularly in Liúlichǎng and Dàzhàlán Jiē. This is relatively harmless but wastes your time by dragging you into a shop so that you can be monstrously overcharged for 'unique' paintings. Worse is the person who purports to want to practise their English and takes you to a private room at the back of a bar where a pretty girl comes and sings karaoke. The bill may run to four digits.

Běijīng Tourism Authority now issues ID cards to bonafide guides, which you should ask to inspect if someone describes themselves as a professional guide.

Health

'They say it's a very healthy post, and perfectly suitable for children,'
replied Grant-Howard in the completely colourless tone which in diplo-
macy implies doubt. 'The riding,' he went on more briskly, 'is first class,
and the cheapest in the world. Quite average ponies for a tenner, and
plenty of polo.'

Ann Bridge, *The Ginger Griffin*, 1934

At least the main characters in this particular novel survived, but in *Peking Picnic*, another Bridge novel, one falls ill and is dead in 24 hours, an event treated as regrettable but commonplace by the diplomatic community of her day.

What follows is a general introduction to the health problems you may encounter and how to avoid or deal with them. But remember that new medicines are constantly being developed, medical opinion about the best method of treatment sometimes changes, and the health problems themselves change. Family doctors are rarely right up-to-date on travel medicine, but should be able to point you to specialist travel clinics and hospital tropical medicine departments. Consulting a specialist is absolutely vital, especially if you are pregnant or travelling with children. As some vaccinations cannot be taken together or involve multiple injections, make contact at least three months before you plan to travel. In most developed countries these injections are no longer free, if they ever were, and if you need to have several the expense can be considerable. None is absolutely 100% effective, and reducing risk by cautious eating, attention to hygiene, and the use of insect repellents is also important. However, keep risks in proportion: You are far more likely to die in a road accident within in mile or two of your own home than from any disease picked up in or around Běijīng.

The Center for Disease Control in Atlanta maintains a website with up-to-date information set out country by country, <*http://www.cdc.gov/*>.

Before You Leave

Immunization against typhus in 1935 Běijīng:

They were thin, wrinkled, resigned old men; beggars by profession.
They sat on three hard chairs in a small room opening off a laboratory
and full of guinea-pigs in cages. Their ragged trousers were rolled up

above their knees and to the dwindled calves of each were clamped a number of little shallow boxes. The sides of the boxes which pressed against the flesh were made of gauze, or something like it; and each box contained 500 lice. For two hours every day, and for the wage of twelve Chinese dollars a month, the three old men pastured, between them, some 18,000 lice.

Peter Fleming, *News from Tartary*, 1936

The essence of 30 lice went into each of the three necessary anti-typhus injections. Although Fleming is here describing a Western clinic, some believe that the idea of variolation, the transmission of matter from one human to another to prevent disease, was in use in China in the late Míng, and perhaps even earlier.

Begin by making sure that the basic immunizations you should have even at home are up to date, and get boosters if necessary. These include **polio, diphtheria** and **tetanus.**

In China it is best to carry as much paperwork as possible, including one of the internationally recognized yellow booklets giving a record of vaccinations, the *International Certificate of Vaccination*. Health checks are rarely made except at land borders, and even there are usually perfunctory for visitors from developed nations.

The need for other inoculations will depend on exactly where you travel in China and the time of year. If you plan to stay mainly in urban areas, mosquito-borne diseases such as malaria and Japanese B Encephalitis are best avoided by use of clothing, repellent, and insecticide impregnated nets on short trips out of town, although there is no malaria risk in any town discussed in this book. However, inoculation may be advised for the following:

Typhoid fever, caught from contaminated food and water. There are two possible regimens. A single injection, which requires a booster every three years if you will be repeatedly travelling in affected areas, or an oral vaccine in three doses taken on alternate days with a validity of one to three years depending on exposure.

Meningococcal meningitis, an infection of the lining of the brain caught from others with the disease in the same way you catch a cold. A single injection covers you for three years.

Cholera, an infection of the intestine from which existing vaccines only provide partial protection, and are now rarely offered.

If you are arriving from a country with **yellow fever,** you may be asked for proof of vaccination, which in some countries is only available from a limited number of specialist centres.

Hepatitis comes in a form communicated quite easily through shared utensils and low hygiene (hepatitis A), and in more dangerous forms that require the exchange of body fluids (mainly hepatitis B). Immunization against hepatitis A is important because of poor hygiene standards, and many doctors recommend immunization against hepatitis B to avoid further complications should you receive emergency treatment with contaminated blood or equipment. Both diseases attack the liver and cause weakness and lassitude, but hepatitis B can be life-threatening. For hepatitis A one injection gives one year's protection, and a second a year later will cover you for at least 10 years. For hepatitis B there are two injections given one month apart and a booster six months later, giving 90% protection for a lifetime. (Fans of alternative medicine may like to know that the Chinese Ministry of Health and the State

Administration of Traditional Chinese Medicine recommend an intravenous drip made from 'sophora-rhubarb' to cure viral hepatitis.)

Japanese B Encephalitis is a severe brain infection carried by mosquitoes to which you may be exposed in rural areas, especially during rainy periods. Three injections are needed over a one-month period to give two years of coverage which can be boosted if necessary.

Mosquito-born **malaria** comes in various forms, and you may need to take two different prophylactic drugs, depending upon the time you travel and whether you venture into rural areas. You must begin to take these drugs two weeks *before* you enter an affected area, and *for four weeks after you leave it.* Dangers vary over time, but at the time of writing, if you are staying within the areas covered by this book, malarial prophylaxis may not be necessary. If venturing into malarial areas, ignore scare stories about side-effects of malarial medication and insist on taking it—in this case the dangers of illness far outweigh the risks, and the medication should be backed up with serious attempts to avoid being bitten. Cover up exposed skin from sundown onwards, wear repellent, and use insecticide impregnated bed nets. Pregnant women need to take particular care.

While You Are There

Colds and sore throats are the common lot of those travelling in China for more than the briefest of periods, so if there is a proprietary medicine you usually use for relief, bring a supply with you. The causes are the general lack of hygiene in China (particularly the spitting, which can also transmit diphtheria, meningitis and other illnesses) and the lack of resistance to unfamiliar versions of these everyday diseases. Spitting has a long history:

> And everyone of the chiefs and nobles carries with him a handsome little vessel to spit in whilst he remain in the Hall of Audience—for no one dares spit on the floor of the hall,—and when he hath spitten he covers it up and puts it aside.

> Marco Polo, *The Travels*, 13th century, Yule-Cordier edition

For some these problems come in the slightly more serious form of upper respiratory tract infections. Chinese doctors will prescribe low doses of antibiotics, sometimes with additional Chinese medicines, or you can ask your doctor at home to prescribe a course of broad spectrum antibiotic to take with you. Remember, however, that Běijīng has one of the highest levels of air pollution on the planet, and although leaded petrol has been banned and substantially cleaner air is promised over the coming years, for now airborne particulates remain as high as 10 times the internationally recommended maximum—enough to give many people respiratory problems for a while which antibiotics won't cure. Westerners have in general taken far too many in the past, and caution should be used. If you do begin, make sure you complete the course. Around 800 million Chinese cook on coal, much of it of extremely low quality and laced with arsenic, fluorine, lead and mercury, contaminants which can also make their way into foods dried over coal, such as peppers, and later added to other dishes. While short-term exposure carries little risk of danger, keep clear of the dense clouds of smoke rising from roughly rigged roadside food stalls and the blueish haze inside some hole-in-the-wall restaurants.

Diarrhoea, vomiting and a variety of **bowel problems** are commonplace, and caused by poor toilet hygiene and bad food. Wash your hands as often as you can (usually not possible at public toilets in the street, so go into hotels and familiar Western fast food outlets) and make use of the bathroom in your room (if you have one) in preference to other options. If faced with ancient gnawed chopsticks demand disposable ones, universally available (small particles of food embedded in chopsticks can also transmit hepatitis A). Do not drink the water—this is no time to be macho, not even local people do. Drink tea, bottled water and soft drinks. Everywhere you go there are thermoses of boiled water to hand, even on trains and in the most undistinguished backwater hotel. Boiling won't get rid of the heavy metals and other contaminants in the water, but is fairly successful at killing bacteria. Upmarket hotels have their own water purification systems with a separate tap for drinking water in the bathroom (notably Běijīng's Palace Hotel), and the others supply a free bottle of local mineral water per person per day (although in recent government tests fewer than 50% of them reached an adequate standard, whatever that may have been).

Remember in China that the waste you deposit in the public lavatory today is tomorrow's fertilizer. Do not swim in China's lakes or rivers. Do not eat salads or any fruit that cannot be peeled and, having touched the outside, don't touch the inside before eating. Avoid fruit with damaged and broken skin, and all water melons. Eat only piping hot food that has been freshly cooked for you. Do not walk around bare foot. All these measures will help you avoid parasitic infections. If you do get diarrhoea, it is essential to replace lost fluids. Take with you a few sachets of oral rehydration salts which can be dissolved in mineral water or in boiled water which has been allowed to cool. This is far better than taking anti-diarrhoea tablets. Seek help if diarrhoea is bloody or extremely profuse.

As mentioned above, cases of **sexually transmitted diseases** are rapidly increasing in China, particularly gonorrhoea and syphilis, both extremely nasty and increasingly resistant to treatment. Visiting students and other long-stayers are asked to provide proof of a recent AIDS test, but not those on tourist visas.

China admitted to 15,088 HIV-positive patients across the country in September 1999, but experts estimated the real number of suffers to be around 400,000, two thirds of them under 30. Amongst China's rapidly increasing numbers of drug addicts the infection rate is estimated at 70%. However, heterosexual sex is now the world's most common method of transmission. Amongst its many other 'greats' and 'betters', China claims to have a wider variety of types of AIDS strains than anywhere else, with eight different types identified so far. There's widespread ignorance about sexually transmitted diseases of all kinds, once known to Chinese medicine by names such as 'plum poison', and 'white mud', and still the subject of rumour, superstition and hearsay. About 750,000 cases are reported per annum, but since embarrassment and the availability of penicillin and other drugs over the counter play a role, the true number is probably far greater.

Inoculated or not, avoid **mosquitoes** by covering up from dusk to dawn and using mosquito repellent. The summer **sun** can quickly damage your skin, and even in China's smoggy cities is potent. Keep yourself well covered with sunscreen, carry the tube with you for topping up, wear sunglasses with proper UV protection and consider a hat, however 'uncool' this may look.

Smoke cannot be avoided in China, where no smoking signs are often purely decorative. The country claims the world's largest number of smokers, with 300 million or 63% of men (it merely seems like 100%) and 20 million or 3.8% of women active smokers, making the country by far the world's largest market for cigarettes, at an average of 1,900 per person per annum. The Chinese are still used to obeying rules, and pointing to no smoking signs is often enough to make them guiltily put out their cigarettes or move to where smoking is permitted, such as at the ends of railway carriages.

It is probably not politically correct to attack **traditional Chinese medicine** (TCM), but there has been almost no rigorous scientific testing of the remedies or the simplistic assumptions behind them (for impotence eat tiger penis). In 1999 the Chinese launched a campaign to promote traditional Chinese medicine overseas, calling on scientists to conduct research to prove the medicines' effectiveness. Only two medicines out of about 50 types on sale overseas have been registered by the US Food and Drug Administration for testing, and the rest are imported either as food or nutritional supplements. While much is herbal, some treatments involve parts of endangered species and substances such as bear bile, extracted under conditions so inhumane as to defy description. If you wish to experiment with acupuncture, ensure that disposable needles are being used or select a more hygienic country in which to turn yourself into a pin cushion. Even in hospitals needles may be reused, so consider taking a needle kit with you in case of need, now widely available at travel shops and specialist clinics.

If you need a **doctor** head for the nearest international hotel, or failing that any other large hotel that accepts foreigners, all of which have clinics and can usually both prescribe and dispense more familiar remedies. Don't take chances with Chinese **hospitals** unless absolutely necessary. Take out travel insurance which covers you for emergency repatriation and call your embassy or consulate for advice (*see* p.114 for telephone numbers). Foreign-run or staffed hospitals and clinics in Běijīng include (prefix telephone numbers with 010 when calling from outside Běijīng):

United Family Hospital (Hémù Jiā Yīyuàn) Jiàngtái Lù 2, close to Holiday Inn Lido on the way to the airport, ✆ 6433 3960. Doctors of Chinese and assorted foreign nationalities.

International Medical Centre, Běijīng Lufthansa Centre Office Building S–106, European and American physicians, 24-hour ambulance service, ✆ 6456 1561, ⊕ 6456 1560. Also dental service in room S–111, ✆ 6456 1384/1394/1328, ⊕ 6456 1984.

Other medical and emergency contact numbers (prefix with 010 when calling from outside Běijīng):

China Emergency Coordinative Organization For Tourists, CNTA Department of General Coordination Affairs, ✆ 6520 1622, 6520 1623 ⊕ 6512 2096.

International Assistance, MOH, ✆ 6400 1746, ⊕ 6400 1737.

International AEA, Building C, BITIC Leasing Center, Běi Jiē 1, Cháoyáng District, ✆ 6462 9100, 6462 9112, ⊕ 6462 9111.

International SOS Assistance (SOS), ✆ 6500 3419, 6500 3388, ⊕ 6501 6048.

China International Travel Assistance (CITA), ✆ 6603 1185; ⊕ 6601 2040.

MEDEX Assistance Corporation, Regus Office 19, Běijīng Lufthansa Center, Liàngmǎ Qiáo 50, ✆ 6465-1264, ⊕ 6465-1240.

Internet and Other Computer Resources

There were an estimated two million Chinese Internet users in 1999, 10 million in 2000, and it's forecast that there will be 33 million by 2003. Internet access is now easy to find in Běijīng and with a little persistence in other towns, too, either at Internet cafés, in the business centres of larger hotels, or the main post office or telecom building. Details are given in the introductions to each city. Those staying in Běijīng for longer periods and with access to a computer and modem while there can now easily set up their own email accounts in a few minutes, and long distance calls within China are cheap.

Although it's often necessary to wade through hundreds of pages of nonsense before finding useful material, the Internet can still be of assistance before your trip, if used critically. Email and web page references are given throughout this book, but below are details of a few more general sources of information.

NB: Booking through travel agents found on the Internet and based in China is extremely unwise, and likely to be both very disappointing and unnecessarily expensive.

Comment on this guide is very welcome, and can be emailed to Cadogan Guides at *becky. kendall@morrispub.co.uk.*

Mailing Lists and News by Email

The Oriental-List is a moderated list for the discussion of travel in China and neighbouring countries run by the author of this guide. List members include experienced travellers, foreign residents of China and several writers of guides and other books on China, as well as those planning their first trips, and answers to detailed queries are usually fulsome and well-informed by recent personal experience. Send a blank email with the word *Subscribe* in the subject line to <*pnh@axion.net*>.

Xiānzài Běijīng is a weekly email newsletter about what's on in Běijīng, concentrating on events likely to be of interest to ex-pats in the bar areas of Sānlǐtún, Cháoyáng Gōngyuán and around the Lufthansa Centre, as well as in the better hotels. There's also information on discount air tickets out of Běijīng, flat share and rental, and social snippets on everything from the Běijīng Airheads motorcycle club to rock bands looking for a new bassist. Send a blank email to <*beijing@xianzai.com*>.

Several relevant web sites allow you to subscribe to emailed notifications of changes of their contents by entering your email address at the site. The Běijīng fortnightly newspaper *City Weekend* has an email brief of the contents of its latest edition with links to the relevant web pages, as does (or did) the weekly *Beijing Scene*. See also the sites for *Inside China Today*, *Sinopolis* and *China Online*, all given below.

China News Digest is published three times a week by a volunteer group of Chinese students mostly in the USA; set up in the wake of the Tiān'ān Mén events of 1989, it contains a summary of news reports about China mostly rewritten from agency sources. Despite occasionally succumbing to we-Chinese-versus-the-world rhetoric, this is a generally balanced and informative source of brief news items about China. For further information on the list server nearest you, and how to subscribe, write to <*cnd-info@cnd.org*>, or visit the web site mentioned below. A Chinese language publication called HXWZ is also available.

Newsgroups

The obvious starting point is *rec.travel.asia.* In amongst peevish complaints about lost credit cards, smutty postings about sex tourism to Bangkok and the inappropriate commercial material of travel agents (please boycott all agents who post there) can be found useful nuggets of information. To make the best of the group, read this book carefully, then post a *detailed* question. With luck there will be informative postings to the group, and you will receive email responses, too. If you post a vague query ('What are the best cities in China to visit?'), you'll be told to read a guide book or that 'Běijīng is kinda cool', which is all you'll deserve. If you are interested in making contact with travel agents and other commercial organizations, post on *rec.travel.marketplace*, which is where this kind of query belongs.

Another obvious news group is *soc.culture.china*, but as only the briefest of readings will tell you, this is the home of people with chips on their shoulders about Taiwanese independence, interracial marriages, the superiority of Chinese people over everybody else, the greatness of the late Dèng Xiǎopíng, and so on. *talk.politics.china* is much the same.

The World Wide Web

The best starting point for information about China on the web is *<http://freenet. buffalo.edu/~cb863/china.html>*, a regularly updated collection of links to reputable sites of all kinds.

For a rosy picture of Běijīng, try Běijīng Tourism Administration, *<http://www.bjta.gov.cn/>* and *<http://www.beijingtour.net.cn/>*. For a less rosy one try the English paper *<http://www.beijing-cityedition.com/>* or the cynical *<http://www.beijingscene.com/>*.

The online versions of Hong Kong's *South China Morning Post* *<http://www.scmp.com/News/Front/>* and *Hong Kong Standard* *<http://online.hkstandard.com/today/>* carry more detailed coverage of Chinese affairs than Western newspapers. The BBC World Service's *East Asia Today* programme can be read and heard (Real Audio format) at *<http://www.bbc. co.uk/worldservice/eastasiatoday/eattn.shtml>*.

The website *Inside China Today* has a wide selection of news about China drawn from publications and news agencies around the world, together with links to other professional sites at *<http://www.insidechina.com/>*. Slightly more business oriented news can be found on the sites of Sinopolis *<http://www.sinopolis.com/>* and China Online *<http://www.chinaon-line.com/>*.

For a preview of *China Daily*, the Chinese government's English-language propaganda sheet, see *<http://www.chinadaily.net/>*, and for a variety of propaganda magazines, such as *China Today* and *Běijīng Review* (sample headlines: 'A Glorious Period Ahead', 'Běijīng Becoming an International Metropolis') as well as papers on government policy and structure, see *<http://www.china.org.cn/English/>*.

CND's website *<http://www.cnd.org/>* has back issues of their publications, pictures and other information, plus a variety of useful software for Macintosh and other platforms, such as that allowing you to see Chinese text in mail and newsgroup postings, and to view and print out their Chinese language HXWZ magazine. There are two main methods of encoding Chinese characters: *gb* which has the simplified characters of Modern Standard Chinese and *big5* which has the full form still in use in Tāiwān and Chinese communities overseas. There's even software which will read out Chinese documents to you, if you have a Macintosh or your other computer is suitably equipped.

One of the areas in which the web shows promise is in last-minute air ticket discounting. Most airlines' web pages are called *www.*name-of-airline*.com*, but some are foolish enough to introduce variations and you'll have to resort to a search engine. For an example with cheap fares for US residents flying to Asia, try *<http://www.cathay-usa.com/>*. These tickets are *only* available to Internet users. For instant access to quotes on multiple airlines flying the same route try *<http://www.travelocity.com/>*. Don't expect internal flights in China to appear here, although some do on *<http://www.flychina.com/>*. It is unnecessary and expensive to book tickets for internal flights over the Internet, however. General news about safety in Asian air travel and related matters can be found at *<http://www.airwise.com/news/headlines/asiatravel.html>* which also has links to airline web pages.

<http://www.travel.com.hk/china/transpor/train.htm> has some general information on rail travel in China, and *<http://severn.dmu.ac.uk/%7emlp/crsg.html>* has not only obsessive levels of detail on how to take steam train tours, but also rail timetables for all four main Běijīng stations (not entirely up to date).

Other useful on-line services include Xenon Laboratories' automatic currency exchanger at *<http://www.xe.net/currency/>* where you can discover the latest value of the Chinese ¥RMB against any hard and many soft currencies.

Those whose brains and computers alike can deal with Mandarin can use the search engines at *<http://www.zhaodaola.com/>* and *<http://www.netease.com/>* to find Chinese language sites of interest. Both sites also have optional English interfaces.

Internet Access in Běijīng

China's attitude to the Internet is confused. In September 1996 the government began experiments with blocking access from within China to various sites outside, particularly those run by Western news organizations. At the same time control of the electronic dissemination of stock market information was put under the control of the monolithic Xīnhuá, the government's official media machine. The following month an intensive programme to educate the Chinese public about the Internet began, and signs appeared in post offices and elsewhere saying 'Internet' in English. A survey at the end of the month reported that only about 3% of high-income owners had Internet accounts, but more than a third had mobile phones. Walking into post offices that had the signs and asking for email access showed that usually no-one behind the counters had the first idea what email was, but this gradually began to change and the rate of growth of Internet use in China has in recent years matched that of the rest of the world despite starting late and from a very small base. Having an email address on one's business card has taken over from the mobile phone as a status symbol. In 2000 the government announced that it would hold ISPs responsible for websites which leaked state secrets, effectively meaning anything that they retrospectively decided they didn't like and thus anything critical of China at all. Simultaneously, they announced controls on encryption likely to hinder the introduction of many Internet technologies.

Despite continuous rapid growth, the number of Internet users in China still only amounts to around 3% of the world total, with China having fewer than one computer for every 300 people, while the EU contries have an average of one for every 55, and the USA one for every 15.

cybercafés

These are plentiful in Běijīng and usually found around the university districts of other cities mentioned in this book—addresses are given in the relevant sections. Rates vary from ¥10 to ¥30 per hour. Access is also available inside the business centres of four- and five-star hotels, but for ¥60 and ¥100, not that this necessarily guarantees you anything other than slow and conventional dial-up access although ISDN connections are available in China. If you plan to use web-based email which does not allow you to use a POP3-client for access (by entering your own information in the mail part of the web browser software), expect to wait a long time for downloads. In smaller towns the last resort is the local telecom office, usually inside or next door to the main post office, but you may find conventional email access is best.

getting your own email account in Běijīng

For those staying longer, dial-up services are available. In Běijīng if you arrive with a laptop of your own, there's completely anonymous access to the Internet at speeds of notionally up to 56kbps, by dialling 2631, or, slightly less well-known and thus a little faster, 2632 (and there are other numbers, too). Set up a new account on your email program with username 263, and password also 263. This will not give you a Chinese email address, but will allow you to use the Web or to get access to your own home smtp and POP3 servers, depending on how your home accounts are set up. You pay for the service through an increased telephone charge, around ¥0.5 per minute. A few of the more upmarket hotels, unable to pass on the charges, block access to these numbers, others add their own charges on top, and your connection will generally be faster if you go to a long-distance telephone booth in the street. Connection speeds tend to drop the more they are routed through switchboards. Nevertheless, in most Běijīng hotels this functions perfectly well, and outside Běijīng you can simply prefix the number with 010 to get the same results, albeit with long-distance call charges, typically ¥2 for three minutes.

To get your own Chinese email address, head for Chinanet at the Běijīng Telecom Building (Běijīng Diànbàojú) on Cháng'ān Xī Jiē (*open Mon–Fri 8.30–8, Sat and Sun 8.30–6*). Go straight ahead past the reception desk and you'll see counters on the right marked Chinanet. You'll need your passport (they will take a photocopy), to provide a Běijīng address including postal code and phone number (your hotel address will do), and to choose a (Roman alphabet) user name. The application form is brief and in English. In a few minutes you will be provided with a pile of instruction materials in Chinese and a print-out showing quite clearly your name, address, account name and, next to that, your password—a jumble of lower case letters and numbers. Below that is your email address in the format <*username@ public.bta.net.cn*>. The domain may also be *public2*, or *public3*, and, presumably, higher numbers in the future. You are asked to sign documents which agree that you won't do anything subversive, and then to go and pay in advance for the time you need. Go back towards the entrance and turn left into the hall on the left (east) side. The counter for paying is towards the far end on the left, no.9. At the time of writing the charges (these went down in 1999 and might drop further) are ¥100 ($12.50) to set up the account, plus ¥4 an hour for 1–60 hours a month and ¥8 for each subsequent hour. Those able to read Chinese should look at <*http://www. bta.net.cn/*> for the latest charges.

For email access only (time unlimited) it's ¥100 to set up and ¥30 a month. (NB: if you have web-based email, such as NetAddress, Hotmail, MailExcite, etc., this is of no use to you unless you have arranged for direct POP3 access to these accounts, allowing you to use an email program to get access to your mail. Web-based 'free' email services generally do not allow this kind of access, or charge for it, although very small sums. Consult your web-based email service operator for further information.)

You pay in advance for the amount of time you feel you wish to use, and must go back to top up the sum before it's all used up.

To set up your software you'll need the telephone number, userid, password, email address and the name of the smtp (sending mail) and POP3 (receiving mail) servers. These are given in the Chinese language manual supplied beneath screen shots of Netscape (page 8) and have the same IP address, but vary according to the first level of your domain name (the first part of your email address after the @ symbol).

public: 202.96.0.97

public2: 202.96.12.17

public3: 202.96.0.193

The telephone numbers are 6306 2266, 2605 0000 (56kpbs) for full Internet access, and 6306 3456 for email only access, up to 56kbps.

There are 25 other Internet service providers in Běijīng, but they all have to buy their Internet time from the same source and in late 1999 as many as 22 of them owed the bureau money. You may as well do as outlined above and buy direct.

Other Computer Resources

CD-ROMs on China are now available, but if produced in China itself are no more reliable than books produced there. There's even a Běijīng map CD-ROM, the *Běijīng Diànzi Dìtú*, available for a mere ¥18 (Windows format only). There are several programmes available for teaching Mandarin, and Chinese versions of various operating systems can be bought in China, although owners of Mac OS9 or better will find full Chinese compatibility built in.

Laundry

Almost all hotels in China have a laundry service, although in cheaper places this may just mean that the staff take it home and charge you what they think you'll pay—don't expect whiter than white results under either circumstances. Familiar Western brands of washing powder, although not in 'green' versions, are available throughout the country in handily portable sachets, and you are better off doing it yourself. Take a universal bath plug and an elastic washing line.

Lavatories

Bring a roll of toilet paper and carry a few sheets with you at all times. Buy a fresh roll well before you run out.

One benefit of the rapid growth of American fast food outlets in Běijīng is the consequent increase in the number of reasonably clean lavatories. Use these or the ones in your hotel whenever possible—the alternatives are not pleasant. Even in booming Shànghǎi only 60% of apartments have flushing toilets and only 43% of city households are connected to modern sewerage. The rest of the populace uses public toilets in the street. There is no guarantee of finding facilities within public buildings either; however, there is no problem identifying public lavatories even at some considerable distance, as the language of the nose is international. One entrance is for women and one for men (*see* language section for the relevant characters). In the countryside and away from the city centres facilities usually consist of a row of slits in a concrete base, which may or may not be separated by waist-high walls, open to the front. You must squat, attempting neither to step in earlier near-misses nor slip into the pit below, which will contain a steaming, maggot-ridden heap of earlier deposits awaiting collection and distribution to the fields. In winter a frozen stalagmite of human faeces may poke its tip through the slit. There is almost never anywhere to wash your hands. Occasionally there may be a ¥0.20 charge at the entrance, especially if the facilities are near a bus or railway station or actually do have running water.

Media

In 213 BC the Qín government ordered the destruction of ethical writings which were critical of authoritarianism. In the Hundred Flowers Movement, a liberation of artistic expression begun in 1956, and of political thought in 1957, the government encouraged intellectuals to speak out. The result was widespread condemnation of the Communist Party's monopoly of power and the absence of human rights. Intellectuals and officials who made their views known were subsequently dismissed from their posts and exiled or imprisoned. In 1997 the Chinese President Jiāng Zémín made speeches encouraging higher ethical standards amongst writers and journalists. This was ominous, since Jiāng's definition of meeting higher ethical standards, as a *People's Daily* article made clear, was that journalists should write bright and upbeat stories supporting the party line and socialism, rather then revealing the failings of society to foreigners. When Hong Kong's first post-reunification administrator Tung Chee-hwa was given the status of 'state leader', one of the perks was that his photograph would be guaranteed to appear larger than those of provincial leaders in Chinese newspapers. No newspaper in China can be put on sale, distributed or sell advertising without a licence from the government for each process. In short, there is no free press in China, nor has there ever been one.

The English language window onto the grey corridors of the political mind is *China Daily*, a dull mix of hypocrisy, cant, propaganda and window dressing, mixed with a few sports results and other items from around the world, which is distributed free to tourist hotels. Production is always up, Western quality standards have always been obtained and the minorities are always happy. China Daily dwells on social problems overseas (particularly in the USA) and will calmly inform you (without intending to suggest that you should do anything other than stay in China and spend your money) that you are involved in a racist conspiracy with other Western nations to suppress China. Meanwhile the native wit, intellectual acumen and high cultural level of the Chinese people will be given regular praise—'Some people even claim using chopsticks explains the high intelligence level of the Chinese people.' Typical headlines are 'Frozen food consumption up in Liáoníng Province' and 'Nation values relationship with Venezuela'. *China Daily* will never report '700 dead in floods', but 'Despite floods, output up'. In theory the paper employs foreigners as sub-editors, but with headlines like the tautological 'Illegal fishing in Yangtze banned', it's not easy to tell. Or perhaps this recognizes the truth that something being illegal and it's actually being restricted are two different matters.

There are a number of more or less legal listings magazines catering principally to Běijīng's sizeable expatriate population, and other rather blander legal publications aimed at visitors, details of which are given on p.116. Foreign news magazines and newspapers are available at the bigger hotels in Běijīng.

There's an English 'news' broadcast in the same vein as *China Daily* at around 12–12.30, 7–7.30, and 11–11.30, on CCTV Channel 4, often followed by other comment or analysis programmes in English, especially on Sunday, such as *Sunday Topics.* Occasionally candid, mostly turgid and full of childish phrases such as, 'A seminar was held to denounce...', 'goes against historical trends', 'refutes anti-China forces', and so on. CCTV4 also has a number of other English-language programmes and will probably eventually turn into the long-delayed English channel. Interested in Chinese traditional remedies? 'Chinese Medicine' on CCTV4 will show you animal testing to prove that it works.

BBC World Service TV can at least be found at the Palace Hotel, the Great Wall Sheraton the St Regis and the Jianguo Hotel, while HK Star TV and CNN are more widely available. Expect to receive a note from the hotel management apologising for a breakdown in service due to necessary repairs, which just happens to coincide with politically sensitive periods such as the Tiān'ān Mén anniversary of 4 June.

For reliable news take a short-wave radio and tune in to the following frequencies at different times of day:

BBC China: 21660, 15360, 15280, 11955, 11945, 9740, 7180, 6120, 6065, 5990, 5965, 5905. For a complete schedule see *<http://www.bbc.co.uk/worldservice>*.

Voice of America: MHz 17.73, 15.42, 11.76, 6.110.

Local English radio includes a talk show called 'Voices from Other Lands', on Joy FM/Easy FM 91.5 every week on Wednesdays at 8.35pm and 11.35pm, and Thursdays at 7.35am and 11.35 am. For general information on other English language programming: *<http://www.beat.com.hk/>*. This is daily 8–11, 12–1, 5–8 and 9–11. This includes English or Mandarin and English music, news, weather and cultural information.

Money and Prices

The Bank of China routinely accepts: Sterling; Euros; US, Canadian, Australian, Singaporean, Hong Kong and Malaysian dollars; Deutsche Marks and Finnish Markka; Austrian Schillings; French, Belgian and Swiss francs; Dutch Guilders; Italian Lire; Swedish, Norwegian and Danish Krone; Japanese Yen; Thai baht; Philippine pisos; Macanese patacas. The rate for travellers' cheques is about 2.4% better than that for cash, but attracts a commission charge of 0.75%. Scottish and Northern Irish bank notes are not accepted.

China has expressed its intention of floating the ¥RMB, but for now such plans are on hold. While bullish talk in the late 1990s suggested the currency would hold its own, the end of the decade saw fears that it would plummet once released, and the demands of face meant that China decided to ride out the Asian financial crisis of 1998–9, the year of the 50th anniversary of the People's Republic, without devaluing the currency, despite a consequent fall in competitiveness, declining exports and sluggish domestic growth. According to one MIT economist, a full flotation is likely to take another decade, since China lacks a credible domestic banking system or proper financial supervision of the large chunk of the economy still represented by state-owned enterprises, let alone adequate assessment of all the new cowboys. The currency remains linked to the US dollar at approximately ¥8.27 (cheques) and ¥8.07 (cash), and the purchasing power of other currencies in China is a matter of how they are doing against the US dollar.

Conversions in this book, where given, take a pessimistic view of only ¥8 to the dollar, and tend to round down. If the monthly price deflation that ran into 2000 continues then prices may well be lower than quoted in this book. China's currency is stable, but state-run institutions often increase their prices arbitrarily, and as double prices for foreigners are removed in certain sectors, so they arrive in others. The main purpose of quoting prices is for the comparison of competing services, one with another.

Chinese currency is known as *rénmínbì*, which means 'people's money', the unit of which is the *yuán* (¥ or ¥RMB). The most useful notes are ¥50 and smaller, and you should make sure that you have plenty of ¥10 notes for everyday use. There are also smaller notes (in size and value) for *jiào*, or one tenth of a *yuán*, and tiny notes for *fēn*, or 100ths of a *yuán*, which these days are of little use except to make up one *jiào*. A new set of notes, the fifth series, was issued on 1 October 1999, with Máo by himself on a reddish ¥100 note and modern security devices such as coloured threads in the paper and magnetic security lines, designed to make forgery too expensive. Good notes also have watermarks, and the braille dots on the lower left side of the note should be slightly raised. However, there are floods of forged notes, some of very high quality, and you will notice that every ¥50 or ¥100 note you try to spend in shops will be checked under ultra violet to see if various images fluoresce and to see how the paper itself aborbs or reflects the light. If a note is rejected, shred it or give it to the next mean taxi driver you encounter (who will then say that he doesn't have change).

One small problem for the budding scholar of Chinese is that in speech *yuán* are usually called *kuài*, and *jiào* are called *máo*. The numbers used on currency and in financial documents are also different and more complicated from those used in everyday writing, although all money except the *fēn* coins and notes carry arabic numerals, too. The one *fēn* note has a picture of a lorry (truck), two *fēn* a picture of a boat, and five *fēn* a picture of a plane, but these are dying out. Coins for 1 and 5 *máo* and 1 *kuài* are now coming into circulation.

Almost all money exchange is carried out at branches of the Bank of China, or at desks in hotel foyers and some Běijīng department stores which are under the Bank's control. At major branches you can also cash cheques into US dollars, and convert RMB to dollars as long as you can show receipts to prove that you have changed at least the same amount into RMB in the past (or twice that amount, according to some branches). In larger towns you can make over-the-counter withdrawals up to the amount of your credit limit from Visa, Mastercard, American Express and JCB cards, with commission of 4% and a minimum withdrawal of ¥1200 ($145). Allow at least 30 minutes for clearance, and don't leave yourself in the situation where this is your only source of cash, as sometimes the system breaks down or lazy bank staff may simply refuse to go through the hassle. At certain banks in major cities, American Express cardholders can cash personal cheques guaranteed by their Amex card. Some Běijīng locations are listed on p.115, but contact Amex for a complete list. Diners' Club has an office just east of the International Hotel.

There are now ATM machines all over China but still only a tiny number accept foreign cards, and the locations of these are listed for each city. There is no minimum transaction. Some foreign banks in Běijīng accept a wider range of cards. Holders of major cards such as Mastercard and Visa should call their card issuer, or check the websites *<http://www.visa.com/>* and *<http://www.mastercard.com/>* for the latest ATM sites.

Money can also be wired from Western Union. Check with your nearest office for more details or <*http://www.westernunion.com/*>.

China is expected to become the biggest payment card market in the world in the next seven years, but don't be fooled either by the cards you see in people's wallets or the plethora of Visa and Mastercard signs. In most locations only the Chinese versions are accepted, and these cards have 'Only for use in China' printed on them. If foreign cards are accepted then you are going to be paying well over the odds for whatever goods or services you are buying.

You are not allowed to import or export more than ¥6,000 in ¥RMB without special arrangements, and indeed there's little point as convertibility is limited outside China. You can reconvert to hard currencies at branches of the Bank of China, although those not at borders are sometimes reluctant and you'll need to show receipts showing you've exchanged sums in excess of those you wish to reconvert (some will only allow you to exchange sums up to half the value of your receipts, which much be less than three months old). Foreign currencies in excess of $5,000 should be declared on entry, but no-one seems to care very much.

While it was once official government policy to charge foreigners 200–300% more for hotels, train tickets, plane tickets and tours than local Chinese were charged, official policy is that we should now all be charged the same. However, as more and more of the economy becomes private this only adds to the number of individual entrepreneurs looking to separate you from as much cash as possible.

In larger cities a black market in US dollars has sprung up, partly because the Chinese themselves fear that the *yuán* will be devalued and partly because more and more are making trips to Hong Kong or further abroad. The differential is often not enough to make worth while the risk of being cheated by clever tricks with folding money or being given fake notes, however, unless you are staying in Běijīng long enough and don't mind breaking the law. In this case, find out from expatriates which Sānlĭtún stall is currently the one doing the business.

Stories of China becoming the biggest economic superpower in the near future are greatly exaggerated; even the World Bank admitted that it had its sums wrong. The average monthly urban salary in the best 35 cities in China is claimed to be ¥680 ($85) but is probably lower, very little of it truly disposable, and the average income for China less than half that. More than 300 million are thought to live below the poverty line drawn by international standards. The urban population is only 30% of the 1.2 billion total, the rest working on the land. It is generally agreed that the gap between the relatively wealthy and the poor will continue to widen, although if the government finally takes action against loss-making state enterprises the average urban salary will drop, and the greatest fear of many is that membership of the WTO will accelerate this process. The state firms hire two-thirds of the urban workforce, about 120 million people, but yield less than one third of industrial output, losing nearly $7 billion a year. The government estimates that 20 million of the employees are surplus, and already 2.2 million are paid for working in factories which have in fact stopped production. Fear of the unrest which might follow attempts to put things in order has until recently stayed the government's hand, but there are increasing numbers of forced mergers and bankruptcies. To add to the problems, despite the very limited mechanisation of Chinese farming, as many as 100 million peasants are thought to be surplus to requirements. These are increasingly joining the vast armies migrating illegally to the cities to find work, and who are blamed for rising crime there.

With the rarest exceptions, entrance fees to museums, temples, palaces and other ancient monuments are now the same for foreigners and Chinese.

Closing times given in the guide are usually those at which they stop selling tickets. Although in theory (and signs may clearly state) they remain open for a further half an hour to one hour, staff will usually immediately begin to close sections, or turn off lights, or start driving people out, sign or no sign, and whether you were sold a ticket two minutes ago or not. They don't care about anything except going home, so go no later than mid-afternoon.

Few museums have information in any language other than Chinese. Typically, museum collections are also poorly lit, dusty and uncared for, even in Běijīng. Whole sections of the museum may be closed at random because someone hasn't turned up for work, but don't expect a discount or a refund. In museum shops items that you can find much cheaper in local markets are sold for outrageous sums, and books you can find in Xīnhuá bookshops and elsewhere for much less have stickers over their prices. Sections of temples and museums are sometimes turned over to other enterprises, as the members of its work unit look for ways to supplement their incomes.

Most museums follow the same pattern, presenting their collections in date order. As part of the propaganda process, displays are often carefully selected and labelled to promote a viewpoint, such as the willing subservience of a minority group to the imperial court, or the glory of Hàn traditions. Periods when the Hàn withdrew or were repelled, or when the minorities took power over the Hàn, are glossed over. Everywhere there is the sour reek of nationalism. Despite this there are some fine museums in China, and the numbers of these are on the increase.

Misrepresentation of the true history of a site is commonplace, whether for political reasons intended to exalt the Communist Party or put the blame for destruction wholly on foreigners. Credit is demanded by the government for restoration undertaken, without blame being accepted for neglect or deliberate destruction during the regime's time in power, particularly following the occupation of Běijīng by the communists in 1949, during the Great Leap Forward campaign of the late 1950s, or during the Cultural Revolution of 1966–76. And, as Osbert Sitwell put it during his visit to Běijīng in 1934, 'Restoration is often the favourite weapon of Siva the Destroyer, and can achieve more in a few weeks than whole centuries of decay.' Grey cement is slapped on spalled brickwork and scored with lines to represent the original, garish paint replaces lacquer, and strip lighting is mounted in interiors, air conditioning on exteriors. Restoration in China often means complete rebuilding: the replacement of statuary smashed in the Cultural Revolution, the replanting of trees for those hacked down, and even wholly reconstructed buildings are given out to be original. One section of the Great Wall, 'restored' in the last few years, has in fact been wholly rebuilt from the ground up and joins a long list of such '20th-century Míng' artefacts.

In Běijīng those planning to visit several museums can save money by purchasing the Tōngyòng Niánpiào—general annual ticket—which gives free admission to nearly 60 museums around Běijīng. The ticket is good for three person-visits to each museum, which can be made at the same time or separately. A few of the museums, which are listed in an accompanying booklet, are big names, many are obscure, and some are eminently avoidable.

Nevertheless, the cost of the card can easily be recovered by a single three-person visit to some museums, on average one person's visit to four or five. The offer varies from year to year but typically the card is ¥60, dropping to ¥40 later in the year, and available both from museums which participate in the scheme and some which don't (such as the Natural History Museum).

Opening Hours

Never leave anything important until your last opportunity to do it, as this will almost certainly guarantee that the electricity will be off, the one person who can help is sick, the office is closed for a meeting, the flight will be cancelled, the road dug up, or the border closed for an unforeseen holiday. Allow extra time for everything.

Whatever is the most important thing you want to do in a day, do it first. Few premises open on time in China and most close early, unless they are private businesses. Museum staff frequently stop selling tickets an hour or so before the museum closes so as to make sure everyone's out of their hair in plenty of time for going home, and staff of all government offices right down to postal workers may decide that they are *xiàbàn* (off work) up to 30 minutes before closing time, even though they carry on sitting at their desks. Two-hour lunch breaks are also likely to begin early and end late, cutting down the working hours of the officer in charge of issuing visa extensions, for instance, to a very brief period. 'Work', in this and many other cases, means the strenuous labour of reading the newspaper, drinking tea and discussing the price of things with any fellow officer who may happen to drop in.

Most offices, many shops and museums open around 8am and close around 5 or 6pm. Some offices take a break from 12 noon to 2pm. The 1995 introduction of a five-day working week has confused matters. In general you cannot get a visa extension, an English-speaking policeman or any other government service on Saturday or Sunday. Banks are usually open, but their foreign exchange counters usually not. Most museums and tourist sites stay open seven days, but some, particularly in Běijīng, shut on Mondays. Post offices are open seven days, but particular services you may require, such as stamps for overseas letters or *poste restante*, may be unavailable if the one person whose job it is to deal with them is not in that day, or has gone off for lunch.

Until only a few years ago, most of China had shut down by 6pm and the rest by 8pm, but now private stores stay open into the evening and private restaurants stay open until 10pm or later. Běijīng has plenty of numerous fast food outlets which stay open 24 hours a day, but in smaller towns the choice of places to eat will shrink after 7pm or 8pm—most ordinary Chinese will have eaten well before then.

Packing

There was a crowd perpetually round the tent: all our actions, all our belongings, were closely scrutinised—by the Mongols with vacant gravity, by the Chinese with magpie curiosity. 'How much did this cost, Mr. Fu? How much did this cost?' It was laughable to recall that we had brought with us a tiny portable gramophone (and three records) because it would be so useful to attract the natives; there were times, at this period, when we would gladly have exchanged the gramophone for its weight in tear-gas bombs.

Peter Fleming, *News from Tartary*, 1936

The best policy is to take as little as you can, and restrict it to what cannot be cheaply and easily obtained in China itself.

Clothes. Light, loose, natural fibre, hand-washable clothes are best, plus one heavy jumper and a light waterproof jacket with a hood. Take stout walking shoes or boots with good support, and a pair of flip-flops for use in hotel bedrooms and showers. Include something with long sleeves and a high collar for covering up against mosquitoes in the evenings. Despite the heat, sturdy jeans are a good choice for long bus journeys, due to the dirt and hard-edged metal surfaces of some public transport. Cheap, casual clothing such as T-shirts can be found in Běijīng without difficulty, as well as fake brand-name down jackets, raincoats and other outdoor gear.

Cheap, if aesthetically unappealing, warm clothing is also widely available in China, particularly shaggy, sheepskin-lined army great coats, which will see you through even a bitter Běijīng winter.

Toiletries. Many popular brands are now available throughout China, with more choice in the bigger cities. Good toothpaste is a little harder to find than familiar brands of soap or shampoo. Bring plenty of good sunblock and small quantities of whatever upmarket moisturiser or other cosmetics you can't live without, as while these can be found in Běijīng they usually cost more than they do at home. Familiar feminine hygiene products are also widely available as well as Chinese copies, although the panty-liner is more favoured than the tampon.

Wearers of **soft contact lenses** will find solutions on sale on everywhere, but for **hard lenses** there's only one source of supply in Běijīng—the eye clinic at Tòngrén Hospital in Chóngwén Mén Nèi Dàjiē south of Dōng Dān which has a Japanese brand called SEED, ✆ 6513 5364. There's an English sign saying Contact Lens Centre and it's *open 8.30–5.*

Other items: A Swiss army knife or other multi-purpose tool, an unbreakable mug for drinking hot water and making tea on Chinese trains (both mug and tea can be bought there, however), good UV-proof sunglasses, a universal bath plug, an elastic washing line for drying your hand-washing, a North American to European adaptor or vice versa (just in case), a basic first aid kit (*see* 'Health' *above*) and a paperback or two for exchange with other travellers when read. Streets in all the towns in this book are either unlit or very poorly lit, have uneven pavements, unguarded trenches and uncovered manholes. A small torch is useful at night, on trains after lights out, and for those times when the electricity has failed and the hotel staff can't be bothered to bring you a candle. Photocopy the information pages of your passport and those holding the visas for your trip; if you are travelling with a companion, each should carry the other's copies. Also take or copy a bilingual menu from your local Chinese restaurant to help with ordering food. Take a small day pack for holding a guide book, sunblock and other daytime necessities, as well as for use on buses when your main luggage is out of reach on the roof.

Small gifts of obviously Western origin are nice to offer with discretion in exchange for personal kindnesses received (*not* as tips for services rendered professionally).

Photography

Fuji and Kodak dominate the Chinese market along with Konica, mostly in the form of standard 35mm ISO100 print stock. Konica film is also available, but don't expect to find slide film, high speed film or the latest formats anywhere outside the major cities. Care of film is not widely understood and it's often left to bake in the sun at stalls near tourist sites, so buy in dark department stores or specialist shops with fridges. The latter are very rare outside Běijīng, but there are a few in the capital which do also have a wide range of professional films in various formats.

X-ray machinery is found at railway stations as well as airports in China, but smaller bags are not X-rayed at stations, so carry your film there or in your pockets to avoid the cumulative effects of multiple X-ray exposure.

Photography is never allowed inside museums and temples, and in some Lamaist monasteries strips of exposed film have been nailed to the wall as a warning. Resist the temptation to photograph anything remotely military that's obviously been photographed in great detail from satellites already.

From mid-morning to mid-afternoon the glare renders all subjects washed out and flat, so choose your time to visit major monuments appropriately. Be aware, too, that you are unlikely to see much blue sky, and consider taking a polarising filter to compensate. Ask permission before taking photographs of people, but *do not pay them.*

Police

Policemen in China are generally to be avoided, not because they pose as much of a threat to visitors as they do to their own countrymen, but because they tend to be more of a hindrance than a help. Effectively in China the law is what a policeman says is it, and like most other officials policemen are assumed to be corrupt until proven honest. There are honest policemen, but the response of ordinary Chinese is to keep as far away from the police as possible and to flatter and bribe when necessary. Visitors to China, although they can potentially yield far more cash, cannot so easily be made into victims and are mostly left alone by police. However, they are often reluctant to do their jobs, and will frequently refuse to help visitors by investigating frauds or petty assaults, for instance, or registering thefts for the purpose of insurance reports. Some persistence is necessary.

As with other areas of Chinese administration the left hand is unaware of the right hand's existence. Officials in two neighbouring areas may give completely different answers to a question and one may refuse to honour documents issued by the other. Two different policemen on different days at the same station may also give different answers, but always with the tendency to say 'no', because this involves both less work and less responsibility than saying 'yes'. Policemen generally have a poor understanding of their own rules and regulations, and a low level of education.

There are two main types of policemen in China, those of the Public Security Bureau, and of the People's Armed Police. Visitors to China usually encounter only the first, known as the

PSB (*gōng'ān*), and then only when applying for an extension to their visas. Occasionally it's also necessary to buy a permit to visit certain areas, but this is increasingly rare and applies to none of the destinations mentioned in this book. In general the PSB officers have little interest in foreigners, although the police stations in larger towns have at least one person with a theoretical knowledge of English.

When faced with unreasonable rulings, the Chinese response is never to challenge the fairness or legality of the decision, but simply to decide which is the least harmful of the options open to them. Police can detain people for 30 days without charge (in practice for unlimited periods) and can sentence them to years of 'administrative detention' without resort to the courts. Neither is very likely to happen to you.

When you are inadvertently guilty of a misdemeanour, politely refuse to pay 'fines'. If you become involved in a dispute with a policeman, always leave him room to back down, and search for an excuse that he can use to do so, once he understands that you are not going to pay the sum he mentioned. *Do not offer a bribe.* When you really have been in the wrong, haggle. Even if the policeman can show that you should pay a fine of ¥2,000, haggle it down to ¥50 or so, and ask for a receipt.

Post Offices

The Chinese post office is a fine example of state-owned monolithic industry, employing 500,000 people who are better paid than those in any other state-owned industry except financial ones, and comprise about one thirteenth of all the people in postal services for the whole world. They process approximately 14,000 pieces of mail per person per annum, whereas the average for those in the rest of the world is 67,000 per person. The fact that these figures have been published in the Chinese media suggests that there may be many redundancies before long.

Glue the stamps on with the adhesive provided in pots or on a roller, rather then licking them. Take them back to the counter for franking in front of your face; in China this isn't really necessary at post offices, but at postal counters in hotels there are occasionally problems with theft or just laziness.

Chinese post offices are mostly open seven days a week and for the same hours every day, although some variations are creeping in as China slowly adapts to the introduction of a five-day working week (from six-day). Individual counters may close unexpectedly, however, while the clerk takes a lunch break, and no-one else will cover his or her job. There's also a tendency for clerks to refuse to serve people up to 30mins before closing time. Their jobs are still 'iron rice bowl' (guaranteed for life) and they don't care about service. Watch out for a tendency to round up the prices to avoid having to look for smaller denominations of stamps or give change. As with ticket buying there's often a bit of a scrum, with everybody talking over the top of everybody else in their attempt to get service from the scowling clerk. Join in, or send your postcards when you get home.

Take parcels unwrapped, so the contents can be checked, and then wrap them in front of the clerk. Some clerks will assume that you want EMS, the equivalent of a courier service, because you are a rich foreigner. There are considerably lower rates for airmail, surface mail and mail that contains only printed matter. Occasionally post offices may insist that you buy a tailor-made box from them, and very occasionally that you sew up your parcel in white cloth. Registration can be added for a small fee, is computerized and efficient, and requires you to fill out a small form which is in Chinese and French only. Adding the name of the destination country in Chinese characters will speed things up.

Postcards are only found in hotels and at tourist sites, and usually only in sets.

Poste restante. Available in major cities where advised in the 'Tourist Information' section that the system works. Using the postcodes quoted and adding the characters for *poste restante* given in the language section (*see* p.396) will speed things up, but in general anything addressed in a foreign language tends to end up in the *poste restante* box anyway. There is a charge of ¥1.50 for every item picked up in China. Ask for a receipt.

Express mail and courier. In theory EMS is the only service that can handle private letters, and the only one which operates within China itself. FedEx and DHL are both in Běijīng, but don't expect things to run as smoothly with either as they do at home. There can be problems with using foreign account numbers and with packaging. For up to 500g: to Western Europe EMS costs from ¥232 for documents and from ¥307 for parcels, to North America ¥217 and ¥292, and to Australasia ¥195 and ¥270. *See* p.117 for contact details.

Shopping

> *I have lived a great deal in Italy, and can remember the hundreds of antique shops, full of lovely objects, in Rome and Venice and Florence, and the scores in the smaller provincial towns: but I have never seen so many as in Peking; at least ten thousand, I should hazard at a guess, all equipped with enormous staffs. How these establishments carry their overhead charges, by what means they pay their assistants, I cannot imagine.*
>
> Osbert Sitwell, *Escape with Me!*, 1939

The tradition continues, and some establishments have come to the same conclusion as Sitwell. In late 1999 one department store in Tiān Qiáo proposed to lay off 280 of its 600 workers who then occupied the store, forcing it to close for a week. A peaceful solution was negotiated, but elsewhere police have sometimes been brought in to disperse similar demonstrations.

Take the usual common sense measures of shopping around, bargaining *very* hard (but with a smile), and not buying souvenirs in hotel foyers or souvenir shops. The sign 'authorized tour unit' is only a guarantee that what you are buying will be highly priced, and not that the goods that you are buying are of particularly high quality or even genuine at all. Some visitors are under the illusion that vendors in markets standardly ask double the normal price for their goods, that the correct response is to offer one third, and finally to pay half the original asking price. In fact first asking prices are not untypically 10 to 15 times the proper price, and there is no shame whatsoever in offering 10% of the first price, however cheap that may appear in developed country terms. Some vendors will be unwilling to deal with any foreigner who is not prepared to pay vastly too much money (after all, that is what foreigners are *for*, in the opinion of many) and would otherwise rather lose the sale, but these are few. If the bargaining has been good-natured, and you are allowed to walk away without being offered a lower price, you've got as low as you're going to get. At that point it is up to you to decide how much you want to compromise. Never accept the advice of a tour guide, however pleasant, as he or she will almost certainly be on commission.

State-run department stores are struggling to compete with the new private enterprises. In the one, customers are served grudgingly if at all, and the stock includes volleyball nets, Bakelite slide projectors, and very low quality exercise books, but little that you might want. In the new stores the idea of customer service is catching on. Staff have been taught to look alert, dress smartly, and smile. Goods are fairly well displayed and lit, and imported snacks, toiletries, batteries, tapes and other items useful to the traveller are available. Everything is labelled in price, and if not then shop elsewhere or you will certainly be overcharged. Haggling is for markets, not stores, and what you have found is an indoor market. The 'Friendship Stores', which used to stock the best souvenirs for hard currency vouchers only, have mostly disappeared, but some have continued to garner the best of local products. Marked prices are for haggling over at all tourist stores, including these. A 10% discount is the minimum, and you should be able to do better than that.

In most cases, having identified what you want to buy, you are given a receipt to take to a cashier nearby, where you pay and have the receipt stamped, returning to exchange it for the goods you selected. When you buy books, these too receive a stamp. The Chinese do produce a number of attractive art books, but note that all have their correct price as set by the publisher printed on them, usually not far inside the back cover and easily identifiable by the Chinese *yuán* character, or the ¥ symbol. Others simply have a string of five digits found in the same place under the publication date and ISBN number, which expresses the price in *fēn*. 01580, for instance, is only ¥15.80. If the price has been obliterated or stickered over you are being cheated and should shop elsewhere. Publishers also consider foreigners fair game, and the few books made for the tourist market with text in English are not priced, to the delight of museum souvenir shops.

No-one without a serious understanding of Chinese art should consider buying antiques. These are being manufactured daily, and the few real pieces may need export licences. If you are considering buying a carpet, gems or jewellery, you should not do so without having thoroughly familiarized yourself with quality and prices back home, to be sure that you are buying a genuine item, and for a price considerably less. Even if a store has some kind of authorized or official status, under no circumstances take it for granted that you are being told the truth, or that it is any less likely that you are being sold a fake. If some imperfection is discovered after purchase, or even if the item turns out to be manifestly other than what it was sold as being, don't expect a refund, or sympathy from the police.

Chinese quality control is poor, and the idea of commerce is to obtain money; giving customer satisfaction is not regarded as essential. So stick to buying simple objects with no pretensions to sophistication: chopstick sets, fans, silk (but check carefully), political posters (found in many Xīnhuá bookshops) and soapstone seals (jade? Ha!).

The word 'jade' is commonly used to refer to what are in fact two different stones very similar in appearance: nephrite and jadeite. Although they have different chemical compositions, they are difficult to tell apart even after carving and polishing. Khotan and Yarkand in China's far northwest have long been the principal sources of supply of nephrite, while jadeite has been imported from Burma and sometimes Siberia.

Silk should generally be bought in lengths rather than as made-up goods, Western sizes and styles not usually being available, but Běijīng's silk markets are worth checking. Chinese paintings are light to carry, if fragile, but ignore claims of the fame of the artist and the uniqueness of the work. Anything that tourists will buy is repainted thousands of times, and many paintings on sale are simply copies of famous classical paintings. There's nothing wrong with this, so long as you accept that you're buying a copy because it appeals to you and not some original masterpiece. Markets catering to tourists in Běijīng and Tiānjīn offer Máo watches and clocks, 'little red books' (of his sayings), old photographs and old *májiàng* (mahjong) sets made from bone and bamboo. First asking prices are at least five times what you should pay, and often ten times or more.

For those with luggage space to spare, and about to leave the country, China is good for acquiring hundreds of simple items at a fraction of the cost you pay for them in repackaged forms at home. Pots and pans, woks, spatulas, sieves, knives, choppers and small household implements of all kinds are examples, as well as toys, blank tapes, calculators, packs of cards, wooden coathangers and everything else that's marked 'made in China' in your local shops.

Then there is the extravagantly kitsch, and the outdated but interesting. In department stores look for items such as fluorescent plastic *májiàng* sets, plastic mosques with little lights at the top of their minarets which are actually tape players, and watches which speak the time in Mandarin. Reliable, non-electronic full plate cameras of ancient design (Seagull brand) can be bought very cheaply by those who've always wanted to experiment in the medium but been put off by cost. Check aperture, shutter and winder carefully before purchase.

Social Niceties

Having an introduction to a Chinese person or family is a joy to be looked for. Their generosity knows no bounds and can quickly reach embarrassing levels if disposable incomes are compared. If you are invited to stay with someone, still a delicate proposition politically, consider carefully that you will be enveloped in a way which may be a major economic drain on the family and behave accordingly. If you are taken out for a meal, insist on returning the favour. They will say no for at least half an hour, because this is polite. *Insist.* It will be very unlikely that you will be able to get any indication from them what kind of food they would like to eat, although you may be able to get some indication of what they don't like. Use caution, however: if you suggest Běijīng duck, for example, and they say they don't like it, the real reason may be that they think that it's too expensive. Most families eat out rarely. Be as attentive to them as they were to you, insisting they take the best morsels, topping up their tea cups or glasses and dealing with the bill swiftly and unobtrusively.

If you are invited to eat in someone's home always take something to eat, perhaps fruit, and something to drink, preferably a relatively expensive (but not for you) type of white spirit. Most localities have their own special brand, often made from sorghum, such as Běijīng's *Běijīng Chún*, at ¥30 to ¥40 ($4–5) per bottle. If you have anything from your own country, this, too, will be highly appreciated. They may attempt not to accept your gifts (multiple cries of 'not acceptable'—meaning that you shouldn't have bothered, or 'not necessary', or 'no need to be polite'), all of which you should ignore and gently but firmly persist. Under no circumstances take any part of your gifts away again. You will yourself be given fruit or something else to take away. Politely decline several times but finally accept, unless there is a genuine reason why you cannot, in which case do your best to explain this and it will be accepted.

More likely, if your acquaintances are not entirely without funds or if you are on business, you will be invited out to eat, your host choosing the dishes. In either case the host will likely apologise for the poverty of the fare and for how little food there is (even if the table is groaning). Your job is to disagree politely, try everything and praise everything, taking an intelligent interest and enjoyment in the dishes. As everywhere else in the world, young people and especially those who have an interest in the West, are much less formal.

Drinking is usually undertaken collectively, rather than at your own individual pace, and through a succession of toasts. Don't forget to propose your own in praise of the food, your hosts and the hospitality in general. The local equivalent of 'cheers', frequently heard, is *gān bēi* ('dry cup'—empty your glass). In more casual settings, drinking beer, for instance, replenish others' cups before topping up your own. Should you be eating out, or if you are participating in an official banquet, note that there is no dithering at the end of the meal. All participants quickly vanish.

A few other points: remove your shoes when entering someone's house, despite cries of 'no need, no need', unless you can see that everyone else is wearing street shoes, too. You'll be offered slippers probably too small for your feet. Despite the freedom with phlegm in public places, note that it is very bad form to blow your nose at the table. If you feel the need to sneeze, turn completely away or leave the table if you can. Only help yourself to small amounts of food at a time and don't refill the rice in your bowl until you have eaten completely what you have. Don't wave your chopsticks around, but note that picking up your bowl and cupping it in one hand is perfectly normal, as is noisy eating, particularly of noodles. It is also perfectly acceptable to drink your soup straight from the bowl. Your tea will be topped up by someone (almost as soon as you drink any, so when you've had enough leave the glass full. Cleaning your bowl is also a direct invitation to refill it, so start protesting about your repletion well in advance ('*Wǒ chībǎo le*'—I've eaten-to-fullness) and leave a little in it.

Losing your temper in China is rarely a good idea, although your patience may frequently be tried to the limit. When dealing with people behind a counter, try to avoid getting them into a situation where they give you a flat 'no'. If you get a 'no' straight away such as 'no discounts at this hotel', you'll need to offer them an excuse to change their minds, otherwise they cannot do so without losing face. The excuse can be entirely spurious, such as offering them some completely irrelevant piece of identification and saying, 'I'm a student,' or saying 'I plan to stay for three days,' which would normally make no difference at all. This is particularly important if the 'no' has been given publicly.

Be unswervingly polite until it's absolutely clear that it will get you nowhere. At times, however, you may need to make a scene just to get service at all, such as when the bank teller simply can't be bothered to fetch the notes you want. Simply make it clear that you are not going away until you get service, and usually (but not always) you will win. You may also find that all the Chinese on your side of the counter, as sick of bad service as you are, are cheering you on. Beware, however, of causing someone able to have the last laugh to lose face.

Receipts are very important in China. If you spend 30 minutes gradually winning a refund for some non-performance then are unable to produce your receipt, your cause is lost. It does not matter if it is undeniable that you paid. It does not matter that the clerk is not denying that you paid. It does not matter that you offer to write a receipt for the refund yourself. If you don't have the original, then you can't have a refund. You will quickly accumulate piles of tissue paper receipts in China. Keep *all* of them until you are well clear of the city in which you got them. You never know.

Tipping does not exist in China outside of the top-range joint-venture hotels and only there because foreign guest have brought it with them—there is no need to follow suit. There used to be signs up in hotels informing guests that tipping was unnecessary and even offensive. Bribery exists in China, tipping does not. Neither should be encouraged to spread. The Chinese very rarely tip each other. Foreigners are already overcharged wherever possible and further donations are unnecessary. Furthermore, the individuals with whom you do business, including hotel employees, are already some of the better off. If you want to give charity, choose the obviously starving, ill, deformed and injured who really need it. There are unfortunately all too many of these to choose from.

Telephones

If you use a phone at a shop or on a table in the street, the cost is usually ¥0.30 for three minutes (which, since there's almost always someone waiting, is usually about all you should take), but ¥0.50 at some places and at (relatively rare) coin phones which require a ¥0.50 coin. If you beep someone to get a call back expect to pay at least ¥0.60, even if that person doesn't actually call back.

Mobile phones in China work on both GSM and CDMA systems, with the most popular phones being Nokia and Ericsson, of the kind where you can have a chip for billing at each location from which you operate. Before you arrive in China the rules will have changed several times, but in 2000 phones were as little as ¥1,400 including local chip and ¥50 a month for calling. In China, you pay when you call a mobile phone, and the person receiving the call pays too. The problem for foreigners is that there's now a required ¥8,000 deposit, since too many had skipped the country without paying their bills. Residents get local Chinese to open the account on their behalf.

For those dialling into China, the country code is 86 and the leading zero on the city code should be omitted when dialling the rest of the number. When dialling internationally out of China, first dial 00 then the code of the country you want to reach.

IC (integrated circuit) cards are all the rage in China; their most common form is as telephone cards which can be used in public phones country-wide, and have a face value of between ¥30 and ¥200. These are sold at post and telephone offices, at the information counters of department stores, at hotel receptions (with a mark-up of as much as 10%), at tiny *hútòng* corner stores and by canny students who split their commission with you, giving a discount of up to 5%. Look for signs which include the letters *IC*.

You'll also see in Běijīng, and soon further afield too, the letters *IP*. These cards route your long-distance call from any telephone via the Internet for rates considerably lower than those of conventional telephones. Voice quality is reported to be very good for now, but will no doubt deteriorate as bandwidth is absorbed.

As a result of these changes, and no doubt anticipating the increased competition from foreign companies, telephone and Internet charges have been falling and are expected to continue to do so. In the spring of 2000 a special offer from Běijīng Telecom temporarily brought the cost of calling the USA from China below the cost of calling China from the USA for the first time in history.

Even the tiniest towns in China have post and telephone offices with satellite uplinks, and connections to overseas countries and long-distance calls within China are quick and clear, often better in fact than local calls. While it was once best to make your international calls from long-distance telephone booths at the city's largest post office or separate telephone office, now in larger cities IDD public telephones on the street, in department stores and malls, and in hotels, all accept the IC Telephone Card (*IC kǎ*).

There will be further downward pressure on call prices as China's telecommunications market opens up to foreign joint-ventures over the coming years. AT&T already plans to use the fibre-optic systems of the Ministry of Railways and State Administration of Radio, Film and Television to set up a new network.

International call prices dropped 30% as this book went to press, so you'll probably find most calls cheaper than quoted. Probably the charges will have dropped at the telephone offices but stayed the same at the hotels. International calls made between midnight and 7am are 40% cheaper, Mon–Fri 9pm–midnight 20% cheaper, and Sat, Sun and public holidays 7am–midnight 20% cheaper, but these discounts do not always apply to public telephones.

Time

Běijīng time is GMT+8 hours with no summer time (daylight saving time); the whole country is in a single time zone.

Tourist Information

in China

China's three big state travel agencies are CITS, CTS and CYTS, originally designed to deal respectively with foreigners, foreigners of Chinese descent and young people (but without offering any discount). Now to a certain degree deregulated, they compete in offering the same services, but remain by-words for cupidity, insolence and non-performance. Occasional exceptions are noted in the relevant city sections. With increasing deregulation, a fog of equally unreliable private travel operators is seeping into all major towns. Even the government has become alarmed at the damage to the country's image these cause and periodically cancels licences.

All depend on your unwillingness to try and do things for yourself, and on contacts within ticket offices that may get them access to seats and beds that you can't get. They depend on the language barrier to fix up transport for you that you could fix for yourself for half the price or much less. Some run one-day tours that are worthwhile for their convenience, and many travellers find it's worth paying ¥20–50 more for a railway ticket to be spared the confusion and crush of railway stations. This, however, should be the limit of your involvement with these organizations.

There are now tours run by private operators aimed at Chinese. At little booths in Tiān'ān Mén and Wángfǔjǐng, for instance, it's possible to book a four-day trip to Wǔtái Shān and Dàtóng for ¥760 for a pair of beds, or a trip to Qūfù for the same price. The 'pair of beds' may mean that you'll be on an ancient sleeper bus with double width beds, and that's where you may spend the night. Any nights spent at hotels may be in those which don't accept foreigners, and even if you can persuade the tour company to take you, you'll be harassed by megaphone-wielding guides from point to point at haste, overcharged for food and other auxiliary services, and (because that's what the Chinese market wants) spend far too much time at amusement parks and far too little at historic sites.

in Australia

China National Tourist Office: 19th Floor, 44 Market St, Sydney NSW 2000, ✆ (2) 299 4057, ✉ 290 1958.

in Canada

China National Tourist Office: 480 University Ave, Suite 806, 28013 Toronto, Ontario, M5G 1V2, ✆ (416) 599 6636, ✉ 599 6382.

in France

Office du Tourisme du Chine: 15, rue de Berri, 75008 Paris, ✆ 01-56-59-10-10, ✉ 53-75-32-88.

in Germany

Fremdenverkehrsamt de Volksrepublik China: Ilkenhans Strasse 6, 6000 Frankfurt M50, ✆ (069) 528465, ✉ 528490.

in Hong Kong

China International Travel Service: 6/F, Tower 2, South Seas Centre, 75 Mody Road, Tsim Sha Tsui, Kowloon, ✆ 2732 5888, ✉ 2721 7154.

in Japan

China National Tourism Administration: 8F Air China Bldg, 2-5-2 Toranomon, Minato-ku, Tokyo, ✆ & ✉ 3-3691 8686.

China National Tourism Administration: 4F OCAT Building, 1-4-1 Minatomachi, Naniwa-ku, Osaka, ✆ 6-635 3280, ✉ 6-635 3281.

in Singapore

China National Tourist Office: 1 Shenton Way, #17-05 Robina House, Singapore 0106, ✆ 221 8681, ✉ 221 9267.

in Spain

China National Tourist Office: Gran Via 88, Grupo 2, Planta 16, 28013 Madrid, ✆ 1-548 0011, ✉ 548 0597.

in the UK

China National Tourist Office: 4 Glentworth Street, London NW1 5PG, ✆ (020) 7935 9787, ✉ (020) 7487 5842.

China Travel Service Information Centre: 124 Euston Road, London NW1 2AL, ✆ (020) 7388 8838.

in the USA

China National Tourist Office: 350 5th Avenue, Suite 6413, New York, NY 10118, ✆ (212) 760 8218 (information), ✉ 760 8809, <*cntony@aol.com*>.

China National Tourist Office: 333 West Broadway, Suite 210, Glendale California 91204, ☏ (818) 545 7507, 🖷 545 7506.

Where to Stay

This nation, which so enjoys the possession of physical property, takes abominable care of it. Upkeep, in general, is simply non-existent. There are almost no exceptions to this.

Anyone who has kept house in China knows how unceasing is the exhortation necessary for the simplest tasks demanding routine effort. If the project is new, and therefore interesting, the dragon's head will appear at once, all splendid with horns and fangs, the beast curvetting and breathing noble vapor! Yet ask to have a foreign-style hardwood floor regularly waxed, as did my missionary friends, or order that a piece of machinery be carefully wiped so that it will not rust in damp weather, and the snake's tale will slide away under the door.

George Kates, *The Years that were Fat*, 1952

Pity the poor foreign manager of the Sino-foreign joint-venture hotel, for the problems once faced by expat matrons are now his, as he attempts to cajole staff into taking proper care of unfamiliar surfaces and materials in unfamiliar surroundings.

You may find that the bathroom has no toiletries, and, having called housekeeping to bring them up, you may find that on subsequent days you have three of some things. It would be to misunderstand the Chinese to view this as intentional irony, but you are free to form a theory as to whether it's due to laziness or cluelessness.

In a higher-class hotel, accepting a turn-down service will mean the housekeeper moving around carrying out a check-list of items as if you weren't there, turning on several lights you aren't using and perhaps turning off the one you are.

Hotels in China range from the luxury international chains of the bigger eastern cities, and Chinese attempts at the same thing, to the grim transit hotels of small towns on long bus routes in remote areas. In theory only a hotel which is an 'authorized tour unit' or otherwise endorsed by the local tourism administration, usually with a brass sign outside, can accept you; others are for Chinese only. If you meet with real resistance, ask the PSB (Public Security Bureau or police) to help you. The problem may lie in the Chinese system of selling individual beds. In effect all rooms except doubles, and quite often those too, can function as dormitories. The fewer beds there are in a room, the higher the price per bed. Although reception staff may refuse to give rooms to Chinese couples who cannot prove their married state, male and female foreigners who just buy individual beds are often put in the same room. However, mainland Chinese are never put in the same room as foreigners, so if you are the only foreigner in a busy hotel that only has four-bed rooms available, you may occasionally have to pay for all four beds.

Until very recent times, all double rooms in China, except those in four- and five-star hotels that were either joint ventures or aspiring to be, were twins. The majority of rooms still are, but even some three-star hotels are now installing big beds. Unless particularly detailed coverage is given, expect 'double' to mean 'twin', but the use of the word 'twin' doesn't mean that the hotel hasn't recently installed double beds.

The upmarket hotels in China which are Chinese enterprises tend to be overpriced. Everything glitters, but the knobs come off in your hand, the service lacks polish and so does the room. There may be automatic lifts, but someone is employed to work them and when that person goes to lunch the lifts are switched off. You may discover a dimly-lit cocktail bar on the top floor, for instance, with background jazz, smartly uniformed Hong Kong-trained waitresses and an impressive drinks menu. However, key cocktail ingredients such as gin will be unavailable. If you don't expect too much, stays at these hotels can be highly entertaining. Any hotel with pretensions, including many cheaper ones, will have a row of clocks on the wall each with the name of a capital city underneath. There will be at least six, and sometimes as many as ten. Only the one for Běijīng will usually be correct. When they are taken down for dusting or (rare) redecoration, no-one notes in what order they should go back up, and foreign summer time (daylight-saving time) is not understood, although it was briefly experimented with in China. Complain that the fan in your bathroom isn't working and you'll be told the reason why. 'It's broken.'

China's star rating system is arbitrary and not to be trusted, since hotels begin to deteriorate quickly from the moment they are completed (although stars are never subtracted as they go downhill). For real quality stay at familiar Western or Japanese names or joint-venture hotels, which are usually no more expensive than the Chinese ones. It takes at least three years before star classifications are awarded, and since most Chinese-run hotels are at their best in the first year of operation, many of the best hotels are unclassified.

In even the meanest guest house, a thermos of boiled water (*kāi shuǐ*) is provided for making tea or drinking straight. This is brought to the room every morning, sometimes very early, and topped up in the evening or occasionally during the day if requested. Often tea and cups are provided too, but it is wise to carry your own. Hot water for washing may only be available part time, especially off the beaten track. In the traffic hotels at the bottom of the scale there may be only shared toilets consisting of little more than a trough, which is flushed out only once or twice a day. You will usually not be given a key to your room. Instead you may be asked to pay a deposit for a little plastic envelope with your room number, which you show to a *fúwùyuán* 'service person' on your floor. She will then open the door whenever you want to enter your room. If you can't find her she is sitting, knitting and chatting with the floor lady of the floor below or above, or in the common bathroom doing her washing.

When checking in you are always asked to complete a form with your name, nationality, passport number, visa number, date of validity, occupation, why you're here, where you've come from, where you're going to and when. Leave the latter blank if you don't know. The staff will attempt to check that what you have written correlates with what's in your passport. Almost all hotels insist that you pay in advance. It's best to pay day by day as what seems to be a pleasant hotel may turn out to be without functioning plumbing or some other promised service. If you decide to leave town earlier than expected you may have difficulties obtaining a refund.

Hotel staff frequently make mistakes in copying payments into their accounts, whether computerized or not, so it is important to retain your receipts, as without these they will never accept that the mistake is theirs and not yours. Your room will usually be carefully inspected to make sure that you haven't stolen a threadbare towel or cracked cup before you leave, so allow time for this when checking out. Speed things up by leaving towels and cups in the places where you found them.

Hotel managements never seem to allow funds for maintenance, and the shiny newness of hotels wears off with remarkable speed. Where staff make an effort to keep the rooms clean it's often with wholly inappropriate methods and materials that leave fabrics faded and surfaces scratched and dull. Even in mid-price hotels it is unlikely that all the bathroom fitments will work, and the carpet in the room will usually be marked by ancient cigarette burns and other substances about which it is best not to speculate. Slippers are provided, but it is better to take your own, suitable for wearing in the shower, too, since the bath may have more rings than a sequoia. The heating comes on on a specific day of the year, usually in November, and goes off again in March. The dates vary slightly across the country and are respectively rather later and earlier than you would like, but are set by government regulation and ignore the actual weather conditions. Hotel managements often adopt the same policy towards air conditioning where this is a central system, and will leave it as late as possible to turn it on.

However, service industries in China are improving rapidly, and the days when requests for a room at a half-empty hotel routinely met with the response, 'All full', are gone. Receptionists may prefer to finish the social chat they are having before dealing with you, but at least they usually no longer just carry on with their knitting, newspaper reading and tea drinking, and ignore you completely. The semi-privatization of some hotels has helped, together with specific government instructions issued in 1995 outlawing 50 phrases such as, 'Can't you see I'm busy? Ask someone else!' At the same time it became possible for service industry employees to lose their jobs, at least theoretically—enough to concentrate the mind of even the most die-hard timeserver, given China's rising unemployment and erratic progress towards a market economy.

New hotels are going up all the time, many of which have more of a sense of competition than long-established places, are trying to work out how to please and have been selected for mention in this book. Many also have cheaper promotional rates for the first few months, and even if travelling on a limited budget it's worth looking at any brand new hotel you see that's not obviously four or five star.

Dorm beds with shared bath can cost as little as ¥25 ($3) and doubles with bath as little as ¥40 ($5) per bed outside the busiest tourist areas.

apartments

Forget it. Short of staying with permanently resident friends or arranging to house-sit for a temporarily departing expat, it's considerably cheaper for budget travellers to stay in budget hotels. Stays of less than six months are in any case even more difficult to arrange than residence usually is, and for those without the proper support of their work unit or joint-venture employer it's only marginally legal anyway.

It was widely believed that foreigners were only allowed to live in specially designated (and, needless to say, very expensive) apartment buildings. Nevertheless, given that the law is only the law in China if you're caught, and you'll only be caught if it's financially worth the effort or more tiresome not to catch you, by the end of the '90s several thousand foreigners were living in Chinese apartments in Běijīng. Just prior to 1 October 1999 the police suddenly conducted a sweep, informing startled foreigners that they should register, and fining them random amounts of money for not having done so sooner. Those that then tried voluntarily to go and register sometimes found themselves refused, and their landlords forced to evict them.

In short, the position on renting an apartment directly from a Chinese varies according to the rapacity of the policeman you happen to speak to. Talk to expats for the latest situation, and look for flatshare ads in the free newspapers and in the email newsletter *Xiànzài Běijīng*. Whether you are on an L (tourist), F (temporary business) or Z (permanent employment) visa, you can go with your landlord to register at the nearest police station, and be told which district station to go to get your temporary residence card, which is only valid as long as your visa is. You may simply be denied permission, of course, but at least your landlord and you will both be on the right side of the law and spared the possibility of large fines.

Long stayers expecting employment and wanting to stay legally can get some idea of prices from Wanhai Real Estate's monthly newsletter, © 6599 1618, @ 6539 1610, <*zxb_99@ yahoo.com*>, or look at <*http://www.roofinder.com/*>. Also look in *City Weekend* and *Běijīng Scene*, although few people want short-term occupants.

Camping in China is generally problematic. There are few official campsites of any kind, and in general foreigners are supposed to stay in a hotel which will record their passport details and check that their visas are valid.

History

Běijīng, a city whose name is now synonymous with Chinese power, is nevertheless an odd choice as the heartland of Chinese self-admiration and conservatism. Founded by foreigners more than 700 years ago, it has spent over half of that time under foreign control, and more than a further 50 years under the control of Chinese promoters of foreign ideology. Xī'ān, the capital during most of the rest of China's history, and in particular during the golden age at the height of the Táng dynasty, would make a better choice; a more *Chinese* choice. But just as Běijīng was the choice of foreign dynasties, being closer to their northern points of origin, so it became the choice of Chinese ones as the appropriate place from which to resist further foreign invaders.

Mongolian Beginnings

Probably the earliest predecessor of Běijīng was the nearby market town of Jì 2,000 years ago, and which for a few hundred years before the unification of China under the Qín dynasty was the capital of the small state of Yán. It was also known as Yánjīng, a name still occasionally used for Běijīng today in literary contexts, as well as the name of one of its most popular beers.

A minor capital of lesser non-Hàn (non-Chinese) dynasties, such as the Khitan Mongol Liáo (907–1125), and the Jurchen Tartar Jīn (1115–1234), who ruled the north while the Sòng dynasty ruled the south, it was under the Mongol Yuán dynasty, which swept all the others away, that Běijīng finally became the full-scale capital of a large empire and on the current site. Captured by Genghis Khan in 1215, it was adopted as his chief residence by his grandson Khubilai Khan in 1264, and the new city was founded in 1271. Known as Dàdū (Great Capital) by the Chinese, it was called Khanbalik by its Mongol founders. All roads led to Dàdū in the winter, and to the summer capital of Shàngdū (the Xanadu of Coleridge, and today's Dolon Nor in Inner Mongolia) when the Great Khan was there.

The Mongol design roughly gave the shape to modern-day Běijīng, a rectangle with a north–south central axis, of which the Imperial residence was the heart. An immense wall ran round the city with corner turrets and three gates to each side, topped with 'palaces' according to Marco Polo, although its construction was only of rammed earth topped with reeds to reduce erosion by rainfall.

After the expulsion of the Mongols, the Hàn Chinese Míng dynasty set up its capital at Nánjīng, well to the south, and Dàdū was renamed Běipíng (Northern Peace, or The Pacified North). The Yǒnglè emperor, the third of the Míng (reigned 1403–25), had previously served in the north fighting attempts by the Mongols to return, and rebuilt the city on a slightly smaller scale, moving the capital back there in 1420. It was named both Shùntiān, 'Obeying Heaven', and Běijīng, 'Northern Capital'. Yǒnglè repaired the existing walls, but reduced their overall length by cutting off part of the northern side of the Mongol city with a new wall, leaving the traditionally central bell and drum towers north of the new focal point. He also moved the southern wall slightly south to the line of the modern Qián Mén, and the original buildings of the Forbidden City and several other major monuments date from his reign.

The broader extension south of Qián Mén, with lower walls, was built in the reign of the Zhèngtǒng emperor (1436–49), and the whole system was clad in stone and brick by the Jiājìng emperor (1522–66), who added towers and enceintes. Although the next 400 years did not pass without demolition and new construction, Běijīng remained essentially the same in plan until the destruction begun randomly under the Republic from 1912 became organized vandalism under the People's Republic from 1949. Even in the 1940s the gates were still locked against bandits each night, as in medieval Europe, and little more than 40 years ago visitors could still see an essentially Míng and Qīng Běijīng.

Northern Barbarians

Corruption, ineptitude and poor responses to a series of natural disasters brought down the Míng, who had also been weakened by the attacks of the mounted Manchus to the northeast. However, it was a rebellion of peasant Chinese which stormed Běijīng and overthrew the Míng, the rebel leader declaring himself the first emperor of a new dynasty, which collapsed almost immediately as armies guarding the passes at Shānhǎiguān allowed the Manchus into China and went with them to Běijīng to expel him.

The Manchus installed themselves as the Qīng dynasty in 1644, but left the Míng city much as it was, a series of walls within walls. At the heart lay the walled Imperial Palace or 'Forbidden City', surrounded by the Imperial City whose walls enclosed what is now Běi Hǎi Gōngyuán (park) and the still inaccessible Zhōngnán Hǎi government compound to the west. Its Hòu Mén (rear gate) was halfway to the bell and drum towers to the north, and the walls ran down modern-day Běihéyán Dàjiē to the east and halfway down what is now Tiān'ān Mén Guǎngchǎng (Square) to a gate which survived in the middle of the square until it was pulled down for the construction of the mausoleum for Máo Zédōng in 1976. Around all of this stood the massive outer walls of what foreigners later called the Tartar City, which the Manchus had taken for themselves and their troops. The southern city south of Qián Mén became the Chinese quarter of Běijīng.

Western Ocean Barbarians

Two hundred years later, the Manchu-ordered suppression of the import of opium gave Britain an excuse to go to war with the Great Qīng Empire, which had expanded as far as Central Asia. The Chinese had continued through the 18th and 19th centuries to regard foreigners as inferior, an attitude also adopted by the Sinified Qīng, and all trade was seen as merely the offering of tribute. The country was closed to outsiders and going abroad was forbidden without special permission, as was the teaching of Chinese languages to foreigners. The country's Qīng-enforced purdah left it ignorant of foreign technological developments and militarily backward, so the Opium War of 1840–42 was largely a string of easy victories for the British. It ended with Qīng capitulation and the Treaty of Nánjīng, which forced China to open up yet further to contact with the despised foreigners at designated treaty ports. This was also the agreement which gave Britain Hong Kong, and marked the beginning of a century of 'unequal' treaties with foreign powers.

The Qīng were reluctant to enforce their side, and a petty incident involving the boarding of a ship suspected of piracy in 1856 led to the Arrow War (named after the ship in question), in which further British military activity forced on the Qīng the Treaty of Tiānjīn of 1858. This opened up yet further areas for trade, and compelled the Qīng to accept the residence of foreign diplomats in Běijīng. (Another clause forbade the Chinese from using the character *yí*, 'barbarian', in documents relating to the British.) Reluctance on the part of the Manchus to sign the treaty in Běijīng and to accept the permanent residence of foreign diplomats to which they had already agreed led to further engagements, and after the imprisonment of some foreign emissaries sent to complete arrangements, and the execution of others, the barbarians came to the gates: Anglo-French forces retaliated by occupying Běijīng in 1860. Realizing that destroying the Forbidden City would lose the Qīng so much face the house would fall, they instead burned down the Summer Palace and drove the Xiánfēng emperor into exile at his summer resort at Chéngdé (where tradition has it he was later struck dead by lightning). Another agreement, the Conventions of Běijīng, reduced Manchu sovereignty over China yet further, and added Tiānjīn, through which the invading forces had had to fight, as a further 'treaty port' where foreigners could reside and trade.

The Boxer Rebellion

Foreign powers continued to gnaw both at China's remoter inland regions and its coastline. Territory was annexed by Britain, France, Russia, Germany and Japan, and Portugal gained confirmation of its control of Macao, occupied since the 16th century. The Japanese inflicted a major military defeat in 1898, and took control of the entire island of Formosa (Tāiwān) which the Qīng had incorporated as part of their empire. The foreign powers also fell out with each other, and in 1904–5 Japan surprised almost everyone except *The Times* correspondent G. E. Morrison by defeating the Russians and driving them from the Qīng ancestral homeland of Manchuria, over which the Russians had gained almost complete control. A series of 'unequal' treaties allowed foreigners to travel where they pleased, only responsible to the laws of their own governments and not to those of China or its officials.

Like the modern-day communist government, the Manchus, ruling a country of around 350 million people to whom they were greatly inferior in numbers, deliberately kept the population ignorant of the outside world. The average Chinese peasant may not have known of the scale of China's military and diplomatic defeats, but he did encounter their effects in the arrival of foreign missionaries. If the Manchu and Chinese elite were arrogant, superior, self-righteous and intolerant, these 'foreign devils' were scarcely less so. Relying on officaldom to protect them, they seemed to common people to be allies of the often oppressive and corrupt local administrators. They preached against ancestor worship and took valuable land to build churches, whose pointed spires poked threateningly aloft in opposition to the otherwise harmonious *fēngshuǐ* (geomancy) of a town or village. Even more violence was offered to the gods by foreign railway construction and mining operations, and the new lines threatened the livelihoods of those operating water and land transport.

First heard of in 1898, The Harmonious Fists, or Boxers (a label given them by a missionary), seemed just another secret society in a country riddled with such peasant-level masonry, but one violently opposed to foreigners, and in particular to missionaries. Its mumbo-jumbo rituals included stamping on a cross and were believed to induce a state of invulnerability to sword-cuts and bullets alike. In a rare moment of forthrightness, Yuán Shìkǎi, then governor of Shāndōng Province, lined up a few Boxers and had them shot. When they survived execution the watching crowd became wildly excited. Yuán then had them shot again, but this time used real bullets not blanks, and in Shāndōng kept the peace, earning him the gratitude and support of the foreigners resident in China.

Elsewhere the Boxers began with rioting, continued with looting, then moved on to the destruction of churches and the murder of Chinese converts to Christianity, until they finally dared to kill their first foreigner, an Englishman, on 31 December 1899. The perpetrators were executed under the eye of a consular representative, and official apologies were made. However, edicts from the court urging general restraint on local officials who wished to suppress the Boxers caused alarm amongst both the more far-sighted foreigners and the more steady of the Chinese government advisors. By May 1900 the Boxers were on the edge of Běijīng, and even the foreign diplomats, whose contempt for the Chinese was nearly as great as that of the Chinese for them, began to take note.

The foreign community in Běijīng lived mostly in what was known as the Legation Quarter, although not formally organized as such, within the Tartar City wall east of Qián Mén, behind the location of the modern History Museum. In addition to the legations, there were two European-run shops with imported provisions, and the original Hôtel de Pékin, run by a Swiss. The first Boxer activity near Běijīng was the firing of the railway junction at Fēngtái in May, and during June all Europeans in the area and a large quantity of Christian converts withdrew either to the Legation Quarter or the city's cathedrals, to be joined by a small body of troops from the foreign warships standing off the coast beyond Tiānjīn. Reinforcements coming by rail later that month found the tracks damaged and were forced to retreat, but the chancellor of the Japanese embassy, riding alone to the station to greet them, was dragged from his horse and hacked to death. On 13 June there was a general firing of foreign property outside the Legation Quarter including the East Cathedral, and a massacre of converts. Following the rescue of a party of nuns and converts from the South Cathedral, that too was put to the flames.

In the first few days non-Christian retainers wisely left, and occasional sallies were made to bring in groups of Chinese Christians who were being attacked. Imperial troops stood by and watched, yet messages were received from the Manchu court which expressed concern for the safety of the foreign community and suggested a retreat guarded by the very troops who were currently doing nothing to protect them. Nevertheless, a majority of the ministers were in favour of accepting this offer, which would almost certainly have led to a general massacre en route, but sent a reply requesting a meeting to discuss logistics. Tiring of the wait for a reply, the forceful German minister, von Ketteler, set out on 19 June for face-to-face discussions at the Zǒnglǐ Yámen (Foreign Office), only to be shot dead in the street by a Manchu soldier.

The next day the fight began in earnest. In the weeks that followed, the besieged withdrew mostly into a moderately defensible area around the British Legation, expanding only to take over an area of city wall that overlooked it. The multi-national defenders, after some jostling, fell under the overall leadership of the British minister, Sir Claude MacDonald. Instructions were issued and requests for reinforcements received in the form of polite written notes quite in keeping with the usual occupation of the more senior defenders. Ill-prepared for a siege, the community, mostly crammed into the British buildings, had to live on the meat of their Mongolian ponies, washed down with champagne from the ample cellars of one of the European shops. After only a few days the pretence that it was the supposedly uncontrollable Boxers who attacked the legations was given up, and both Imperial troops and a Muslim army from the northwest could be seen to take part in the attacks. The Muslim army, in order to burn out the foreigners, set fire to China's greatest library in the Hànlín Shū Yuán (literally, 'Hanlin Book Garden') just to the north of the British Legation, but the wind did not blow the fire in the right direction. What little was saved of the immense literary treasures inside ended up in the libraries of European capitals. Amongst the volumes lost were most of one copy of an extremely rare 22,877-chapter compendium of Chinese learning, known as the *Yǒnglè Dàdiǎn*, after the Míng emperor who commissioned it.

At one point the Qīng declared a truce, and fruit was sent in to the foreigners, together with news from home, and messages of condolence when that news was bad. Some authorities have it that the Empress Cíxī merely wished to pass some time in Běi Hǎi without the sound of gunfire to disturb her.

Communication by telegraph was once again allowed with the outside world, enabling the foreigners to send messages concerning their plight, directly contrary to those sent by the Qīng assuring their governments that every possible assistance was being given. But of all the bizarre aspects of the siege, perhaps the strangest was that the besiegers, even when after a few days hostilities were resumed, and with all the advantages of numerical superiority and of the high ground of the Qián Mén, did not press home the attack and massacre the besieged, which with a little firm leadership they might easily have done. An American woman who lived through the siege, writing under the name Mary Hooker, put it down, without complaint, to a 'national fear of attacking'.

Relief eventually came from a multi-national force of Russians, Americans, French, Japanese and British, which encountered little organized resistance on the way from Tiānjīn. Having been slow to set off, and not unreasonably fearing a need for far greater numbers than they had, they also feared that they were too late—obituaries of Sir Claude MacDonald and others had already been published. Meeting little credible opposition as they progressed, their tentativeness faded away and was replaced by a spirit of competition for the credit of being the first to relieve the siege, and the political benefit of sitting at the table for negotiations of a partition of China, one possible result of their advance.

The armies camped three miles just outside the city walls to the east, planning a co-ordinated attack on five points on 14 and 15 August, but the Russians got carried away and attacked during the preceding night, eventually taking the Dōngbiàn Mén (now the site of an interchange between Chóngwén Mén Dàjiē and the second ring road, southeast of Běijīng Zhàn), with considerable losses, sometime the next day. The Japanese were held up at a gate further north, halfway up the east side of the Tartar City. Like all the other major gates, its enclosed courtyard design proved remarkably difficult to penetrate, and it was not until the 15th that the majority of the Japanese entered Běijīng. The French got lost, and entered Běijīng last through the Russian-reduced Dōngbiàn Mén. The Americans scaled the wall just south of the Russians. The British found their gate, halfway down the east side of the Chinese City, undefended. Blowing it open with artillery, they advanced cautiously northwest through deserted streets, until they caught sight of a signaller on the wall who semaphored a message telling them to break through a water gate beneath, leading directly into the Legation Quarter. Scarcely a shot was fired, and it was a joint Russian-American charge along the wall itself that later in the day cleared the opposition from the remains of the Qián Mén.

A period of considerable confusion followed. The court had disintegrated, and the Dowager Empress and the Emperor had escaped to Xī'ān. Boxers, Imperial troops and private citizens all fell to looting, followed with gusto by members of both the besieged and relieving forces.

Settlement of reparations was not completed until the following year. The foreign powers insisted on the deaths of leading xenophobic ministers, who were duly instructed by the court to commit suicide. The indemnity claimed was £67,500,000, in yearly payments equivalent to half the Qīng annual budget. This took another 39 years to pay in full, and the British and Americans led the way in returning it to China in the form of educational schemes and other aid. The Qīng court probably considered itself to have got off lightly. The Dowager Empress, known by all to be the real power in China, returned to Běijīng, completing her journey by a Belgian train, changing at the Fēngtái junction near the Marco Polo Bridge to a British train, which brought her along a newly built extension to just outside Yǒngdìng Mén, still the site of Běijīng South Railway Station (Nán Zhàn). She and the Emperor proceeded directly north by palanquin to Qián Mén where large numbers of foreigners had gathered on the remains of the gate to watch the Imperial progress. Their presence was acknowledged with a series of little bows, which so amazed them that a spontaneous round of applause broke out for the woman who only a few months before had connived at the destruction of themselves and their compatriots.

The Manchus were also forced to agree to a permanent foreign military presence to guarantee the link to the coast and to protect a brand new Legation Quarter. The remains of the private residences of both rich and poor, as well as neighbouring temples and the remains of the ancient academy which had been set alight by the Huí (Muslim) troops, were absorbed into the area, which then became yet another walled sector. The section of the Tartar City wall between the Qián Mén and what is now known as Chóngwén Mén overlooking the Legation Quarter was also taken over and, while the rest disappeared under weeds, was kept in good repair. The streets were given foreign names (Legation Street, Rue Marco Polo), and most countries erected buildings in imitation of styles from home, like an early Expo. Instead of driving away the foreigners, the foreign Qīng had only succeeded in giving them an even greater presence in the capital.

Cíxī was probably astonished that once again a successful foreign invasion of Běijīng had nevertheless left the Qīng in power, but then as now, foreign big business preferred stability, under which they might make profits, to an unknown alternative, however murderous and distasteful the current government might be. Reginald Johnston, writing his memoir of his long relationship with the last Manchu emperor, likened the Boxers' policies to those of the Hitler government—whose power was on the rise as he wrote—towards non-Nordic peoples on German territory, and suggested that the ever-louder rhetoric of Chinese revolutionaries was drawn as much from these speeches as from those of the newly communist USSR to the north.

Modern Běijīng

The 20th century brought further uprisings and rebellions following those which had plagued the Qīng in the 19th century. Following her return to Běijīng the Dowager Empress began a number of conciliatory reforms of the kind started decades earlier by the Guǎngxù emperor, and which she had crushed, retaking power in a coup. She was now forced to consider moves towards a written constitution and perhaps some more limited form of monarchy. There were steps, too, continued after her death in 1908, to dissolve the remaining barriers of status between Manchu and Hàn Chinese (the main Chinese ethnic group) and Manchus were now permitted to marry Hàn. But the Qīng's failures were too many and too longstanding. As George III's emissary to the Qiánlóng emperor, Lord Macartney, had put it in 1793–4:

The Empire of China is an old, crazy, First rate man-of-war, which a fortunate succession of able and vigilant officers has contrived to keep afloat for these one hundred and fifty years past, and to overawe their neighbours merely by her bulk and appearance, but whenever an insufficient man happens to have the command up on deck, adieu to the discipline and safety of the ship. She may perhaps not sink outright; she may drift some time as a wreck, and will then be dashed to pieces on the shore; but she can never be rebuilt on the old bottom.

Lord Macartney, *An Embassy to China,*
J. L. Cranmer-Byng [Ed.], 1962

Although there had been a succession of undistinguished captains since the Qiánlóng emperor of Macartney's day, the 'insufficient man' turned out to be a forceful woman. The greatest failure of the Qīng throughout the 19th century, and especially during the serial regencies of the Dowager Empress Cíxī, was the failure to throw off the anti-foreign prejudice they had absorbed from the Chinese, and deal realistically with the challenges and opportunities presented by the high-tech, expansionist West. These failures were to be repeated both by those who rose against the Qīng, and by those who finally took power over the whole country in 1949. Foreigners remain to this day a handy scapegoat for the failures of government policy, and whipping up anti-foreign sentiment a useful diversion for domestic discontent.

The Qīng's failure to control the Western barbarians was held against them by both those Chinese who despised the Qīng as also foreign and barbarian and by those who accepted their rule but criticized their failure to resist the foreigners by adopting their technologies and institutions. A Qīng duke who was going overseas to study foreign methods of government was wounded by a bomb thrown at him on the platform of the station at Qián Mén. In 1907 the foreign-educated Sun Yat-sen (Sūn Zhōngshān) launched a failed uprising in the south, and returned to exile. In 1910, the Prince-Regent, the infant emperor's father, issued an edict announcing the creation of a two-chamber parliament to begin work in 1913, and in the same year survived an assassination attempt. His assailant, to whom he generously only gave a life sentence, survived to become an important Nationalist Party official.

The Prince-Regent's biggest mistake, however, was to summon Yuán Shìkǎi back to suppress a rebellion which almost accidentally took the industrial tri-city complex of Wǔhàn in 1911, and spread rapidly from there. Yuán had earlier betrayed the Guǎnxù emperor's attempts at reforms, which might have spared the Qīng their current dangers, and had been banished from the court following the accession of the infant Pǔyí. He was the only credible military commander the Qīng had, however, and the forces under his control were the most disciplined. He reduced rebel forces just enough to show who was in charge and, had he wished to do so, he could have saved the dynasty by crushing them. Instead he brought Qīng representatives and rebels to a peace conference in Shànghǎi at which he negotiated the 'Articles Providing for the Favourable Treatment of the Great Ch'ing [Qīng] Emperor after his Abdication'. The emperor was to continue living in the Forbidden City for the time being, and then to move to the Summer Palace, powerless but assured of an annual government stipend of four million taels of silver. He remained there until driven out by another warlord in 1924. Yuán's price to the rebels for completing their revolution was that he, not Sun Yat-sen, become the first President of China.

The term 'the Chinese empire' was one used by foreigners rather than Chinese, who referred to the Great Qīng Empire, and before that the Great Míng Empire. The Qīng might easily have retired to their ancestral homelands in Manchuria, never part of China, and the revolutionaries might have found them very hard to dislodge, and it might not even have occurred to them to try. But thanks to Yuán both empires were lost to the Qīng, although Europeans hailed the terms as remarkably generous compared to those offered to their own deposed monarchs in recent centuries. However Yuán subsequently looted what funds he could, borrowed sums from the imperial house he never repaid, and the imperial stipend was itself never paid in full. The Republic also took on loan from the emperor a vast collection of treasures until such time as it could afford to pay an agreed seven-figure purchase price. The treasures were subsequently confiscated without a penny being paid.

In the early period of the Republic there was widespread looting by soldiers who largely went unpaid (Yuán himself had one million men under arms) and recompensed themselves by force of arms instead. Foreigners found themselves being offered great treasures for minimal sums, and vast quantities of texts and objets d'art left China forever to join private collections and those of museums. The Chinese authorities, even if they had shown interest, would have been unable to pay in funds the owners would accept, and while the current regime wishes to portray this as yet another period of foreign plunder, many express thanks that at least the items were preserved.

Yuán's final betrayal was his own preparations to adopt imperial status just three years later in 1915. Once President he had immediately banned Sun Yat-sen's supporters, the Nationalist Party, but a revolt in the south—Sun's 'second revolution'—forced him to cancel his plans for a new dynasty and he died the following year. The revolution was nevertheless crushed and Sun once again fled to the safety of Hong Kong and on to Japan.

Yuán's original betrayal of the Guǎngxù emperor's reforms had caused the strengthening of opposition to ineffectual Manchu rule, and his betrayal of the Manchus for his own ends cost them both China and Manchuria. His subsequent betrayal of the ideas of the Republic weakened its own already insubstantial authority, and it is he, as well as Cíxī, who must take some of the blame for the chaos of 20th- and 21st-century China.

Communist China

After Yuán's death other presidents came and went, parliaments and cabinets were summoned and dismissed again, and Běijīng changed hands between various warlords, whose loyalty to a democratic Republic came and went at their convenience. One pro-monarchist even restored the emperor to authority for 12 days in July 1917, but was almost immediately defeated by another warlord who had the military advantage of aeroplanes and who dropped three bombs on the Forbidden City. One fell in a lake and another failed to explode, but it was enough.

In late 1924 the 'Christian General' (who used forcibly to baptise his men with a fire hose) took advantage of battles between other warlords to seize control of Běijīng, and on 5 November expelled the emperor from the Forbidden City and placed him under arrest at his father's house. On 29 November his tutor, Sir Reginald Johnston, engineered a daring escape to the Legation Quarter. He was never to visit the palace again.

Intermittent civil war between the north and south followed. The Nationalist government in the south declared the return of the capital to Nánjīng in 1928, and Běijīng to its old name, Běipíng, and the city went into further decline. The authors of one 1930s guide book complained that many ancient buildings had been vandalized, allowed to fall into disrepair or were now covered in political slogans, and some had been destroyed on official orders.

> The loss by vandalism and utter neglect has been proceeding at such
> a rate that, on repeated occasions, buildings and historical
> monuments have actually disappeared while the authors were still
> writing about them.

L. C. Arlington and William Lewisohn,
In Search of Old Peking, 1935

The Japanese occupied the city between 1937 and the end of the Second World War, but did little damage, revering its remaining palaces and temples, still far more numerous than today, although they treated the Chinese themselves with callous contempt.

Elsewhere in China civil war between the forces of the Communist and Nationalist Parties was temporarily suspended so as to drive out the Japanese, but at the end of the Second World War hostilities were resumed where they left off.

The Republic went from bad to worse and, with illiteracy the norm, only a tiny proportion of the population had the first idea what a republic was, much as only a small number really have any idea what 'democracy' is today. Despite the constant repetition of the idea 'serve the people' few have any idea of putting the state above the needs of their immediate family and those with whom they have connections—*guānxì*—and so it was then.

The communists returned the city to capital status, Máo Zédōng announcing the creation of the People's Republic from atop the Tiān'ān Mén on 1 October 1949, and they then proceeded to destroy most of what was left. During the years that followed ancient temples and halls were turned into military camps and factories. A huge influx of people turned court-yard houses that had once held single families and their servants into homes for dozens. The city walls that had stood since Yuán and Míng times were completely torn down, leaving only the occasional gate tower standing isolated and pointless. The stone from the walls was used to line a system of tunnels into which the population could theoretically run in case of nuclear attack, and no doubt be tidily vaporized all in one place (*see* 'Underground City', p.155), as well as a secret system connecting the Great Hall of the People and the government residential compound of Zhōngnán Hǎi with an escape route to the west. The line of the walls of the Tartar city was replaced below ground by more tunnels, those of the metro's circle line, several of whose stops are named after now-vanished gates. Above ground the perimeter line of the Tartar and Chinese cities is followed by the second ring road, still clearly showing the wider bulge of the Chinese city in the south.

The few English signs at Běijīng's sights are loquacious in their indictment of the foreign troops who inflicted damage in 1860 and 1900, but remarkably reticent about the rather larger scale efforts of the Chinese themselves, who mobilized themselves in large-scale political campaigns aimed at ridding the country of its heritage and set about destroying artefacts, buildings, as well as people with any education about or sympathy for them, particularly during the 1966–76 Cultural Revolution.

The scale of the destruction is indicated by recently announced plans to make Běijīng one of the world's top tourist attractions within 15 years. While much of this plan consists of vague intentions to improve the environment and infrastructure, socialism is never seen to advance without concrete figures. First 45 ancient sites are to be restored at a cost of ¥200 million, bringing the number of officially designated tourist sites from 105 to 150 (24 of 'national level'), although even the most obsessive visitor will currently have difficulty finding more a fraction of that amount, unless he or she includes such joys as the Dōngbiān Mén Overpass, hymned in one Chinese guide book ('821,000 square metres of road surface along with 60 bridges embracing a total length of 97,290 metres').

By 2010 the number of restored sites will supposedly have tripled to 350, demonstrating what a treasure house pre-communist Běijīng must have been. Twenty new museums are to be built, including a new Capital Museum to display the treasures stored beneath the Forbidden City, bringing the city's total to 110, although many are of little or no interest even to the Chinese, and many cannot be found even in Chinese guide books. That new museums at Xī'ān and Shànghǎi have won international attention is undoubtedly a factor in this programme of culture-by-numbers. The modern guidebook writer is faced with a problem exactly opposite to that of Arlington and Lewisohn, quoted above, as numbers of ancient buildings emerge from obscurity as factories, storehouses, and dormitories, and new museums sprout faster than the pen can follow.

'The streets are so straight and wide that you can see right along them from end to end and from gate to the other,' reported Polo of the Mongol city, but if the gates still stood they would now be invisible. The rapid industrialization brought on by the communists has led to Běijīng becoming one of the world's most polluted cities. The number of vehicles on its streets has been growing by 15 per cent per annum, and it has been estimated that 50 per cent of them would fail even the most basic emissions test. In 1996, in a long overdue effort to reduce traffic congestion and pollution, the city's PSB (police) announced that minibuses and jeeps would only be allowed inside the third ring road every other day, based on whether they had odd- or even-numbered licence plates. This ran directly counter to the declared national policy of developing the auto industry into an 'economic pillar', and so the regulation was quietly dropped. Spring is the best time to visit, for although its winds may bring in scouring clouds of Gobi sand they also blow some of the pollution away.

Shànghǎi considers itself far more sophisticated and trendy than Běijīng, but new regulations and changes in the social order are first detected on the capital's seismometers. Běijīng is always the first to see new regulations in operation, sometimes the only place, and sometimes the writ runs little further than Tiān'ān Mén and the neighbouring streets directly under the eyes of senior party officials.

Surveys reveal that Chinese increasingly identify themselves with their home towns, and don't trust those from other parts of the country. Government-approved research showed that while people from Shànghǎi are regarded as astute and stingy, those from Guǎngzhōu as involved in shady deals, and Hong Kongers as smooth and slippery, Běijīng people are rated by others as frank, passionate and cultivated. Asked what they thought about themselves, they replied, 'lazy'. These days their incomes are Běijīng residents' greatest concern, and they are cynical about the government's various campaigns, 54 per cent rarely or never talking about politics.

The gap between rich and poor is widening rapidly, the richest 20 per cent of urban house-holds owning 7.85 times the property of the lowest 20 per cent.

Crowded Běijīng is becoming more so, as permit-less migrant labourers pour into the capital to work on construction projects, and visitors become more and more numerous. Tourism administrators expect 3.23 million overseas tourists per annum by the year 2010, and 93 million domestic visitors as more people take advantage of their growing incomes and new freedom to visit the centre of Chinese power. Meanwhile, the numbers of peasants excess to requirements, already estimated at about 100 million even with the low level of mechaniza-tion currently seen on China's farmland, is only likely to grow as entry to international trade organizations forces China to allow food imports. This situation again forces them to allow peasants to grow whatever will make a profit, and not what a planned economy determined not to be dependent on others for its food makes them plant, whatever the soil suitability. This will only increase migration.

Topics

Two hundred years ago, she told us, the Ch'ien Lung [Qiánlōng]
Emperor traveled in disguise to the south of China by ship, and on the
way a magic storm arose, during which the water devils... rose up and
held the ship fast, intending to sink it then and there. But the emperor,
revealing his true identity to them, promised that if they let the ship
proceed, they would all become government officials in a future incar-
nation, two hundred years later. This satisfied them, and they released
the ship and sank down into the sea again. The storm subsided, and
the emperor continued on his way, thinking no more of the incident.
Nevertheless, an emperor's promise is sacred and may not be broken.
Aunt Chin laughed. "They've all become Communist officials," she
said. "But they're really water devils, and that's why it rains every time
they come out."

David Kidd, *Peking Story*, London 1996

The overnight disappearance of Marxism worldwide in all but the tiniest and least influential places took the leadership by surprise. But even as the popular rejection of self-perpetuating communist oligarchy and its corruption, inefficiency and inability to deliver a decent standard of living gathered pace, the growing anarchy and shortages, the decline in life expectancy and further decline in living standards, and the increase in crime that followed the installation of democracy in Russia provided the hysterical irony of Chinese 'revolutionaries' donning the mantle of reactionary Madame de Pompadour and threatening, '*Après nous le déluge*.'

The regime's current love affair with free-market capitalism has had to be carried out while claiming it to be a natural and inevitable progression from its seizure of power in 1949, although many view it as a final realization that without giving politics a back seat and putting material comforts to the fore, the Communist Party of China might finally lose its monopoly on power. Basing its claims to legitimacy on popular support for the policies of Marx and Máo, it cannot admit to turning its back on these without also admitting the possibility that it might itself disappear, and so its current policies are not anti-collectivist and anti-Marxist, but 'socialism with Chinese characteristics'. But the cuts in state support for enterprises and social programmes are as rapid and deep as die-hards in the Party will permit the current leadership to make. These include dismantling the cradle-to-grave employment system and the cheap housing, free healthcare and free education that go with it. Black, 'with Chinese characteristics', is white.

The Party performs a difficult balancing act in which a freeing of incomes allows some to get very rich very quickly as the new private sector booms, and earns the (albeit lukewarm) support of those who benefit, while there are daily demonstrations by those whose spending power has dropped as the success of the more efficient and customer-oriented private businesses has reduced demand yet further for the low-quality goods and services of their state-owned employers, and they are sent home on part pay, or see their livelihood disappear altogether.

In 1999 these factors came together to create significant changes to the very experience of visiting Běijīng, partially due to a tricky conjunction of anniversaries. It was the 80th anniversary of the 4 May protests of 1919, officially adopted as pro-revolutionary, but which also contained calls for greater democracy. It was the 10th anniversary of the crushing of the 4 June 1989 democracy movement, the cause of annual irritation to the Party, and the world would almost be expecting some kind of protest activity. But it was also the 50th anniversary of the founding of the People's Republic itself—an occasion to mark the glorious, unwavering, unidirectional, irreversible progress in the well-being of the Chinese people brought about by 50 years of communist rule.

Tiān'ān Mén Square being the focus both for protest and the centre of officially sponsored celebrations of all kinds, the government decided to close it off for repairs until the 4 May and 4 June anniversaries were safely past, and then on 1 October to hold the biggest party the country had ever seen. To make sure the message about the successes of the last 50 years got across, the jowls of communism were given a face-lift.

Tiān'ān Mén square was repaved in granite, given a new PA system, lighting, and, of course, security cameras. The grime of the surrounding buildings was sandblasted away. Even the symbols of imperial authority got an overhaul, with the two Qián Mén gates at the south end of the square and the Tiān'ān Mén at the north touched up, as if even they had been improved by 50 years of communist disasters and mismanagement.

Hoardings and signage along an extended section of Cháng'ān Dàjiē (nearly all of them triumphantly advertising foreign goods and services) were forcibly removed, regardless of contracts between the advertisers, the owners of the hoardings, and the owners of the buildings. Beneath the street, the construction of a long-overdue metro system extension (its funds siphoned away by corruption), was accelerated to meet the 1 October deadline, while all along the avenue shiny new buildings went up and older ones were given a new coat of paint. Shopping streets were pedestrianized, new gardens planted, the canal system and Forbidden City moat cleaned out and relined. For a long period leading up to the great celebration, Běijīng became a giant building site.

If it didn't rain on the communists' parade, it was probably because they had somehow made arrangements that it shouldn't, and because like other dissident elements and disgraced former party members, anything resembling a water devil had been hustled out of Běijīng for the duration and put under arrest elsewhere.

Certainly nothing else was left to chance. On several weekends before the great day, martial law was imposed in central Běijīng while rehearsals were carried out. Twenty-five factories were told to cease production for 10 days so that the sky would be clear enough to see the flypast by military aircraft. Mobile phone and pager systems were shut down for two hours. Foreigners weren't allowed hotel rooms looking towards Tiān'ān Mén, and residents of many buildings along Cháng'ān were told they could not leave their homes on the day of the event, while others were warned they could not have guests to stay during the period leading up to the great day.

For weeks beforehand tour groups were also banned; even private individuals who stepped off trains were questioned, and if they couldn't provide a satisfactory reason for being in town were sent away again. The goal was also to reduce the city's population by 300,000. Beggars, itinerant labourers and the homeless were rounded up and put on trains to the countryside. Prostitutes and bar hostesses were also targeted, papers claiming that in a single raid the police had closed 6,000 saunas and beauty parlours providing illegal sexual services. Street vendors were cleared away from the centre and, beyond Běijīng itself, across the country dissidents were locked up.

But in addition to the promised circus, others more in a position to make trouble for the government also received bread. A few days before the big day companies were suddenly instructed their staff would have several days' paid public holiday, and government employees suddenly gained 30 per cent pay rises, a backdated six-month lump sum being handed over on the spot.

Only 100,000 observers hand-picked as reliable were allowed to become the enthusiastic audience and the rest of China was told to watch TV, but many couldn't be bothered. Those who attended were instructed in exactly how to be enthusiastic, and given 50 slogans to yell, including 'Long live Marxism-Leninism, Máo Zédōng thought, and Dèng Xiǎopíng Theory', 'Wholeheartedly depend on the working class' (who are in fact once again as despised in China as they ever were), and the snappy 'Use your own strength to change your life, struggle arduously, with hard work and thrift build the nation, with hard work and thrift accomplish all tasks.'

'Thrift' was hardly a factor in the celebrations themselves. Estimates of the cost vary wildly, the government having co-opted many schemes, such as the construction of the giant shopping-office-hotel complex of Oriental Plaza on Cháng'ān, into the general celebrations. The Běijīng municipal government claimed to have invested ¥116.5 billion (about US$14 billion) to complete 67 large-scale projects in time for the anniversary. The urban waterways beautification project alone cost ¥1 billion ($125 million) according to *China Daily*, but ¥30 billion ($3.75 billion) according to another source published at the same time. Meanwhile, at the end of that year, tens of thousands of people made homeless by the Yangtze River's annual floods were left without any government support and were being fed by the Red Cross.

China receives an estimated $6 billion in aid from foreigners every year, a fraction of the cost of the Party's big party.

Hútòng Walking

'Where,' demands the visitor, alternatively squinting at the fine mesh of streets marked on his map and waving it in the face of the puzzled concierge, 'is *The Hútòng?*'

The *hútòng* once provided instant 'I'm a traveller—you're just a tourist' credibility, conveniently gained with minimum discomfort by merely turning a corner when organized tours went straight on. But now the beaten-up backstreets of Běijīng have joined the list of 'must-sees' for even the most opulent of tours.

Hútòng, singular and plural, a Mandarin word derived from the languages of the capital's Mongol founders, means nothing more than 'alley', and no map or guide, and certainly no 100-yuán half-day tour in some Cadillac version of a bicycle rickshaw is needed. Simply turn off almost any of the main streets boulevardized by communism, and you're in a different world.

But if beauty is in the eye of the beholder, charm certainly is, too, as well as in the nose. The careful stage management of early China tourism kept foreigners well away from all but carefully sanitized poverty, but the authorities now seem resigned to the fact that they can't hide the slums, and have learned that 'where there's muck, there's brass', as the increasing numbers of coffee table books of *hútòng* photography, each the cost of a week or two's salary for the average Běijīng worker, testify. But if you want to see 'real' China—or, at least, real Běijīng, here it is.

This is the setting for Chinese television's equivalent to *Coronation Street*. Families live crowded together in a jumble of ancient courtyard houses called *sìhéyuàn*, hundreds of years old, mixed with grim and grimy dormitory blocks, workshops and factories. Few have proper running water, and washrooms and toilets are both public. Nevertheless, air-conditioning units are stuck on crumbling walls which sometimes seem like parcels tied together by cable television wiring with junction boxes as knots.

Here cars are relatively few compared to bicycles, cycle rickshaws, and HGV tricycles working as delivery vans, their flat beds overloaded with furniture or televisions and with limited braking power. Small guardian lion statues or drum stones on doorsteps, carved lintels and roofs of ancient tile give clues to the history now covered with a patina of small scale commerce.

Walls have been knocked out to turn rooms into tiny shops. Seamstresses bend over wedding dress commissions; an old woman sits patiently next to her speak-your-weight machine; a man selling vegetables feeds baby rabbits which sit placidly amongst his produce; a woman in a highly slit cheongsam and vertigo-inducing high heels beckons at the entrance of a dubious hairdressing salon; piles of bamboo steamers sit on miniature coal-fired stoves, offering tasty and filling dumplings for ridiculously low prices.

The dominant colour is grey—that of the brick and the coal smoke. Colour is provided by red peppers drying on a windowsill, by a woman cycling by with difficulty in a sheath dress of metallic blue sequins, by the partly knitted baby clothes of a row of mothers seated on small stools along a wall, or by a public toilet whose exterior is painted in a pink nearly as unpleasant as its smell. The lanes are playgrounds for children, a marketplace for adults, and, at night, for lives in which privacy is almost completely unknown, the place for trysts behind tree trunks.

In the quieter *hútòng*, the day may begin with the fluid slow-motion exercises of *tàijíquán* ('tai chi'), sometimes in the tiny parks that dot the city, sometimes in the streets themselves. As the day heats up, retired old men may be seen walking to meeting places under trees, carrying bamboo birdcages containing songbirds, which they uncover and suspend from wires strung between the branches, next to those of their friends. Both species proceed to chat.

As the day progresses, the shade also collects groups of chess, mah-jong and go players, and numerous onlookers. In the afternoon, back from school, children in Manchester United kit kick around a ball, or play netless badminton. Once again allowed to own dogs (there's a black market in the licences), Běijīng people have returned, appropriately, to keeping snuffling Pekinese, which are known in local slang as 'capital barks' (*Jīngbā*) but which they are only allowed to walk in the evening. As night falls in larger open spaces older ladies gather for sessions of yangko (*yāngge*) folk dancing to the beat of drum and cymbal, and process, conga-like, waving fans. An electronic folk tune heard repeating itself at various distances comes from a sewage truck, or from one spraying the road with water to reduce the dust.

From the higher floors of any of the better central hotels you can look down on much the same views as the first diplomats to reside in Běijīng might have seen, only the housing is now 150 years older and the roofs are often corrugated sheets held down with piles of bricks, random pieces of lumber and other debris, the houses huddled as close together as if in a rugby scrum.

Otherwise views are surprisingly green, and not only because roofs themselves are often over-grown. There are more than 130 parks of 16 acres or more around the town centre. Each spring massive planting campaigns can add as many as 11 million saplings to Běijīng's tree count. The most popular varieties in and around the city are the Chinese scholar tree, which has low resistance to pests, and the poplar and willow, whose feathery seeds blow around the streets in spring and early summer. Běijīng is now planting ginkgoes in the city, and persimmons, peaches and walnuts in the surrounding countryside, with the hope of developing a viable fruit and nut industry.

The trees also help to reduce Běijīng's dreadful dustiness, but even so, whereas the international standard for dust fall is less than eight tonnes per square kilometre, Běijīng has 18.5 tonnes, most of it blown in by spring winds from 1.1 million acres of sandy wastes outside the centre, and particularly from one county to the northwest which is 300 metres higher than the city. The general pollution and the dust from continuous construction mean the sky is rarely blue, and in windy spring time many wear masks.

The *hútòng* are also seeing a gradual return of more traditions than simply once-banned board games. The resumption of permission to own private businesses has brought a return of the itinerant street vendors' cries for which the city was once famous. The literary English eccentric Sir Osbert Sitwell, visiting Běijīng in 1934, noted cries including 'I will give money for foreign bottles. I also buy scrap iron and broken glass,' and a toy seller with 'Buy, Small Man, they are lifelike, they have eyes and arms,' as well as an orchestra's worth of different percussion instruments identifying everything from hat sellers to porcelain menders. You can now hear pear sellers yelling, 'Sweet and crunchy!', and may be woken in the morning by the long-drawn out '*Mó jiǎnzi le, qiǎng cài dāo*', advertising a willingness to sharpen knives and scissors. Hand-painted signs at narrow entrances hint at more modern and less mobile occupations: 'I fix VCD players.'

Kite-flying traditionally dates back to the time of Confucius, and the Chinese once produced a wide variety of flying dragons, centipedes and goldfish from paper or silk and bamboo. The imperial family were once the buyers of the most expensive kites, and after the downfall of the Qīng they were popular with rich actors. Méi Lánfāng himself (*see* p.179) is said to have been an expert flyer. The kites of modern Běijīng more resemble Western ones, although their plastic is still printed with images of birds and dragons, although exactly what can be hard to discern—great altitudes are often obtained, particularly from the bridges over the second ring road, and the kites are mere specks.

Tradition has it that keeping birds in China dates back to a goose-loving calligrapher of the third century BCE. Bird ownership was once so popular, and the morning airing of the birds thought so important, that bird walkers were employed much in the way of dog walkers in developed countries today. Flocks of pigeons can commonly be seen whirling in ragged formation over the *hútòng* and until a few years ago, before the rapid growth of traffic and karaoke, the eerie moan made by bamboo whistles attached to the roots of their tail feathers could also be heard.

Although pigeons and caged songbirds were the first pets to return after the Cultural Revolution of 1966–76 (during which it was dangerous to be connected with anything remotely amusing or bourgeois), the Chinese have also long trained birds to perform tricks and act as retrievers. Particularly in the autumn you may come across a small crowd gathered around a bicycle rickshaw with extra attachments to its handlebars on which sit a small flock of grey, black-capped, yellow-beaked birds, a string from a chest feather tying each to its perch, and a man who suddenly throws one bird up in the air together with a small bead, which the bird intercepts. But even as it does so, the owner quickly presses a blowpipe to his lips and fires a second bead high into the sky which the bird also intercepts, and then perhaps performs a little mid-air gambol as it returns to drop the beads into the palm of its owner and be rewarded with some flax seeds.

The trick is called *dǎ dànr*, 'fetch balls', said to have been a pastime popular with the imperial eunuchs, and the amiable bird is the *wútóng*, or masked grosbeak. Perhaps the redpolls, cross-bills, waxwings and other birds the Chinese used to train to do different tricks will reappear before long.

As in the past, some train the birds and fly them for pleasure, others train them to sell for up to eight times the price of an untrained chick. The birds used once to be found at the temple fairs which have also recently been revived, often as a way of attracting visitors to otherwise over-looked locations, many now staging fairs they never had before and limiting them mostly to the spring. The biggest fairs were once at the Lóngfú Sì just east of the top of Wángfǔjǐng, its site now covered by the Lóngfú Dàshà department store with a token temple built on the roof, followed by that of the Hùguó Sì in a corresponding position on the west side of the city, of which only a single dilapidated hall remains (*see* p.179). Another fair was held at the Bàoguó Sì, now completely turned over to the selling of antiques and bric-à-brac (*see* p.237). In spring, look for details of fairs at Báiyún Guàn, Dì Tán and Dōng Yuè Miào, and outside Běijīng at the Red Conch Temple and Tánzhè Sì. These often amount to little more than impromptu street markets, but at some there's now a comeback of traditional street performers, too: acrobats, musicians and conjurers.

Many *hútòng* names give away the former presence of long-vanished landmarks, such as Three Palaces Hútòng, Three Wells Hútòng, Sleeping Buddha Temple Hútòng, or those named for grain warehouses. Some, such as Shí Family Hútòng, were named for former residents; other names merely confuse, such as Big Ear Hútòng.

Despite all the fuss about new tourist attractions, destruction of old Běijīng continues, particu-larly as the ancient alleys are bulldozed for more of the windy totalitarianism of immense boulevards, and for foreign-funded squeaky-clean shopping complexes and hotels. The govern-ment has been pulling down ancient housing almost since the day it took power and putting up first hideous six-storey brick blocks, then equally hideous concrete towers, and finally the ramshackle collection of aesthetically challenged office towers which prick the grey skies today. Estimates of the numbers of *hútòng* vary, but there are said to have been several thou-sand in the Míng and Qīng dynasties, and still 3,200 in 1944, but well under a thousand now, nearly 300 having disappeared since the '60s alone.

But only recently has the smashing down of a large area for a new cross-city highway, Píng'ān Dà Dào, attracted much in the way of protest. Eight thousand displaced residents were promised accommodation in new towers and apartments with private bathrooms. These turned out to be poorly constructed, and far from both the centre of town and from friends. Furthermore, although some of the residents had owned their homes since the 1940s, many were moved without compensation into rented property in violation both of the constitution and more recent housing law. Unsurprisingly, suing the govenment brought no relief.

Other areas of *hútòng* are cleared because planners envision a modern capital, effectively indistinguishable from any other metropolis, and which can accommodate the city's rapidly growing fleet of 1.5 million vehicles. The narrow *hútòng* get in their way, and in 1999 alone 600 acres of *hútòng* housing was cleared for 'safety' reasons. Once the dreaded character *chāi* ('demolish') appears daubed in red on the side of a house, its fate is sealed. Yet more land has been cleared for the construction of the new National Theatre behind the Great Hall of the People, the residents just given small sums in cash and told to go. The hideously expensive building will act as a showcase for the 'superiority of Chinese culture', say officials, obviously feeling that they are sweeping away much of the inferior side to do it.

The pressure for construction is not only due to government vanity, but also to the increase in the number of residents. According to Chinese figures the population of China passed 1.3bn in 2000, but some foreign commentators believe it in fact to be as much as 1.5bn already. The numbers of migrants moving around the country looking for work may soon reach 120 million, and some expect 20 per cent of the population to move from the countryside into the cities during the first half of this century.

There's frightening talk of preserving a few *hútòng* for posterity—in a city where preservation usually means complete reconstruction and prettification. Better take that quiet turning now while it's still there to take.

How Chinese Works

妈

mā

'I speak Chinese' is a statement that carries less meaning than might at first appear. There are several groups of Chinese dialects so different from each other that they are often spoken of as different languages. The Cantonese speaker at your local Chinese restaurant would not be understood by a speaker of Mandarin, for instance, nor vice versa.

麻

má

Mandarin, also known as Modern Standard Chinese or *Pǔtōnghuà*, 'common speech', is the official language of the People's Republic, and used in schools. It's commonly assumed by foreigners that Mandarin must be very difficult to learn, but in fact it is in many ways simpler than European languages. The basic sentence structure is subject–verb–object, just as in English. Verbs have a single form for all persons, and there are no tenses. Nouns have no plural forms or genders, and there are no articles, definite or indefinite. The apparent complexity of Chinese lies in the unfamiliar nature of its sounds, and its apparently inscrutable writing system.

马

mǎ

Tones

吗

mà

Mandarin, like other forms of Chinese and several other Asian tongues, is a tonal language. Most of its sounds begin with a simple consonant and end with a vowel, or a vowel with a nasal finish *n*, or *ng*. Some are just vowel sounds on their own, but there are no combinations of consonants like the *str* in 'straight'. To expand its limited range of noises, it has developed four different ways of pitching them (Cantonese, by the way, has eight).

吗

ma

1st: *Mā*, said with a high, sustained tone ('Mum')

2nd: *Má*, said with a rising tone ('to tingle')

3rd: *Mǎ*, said with a falling and then rising tone ('horse')

4th: *Mà*, said with an abrupt falling tone ('to swear')

Some sounds can also be said neutrally. *Ma* (toneless) at the end of a sentence indicates it's a question rather than a statement.

If this seems bizarre, consider that many languages use tone or pitch to convey meaning, but in a different way. For instance:

Mm? (Sorry, what was that you said—I wasn't paying attention)

Mm. (I'm listening to what you're saying and I agree)

Mmmm. (That was nice. Do it again)

Unfortunately Mandarin still has too many homophones (words that sound the same but have different meanings). *Mā* can also mean 'to wipe' and *mǎ* can also mean 'yard', but each is *written* differently. Context is usually enough in speech to make it clear what is meant—there aren't many sentences in which you could substitute 'yard' for 'horse' and still make sense. Where there is confusion during a conversation the speaker will describe the component parts of the character he means, sketch it in his palm with a finger, or give another example of its use. Just as the word 'horse' can be combined with others in English to make new ideas (e.g. horseback, horse trough, horse hair) so can *mǎ* and other Chinese characters. *Mǎ'ān* is 'saddle', and *mǎkù* are jodhpurs or riding breeches ('horse trousers'). Entertainingly *mǎhū* ('horse tiger') is 'careless', *mǎmǎhūhū* ('horse horse tiger tiger') is 'not so bad, so-so', and *mǎshàng* ('on horseback') is 'immediately', which may tell you something about how quickly things get done in China.

Characters

Chinese is not written phonetically. If you see an unfamiliar character you can sometimes see a hint as to how it should be pronounced (one character equals one syllable), but only a hint. On closer examination, what at first seems to be an infinite variety of forms turns out to be constructed from a limited number of elements put together in different combinations. All but

fēng

the simplest characters can be divided into two parts, the *radical* and the *phonetic*. The radical may give some indication of the class of idea with which the whole character is dealing, while the phonetic part may indicate that the whole character sounds something like the phonetic part would if it stood on its own. Take the five *ma* examples:

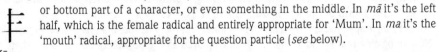

fēnghuǒ tái

Mǎ (horse) is functioning as the phonetic element in *mā* ('Mum') and *ma* (question particle), standing on the right in each case. It's also the bottom half of *mà* (to swear). The radical element can also be the left, right, top or bottom part of a character, or even something in the middle. In *mā* it's the left half, which is the female radical and entirely appropriate for 'Mum'. In *ma* it's the 'mouth' radical, appropriate for the question particle (*see* below).

fēng

The character *fēng* means 'beacon'. The left-hand side of *fēng* is the fire radical *huǒ*, and together with *huǒ* by itself, meaning 'fire', and *tái* meaning 'tower', 'platform' or 'terrace', it makes up the word for the beacon towers that dot the landscape on both sides of the Great Wall, and in some cases replace it (*fēnghuǒ tái*). The lower right-hand side is pronounced *fēng* when standing by itself (meaning 'plentiful'), and is a

fēng

fēngmì

fēng

fēng

qián

zhōng

tiě

铁路
tiělù

口
kǒu

phonetic element in several other characters. It shows up in *fēng* meaning 'bee', where the radical (on the left) is the one for insects. You are most likely to see it on menus—*fēngmì* is 'honey'. Reverse the characters to *mìfēng* and you get 'honey bee'. Note the slightly squashed version of the insect radical at the bottom of the *mì* character. In the next *fēng* the radical is the one for mountains, and this character means 'peak' or 'summit'. Yet another *fēng* has the metal radical, and means 'cutting edge' (of a sword, for instance). While you're not likely to see this character often, the metal radical is commonplace for the traveller, appearing in *qián* meaning 'money', *zhōng* meaning 'bell' (in bell tower) and *tiě* meaning 'iron'. *Tiělù*, 'iron road', is railway line.

Using Dictionaries

It's impossible to use a dictionary to look up a character you don't know how to say unless you know how to write Chinese characters. It's only necessary to master a small number of strokes to be able to write Chinese, but everyone is expected to make these strokes in the same way and in the same order when writing a character. In everyday handwriting the pen may not be lifted from the paper between every stroke, and unless everyone used the same order and direction a wide variety of different squiggles would result although the same character was intended. Writing clear characters with individual strokes is like block printing (using capital letters) with the Roman alphabet. The number of strokes is fairly well hidden in most printed forms. *Kǒu*, for instance, takes three strokes to write, not four. The first is the left side of the box, drawn downwards, the second is drawn across the top from left to right and then down the right side in a single stroke. The third closes the box from left to right.

The first task when using a dictionary is to identify the radical of the character you want to interpret. At the front of the Chinese–English section you'll find a table listing all the radicals in order of the number of strokes it takes to write them. To look up *mā*, with experience you'd be confident that the radical was the female part on the left, which takes three strokes to write. Turning to the part of the table that lists three-stroke radicals and running your finger down the 39 possibilities until you saw the female character, you'd be referred to another table on the following pages, which would list all the characters which have the female radical, in order of the number of strokes it takes to complete them. In the case of *mā* this would be three more strokes, and it would not be difficult to spot the right character amongst the eleven or so possibilities (depending on the size of your dictionary). You would now be given the number of the page on which to find it in the main body of the dictionary, or the pronunciation, written in the official Romanized form of Chinese known as *pīnyīn*. The rest of the dictionary is in alphabetical order of *pīnyīn* spelling, and then in order of tone: *luò, mā, má, mǎ, mà, ma, maí*, for example. (Note in passing that Mandarin hasn't even employed all the possibilities open to it—there is no first tone *māi*, for instance.)

This procedure sounds complex, but a little familiarity with Chinese makes it swift and fairly straightforward, although there are many inconsistencies. *Mà* ('to swear'), for instance, might be expected to have one of the little mouths as its radical, but in dictionaries it's found under the horse radical, although that is also apparently the phonetic element, and the connection between horses and swearing is probably only apparent to jockeys and gamblers. To confuse matters further, dictionaries may differ on which is the radical for a particular character.

Simplification

Originally, although Chinese people spoke several mutually incomprehensible languages (or dialects—the debate is between linguists, and in Běijīng has political overtones to do with the gospel of Hàn unity)—they could at least write to each other, since barring a few localizations and shorthand variations, they all wrote the same characters, and at least amongst educated people employed largely the same grammar. The harmonization of the writing systems of individual kingdoms was enforced following the unification of China under the Qín dynasty (221–207 BCE). After the communist victory of CE 1949 this unity began to be dismantled, for the laudable purpose of increasing literacy by reducing the number of characters and making them easier to write. The result is that many of the characters in your local restaurant's menu are often more complicated than the ones that you will see in mainland China, since most ex-patriate Chinese left long before the simplification began, or came from Hong Kong which despite the handover from British rule in 1997 has so far escaped it. Take the character for 'meal', or 'cooked rice', for example: *fàn*. In Modern Standard Chinese it takes a mere seven strokes to write, but in the original full form it took nine to write the radical alone (the left-hand side). This still appears in its original form when it stands by itself as *shí*, meaning 'meal' or 'food'.

饭
fàn

食
fàn

Full form characters are making a come-back in the giant brass letters on new shop, hotel and restaurant signs. These, incidentally, are usually read from left to right, but some, like many older inscriptions on temples and gates, are read from right to left.

Mandarin in Roman Characters

The modern official Romanization system is *Hànyǔ Pīnyīn*, which means 'Chinese language combine sounds', and has largely replaced a bewildering variety of alternative systems. The most popular of the earlier versions was Wade-Giles, still preferred by those who studied Chinese before the sixties, and still in use in many important text books. It's usually easy to identify because it uses apostrophes to indicate hard frontal sounds by placing them after consonants that would otherwise be relatively soft. For instance, *p* is sounded as *b*, unless it appears as *p'*. It may suddenly seem clear why Běijīng ended up as Peking in English—that's how it was written in Wade-Giles, and only the language student would know to soften the initial *p* to a *b*, and the *k* to a *j*. The French developed the official Post Office Romanization of place names, influenced by the values of Roman characters in the French language, and this, too, contributed to the confusion.

A familiarity with *pīnyīn* is considerably easier to master than written Chinese and, since all important Chinese names and places are given in *pīnyīn* in this book, will be a great aid to communication. Unlike in earlier systems, most letters have values similar to those the English speaker would expect, although Chinese does have some noises that are not found in English. It's particularly important to grasp, for instance, that the *zh* in Gānsù Province's capital *Lánzhōu* is a soft kind of *j*, and the *ou* is the *ough* of *dough*. Ticket-sellers hearing 'Lan-zoo' or 'Lan-chow', common mispronunciations amongst foreign visitors, are not likely to understand. Something resembling 'Lan-joe' has a chance of success, even if your tones are less than accurate. A guide to *pīnyīn* is given in **Language**, *see* p.392.

Apostrophes also appear in *pīnyīn* but only to make it clear where breaks in sound should come. The name of Cháng'ān Dàjiē, the Avenue of Eternal Peace in central Běijīng, is made from two characters for *cháng* (long) and *ān* (peace), not any form of *chan* and *gan*. The name of the ancient capital Xī'ān needs the apostrophe to show that it's made from two characters and syllables, *xī* (west) and *ān* (peace), not a single *xiān* (pronounced differently and meaning 'first'). Although there are rules for the application of the apostrophe, there's little consistency in how it is used in real life. In this book apostrophes are added wherever it helps to make the word clearer to those unfamiliar with Mandarin. Oddly, *pīnyīn* is rarely tone-marked except in language texts, rather defeating its object of helping you to say the right sound (but in this book every *pīnyīn* word is tone-marked).

There's a lot of variation, too, as to how *pīnyīn* should represent longer strings of syllables— what should be joined together, and what separated. This book breaks things up whenever it will aid clarity. You'll occasionally see *pīnyīn* on street signs and shop signs, sometimes written as long strings and perhaps broken in the middle of a word to go to the next line. At other times it appears as a row of monosyllables.

Pīnyīn has been introduced to primary schools to aid children in producing the same sounds. Mandarin has only been the national language of China since the time of the Republic, although it became the official language of administration under the Manchu Qīng dynasty and is essentially just the Běijīng dialect of the language. Even today, a mere 100km from the capital, the sounds made when speaking at home may vary quite widely from those of the schoolroom, and the introduction of the foreign alphabet has increased the likelihood of Modern Standard Chinese becoming truly standard. However, only younger adults educated after 1976 are likely to have any grasp of *pīnyīn*, and it plays no significant role in life after school.

Everyday Grammar

Questions

There are three main ways of asking questions in Chinese, and since you'll want to ask quite a few, and will be asked many yourself, it's worth at least learning to recognize a question from a statement. As in English, one way of asking questions is to use question words such as 'who', 'what' and 'where'. You'll frequently hear: *Nǐ shì nǎguó rén?* 'You are which country person?', to which the answer is *Wǒ shì Yīngguó rén*, 'I am Britain person' (a list of other nationalities is given in the Language section). Note that for all persons, singular or plural, the verb to be is *shì*. There's no memorizing the conjugations of regular and irregular verbs in Mandarin: every one is of this one-size-fits-all kind.

Questions are also frequently asked by offering you a choice: *Nǐ shì bú shì Měiguó rén?*, 'You are not are America person?'. If you are, the response is *shì*, 'am', and if you aren't, the response is *bú shì*, 'not am'. You'll also often hear, *Nǐ dǒng bù dǒng*, 'You understand not understand?'. If you did, say *dǒng*, and if not, *bù dǒng*. Chinese doesn't really have words for 'yes' or 'no'. The tendency is to concentrate on the main verb and affirm or deny it. *Duì*, meaning 'correct' is the nearest thing to 'yes', and *bù* (sometimes *bú*, often toneless) is used in most cases to make verbs negative. The exception is the verb 'to have', *yǒu*, which is negated by *méi*. *Méi yǒu* is the Mandarin expression you will hear more frequently than any other during your trip: 'There aren't any', 'We don't have any', and 'Whatever you want to happen isn't going to come to pass', although '*Xiǎo děng yí huǐ*', 'Wait a moment', is becoming more popular.

The third main way of asking questions is to use the question particle, *ma*. Add it to the end of any statement and you have a question. *Tā shì Jiānádà rén ma?* 'He is Canada person [question]?' Chinese has several useful particles which go at the ends of sentences, such as *ba*, used for making suggestions or propositions, and *ne*, indicating that there's a continuing subject of conversation. For instance, *Nǐ hǎo ma?*, a standard greeting, 'You well [question]?', is often answered, *Wǒ hěn hǎo. Nǐ ne?*, 'I very well. You [same topic]?'

Time

Particles after verbs and sentences play a role in indicating time, since verbs don't modify to show tense. *Tā qù Zhōngguó*, 'He is going to China', is also 'He will go', 'He went', etc. Extra terms such as 'tomorrow' and 'before' are usually added to give a sense of time: *Zuótiān tā qù Zhōngguó le*, 'Yesterday he went to China'. Suffixes called aspect-particles, such as *le* and *guo*, clarify matters further. Chinese is mostly concerned with putting events in order, and with whether they are over and done with yet, or still continuing: *Tā qùle Zhōngguó*, 'He's gone to China' (at a specific time, but he hasn't come back yet), or *Tā qùguo Zhōngguó*, 'He's been to China' (at some unspecified time and returned). Roughly, *le* at the end of a sentence or after a verb gives a sense of change or completion, and *guo* after a verb indicates that something happened over a period of time but it's now finished. Another particle *zhe* is used to indicate that two actions are happening at the same time. This may sound odd at first, but with a little familiarity it makes English, French and German look unnecessarily complicated.

Quantities

There's no plural form for nouns, so indications of quantity are important, as are expressions such as 'some', 'many' and 'a set of'. *Tā mǎi shū ma?* means 'Is he buying books?' *Tā mǎi yì běn shū ma?* means 'Is he buying a book?' All expressions of quantity require the use of a *measure word*. You can't say 'a fish' or 'two fish' in Chinese; the required structure is number + measure word + noun. This is like saying 'a slice of toast' or 'a round of ammunition' in English, using simple expressions of quantity like 'a cup of', 'a kilo of', and using collective nouns like 'flock' or 'shoal'. There's no real translation of *běn* in the sentence above that works in this context: 'Is he buying one volume book?' is like the pidgin English that was used in the early days of British trade in Canton.

Objects with similar characteristics use the same measure word. Most things that are flat use *zhāng*, for example. Three tickets are *sān zhāng piào*, two tables *liǎng zhāng zhuōzi*. Long and flexible things use *tiáo*. *Sì tiáo yú* are four fish, *yì tiáo lù* is a road. One of the pleasures of learning Mandarin is that since the Chinese have had little contact with the West they do not share the same metaphors or link ideas in the same way. To learn the language is also to learn new and often entertaining ways of looking at the world—you probably never thought of roads and fish being alike before.

Although there are large numbers of measure words, only a limited number are in everyday use and some can be replaced by the all-purpose *ge*. Most useful to the traveller are quantitive expressions like *yì bēi chá* 'a *cup of* tea', *liǎng wǎn bǎifàn* 'two *bowls of* rice', and *qǐng lái yí fèn huíguō ruò* 'please bring a *portion of* "return-to-the-pot pork".'

A Few Sayings

Mandarin is a very pictorial language, not only in the sense that its writing system was long ago derived from pictures, but because of the vibrant imagery of its everyday expressions, called *chéngyǔ* (idioms or proverbs). Some refer to events in traditional myths and legends, but still pithily and unsentimentally capture the struggle of daily life, and human failings in general. *Hǔ tóu shé wěi*, 'tiger head, snake tail', describes those who start projects enthusiastically but fail to finish them off. A person with limited experience or narrow views is described as *jǐng dǐ zhī wā*, 'a frog at the bottom of a well'. Those who practise self-deception are neatly captured in *yǎn ěr dào líng*, 'cover ears to steal bell'—everyone is aware of the noise except the thief. An expression describing those who take action without noticing changes in circumstances is derived from the story of a man whose sword accidentally fell overboard during a river trip, so he made a mark on the boat to help him find it again. This idiom, *kè zhōu qiú jiàn*, 'cut boat seek sword', also indicates absurd levels of stupidity.

Learning More

A far more erudite and complete introduction to Chinese both for those who intend to study the language and those who are just curious about how it works can be found in *About Chinese* by Richard Newnham (Pelican Books, revised edition 1987). Your local China friendship society is usually a good source of information on where to find classes and other information about China. In the UK try the Great Britain–China Centre, 15 Belgrave Sq., London SW1X 8PS, ✆ (020) 7235 6696, ✉ (020) 7245 6885, <*gbcc@gn.apc.org*>, which offers classes, lectures, social events, a specialist library and an excellent magazine.

Běijīng

北京

Landing at Běijīng's Capital Airport and driving down the highway into the smoggy, stationary city, it may occur to modern Marco Polos that the only similarity between their situation and that of those who once arrived by camel caravan is that their vehicles are nose-to-tail. Where is *real* China?

Of course, the Běijīng of traffic jams and 24-hour, seven-day construction is a reflection of modern China's slow transformation to a 'socialist market economy', and as 'real' as it gets. Whereas political motives once led to the levelling of historic buildings as symbols of old ways of thought, now the old-fashioned profit motive works both to the same end and to restore some of the few ancient sites that remain in order to attract tourist hard currency. Whether they like it or not, Běijīng residents are being given new apartments with private toilets, and the picturesque remnants of their courtyard houses with overly aromatic public facilities are gradually being demolished. But tucked away behind shoddily built towers, in the shadow of on-ramps and overpasses, round the corner from a branch of McDonald's, down a lane too narrow for cars, a glimpse of a steep tiled roof or of a carved lintel over a sagging doorway shows the sufficiently inquisitive visitor that not all traces of ancient Běijīng have passed away.

Then there are the great icons of Chinese tourism—the Imperial Palace, the Temple of Heaven, and the Great Wall, all far from hidden, and all not to be missed. Stuffed, mounted and on display, like trophies that have been through the hands of an inept taxidermist, they have a rigidity and artificiality about them that scarcely seems 'real' either. But peering through windows, investigating the remoter corners of even busy tourist sites, and always taking the smaller turning can produce surprises. In Běijīng atmosphere must be stalked and hunted down.

Getting to and from Běijīng
by air

And here—what a contrast!—passengers and friends sit sipping tea while somewhere passports are being checked and luggage is carried out to waiting cars. And—blessed thought—no worry about how much to tip. No one fusses and no one hurries. And why hurry? For this is Peking, the end of the line, and who wants to hurry on from here?

Felix Greene, *Peking*, 1978

Greene was in China for the BBC at a time when the only journalists who got in were ones who would oblige by finding everything perfect, even immediately following the Cultural Revolution, and Greene obliged by praising not just the airport but even the air itself.

The Capital Airport, which lies to the northeast of the city, is reached by an expressway beginning at the second ring road and fed by the third and fourth. For several years it remained much the same as when Greene saw it, something which would embarrass even the most provincial North American or European town, until

1999 when a second terminal, four times the size of the old one, was opened (just in time for 1 October, of course). This will handle 35 million passengers per annum by 2005, and has capacity for 190,000 flights annually. It's still no Narita, JFK or Heathrow, but at least it's fairly comfortable, well laid-out and efficient. What will happen to the old Terminal 1, which is undergoing renovation, is not clear, but it will probably reopen to increase capacity further in a few years.

Airport information, ✆ 6456 3604/3107. Domestic ticketing, ✆ 6601 3336. International ticketing, ✆ 6601 6667. Some English spoken. The timetable for all domestic and international flights, a fat book, can be bought at counters at the airport, and at the Aviation Building (Mínháng Dàlóu) just east of Ⓜ Xī Dān on the north side of the road, ¥29, or domestic flights only ¥12.

Arrivals

The arrivals hall contains everything you are likely to need, and there's plenty of English signage to get you around the building and announcements are also in English. Avoid 'tourist information' which doesn't have any (not even maps) and only sells expensive hotels, and even those at rates you can beat yourself. Avoid all other counters offering hotel booking services for the same reason (*see* 'Where to stay', p.241). Use these people solely to get an idea of what's available, then head down town to beat their prices.

There are public telephones at the right- and left-hand ends of the building. You'll need Chinese cash straight away—very few operations are legally allowed to accept foreign currency, and very few want it. For **foreign exchange** there are enough machines to make using a credit card or ATM card a safe bet. There are ATMs belonging to the Agricultural Bank of China and to the Bank of China which take Visa, Plus, Mastercard, Maestro, Cirrus, and JCB cards. ETC. cards and their successors from Hong Kong also work in this and most other airport machines. There are two more machines upstairs. The Agricultural Bank of China and the Industrial and Commercial Bank of China both have counters which are open 24 hours a day, and the latter offers very fractionally better rates than the Bank of China and Construction Bank of China counters upstairs at departures level. For the rest of your trip expect only to be able to exchange money at the Bank of China or at counters under its control, at least legally, and to be able to use a very limited number of its ATMs. Turn towards the centre of the hall to find the exchange counters on the near side, and the ATMs on the far side, at the front of the building.

There are also **left luggage** counters at ¥5–20, or ¥30–50 for a day, depending on size of bag and length of time.

Counters for **hotel shuttles** are to the left, and the **airport express bus services** are over on the far right as you emerge. Even if you usually jump into a **taxi** without thinking twice about the cost, you should consider taking the airport bus down town, and then taking the metro or a taxi from there. The speed of the traffic is one reason, and dishonesty is another. If you are going to find attempts to haggle the price, refusals to start the meter, attempts to levy extra charges, and drivers who take figure of 888 routes, it will be here. If you are confident you can handle this, then the taxi rank is right outside the building. Do not under any circumstances deal with drivers who approach you in the hall.

There are three air-conditioned frequent bus services into town with the first service at 6am, and the last at 9pm, all costing ¥16 ($2):

1st line (A) Bus to Sānyuán Qiáo (where the airport expressway meets the third ring), Ⓜ Dōng Zhí Mén, Ⓜ Dōng Sìshí Tiáo, Cháoyáng Mén, Běijīng Zhàn Kǒu (just north of the station), and the Aviation Building next to Ⓜ Xī Dān.

2nd line (B), to Ⓜ Gōngzhǔfén, Hépíng Lǐ and the Běijīng Xī Zhàn (West Station).

3rd line (C) to the east side of Měishù Guǎn (National Art Gallery) at the top of Wángfǔjǐng.

The journey time is usually about 45mins but can extend to nearly two hours if you travel mid-afternoon to early evening.

Budget travellers can take regular bus 359 to its terminus near Ⓜ Dōng Zhí Mén for about ¥3. There's also a bus direct to Tiānjīn for ¥70 ($8.75).

Next to the bus ticket counter is an office of New Concept **Car Hire** (BCNC), but don't imagine that driving yourself is as easy as in most other countries. You'll need an international driving licence, your air ticket, your passport, a lot of money, and a great deal of nerve—*see* 'Self-drive', p.111).

Departures

The best way to get to the airport is by airport bus—*see* routes above. Services are generally from 6.30am to 7.30pm, every half an hour, but in many cases buses leave as soon as they are full, and are immediately replaced by another. The most convenient boarding point is outside the Aviation Building (Mínháng Dàlóu), Xī Cháng'ān Jiē 15, Ⓜ Xī Dān, just east on the north side of the road. Buy your ticket at the building's far right-hand entrance. There's also a service from outside the Silver Swallow Air Services Inc. office (✆ 6433 5878), also 6.30am to 7.30pm and every half an hour, ¥16, tickets from the right-hand entrance. This is opposite the east side of the National Art Gallery in Měishù Guǎn Dōng Jiē just north of Wángfǔjǐng, bus 106, stop Měishù Guǎn. The large modern building immediately behind it is the CAAC (Civil Aviation Administration of China) headquarters in Běijīng, and services may later start running from here instead. You can also catch an airport bus from outside Běijīng West Station.

Board your bus to the airport absolutely no later than 2½hrs before departure, earlier still for international flights—ask the airlines for advice. Although the journey is usually 45mins, it can extend to as much as two hours in the second half of the afternoon. Don't forget to reconfirm at least once, or you will stand a good chance of being bumped off your flight.

At the airport the departures level is one floor up from the arrivals one, and has all the same facilities (*see* above), as well as a post office. All floors have shops, including the one above departures, but don't expect to be able to pick up an airport paperback. International departures are to the right, and domestic ones to the left. You can change excess RMB back to other hard currencies at the bank counters here as long as you are carrying sufficient receipts demonstrating earlier purchases of RMB, and within certain limitations (see 'Money and Prices', p.45).

Don't forget to pay your airport tax ('Administration and Construction Fee') at the central counter before proceeding through to check-in. This is ¥90 ($11) for international and ¥50 ($6) for domestic departures, and is the same at every airport in China. There are signs that the domestic fee may soon be incorporated in the air ticket price.

Airlines

Almost all the world's major airlines and many of the minor ones now fly to Běijīng. The following list is fairly exhaustive, but the frequencies when given are for the summer peak, and there may be fewer flights at other times, or more as the economy rebounds. These are local contact numbers. For Web addresses and offices overseas, see **Travel**, p.2. For special offers on flights out of Běijīng, see the email newsletter *Xiànzài Běijīng* (see 'Internet', p.38), and the local media (see p.115)

If your hotel insists on charging a ticket fee, or if no contact information is given below, go directly to Airtrans Service Co. Ltd, just to the left of the main entrance to the Jiànguó Hotel, ✆ 6595 2255, <*mak@public.bta.net.cn*>, or to the Silver Swallow agency Měishù Guǎn Dōng Jiē 30 opposite the east side of the National Art Gallery, ✆ 6404 9730 just beyond the top of Wángfǔjǐng, or to China Air International Travel Service, just north of the Great Wall Sheraton on the east third ring north, ✆ 6508 2172.

Domestic airline and **Chinese airline international tickets** can be bought through agents or at the Aviation Building (Mínháng Dàlóu), Xī Cháng'ān Jiē 15 (🚇 Xīdān, just east on the north side of the road), ✆ 6601 7755, 🖷 6601 7585. International ticketing is on the right and domestic to the left (*open 24 hours*). There are flights to almost every city in the country, often with several of China's few dozen airlines nominally competing, but with rates fixed by the government. There is a branch of the Bank of China upstairs, too (*open Mon–Sat, 9–5*), but you can also pay by credit card here. You can buy a complete domestic and international timetable for ¥29 ($3.50) which includes the flights of foreign airlines. Turn left as you enter and ask at the counter on the left. Two further booking numbers for Chinese airlines: domestic ✆ 6601 3336, international ✆ 6601 6667.

It's now finally possible to buy return air tickets in China, but be scrupulous about reconfirmation. Holders of Peony Cards (a Chinese credit card) can buy tickets from 12 automatic outlets around Beijing for one way and round trip flights departing from the capital. Perhaps this service will be extended to other card holders in the future.

There's also a **second airport** with domestic services only 18km south of Qián Mén—a former military airfield called **Nányuàn Jīchǎng** from which services of China United Airlines (Liánhé Hángkōng Gōngsī) operate routes on Russian aircraft to some surprising spots served by no one else including Sūzhōu (otherwise reached via Shànghǎi), and reportedly cheaper flights on some other routes. The ticket office is in the Aviation Building (*see* above), ground floor west, but has announced its intention to move to the ground floor of the neighbouring Telegraph Building. ✆ 6691 5118 / 6340 2590, but don't expect English to be spoken. These flights do not appear in the

Airlines

Aeroflot flies to Moscow five times a week and on to almost everywhere. Hotel Běijīng-Toronto, Jiànguó Mén Wài Dàjiē, ✆ 6500 2980.

Air China flies to Bangkok, Copenhagen, Frankfurt, Fukuoka, Hiroshima, Hong Kong, Karachi, Kuwait, London, Los Angeles, Melbourne, Milan, Moscow, Paris, Rangoon, Rome, San Francisco, Sendai, Seoul, Singapore, Sydney, Tokyo, Ulaan Baatar, Vancouver, Vienna, Zürich. Aviation Building, Xī Cháng'ān Jiē 15, ✆ 6601 6667.

Air France flies to Paris daily except Tuesday. ✆ 6512–5155. Full Link Plaza, Cháoyáng Mén Wài Dàjiē 18, ✆ 6588 1388.

Air Koryo flies on Tuesdays and Saturdays to Pyongyang, but for now you won't be flying with them unless on a package tour—*see* 'by train' *below*). Swissôtel, Ⓜ Dōng Sì Shí Tiáo, ✆ 6501 1557.

Air Macau flies daily to Macau. SCITECH office building, Jiànguó Mén Wài Dàjiē,✆ 6512 2288 ext 807.

Air New Zealand flies to Aukland three times weekly from *Hong Kong*; call in HK ✆ (852) 2524 8606.

Air Ukraine flies to Kyiv (Kyev) and on to various central Asian capitals and Istanbul, Helsinki and Toronto. It also has a complex series of codeshares to Amsterdam, Athens, Bangkok, Belgrade, Berlin, Brussels, Vienna, Hamburg, Dusseldorf, Copenhagen, London, New York, Milan, Munich, Osaka, Paris, Rome, Singapore, Stockholm, Toronto, Frankfurt, Saigon (Ho Chi Minh City), and Zurich, usually via Sofia, Warsaw, or Budapest. Poly Plaza Hotel, northeast side of Ⓜ Dōng Sì Shí Tiáo, ✆ 6501 0282.

ANA flies daily to Tokyo, and twice a week to Osaka with connections to Europe, Australia, and the US east and west coasts. China World Trade Centre, ✆ 6505 3311.

Alitalia flies twice weekly to Milan and on to multiple European destinations. Jiànguó Fàndiàn, Jiànguó Mén Wài Dàjiē, ✆ 6591 8468.

Asiana flies daily to Seoul, and on to eight US destinations. There's also a daily flight to Pusan. Kempinski Hotel, ✆ 6468 4000.

Austrian flies twice weekly to Vienna, and on to most European capitals. Lufthansa Centre, ✆ 6462 2161-4.

British Airways flies to London Heathrow three times a week, with connections worldwide. SCITECH Tower, Room 210, 2nd Floor, Jiànguǒ Mén Wài Dàjiē, ✆ 6512 4070.

Canadian Airlines flies to Vancouver four times weekly with connections to major Canadian and other North American cities. Lufthansa Centre, ✆ 6468 2001.

China Eastern Airlines flies to Fukuoka, Los Angeles, Munich, Paris, San Francisco, Sydney. Aviation Building, ✆ 6601 7755.

China Southern Airlines flies to Amsterdam, Hanoi, Hong Kong, Kuala Lumpur, Manila, Sharjah, Singapore. Aviation Building, ✆ 6601 7755.

Dragonair flies to Hong Kong three times daily with Cathay Pacific connections to Australia, New Zealand, Europe and North America. China World Trade Centre, ✆ 6505 4343.

El Al flies to Tel Aviv on Tuesdays. Jīngguǎng Centre at Cháoyáng Lù and third ring, ✆ 6501 4512.

Ethiopian Airlines flies to Addis Ababa via Bangkok and Delhi on Mondays. China World Trade Centre, ✆ 6505 0314.

Finnair flies to Helsinki on Mondays and Fridays with connections all over Europe. Scitech Tower Room 204, Jiànguó Mén Wài Dàjiē 22, ✆ 6512 7180/1.

Garuda Indonesia flies twice weekly to Jakarta via Guǎngzhōu. China World Trade Centre, ✆ 6505 2901–3.

Iran Air flies to Tehran on Mondays and Thursdays. CITIC building (west of the Jiànguó Mén Friendship Store), ✆ 6512 4940. It also has flights to Tokyo on the same days.

Japan Airlines has flights to Tokyo and Osaka, has a large international network and is a good choice for onward flights to Australia. Chángfùgōng Fàndiàn (Hotel New Otani) office section, Jiànguó Mén Wài Dàjiē 26, ✆ 6513 0888.

Kazakhstan Airlines flies to Almaty on Tuesdays and Thursdays, with slightly unpredictable onward links to Central Asian and some European destinations.

KLM flies to Amsterdam on Thursdays and Sundays with rapid connections at Schipol airport to a wide range of destinations worldwide. China World Trade Centre, ✆ 6505 3505.

Korean Airlines flies daily to Seoul with connections to Europe, North America and Australasia. China World Trade Centre, ✆ 6505 0088.

Kyrgyzstan Airlines flies to Bishkek every Wednesday, and on to other Central Asian capitals and Russian cities, as well as Birmingham, London (BA codeshare), Delhi, Karachi, Frankfurt, Hannover and Istanbul. Běijīng International Hotel, ✆ 6522 9799, 138 128 7477.

Lufthansa flies to Frankfurt daily with connections to an immense worldwide network. Lufthansa Centre, ✆ 6465 4488, <*lhbjsgp@eastnet.cam.cn*>.

Malaysian Airlines flies five times a week to Kuala Lumpur, with connections to Europe. China World Trade Centre, ✆ 6505 2681.

Malev Hungarian Airlines flies to Budapest on Sundays and on to most European capitals. Rm 1410, Tower B, COFCO Plaza, ✆ 6526 3091/2.

MIAT Mongolian Airlines flies to Ulaan Baatar, and on to Berlin, Moscow, Seoul and Osaka. Jīn Qiáo (Golden Bridge) Tower, just west of the China World Trade Centre, ✆ 6507 9297.

Northwest Airlines flies daily to Detroit, and on to New York four times a week, ✆ 6505 3505. Three flights a week stop in Tokyo.

PIA flies to Islamabad and on to Karachi every Monday and Friday, with connections to Europe. China World Trade Centre, ✆ 6505 2256. It also has flights to Tokyo on Mondays and Fridays.

Qantas flies three times a week to Sydney via Shànghǎi—the Běijīng–Shànghǎi leg is with China Eastern. Lufthansa Centre Suite S120, ✆ 6467 3337.

Royal Brunei Airlines flies to Seri Begawan on Thurs and Sun. China World Trade Centre, ✆ 6505 5071.

SAS flies six times weekly to Copenhagen. 1403 Office Tower 1, Henderson Centre, ✆ 6518 3738.

Siberia Airlines flies to Novosibirsk on Wednesdays and Fridays.

Singapore Airlines flies twice daily to Singapore with connections to London, Paris, Amsterdam, Australasia and US west and east coasts. East Wing, China World Trade Centre, ✆ 6505 2233.

Swissair flies five times a week to Zürich and beyond. SCITECH office building, ✆ 6512 7481, <*swissair@ public3.bta.net.cn*>.

Tarom Romanian Air Transport flies to Bucharest on Tuesdays and Sundays, with connections to the main European capitals, Chicago, New York and Montreal. Jiànguó Hotel, ✆ 6500 2233 ext 109.

Thai Airways International daily to Bangkok with good onwards connections. Lufthansa Centre, Suite S102B, ✆ 6512 3881 / 6460 8899.

Turkish Airlines flies to Istanbul on Thursdays and Sundays, and on to more than 100 cities in Europe, the Middle East and South Africa. C308 Lufthansa Centre, ✆ 6456 1867-9, <*thybjs@public3.bta.net.cn*>.

Ukraine International flies to Kiev (Kyiv) via Novosibirsk on Wednesdays and Saturdays. Poly Plaza, Ⓜ Dōng Sìshí Tiáo, ✆ 6501 0282.

United Airlines flies to San Francisco via Tokyo daily, and on to major US cities. Lufthansa Centre, ✆ 6463 1111, <*flyua@public.bta.net.cn*>.

Uzbekistan Airways flies to Tashkent on Wed and Sat, and on to some European cities and New York.

CITS offices also act as ticket agents for Chinese airlines and for JAL, ANA, Northwest and United. CITS is at 103 Fùxīngmén Wài Dàjiē, ✆ 6603 9321; China World Trade Centre, ✆ 6505 3775. There is no commission on airline ticket sales when the agent has a terminal for the Chinese ticketing system. Further numbers, ✆ 6515 7515 / 6515 8575.

main airline timetable, and it's possible that some agents may deny their existence. The company runs a shuttle bus to the airport at 6.30am, for ¥5, which starts from their Gōngzhǔfén office, Ⓜ Gōngzhǔfén—ask for details.

by train

Běijīng is rather more advanced than anywhere else mentioned in this book as yet, having a fully computerized ticketing system. Some English is spoken at foreigners' ticket windows, but none on the telephone. It's neither difficult nor too time-consuming to do your own booking at the main stations, particularly at Běijīng Xī Zhàn and Běijīng Zhàn, both of which have special offices for foreigners. Běijīng Zhàn also has its own metro station, and is thus easy to reach.

Mandarin speakers can get limited information and book tickets by phone, ✆ 6321 7188. There's also ✆ 2586, a premium rate line (¥1 per minute if you do the whole thing automatically with touch-tone menus, ¥2 per minute if you have to speak to an operator) with fuller information. Tickets can be booked through both numbers 2–5 days ahead. Discuss collection arrangements with the *fúwùyuán* on the telephone (if you speak Mandarin), but usually tickets must be collected within 48 hours. Seat availability information for three days ahead is available on ✆ 2585 (also premium rate). These lines may not work from hotel rooms.

There are more than 100 railway offices and agencies around Běijīng where advance bookings can be made (Mandarin speakers can choose one from the website <*http://train.cei.gov.cn/index8.htm*>). Most useful to the visitor are likely to be the Qián Mén office on the southeast side of the half moon at the top of Qián Mén Dàjiē, Xī Zhí Mén just northwest of Ⓜ Xī Zhí Mén, just south of the Fùchéng Mén overpass, and inside the Xī Dān Department Store on Xīdān Běi Jiē. The Silver Swallow agency, Měishù Guǎn Dōng Jiē 30, ✆ 6404 9730 (*open 8–5*), has an online terminal and only charges ¥5 per ticket booked, which is actually the legal maximum, but expect charges of ¥30–50 per ticket from ticket agencies and hotel receptions.

Booking via the Internet <*http://train.cei.gov.cn/*>. This is only for those who read Mandarin or who can borrow someone who does, those with access to computers which are able both to read *and to enter* Chinese text, and only works for departures from Běijīng stations but *not* international trains or those to Hong Kong. However, those suitably equipped can book departures from any Běijīng station 5–10 days in advance. Those whose web browsers are equipped to read Chinese (go to the preferences section and change the character set to simplified Chinese, then reload the page) but who can't enter text can get train schedules and ticket availability charts (right down to the exact number of tickets remaining in each class) by using pull-down menus. Knowing the train number is an advantage, but this can be looked up on the site, too.

Ideally, for those on tight schedules, this system could be used to book tickets before leaving for China. But bookings must be checked after noon the next day to see if they have been accepted, and tickets must be picked up from a designated office within the following 48 hours. This might be possible if you are gaining time by flying east from Europe, you get the booking confirmation just before you leave, and you go straight to the office on arrival. There are 10 offices able to issue your ticket scattered around the suburbs, but you'd do better to go to one of the four main stations, and, best of all, to either Běijīng Zhàn or Běijīng Xī Zhàn (however, *see <http://infonavi.cei.gov.cn/ train/direction.htm>* for a list of offices in Mandarin). The whole system is clearly experimental, and rules may change. For an extra ¥10 per ticket you can also arrange to have your Internet-booked ticket delivered to your hotel; call ✆ 6321 7799 to make the arrangements.

Ticket touts (scalpers) are very active at holiday periods and, computer system or not, bribe the ticket staff to give them access to the tickets. Buying tickets for any domestic destination is impossible at Chinese New Year, unless you buy from a tout or have other *guānxi* (connections, special relationship) with railway staff. It's also difficult to buy tickets for important destinations such as Shànghǎi during the May and October national holidays, too, and at these periods fake tickets tend to appear. The touts are not hard to find—just look for groups of men hanging around station forecourts at points where people alight from buses and taxis or emerge from the metro. Expect to pay as much as 50% more than the price on the ticket. Prices do not drop as departure time approaches, but instead tend to go up. Unsold tickets are simply taken back to ticket office contacts, and re-entered into the computer as unsold.

Běijīng has two major stations of importance to visitors, **Běijīng Zhàn** and **Běijīng Xī Zhàn** (west), and two minor ones of equally minor importance, **Běijīng Běi Zhàn** (north, also known as Xī Zhí Mén Zhàn), and **Běijīng Nán Zhàn** (south, also known as Yǒngdìng Mén Zhàn), although the numbers of departures from these last two are growing.

Běijīng Zhàn

Běijīng Zhàn is gradually being overtaken by the West Station as main Běijīng station, but remains the one nearest the centre. Built in 1959 with Soviet assistance, it's a slightly Sinified version of their own socialist palaces, and was musty and decaying until a complete refurbishment in 1999 as part of the general sprucing up of Běijīng for the 50th anniversary of the founding of the People's Republic. The broad space in front of the station, often occupied by a sea of peasants, has now been repaved expensively in granite and marble, and the peasants largely cleared away. The station clock chimes the opening to 'The East is Red' on the hour.

Baggage is X-rayed upon entering the building, so keep film in your pockets. The **ticket office for foreigners** (formerly snappily known as The Ticket Office for the Foreign Guests, Journalists and the Deputies to the National People's Congress and the Chinese People's Political Consultative Conference) is at the rear of the main hall on the left and through the international waiting room (*open 5.30–7.40, 8–12, 1–6.40, and 7–11.20*).

Advance bookings can be made in person a maximum of four days ahead including the day of booking and the day of travel. Occasionally you may be handed a ticket booking form to complete, but this rarely seems necessary now. Refunds are available up to two hours before departure, with a deduction of 20% of the ticket value (minimum ¥10/$1.25). The windows for this (*tuì piào*) are outside the front of the station, as is the one for platform tickets (*zhàntái piào*) if you are going to meet a friend.

Full national timetables in Chinese are sold for ¥8 at the desk at the entrance to the international waiting room and other stalls around the concourse, but the small ¥2 booklet which only contains trains to and from Běijīng, although also in Mandarin, is far easier to digest. Neither, although published by the railways themselves, is accurate.

When you arrive to take any domestic train, show your ticket to someone at the top or bottom of the escalators in the main hall to be pointed to the right waiting room or platform entrance for your train. Most are upstairs.

Of the destinations outside Běijīng mentioned in this book, Běijīng Zhàn has trains to Tiānjīn, Qínhuángdǎo, Shānhǎiguān and Chéngdé.

There are **left luggage** lockers in the international waiting room for ¥10 ($1.25) per day (*open 5am–12 midnight*). An office across the road from the main entrance and to the right of the Paragon Hotel also offers a secure service for the same prices (*open 24hrs*). There's another to the left as you leave the station with a sign, 'State-owned dagage safe keeping' (*sic*).

Getting to and from Běijīng Zhàn. The station has its own metro station (Ⓜ Běijīng Zhàn), and whatever your destination you should use the metro to go as far as you can towards it. The second and third stops to the west, Qián Mén and Hépíng Mén, are handy for shopping, eating and moderate hotels, and Qián Mén offers an interchange to buses running to the southern dormitory accommodation. One stop east, Jiànguó Mén, is near a number of more expensive hotels and the Friendship Store, and an interchange for the line crossing Běijīng east–west. Useful buses include the 209 which goes to Běijīng Xī Zhàn via Qián Mén and Hépíng Mén, and there are direct minibus alternatives at the far left-hand corner of the forecourt as you exit which will take you directly to the Xī Zhàn for ¥5. The tè1 ('special 1') runs from just north of Běijīng Zhàn (straight ahead as you exit) along Jiànguǒ Mén Wài Dàjiē past several major hotels. The 20 (stop to the right of the station as you emerge) runs down Qián Mén to the Nán Zhàn, not far from many of the moderate and budget hotels. Go to the far left-hand side of the courtyard and keep going left to find bus 104 to Wángfǔjǐng, with stops at Xīn Dōng'ān and Měishùguǎn. Bus 103 runs via Wángfǔjǐng to the Zoo. Other buses run directly to Tiānjīn and other destinations outside Běijīng. Your best bet for an honest **taxi** is to avoid the rank and cross the road (use the metro station entrance if you don't want to brave the traffic). If westbound get in a cab that's just dropping someone off on the north side of the road, and if eastbound walk to the right and up past the front entrance to the Paragon Hotel. Taxis here will go north and turn right along Jiànguó Mén.

International departures all go from Běijīng Zhàn except those to Hong Kong (still administered as if international) and Hanoi, but the sign saying 'international passengers' means foreigners travelling within China, and international tickets are not sold here. Some travel agencies will lead you to believe either that access to international tickets is difficult to get, or that only they have access. In fact it's usually easy to buy tickets for yourself often right up to the day of departure, even in the summer, and several of the international ticket office staff speak reasonable English. The busiest periods are June, July and August. **International Train Booking Office** (Guójì Zǒngshè Piào Wù Zhōngxīn) is in the Běijīng Guójì Fàndiàn (Běijīng International

Hotel, ☎ 6512 0507, ✉ 6512 0503, <wuxx@cits.com.cn>, <http://www.ctn.com.cn/> (open Mon–Fri, 8.30–12, 1.30–5; Sat, Sun and public holidays, 9–11, 2–4). On entering the hotel keep to the left and look for signs. The rules for international ticket booking are completely different. You can book well in advance, in person, by phone (some English spoken), by email or via the website, but tickets must usually be paid for seven days in advance. It's not always asked for, but it's a good idea to carry your passport whenever you go to book international tickets.

On international trains the lowest level of accommodation is equivalent to soft sleeper in China (but sometimes referred to as hard), and the luxury class has two berths in a compartment with a comfy chair and a washroom shared between each two compartments. Where there are three classes, the middle one is simply soft sleeper plus a few decorative details, and both the cheaper and the more expensive classes are better value for money. There are lower rates for groups of 20 or more. The prices quoted below (which will probably have changed) include a ¥50 booking fee.

The no.19 **Trans-Manchurian to Moscow** heads to China's northeast before crossing directly to Russian territory. The trains are Russian and leave at 23.10 on Sats, arriving the following Fri, for ¥1825 ($228) 'hard' sleeper, ¥2,900 ($363) deluxe, arriving in Moscow the following Friday 9025km later at 19.50.

The Chinese-run no. 3 **Trans-Mongolian to Moscow** heads more directly north, passing through Outer Mongolia before entering Russia, and departs at 07.40 on Weds for ¥1,602 ($200) 'hard' sleeper, ¥2,306 ($288.25) soft, and ¥2,782 ($348) deluxe, arriving in Moscow the following Monday at 16.32.

The Mongolians are easy-going about visas, and both transit and tourist visas can be obtained in a few days without difficulty. A tourist visa is typically $40. One photo is needed. The Russians are less easy-going and you'll need to get a receipt for your booking to show them when you make the visa application.

Ulaan Baatar (Wūlánbātuō) can by reached by the Trans-Manchurian, or by its own train no. 23 at 7.40am on Saturdays, which may be Chinese or Mongolian, for ¥559 ($70) 'hard' sleeper, ¥778 ($97) soft, and ¥949 ($105) deluxe, arriving the next day, 1,561km later at 13.10. If the train is Mongolian the deluxe is slightly cheaper, the 'hard' slightly more expensive, and the soft class non-existent.

Trans-Manchurian and Trans-Mongolian tickets can also be arranged through the company known as Moonsky Star or Monkey Business, ☎ 6356 2126, ✉ 6356 2127, <monkeychina@compuserve.com>, <http://www.monkeyshrine.com/>. This company, despite being European-owned and operated, offers levels of surliness to rival CITS, and has been known to suggest that it is the only source of railway tickets to **Mongolia** and **Russia**. What is true is that the company can offer tickets with breaks in the journey, and tours of Mongolia and the Baikal area of Siberia, although these are expensive, and even after subtracting the cost of one night at a Moscow hotel it includes in its packages, a ticket will cost you in excess of ¥1,000 ($125) more than it will cost you to buy it yourself. The company will also do the running around with your passport to obtain the necessary visas (although you can do this for yourself, too), but visa fees are extra, and there are single occupancy supplements for the hotel, too. Sample prices include $395 Běijīng to Moscow through Mongolia including the first night's accommodation, or $840 including a six-day stopover in Mongolia.

A better choice of agent for activities in **Mongolia** and for buying a return ticket to Běijīng or onward ticket to Russia would be Aussie-run Karakorum Expeditions, *<graham@gomongolia.com>*, *<http://www.gomongolia.com/>*. A side trip to Mongolia is highly recommended during its brief period of comfortable weather from late May to early September, but rare public transport and fuel shortages mean that those without a lot of time to spare, and who want to get out of Ulaan Baatar to the Gobi or the Steppe, will need to organize a jeep and a route in advance.

Pyongyang (Píngrǎng) is reached by train no. 27, which may be Chinese or Korean, leaving on Mon, Wed, Thurs and Sat at 17.25 and arriving the next day at 18.50 after 1371km. The Chinese train has two classes for ¥467 ($58) and ¥652 ($82), and the Korean three classes for ¥384 ($48), ¥521 ($65) and ¥642 ($80). You won't be allowed to purchase this ticket without a North Korean visa, which you are very unlikely to get unless you go on a tour.

Bizarre as it may seem, Koryo Tours, *<http://www.koryogroup.com/>*, run by Běijīng expat Nicholas Bonner, *<northkorea8@hotmail.com>*, offers five-day (flight in and out) and eight-day (train in, flight out) escorted and unescorted tours (although there are always Korean guides and a fixed schedule), which include a compulsory trip to lay flowers before a statue of 'Great Leader' Kim Il Sung. The costs are between $1,590 and $2,170 per person, depending on the kind of tour taken and room occupancy. The absolute seclusion of the country from the rest of the world has made it the last home of sealed communist reality-denial, worse even than the China of the '50s and '60s, and making modern China look like a completely open society by comparison. Visitors are well-fed, allowed no free time to wander on their own, and kept away from any sight of poverty and famine. As a condition of being accepted on a tour you must guarantee not to report on your trip in the media.

Běijīng Xī Zhàn

The new Běijīng Xī Zhàn (West Station) is one of the most impressive and most vulgar buildings in Běijīng—a post-modern assemblage of popular motifs from China's architectural past, with hints of arrow tower and Forbidden City all out of scale both with each other and with a vast arch in the centre. Opened in early 1996 after three years' construction work by 20,000 people at a cost of ¥5 billion (more than $600 million—equivalent to about two thirds of China's total annual spending on education at the time), this is the kind of building that makes the visitor wonder whether giving aid to China would be necessary if the government altered its priorities. In the great tradition of modern Chinese 'all fur coat and no knickers' jerry building the roof already leaks onto its vast acreage of marble floor, sections have been known to fall off, and platforms have all had to be rebuilt. Even the Chinese press has commented on interior flooding and much sub-standard workmanship. Eventually the station is expected to handle about three times the capacity of Běijīng Zhàn. Trains from here now run mainly to the southwest and west.

Getting to and from Běijīng Xī Zhàn. The nearest metro station for the Xī Zhàn is ⓜ Jūnshì Bówùguǎn, three stops west of the ⓜ Fùxīng Mén exchange station. Take the east exit on south side and walk west, taking the first left turn at the lights down Yángfángdiàn Lù—about 15mins walk altogether, or catch any bus on the opposite side of Yángfángdiàn Lù. There's talk of building a new metro line from here to the airport, but this will not appear for many years, if ever.

Several buses start from stands signposted to your right in English and Chinese as you leave the station, well below ground level. The 52 runs straight along Cháng'an Jiē across the top of Tiān'ān Mén and along Jiànguó Mén Dàjiē. The 21 runs to Xīzhí Mén Nán Dàjiē just south of Bĕijīng Bĕi Zhàn. There's also a minibus direct to the Summer Palace. The 102 runs to Tiāntán Nán Mén (south gate), and along with the 40 runs to the South Station (Nán Zhàn) close to several backpacker dorms. The 320 double decker runs up through Zhōngguān Cūn to Rénmín Dàxué (People's University). The tè1 also passes Tiān'ān Mén and Bĕijīng Zhàn Kŏu. All of these go from a terminus signposted as you leave the station, but you can then U-turn as you emerge from the stairs to find the minibus equivalents or and special routes waiting behind you. Most of these routes run 5.30am–11pm, but if you arrive at night you can take the 212 to Qián Mén. There's also still a direct connection to Bĕijīng Zhàn at night between 10pm and 5am.

Outside the station at ground level (reached by a spiral ramp) the 212 goes to Qián Mén (marked 'to square'). The tè5 ('special 5') is an express double-decker which runs to the Zoo in one direction (where you can change for most of the universities and the Summer Palace) and to Bĕijīng Nán Zhàn in the other. Going south, it passes usefully close to the some of the moderate and cheaper hotels south of Qián Mén, stopping near the junction of Nán Xīnhuá Jiē and Zhūshìkŏu Xī Dàjiē. The 48 runs to Hépíng Mén, Qián Mén and along Jiànguó Mén Wài straight east. The 209 goes to Bĕijīng Zhàn via Hépíng Mén and Qián Mén. The tè1 runs to just north of Bĕijīng Zhàn and on down Jiànguŏ Mén Wài Dàjiē past several major hotels. 15mins' walk west at the junction with the third ring road, the 324 travels around it south to the Jīnghuá Fàndiàn (although taking the tè5 to the south station and changing to the 40 on the opposite side of the canalized river may be more reliable).

Arriving by **taxi**, whether you already hold a ticket or whether you want to go to the foreigners' ticket window to buy one, have the taxi climb the spiral ramp to one floor up from the roadway (actually the sixth floor according to the railway station). All platforms are at this level except platform 1, which is down the escalators and to the left. This is also the safest place to get a taxi, picking up one that's dropping off other passengers, if it will let you, and not one that's hanging around the station waiting to feed off naïve new arrivals. Or walk across the forecourt and flag down one that's passing, not waiting. A ¥1.6 per km vehicle should cost about ¥20–¥24 to Wángfŭjǐng, for instance.

The **left luggage** office is straight in front of you as you emerge from the platforms, and there's another at ground level at the east end of the station frontage.

The **main ticket office** to the left of the entrance on the ground floor has a useful sign with ticket availability up to three days ahead for those who read Mandarin or who can recognize at least the characters for different kinds of seat (the columns from left to right are soft sleeper, hard sleeper, soft seat, hard seat and unnumbered) and the train numbers (*see* Language p.391). These electronic signs can now be found at all the main Běijīng stations. If you do shop here, just about any window can help you, except that tickets for the K97 to Hong Kong can only be bought at the **foreigners' ticket office** upstairs, which should anyway be your first choice for buying tickets. K97 tickets cannot be ordered by phone, either, but other telephone-ordered tickets can also be picked up at window 6 in the foreigners' ticket office. This is through the main entrance, where all baggage is X-rayed, and at departures level. Go up the escalators ahead of you (unless you are already at departures level) and turn left (*open 8–12, 1–6, and right through the night 7.30pm–7am*). The soft sleeper waiting room is also at this level. If you've come to meet friends, platform tickets are from a separate window outside the main entrance at ground level. There are several fast food outlets, not particularly recommended, but open 24 hours, and there are lots of under ¥10 meals for budget travellers.

Tickets for the K5 to **Hanoi** (Hénèi) and the K97 to **Kowloon** (Jiǔlóng) in Hong Kong must be bought at Běijīng Xī Zhàn, which is the departure point for these two services. The K5 leaves on Mon and Fri at 10.51, arriving Wed and Sun at 11.30. It's 2,786km to the Chinese border but the Vietnamese are cagey about the remaining distance. The K97 leaves on alternate days at 09.11, arriving at 13.10 the next day after 2,476km. Hard is not as high-class as on the fully international trains, still being three berths high in a largely open compartment, but is of higher standard and has a little more privacy. Hard ¥601 ($75), soft ¥934 ($117) and 'high class' soft (two beds in a compartment but bathroom at the end of the carriage) ¥1,191 ($149).

There are ticketing problems for the Hanoi train. Start at the foreigners' ticket office at the station, but you may be sent to a travel agent in the railway branch of the Construction Bank, on the east side of the West Station, ✆ 6321 6541, which claims to be the source of tickets for this train, and also claims that there is only one class—the most expensive, inevitably—which costs ¥1,023 ($128), including a ¥50 booking fee. However, the Inner Mongolia Autonomous Regional Government Beijing Representative Office, in the same Xī Zhí Mén back street as the Běi Zhàn (North Station), Běi Bīn Hé Lù 8, ✆ 6223 3477, offers hard seat for ¥306 ($38), hard sleeper ¥529 ($66), and soft sleeper ¥800 ($100), all including ¥30 booking fee. Don't expect to get to the bottom of whatever scam is going on here.

Běijīng Běi Zhàn

Běijīng Běi Zhàn (north, also known as Xī Zhí Mén Zhàn) is on the circle line at Ⓜ Xīzhí Mén and has an early morning train to the Bā Dá Lǐng Great Wall, and the occasional train to Dàtóng and beyond. From the northwestern exit of the metro, walk down to a lower road and turn right (north). The station, a small brick building, is a minute's walk up on your left, across a yard. The ticket windows are open with short breaks throughout the day from 6am, tickets on sale up to four days ahead (including day of travel) and you can buy them for departures from the other Běijīng stations, too. There's rarely much activity, so if you find yourself in this area consider buying your ticket here. Stations in smaller towns around China look like this, with the same cluster of cheap eating.

Běijīng Nán Zhàn

The Běijīng Nán Zhàn (south, also known as Yǒngdìng Mén Zhàn) is reached by the tè5 from Běijīng Xī Zhàn, and the 20 and 106 trolley from Běijīng Zhàn. There are minibus services to and from Tiān'ān Mén, Běijīng Zhàn and Běijīng Xī Zhàn too. For those staying in budget accommodation in the south, it may also be worth considering one of the trains that leave from here, and the station, despite being moderately busy with no foreigners' window, might be more convenient for buying rail tickets for departures from any Běijīng station. The station is growing in importance; it is now used for a much larger amount of traffic than was originally envisaged, and there are several barn-like waiting rooms.

Amongst the places mentioned in this book, there are trains to Chéngdé, Qínhuángdǎo and Tiānjīn, mostly slower (and therefore cheaper) than those from Běijīng Zhàn or Xī Zhàn. The ticket office is well over to the right of the main entrance in a separate building, and there's a lively market probably going all night long with peasants sitting around disconsolately on sacks in the square, smoking, a bit like Běijīng Zhàn used to be. You need windows 5–15 (*open 24 hours more or less*). Use window 16 to return tickets, and the electronic signs to find out about seat availability on all trains from Běijīng for the next three days, if you can read Chinese. There's an unhelpful **left luggage office** on the right of the square opposite the ticket office sign, *open 24 hours.*

Tourist Trains

Trains to the stations around Bā Dá Lǐng Great Wall have run for several years, first from the Běijīng Běi Zhàn and then also from Běijīng Zhàn, but new highways and rapid a/c buses have made these irrelevant. However, experiments have recently begun with opening goods and long-distance traffic lines to tourist trains to sights north and west of the capital, and opening tiny stations to do this. The government has announced its intention to use the network of more than 200 lines around Běijīng for tourism purposes. The first of these began in June 1999 from **Píngguǒ Yuán Dìtiě** (*opposite* the metro station), a tiny station that's nothing more than a pair of platforms on either side of a single track line designed to serve the Capital Iron and Steel Works. There are only a handful of departures a day. At the time of writing the only destination served likely to be of interest to foreign visitors was the temple Dà Jué Sì (*see* p.333) and more details of trains are given there. There are other departures from Běijīng Běi Zhàn. A new line to stretch in a large loop north from Xī Zhí Mén (Běijīng Běi Zhàn) to Dōng Zhí Mén is under construction, intended both to make rail commuting possible to the new northern suburbs and to give further tourist access to northern sites. To check times and services in the coming years, for Běijīng Běi Zhàn call ✆ 6512 8931, and also ask about Píngguǒ Yuán (no English spoken). Píngguǒ Yuán service number ✆ 6984 5542, or ✆ 6828 9988 and beep 11532.

by bus

Běijīng has several bus stations scattered around its third and occasionally second ring roads, and as China has finally begun to develop a credible national highway network, long-distance buses are now sometimes quicker or more convenient than the train.

The same bus stations also have buses to day trip destinations, and there are special tourist buses from a number of sites around the city's centre, most of which run on summer Saturdays and Sundays only, but which are the most convenient way to visit the major Great Wall sights and various other destinations.

The **Dōng Zhí Mén** Chángtú Qìchēzhàn, ✆ 6467 4995, has buses which will take you close to the **Sīmǎtái** and **Jīnshānlíng** Great Wall sites, and direct minbuses, both Iveco and less modern varieties, to **Chéngdé**. It's on the northeast side of Ⓜ Dōng Zhí Mén. Leave the metro at the northeast exit and turn right up the final steps. Turn first left and swing to right. The recessed entrance is not far past Domino's Pizza.

The **Liánhuā Chí** Chángtú Qìchē Zhàn, ✆ 6327 1467, has buses for Shíjiāzhuāng. Avoid the touts and buy from the computerized ticket window. Take bus 300 to Liù Lǐ Qiáo Nánlǐ and take pedestrian underpasses (full of people selling live fish from plastic buckets) to the east side of the third ring road. Walk north and fork right up Guǎng'ān Lù. The bus station is on the north side two minutes' walk further, fairly smart and clean by Běijīng bus station standards. You can also take all the buses mentioned for Liùlǐ Qiáo bus station below.

The **Liù Lǐ Qiáo** Chángtú Kèyùn Zhàn has big comfy Volvo buses and reasonable Chinese copies to Shíjiāzhuāng and a few buses to Yìxiàn near the **Western Qīng Tombs**. Take 300 to Liù Lǐ Qiáo Nánlǐ (the suburban 339 to Lúgōu Qiáo goes from here), walk north and cross one turning to turn left into the entrance to the Jīng Shí Gōnglù expressway. The station is three minutes' walk on the south side of the road. Bus 1 comes to Liù Lǐ Qiáo Běi Lǐ, just north of the station on the third ring road, from Jiànguó Mén, past Dōng Dān, Xī Dān and Fùxīng Mén, and bus 4 has regular stops along Jiànguó Mén and Cháng'ān between the China World Trade Centre (Dabeigou) and Xī Dān, also to Liù Lǐ Qiáo Běi Lǐ. Bus 6 comes to Liù Lǐ Qiáo from Hóng Qiáo and Tiāntán north gate. Also served by night bus 201 which comes from Qián Mén.

The **Lízé Qiáo** Chángtú Qìchē Zhàn has Volvo and Volvo-like buses to Tàiyuán every 15mins throughout the day, and one per hour after 5.45pm, a better way to travel than taking the train, and to Shíjiāzhuāng. It also has buses to Jǐ'nán and to Yìxiàn in the vicinity of the **Western Qīng Tombs** (Qīng Xī Líng). Take the 324 to Lízé Qiáo from Ⓜ Gōngzhǔfén, then walk back under the bridge and turn right. The station is slightly east on the north side of the road.

The **Mǎjuàn** Chángtú Qìchēzhàn, ✆ 6771 7622, has buses to **Tiānjīn**, **Chéngdé** and **Qínhuángdǎo**, mostly leaving early in the morning, and isn't your best choice for any of these destinations. However, it does have buses to Zūnhuá, in the vicinity of the **Eastern Qīng Tombs** (Qīng Dōng Líng), the cheapest way to reach the site. The station is one of the more central, in Guǎngqú Mén Wài Dàjiē just outside the second ring, reached by bus 23 east from Zhūshìkǒu, which is the first major junction south of Qián Mén, to stop Mǎjuàn (which means 'paddock' or 'horse enclosure'). Or take any bus down the east side of the second ring, get off at Guǎngqú Mén Qiáo and walk east.

The **Mùxī Yuán** Chángtú Qìchē Zhàn (which Beijing people like to call Mùxū Yuán), ✆ 6726 7147, has older, cheaper, slower buses to Jǐ'nán, and Shíjiāzhuāng, and is usefully located for those in southern budget accommodation (the Sea Star is just to the west), just next to the southern terminus of bus 2 from Tiān'ān Mén and Qián Mén.

Walk out of the east gate where the bus has just entered and turn right, and the next gate on the right is the long-distance bus station. The ticket office is in the basement. The **Tiān Qiáo** Chángtú Qìchē Zhàn, ✆ 6303 7770, has a bus route to **Shídù** via **Yúnjū Sì**, ¥15. The station is a short walk west of the Natural History Museum, and reached by buses south from Qián Mén to Tiān Qiáo, or bus 15 from the Zoo and Xī Dān.

The **Yǒngdìng Mén** Chángtú Qìchē Zhàn, ✆ 6303 6323, is another worth trying for its proximity to southern budget accommodation, with buses to Tiānjīn, Shíjiāzhuāng and Tàiyuán, although those wanting more comfortable and faster buses should look elsewhere. The station is in the forecourt of Běijīng Nán Zhàn (South Railway Station), *see above*.

The **Xī Zhí Mén** Chángtú Qìchē Kèyùn Zhàn, ✆ 6217 8742, is the best choice for buses to **Chéngdé** with speedy and comfortable departures about every 30 minutes, although you can also try Dōng Zhí Mén, which has fewer departures and fewer Iveco buses. All these services can take you to near Sīmǎtái and Jīnshānlǐng Great Wall sites. There's also one departure a day to Yīngxiàn outside Dàtóng, and two to **Qínhuángdǎo**. From Ⓜ Xī Zhí Mén walk west along Xī Zhí Mén Wài Dàjiē, and take the first major right turn into Gāoliang Qiáo Lù ('sorghum bridge road'—not so many years ago this was green space). The bus station is five minutes' walk up on the left.

Zhàogōng Kǒu Chángtú Kèyùn Qìchē Zhàn, ✆ 6723 7328 (can accept advance bookings), is the principal bus station for express buses to **Tiānjīn** at several levels of comfort and price, departing every few minutes all day, some continuing to the port at **Tánggū**, which has ships to Inchon in South Korea. There are also buses to Chéngdé, Shíjiāzhuāng and Jǐ'nán. Take bus 300 round the third ring to Liú Jiā Yáo Qiáo and walk west to Zhàogōngkǒu Qiáo then south a few minutes and take the first right. Advance booking at this station is on ✆ 6723 7328; turn right through white gates and you'll see a sign in English saying Ticket Office. Tánggū is cleaner and brighter than most stations. The 25 comes to Zhàogōngkǒu Qiáo from Xuānwǔ Mén, Fùxīng Mén and Yǒngdìng Mén.

Běijīng Zoo is also a useful starting point for out-of-town trips. Buses run from there and the bus station opposite to the university district, and on to the old and new summer palaces, from where further buses can take you to sights to the west of the city, such as Xiāng Shān. From **Déshèng Mén**, ✆ 6204 7096, 10mins walk east of Ⓜ Jīshuǐtán, there are buses to the Jūyōng Guān and Bā Dá Lǐng Great Wall sites, and to Sōng Shān.

Special Tourist Bus Routes

There are special buses which run day trips to an assortment of sights outside Běijīng in an assortment of combinations for a flat fee which combines cheapness and convenience. These are designed for Chinese tourists but happily accept foreigners' money without problems, although because they are designed for Chinese they do tend to stop at *lè yuán* (amusement parks) and *fēngjǐng qū* (scenic areas which were nice *before* they were so labelled, and now spoilt by loudspeakers in the trees, endless souvenir stalls and more amusement rides), as well as the genuine historical sights of more interest to visitors, many of which nestle in unspoilt scenery of their own.

Starting points include: just east of **Qián Mén** on the north side of Qián Mén Dōng Dàjiē opposite Macdonald's; on the west side of **Běijīng Zhàn** near the 104 bus stop; outside the main entrance of the **History Museum** in Tiān'ān Mén; northeast of Ⓜ **Xuānwǔ Mén** near the South Church; **Dōng Dà Qiáo** near the 350 bus stop; opposite the **Zoo** near 27 bus stop; northwest exit of Ⓜ **Xī Zhí Mén** near 16 bus stop; Ⓜ **Píngguǒ Yuán** near 326 bus stop; southwest exit of Ⓜ **Fùchéng Mén** near 335/6 bus stop, northwest exit of Ⓜ **Āndìng Mén** near 328 bus stop; 42 bus stop near Ⓜ **Dōng Shìshí Tiáo**; northwest of Ⓜ **Chóngwén Mén** near 111 bus stop.

The most convenient for visitors, and the points with the most departures, are Qián Mén and Xuānwǔ Mén. Starting times are given below, but at least 20 people are needed for a bus to depart, and 10 for a minibus, where such an alternative exists. The Chinese start early and so should you, and except for the Bā Dá Lǐng routes you should aim to be at the departure point by 7.30am, or better still 7am, although you may have to wait around until a bus fills. Some locations have a hut selling tickets, but conductors board the bus to sell tickets before departure. Use the routes and prices listed below as a general guide—these are constantly changing, but ticket prices are clearly marked and there are no problems with overcharging. The buses are fairly comfortable, and the higher price given is for those with air conditioning, although these are not always available.

Yóu1–4	Bā Dá Lǐng (*see* p.302), Shíshān Líng (Dìng Líng, *see* p.315), ¥36–4
Yóu5	Bā Dá Lǐng, Shíshān Líng (Dìng Líng, Cháng Líng), Jūyōng Guān (*see* p.304), ¥50
Yóu6	Mùtiányù (*see* p.304), Hóngluó Sì (*see* p.336), Yànqī Hú (amusement park with lake), ¥50–60
Yóu7	Shíhuā Dòng (caves made lurid by artificial lighting), Tánzhè Sì (*see* p.324), Jiétài Sì (*see* p.327), ¥30–36
Yóu8	Lóngqìng Xiá (scenic gorges), Jūyōng Guān, ¥40–50
Yóu10	Shí Dù (*see* p.334),Yúnjū Sì (*see* p.335), ¥43–50
Yóu12	Bái Lóng Tán (scenic area), Sīmǎtái (*see* p.305), ¥50–60

Routes 1–5 (including 'zhī' alternative routes) run daily all year round, but last departures are about 30mins earlier 16 Sept–14 April.

Routes	Departure times	From
Yóu1	6am–11am	Qián Mén
Yóu2	6am–10am	Běijīng Zhàn
Yóu2zhī	6am–9.30am	History Museum, Xuānwǔ Mén
Yóu3	6am–10am	Dōng Dà Qiáo near 350 bus stop
Yóu3zhī	6.30am–8.30am	Qián Mén
Yóu4	6am–11am	The Zoo, Xī Zhí Mén
Yóu4zhī	6am–8am	Píngguǒ Yuán
Yóu5	6am–10am	Qián Mén (southwest corner)

The remaining routes only run 15 April–15 Sept, and only on Saturdays, Sundays and public holidays.

Yóu6	7am–8.30am	Xuānwǔ Mén, outside the South Cathedral

Yóu7	7am–8.30am	Fùchéng Mén, Qián Mén
Yóu8	7am–8.30am	Āndìng Mén
Yóu10	7am–8.30am	Fùchéng Mén, Qián Mén
Yóu12	7am–8.30am	Dōng Shìshí Tiáo, Chóngwén Mén, Xuānwǔ Mén

There are other buses named only by their destinations, of which the most interesting are those to Shí Dù (*see* p.334) ¥43, to Jīnshānlǐng (*see* p.306) ¥50, and to Qīng Dōng Líng (Eastern Qīng Tombs, *see* p.313) ¥80 all from Xuānwǔ Mén, but the latter two rarely seem to attract enough passengers except right at the end of the summer when Chinese tourism is at its peak. Try and get together a large enough group to make the trip viable and show up early, 7am–8am. It's worthwhile, since the Eastern Qīng Tombs are difficult to see in a day using public transport.

Several bus companies now run comfortable services aimed at the four-and five-star hotel trade, such as Dragon Bus, which has various half-day and one-day tours within and near the city for around ¥300 (including lunch) and further afield to Bā Dá Lǐng Great Wall (*see* p.302), the Míng Tombs (*see* p.309), Mùtiányù Great Wall, the Dàbǎotái Han Tomb (*see* p.323), and the Marco Polo Bridge (*see* p.336). Ticketing and pick up points include: Jiànguó Fàndiàn, ✆ 6500 2233 ext 2186, and Wángfǔjǐng Grand Hotel, ✆ 6522 3981. Also try Panda Bus, ✆ 6803 7045.

Getting Around

The budget traveller takes public transport, mixes with the Chinese and pays a fraction of the price that everyone else does, but often spends much more time getting to a destination. For out-of-town sites, walk-up bus tours run for Chinese tourists are more expensive but still very cheap, and offer two or three sites in a day for around ¥50 (*see* 'Special tourist bus routes', *above*).

The canny traveller gets together with two or three others and charters a taxi which he or she flags down in the street. There can be hassles and the cost is a little higher, but at ¥1.2 per km or often less for one-day hires or long trips outside the city (depending on distance and negotiating skills) is affordable even by many budget travellers, providing door-to-door convenience and complete control over route and time at each stop.

Those for whom comfort and convenience is more important choose foreigner-oriented comfortable bus tours which pick up from five-star hotels, for around ¥300 ($37.50).

Those who pay most use the transport desks of their five-star hotels to organize a car, and pay as much as three or four times the going rate—as much as ¥1,500 ($188) per day for Santana and driver. Details of all these options are given below.

Běijīng's heart is Tiān'ān Mén and the vast square to its south, surrounded by four concentric ring roads, the fourth of which is still under construction, a few kilometres out in partially green space. Most of the main sights are within the second ring road, much budget accommodation is out on the third, and the fourth will only be crossed when venturing out on day trips to the Great Wall, the Marco Polo Bridge, the Summer Palaces and other sights. Most major streets run north to south or east to west, parallel to the sides of Tiān'ān Mén Square, often running straight for several kilometres and changing name several times. If a little attention is paid to these names, they help with orientation. Those called '*Wài*' meaning 'outside' are further out from the centre than those called '*Nèi*', 'inside', and many have compass points in their names: *Dōng* (East), *Nán* (South), *Xī* (West) and *Běi* (North). In fact *wài* usually indicates 'outside' the second ring road which follows the line of city walls, pulled down by Máo, and *nèi* inside it. The avenue passing the northern side of Tiān'ān Mén Square is a good example. Beginning in the west outside the second ring road it's called:

Fùxīng Mén Wài Dàjiē	Avenue (*dàjiē*) outside (*wài*) Fùxīng gate (*mén*)
Fùxīng Mén Nèi Dàjiē	Avenue inside (*nèi*) Fùxīng gate
Xī Cháng'ān Jiē	Cháng'ān Street West (*xī*)
Dōng Cháng'ān Jiē	Cháng'ān Street East (*dōng*)
Jiànguǒ Mén Nèi Dàjiē	Avenue inside Jiànguǒ gate
Jiànguǒ Mén Wài Dàjiē	Avenue outside Jiànguǒ gate.

This Cháng'ān Jiē is more commonly known in English as the Avenue of Eternal Peace. En route it passes many hotels and restaurants, the Aviation Building, the main Běijīng Telecom office, Tiān'ān Mén, several major shopping malls, the Rìtán embassy areas, the observatory, a Friendship Store, a silk market, several upmarket hotels and much more. The north–south Qián Mén Dàjiē runs directly south from Tiān'ān Mén Square. Its top is the departure point for public bus trips to Bādálǐng Chángchéng (Great Wall) and elsewhere, and it has endless fast food operations, both Chinese and Western, messily mixed with a street market. It runs south through seething shopping areas, and a maze of alleys known as *hútòng*.

by metro

Unless it means going absurdly far out of your way, always use the metro to travel as much of your route as possible. There are two lines: an east–west 17km 'First Line', which opened in 1970, and a circle line which follows the route of the second ring road, opened in 1984. Later it occurred to someone that since these lines cross there should be an interchange between them and this opened three years later (⊕ Fùxīng Mén). In 1999, just in time for 1 October, a new 13½km section opened continuing the First Line to the east, but not actually connected to the earlier part until mid-2000, and with a second interchange in the east at ⊕ Jiànguó Mén, altogether costing ¥7.57 billion. This finally put major central sights such as Tiān'ān Mén on the system (the Tiān'ān Mén West and East station buildings Forbidden City-ized with yellow eaves and some gold trim) and connected them to some of the main shopping and hotel areas on or off Cháng'ān Dōng Jiē, and Jiànguó Mén Nèi and Wài.

Signs in pīnyīn indicate exits and the nearest sights, cross-track signs tell you the next station in each direction, and on the trains long announcements in Mandarin end with the name of the next stop in English. Buy your ticket at a window below ground just before the final stairs to the platform, and have it torn by offering the short end to the ticket collector and hanging on to the rest. Make sure you get your half back. There is a ¥3 flat fare, and exchange between lines is permitted without further charge. Since the tickets are not dated, save time by buying a handful and using them at will.

The metro runs 5.30am–11pm and should be your first choice for getting around reasonably swiftly. An overhead extension further east is planned for some time in the indefinite future, and a new line running from Běijīng Xī Zhàn to the airport is already mooted. Come back in 10 years at the earliest.

by bus

At present, more than 8,200 buses are running on 363 bus routes throughout the city, with a total length of 7,180km. The government announced its intention to convert 'up to' 50,000 buses and taxis to liquefied petroleum gas and compressed natural gas by the end of 2000, not surprisingly concentrating their efforts at first in the heart of the city. But the largely ancient fleet will continue to make a significant contribution to atmospheric pollution for a while yet.

Read bus stop signs with caution. Where the stop doesn't have a name (or even if it does in many cases) the black number in the top left-hand corner is the route number, and any number in red is the *stop* number. The stop name is often given in pīnyīn as well as Chinese characters, but the rest of the route is usually only in vertical columns of characters. The present stop is marked along with an arrow to show direction of travel. To the left, beneath the bus number, you'll find the time of the first and last buses, and at the bottom the cost of a ticket.

Buses within the city and with numbers lower than 100 have a flat fare of ¥1 for all but the longest trips. Trolleybuses, numbering 101 upwards, are the same. Some trolley routes are doubled by limited stop bus versions of the same routes (*kuài chē*). Other buses in the 200 series which are night buses, and the 300+ series for suburban transport, begin at ¥1 for up to 12km, ¥1.5 up to 15km, ¥2 up to 22km, ¥2.5 up to 27km, and so on. Express buses *tè* (special) 1–5 have flat fares of around ¥2–5 depending on route (these are sometimes double-deckers), as do green and yellow a/c single-decker buses. Minibuses running in parallel with conventional city routes and displaying the same numbers charge ¥2, although locals haggle for ¥1 for shorter trips. Usually the conductor is leaning out of the window yelling the price.

Běijīng blocks are exhaustingly long, and bus stops far apart. Small wars sometimes break out in the search for seats, but unless you are willing to pile in and crush your share of children and old ladies (both capable of looking after themselves, as your ribs will discover), you may not get on. The pressure has been relieved a little by a recent increase in price and the arrival of the minibuses.

On most buses you pay the conductor and get change (although it's better to have the exact money ready to avoid argument), but on newer ones a picture of a hand dropping a coin into a slot on the bus stop indicates exact fare only. Times vary, but most services run from around 5am to 11pm, with a completely different set of night routes starting up from around 10pm. Times are given on the stop signs.

by taxi

The once legion yellow or white minivans (*miàndī*), which were the cheapest cabs, were told to disappear before the 1 October 1999 anniversary on the grounds of pollution (which simply meant that some went to pollute other cities, while their drivers acquired the only marginally better *Xiàlì—see* below). However, in late 1998 prices on all other cabs were reduced to compensate. The majority are small, usually red cars both in hatchback and 'three box' form (*Xiàlì*), but there are also longer estates (station wagons) called *bullets*, and the occasional Lada or other oddities. For all of these the flag-fall is ¥10, which includes 4km. For each subsequent km the rate is ¥1.20. The rate per km jumps by 20% after 11pm and before 5am, although this may happen a little early in some taxis as the meter's clock may not be accurate. The rate per km is written clearly on the side of all cabs, and this will help you tell the Fùkāng (a Citroën joint venture in Wǔhàn) from the Xiàlì (made in Tiānjīn), since these are ¥1.6 per km, as are a handful of Mazda 323s, and Shànghǎi Santanas (a Volkswagen Jetta made in Shànghǎi). The larger Santana 2000 is ¥2 per km, as are Toyota Crowns and a limited number of other older vehicles. These mostly do not ply for hire, but hang around the five-star hotels waiting to be called forward by the staff (who will have been suitably squared).

As usual, do not accept rides from independent taxi drivers who approach you at the airport, principal tourist sites, larger hotels, the Aviation Building or railway stations, and where possible walk out a little distance before flagging a cab. Otherwise be prepared to face all the range of tricks—speedy meters, 'broken' meters, getting 'lost', 'misunderstanding', 'no change', and, most shockingly for those who remember the China of only a few years ago, 'You want girl? Drugs?' Taxi drivers who head out of town towards ring roads and then travel around these usually know what they are doing in terms of getting you to your destination fairly quickly, but with a consequent increase in distance travelled. Always sit in the front and carry an open map on your lap so that the driver thinks you are following the route, even if you are not. Mandarin speakers only occasionally encounter difficulties.

If you are going one way out of Běijīng the driver is entitled to push a button on the meter which adds 50% to the kilometre rate after 15km. Some drivers push this button whenever they reset the meter, but around town they should not do so.

If you do have a bad experience try ostentatiously noting the complaints telephone number displayed on a card with the driver's picture posted on the dashboard, and the driver's own number and the cab number plate. Better hotels give you a card with the cab number written on it when you board at the hotel entrance, so that if you subsequently have any complaint they can (at least in theory) take action.

There are 500 cabs fitted with the satellite GPS system which can be called by phone, © 6837 3399, 24hrs. These are all of the ¥2 per km persuasion, and there's a ¥3 charge for the booking service, payable to the driver. As with most numbers, no English is spoken, however, so you'll need help.

by bicycle or cycle rickshaw

Bicycles are usually available for hire at the cheaper hotels, typically for ¥10 ($1.25) per day, but Běijīng's heavy traffic means that you are risking your life, although doing so with millions of Chinese. If you stay in Běijīng for a week it is very likely that you will see an accident involving a cyclist and a vehicle. Always park in designated spots (wherever you see a vista of bicycles in a roped-off part of the pavement, ¥0.20), and nowhere else, or your bike is unlikely to be there when you get back. A basic Chinese boneshaker only costs about ¥300, and those staying a few weeks, and with contacts through which to sell the bike at the end of their stay, might find buying one a good idea—*see* 'Shopping, p.228.

While decrying the pollution caused by vehicles and theoretically trying to do something about it, Běijīng seems to be marching firmly backwards. In 1998 for the first time a street was *closed* to bicycles to enable cars to flow more freely, and in 1999 an official was quoted in *China Daily* calling for road building to be put above house building.

For a foreign visitor a ride in a **cycle rickshaw** (pedicab) *always* ends in tears. If you don't fix a price in advance, ¥200 ($25) will be demanded for half a kilometre. If you do fix a price, either you will not be taken to your destination or a much higher price will be demanded for an incomprehensible reason when you arrive. The average worker is being paid as little as ¥5–600 per month, not per 15mins. A typical price quoted to a Chinese for the run from Qián Mén to Wángfǔjǐng is ¥10 ($1.25), but for foreigners never less than ¥30, with probable added difficulties. Why waste your time when a *Xiàlì* will take you there much quicker for only ¥10 and be happy to take your money for such a short run? Spare yourself.

by boat

Part of the mammoth beautification of Běijīng prior to the 1999 50th anniversary of the founding of the People's Republic involved draining several of the many rivers and canals that lace the city, including the moat around the Palace, and lining them with stone. Banks were cleaned up and balustrades and electrically lit walkways constructed. The work will continue for a few years, but at the time of writing two boat routes had already opened up connecting the city with the Summer Palace: line A starting from Bā Yī Hù (in Yùyuán Tán Park, behind the Military Museum), and line B with less frequent services from near the Zoo. *See* Summer Palace p.290 for full details. Eventually there will be a network of boat services around the city, and while it won't be Venice or Amsterdam, it will make a pleasant change from the noisy and polluted streets.

self-drive

This has never been straightforward even for those with residence permits, and is a brand new option for visitors. Cars have formerly come with drivers, or not at all. Frankly, you prefer it that way, and there are few countries in the world whose roads can possibly prepare you for the blind selfish manic stupidity of driving in China, where drivers mostly ignore common sense and put their vehicles anywhere physics will allow them, including some places physics will not allow them intact. The only rule of the road is that there are no rules unless someone with an ability to charge a fine is watching, and if a car is carrying a plate indicating that it is from the military or belongs to a resident of certain government compounds it can and will ignore traffic signs, which are only for the proles, at will. You may consider joining the fray, but you'd be much better to do so after a week or so of getting used to the place.

However, the easiest place for a foreign visitor to rent a car is at the new Terminal 2 arrivals lounge counter of BCNC car rental (well over to the right after you pass through customs), toll-free in China ✆ 800 810 9001, ✆ 6457 5566, <*http://www.bcnc.com.cn/*>. You will need your air ticket, passport, an international driving licence (ignore public information which says that your national licence is sufficient), plus a credit card to cover the ¥8,000 ($1,000) deposit (¥10,000 on larger vehicles). Visa, Mastercard, Diners' Club, American Express, and JCB accepted.

Cars range from small Citroëns to large Audis. The Citroën is ¥400 ($50) per day (reductions for rentals of more than two weeks), including 180km per day, plus ¥3 per kilometre over that. The charges include insurance, but not personal accident insurance which is available for an extra charge, and allow a single named driver to drive in Běijīng (which means that you can reach some Great Wall sites but not others, for instance) unless you pay a further ¥10,000 deposit and ¥100 per day extra for rental, and ¥100 for each extra driver.

BCNC has six further locations in Běijīng, but at all of these you'll have to ask a permanent Běijīng resident to take his or her residence papers and act as your guarantor. It's also possible to acquire a membership of BCNC in which they clear all your paperwork and then act as guarantor when you want to rent a car from selected companies in other Chinese cities.

Běijīng ℡ (010)   **Tourist Information**

Police ℡ 110 (may speak English), fire ℡ 119, ambulance ℡ 120.

Directory enquiries 114 (won't speak English); English directory enquiries ℡ 2689 0114 (¥3 per minute premium line—may not work from your hotel room). For numbers outside Běijīng dial the city code plus 114 (definitely won't speak English).

Time in Mandarin and English ℡ 118; weather forecast, also in both languages, ℡ 121.

Don't expect English on any of the following numbers: Taxicab Administration (use for complaints) ℡ 6601 2620; Airport Information ℡ 6655 2515; Railway Information ℡ 6512 8931.

Complaints about guides and travel agents: Supervisory Office of Tourism Quality of CNTA, in the Běijīng International Hotel (*open 8.30–1 and 2.30–5*), ℡ 6512 6688, ext 4040; Supervisory Office of Travel Agencies Service Quality of Běijīng Municipality, Běijīng Lǚyóu Building, Jiànguó Mén Wài Dàjiē 28 (*open 8.30–12 and 2.30–5*), ℡ 6513 0828.

Běijīng has an English- and Japanese-language Tourist Hotline, open 24 hours, ℡ 6513 0828, which is for assistance and complaints, but don't expect miracles. In fact those who reply seem to have very little useful information.

discounted culture and entertainment

Those planning to spend a lot of time in nightclubs (not Běijīng's strongest attraction) and other expat-oriented entertainments can save money by buying an **Asian Hospitality Associates (AHA) Card**, which allows free or discounted entrance and discounts on shopping and off restaurant bills. The list of more than 200 participants changes from year to year; contact ℡ 6538 1775, @ 6538 1776 or <*aha@public. bta.net.cn*> for the latest details of cost and benefits. The Card can be bought at expat locations or at upmarket department stores such as Full Link and COFCO.

Those planning to visit several **museums** can save money by purchasing the Tōngyòng Niánpiào—**general annual ticket**—which gives free admission to nearly 60 museums around Běijīng. The ticket is good for three person-visits to each museum, which can be made at the same time or separately. A few of the museums, which are listed in Mandarin in an accompanying booklet, are big names, many are obscure and some are eminently avoidable. Nevertheless, the cost of the card can easily be recovered by a single three-person visit to some museums, or, on average, one person's visit to four or five. The offer varies from year to year but typically the card is ¥60, dropping to ¥40 later in the year, and available both from museums which participate in the scheme, and some which don't (such as the Natural History Museum). *See* individual site descriptions—29 of those covered in this book accept the pass.

embassies

There are two principal diplomatic enclaves: the Rìtán Embassy Area (Rìtán Shǐguānqū), which is north of the Friendship Store, and the Sānlǐtún Embassy Area (Sānlǐtún Shǐguānqū), which is further to the northeast towards the Lufthansa Centre, although there are now increasing numbers of escapees, especially to the east of Sānlǐtún. Almost every country in the world has an embassy in Běijīng.

For **onward visas,** contact the following:

Cambodia: Dōng Zhí Mén Wài Dàjiē 9, ✆ 6532 1889, ✉ 6532 3507, but one month tourist visas are granted on arrival for $20. One photograph is needed.

Kazakhstan: Sānlǐtún Dōng Liù Jiē 9, Sānlǐtún, ✆ 6532 6182, ✉ 6532 6183 (*open Tues and Fri, 8.30am–12 noon*). Transit visas available if you hold another CIS visa or an air ticket from Almaty, $15. Tourist visas $25 for 2 weeks, but only with an invitation. Payment in 1990 or later $US cash only. One photograph is needed.

Kyrgyzstan: Tǎyuán Diplomatic Office Building, Liàngmǎhé Nánlù 14, Sānlǐtún, ✆ 6532 6458, ✉ 6532 6459 (*open Mon–Fri, 8–6*). Tourist visas are valid for up to two months, and cost $60. Two photographs are needed.

Laos: Dōng Sì Jiē, Sānlǐtún, ✆ 6532 1224, ✉ 6532 6748.

Mongolia: Xiùshuǐ Běidàjiē 2, Rìtán, ✆ 6532 1203, ✉ 6532 5045. Another country requiring perfect post-1990 $US, although RMB can also be used to pay for visas, which are easily available. Tourist visas are $40 or ¥400. One photograph is needed.

North Korea: Rìtán Běi Lù, Rìtán, ✆ 6532 2558. It is possible to visit North Korea, but only in an organized way. *See above* under Běijīng Xī Zhàn, p.100.

Pakistan: Dōng Zhí Mén Wài Dàjiē 1, Sānlǐtún, ✆ 6532 2558, ✉ 6532 2715 (*open Mon–Fri, 9–4*). Visa fees vary according to nationality (can be as much as ¥500, $60) and are usually available later the same day. Two photographs are needed.

Russia: Dōng Zhí Mén Běi Zhōngjiē 4, ✆ 6532 1267, ✉ 6532 4853 (*open Mon–Fri, 9–1*). To buy a tourist visa you must prove that you have booked accommodation. No visa is required if you simply change planes at Moscow, but if you have an onward ticket and want to see the city, transit visas can be purchased in the transit lounge in Moscow's Sheremetyevo Airport. They start from $18 for 6 hours, running up to $110 for 72 hours, but ask Aeroflot for the latest prices since these are liable to change at short notice. It is also possible to buy tourist visas at the airport if accommodation is purchased at the same time, although this will be very expensive. Aeroflot staff advise making visa arrangements before leaving Běijīng if possible. A three-day transit will only cost $40 if bought in Běijīng, a tourist visa $50. You will need three photographs.

South Korea: China World Trade Centre, Jiànguó Mén Wài Dàjiē, ✆ 6505 2608, 🖷 6505 3067.

Vietnam: Guǎnghuá Lù 37, ✆ 6532 1155, 🖷 6532 5270.

In **emergencies**, contact the following:

Australia: Dōng Zhí Mén Wài Dàjiē 19, Sānlǐtún, ✆ 6532 2331–7, 🖷 6532 4605.

Austria: Dōng Wǔ Jiē 5, Rìtán, ✆ 6532 2061, 🖷 6532 1505.

Belgium: Sānlǐtún Lù 6, Sānlǐtún, ✆ 6532 1736, 🖷 6532 5097.

Canada: Dōng Zhí Mén Wài Dàjiē 19, Sānlǐtún, ✆ 6532 3536, 🖷 6532 4072.

Denmark: Dōng Wǔ Jiē 1, Sānlǐtún, ✆ 6532 2431, 🖷 6532 2439.

Finland: Tǎyuán Diplomatic Office Building, Liàngmǎhé Nánlù 14, Sānlǐtún, ✆ 6532 1817, 🖷 6532 1884.

France: Dōng Sān Jiē 3, Sānlǐtún, ✆ 6532 1331, 🖷 6501 4872.

Germany: Dōng Zhí Mén Wài Dàjiē 5, Sānlǐtún, ✆ 6532 2161, 🖷 6532 5336.

Ireland: Rìtán Dōng Lù, Rìtán, ✆ 6532 2691, 🖷 6532 6857.

Italy: Dōng Èr Jiē 2, Sānlǐtún, ✆ 6532 2131.

Japan: Rìtán Lù 7, Rìtán, ✆ 6532 2361.

New Zealand: Rìtán Dōng Èr Jiē 1, Rìtán, ✆ 6532 2731–4, 🖷 6532 4317.

Norway: Dōng Yī Sān Jiē, Sānlǐtún, ✆ 6532 2261, 🖷 6532 2392.

Portugal: Tǎyuán Diplomatic Office Building, Liàngmǎhé Nánlù 14, Sānlǐtún, ✆ 6532 3497, 🖷 6532 4637.

Singapore: Xiùshuǐ Běi Jiē 1, Rìtán, ✆ 6532 3926, 🖷 6532 2215.

Spain: Sānlǐtún Lù 9, Sānlǐtún, ✆ 6532 1986, 🖷 6532 3401.

Sweden: Dōng Zhí Mén Wài Dàjiē 3, ✆ 6532 3331, 🖷 6532 5008.

Switzerland: Dōng Wǔ Jiē 3, Sānlǐtún, ✆ 6532 2736, 🖷 6532 4353.

UK: Guānghuá Lù 11, Rìtán, ✆ 6532 1961–5, 🖷 6532 1939 ext 239.

USA: Xiùshuǐ Běi Jiē 3, Rìtán, ✆ 6532 3431, 🖷 6532 3831.

maps and books

Maps in English and Chinese or Chinese only are available in bookshops throughout the city, from street vendors at railway stations and at tourist sites for ¥2.5 to ¥3. The clearest of these is the Hong Kong produced *Běijīng—The Latest Tourist Map*, which also has an English key. There are also much more detailed Chinese-only street directories such as the *Běijīng Shēnghuó Dìtúcé*, ¥14.60, in a fresh edition every year, more or less. The four-storey Foreign Languages Bookstore (Wàiwén Shūdiàn) on the west side of Wángfǔjǐng (no.235) has a large stock of **novels** and other materials in English and other languages on the fourth floor. The Běijīng Book Centre at Ⓜ Xī Dān has postcard sets, books in English, books on learning Chinese, and an extensive map section including maps for various cities and provinces around China upstairs and to the right. *See also* 'Shopping', p.228.

Foreign exchange. Travellers' cheques and cash can be most easily exchanged at the Friendship Store (*open daily, 9 –9*) in Jiànguó Mén, ⓜ Yŏng'ān Lǐ, and the One World Department Store (Shì Dū Bǎihuò) in Wángfǔjǐng, ⓜ Wángfǔjǐng (*open daily 10–9.30*), both with much longer hours than banks.

Bank of China branches with longer hours include upstairs in the Aviation Building, ⓜ Xī Dān (*open Mon–Sat, 9–5*), and the building with a clock on top directly south of the Great Hall of the People in Tiān'ān Mén Square with long opening hours during all of which it claims to change money (*Mon–Sun, 9–5*) and with an ATM inside. Other useful branches with foreign exchange counters include: just south of ⓜ Hépíng Mén (*open Mon–Fri, 9–12 and 1.30–5*); the ground floor of the SCITECH building on the south side of Jiànguǒ Mén Wài Dàjiē west of the Friendship Store (*open daily 9–12 and 1–6.30*); in the Landmark Building next to the Great Wall Sheraton (*open Mon–Fri, 9-4.30*), with ATM outside; ground level near the northernmost entrance of Sun Dong Plaza (*open Mon–Fri, 9–12 and 1.30–5*), with an ATM outside in Wángfǔjǐng Dàjiē; and one in the basement (next to three others which don't take foreign cards) in Dōng'ān Mén Dàjiē west off Wángfǔjǐng (*open Mon–Fri, 9–5*) with an ATM outside; and an ATM in Lándǎo Dàshà in Cháoyáng Mén Wài Dàjiē (*open daily 9–9*). You can experiment with other ATMs around Běijīng, but only Bank of China ones will work, and only a few of those. You'll need a Mastercard, Visa, Cirrus, Plus, JCB and ETC (or successors) card.

Non Bank of China ATMs include those of two other Chinese banks at the Capital Airport, and of Citibank and Hong Kong and Shanghai Bank in central Běijīng, opposite one another in Jiànguó Mén Nèi Dàjiē, just north of Běijīng Zhàn. The Citibank cash machines are east of the International Hotel and seem to take just about anything. There's also a Diner's Club office here, and a Bank of China ATM in the lobby of neighbouring Cháng'ān Grand Theatre, too. The HSBC is in COFCO Plaza, opposite, with an ATM also accepting a wide range of cards, and also accessible 24hrs. American Express is on the 11th floor of the China World Trade Centre (*open Mon–Fri, 9–5, Sat 9–12*), ✆ 6505 2888, and has its own teller machine in the China World Hotel nearby.

Personal cheques guaranteed by an Amex card can be cashed at major branches of the Bank of China, including branches of the Bank of China at Fùchéng Mén Dàjiē 410, ✆ 6601 6699, Xī Jiāo Mín Xiàng 17 (on west side of Tiān'ān Mén Square), in the Lufthansa Centre, on the second floor of the first tower at the China World Trade Centre, and Citic Industrial Bank on the ground floor of the Citic Building just west of the Friendship Store on Jiànguó Mén Wài. All of these are open Mon-Fri, 9–12, 1–4. You'll need your passport and credit card, but counter cheques are available of you haven't brought any.

Money can be **wired** to Běijīng via Western Union. Receiving offices include the Jiànguó Mén Post Office (*see* below). For more details: ✆ 6318 4313.

newspapers and magazines

For detailed listings of events, reviews of the latest restaurants and notes on every possible kind of service of interest to resident foreigners, see the highly competitive, but all free, foreigner-produced local English-language media mostly appearing on Thursdays at better hotels and bar and shopping locations popular with foreign residents.

The longest running and most outspoken (and often shut down by the authorities) is the weekly *Běijīng Scene*. This has a smart-alec and occasionally spiteful, bored-of-Běijīng tone, at its best in the columns *Comrade Language* and *Ask Ayi* (the maid-housekeeper-'woman what does' common in many expat households), which under the guise of teaching fresh, slangy vocabulary or offering helpful advice, engages in savage satire of many aspects of Chinese society and the experience of living in Běijīng as a foreigner. The paper also carries interviews with underground artists, film-makers and bands, many of whom would not be covered elsewhere.

Fortnightly *City Weekend* has many similar elements but is generally a better read and in better taste, though also not unwilling to laugh at the regime and various absurdities of Chinese society where warranted. There are often very readable pieces on the grind of daily life from a Chinese perspective. Twice-a-month *Metro* is again similar in content, but considerably more amateurish and sometimes barely literate. It does, however, contain a free colour map showing the locations of most of the popular Westerner-oriented entertainment venues.

China Daily, free at larger hotels and now *on sale* at the Friendship Store, has information on what's on in Běijīng, as does the weekly *Běijīng Weekend* published by *China Daily* and available on Fridays in the same locations, which has almost no news or politics, just entertainment features. All of these publications have websites (*see* p.39).

The official guide to what's on is *Běijīng This Month*, issued at larger hotels at the beginning of each month, which is good for coverage of seasonal events, and news of the latest government-reopened temples, etc., although as completely uncritical as *China Daily*, and often, like that publication, omitting key geographical, transport and contact information. The official reference work to Běijīng is the *Běijīng Official Guide*—a small paperback published twice a year under the auspices of the Běijīng Tourism Administration, which contains as unsophisticated a government-approved view of Běijīng as one might expect. With a nominal cover price of ¥20, it is usually in fact given away at the desks of major hotels.

Travel China comes out weekly with stories of ever-increasing tourist numbers, ever-increasing tourist satisfaction, and the enforced beautification of otherwise pleasant wild places. This magazine can also sometimes be picked up at the offices overseas listed on p.58.

photography

Film and camera shops are numerous in every major shopping street, and passport photos are widely available from various Polaroid-sign-sprouting sites. There's an excellent photography specialist at the side of the Sānlián Bookstore north of the National Art Gallery, with large refrigerators full of a wide variety of amateur and specialist film, in many formats. Reasonably reliable slide and print developing is also widely available here, and also at SCITECH in Jiànguó Mén Wài and at other upmarket department stores, as well as at higher prices in the five-star hotels.

post offices, telecommunications, Internet

The Jiànguǒ Mén Post and Telecommunication Office (Jiànguǒ Mén Yóudiànjú), a block north of ⑩ Jiànguǒ Mén up Jiànguǒ Mén Běi Dàjiē, (*open 8–7*) is the one where *poste restante* mail ends up. The counter is half way down on the left where incoming mail sits on a desk in three boxes. There is a ¥1.5 charge per item to pick up. The postcode is 100600. To claim parcels you must show your passport, and you may have to open the parcel in front of the staff if requested. The parcel counter is at the rear on the right (*open Mon–Fri, 9–5*).

The main post office is on Jiànguó Mén Nèi Dàjiē on the corner of the approach to the station, (*open 8–7*). There are numerous useful small post offices dotted around, including in the basement of the China World Trade Centre (*open 9–6*), in Dōng'ān Mén Dàjiē west of Wángfǔjīng Dàjiē with a useful parcel wrapping service (although some reports of overcharging foreigners here—*open 8–7*), just east of the Telegraph Building on the south side of Xī Cháng'ān Jiē (*open 8.30–7*), just to the east of the Hépíng Mén roast duck restaurant on the south side of Qián Mén Xī Dàjiē (*open 8.30–6.30*), in the Landmark Building next to the Great Wall Sheraton (*open 9–12, 1–5, closed Sat and Sun*) and to the east of the main entrance at Běijīng Xī Zhàn (*open 9–5*).

Couriers: DHL has an office on the ground floor of COFCO (*open 8–6, Sat 8–4.30, closed Sun and public holidays*), ✆ 6526 6666 ext 2117/8. The main office for EMS (Běijīng Shì Yóuzhèng Sùdì Jú) is at Qián Mén Dōng Dàjiē 7, ✆ 185, or ✆ 6512 9948. Federal Express, ✆ 6468 5566. DHL-Sinotrans Ltd, ✆ 6466 2211. UPS, ✆ 6593 2932. Upmarket hotels have the paperwork for some or all of these services in their business centres or at reception.

International telephone services are offered by even the cheapest hotels in Běijīng, although occasionally only from a cabin in the foyer, and at substantial mark-ups above the already expensive International Telegraph and Telephone Service Hall (Diànbào Diànhuà Gōngyètīng), which is at ⑩ Xīdān, just east of the Aviation building on the north side of Qián Mén Xī Dàjiē (*open 8.30–8*). Typical call charges per minute: ¥15 to Europe, North America and Africa, ¥12 to Asia, ¥5 to HK, Macau and Taiwan. Subtract 40% between midnight and 7am daily. Subtract 20% Mon–Fri 9pm–12 midnight; Sat, Sun and stat holidays 7am–12 midnight. To HK, Macau and Taiwan subtract 20% all day on public holidays. But many of these discounts do not work from pay phones, to use most of which you need to buy a card, although a temporary further cut in rates from early 2000 may be extended and in general telephone call prices are falling fast. The cheapest method of all remains to buy an IP card to route your call through the Internet, although the results are patchy, for ¥4.8 per minute.

Internet. To open your own email only or full Internet account in Běijīng (a surprisingly easy and cheap proposition), *see* 'Internet', p.41. Most hotels big enough to have a business centre now have **email** access, but most haven't made an adequate investment in the infrastructure and have hopelessly slow dial-up connections for which they charge anything between ¥1 and ¥7 per minute.

Amongst **cyber-cafés** try Sparkice at Capital Stadium west gate, ✆ 6833 5225; China World Trade Centre, 2nd floor, ✆ 6505 2288 ext 8209, near Qīnghuá University,

© 6236 2505; Wàntōng, © 234 3388, and two other branches in Běijīng. Each branch has plenty of machines and reasonably fast connections within the limits of China's Internet infrastructure. ¥30 per hour, ¥15 for 30mins or buy a ¥100 'tiger' card which includes five hours and gives further hours at a cheaper rate, *<http://www.sparkice.com.cn/>*. Try also Compaq Cyber Café in the basement of Full Link Plaza, *<http://www.cc-cafe.com/>* and Beak Internet Café just round the corner from the Silk Market (¥15 per hour). Others include: Sānlián Bookstore north of National Art Gallery, which has Internet on the second floor but pretty slow dial-up, ¥20 per hour, ¥10 for 30mins; the Grand Skylight Hotel, just north of ⓜ Hépíng Mén, with Internet access to non-residents for ¥15 per hour; Běijīng Bohong Technology (look for 'Internet' sign), Lángfáng Tóutiáo 63, west of Dàzhàlán Jiē, which has four online machines (*open 24 hrs*), ¥10 for 20mins, ¥20 for one hour. The supposedly budget hotels in the south have Internet access at upmarket prices to match those of Sparkice.

tours

Even the cheapest hotels in Běijīng have **travel agents** who can make local travel arrangements, although often at a higher price than they charge Chinese for the same service and often at many multiples of the cost of using local transport for the same purpose. A tour to the Míng Tombs and Bādálǐng Great Wall, for instance, can cost up to ¥500 ($63) per person, including entrance tickets and lunch, but you can do much the same thing yourself by bus for only ¥25 ($3) in bus fares, ¥60 ($7.50) or so in entrance tickets (depending on which tombs you decide to enter) and whatever you choose to spend on lunch (take a picnic). These agents can also book air and train tickets for commissions ranging from nothing (usually air tickets) to ¥100 ($12) per ticket, which it's also easy to do for yourself in Běijīng.

If you are in search of the best deal for any kind of organized transport it might be worth going to **Běijīng Tourism Street** which is behind the State Tourism Administration office, just to the north of the Běijīng International Hotel on Jiànguó Mén Nèi Dàjiē, ⓜ Běijīng Zhàn and walk north. This has been slow to take off, although about 30 agents now have offices there. Competition is supposed to make bargaining possible, but they are busy enough with Chinese business not to feel the need to open at weekends.

The **Beijing International Society** runs a programme of lectures, demonstrations, films, performances and outings about four times a month (there's a summer break) for those expatriates who maintain an interest in Chinese culture. Not infrequently the Society manages to gain access for its members to sites otherwise closed to the public. Expat members are allowed occasionally to bring one or two friends to meetings other than excursions (for which there are extra charges and which must be booked in advance). Annual membership is ¥200, which could be considered worthwhile for those staying in and around Běijīng for a few weeks. For programme details see: *<http://www.wayx.com/bis/>*.

visa extensions

Visa extensions are no longer available from the PSB's Wàiguórén Qiānzhèng Bàngōngshì (Foreigner Visa Office) in Běi Chízǐ Dàjiē, but now at the Division of

Aliens Exit-Entry, Āndìng Mén Dōng Dàjiē 2, ℃ 8401 5292 or ℃ 8402 5292 (open Mon–Fri, 8.30–12 and 1–5.30). (There's a visa information hotline on ℃ 2661 1266 which is supposed to have an English option, but didn't at the time of writing, and is a premium line costing ¥30 to call.) Go to ⓂYōnghé Gōng and walk east 100m on the south side of the street.

This should be the only contact you have with the police or 'Public Security Bureau', who already have enough problems. In 1999 Police Chief Zhāng, known as the 'Sherlock Holmes of Běijīng', was accused of issuing registrations for 70,000 smuggled cars.

The Imperial City and Tiān'ān Mén Square

The wall of the Míng Imperial City once ran for 11km, passing across the top of what's now Běi Hǎi Park and about halfway between Jǐng Shān Park and the Drum and Bell Towers. It enclosed the imperial pleasure grounds of three lakes to the west of the Forbidden City built by earlier dynasties, the Běi, Zhōng and Nán Hǎi, and on the east ran down modern Běi and Nán Hé Yán, halfway between the palace walls and the Wángfǔjǐng shopping street. The two sides met at Tiān'ān Mén—the Gate of Heavenly Peace. This enclosure was the haunt of the emperor, his family, his servants and administrators, and at its heart lay the palace, the southern half of which was for imperial audiences and administration of the state, and the northern half for the emperor, his empresses and concubines, and the eunuchs who served them.

The area around the Zhōng (Middle) and Nán (South) lakes has become the compound of the new government, and is as closed to the public now as it has been for centuries. The space around the palace has been invaded by plebian modern construction, and many of the ancient buildings have been pulled down. But the Forbidden City, or Palace Museum, remains the greatest complex of ancient buildings still surviving in China, and its neighbouring temples and administrative buildings, many around 500 years old, are still magnificent.

A spur of the Imperial City walls ran straight south from the Tiān'ān Mén to the Dà Míng Mén, the Gate of the Great Míng, renamed Gate of Great Qīng after the fall of the Míng, and the Zhōnghuá Mén (China Gate) after the creation of the Republic. This narrow stone-flagged way, known as the Thousand Steps Passage, was lined with imperial storehouses. Clearance of the buildings began after the end of the Qīng, but the modern vast 49-hectare expanse of Tiān'ān Mén Square (or 44-hectare depending on who you read—as with all figures in China, estimates vary) is a communist creation, and a showplace for the images the Party would like you to believe. The square and its contents are utterly fascinating as propaganda through town planning and a sobering lesson in modern Chinese history.

Since 4 June 1989 Tiān'ān Mén Square has become as famous outside China as the Great Wall, but not for reasons which give much pleasure to the Chinese authorities. The remainder of the Imperial City walls have mostly vanished, except those parts which still form the perimeter of the Zhōngnán Hǎi government compound, and a little section at the entrance to Nán Chízi, just to the east of the Tiān'ān Mén, which had an arch put in during the Republic to allow traffic to enter from Cháng'ān Dàjiē.

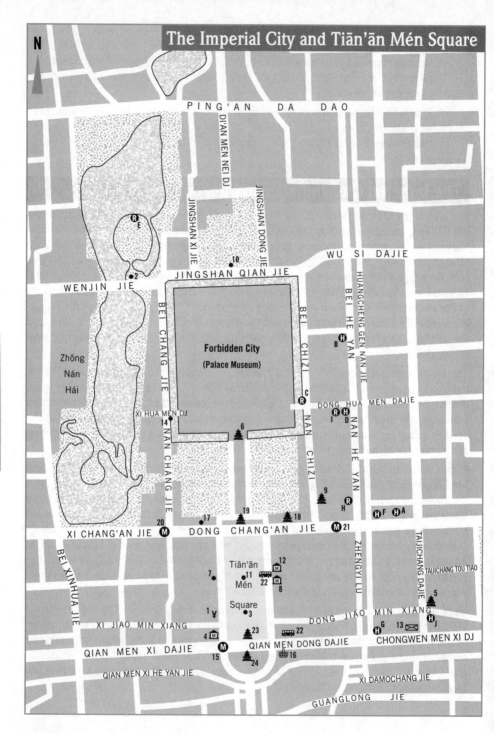

N

PING'AN DA DAO

DI'AN MEN NEI DJ

JINGSHAN DONG JIE

JINGSHAN XI JIE

R
E

10

WU SI DAJIE

2

JINGSHAN QIAN JIE

WENJIN JIE

BEI CHANG JIE

Forbidden City

(Palace Museum)

Zhōng

Nán

Hái

BEI CHIZI

BEI HE YAN

HUANGCHENG GEN NAN JIE

B H

R

C

DONG HUA MEN DAJIE

XI HUA MEN DJ

NAN CHANG JIE

14

6

I R H
D

NAN CHIZI

NAN HE YAN

9

R
H

H F H A

19

17

18

20

XI CHANG'AN JIE M

DONG CHANG'AN JIE

M 21

ZHENGYI LU

TAIJICHANG DAJIE

TAIJICHANG TOU TIAO

BEI XINHUA JIE

Tiān'ān

12

7

11

Mén

22

8

Square

1 ¥

3

DONG JIAO MIN XIANG

5

H J

XI JIAO MIN XIANG

4

G

23

22

G 13

H

CHONGWEN MEN XI DJ

QIAN MEN XI DAJIE

15

M

QIAN MEN DONG DAJIE

16

24

QIAN MEN XI HE YAN JIE

XI DAMOCHANG JIE

GUANGLONG JIE

Key

中国银行	1	Bank of China (Zhōngguó Yínháng)
北海公园	2	Běi Hǎi Gōngyuán (Běi Hǎi Park)
毛主席纪念堂	3	Chairman Mao Memorial Hall (Máo Zhǔxí Jìniàntáng)
中国钱币博物	4	China Numismatic Museum (Zhōngguó Qiánbì Bówùguǎn)
东交民巷天主堂	5	Dōng Jiāo Mín Xiàng Tiānzhǔ Táng (St. Michael's Church)
故宫博物院	6	Forbidden City, Palace Museum (Gùgōng Bówùyuàn)
人民大会堂	7	Great Hall of the People (Rénmín Dàhuìtáng)
中国历史博物馆	8	History Museum (Zhōngguó Lìshǐ Bówùguǎn)
皇史宬	9	Imperial Archive (Huáng Shǐ Chéng)
景山公园	10	Jǐngshān Gōngyuán
人民英雄纪念碑	11	Monument to the People's Heroes (Rénmín Yīngxióng Jìniànbēi)
中国革命博物馆	12	Museum of the Revolution (Zhōngguó Gémìng Bówùguǎn)
北京邮政速递局	13	EMS (Běijīng Shì Yóuzhèng Sùdì Jú)
紫藤庐	14	Purple Vine Teahouse (Zǐténg Lú)
前门	15	Qián Mén Metro
老车站商场	16	The Station (Lǎo Chē Zhàn Shāngchǎng)
中山公园	17	Zhōngshān Gōngyuán (Sun Yat-sen Park)
太庙	18	Tài Miào (Workers' Cultural Palace)
天安门	19	Tiān'ān Mén (Gate of Heavenly Peace)
天安门东	20	Tiān'ān Mén Dōng Metro
天安门西	21	Tiān'ān Mén Xī Metro
	22	Tour buses to outside Běijīng
正阳门	23	Zhèngyáng Mén
正阳门箭楼	24	Zhèngyáng Mén Jiànlóu

Hotels and Restaurants

北京饭店	A	Běijīng Fàndiàn (Běijīng Hotel)
北京工商宾馆	B	Běijīng Gōngshāng Bīnguǎn
四合轩	C	The Courtyard Restaurant and Gallery (Sìhéxuān)
翠明庄宾馆	D	Cuìmíng Zhuāng Bīnguǎn (Cuìmíng Manor)
仿膳饭庄	E	Fǎng Shàn Fàn Zhuāng
贵宾楼	F	Grand Hotel Běijīng (Guì Bīn Lóu)
华风宾馆	G	Huáfēng Bīnguǎn
欧美食府	H	Ōuměi Shí Fǔ (Royal Park Restaurant)
烧鹅仔	I	Shāo'ézǎi
紫金宾馆	J	Zǐjīn Bīnguǎn

Street Names and Bus Stops

北长街	Běi Cháng Jiē		南池子	Nán Chízi
北池子	Běi Chízi		南河沿	Nán Hé Yán
北河沿	Běi Hé Yán		平安大道	Píng'ān Dà Dào
地安门内大街	Dì'ān Mén Nèi Dàjiē		前门东大街	Qián Mén Dōng Dàjiē
东长安街	Dōng Cháng'ān Jiē		台基厂大街	Tāijīchǎng Dàjiē
东华门大街	Dōng Huá Mén Dàjiē		台基厂头条	Tāijīchǎng Tóu Tiáo
东交民巷	Dōng Jiāo Mín Xiàng		五四大街	Wǔ Sì Dàjiē
黄城根南街	Huángchéng Gēn Nán Jiē		西长安街	Xī Cháng'ān Jiē
景山前街	Jǐngshān Qián Jiē		西华门大街	Xī Huá Mén Dàjiē
景山西、东街	Jǐngshān Xī/Dōng Jiē		西交民巷	Xī Jiāo Mín Xiàng
南长街	Nán Cháng Jiē		文津街	Wénjīn Jiē
			正义路	Zhèngyì Lù

天安门广场

See map p.120. An agoraphobic's nightmare, Tiān'ān Mén Square, one of the world's largest man-made open spaces, is full for most of the day with happy holiday-making crowds flying kites, taking each other's photographs and, in the case of those from out of town, marvelling to find themselves at the country's very heart. A kite-tail of a queue to see China's one-man Madame Tussaud's, the embalmed Máo, edges slowly forward. Around its rim crowds gape both at the grim buildings symbolizing the current 'dictatorship of the proletariat', and at the ornate relics of the imperial past.

On the north side of the vast open space stands the **Tiān'ān Mén** (Gate of Heavenly Peace) after which the square in named, the entrance to the 800-year-old palace of the emperors, and from the balcony of which Máo declared the formation of the People's Republic of China on 1 October 1949. On the west side lies the **Great Hall of the People** (Rénmín Dàhuìtáng), the venue for set-piece government meetings where, in a mockery of consultation and democracy, delegates largely rubber-stamp what has been decided for them. On the east side the **Museum of Chinese History** and the **Museum of the Revolution** enshrine the official view of what happened in Chinese ancient and modern history (subject to revision without notice). The south side has some of the few remains still standing of the ancient city walls destroyed in the 1960s as part of Máo's 'Great Leap Forward' campaign, victims of the communists' desire to make their own mark on Běijīng. These, the double towers of the **Zhèngyáng Mén**, are more commonly known as the Qián Mén or 'Front Gate'. Within the square are the **Monument to the People's Heroes** (Rénmín Yīngxióng Jìniànbēi), an involuntary tribute to the manipulation of history the government would have the masses think important, and the **Chairman Máo Memorial Hall**, containing the embalmed corpse of the 'Great Helmsman' who so often directed the ship onto the rocks.

The square has long been the venue both for carefully staged political set pieces (military reviews, demonstrations in support of Máo, celebrations of National Day), and spontaneous outbursts of dissent. Long before the violent suppression of the Democracy Movement was beamed around the world by television on 4 June 1989, the square had a history of mass political protest.

The May Fourth movement of 1919 (known as Wǔ Sì—'Five-Four') saw 3,000 students gathered to protest at the provision of the Treaty of Versailles which at the settlement conference at the end of the First World War had given Shāndōng Province, formerly occupied by Germany, to Japan. While not being able to send troops, China had sent several thousand labourers to France, thus freeing Europeans to go to the front. Expecting the return of occupied territory, they were betrayed by an earlier secret agreement between the British and French guaranteeing Japanese possession after the war in return for Japanese naval support during it (which never actually came). The USA, which had promised to support China at the conference, acquiesced to the handover and was regarded as the greater betrayer, although the Chinese also roundly condemned the weakness of their own government. President Wilson had given in to Japanese threats not to participate in the formation of the League of Nations, precursor to the UN. The students marched on the Legation Quarter where gates and foreign guards barred them from entry.

On 9 December 1935 thousands of students rallied to protest against the Republican government's impotence against Japanese aggression and ever-increasing expansion from their Shāndōng base. The students were hosed with water and clubbed, but the following week almost 30,000 people reappeared.

In mid-March 1976 people began to come daily to lay wreaths at the base of the Monument to the People's Heroes in a spontaneous outpouring of affection for the memory of the popular moderate Premier Zhōu Ēnlái, who had recently died. Partly they also represented an outpouring of support for pragmatist Dèng Xiǎopíng, who was being persecuted by Máo's wife and her cronies, known as the 'Gang of Four', who were running the Cultural Revolution (see 'History', p.72). On 4 April, which that year was the date of the traditional Qīngmíng festival for honouring the dead, tens of thousands entered the square and left floral tributes, poetry and other messages at the monument. This spontaneous 'mass movement' was labelled counter-revolutionary, and everything was cleared away overnight. On 5 April 1976 numbers swelled to over 100,000 demonstrating their anger at the removal of the tributes. Placards compared the current leadership to the cruel and tyrannical first emperor of all China, Qín Shǐ Huángdì, and called for a return to 'genuine' Marxism-Leninism. Threats over loudspeakers frightened most away, but in the evening several hundred of those still in the square were beaten, arrested and later sent to prison camps.

Máo's reaction was to blame the relatively moderate Dèng Xiǎopíng, whose ideas on opening up the economy were both popular and opposed to his own, and have him removed from all of his several posts. But Máo's death in September eventually allowed a groundswell of public support to restore Dèng and make him paramount leader a few months later.

Dèng 'reversed the verdict' on the 1976 demonstrators, who had been branded counter-revolutionary, but by 1986 faced student demonstrations against his own slow progress towards democracy, and in January 1987, despite police bans, Běijīng students held massive rallies in Tiān'ān Mén Square. Now taking Máo's role, Dèng in turn used the demonstrations as an excuse to remove another moderate, Party Secretary-General Hú Yàobāng, and to blame the pernicious influence of foreign ideas. Professors known for their liberal views such as internationally respected astrophysicist Fāng Lìzhī bore the brunt of the attacks rather than the students, whose protests sputtered in the face of imminent exams.

It was Hú Yàobāng's sudden death from a heart attack on 15 April 1989 which set off the most widely attended, most widely watched (due to the efforts of foreign television crews) and most bloodily suppressed demonstrations in the square's history. Student demonstrators wanted Dèng to reverse the verdict on Hú as he had the one on the 1976 demonstrations, and revived the anti-corruption and pro-democracy issues of those earlier protests. The government was taken aback, and initially prevented from taking firm action by the presence of Mikhail Gorbachev, then leader of the Soviet Union, on a state visit. Once he had departed tanks and soldiers were sent into the square on the night of 4 June, an incident known as Liù Sì ('Six-Four'). Party members who had expressed sympathy with the students and workers in the square were purged, and Zhào Zǐyáng, Dèng's hand-picked successor, who had gone out into the square to apologise to the students, was sacked and put under house arrest which continues until this day.

As with every other figure ever quoted about China, the numbers of those who died in the square vary, from thousands (supporters of the movement) to none (the Chinese government—on the grounds that if any died it was in Cháng'ān Dàjiē, which runs across the top of the square and along which many fled). In the days leading up to the anniversary each year the military presence in the square increases, and access to Běijīng Dàxué and other university campuses is more tightly controlled.

In 1999 the authorities handled a worrying conjunction of political anniversaries with an aplomb extremely rare in official public relations. The year marked the 80th anniversary of the 4 May democracy movement, the 50th anniversary of the Communist Party's rule over China (1 October—Bā-Yī) and the 10th anniversary of the Tiān'ān Mén Massacre of democracy protestors, all focused on Tiān'ān Mén Square. They closed the square in October 1998 for repaving and spent vast sums covering all 170,000sqm (about 1.83 million square feet—yet another different figure) with granite—better able to support the weight of tanks, said some wags. Unsurprisingly the repairs continued until the dangerous anniversaries were past, and were completed just in time for the 1 October celebrations. On the night of 4 June, the only figures hovering at the edge of the square were a few tourists and plain clothes police.

Dèng Xiǎopíng may have reversed the verdict on the 1976 demonstrators, but refused to do so on the 1989 ones before his death in 1997, and the square remains the epicentre of dissent. Plain clothes and uniformed police hover all day, and within moments of some protester whipping out a placard, or as soon as members of some banned sect take a deep breath and stand on one leg, the heavies appear, and the guilty (no room for debate here) are in the back of vans and on their way to a beating or lengthy detention without trial.

People gawp, but quickly go back to other occupations such as flying kites in the form of birds, butterflies and carp, some of which (whisper it) are for sale. In 1999 the authorities, in a fine example of the insidious growth of tiny taxes which cause far more resentment than the lack of grand and only half-grasped ideals like democracy or freedom of religion, tried to institute a kite management office which would charge ¥20 for an annual permit to fly kites in the square. There were protests, and this time the decision *was* reversed.

Tiān'ān Mén   天安门

Open 8.30–4.30; adm ¥15.

See map p.120, no.19. There's a compulsory bag deposit for ¥1–2 just to the left of the ticket office. The ticket staff will want to be sure that it's the gate you want to see, and not the Palace Museum or 'Forbidden City', which doesn't begin until the Wǔ Mén, further north. Many visitors make this mistake.

Since the source of all power in China once resided behind this gate, it's not surprising that it has become a symbol of power itself. At times of important celebrations edicts were promulgated from its terrace by being placed in the mouth of a gilded wooden phoenix and lowered to a waiting official who took them away for copying and dispatch.

Those who have replaced the emperors have felt the need to be seen here, and the gate appears on coins, official seals and insignia, and other symbols of power. It has a history similar to most of the wooden buildings in Běijīng (and indeed in China as a whole). Originally built in 1417, it burned down 1456, was rebuilt in 1651, and was set ablaze again in 1644 by the peasant armies who had ended the Míng as they were chased out by the Qīng. Rebuilt in 1651 it no doubt went through numerous further restorations up to a complete replacement of the roof in 1984, and a total refurbishment in 1999 in time for it to take up its usual function as a reviewing stand on 1 October.

Of the five arched bridges leading to it from the square, the middle one was for the emperor alone, as was the central door, above which Máo's portrait now hangs. That to the right was for senior officials and the left for military advisors. The way in is often blocked by Chinese trying to stick coins to the doors for luck, but beyond on the left is an office for tickets to climb the gate. You can look across the square (although this can be done considerably more cheaply from the Zhèngyáng Mén to the south) and pretend to be China's first president Yuán Shìkǎi reviewing celebrations of his appointment in 1912. Alternatively you can be Máo announcing the formation of the People's Republic in 1949 or reviewing the Red Guards who during the Cultural Revolution of 1966–76 were to damage or destroy most of what you will want to see while in China.

Two dragon-carved pillars called *huábiǎo* stand in front of the gate and two behind, which you get a chance to examine more closely on your way to the staircase to climb the gate. These are often to be found at important sites (there are two at the Marco Polo bridge) and imperial residences. Topped either with a mythical animal called a *hòu*, or with Chinese lions, and with cloud-shaped projections, they are ornamental descendents of boards established by early emperors inviting criticism and comment on their policies. Here tradition has it that the animals facing south on top of the outer pair have their mouths open, supposedly to report to the emperor any misdeeds of his officials when he returned. The inner pair face north to the interior of the palace with closed mouths to indicate the need for silence on the emperor's whereabouts when he left the palace incognito. It is said that one of the last Qīng emperors, Tóngzhì (reigned 1862–74), would go secretly to the pleasure quarters of the Chinese city and later died of syphilis, which was indeed hushed up. Another variation of the pillar story has the inner pair watching the emperor to make sure that he did not spend too much time with his concubines rather then in government, and the outer pair watching that imperial tours did not last too long.

Inside the hall on top of the gate sit the dragon-carved chairs where the gerontocracy rests between trips to the rostrum. Historic footage of soldierly march pasts plays on video screens, with optimistic swirling string accompaniment and heavenly choirs worthy of the Hollywood productions of the same period, and in which you can clearly see the original outer walls of the square and some of the older buildings, later demolished for the construction of the Great Hall of the People and the Museum of History.

Oddly, there's a post box at the foot of the opposite stairs. Perhaps the Party leaders get bored of the parades and sneak off to write postcards.

Monument to the People's Heroes (Rénmín Yīngxióng Jìniànbēi) 人民英雄纪念碑

See map p.120, no.11. One of the first acts of the communists following their occupation of Běijīng in 1949 was to ordain the construction of this 14.7m-high monument, although it took until 1958 to complete. Official policy says that the story of modern China is that of revolution and anti-imperialist struggle, but the government has had to distort history to find enough heroes to fill the monument's eight relief panels. One portrays the campaign to prevent the importation of opium in 1840, seen as marking the beginning of modern history. The destruction of opium at Canton was undertaken by anti-opium commissioner Lín Zéxú on the orders of the Qīng emperor, member of a then 200-year-old foreign dynasty, and thus hardly a revolutionary or an anti-imperialist. Another panel celebrates the Tàipíng Rebellion which, while certainly anti-Manchu, lacked populist revolutionary qualities. There was a pooling of funds and common granaries in the large areas of southern China which they ruled from Nánjīng between 1853 and 1864, but the movement was pseudo-Christian, formed by one Hóng Xiùquán, who believed himself to be the younger son of Jesus Christ. It was led entirely by members of the Hakka minority, who were often discriminated against by the Hàn (as the Chinese call themselves), and faced passive resistance from them. In the best imperial traditions, paranoid Hóng Xiùquán had his best advisers killed, and retired to a life of luxury with multiple concubines. The rebellion was only crushed when foreigners stepped in to help, training the 'Ever Victorious Army' (which until then had been anything but) led first by an American and then by British General 'Chinese' Gordon (who later died at the siege of Khartoum).

You are no longer allowed to mount the plinth and view the friezes close up, and signs make clear that you may not lay floral tributes here without special permission, presumably for fear of a replay of earlier events. The monument is suitably two-faced—lively characters on the north face are in Mao's calligraphy, stating that the fame of the people's heroes will last forever, and on the south are those of Premier Zhōu Ēnlái, whom Máo later came to distrust.

Chairman Mao Memorial Hall (Máo Zhǔxí Jìniàntáng) 毛主席纪念堂

Open Mon–Sat. 8.30–11.30 and Mon, Wed, Fri, 2–4; adm free.

See map p.120. Left isolated in the centre of the square when the surrounding walls were pulled down, the 450-year-old Dà Míng Mén finally disappeared in 1976 to make way for the mausoleum to hold Máo. The building's design matches the surrounding edifices, but with a motif of vertical lines found in the tombs of Lenin in Moscow, Suk Bataar in Ulaan Bataar and Ho Chi Minh in Hanoi, although it dwarfs all of these.

The 'Máo-soleum' is grotesquely popular so go very early, and without bags or cameras, which you can deposit at the entrances to the museums on the west and east sides of the square, or at the entrance to the Great Hall of the People. It's a long slow shuffle to enter, which seems to turn into a brisker shuffle when you finally get to Máo, and you quickly find yourself out in the sunshine again with the souvenir vendors. Máo died in 1976, having caused, according to one estimate, nearly 38 million people to predecease him—beating Hitler, but exceeded by Stalin. Pumped with 22 litres of formaldehyde after his death and now kept underground and refrigerated, he's hydraulically brought up for the adoration of the masses during opening hours, visible through a crystal coffin, which is fortunately air-tight.

Máo's current status is ambiguous. The oft-parroted official position is incomprehensible: Máo was 70 per cent right and 30 per cent wrong. This is the nearest that there will probably ever be to public criticism of the Communist Party's pin-up boy, a man whose social experiments caused so much misery, death and destruction. Officially Máo's writings, once almost the only books in print in China, are still bestsellers. New editions are still being produced, but the emphasis is now on the poetry and the letters, rather than on the political campaigns. Today Máo, the great suppressor of all who disagreed with him, has become a useful tool for dissent against his heirs. In Máo's day there was little conventional crime, prostitution or drug use, and jobs were guaranteed for life. There are those who loudly praise these achievements, and express nostalgia for purer, simpler times: a safe way to criticize the current leaders for the rise in criminal activity, heroin addiction, unemployment, corruption and naked greed. It was notable that in 1999's great celebrations of 50 years of communist rule, he got only a passing mention.

Despite his waxen rigidity, Máo lives on. While a recent revival of his cult is ebbing, double-sided images of him can still sometimes be found hanging from the rear-view mirrors of minibuses and taxis—one the familiar plump face, the other a younger, slimmer figure, but still with the trademark mole on his chin. He functions as a St Christopher, although the appalling death rate on China's roads might be said to demonstrate that he is as effective in death as in life. Peasants in one Shǎnxī village even built a temple to Máo, which was closed down by outraged officials. Until fashions change again there are many Běijīng restaurants named after or dedicated to him which serve the peppery food of his home province, Húnán (see p.259).

There's ghoulish comedy in the account of Máo's doctor, Li Zhisui, concerning the panic amongst his medical staff when the politburo ordered that Máo's body be preserved. As there was no longer any amity between the Chinese and Soviet Communist Parties, it was impossible to ask how Lenin had been embalmed and Dr Lǐ had anyway visited the bodies of Lenin and Stalin on a trip to Moscow with Máo, where he had been told that their extremities had rotted and been patched with wax. Colleagues were sent to Hanoi, but were refused sight of Ho Chi Minh, being told, however, that both his nose and beard had fallen off. Two researchers sent to Madame Tussaud's waxwork in London concluded that in this area, one of preserving rather than progressing, the Chinese were appropriately ahead of foreign science. (However, in 1999 during a state visit to Britain, President Jiāng Zémín found time to visit the famous waxworks to be photographed and measured up for an image. An image of the Dalai Lama was temporarily removed for the period of his visit, although any political motivation was denied.)

Eventually a preservation method was concocted from readings in medical journals. Most of Máo's organs were removed and he was pumped full of formaldehyde, but too much was injected and the body swelled grotesquely, the face and neck bulging and the ears sticking out. Careful massaging and the help of make-up sorted out the problem, but a wax copy of the body was also prepared just in case, and the two were kept underground and carefully monitored for more than a year while the mausoleum was prepared. You may ask yourself after your visit, 'Which of the two did I just see?'

History Museum (Zhōngguó Lìshǐ Bówùguǎn) 中国历史博物馆

Open 8.30–3.30; closed Mon; adm ¥5, annual ticket accepted.

See map p.120, no.8. The History and Revolution Museums are together on the east side of the square, Ⓜ Tiān'ān Mén Dōng, and the History Museum ticket office is on the right under the arches. You must leave any bags at the neighbouring bag deposit office. The Museum also occasionally houses special exhibitions which may have their own separate entrance fees of up to ¥20. The museum closes at 4.30pm, but you are not allowed to the upper storey after 4pm. Bus 22 from Xī Dān, and bus 120 from Tiān Tán south gate both stop outside, stop name Lìshǐ Bówùguǎn, but any bus to Qián Mén or along Cháng'ān Dàjiē will put you in walking distance.

This is the museum of China's greatest hits, with a total of 6000sqm of exhibition space, so it is unfortunate the gloomy interior with its poorly lit exhibits makes you more conscious of

China's impoverishment than of the splendours of its cultural achievements, and creates the kind of atmosphere that may have driven you out of museums as a child.

The exterior was cleaned up for the 50th anniversary, but progress on modernizing the interior remains slow, although a few exhibits have finally received English labels. Regardless of these drawbacks, there are many individual items on display which it would be worth ¥5 to see in their own right, such as a remarkable burial suit made from hundreds of pieces of jade linked together by gold wire (sometimes the only illuminated item in the whole museum).

Other magnificent artefacts on the ground floor include a 12-branched Hàn dynasty lamp, a replica of what is supposed to be the world's earliest seismometer, and funeral objects which include clay figurines (and some samples of the near life-size warriors from Xī'ān), and complicated glazed ceramic towers and mansions.

Upstairs (where there's better lighting and presentation) Táng ceramics include a tri-coloured horse and a particularly fine camel, and twelve unusual animal-headed figurines about one foot high, amongst them a chicken, goat, duck and horse, each with a half-pensive, half-quizzical expression on its face which probably reflects your own reaction, and other fine figurines of a fish with the head of a man, musicians, etc.

Other items of interest include the chance to get close to a bug-eyed water dragon of the kind usually remote on the spine of temples, an early photograph of the Lúgōu Qiáo (the Marco Polo Bridge, *see* p.336) looking particularly delapidated, and fine examples of ancient cloisonné to compare with what's offered to you for sale in souvenir shops.

In the Míng section there are parts of a copy of the Yŏnglè Dàdiǎn, a huge compendium of Chinese knowledge compiled during the Míng dynasty, mostly destroyed in the fire which consumed one of the world's greatest libraries, the Hànlín Academy (Hànlín Shū Yuán—'book garden') in 1900.

The labelling in Chinese museums is always happy to forgo accuracy in the service of politics and national pride, so the destruction of the Academy is here blamed on foreign powers. In fact it was Chinese troops who were the arsonists, hoping the fire would carry to the neighbouring Legation Quarter buildings occupied by besieged fireigners. According to Mary Hooker who chronicled the siege, the defenders had already discussed setting fire to the building for their own protection but could not bear to do it. As the *Times* correspondent, Australian G. E. Morrison put it, 'Other great libraries, the Alexandrian and in Rome, had been destroyed by the victorious invader, but what can we think of a nation that sacrifices its most sacred edifice, the pride and glory of its country and learned men for hundred of years, in order to be revenged upon foreigners?' Perhaps the Chinese feel the sting of this. Neither at the sites concerned nor in museums is there ever mention that thousands of armed Chinese had surrounded the quarter, and without any formal declaration of hostilities were attempting to kill every foreigner and every Chinese Christian in Běijīng (*see* 'The Boxer Rebellion', p.66).

There's further treatment of foreign contact with China (rarely flattering), and there are images of the pre-1860 Yuánmíng Yuán ('Old Summer Palace' *see* p.293), including the recently rebuilt maze in its original boxwood form, and a photograph of the troops of the Eight Allied Powers who eventually came to the relief of the legations parading in the space now occupied by Tiān'ān Mén Square.

For a partial preview of the museum, see <*http://www.nmch.gov.cn/*>.

Museum of the Revolution
(Zhōngguó Gémìng Bówùguǎn)

中国革命博物馆

Open 8.30–4; closed Mon; adm ¥5, annual ticket accepted.

See map p.120, no.12. The ticket office is to the left under the arches on the east side of the square, opposite that for the History Museum, and bags must be deposited in a neighbouring hut.

The exhibition begins with the guns which fired salutes at the ceremony for the founding of the People's Republic, and the flag which was hoisted on that day; after that the *propagandafest* begins in earnest. Successive displays deal with opium importation, naval battles, the destruction of the Yuánmíng Yuán by the British and French, and the later invasion of Běijīng by the Eight Allied Powers. There's a statue of Opium Commissioner Lín Zéxú (*see* the Monument to the People's Heroes, above), but nothing on the Chinese growing their own opium or on their own eagerness to import and distribute the drug to make big profits, and nothing on the willingness of coastal ports to supply British ships while the two countries were fighting. History is never complex in the communist mind, but a matter of black and white. It's a shame to undermine a perfectly telling case against the slicing up of China by foreign powers in the 19th and 20th centuries by distorting the truth.

However, the material used is fascinating, including lithographs and prints from the period (such as one of the Congress of Peking in 1901 in which the diplomatic envoys of eleven powers forced a ruinous settlement on the Qīng), reproductions of imperial memorials, and period costume. Some bring the treaty ports such as Tiānjīn (*see* p.345) to life, showing documents giving Chinese positions as watchmen or policemen in areas under foreign occupation, copies of various treaties made with foreign powers, as well as maps, photographs of atrocities, and some fine examples of early advertising. There's also the insignia of a stationmaster on the British-built Shànghǎi–Nánjīng railway, and a picture of Ulsterman Sir Robert Hart, after whom one of the streets in the neighbouring Legation Quarter was named, and who was controller of the Chinese Imperial Customs for 48 years. Paper money issued by foreign banks in China is among other evidence that the foreign concessions operated as mini-states within a state. There's also a display concerning the Ever Victorious Army which eventually defeated the rebels known as the Tàipíng Heavenly Kingdom, including some reproductions of Tàipíng documents and a picture of 'Chinese' Gordon, the British general who led those forces to victory only to die a famous death later in the siege of Khartoum.

The English labels are not as loquacious as the Chinese ones, nor do they always contain the same 'information', but there are more of them than in most Běijīng museums.

Further on the exhibition discusses the very gradual adoption of Western technology and manufacturing methods, with examples of early imported factory machinery. Post-revolutionary items include a gun from the Wǔchāng uprising, a reproduction of Sun Yat-sen's office and of the room where the first meeting of the Chinese Communist Party took place (in Shànghǎi), right down to the tea cups on the tables.

Whatever you may think of the interpretation, the key events of modern Chinese history are documented here, with period photographs, military equipment and scale models of key locations, through the Long March period and onwards, the Anti-Japanese (Second World) War, the Nánjīng Massacre, to a boat used in the crossing of the Yangtze during the final defeat of the Guómíndǎng (Kuomintang or Nationalist Party—their continued existence as an opposition party in Táiwān excepted) on 20 April 1949 when Nánjīng was taken.

Great Hall of the People (Rénmín Dàhuìtáng)

人民大会堂

Opening hours vary and are posted on a sign on the south side of the hall in Rénmín Dàhuìtáng Xī Lù for up to three days ahead; adm ¥15.

See map p.120, no.7. Bags cannot be taken in but must be left at a window to the left of the ticket office, ¥2–5. Cameras may be taken in, but you'll have to ask very nicely for a hand inspection if you want to avoid the X-ray machines inside.

The building was constructed in 1958/9 as one of ten mega-projects which included the museums opposite and the establishment of Tiān'ān Mén Square in its modern form. The Chinese seem to come here because the building has an 'as seen on TV' fame (almost nightly) but would admit that despite the cavernous interior spaces the modern palaces to commerce in Wángfǔjǐng and elsewhere are now more impressive. Not that commerce has been expelled from this supposed bastion of public ownership—you can pay to have your photograph taken in front of a mural in one room (¥16), and a café on the balcony of the entrance hall sells the Coca-Cola of the hated imperialists. Perhaps a resurrected Máo would storm across the road to drive the moneylenders from the temple.

There's a clear roped route around the building, and you do not wander at will. There's a whiff of left-over communism in the antimaccassared armchairs arranged in circles, broad staircases with slightly tatty red carpets, vast marbled interior spaces without quite enough electricity to light them, with one hall for every province, one for each of the cities reporting directly to Běijīng, and one for each of the two Special Administrative Regions—Hong Kong and Macau. One has a large mural showing Máo with representatives of every minority and attempting to look jolly (which he doesn't do very well), and large Chinese ceramics and screens standing around in various corners. It's all a colossal exercise in bad taste with shoddy chandeliers and other micron-thin glitz.

Upstairs there's a huge red relief of the minorities being positively frisky in their joy at uniting with the Hàn, after which you pass the Běijīng hall with its mural of the Great Wall, then into the banqueting hall, a large gloomy space, where you can buy a lunch ticket and eat set meals for ¥5–10. But in the classic traditions of communist 'service' the place seems to close for lunch.

In the Shànghǎi room the mural of the skyline has been updated to include the new tower which is the third highest in the world, but also over-optimistically another, yet higher one, which hasn't been built and is on permanent hold. Returning to the ground floor you pass a large model in oxidised green copper of the Hall of Prayer for Good Harvests from the Temple of Heaven.

You leave down the main stairs, but have to take a tunnel full of souvenir stalls and other merchandise and end up in the main square, presumably on your way to see Máo, having acquired fake jade or a polyester raincoat en route.

China Numismatic Museum
(Zhōngguó Qiánbì Bówùguǎn)

中国钱币博物馆

Open 9–4, closed Mon; ¥2.

See map p.120, no.4. Bags must be deposited at the ticket window on the left.

This is a recent museum in what appears to be a very Western-influenced late-Qīng building on the southwest side of the square on the corner of Xī Jiāo Mín Xiàng. It's the modern counterpart of the Ancient Coin Exhibition Hall in the Déshèng Mén Jiànlóu (*see* p.178) and has changing exhibitions dealing with post-revolutionary money, such as the release of the fifth series of notes, which in 1999 introduced the first ever ¥20, and exchanged the four heroes of the ¥100 bill with Máo by himself. Numismatists should see both this and the Ancient Coin Exhibition Hall, which has a lively coin and note market around it.

Zhèngyáng Mén and Zhèngyáng Mén Jiànlóu

正阳门, 正阳门箭楼

Open 8.30–4; adm ¥5, and open 8.30–4; adm ¥3, respectively, annual ticket accepted.

See map p.120, nos.23 and 24. Enter Zhèngyáng Mén from the west side if using the museum annual ticket (*see* p.112).

The 'Straight Towards the Sun Gate', more commonly known as the Qián Mén or 'Front Gate', was once part of the Tartar City wall separating the north and south sections of Běijīng. The Jiànlóu (Arrow Tower) stood on a semi-circular projection, which had side gates for the common people and a central gate for the emperor's use only. The existing Qián Mén road loop was the result of Qián Mén Dàjiē splitting into two roads which ran round either side of the semi-circular enceinte, and turned into the lesser gates. The two towers still stand in line with Tiān'ān Mén and the key buildings of the Forbidden City, and formed one of three entrances from the Chinese City to the Tartar City. Any invader fighting his way into the interior courtyard would face fire from both towers while he attempted to break down the second gate.

The originals were constructed in 1420 and 1439, but the outer Jiànlóu was burned down by the Boxers in 1900 as the result of their setting fire to some neighbouring shops with foreign connections. The inner Zhèngyáng Mén looked down into the besieged part of the Legation Quarter. In the final hours of the siege, the glint of brass mountings having been spotted at a window, bearings were taken by the defenders. Once night fell and a field gun opened up from the tower it was silenced after only its seventh round, and the tower was later accidentally reduced to ashes by the relieving forces driving out a last pocket of resistance.

Since the Qián Mén was the main gate of the Tartar City, the towers were promptly rebuilt, but increasing motor traffic led to adjustments in 1916, in which the outer enceinte and tower were completely torn down and replaced by the modern tower, which even by the '30s was being used to display local handicrafts, as today. By that time, too, railway termini had been built by foreign companies on either side of Qián Mén, which were in use until the construction of Běijīng Zhàn with Soviet help in 1959. The eastern terminus still stands although it was hidden behind a patina of modern contruction until a renovation in 1999, when it reopened as a shopping mall. The noose of railway track the foreigners threw around the outside of the

Tartar City in 1911 is gone (other enceintes were destroyed so that it could run along the base of the wall), but the route now taken underground by the modern metro's circle line is similar.

All the main gates were arranged in the same way, and within the enceintes each had a daoist temple, except the Zhèngyàng Mén which had two, always visited by the emperors when they returned to Běijīng this way or came back from ceremonies at the Temple of Heaven or Altar of Agriculture. These were pulled down in 1967.

Běijīng's gates were closed at dusk with the beating of gongs and loud cries from the guards to alert those who wanted to pass through. Alone amongst them, the Zhèngyáng Mén was re-opened for a few minutes after midnight to allow officials to return from the theatres, tea houses and the more sensual pleasures of Dàzhàlán Jiē in time for the imperial audience, which would take place in the small hours of the morning. (That later emperor, Máo, also often summoned his subordinates at 2 or 3am.)

A 1999 refurbishment cleared away an electronic rifle range and other amusements at gallery level and thoroughly modernized the interior, which contains models of various towers and gates, and an illuminated table plan of the Qiánlōng's emperor's Běijīng of 1750. This shows the city walls intact as well as many long since disappeared temples. (The largest and most detailed model of this kind is at the Museum of Ancient Architecture—*see* p.164.) Black and white photos, some labelled in English, show Běijīng before its destruction in the modern era, also serving as an introduction to an old Běijīng many visitors would like to find now—a much more *Chinese* one. There are images of the old British-built Qián Mén station, until recently unidentifiable except to the sharp-eyed who knew of its existence and to look for the tower; it is now a shopping mall. There's a view of the Zhèngyáng Mén at the conclusion of the Boxer Rebellion with its top missing (again blamed on the Eight Allied Powers), a view to the west of the other railway station which has now disappeared, and a picture of the Eight Allied Powers marching into the city. One aerial photo shows the time when the enceinte had been torn down but the rest of the walls still existed, and a wall map compares clearly the layout of the Jin Zhōngdū, Yuán Dàdū, then Míng and subsequently Qīng Běijīng including the wall and layout of the Imperial City. There's a picture of the first locomotive to reach the heart of Běijīng at Qián Mén on 1 November 1901, one of Chinese wearing the hated top-hatted costume of the capitalists at the Dōngbiān Mén station, and a picture of a level crossing by Déshèng Mén from the line that the foreigners threw around the city. Upstairs is an exhibition of the long-vanished streetlife of Běijīng, the vigour of which has only recently returned: shop signs, photos of *hútòng* and their occupants, and samples of street vendor wares.

The 38m-high **Jiànlóu**, with its 94 windows for shooting arrows, gives you better views over Qián Mén but usually contains only exhibitions of paintings for sale, and it is not possible to climb higher. It had a similar role in the 1930s when it was a shop, and then a cinema until 1945. The ground around its base was a bus station until 1999, when it was turfed with what is claimed to be Běijīng's largest ever lawn, although not of any great size. The eaves and narrow brick windows are the favoured homes of so many swallows you may wonder if it supplies the nests for the soup of local restaurants. (The genuine nest is actually that of a kind of sea swallow, and usually imported from Malaysia.) The tower was only reopened to the public in 1990 and, although thoroughly refurbished in 1999, still receives fewer visitors than its neighbour. Enter from the south side, buying a ticket on the left and then walking around the left-hand side of the tower to find the stairs.

Very little else of the city wall remains, although a small section of its earthen core can still be glimpsed on the north side of Chóngwén Mén Dōng Dàjiē south of Běijīng Station. You can also climb the Déshèng Mén, *see* p.178, and the Dōngbiān Mén corner tower (*open Mon–Sat, 9–3.30; adm ¥8*), clearly visible from trains coming to Běijīng Zhàn; call ✆ 6512 1554 for details of current exhibitions inside the tower.

Legation Quarter

I dined that evening in the stuffy atmosphere of the British Legation. The compound of the English Palace with its Chinese-style hall of ceremony, its low white houses and broad English lawns formed a spacious setting unsymbolic (except for the surrounding walls) of the legation officials' narrow, cut-off lives.

John Blofeld, *City of Lingering Splendour,* 1961

They talked of racing and golf and shooting. They would have thought it bad form to touch upon the abstract and there were no politics for them to discuss. China bored them all, they did not want to speak of that; they only knew just so much about it as was necessary to their business, and they looked with distrust upon any man who studied the Chinese language. Why should he unless he were a missionary or a Chinese Secretary at the Legation? You could hire an interpreter for 25 dollars a month and it was well known that all those fellows who went in for Chinese grew queer in the head.

Somerset Maugham, *On a Chinese Screen,* 1922

Having examined the photographs in the Zhèngyáng Mén, take the stairs just south of the Museum of History which lead up into Dōng Jiāo Mín Xiàng, 'Communicate with the People Lane (East)', once known to its foreign residents as Legation Street. This was the lodging area for visiting tributaries to the Qīng state from Korea, Tibet and Mongolia, long before the 'Western Ocean barbarians' appeared and forced the Qīng to accept the permanent residence of their representatives. The Qīng proposed to put the foreigners well out of the way at the Summer Palace they had ruined, but they insisted on being much closer to the source of power. It probably amused Qīng vanity that the new arrivals were instead put in an area long reserved for barbarians, and they also retaliated by placing the foreign office they were reluctantly forced to create, the Zǒnglǐ Yámen, inconveniently distant in the northeast of the Tartar City. There was a foreign diplomatic presence here well into the 1950s; the premises of those countries which did not immediately recognize the People's Republic were confiscated and handed to those which did.

The first foreign legations appeared in 1861, in what was then an area of temples, princely palaces and more plebian private dwellings, as well as an open space famous for annual fairs held by Mongolian traders. Following the destruction during the siege of 1900 (*see* 'The Boxer Rebellion' p.66) there was extensive rebuilding, and the foreigners took control of a stretch of city wall east of Qián Mén which bordered the area, built walls around the other three sides with eight entrances and large gates, and surrounded this with an area cleared of buildings—a glacis—to prevent future surprise attacks. As tensions lessened these were gradually given over to sporting activities, the last remaining part being Dōng Dān Gōngyuán in the northeastern corner of the quarter, which was used as a polo ground. Eventually some construction of leisure facilities was permitted, which included even a licensed brothel.

Chinese were no longer allowed to live in the area, and some of the few buildings not destroyed or severely damaged by the attacking forces were pulled down to make space for new embassies, then known as legations. Compensation was given to Chinese who could produce deeds to prove ownership of land inside the legation quarter, which started a brisk industry in fake documents. At first no Chinese could even enter without a pass or a formal letter of invitation, but as tensions dropped these rules were later relaxed. By the 1920s 20 countries maintained legations, and the day to day running of the quarter was handled by a committee of mixed diplomatic and non-diplomatic representatives. This levied taxes to provide, amongst other necessities, for the maintenance of the roads inside the quarter, which were the only decent ones in the capital.

The Qīng tried to prevent the opening of shops to serve the foreign community on the grounds that unlike treaty ports such as Tiānjīn, Běijīng had not been opened for foreign trade. But they were the first through the doors when the shops opened anyway. Towards the end of the Qīng and up until 1949, warlords and Nationalist Party officials often incited hatred of foreigners and adopted populist anti-foreign policies, but were the first through the gates for protection when their coups failed or they were defeated by a rival. Pǔyí, the last Qīng emperor, fled here shortly after being evicted from the Forbidden City in 1925. Warlords and other wealthy Chinese were also allowed to come to use the facilities of the German hospital.

The foreign architects used representative national styles, like an early Expo, and it's startling so close to the heart of China to find alien neoclassical porticoes, arched brick and wrought iron balconies. On every side, sometimes behind high brick walls, stand imposing façades, now housing government organs of assorted benign and sinister kinds. Until recently this area was left blank on maps, and there are still suspiciously large areas of white space, indicating the homes of senior cadres and truly secret policemen.

The British did not build their own embassy but occupied the palace of a Manchu duke who had fallen on hard times, only building some residences in the garden, and up until 1900 annually sending £500 in rent by horse cart to the Zǒnglǐ Yámen, accompanied by the legation's Chinese-speaking secretary wearing a special silk top hat. After 1949 the site spent some time as the headquarters of the Ministry of State Security (Ānquán Bù), a highly secret part of the security apparatus, sometimes known as 'China's KGB', reporting directly to the President, and whose sign can still be found at the compound entrance. Bizarrely, there's also a shop selling military equipment such as gas masks and uniforms.

As you walk east from Tiān'ān Mén Square, on the north side of the street is a handsome French hospital building, which became law offices and is now a hotel (which, ironically, doesn't accept foreigners), and then on the corner of a north turning the red-brick frontage and wrought iron balconies of what was once the Chartered Bank of India, Australia and China, later accommodation for the Public Security Bureau. The glacis and then the main wall were just beyond this turning, and on the right you can find the bricked-up gate to the Dutch Legation, and beyond the colonnaded frontage of the former National City Bank of New York, and the neoclassical pile of the Banque de l'Indochine et de Suez. The rest of the block on the north side was taken up with the Russian barracks and Russian Legation, razed in the 1980s to build a courthouse. A passage between them once ran up to the British Legation, the largest of all, whose main entrance was in the next turning, Zhèngyì Lù. The near lane of this was renamed British Road and the far one the Rue Meiji, which bordered the Japanese barracks and Legation, and whose gatehouse still stands, now the entrance to the Běijīng city government offices. The ornate building on the corner on the Japanese side was the Yokohama Specie Bank. Its original interior is quite well preserved. Opposite on the south side was the Hôtel des Wagons-Lits, which was seen as a barometer of political unrest—wealthier Chinese and their families would suddenly move in whenever some upheaval was in the air, such as the departure of one warlord ruler and the arrival of another. The site is now occupied by the Huáfēng Bīnguǎn, another hotel.

A drainage channel of Yuán dynasty construction, the Imperial Canal, ran down the middle of the street carrying noisome waste from the heart of Běijīng to the 'water gate' in the base of the city wall, which was the point of access for the relieving forces at the end of the siege in 1900. Later the foreigners covered it over to stop the smell, and opened a full scale gate in the city walls to give them direct access to the station they had built at Qián Mén.

Beyond, on the north side, the former French Post Office (at one time three different legations ran postal services) has become a restaurant specializing in 'red cooked lamb meat', its interior now revamped. On the south side the Capital Hotel (Dōngdū Bīnguǎn) has doubles of moderate quality for ¥360 ($45) and sprawls across a large area once occupied by the German Legation and two banks, both pulled down in the mid-'80s. After the siege legations on this side were supposed to take responsibility for the defence of the section of the now vanished city wall, the only one kept in good repair and a favourite promenade of foreign residents. There was some bickering between the Germans and the Belgians, further east, as to whether the latter were making a fair contribution to defence efforts.

Further on, across Tàijīchǎng Dàjiē, which the foreigners named the Rue Marco Polo, the Belgian Legation, a self-conciously Flemish pile, is the last of the original legations to be easily accessible to foreigners, having been handed over to the Burmese after the revolution. It is now a hotel, the Zǐjīn Bīnguǎn (*see* p.247). The interior of the main building is a perfect example of the approach taken by all nationalities in construction; they used local brick and stone, but imported all interior fittings directly from home.

Opposite stands a neo-Gothic Catholic church, formerly St Michael's and now the Dōng Jiāo Mín Xiàng Tiānzhǔ Táng, looking like a refugee from the suburban wasteland of some harsh manufacturing town, and which in Britain would by now have become an arts centre or flats. Niched saints, their Chinese names incongruous and bright in gold, look down on a scruffy courtyard. The interior is at first just as expected: antique radiators, dark pews and confessional, small painted and stained panels in the otherwise clear windows, and the aromas of floor polish, dust and incense. Yet the pillars are tinted red in a reminder of Chinese temples, and long white banners to either side of the altar carry the creed in strong red Chinese characters. Its cool interior welcomes 300 members of the Chinese Catholic Patriotic Church on Sundays, under firm government control; it does not recognize the authority of the Pope.

Walking up the north turnings, taking other side streets and peering over walls will reveal the remains of many other legation and trade buildings, as well as small details such as the original cement nameplate saying 'Rue Hart', named for the foreign head of the Imperial Customs, Sir Robert Hart, at the junction of Tàijīchǎng Dàjiē and Tàijīchǎng Tóu Tiáo.

Open 8.30–3.30; adm ¥50 ($7).

故宫博物院   *See* map p.120, no.6. The last ticket is sold at 3.30pm, and there's a further 30mins to look around, but 3.30pm is also the time the special exhibition halls close and no warning or refund will be given. Begin the day here: the light is better for photography, and seeing all the corners of the palace open to the public and admiring all the exhibitions can take several hours.

Your ¥50 is for a *tào piào* or set ticket which gives you admission to all exhibitions within the complex at no further cost. You may also be given a little booklet whether you like if or not and charged ¥5. Give it back if you don't want it. You can also buy a *mén piào* for ¥30 and pay extra for those exhibitions and halls requiring an extra ticket. Rules change frequently, but the exhibitions, some of which are essential viewing, cost between ¥5 and ¥10, and some are housed in magnificent side halls worth seeing in their own right, so buy the *tào piào*.

It's also possible to pay a further ¥30 ($4) plus ¥100 deposit (or a passport or driving licence) for an Acoustiguide with up to two headsets and a wide choice of European and Asian languages. In English the voice is that of Roger Moore at his most lugubrious. The audio tour takes about 1.5 hours, and the route follows the tour groups (including Chinese ones wearing little round Manchu hats with attached pigtail) up the central axis of the palace (and of Běijīng) through the largest ceremonial halls; the audio equipment can be returned at the rear entrance. However, even if you take the tour you should return to the exhibition halls it does not cover, and to the smaller halls on either side which were offices or the residences of concubines.

Having passed through the Tiān'ān Mén don't be confused into buying a ticket at the first booth you see on the left, unless you want to climb it (*see* above). The ticket office for the Palace Museum is some way ahead, down a path lined with souvenir vendors, entrances to ridiculous exhibitions, dress-up photo opportunities, and boyish soldiers doing exercises in uniforms a few sizes too large as if their mothers had bought them for them to grow into. You pass through another gate (the Duān Mén—Gate of Correct Deportment), and across the moat, to the right of the enormous Wǔ Mén (Meridian Gate), which is the main entrance. Guides will hassle you to take their services, but few have much grasp of their subject and they are not recommended. One benefit of your ¥50 ticket is that you have an express entrance, the far right-hand door of the Wǔ Mén, where you can also pick up your audio-tour, Forbidden City baseball cap, mug or CD-ROM. On the right just before entering there is a place to deposit bags, but this is not compulsory.

The Imperial Palace was originally constructed over a period of 14 years, and is said to have involved 100,000 artisans (but this is the kind of round figure the Chinese love to use when they just mean 'many'). The palace was completed in 1420 and the Míng emperor Yǒnglè moved here shortly afterwards, the first of 24 Míng and Qīng emperors to live there up to 1924, kept secure by its 10m-high walls, surrounded by a moat. Wild figures of up to 9,000 are given for the number of rooms in what is still the largest and best preserved group of historic buildings in China, occupying approximately 1km by 0.75km.

Encouraged to visit China by the American archaeologist and art historian Langdon Warner, Sinophile George Kates lived in Běijīng between 1933 and 1941, in the style of a member of the Chinese scholarly class. While there, he was determined to see as much as possible of the

Forbidden City, which then had only small areas open to the public, entered separately from the north and south ends.

It was a pursuit, almost a wooing; it carried me through the seasons; it became an absorption. After two or three years, some weed-overgrown courtyard, apparently destined to remain sealed for ever with a rusty Chinese padlock, through chinks in whose rotting doorways I had long peered in vain, would one day be wide open, while unconcerned masons went about some simple task. My reward would then be great.

George N. Kates, *The Years that Were Fat*, 1952

Kates eventually obtained a pass to use the two libraries then located in the palace, which allowed him a quarter of a mile further in than most visitors, he estimated. Few today will have the time that Kates did to devote to sleuthing, but by following him around the edges of courtyards, by peering through windows and loosely chained doors, and by taking every side turning that you find, you will discover dusty rooms and overgrown peeling corners with crumbling stonework. In 1999 the Forbidden City got a long overdue but only partial touch-up with some courtyards re-flagstoned and roofs mown, but many of those freshly arrived in China will be shocked that such a major monument could be allowed to decay. The heavily restored towering palaces and broad open spaces on the main axis, however, impressive as they are, are comparatively lacking in atmosphere. It is in the smaller, more human spaces of the residential quarters, a more luxurious version of the *hùtóng* of the outside world, that the ghosts of drowned concubines and Machiavellian eunuchs must reside. Vast areas remain out of bounds to visitors, and dragon-topped pavilions are glimpsed intriguingly over the tops of lower buildings that block access to them. One northwest section is said to contain solely the remains of buildings deliberately set alight by eunuchs to prevent an inventory from discovering how much they had stolen of the palace's resources, and this seems to be undergoing restoration and may open during the life of this book. Another section is used for above- and below-ground storage of a claimed one million relics (in nine underground storeys) and it has recently been announced that this will eventually open to the public, but no date has been given—ask for news.

Most of the palace's original treasures are long gone, however. In 1928 the Nationalist government took those neither previously looted or removed by the departing imperial household for safe-keeping in the new capital of Nánjīng, ignoring the terms of the articles of 'favourable treatment' which required them to pay an agreed purchase price to the imperial family. When, following their defeat in the civil war, the Nationalists retreated to Tāiwān, the treasures retreated too, and are now on display in the world's finest museum of oriental art in Tāiběi (Taipei). What is now on display in the palace has mostly been gathered from other sources, and much is poorly displayed behind glass in dimly-lit interiors, obscured by smears from the noses of every visitor since the place was opened.

The palace itself is an architectural reference work, full of elements that you will see repeated in palace after palace, and in other imperial buildings across Běijīng and elsewhere.

Most of the halls have yellow **roof tiles**, a colour that could only be used with imperial consent. Green tiled buildings belonged to princes, although upon attaining maturity they were usually required to live elsewhere. The palace libraries had black tiled roofs, the colour being associated with water and seen as an aid to fire-fighting. Those buildings reserved for functionaries had the same grey tiles as buildings throughout the rest of China.

The huge wooden doors from the Tiān'ān Mén onwards are studded with large golden **knobs**. These have been likened to golden fish eyes, bowls, mushrooms and *mántou*, Chinese steamed bread rolls. One story has it that they were inspired by conches, symbols of tightness and security. The number of knobs, usually arranged nine by nine, seven by seven or five by five, indicates the rank of the door.

Looking up you'll see **ceramic figures** on the spine and eaves of the roof of each building. The two beasts facing inwards along the spine of each roof are water dragons, supposed to resist the attacks of lightning and fire. A row of ceramic figures runs down the eaves; at the tip is the figure of a man followed by a succession of animal figures. Traditionally the figure is the tyrannical prince of an early pre-Qín state who was overthrown by the combined forces of his neighbours and hanged from the roof of his palace. The people erected images of the prince on their roofs, mounted on a chicken unable to fly down to the ground below, and with a fearsome dragon (called a *chīwěn*) at his back to prevent escape over the roof. The other figures are said to date from the time of the Forbidden City's builder, Yǒnglè, and can include another lesser dragon, phoenix, lion, unicorn (*kylín*) and celestial horse, with the *chīwěn* always last. Often the middle figures are all lions.

The large dog-like creatures to either side of the main entrances of major buildings throughout China are **guardian lions.** The beast on the right is male, his right paw placed on top of a ball, said either to represent the world or to be full of milk supplied by the female. She sits on the left, a cub lying on its back beneath her left paw, apparently taking suck from one of her claws. Most of these lions are stone, but look out for a particularly fine bronze pair within the Forbidden City.

Several of the palaces sit atop marble plinths of up to three layers, with beautifully carved balustrades and projecting water spouts carved in the shape of dragons. The main pillars are single tree trunks, heavily lacquered in red, the colour of prosperity, used also for the walls. All the important buildings on the main axis face south, giving them maximum sunshine and turning their backs to baleful northern influences. They were heated with braziers of charcoal, different quantities allotted to members of the imperial household according to rank, the careless handling of which caused many fires.

The major halls are arranged ahead of you along the north-south axis which bisects the entire city from the Yǒngdìng Mén, now vanished except in name, in the middle of the southern wall of the Chinese city, through the gates of the Qián Mén, Tiān'ān Mén and north of the Forbidden City through the Drum and Bell Towers. These halls have brief introduction signs in English.

Where Are They Now?

 Emperors went through several names in their lifetimes, but to foreigners and to modern Chinese the one by which each is usually known is not his at all, but that of his reign. This was different from his personal name (which it was forbidden to speak during his reign), his 'temple name', or his posthumous name. It's more correct to speak of the Yǒnglè emperor, rather than the Emperor Yǒnglè ('eternal happiness').

The Hóngwǔ emperor ('vast military accomplishment'), the first of the Míng, who established himself after pushing back the Mongol Yuán dynasty court into Inner Mongolia in 1368, renamed the conquered capital Běipíng (northern peace—or 'the north pacified') and settled the Chinese court at Nánjīng instead. The Yǒnglè emperor, formerly prince of a northern region, believed that China could better be defended from the north, and after massive reconstruction which gave the central capital its modern layout, gave it the name Běijīng (Northern Capital) for the first time, moving the court there in 1421.

The Míng emperors who lived in the Forbidden City and who were buried in the Shísān Líng (Míng Tombs), were:

Yǒnglè	1403–24
Hóngxī	1425
Xuāndé	1426–35
Zhèngtǒng	1436–49
Jǐngtài	1450–57
Tiānshùn	1457–64.

The Zhèngtǒng and Tiānshùn emperors were the same person. The luckless Zhèngtǒng emperor was captured by the Mongols and held as a prisoner of war 1450–51, led a secluded life in Běijīng for seven years since in his absence his brother, the Jǐngtài emperor, had usurped the throne and was not therefore buried with the rest of the family.

Chénghuà	1465–87
Hóngzhì	1488–1505
Zhèngdé	1506–21
Jiājìng	1522–66
Lóngqìng	1567–72
Wànlì	1573–1620
Tàichāng	1620
Tiānqǐ	1621–27
Chóngzhēn	1628–44.

Emperors usually stayed in harness until death, most commonly of natural causes although the Yǒnglè emperor deposed the second Míng emperor (who was his nephew and the founding emperor Hóngwǔ's grandson), and as peasant armies entered Běijīng the last of the Míng emperors committed suicide by hanging himself from the 'Guilty Sophora' in Jǐng Shān Gōngyuán (*see* p.149).

The Qīng Qiánlóng emperor retired so as not to show disrespect to his grandfather, the Kāngxī emperor, by reigning for a yet longer period. The last of the Qīng, Henry Aisin-Gioro Pǔyí, abdicated (or rather his regent father did so on his behalf), and is rarely known by his reign title since he never completed his reign and died a citizen at the height of the Cultural Revolution.

The Qīng had emperors before they took over China, buried in a tomb complex at Shěnyáng in Manchuria, in territory which never belonged to China but which has been absorbed into it now (*see* 'The Last of the Emperors' *below*). Those who reigned from Běijīng were:

Shùnzhì	1644–61	Xiào Líng (Dōng—Eastern Qīng Tombs)
Kāngxī	1662–1722	Jǐng Líng (Dōng)
Yōngzhèng	1723–35	Tài Líng (Xī—Western Qīng Tombs)
Qiánlōng	1736–95	Yù Líng (Dōng)
Jiāqìng	1796–1820	Chāng Ling (Xī)
Dàoguāng	1821–50	Mù Líng (Xī)
Xiánfēng	1851–61	Dìng Ling (Dōng)
Tóngzhì	1862–74	Huì Líng (Dōng)
Guāngxù	1874–1908	Chóng Líng (Xī)
Xūantǒng	1909–12	Henry Aisin Gioro Pǔyí was cremated—his ashes originally stored at the Bā Bǎo Shān mausoleum with various heroes of the revolution, but now in a small plot at the Western Qīng Tombs.

The **Wǔ Mén** or Meridian Gate where you buy your ticket is the main entrance to the Forbidden City proper, also called Five Phoenix Tower, with five pavilions on top. In the early days of the Palace Museum these were used as exhibition spaces, but the gate cannot be climbed now. Drums on top were struck when the emperors visited the ancestral temple (the Tài Miào—on the right as you walk up from Tiān'ān Mén and now converted into the Working People's Cultural Palace—*see below*, p.150). Trips to the Temple of Heaven were marked with the striking of bells. Ceremonies performed here included the announcement of the calendar, and the punishment of lax or unfortunate officials, many of whom would die from their beatings. Of the five doors, the middle was for the emperor alone, the right for senior civil officials, the left for senior military advisers, and the outer gates for the few others allowed in.

Beyond the Meridian Gate, offices on the right originally housed the imperial secretariat and historians, and those on the left translators. Behind them were the only other two side gates, used by civil and military officials when coming for the emperor's pre-dawn audiences. Crossing a stream by one of five bridges matching the gate's five doors, you reach the **Tàihé Mén**, or Gate of Supreme Harmony. During the Míng dynasty this was used for imperial consultations, which under the Qīng were handled further into the city.

Beyond the gate is the largest courtyard in the palace, capable of holding a vast throng of officials and administrators on ceremonial occasions. The paving tiles are said to be 15 layers deep to prevent anyone tunnelling in from the outside. Storage areas run down either side, and around the courtyard are large vats for storing water to aid in fire fighting, which are numerous throughout the palace. Fires were not always accidental, the eunuchs able to benefit by stealing the contents of buildings before setting them alight and by fiddling the repair bills.

Across the courtyard is the first of three halls that form the palace's centrepiece, raised on triple-layer plinths, on which stand large, bronze incense burners. The **Tàihé Diàn** or Hall of Supreme Harmony was where the emperor sat to review the prostrations of his court at the celebrations of solstices, birthdays, the new year, etc. Behind it, the smaller **Zhōnghé Diàn** (Hall of Middle Harmony) was the antechamber where the emperor made his preparations for the ceremonies. The Emperor Guāngxù was arrested here on the orders of Dowager Empress Cīxī.

Behind this is the **Bǎohé Diàn** (Hall of Preserving Harmony), which was used to receive the princes of vassal states, on New Year's Eve for banquets for high officials, and for the highest level imperial civil service examinations, which began during the Táng and were held every three years until cancelled on the orders of the Eight Allied Powers from 1901 and abolished altogether in 1905. At the rear of the hall is the most magnificent of the marble ramps that run up the middle of the stairs to the palaces. These are carved with intertwined dragons of remarkable complexity, and this one is nearly 17m long and said to weigh as much as 200 tons. It was made in the Míng and brought to Běijīng on a combination of rollers and a path made from ice. It was recarved during the Qīng in 1761.

The buildings straddling the Bǎohé Diàn are often used for exhibitions of art from various dynasties, including ceramics, bronzes and stonework from other imperial palaces, as well as calligraphy, watercolours, Buddhist statuary and terracotta warriors from the tomb of the first emperor of all China in Xī'ān. These are not well signposted and are easily missed. Start on the right-hand (east) side as you face the hall. Making your way from room to room you pass from one courtyard to the next.

At this point the audio tour will take you straight on, but it's better to turn left (west) into an area of smaller halls that function as offices and residences where the scale is more human. There is considerably more atmosphere in these labyrinthine corridors and interconnected courtyards which echo in a more luxurious and orderly fashion the *hútòng* (alleys) outside. Several residences have been refurnished roughly in the style of the late Qīng, but the original materials are mostly in Taipei. Amongst them, the **Yǎngxīn Diàn** (Hall of Mental Cultivation) was the main living and working space for the emperors and has a magnificent ceiling sculpture of a dragon playing with a pearl. While some of the last Qīng emperors gave audiences to officials in this room, the Dowager Empress Cíxī controlled matters from behind a screen.

The End of the Emperors

Cíxī was born in 1835, the daughter of a minor Qīng official, and was one of 28 Manchu girls selected for the Xiánfēng emperor (reigned 1851–61). She was made a concubine of the fifth rank at the age of 17 and later gave birth to a son, something the Empress Cí'ān had failed to do, and was raised to the second rank. Following the emperor's death in 1861, Cíxī, Cí'ān, and the dead emperor's brother perpetrated a coup which installed the six-year-old Tóngzhì emperor in 1862 and named Cíxī Dowager Empress. The two women both sat behind the screen, but Cí'ān died suddenly in 1881 after eating some cakes sent to her by Cíxī, who then became sole puppet-mistress. When the Tóngzhì emperor died in 1874, a victim, it was said, of smallpox and other diseases resulting from the licentiousness in which she encouraged him, and rather conveniently just as he was just attaining the majority which would have left her with less power, she manoeuvred her sister's child onto the throne so that she could remain as regent. The Tóngzhì emperor's pregnant widow, who might have been carrying an heir, officially committed suicide shortly afterwards, but Cíxī is not surprisingly suspected of having had a hand in this too.

The choice of the boy who became the Guāngxù emperor broke the dynastic house law that emperors should only be succeeded by someone from the next generation (although the emperors chose which of their numerous sons seemed most fitting) and there was much dissent in the court. The new emperor was only four years old. He eventually came of age in 1888, 13 years after taking the throne, and at the beginning of 1889 took up his duties. With the encouragement of forward-looking scholars he began in the summer of 1898 a rapid series of political and administrative reforms called the 'Hundred Days' which might have saved the Qīng but which were resisted by Cíxī. Guāngxù planned to throw off Cíxī's control and asked Yuán Shìkǎi, creator of a new and relatively modern and efficient Chinese army, to arrest her. Instead Yuán betrayed his plans, and Guāngxù was imprisoned on an island in the Nán Hǎi in 1898 (now part of the government compound of Zhōng Nán Hǎi, and not open to visitors).

Cíxī wrote an edict for him to sign claiming that on the grounds of illness and incompetence he had asked her to retake control, and she promptly reversed his reforms and put several of his advisors to death. Guāngxù's own life was no doubt in jeopardy, but the British minister let it be known that foreign powers would take a dim view of the emperor's death, and he spent the rest of his life either locked up in the Nán Hǎi or in the Hall of Jade Ripples at the Summer Palace when the court travelled there, forced to make regular obeisance to Cíxī. He met an early end in 1908 from various illnesses, possibly in the Hall of Mental Cultivation, although the Palace of Heavenly Purity is also named as the place.

Cíxī placed the three-year-old infant Pǔyí on the throne as the Xuāntǒng emperor, ensuring her continuing regency, but died herself a few hours later, aged 73. Some suspect that Cíxī decided to end the Guāngxù emperor's life before her own, and others that the eunuchs who had supported her imprisonment of the emperor poisoned him to prevent his regaining power after her death, which would likely have ensured the end of their own lives. In death Guāngxù and Cíxī remained separated, since he was buried in the Western Tombs, and she at the Eastern set.

Pǔyí's reign was short, and it was in the Hall of Mental Cultivation on 12 February 1912 that an edict of abdication was issued recognizing the Republic of China.

After wandering around various smaller halls you can return to the rear of the Hall of Preserving Harmony and continue north up the main axis. The **Qiánqīng Mén** (Gate of Heavenly Purity) leading to the inner court and built in 1429, was rebuilt in 1655, but it said to have been the only building not to have been destroyed at least once since then, and thus the oldest in the whole palace. Sometimes used for giving audiences by the Míng emperors, the gate did not originally form such a solid block between the larger ceremonial halls and the inner palace. The connecting walls to either side were extended by Yuán Shìkǎi once the emperor had abdicated and been confined to the residential quarters, and two halls, one in the southeast and one in the southwest, were stocked with some of the 70,000 items brought down from the imperial palaces at Chéngdé and the former Qīng capital in Manchuria, and opened as museums.

Unlike its luckier neighbour, the **Qiánqīng Gōng** (Palace of Heavenly Purity), through the gate, is said to have burned down and been rebuilt at least three times. Living quarters for emperors during the Míng and early Qīng, they were later used as an audience chamber. The Guāngxù emperor's secret discussions about reform are said to have taken place here, as well as his fatal briefing to Yuán Shìkǎi, and under the terms of the post-Boxer protocol foreign envoys were given audiences. Being barbarians, they had not previously been allowed to sully the Imperial Palace, and had been received in a hall in what is now Zhōngnán Hǎi. The last emperor carried out all his ceremonial duties here and it was also the site of his wedding ceremony in December 1922. This and the following two halls have the same relationship as the three large 'Harmony' ceremonial halls, but on a much smaller scale and in reverse order.

The **Jiāotài Diàn** (Hall of Union and Peace or Hall of Vigorous Fertility) was the throne room of the empresses, who held various celebrations here. The hall also housed the 25 jade seals of imperial authority from the time of Qiánlōng onwards.

The **Kūnníng Gōng** (The Palace of Earthly Tranquility) was the living quarters of the Míng empresses. It was reconstructed and divided under the Qīng for use in Manchu shaman religious ceremonies.

At the **Kūnníng Diàn** (Gate of Earthly Tranquility) behind the Palace there's an exhibition of Qīng toys on the right. These are mostly musical boxes and automata, and some are exquisite steam-powered contraptions which must have been the most expensive of their time.

The rear courtyard is known as **Yùhuā Yuán** (Imperial Flower Garden) with small temples, ancient bamboo, and an enormous rock garden topped by a small pavilion. One pavilion on the west side was the schoolroom used by the British tutor of the last emperor, Sir Reginald Johnston, and furnished with heavy Victorian furniture, Nottingham lace curtains, and Axminster carpets to make him comfortable. Johnston, Isabel Ingram (the American tutor of the empress) and the imperial couple would have *al fresco* lunches here in the garden.

The Last Occupant of the Forbidden City

 Johnston, played unforgettably by Peter O'Toole in Bertolucci's film *The Last Emperor*, was an Oxford-educated Scot turned Confucian, with fluent Mandarin and a deep love of China, had worked in the British administration of both Hong Kong and a treaty port in Shāndōng, before being invited to take up the post of Western tutor to the 13-year-old emperor Xūantŏng, Henry Aisin Gioro Pŭyí, in 1919. The abdication treaty had been signed seven years earlier, but Johnston's post was created to broaden the emperor's knowledge of foreign things, should the Republic, which tottered from its first day, ever actually fall. One pro-monarchist warlord took temporary control of the capital in July 1917 and engineered a restoration which lasted all of 12 days before the warlord was himself driven out and took refuge in the Legation Quarter.

Granted leave from the Foreign and Colonial Office, Johnston gave Pŭyí two-hour tutorials almost daily until the emperor's marriage in 1922, and far from restricting himself to English, which the emperor never learned to speak well, took on a broader counselling role, eventually influencing him both to end the eunuch system and to undertake a complete financial overhaul of the Imperial Household Department, both of which were corrupt and an immense drain on the emperor's now (relatively) limited resources. These reforms were instituted in 1923, but before they could have much effect the emperor was arrested the following year by the 'Christian general', the warlord Féng Yùxiáng, who had taken Běijīng in one of several changes of control which took place between 1912 and 1949.

Johnston engineered a daring escape to the Legation Quarter, where he lodged the emperor at the Japanese legation, a move that was to prove fateful, putting the impressionable and weak young monarch increasingly under Japanese influence. There he stayed until 1925 when he moved to the Japanese concession in Tiānjīn, and then on to the state of Manchukuo, which the Japanese had set up in occupied Manchuria, eventually accepting the puppet position of Emperor there.

Johnston's modern Confucianism made him firmly in favour of consitutional monarchy, and he seems to have imagined that if the Guāngxù emperor's reforms had continued that China might have followed the same path followed by Japan after it had been opened up by the USA in adopting Western institutions and inventions. He had a rosy view of Japan's intentions in Asia, too, and imagined that an ever-stronger Japan might restore the Qīng monarchy. But Pǔyí never returned to live in the Forbidden City, and his collaboration with the Japanese left him lucky to escape with his life after Japan's defeat at the end of the Second World War.

The **Shénwǔ Mén** (Gate of Military Prowess) is now the rear gate of the Forbidden City, and unlike the rest can be climbed. The well constructed exhibition on top has photographs of less accessible parts of the complex, cut-away models showing the internal construction of some of the buildings, and a complete scale model allowing you to work out where you've just been, and just how much is still not open to the public. The palace wall stretches away, overgrown and inaccessible, to the corner arrow towers. Looking back into the city you can see an area of smaller halls and pavilions on the left (east) containing exhibitions, and small, secluded court-yards and gardens which are perhaps the most attractive parts of the whole complex.

Returning south down the east side of the Earthly Tranquility section, there are various exhibitions in halls formerly functioning as the residences of concubines, each group contained within its own walls.

The **Hall of Arts and Crafts** (Yìměishù Guǎn) is in fact two halls with displays of finely carved jade, and two further halls to the east containing enamel ware.

The **Clock and Watch Exhibition Hall** (Zhōngbiǎo Guǎn, formerly the Palace of Eternal Harmony) contains 185 timepieces of which 51 are Chinese and 83 British, mostly 18th-century, with US and French contributions. Some of the emperors were avid collectors (at one point a clock factory was set up in the palace), and many of the clocks were gifts from those hoping to gain favour at court. While the Chinese were probably the inventors of the world's first escapement mechanism, during their self-imposed isolation they slipped behind Western technology. The clocks are now well-lit and displayed, and a video shows them in operation, many being more automata than clock. Perhaps the most impressive is a British clock with the figure of a man holding a calligraphy brush, who writes eight characters meaning 'People come from various places to pay their respects to the emperor'. Another clock is towed in a circle by an exquisite miniature mechanical elephant, which waves its trunk and rolls its eyes. Some clocks are miniature palaces or pagodas of silver, gold, enamel and precious stones.

Tào piào or no, there is a separate charge of ¥2 for compulsory polystyrene overshoes supposedly to protect the floor (and which you can keep for use at the Hall of Jewellery where the same rule applies). The interior floors of this and many other halls are made of 'gold bricks', named for the cost of their production rather than their grey colour. Manufactured at special imperial kilns at Sūzhōu outside Shànghǎi, the bricks spent 230 days in the kiln, and from collecting the mud from which they were made to delivery to the palace via the Grand Canal took nearly a year altogether. The same kiln still supplies replacements to the palace, but the original techniques of production have been lost. After the bricks were laid, they were coated with a mixture of ink and alcohol, then a layer of paraffin wax, and finally polished with a little sesame oil. They are now supposed to receive a daily polishing with kerosene, but if this happens it leaves no smell. Whether the overshoes have any real success in protecting the bricks is moot, since the staff are only interested in collecting the money not in making visitors wear them, and many just carry the shoes to show they have paid.

When restoration takes place of certain sections, exhibitions move elsewhere. In 2000 the clock exhibition was temporarily on the east side of the Bǎohé Diàn and the emphasis had changed to clock production within the Forbidden City from the Yōngzhèng period (1723–35) to that of Qiánlōng (1736–95), and clocks produced in Guǎngzhōu during the 18th century, in an early example of the technology transfer the government now frequently requires from foreign companies wishing to set up business in China. However, the English explanations imply that all is Chinese ingenuity. Some clocks are wound up by attendants to demonstrate their movements at 11am and 2pm, with different clocks wound on different days. Miniature jewelled pagodas go up and down, and mechanical lotuses bloom to reveal praying figures.

Further to the south and east are the Treasure Halls, labelled **Hall of Jewellery** (Zhēnbǎoguǎn), occupying a number of halls constructed for the retirement of the Qiánlōng emperor (reigned 1736–95) who abdicated at the age of 85 in favour of his son. These buildings have suitable names such as Hall of Imperial Zenith and Palace of Peaceful Old Age, but Qiánlōng did not have long to enjoy them; like many another Chief Executive Officer, he died only a few years out of harness, four years later. They remained unused for 100 years until Cīxī nominally retired to them when Guāngxù reached his majority in 1899. It was here, too, that her body rested for a year after her death, awaiting an auspicious burial date.

On the way in you pass the **Jiǔlóngbì** or Nine Dragon Screen, 6m high and 31m long, originally built in 1773. The blue, yellow, white and purple dragons writhe in relief from an assemblage of large tiles, one of which is said to be a wooden copy hurriedly created to replace a tile broken during assembly, but which could not be replaced before inspection. There's another nine dragon screen in Běi Hǎi Park.

The two jewellery halls have ornate swords, knives, saddles, costume, musical instruments, miniature jewelled pagodas, imperial seals, tea sets and dinner sets, S-shaped ceremonial sceptres called *rúyì* (perhaps similar to the one given by the Qiánlōng emperor to British envoy Lord Macartney to take to King George III), perfume holders and other extravagant items, including an extraordinary woven ivory mat, and jewellery made from sapphires and kingfisher feathers (using kingfisher feathers as decoration is a traditional craft in China, called *diǎncuì*). Three halls beyond these to the north contain other treasures that are also worth inspecting in their own right, and are preserved much as they were in Qiánlōng's day. The first has magnificently carved doors on either side of its interior, and the second houses two enormous pieces of jade, one carved into a dragon-covered bowl, the other into a mountain scene nearly 2m high which is said to have taken 10 years to make. Intricate screen doors with inset painted panels run round the interior on two levels. Behind the third hall lies an area of several small courtyards, where the visitor can search out details such as a moon gate (circular entranceway) inset with mother of pearl, and stelae carved with Qiánlōng's poetry set into courtyard walls. On the left (west) side is the **Níngshòu Gōng Huáyuán** (Flower Garden of the Palace of Peaceful Old Age), with paths winding between small, secluded pavilions, trees and rockeries—one of the most pleasant areas of the entire complex. One of the pavilions contains a snaking water channel for floating wine cups, where the nominally retired emperor played literary drinking games.

Not Feeling Well

 It was in these halls that the hurried conferences of Cíxī and her court took place as the foreign armies approached Běijīng during the Boxer Rebellion of 1900. At the rear (north) side is the gate she used to flee her quarters along with the Guāngxù emperor, called the Zhēnshùn Mén (Gate of Faithful Obedience), and on the way lies what is now known as the Well of the Pearl Concubine.

Guāngxù's wedding, arranged by Cíxī, was said, despite the decayed state of the dynasty, to have cost 5.5 million taels of silver (1 tael = 38g). Nevertheless, Guāngxù is said to have slept with his wife only once, preferring a concubine called the Zhēn Fēi, usually known as the Pearl Concubine. As Cíxī was leaving for Xī'ān, she informed all the imperial concubines that they would stay behind, but the Zhēn Fēi dared to protest. There are several versions of what happened next, some of which are derived from the now discredited Sir Edmund Backhouse's translation of the diary of a Manchu official. Backhouse, quite brilliantly, wrote the fake diary in Chinese himself, and it was long considered primary source material for histories of the Qīng court's behaviour at the time:

> The Pearl Concubine, who had always been insubordinate to the Old Buddha, came with the rest and actually dared to suggest that the Emperor should remain in Peking. The Empress was in no mood for argument. Without a moment's hesitation, she shouted to the eunuchs on duty: 'Throw this wretched minion down the well!' At this the Emperor, who was greatly grieved, fell on his knees in supplication, but the Empress angrily bade him desist, saying that this was no time for bandying words. 'Let her die at once,' she said, 'as a warning to all undutiful children, and to those "xiao" birds who, when fledged, peck out their own mother's eyes.'

> J. O. P. Bland and E. Backhouse, *China Under the Empress Dowager,* 1921

Johnston offers another version, equally colourful, which he claims to have had directly from eunuchs, although none would admit to having been present. In this one the concubine pleaded with Cíxī to let the emperor stay behind to face the imminent foreign troops, an honourable course of action in which he would have been perfectly safe, since it was known that he had no power at court. The Empress Dowager responded:

> 'We will all stay where we are, but we cannot allow ourselves to be taken alive by Western Barbarians. There is only one way out for you and me—we must both die. It is easy. You go first—I promise to follow you.' Then at a sign from her mistress the eunuchs seized the girl and hurled her into the well, where she was left to drown—alone.

> Reginald F. Johnston, *Twilight in the Forbidden City,* 1934

The official version of the Communist Party has her a martyr to her comparatively enlightened political views and especially her support of the emperor's moves for reform, which Cíxī strangled. While the terms of reparations were being worked out with foreign powers during the following months, Cíxī issued a decree praising the Zhēn Fēi for her loyalty in committing suicide when unable to catch up with the departing court.

The far northeastern corner of the palace has the recently opened Exhibition of Opera of the Qīng Court in the **Chàngyīn Gé** (Pavilion of Pleasant Sounds—¥10 without the *tào piào*) in a three-storeyed theatre built in 1776. There are sumptuous costumes with extravagantly beautiful embroidery, photographs of Cíxī dressed up as if to take part herself, gaudy sequinned head dresses, and photographs of how the halls used to look in her day. Cíxī used to sit in the two storey Wèi Shì Lóu (Tower of the Inspection of Truth) and what are now side corridors were divided into boxes.

Behind the Zhēnshùn Mén a passage leads west to the main exit on the north side, and you can leave the palace and cross the road to see the Jǐngshān Gōngyuán. Alternatively when you reach the **Yùhuā Yuán** you can leave from the southwest corner and head south through a long series of halls on two parallel axes, separated by north-south and east-west long red arteries. These were mostly the residences of various concubines and empresses at different times, and lead eventually to the Hall of Mental Cultivation, mentioned above. Particularly notable is the **Cháng Chūn Gōng** (Palace of Enternal Spring), the former residence of several well-known concubines, including those of the Guāngxù and Xūantǒng emperors. Stand at the door with your back to the hall, and look to the right and left along the passage to see clever trompe-l'oeil paintings at either end, which make the passageway appear infinitely extended. In other parts of the courtyard are paintings of scenes from the classic novel, *A Dream of Red Mansions* (*see* Grand View Garden, p.170).

Going south you'll find further exhibitions of ceramics and paintings in the halls running down the west side of the courtyards containing the 'Harmony' halls. Look to your right for a marvellous three-storey pavilion, with huge golden coiled scampering dragons on its roof, beautifully blue tiles, and subsidiary dragons emerging from its eaves, only matched at Chéngdé. Sounds of repair work from this quarter suggest that this long inaccessible tower, in a section badly damaged by fire at a time when the Guǎngxù emperor attempted to reduce the power of the eunuchs by taking a detailed inventory of his possessions, might open during the life of this book.

The Ends of the Eunuchs

After his abdication the Xūantǒng emperor, Pǔyí, was left with the enormous financial burden of the Imperial Household, including 1,000 eunuchs, far fewer than their numbers under the Míng, but still in the opinion of Johnston an organization existing to promote its own survival rather than that of the emperor, and of little use to him. Under Johnston's influence Pǔyí abolished the eunuch system altogether in 1923.

The earliest records of the existence of eunuchs in China date back to at least 3,200 years before the system was ended in the palace. Early mutilations were mostly punishment for adultery or a way of quietening the unruly, or a humiliating expression of complete victory over captured enemies. However, the use of eunuchs as servants to the court, and particularly to the imperial bedchamber, also has a long history, eventually resulting in a situation where the eunuchs, who could be relied upon to manage the imperial harem without impregnating any of it, became the only 'male' servants, forming a barrier between the humanity of the emperor and his ministers, who needed only to believe in his divinity.

The constant proximity of the senior eunuchs to the emperors tended to give them immense influence over the weaker monarchs, and in the worst cases those who found the contents of their seraglios more interesting than affairs of state allowed the eunuchs to run the country for them, a habit blamed for the collapse of more than one dynasty. Emperors grew up surrounded by these plump, timid, soft- or screechy-voiced part-men who tended to all their needs and to whom they were completely accustomed. Consorts and concubines sometimes ran into the thousands, and at the height of their power under the Míng as many as 5,000 eunuchs were employed in the palace. Their ability to acquire great power and vast fortunes through selling their influence and through fiddling the imperial accounts led men to self-mutilation and the eventual rise of professionals in the field of preparing men surgically for court service. The only other route to influence was through years, sometimes decades, of study to pass several levels of Confucian examinations (*see* p.192), and the giving up of one small pleasure through a little operation, refined by the time of the Qīng so as to have a very low mortality rate, seemed the loss of little for the potential gain of much.

Undoubtedly, with the kind of double-think which is common in Chinese society even today, the operation was anti-Confucian, but honoured because it was also an ancient custom and therefore good. Filial piety, a key Confucian doctrine, required each person to take care of the body his parents had provided, which presumably did not include lopping bits off, and especially not the bits involved in another major Confucian duty, that of reproducing so as to continue the family line and provide offspring to tend the ancestors' shrines. But a significant part of the male population was likely to remain too poor ever to have a bride, and so neither the loss of those parts a bride might value, nor the loss of the prospect of putting them to use to make children, seemed much to the point.

Male readers may wish to cross their legs before going on.

Having had his parts washed with pepper water and being held down tightly by the surgeon's assistants, the candidate eunuch was asked whether he would regret the operation afterwards. Those showing the slightest hesitation were sent away. Those steadfast in their desires had both penis and testicles cut off, a plug inserted, their wound bound tightly with cloths soaked in cold water, and were then made to walk around for two or three hours with the help of the assistants. They were permitted no food or drink for three days, after which time the plug was removed. If some urine ran out, the patient would live, and his wounds would heal completely in about three months. If not, he would suffer a lingering death.

Those who survived made sure to keep their organs in a pouch or jar, both because they had to be presented at the time of promotion and because they hoped to be restored to wholeness in the afterlife. For those unfortunate enough to lose track of their *bǎo*, or 'treasure', there was a business in renting or buying parts from others.

Oddly, having climbed their way to wealth through the opportunities for graft provided by being in imperial service, but feeling very much the disdain of other men, some married court ladies, thus achieving solace. On retirement, the richer ones constructed temples and large mansions for themselves to the northwest, and 1930s guides to Běijīng describe a cemetery for eunuchs to the north of Bā Bǎo Shān and a temple for them, both now long disappeared.

Jǐngshān Gōngyuán 景山公园

Open 6am–9pm; adm ¥3.

See map p.120, no.10. 'Prospect Park' is directly behind the Forbidden City's rear entrance, and reached by bus 5 from Qián Mén, but for those who haven't been exhausted by traversing the vast interior of the palace it's simpler to cross to the park directly from there. It can also be seen first, the palace being entered by the rear gate. Until this century it was connected directly to the palace, but the walls were pulled down and a road driven through during the Republic, destroying several gates and other buildings which stood between the hill and what is now the rear entrance of the palace.

Different stories have the hill either constructed on a base of coal or used as a storage place for it, and it is often known as Méi Shān, or Coal Hill. Built by the Míng emperor Yǒnglè (reigned 1403–24), it is mostly made from the earth excavated to make the palace's moat and protects the palace from baleful northern influences. The responsibility for the 'coal' error is sometimes placed on foreigners' inability to recognize the difference between 'méi' meaning 'coal', and 'měi' meaning 'beautiful', which seems to make no sense at all. Surely the word for beauty is learned before the word for coal in any language, and 'coal' is hardly the word that springs to mind when looking at the hill. It's topped by five pavilions which originally date from 1750, once holding Buddha statues, all but one of which were looted in 1900 and the last one smashed during the Cultural Revolution.

For a fee you can be borne around the space immediately inside the main gate in a palanquin, while the costumed bearers try to make you sick by bouncing it up and down, and musicians play adaptations of the latest pop hits on traditional instruments. A variety of paths climb the green and shady hillside, and the central pavilion at the top gives views south over the yellow roofscape of the Forbidden City and to Běi Hǎi ('North Sea', actually a lake) with its stupa to the west. Between the two stands Zhōngnán Hǎi ('Middle and South Seas'), where the Chinese leaders, although so much loved by the people, have always felt it necessary to lock themselves safely away. Originally of a piece with Běi Hǎi, and within the walls of the Imperial City, the lakes were the playground of Liáo, Jīn, Yuán, Míng and Qīng dynasty emperors. Now the southern two lakes and their pavilions are separated by a road and high walls and are the closely guarded headquarters of the Central Committee of the Chinese Communist Party and the State Council of the People's Republic of China.

The hall below on the north side once housed portraits of the emperors and is now part of the Běijīng's Children's Palace. Its neighbour to the east is where the bodies of the emperors lay in state while final preparations were made for their burial. Further to the north and directly on the same axis or meridian line lie the bell and drum towers (*see* below, p.175).

On the east side of the hill's base can be found the stump of a locust tree (a *sophora*, *cassia* or *acacia*, depending on whose view you take, also known as a scholar tree). The last Míng emperor, Chóngzhēn, hanged himself here using his own belt on 25 April 1644 as rebel peasants took over Běijīng, shortly before they were evicted again by the Qīng armies arriving from Manchuria. During the Qīng dynasty the tree was treated like a criminal since it had been an accessory to the death of an emperor, and a large iron chain was placed around it. It was known as the *zuì huái*—'guilty *sophora*'.

One of the gates at the rear of the palace also used to carry a wooden scaffold resembling a *cangue*, the heavy board placed around the necks of certain criminals, a punishment for having allowed the emperor to leave to go to his death. The chain is said to have been removed in the looting following the Boxer Rebellion, but the tree survived until the Cultural Revolution when it was hacked to pieces, only the stunted stump remaining. A new tree was planted in 1981, although how this is supposed to replace the historical authenticity of the original is not clear.

Tài Miào (Workers' Cultural Palace)

太庙

Open 6–8; adm ¥2.

See map p.120, no.18. The Tian'an Men is flanked by two parks which are almost always overlooked by visitors, particularly the one containing the Tài Miào or 'Supreme Temple', its entrance only a few metres to the east. The magnificent halls here are of the same period as the main palaces and are where the emperors came to kneel before wooden tablets representing their ancestors, to pay their respects and to report important events. When in 1644 the Manchu Qīng replaced the Míng (whose third emperor built the whole complex), they consigned the Míng tablets to the flames and added their own.

To the emperors this was the most sacred temple in Běijīng, but under Máo it was deliberately put to plebeian purposes as the Workers' Cultural Palace. Běijīng's citizens are now more interested in *Titanic* and other Hollywood blockbusters than the worthy and politically correct events organized for them here. So it's often almost deserted, and despite the closure of the heronry and the conversion of side halls to offices, there's more atmosphere here than in all but the remoter corners of the palace complex itself.

Through the entrance lies a large open area of gnarled and twisted cypresses seemingly as old as the buildings themselves (originally constructed in 1420 and rebuilt in 1544), each helpfully labelled 'old tree' in Chinese, followed by their Latin names. Stalls sell snacks, dried fruit and seeds. Beyond, a large gate into a vermilion-walled enclosure is followed by five ornate marble bridges over a man-made stream in direct imitation of the entrance to the Forbidden City itself. The main halls with their great sweeps of yellow roof, and which formerly held the thrones of dead emperors and their principle consorts, are nearly as grand as the palace's centrepiece Halls of Harmony.

Only the rear hall can be entered, and that has been converted into studios and classrooms. Formerly it held the spirit tablets which still stood here, albeit dusty, neglected and without receiving sacrifices, in the 1930s. From a distant corner may come the tinkling of a piano for a ballet class, reinforcing the church hall atmosphere, and outside perhaps a mother demonstrates dance steps to her daughter in the unforgiving stone-flagged courtyard. To one side boys play football using the ancient marble balustrades as a goal-mouth and, despite the offence to his ancestors, perhaps the bicycling boy-emperor Pǔyí, the last of the Qīng, might have approved.

This combination of Western domesticity and shabby oriental splendour ends at the rear with open space and park benches on the edge of the moat. Exiting to the left brings you out in front of the Wǔ Mén, the main entrance to the Forbidden City. Straight ahead is the rear entrance to Zhōngshān Gōngyuán.

Zhōngshān Gōngyuán (Sun Yat-sen Park) 中山公园

Open 6–8, adm ¥3.

See map p.120, no.17. Immediately west of Tiān'ān Mén (Ⓜ Tiān'ān Mén Xī), the park was originally a Liáo dynasty temple, and then from 1421 the Altar of Land and Grain where the emperors made sacrifices in thanks for good harvests. The altar is a square raised marble terrace, covered with earths of five colours representing the five directions (the fifth is the centre, China itself). Further ancient trees are labelled so that you can tell your *ginkgo bibola L.* from your other ginkgos.

The writers who visited or lived in Běijīng during the '20s and '30s were lyrical about the colourful use of potted plants in courtyards throughout the year and these are everywhere here, the park also being used for a special exhibition of tulips and other imported plants in season. The altar became Central Park in 1914, and was renamed for Sun Yat-sen after his death.

In the park there's also a monument to a long-forgotten German minister, Baron von Ketteler. Arches of wood or stone called *páilou* were erected to commemorate filial children, widows who refused to remarry, and other exemplars of Confucian virtues. In 1901 the representatives of 11 allied powers forced a settlement which, in addition to annual compensation payments equivalent to half the Qīng budget, shrewdly demanded the commemoration of von Ketteler, murdered as he rode to the Qīng Foreign Office, and in a form which the Chinese would view as a high honour. It bore an inscription rather vaguely expressing the emperor's contrition in Chinese, Latin, and German: 'This monument is erected in order to point out that what is good, is good; and what is evil, is evil. Let all our subjects learn from the past occurrences and never forget them. We order this.' Local people, mostly illiterate and innately foreigner-hating, assumed it to be in honour of the assassin rather than the assassinated. Following the defeat of Germany in 1918 and at the suggestion of former *Times* correspondent G. E. Morrison, by then an employee of the (northern) Chinese government, the triple-arched blue-roofed stone *páilou* was moved here. Its expression of apology was replaced by a general comment on peace, and in 1952 replaced with another version by palatable-to-communists author Guō Mòruò (*see* p.174).

Poor von Ketteler—the strangled rhetoric of the nearby sign can't even get his name right. The forgotten legation quarter itself is a better memorial, expanded after his death as the victorious foreigners demanded and received the right to take outright ownership of land, and to station their own military forces within a walled area on the very doorstep of the palace itself.

Imperial Archive (Huáng Shǐ Chéng) 皇史宬

Open 9–7; adm free.

See map p.120, no.9. The Archive is in Nán Chízi (Ⓜ Tiān'ān Mén Dōng), the first northbound street east of the main entrance to the Forbidden City, and a short walk from the east entrance just south of the Wǔ Mén. There's a sign for the Wan Fung Art Gallery at the entrance.

For those who want to avoid the busyness of the Forbidden City, this joins the Tài Miào in offering similar buildings of the same period in relative peace, if not on the same scale, and the wall around the compound screens out a surprising amount of street noise.

Built in 1534–6, the main hall, which has a number of shrubs growing out of its roof, sits on a single layer terrace and is mostly of stone and brick, constructed without beams or pillars, and thus is relatively fireproof. The main hall cannot now be entered, but inside there are 150 dusty camphorwood cabinets covered in gold-plated beaten copper sheets with a pattern of dragons. The chests held historical records, genealogies (important since the emperors had numerous sons), edicts, and a copy of the Yǒnglè Dàdiǎn encyclopaedia. Some of the chests have been roughly stacked in the right-hand stele pavilion as you face the building, which, as the gates behind you show, like almost all buildings of importance in China was originally approached from the south.

The side halls have mostly been converted into 'free art galleries', which, of course, means shops and you can sit under parasols in the courtyard drinking chilled drinks.

Běi Hǎi Gōngyuán (Běi Hǎi Park)　　　北海公园

Park open 6–9; adm ¥5; halls and temples open 9–4;
adm ¥10.

See map p.120, no.2. The ¥10 ticket is an all-inclusive *tào piào*, allowing access to the whole site. The main south entrance to the park is a few minutes' walk west of Jǐngshān Gōngyuán, and just northwest of the Forbidden City, and there's an east entrance in Jǐngshān Xī Jiē, a west entrance which is also on the south side just across the bridge from the main entrance, and a north entrance from Píng'ān Dà Dào.

This is the oldest section of the entire Imperial City. A lake called the 'North Sea' was first dug out and the artificial hills created during the Tartar Jīn dynasty in about 1179, and remodelled during the Yuán by Khubilai Khan (the white dagoba is mentioned by Marco Polo). Extensive buildings were added by the Míng emperor Yǒnglè during Běijīng's overall redesign, and it was further adapted by the Qīng emperors, particularly Qiánlóng. Originally of a piece with the Middle and South Seas (Zhōngnán Hǎi), this giant imperial pleasure ground was bisected by a road during the republic, and the southern section became the home of the president (although all three lakes were later opened to the public in 1925). The southern two lakes have now been separately enclosed as the 'new Forbidden City' of the modern emperors, but the Běi Hǎi is now a very popular park for local people, with boating activities (¥200 deposit and ¥20 for an hour) and radio-controlled model speedboats on the lake. It is not a place for quiet contemplation. In winter the lake was once guaranteed to freeze, but is now less predictable, though early photographs show skating scenes which would have attracted the brush of an oriental Brueghel, and winter visitors may see the same.

Inside the south entrance and just to the left, the **Tuánchéng** (Round City), in a mixed state of repair, is a raised circular terrace, topped with several small buildings. A pavilion contains an enormous jade urn, claimed to weigh 3,500 kilos, and carved with sea monsters on the outside and poetry on the inside. Used as a wine jar by Khubilai Khan, it was somehow purged during the Míng, and ended up as a pickling vat. Rediscovered and rehabilitated by Qiánlóng who bought it for 1,000 ounces of silver, it was placed in its present position in 1749. Also worth noting is the **Chéngguāng Diàn** (Hall for Receiving Light), which houses a 1½m-high statue of Buddha made from 'white jade' and which originated in Burma. There are several cypresses around the city thought to be as much as 800 years old.

The striking white flask-shaped dagoba, visible from various high points around Běijīng, was first built in 1651 by the first Qīng emperor to reign in Běijīng, Shùnzhì, in a style still common to Tibet and Mongolia to welcome a visit from Tibet by the Dalai Lama of the day, and stands atop an island reached by a bridge from near the south entrance. A steep climb through the halls of the **Yǒng'ān Sì** (Temple of Eternal Peace) leads to the dagoba, which was originally built in 1651 and twice reconstructed following earthquake damage. The temple buildings have bronze and wooden statues of Buddhas, bodhisattvas, arhats, Panchen and Dalai Lamas, as well as the guardian deity of Běijīng (who clearly hasn't been doing much of a job), and are said to be partly dedicated to the mythical empress who taught the Chinese sericulture. In front of the dagoba stands a small hall coated in ceramic tiles studded with Buddha heads.

Paths down the other side of the hill are confusing and often lead to dead ends, so it's best to return the way you came and walk around the base of the hill to find various other dotted pavilions, a stele with Qiánlōng's calligraphy from 1751 identifying this as one of his 'Eight Scenic Spots' and a long corridor around the north side, said have been beloved of Cīxī, passing the upmarket Fǎng Shàn ('copy meals') restaurant which has been reproducing banquets from the Imperial kitchens since 1964 (*see* 'Eating Out' p.261). The proletariat eats at the park's own branch of KFC on the south side of the island (until ejected in 2002).

Most visitors end their visits here, but the north shore of the lake has more to see and the walk up its east side is pleasant. You may see people using the flagstones as squared paper was once used for calligraphy, wielding giant brushes to fill each space with a single character then stepping back to do the next, and using water rather than ink.

The **north shore** has several series of halls of different purposes and dates. Approaching from the east the first is a favourite hall of Qiánlōng's with pools in front and behind, now containing exhibitions of period furniture and ceramics. A gallery at the rear runs behind and above a decorative rockery giving views down to the newly widened Píng'ān Dà Dào below and further lakes to the north. You can connect directly to a striking Míng unpainted two-storey cedarwood hall on a marble plinth, the Xiǎo Xī Tiān (Little Western Heaven) with a black roof with yellow trim, containing three Buddhas and 18 bronze arhats. Further west still a magnificent double-sided Nine Dragon Screen, worth coming to see in itself, once guarded the entrance of a temple which has disappeared, and beyond that a labyrinth of more halls and galleries.

Just behind the easternmost of the five fishing pavilions at the water's edge stands the Iron Screen of the Yuán Dynasty, which until modern times was to be found in a small *hútòng* named after it—a kind of igneous rock carved with strange creatures.

The most substantial structure was the 10,000 Buddha Tower whose destruction is blamed on foreign troops, but which was in fact destroyed in a fire in 1917. The site still has very large and fine tiled *páilou*, and the Dà Xī Tiān, or Large Western Heaven, is reached by bridges over a dry moat. It's an unusual, high-ceilinged square building containing a golden dragon towering over a garish hill of several layers, covered in plaster figures of Buddhist saints.

Leaving via the north gate and crossing Píng'ān Dà Dào brings you to the Back Lakes, which were outside the Imperial City, and a short walk will bring you to **Prince Gōng's Palace**, some pleasant walking in *hútòng* around the lakes, and other sights discussed in 'North, Around the Back Lakes' (*see* p.171).

South of Qián Mén—the Old Chinese City

Upon establishing their control over China in 1644 the Manchus took the main northern part of the city for themselves, relegating the Chinese mostly to the part south of the Qián Mén, which came to be known (to foreigners at least) as the Chinese City—the Chinese Quarter of Běijīng. Much of the city's best shopping was here, as well as various places of entertainment, key ceremonial altars, and, even up to the late 1940s, large areas of agricultural green space to the southeast and southwest, now long filled up with hideous modern construction. But the older area around Qián Mén has one of the best warrens of ancient *hútòng*, at least for now.

The city's principle daoist temple and main mosque are here, with a small Muslim quarter gathered around it, as well as what is viewed by many as the greatest glory of Míng architecture, the Hall of Prayer for Good Harvests at the Temple of Heaven, where the emperors came to make sacrifices and pray for abundant crops.

Today there's been a revival in the commercial activity for which the quarter was once famous, and Dàzhàlán Jiē, which runs west from Qián Mén Dàjiē not far south of Qián Mén, throngs with those looking for a bargain in cheap clothes and accessories, as well as tea, traditional medicine and other necessities, in shops with late Qīng-era fronts and modern interiors, several claiming histories of hundreds of years. Liúlichǎng is another more or less pedestrianized street recreated in an earlier style to please the visitor, with two-storey traditional buildings selling antiques, 'antiques', curios, bric-à-brac, art, artists' materials and books. This is worth a browse of an hour or two although it's too well known to the mass of visitors to be good value for shopping. Beware the plethora of credit card stickers in the windows, and look at the other main antique and curios markets, which are all in this area (*see* 'Shopping', p.227).

The city-wide renovations of 1999 took out the half moon of ramshackle stores around the Zhèngyáng Mén towers that once formed the main gate between the Tartar and Chinese cities, and replaced them with two-storeyed late 20th-century Qīng architecture, but this prettification is merely skin-deep and a few metres back the crowded and earthy *hútòng* begin, with street markets, tiny mosques, lean-to stores, restaurants and some budget accommodation.

Forbidden Pleasures

Just as I was getting into my rickshaw I heard him engage another to take him to Ch'ien Mên Wai! At some other time Ch'ien Mên Wai might have meant anywhere at all beyond the great central gate leading into the southern part of the city; but so late at night, with the shops shut, the restaurants closed and the operas drawing to their noisy climax, it clearly meant that Pao was bound for the lanes of 'flowers and willows' where people go only to enjoy the companionship of courtesans and the pleasures of 'clouds and rain'.

John Blofeld, *City of Lingering Splendour,* 1961

In the early days of the Republic, before President Yuán Shìkǎi decided to remount the throne and the National Assembly still met, there was a discussion as to what allowances for expenses should be given to its members. The foreign-run *Peking Daily*

News gleefully suggested a long list which would not be inappropriate for many cadres (officials) today, including the latest carriage, and immense sums for feasting and drinking, mistresses and prostitutes. The Chinese press, which clearly found none of this surprising, reported with approval that a bell-ringer was sent daily round the Qián Mén brothels to call the members back to their duties.

The detailed accounts of Blofeld and others suggest that while facilities at these houses, which came in three grades, might be modest, at best the girls were highly educated and knowledgeable, and had a limited number of long-term customers who came to them for their wit and culture, as well as for other services, and a certain courtship was necessary before these were made available. There are many accounts in novels and memoirs of groups of foreigners who, in the company of some Mandarin-speaking friend, went to the lanes just as 'tea guests', which meant that they were given fleeting introductions to the house's pool of talent—the 'flowers and willows'—without moving on to any activity requiring meteorological metaphors. Blofeld himself apparently took on the role of guide on more than one occasion, and appears as such in others' books.

In a society in which unwanted daughters were often sold, the picture of the happy, pampered, cultured courtesan must have been a tiny part of a truth less palatable as a whole, as some of Blofeld's companions admitted. The new communist rulers of China decided that prostitutes were most exploited class of all, and engineered an upswell of demand for their emancipation on which they could then righteously take action. The girls were rounded up and sent for re-education. Once another triumph of socialist progress had been announced and a propaganda victory scored, many went back to their old profession, albeit more independently. Today less decorous prostitution is commonplace, and its 'return', as well as the increase in divorce and the keeping of mistresses, is blamed on Western 'spiritual pollution', as if the Chinese' supposed '5,000 years of culture' hadn't included at least 4,950 of legal polygamy, concubine-keeping, and, just like other cultures, prostitution.

The new rich (*dà kuǎn*) graze on the meadows of young girls who are always at the bottom of the income ladder, who face increasing difficulties with employment as state-run enterprises are shut down, but who are desperate for the formerly forbidden glittering girly goodies the new economy has brought to the shelves of shops. Becoming some rich punk's *xiǎo mì* (little honey) is one way to achieve this.

Why, you may wonder as you wander the *hútòng* here and in other parts of the city, do there seem to be almost as many hairdressing salons in Běijīng as there are heads of hair to cut? For the working class, the question, 'Have you had your hair cut recently?' may have more than one meaning.

Underground City (Dìxia Chéng) 地下城

Open 8.30–5; adm ¥20.

See map p.156–7, no.44. From ⓜ Qián Mén walk east on the south side of Qián Mén Dōng Dàjiē and turn first right into Zhèngyì Lù. At the end turn right and then left following the English sign towards the Lìjùn Roast Duck restaurant, left at the T-junction and you'll find the entrance along on the right. Alternatively at the bottom of Zhèngyì Lù turn left, first right, then left at the T. The 'City' is below Xī Dǎmóchǎng Jiē 62.

N

XIZHONG HUTONG

BEI XINHUA JIE

43 ▲35 B L
47 ▣ H
M XUANWU MEN DONG DJ
10 ● M XUANWU MEN XI JIE
● CHANGCHUN JIE ● H HOU HE YAN AB LANGFANG TOUTIAO
A I

NAN XINHUA JIE

34
17 ▣
LIULICHANG
XI JIE
24 ▣

XUANWU MEN XI DAJIE

LIANHUA CHI DONG LU

7

40

2

GUANG'AN MEN WAI DAJIE

GUANG'AN MEN NEI DAJIE
LUOMA SHI DJ
21 ●
6

HUFANG LU

23
GUANG'AN LU

MALIAN DAO LU

GUANG'AN MEN BIN HE LU

NIU JIE
30 15
SHALAN HUTONG

25

37

NAN CAI YUAN JIE

E
M 18
13
YOU'AN MEN XI JIE

YOU'AN MEN DONG JIE
YOU'AN MEN XI BIN HE LU

26
FENGTAI BEI LU

W H 48
3

XI SAN HUAN NAN LU

NAN SAN HUAN XI LU

S

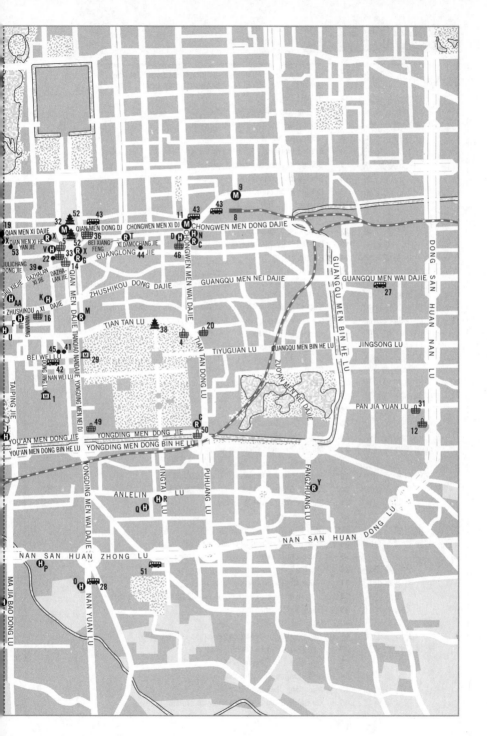

先农坛，北京	1	Altar of Agriculture and Museum of Ancient Architecture (Xiānnóng Tán, Běijīng Gǔdài Jiànzhù Bówùguǎn)
报国寺	2	Bàoguó Sì
北京南站	3	Běijīng Nán Zhàn (south station)
北京市园林花卉市场	4	Běijīng Shì Yuánlín Huāhuì Shìchǎng
北京丝绸商店	5	Běijīng Sīchóu Shāngdiàn
北京工人俱乐部	6	Běijīng Workers' Club (Běijīng Gōngrén Jùlèbù)
北京西站	7	Běijīng Xī Zhàn (west station)
北京站	8	Běijīng Zhàn (station)
北京站	9	Běijīng Zhàn Metro
长春街	10	Chángchūn Jiē Metro
崇文门	11	Chóngwén Mén Metro
古玩城	12	Curio City (Gǔwán Chéng)
大观园	13	Dà Guān Yuán (Grand View Garden—south gate)
大栅栏街	14	Dà Zhàlán Jiē
法源寺	15	Fǎyuán Sì
甘肃临下飞马毛纺地毯专营店	16	Gānsù Línxià Fēimǎ Máofǎng Dìtǎn Zhuānyíngdiàn (Línxià Flying Horse Carpet Co. Ltd)
观复古典艺术博物馆	17	Guānfù Classic Art Museum (Guānfù Gǔdiǎn Yìshù Bówùguǎn)
古陶文明博物院	18	Gǔ Táo Wénmíng Bówùguǎn (Museum of Ancient Pottery Civilisation)
和平门	19	Hépíng Mén Metro
红桥集贸市场	20	Hóng Qiáo Jímào Shìchǎng
湖广会馆古戏楼，北京戏曲博物馆	21	Huguang Guildhall, Traditional Opera Museum (Húguǎng Huìguǎn Gǔ Xìlóu, Běijīng Xìqǔ Bówùguǎn)
北京博宏公司	22	Internet Café Běijīng Bohong Co. Ltd.
莲花池长途汽车站	23	Liánhuā Chí Chángtú Qìchē Zhàn
琉璃厂	24	Liúlichǎng
六里桥长途客运站	25	Liù Lǐ Qiáo Chángtú Kèyùn Zhàn
丽泽桥汽车站	26	Lízé Qiáo Chángtú Qìchē Zhàn
马圈长途汽车站	27	Mǎjuàn Chángtú Qìchē Zhàn
木樨园长途汽车站	28	Mùxī Yuán Chángtú Qìchē Zhàn
自然博物馆	29	Natural History Museum (Zìrán Bówùguǎn)
牛街清真寺	30	Niú Jiē Qīngzhēnsì ('Cow Street Mosque')
潘家园旧货市场	31	Pān Jiā Yuán Jiù Huò Shìchǎng
前门	32	Qián Mén Metro
前门邮品市场	33	Qián Mén Yóu Pǐn Shìchǎng
庄胜崇光百货	34	Sogo (Zhuāngshèng Chóngguāng Bǎihuò)
南堂	35	South Church (Nán Táng)
老车站商场	36	The Station (Lǎo Chē Zhàn Shāngchǎng)
陶然亭公园	37	Táorántíng Gōngyuán (north gate)
天坛公园	38	Temple of Heaven Park (Tiān Tán Gōngyuán—north gate)
天海美食厅	39	Tiān Hǎi Měi Shí Tīng
天宁寺	40	Tiānníng Sì
天桥乐茶馆	41	Tiānqiáo Happy Teahouse (Tiānqiáo Lè Cháguǎn)
天桥长途汽车站	42	Tiān Qiáo Chángtú Qìchē Zhàn
	43	Tour buses to outside Běijīng
地下城	44	Underground City (Dìxia Chéng)
万胜剧场	45	Wànshèng Jùchǎng (acrobatics)
新世界百货	46	Xīn Shìjiè Bǎihuò (New World Department Store)

宣武门	47	Xuānwǔ Mén Metro
永定门长途汽车站	48	Yǒngdìng Mén Chángtú Qìchē Zhàn
元隆丝绸股份有限司	49	Yuánlóng Sīchóu Gǔfèn Yǒuxiànsī (silk shop)
玉蜓花鸟市场	50	Yùtíng Huā Niǎo Shìchǎng (bird market)
赵公口长途客运汽车站	51	Zhàogōng Kǒu Chángtú Kèyùn Qìchē Zhàn
正阳门	52	Zhèngyáng Mén towers
正乙祠剧场	53	Zhèngyǐcí Theatre (Zhèngyǐcí Jùchǎng)

Hotels and Restaurants

八方来客宾馆	A	Bāfāng Lái Kè Bīnguǎn
北京宁波宾馆	B	Běijīng Níngbō Bīnguǎn
便宜坊烤鸭店	C	Biànyifāng Kǎoyādiàn
崇文门饭店	D	Chóngwén Mén Fàndiàn
大观园酒店	E	Dà Guān Yuán Jiǔdiàn (Grand View Garden Hotel)
东方饭店	F	Dōngfāng Fàndiàn
都一处烧麦馆	G	Dūyīchù Shāomàiguǎn
飞鹰宾馆	I	Fēiyīng Bīnguǎn
凤龙宾馆	J	Fènglóng Bīnguǎn ('Youth Hostel')
丰泽园饭店	K	Fēngzé Yuán Fàndiàn
格兰云天大酒店	L	Gélányún Tiān Dàjiǔdiàn (Grand Skylight Hotel)
功德林饭庄	M	Gōngdélín Fànzhuāng
哈德门饭店	N	Hademen Hotel (Hādé Mén Fàndiàn)
海兴大酒店	O	Hǎixīng Dàjiǔdiàn (Sea Star Hotel)
京华饭店	P	Jīnghuá Fàndiàn
景泰宾馆	Q	Jǐngtài Bīnguǎn
凯华宾馆	R	Kǎihuá Bīnguǎn
丽华饭店	S	Lìhuá Fàndiàn
利群烤鸭店	T	Lìqún Kǎoyādiàn
前门饭店，梨园剧场	U	Qián Mén Hotel (Qián Mén Fàndiàn) and Líyuán Theatre (Líyuán Jùchǎng)
前新宾馆	V	Qiánxīn Bīnguǎn
侨园饭店	W	Qiáoyuán Fàndiàn
全聚德烤鸭店	X	Quánjùdé Kǎoyādiàn
昌泰苑	Y	Thai Garden (Chāng Tài Yuàn)
文轩宾馆	Z	Wénxuān Bīnguǎn
远东饭店	AA	Yuǎn Dōng Fàndiàn (Far East Hotel)
越秀大酒店	AB	Yuèxiù Dàjiǔdiàn

Street Names and Bus Stops

安乐林路	Ānlèlín Lù	东经路	Dōng Jīng Lù
北纬路	Běi Wěi Lù	东三环南路	Dōng Sān Huán Nán Lù (east third ring)
北翔风	Běi Xiáng Fēng		
北新华街	Běi Xīnhuá Jiē	方庄路东	Fāngzhuāng Lù
长春街	Chángchūn Jiē	丰台北路	Fēngtái Běi Lù
崇文门西、东大街	Chóngwén Mén Xī/Dōng Dàjiē	广安路	Guǎng'ān Lù
		广安门滨河路	Guǎng'ān Mén Bīn Hé Lù (second ring)
崇文门外大街	Chóngwén Mén WàiDàjiē	广安门内、外大街	Guǎng'ān Mén Nèi/Wài Dàjiē
大观园	Dà Guān Yuán		
大栅栏街、西街	Dàzhàlán Jiē/Xī Jiē	光隆街	Guǎnglóng Jiē
大栅栏	Dàzhàlán	光明路	Guāngmíng Lù
定安路	Dìng'ān Lù	广渠门滨河路	Guǎngqú Mén Bīn Hé Lù (second ring)

Street Names and Bus Stops

广渠门内大街	Guǎngqú Mén Wài Dàjiē	沙栏胡同	Shālán Hútòng
后河沿	Hòu Hé Yán	太平街	Tàipíng Jiē
虎坊路	Hǔfáng Lù	天桥	Tiān Qiáo
劲松路	Jìngsōng Lù	天桥南大街	Tiānqiáo Nándàjiē
景泰路	Jǐngtài Lù	天坛（东）路	Tiān Tán (Dōng) Lù
廊房头条	Lángfáng Tóutiáo	铁树斜街	Tiěshù Xiéjiē
莲花池东路	Liánhuā Chí Dōng Lù	体育馆路	Tǐyùguǎn Lù
琉璃厂西东街	Liúlichǎng Xī/Dōng Jiē	万明路	Wànmíng Lù
琉璃井	Liúlijǐng	西打磨厂街	Xī Dǎmóchǎng Jiē
骡马市大街	Luómǎ Shì Dàjiē	西三环南路	Xī Sān Huán Nán Lù (third ring)
马家堡东路	Mǎ Jiā Pù Dōng Lù		
马连道路	Mǎlián Dào Lù	西中胡同	Xīzhōng Hútòng
南菜园街	Nán Cài Yuán Jiē	宣武门西、东大街	Xuānwǔ Mén Xī/Dōng Dàjiē
南三环西、中、东路	Nán Sān HuánXī/Zhōng/Dōng Lù (south third ring)	洋桥	Yáng Qiáo
南纬路	Nán Wěi Lù	永安路	Yǒng'ān Lù
南新华街	Nán Xīnhuá Jiē	永定门内、外大街	Yǒngdìng Mén Nèi/Wài Dàjiē
南苑路	Nán Yuàn Lù	永定门东滨河路	Yǒngdìng Mén Dōng Bīn Hé Lù (second ring)
牛街	Niú Jiē	永定门西、东街	Yǒngdìng Mén Xī/Dōng Jiē
牛街礼拜寺	Niú Jiē Lǐbài Sì	右安门西、东滨河路	Yòu'ān Mén Xī/Dōng Bīn Hé Lù (second ring)
潘家园路	Pān Jiā Yuán Lù	右安门西、东街	Yòu'ān Mén Xī/Dōng Jiē
蒲皇榆	Púhuángyú	正义路	Zhèngyì Lù
蒲皇榆路	Púhuángyú Lù	珠宝市	Zhūbǎo Shì
前门大街	Qián Mén Dàjiē	珠市口西、东大街	Zhūshìkǒu Xī/Dōng Dàjiē
前门西、东大街	Qián Mén Xī/Dōng Dàjiē	左安门内大街	Zuǒ'ān Mén Nèi Dàjiē
前门西河沿街	Qián Mén Xī Hé Yán Jiē		

Following the beginning of border conflict with the former USSR in the northeast's Hēilóngjiāng Province, Máo ordered the urban populace across China to dig tunnels in which they could either hide or through which they could escape to the suburbs. Those brought up in the '60s spent time after school 'volunteering' their assistance with this and similar projects, such as tearing down the city's walls. The labyrinth created under Běijīng was once accessible from many points throughout the city, and in the '70s and '80s no foreigner's visit was complete without being shown a hidden trapdoor at the rear of a Wángfǔjǐng or Xī Dān shop, one of many through which it was boasted that the entire population of Běijīng could get underground in three minutes. There was even an underground hotel in operation, which accepted foreign guests at a time when the list of hotels that did was much shorter than today. But the construction of large modern buildings with deeper foundations has penetrated, blocked or destroyed much of the warren, although in theory special permission is still needed before tunnels can be closed.

At the same time army engineers were instructed to build a vast secret underground complex for the Party leaders, with a sub-surface highway large enough for four lorries abreast connecting Zhōng Nán Hǎi, the Great Hall of the People and various other central points with a military command centre in the Western Hills. Visitors to Bā Dà Chù (*see* p.332) will still note the large number of military camps, and indeed this area was off-limits to visitors until relatively recently. The complex had offices and its own hospital, which was where Máo's body was taken for embalming.

At this particular entrance the stairs down at first have the atmosphere of a Victorian public toilet, but passages bring you quite soon to a map of the complex, and past the odd pick and shovel of the kind used to excavate the tunnels, and a section with a stuccoed ceiling and Máo slogans on the wall. Beyond intriguing side turnings used for storage (one has a Christmas tree) and past some vaguely religious display, you reach the end, which seems disappointingly to be a large underground space containing a souvenir shop.

The interesting part is in the far right-hand corner, however, which is the entrance to a series of narrow, dank and dimly lit passages (once the *fúwùyuán* turns on the lights). 'Come back here,' she says, and the meaning of this becomes clear as you pass unlit turnings signposted to familiar points such as Běijīng Station, Tiān'ān Mén, Tiān Tán and beyond. Large steel doors with rusty handles stand ready to block the path of invaders, ancient electrical and telephone cables dangle from the ceilings, and there's odd detritus on the floor, while the dust deadens footfalls as the light fades down the side turnings. It's all rather creepy, and a more fitting monument to Máo than the mausoleum in Tiān'ān Mén Square.

The official illuminated route brings you round in a five-minute circle, but the *fúwùyuán* say if you took one of the turnings you could pop up elsewhere, although that seems unlikely, the air seeming dead (although there's a slight breeze from the Běijīng Station direction). Certainly the once popular entrances at Xī Dan and Wángfǔjǐng have disappeared due to so much new building, but if you brought a torch you could investigate further—at your own risk.

Temple of Heaven Park (Tiān Tán Gōngyuán)　天坛公园

Open 6am–8pm, longer in summer; adm ¥14.

See map p.156–7, no.38. You can buy a ticket for the park alone (*mén piào*, ¥4), but the ¥14 all-inclusive ticket (*tào piào*) allows access to all the halls without further charge. The park can be entered from the north (trolleybus 106 from Dōngdān Běi Dàjiē or Běijīng Nán Zhàn—stop Tiān Tán Běi Mén), west (bus 17, 2 and 20 from the west side of Qián Mén—stop Tiān Qiáo), bus no.120 to Qián Mén Tiān'ān Mén and Wángfǔjǐng, and Běijīng Zhàn Kǒu at the top of the short road opposite the station main entrance.

> *Of all Peking's enchanting sights, the beauty of the Altar of Heaven is the hardest to describe. Its sublime austerity is mocked by words. It is what it is—the most fitting architectual expression of man's highest aspirations in the world.*

John Blofeld, *City of Lingering Splendour*, 1961

Blofeld thought even the Taj Mahal would look fussy and tawdry in comparison. In the 1930s he had the luxury of viewing the deserted altar under snow, with just a few equally appreciative Chinese friends for company. In 1934 Sir Osbert Sitwell thought the altar, 'one of the chief objects of beauty in the whole of the Orient', but expected that due to its extreme simplicity it would disappear within the space of a few years. The great trees in the surrounding land had already been hacked down for firewood by soldiers and peasants, and the temples were being used as offices and a police station. However, he was but repeating the views of the guidebook to which he frequently refers, Arlington and Lewisohn's *In Search of Old Peking*.

Tiān Tán was constructed at the same period as the Forbidden City by the Míng emperor Yŏnglè and completed in around 1420. Tiān Tán actually means 'Altar of Heaven', and it was the site of the emperors' winter solstice sacrifices and prayers for a good harvest, and as much off-limits to ordinary Chinese as the Forbidden City itself. Now it's a recreational facility for the local *lǎobǎixìng* ('old hundred names'—ordinary people) who fly kites, practise *tàijīquán* and martial arts, sing opera and play traditional musical instruments—activities which tend to add to the attraction for the foreign visitor, especially since there's less of the funfair rides and piped music of other parks. The buildings, altars and enclosures have the themes of earth, signified by square shapes, and heaven, signified by round ones. The outer wall of Tiān Tán Gōngyuán is square on the south side and rounded on the north, and some of the interior enclosures follow the same plan.

So important were the rites performed here, that when at the winter solstice of 1915 President of the Republic Yuán Shìkǎi revived them and went to the altar to perform them himself, it was taken as a clear public announcement of his intention to place himself on the imperial throne. As imperial tutor Reginald Johnston sardonically remarked, 'Unfortunately the ceremony was shorn of much of its traditional beauty and stateliness by the fact that Yuán thought it necessary to ensure his own safety by proceeding from the palace to the Altar of Heaven in an armoured car.'

Entering from the north, the first major building is the perfectly circular **Qínián Diàn** (Hall of Prayer for Good Harvests) which is possibly the most beautiful ancient building in Běijīng. Painted in blue, green and gold and with its ground floor surrounded by red latticed doors, the triple-layered roofs are a deep blue, reflecting its heavenly focus, and topped with a large gold knob. It stands on a triple-layered marble terrace and is heavily decorated both internally and externally, a superb dragon-phoenix relief in the centre of the ceiling being mirrored by a natural marble circular slab on the floor. The hall is entirely constructed of wood, supposedly without the use of nails, and its roof is supported by 28 pillars, including four of particularly massive girth, all made from single tree trunks. It was struck by lightning and burned down in 1889, and has been restored several times following its rebuild. The original timber for the main pillars came from Yúnnán province, but the Chinese prefer you not to know that the 19th-century replacements came from Oregon, since by then China no longer had tall enough trees. The hall was used for displaying the tablets of the emperor's ancestors, and for cere-monies before he proceeded to the sacrificial altar. You can stand at the doors, but only swallows enter now, and perform acrobatics around the pillars of the interior, just as they do at a similar building in Chéngdé (*see* p.373).

Small halls on the east and west sides of the compound were once used for the worship of various weather-influencing gods, but now the one to the east houses a small exhibition of Chinese traditional musical instruments, and a model of a Chinese orchestra in full swing with recorded accompaniment. The west one is a gift shop.

Just south of here a path leads to the west entrance and to the **Zhāi Gōng** or Palace of Abstinence, where the emperor, who fasted for three days, spent the night before the ceremo-nial sacrifice. The palace is like a Forbidden City in miniature, walled and moated (although the moat is now dry), and inside you can see a model of an emperor duly abstaining. During the occupation of Běijīng by the forces of the eight allied powers in 1901, this building was the British headquarters, and the emperor's personal apartments became the sleeping quarters of the British officers. In the northeast corner there is a two-storey bell tower, built in 1742, and you can pay ¥1 to climb the short but very narrow staircase and strike the bell.

Returning to the Hall of Prayer for Good Harvests, a broad, raised walk leads south to the second main group of buildings. The **Huángqióngyǔ** (Imperial Vault of Heaven), a lower, round building used for storing material used in the ceremony, is enclosed in a perfectly circular wall. This is said to function in the same way as the Whispering Gallery at St Paul's, London, or that at the Duomo in Florence, reflecting the sound of words spoken near the wall to listeners also near it but some distance away or even on the opposite side of the enclosure. Visitors who have been a few days in China may already be wondering whether there is such a person as a quiet Chinese, and it is impossible to find the conditions to test the effect. Once local visitors pressed their ears against the wall itself making it impossible to hear the effect, but now they are (theoretically) prevented from doing so by a fence. Instead they shout loudly enough at it to ensure that their voices are heard on the other side of Běijīng, let alone the other side of the compound.

Leading from the base of the stairs to the hall is a row of three stones. To stand on one and clap produces the expected single echo, but to repeat the action on the second produces two echoes, and the third three. The compound is full day-long of the sound of desultory applause as many experiment, and none gives way to the others. To have a chance to experience the ghostly acoustics of such circular enclosures, visit the Western Qīng Tombs (*see* p.318).

The final major feature is the **Huán Qiū** (usually known as the Circular Mound, although the *huán* character is not the one for *ring*, but for *mediate*). This, not the visitor-attracting Hall of Prayer, was the focus of the site (Tiān Tán means '*Altar* of Heaven'), where the complicated three-part ceremony of supplication took place, culminating with the burning of a bullock killed earlier. The multiple-layered round altar is enclosed in both round and square walls, symbolizing the earth's appeal to heaven. Buildings to the east held the sacrificial implements, the tents that covered the ceremony itself, and were where the butchering of the animals took place.

Tiān Tán is one of several altars with different purposes at the five compass points around Běijīng (the centre, from the Chinese point of view, being the fifth point), but the only one whose site and attendant buildings have remained largely intact. The foreign-built railway line from Tiānjīn ran right up to its west gate for a while, and the British forces of the multinational army that relieved the legations in 1900 camped there. In 1917, a brief attempt to restore the Qīng dynasty ended bloodily here, and later the Republican government set up a radio station and a medical laboratory in the grounds. According to the Chinese press it was subsequently used as the headquarters of a germ warfare unit during the Japanese occupation.

The Altar of Heaven was the most important of the five Míng-built altars at Běijīng's five compass points, including the Altar of the Moon (Yuè Tán) at the west, the Altar of the Earth to the north (Dì Tán, *see* p.196), of the Sun to the east (Rì Tán, *see* p.199), Tiān Tán to the south and the Altar of Land and Grain in the centre, also regarded as a compass point, in Zhōngshān Park (*see* p.151). There's also the Altar of Agriculture neighbouring Tiān Tán to the west (*see* below), and one brand new communist construction, the China Century Altar of 1999, just behind the Chinese People's Revolutionary Army Museum (*see* p.211).

The Temple of Heaven site is surrounded by other attractions: the Yùtíng Huā Niǎo Shìchǎng flower and bird market on the southeast and Yuánlōng Sīchóu Gǔfèn Yǒuxiànsī silk store on the southwest side (*see* 'Silk' p.232), the Hóng Qiáo Jíhuo Shìchǎng antiques market and Běijīng Shì Yuánlín Huāhuì Shìchǎng for garden-size ceramics at the northeast side (*see* 'Markets', p.236). To the west, the performances at the Tiānqiáo Happy Teahouse (*see* p.273) or acrobatics at the Wànshèng Jùchǎng (*see* p.276) may attract you in the evening, and the Natural History Museum (*see* p.165) is also close to the west entrance. A short walk away the Altar of Agriculture is a recommended quiet alternative to the Temple of Heaven's crowds. There are plenty of standard restaurants around the west entrance, and a lesser-known branch of the Biànyīfāng roast duck restaurant can be found by walking east from the south gate to the southeast corner of the site.

Altar of Agriculture 先农坛，北京古代建筑博物馆
and Museum of Ancient Architecture (Xiānnóng Tán, Běijīng Gǔdài Jiànzhù Bówùguǎn)

Open 9–4; closed Fri; adm ¥10, annual ticket accepted.

See map p.156–7, no.1. Take bus 15 from Xī Dān or Liúlichǎng, getting off at stop Nán Wěi Lù (but if you miss this get off at the terminus and walk back). The site can be reached on foot from Tiān Tán west entrance in about 10mins, or from Liúlichǎng in about 20mins, and the Opera Museum (*see* p.166) in about 15mins. Walk south down Dōng Jīng Lù to a crumbling gate, and the entrance to the museum is down on the right.

Unlike at Tiān Tán, this site has been considerably reduced by modern construction, and once had four altars and several sets of buildings for offerings to different gods.

In a superstitious ceremony dating back to the Sòng, but formalized by the Míng and Qīng and carried out at this site from 1410, the emperor himself, in honour of the first agriculturalist, and to encourage the peasants to be good farmers (although none of them would have been able to see this), would drive a plough to cut eight furrows. Senior city officials carried whips, broadcast seed and cut further furrows, while the emperor watched from a terrace which still exists in the southeast corner of the site along with a hall he used for changing to special leather clothes for the ceremony, now surrounded by sheds and parked cars, right next to a kindergarten and ankle-deep in ducklings.

Much of the rest has been destroyed in modern times (although there's recently been talk of spending a vast sum on rebuilding), and the other altars built on and forgotten. Various store rooms for equipment used in the ceremonies (all yellow in the emperor's case) and halls where the empress waited for the emperor to finish playing farmer, are also now covered in factories, accommodation and an infants' school. However, the halls for sacrifices to Jupiter, the 'Year God', which took place at the end of each year, still stand, and the main hall is particularly magnificent, now containing an excellent exhibition on traditional Chinese architecture which provides a good introduction to what you'll see in Běijīng and elsewhere.

The exhibition contains a history of Chinese architectural method from early earthworks to the construction of major halls. Detailed models show the interior workings of the complicated bracket sets (*dǒugǒng*) which hold up the roofs of every ancient building you enter in China, and are sometimes imitated in brick and stone in memorial archways and elsewhere. While there are some outrageous claims for China's first invention of or exclusive use of some techniques, there are plenty of English explanations, and free English-speaking guides if you wish (many other museums in China could learn something here). Diagrams and explanations of social background include material on the role of geomancy (*fēngshuǐ*) in traditional buildings, the use of mathematics in building construction, and discussions of the use of form, colour, decoration and different jointing methods.

In the second hall, on your left as you proceed, there's a reproduction of a Hàn dynasty tomb (*see also* Dàbǎotái Hàn Tomb, p.323) and a table model of the Míng Tombs (Shísān Líng, *see* p.309), and from the Qīng a model of Dowager Empress Cíxǐ's tomb (Eastern Qīng Tombs, *see* p.313). There are other displays on minority architecture, drum stones, *sìhéyuàn*, and more.

The rearmost hall, the **Tàisuì Diàn** or Hall of Jupiter, the Year God, was built later than much of the site in 1532, and is only exceeded in scale by the main Hall of Supreme Harmony in the Forbidden City. Keeping to a calendrical theme, halls to either side were for the gods of the four seasons and the twelve months. The Hall of Jupiter has substantial models of significant buildings still surviving in China, and fragments of ones now vanished, including the caisson ceiling of the Lóngfú Sì, once famous for its temple fair, and now the site of a large store with a token temple on top (*see* p.234), and others never likely to be open to the public, such as the 'double ring' pavilion inside the Zhōng Nán Hǎi government compound (although two buildings removed from there can be seen at Táoràntíng Gōngyuán, *see* p.166).

There's a detailed survey of religious buildings, which are what you'll spend much of your time in China looking at, including an introduction to the evolution of the Buddhist pagoda (*see also* 'Stupa, Dagoba, *Chorten*, or Pagoda?' p.208), and various altars and ancestral temples. An enormous table model, the largest in Běijīng, shows the city's plan in 1949, including the foreign-built railway line, the fortified Legation Quarter and the locations of various long-disappeared temples and *páilou*.

Natural History Museum (Zìrán Bówùguǎn)　　自然博物馆

Open 9–4.30; adm ¥15.

See map pp.156–7, no.29. The museum is just north of the west entrance of Tiān Tán, directly south of Qián Mén.

The museum became briefly notorious amongst budget travellers with a love of the ghoulish, when it was discovered that the upper floors had pickled people's parts of the kind usually only on show to those attending teaching hospitals in the rest of the world. These have now been removed from display. There's a small aquarium in the basement, a display of skulls together with photographs of the sites where they were found, stuffed animals and dinosaur skeletons (the children of China are as excited about tyrannosaurus rex as those of any other country). They may be amused by the second-rate animatronic dinosaurs with public address system roars, including one t. rex which goes for you as you enter, and a smaller dinosaur which cries out for help in Mandarin as it is being eaten.

The Tiān Qiáo (Heaven Bridge) area just north of the museum was once a lively but dubious market area with food stalls and acrobatic street performers. Now the acrobatics and other street performances have gone indoors, and the prices have gone up (*see* 'Entertainment, Culture and Nightlife', p.276).

Táorántíng Gōngyuán

Open approx. 6am–10pm; park adm ¥1, pavilion adm ¥4.

陶然亭公园

See map pp.156–7, no.37. Bus 102 comes down here from the Zoo via Xī Dān, to stop Tàipíng Jiē, which is at the park's northeast corner. Bus 59 comes from Qián Mén.

The park only dates from 1952, and is named for a pavilion at the southern edge of an island in the middle of one of its lakes, the 'Happy and Carefree Pavilion' which originally dates from 1695, and was itself named from a line in a Táng dynasty poem. The park is now filled with children and with devices for making them sick: funfair rides, water slides, and a boating lake (clogged with boats shaped like cars apparently dating from the time before real life dodgems were an everyday hazard). There's also a peafowl enclosure.

The southwest corner of the park has two pavilions moved from the Zhōng Nán Hǎi government compound and a collection of copies of famous pavilions from elsewhere in China. The Táorántíng itself is part of a group of buildings including a convent, which also have a revolutionary history and is described as 'the most famous of the four famous pavilions in China'. It originally dates from 1695 when it was built by the supervisor of the imperial kiln, and one of the halls in the adjacent Temple of Mercy, a former convent, is said to date from the Mongol Yuán dynasty (1279–1368). There's a rare even earlier relic from the Liáo dynasty in the form of an inscribed pillar.

There was considerable secret revolutionary activity here from 1925, and both Zhōu Ēnlái and Máo Zédōng were photographed under scholar trees which no longer exist but which have been replaced with transplants. There are minor exhibitions of stelae and carved stones, mixing oddly with another of revolutionary photographs, and a shop selling revolutionary memorabilia—not as popular as it once was, since the masses can now have more choice where they shop and what for.

Húguǎng Guildhall, Traditional Opera Museum (Húguǎng Huìguǎn, Běijīng Xìqǔ Bówùguǎn)

湖广会馆，北京戏曲博物馆

Open 9–11 and 3–7.15; adm ¥10, annual ticket accepted.

See map pp.156–7, no.21. Also sometimes known as the Húguǎng Huìguǎn Gǔ Xìlóu (Húguǎng Guildhall Ancient Theatre), the building is a short walk south down Nán Xīnhuá Jiē from the Liúlichǎng antiques street, on the southwest corner of the junction with Zhūshìkǒu Xī/Dōng Dàjiē. It can be reached in about 15mins on foot south from Ⓜ Hépíng Mén, one stop west of Ⓜ Qián Mén on the circle line. It's also near the western end of the *hútòng* continuation of Dàzhàlán Jiē (*see* 'Shopping streets', p.236). The museum closes when performances start in the evenings.

This is one of the last remaining of Běijīng's more than 400 guildhalls, formerly meeting places and temporary residences for people from the same province, county or city, or who practised the same trade. The museum is entered from the east side, and the box office for performances, along with a Shāndōng restaurant, is found on the north side.

Built in 1807, the hall was converted to a theatre with a capacity of about 300 in 1875, then renovated and reopened in 1996. The two-storey side hall with the museum has paperwork and photographs downstairs, and costumes, instruments and props upstairs, along with a group portrait of seven performers including Méi Lánfāng on the right (*see* p.179). Several old 78s displayed are on the Victor label with the HMV dog, no doubt drawn to the horn on this occasion by the very high-pitched sounds.

The theatre is a big square space and impressive, with the usual arrangement of square tables at the stalls level, and surrounding balconies. Sun Yat-sen held a Nationalist Party meeting here in 1912 and gave speeches at other times.

Běijīng is famous for having only 'bitter water', but the well inside one pavilion on the site traditionally has 'sweet water', but only at exactly 2pm. One courtyard doubles as an aviary, with parrots, peacocks, finches, and two extraordinary brown and white relatives of the mynah which fluff up their feathers, bow, and greet you in English and Chinese, 'Hello, *ní hǎo, ní hǎo*'.

For details on booking to see opera performances here and elsewhere, *see* 'Běijīng opera', p.274. Those with a stong interest in opera or theatre architecture might want to try and get into the **Zhèngyǐcí Theatre** (Zhèngyǐcí Jùchǎng—same page), which is a beautifully restored Míng dynasty theatre, more than 340 years old, not too far away in Qián Mén Xī Hé Yán Jiē, a *hútòng* to your right as you walk north, immediately before you reach ⑩ Hépíng Mén. This is occasionally open to visitors in the daytime for ¥5. Also visit Méi Lánfāng's house (*see* p.179), and the Guǎngdōng Guildhall and Theatre Museum in Tiānjīn (*see* p.345).

Guānfù Classic Art Museum (Guānfù Gǔdiǎn Yìshù Bówùguǎn) 观复古典艺术博物馆

Open 9.30–5.30; adm ¥20; annual ticket accepted.

See map pp.156–7, no.17. The museum is in the antiques shopping street of Liúlichǎng Xī Jiē, no. 53, on the north side of the street. Walk south from ⑩ Hépíng Mén and turn left (west).

It claims to be the first registered private museum in China and is one of four private museums in Běijīng, including the Gǔ Táo Wénmíng Bówùguǎn (Museum of Ancient Pottery Civilisation, *see* p.171). Both of these have connections with shops, but both have genuine museum functions, and excellent displays. The Classic Art Museum is run by the long-standing Guānfù Antique Furniture Gallery, not far away, but you'll only be pointed to the store if you ask.

The display is on three floors and begins in the basement, which consists of several small rooms with plain pieces of period furniture of the same kind as you can buy elsewhere in the street, set out with tea cups, the walls papered with pages from old Chinese books, and is elegant and pleasant—a little like being in a tea house. There are screens, tables and books on the ground floor, and furniture and jewellery upstairs. English labelling is limited but is fairly thorough where it does exist, and you may also find displays of handwarmers and items from the study, chopsticks and other domestic things—exhibitions rotate, so don't expect them to be exactly as described here. Other domestic items may include the necklaces given to babies after 100 days, some of which feature the good luck image of a unicorn ridden by a baby boy, or a display of a special kind of carved stone used for pressing shoes and to which babies were sometimes tied to prevent them straying. Some of the staff speak good English and know their material well.

Niú Jiē Qīngzhēnsì ('Cow Street Mosque')

牛街清真寺

Open 7–7 (avoid Friday); adm ¥10.

See map pp.156–7, no.30. Take bus 61 (which starts from Xī Dān) south from ⓦ Chángchūn Jiē to stop Niú Jiē Lǐbài Sì (Lǐbài Sì is the Hàn name for the mosque) in Niú Jiē ('Cow Street'—said to refer to the Muslims' love of meat eating—except pork), or walk, deviating perhaps for a look at the antiques market at Bàoguó Sì (not daily—*see* 'Markets', p.237, for details).

Follow a passage to the right of the main gate to find the ticket office. The exterior appearance of the mosque appears little different from than of any Buddhist or daoist temple, although a low tower at the front had astronomical uses before the Jesuits replaced the Muslims as calendrical advisors to the court in the 17th century. The main worshipping hall has a particularly complicated roof and originally dates from 996, although often restored since, and is splendidly decorated with large red and gold pillars and arches with obvious Muslim motifs, and beams painted blue, green and gold. They carry no images of animals, birds or people, which offend Muslim sensibilities, but of flowers and trees and other inanimate objects. Verses from the Koran in Arabic script are simultaneously decorative and instructive to the faithful.

Attendants here claim there are 200,000 Muslims in Běijīng and altogether 68 mosques of which this is the largest. Long-term resident Juliet Bredon, writing her guide *Peking* early in the 20th century regarded the assertion that there were 40 as an exaggeration. There's a history of the faith in China, and inscriptions commemorating two Arab preachers who were buried here, carved in Arabic and Chinese, can be found on very worn stelae in two pavilions. They insist on calling another two-tiered pavilion a minaret. The other buildings are in active use and not open to the public, so the open area is quite small, but very quiet and dignified.

A shop sells Chinese-style ceramics with Arabic script on them, and the mosque is the heart of a small Muslim Quarter with various specialist shops to serve it, including one next door which offers *Qīngzhēn Kǎoya*—Muslim roast duck.

It's a short walk from here to the Fǎyuán Sì (*see* below).

Islam in China

 Conversion of Chinese peoples to Islam began in the 10th century and by the time of the Mongol invasion of the 13th century was widespread. It had originally arrived at China's southern ports in the 8th century with Arab merchants, but also spread in what is now China's northwest through land contacts. While the Mongol Yuán dynasty (1276–1368) had no religion (Kubilai Khan asked the Pope for religious teachers who never arrived, and had a Tibetan lama as his main religious adviser), it had Muslim allies who undertook the suppression of parts of China on behalf of the Mongols. The vast borderless area that constituted the Mongol empire allowed Muslims from Central Asia to move more freely into China's north- and south-west. Small Uighur states continued to exist during Mongol rule. Educated Uighurs became influential at the Mongol court and taught the Mongols how to write using the Uighur script, although they eventually abandoned this themselves in favour of the Arabic script of the text of their new religion.

From the beginning of the closed and inward-looking Míng period to modern times, Muslims in China have been cut off from the Islamic mainstream and have become

Chinese Muslims. In much of China, Muslim intermarriages with the majority Hàn Chinese and their adoption of Chinese names, customs and language made them almost indistinguishable from other Hàn, and today they are labelled by the government as a separate 'nationality', the Huí. The other Muslim minorities, such as the Uighurs, are mostly of Turki stock, and despite their shared faith do not always have good relations with the Chinese-speaking Huí, who apart from their dietary restrictions and prayer habits seem little different from the Hàn. The decline of the Qīng in the 19th century saw a re-emergence of Muslim sensibilities and a number of revolts, mostly in provinces such as Xīnjiāng and Gānsù where Muslims of all kinds were in the majority.

In general Chinese government policy towards Muslims has tended to fluctuate in relation to its sense of threat from the outside, and Muslim occupation of sensitive border areas has informed a history of intolerance by the Hàn. The Muslim response has varied, those Muslims forming visible minorities in the major cities of China proper tending to be quiescent, and those forming majorities in outlying areas whether Huí or Turki periodically rising up against Hàn oppression. Islam draws no distinction between religious and secular behaviour, and thus is bound to try and obtain Islamic government in order to ensure that the will of Allah is carried out. Muslim minorities therefore suffer strain between loyalty to the countries in which they live and loyalty to Islamic principles. Left to themselves they can submit to the non-Muslim ruler, but when oppression becomes too great, as it has periodically in 19th-, 20th- and 21st-century China, there is a tendency to rise up. This is a lesson that the Hàn have had to learn again and again.

On the other hand, if given a larger voice, Muslims will tend to speak up for secession (as during the 'Hundred Flowers' campaign, the one time when criticism of the Party was invited). However, much play was made of Muslim protests during the Tiān'ān Mén Square demonstrations of 1989 which were directed to the government rather than at it. These were 'good' protesters in contrast to the 'bad' students who had occupied the square. The recent emancipation of Muslim communities in the neighbouring newly independent states of Central Asia has caused the Chinese government some disquiet, fearing that the Uighurs of the northwest will want to emulate their neighbours. There is plentiful talk of emancipation amongst Uighurs, but except for occasional local outbursts of discontent and isolated acts of terrorism, including bomb attacks in Běijīng in the late '90s, this is likely to remain just talk. Secessionists seem to be emotional and impractical, especially considering the lack of defensible borders to Xīnjiāng's east, and the maintenance by the Chinese of more than two million men under arms.

All but the Indo-European Tajiks of western Xīnjiāng are considered Sunnis, although the isolation of Chinese Muslims has meant that perhaps few understand the differences between Sunni and Shia (a matter of argument about descent from the Prophet, and interpretation of his actions). Should you see the Huí at prayer, they will immediately seem to be considerably more serious about it than people of other persuasions you may see in Běijīng's temples and churches, except possibly Tibetan visitors to the Lama Temple.

Fǎyuán Sì

法源寺

Open 8.30-4, closed Wed; adm ¥10.

See map pp.156–7, no.15. Walk south from the Niú Jiē Mosque (*see* above), turning second left (east) into Shālán Hútòng. Follow this for a few minutes and the temple is on the north side, its spirit screen on the south.

The name of this temple dates from 1734 when it became the teaching institution it still is, but it is probably the oldest temple in Běijīng, founded in the 7th century during the Táng dynasty (whose capital was at Xī'ān) to commemorate some heroic soldiers. It was later used by the Tartar Jīn dynasty to imprison a captured Sòng dynasty emperor.

The layout of the temple is conventional, and probably none of the current buildings are much more than 100 years old, but there are six very ancient stele and two very fine bronze lions in the first courtyard, and the four bronze Heavenly Kings guarding a podgy Maitreya in the first hall are Míng. The main hall has the expected Buddha and boddhisattvas and attendant 18 *luóhàn*, but the real treasures are in subsequent halls which include a 5m statue of the Buddhas of the five points of the compass surmounted by a larger figure (accounts disagree on who this is), a substantial reclining Buddha, and a collection of bronzes from the Míng and Qīng.

The site is slightly tatty and pleasantly quiet, but the construction of a new teaching block just to the west suggests continuing support from the faithful.

Dà Guān Yuán (Grand View Garden)

大观园

Open 8.30–4.30; adm ¥10 (or ¥15 including film).

See map pp.156–7, no.13. Take bus 19 from the Zoo, or bus 59 from Qián Mén to stop Dà Guān Yuán.

This was Běijīng's first theme park, a modern recreation of the settings of the three-volume classic novel *A Dream of Red Mansions*, or *The Story of the Stone*, translations of which can be picked up at almost any Xīnhuá Shūdiàn or Wàiwén Shūdiàn (book shops). It was originally built as a set for a highly popular television series based on the book. Many of the settings are believed in fact to have been taken from Prince Gōng's Palace (*see* p.175) which, at the time this park was built, was still not open to the public but occupied by some part of the security apparatus.

This park doesn't greatly differ from many other parks, although it's mercifully free of the funfair factor. In the afternoon (even on weekdays) near the 'Happy Red Court' near the main entrance on the south side, you may see bridal couples having their wedding photographs taken, the brides in the finest Western white wedding dresses and the grooms in tails, not entirely in keeping with the recreated period setting. There are lakes surrounded by willows, which can be viewed from a chair carried by bearers for ¥10.

Various halls around a courtyard with a theatre stage on the northern side of the park have displays of images from the TV series, and there are several expensive restaurants. Alarmingly, the reproduction buildings that you find in this garden are indistinguishable from the real buildings that you find elsewhere. Either the Chinese ability to make copies is very good, or everything you see elsewhere is also fake.

Just outside the south entrance there's a fairly new camel back bridge used for kite flying over a willow-hung section of stinky canal (which will be tidied up and relined during the life of this book). Just north of the west gate is the Museum of Ancient Pottery Civilisation (*see* below), and there are several reasonable restaurants around the neighbouring Grand View Garden Hotel.

Gǔ Táo Wénmíng Bówùguǎn (Museum of Ancient Pottery Civilization) 古陶文明博物院

Open 10–5.30, closed Mon; adm ¥20, annual ticket accepted.

See map pp.156–7, no.18. Leave the Grand View Garden by its west gate and walk north past the Grand View Garden Hotel, and turn first right. The museum is a short walk down the alley on the right, backing onto the garden itself.

In a single large downstairs room there's an excellent collection of clay seals (famous in China), various ornate roof tiles with similar themes grouped together, tomb figures, painted pottery and other ceramics of various dates, with detailed introductions and background information in excellent English, and contextual information on various topics, such as the eunuch system, imperial granaries and chariot driving. Amongst the seals there's one belonging to the supervisor of the David's Deer pasturage (*see* p.343).

This is one of China's first private museums, which may account for the excellent English, the good lighting and the generally friendly atmosphere. It's run by some people with a kiln nearby, and the foyer shop has samples of their work, as well as gift items decorated imaginatively with impressions from the ancient seals.

North, Around the Back Lakes

The Shíchà Hǎi, loosely known as the Back Lakes, lie immediately to the north of Běi Hǎi Park (*see* p.152), beyond the northern wall of the Imperial City and separated from it by a controversial new cross-town highway, Píng'ān Dàdào. Constructed in 1999, this flattened acres of ancient housing, despite the surprisingly loud public protest of residents and even legal challenges—not that the plaintiffs had any chance against the government. The street has now been lined with new walls and late 20th-century Qīng shops, which are having trouble finding tenants since there's little passing trade on foot, and traffic is not (in theory) allowed to stop. Taxi drivers prefer the second ring road further to the north because it has no traffic lights; consequently the traffic here is often light, and movement quicker.

To the north, the area around the three lakes, the Qián Hǎi (Front Lake), Hòu Hǎi (Back Lake), and Xī Hǎi (West Lake), was once full of the mansions of Manchu princes both along the shores and in the *hútòng*, which here forsake the city's rigid grid to become interestingly tangled. There's good walking both here and across to and around the ancient Bell and Drum Towers to the northeast. Old men play mah-jong (*májiàng*) at shady tables near the water's edge.

Some of the mansions have long disappeared, others have been taken over and modified by various government departments with sometimes only the gardens remaining, but the extravagant mansion of Prince Gōng has reappeared from a period as government offices, one house has become a hotel (*see* Bamboo Garden Hotel, p.248), and others the memorial halls for artists and officials beatified by Party decree, one of which was the birthplace of the last Qīng emperor, Púyì.

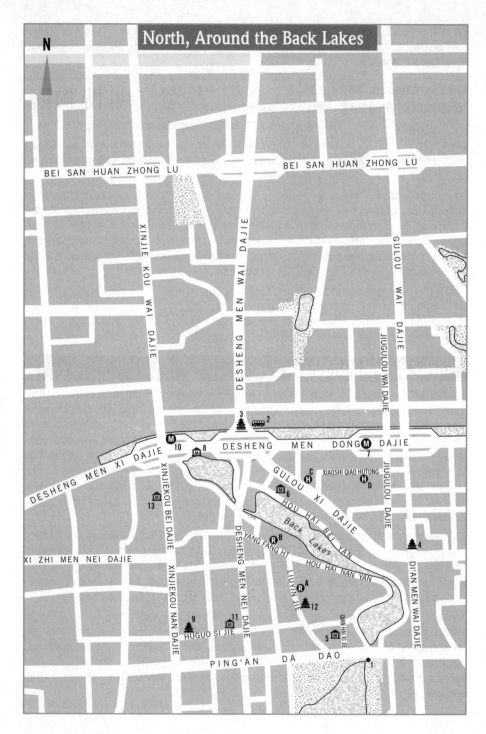

N

BEI SAN HUAN ZHONG LU

BEI SAN HUAN ZHONG LU

XINJIE KOU WAI DAJIE

DESHENG MEN WAI DAJIE

GULOU WAI DAJIE

JIUGULOU WAI DAJIE

3
2

10
8

DESHENG MEN DONG DAJIE

7

DESHENG MEN XI DAJIE

XINJIEKOU BEI DAJIE

GULOU XI DAJIE

C
H
XIAOSHI QIAO HUTONG
H
D

JIUGULOU DAJIE

6

13

HOU HAI BEI YAN

Back Lakes

DESHENG MEN NEI DAJIE

YANG FANG HT

R
B

HOU HAI NAN YAN

4

XI ZHI MEN NEI DAJIE

XINJIEKOU NAN DAJIE

LIUYIN JIE

R
A

DI'AN MEN WAI DAJIE

12

9

11

HUGUO SI JIE

QIAN HAI XI JIE

5

PING'AN DA DAO

1

172

Key

北海公园	1	Běi Hǎi Gōngyuán (north gate)
	2	Buses to Bā Dá Lǐng, Jūyōng Guān Great Wall sites, Sōng Shān
德胜门箭楼, 古代钱币展览馆	3	Déshèng Mén Jiànlóu and Ancient Coin Exhibition Hall (Gǔdài Qiánbì Zhǎnlǎn Guǎn)
鼓楼, 钟楼	4	Drum Tower and Bell Tower (Gǔlóu, Zhōnglóu)
郭沫若故居	5	Former Residence of Guō Mòruò (Guō Mòruò Gù Jū)
宋庆龄故居	6	Former Residence of Soong Ching Ling (Sòng Qìnglíng Gùjū)
鼓楼大街	7	Gǔlóu Dàjiē Metro
郭守敬纪念馆	8	Guō Shǒujìng Jìniànguǎn (Guō Shǒujìng Memorial Hall)
护国寺街	9	Hùguó Sì
积水潭	10	Jīshuǐtán Metro
梅兰芳纪念馆	11	Méi Lánfāng Jìniànguǎn (Méi Lánfāng Memorial Hall)
恭王府	12	Prince Gong's Mansion Gōng Wáng Fǔ
徐悲鸿纪念馆	13	Xú Bēihóng Jìniànguǎn (Xú Bēihóng Memorial Hall)

Hotels and Restaurants

恭王府四川饭店	A	Gōng Wáng Fǔ Sìchuān Fàndiàn
厉家菜	B	Lì Jiā Cài (Lì Family Restaurant)
属穆朗玛宾馆	C	Qomolangma Hotel (Zhūmùlǎngmǎ Bīnguǎn)
竹园宾馆	D	Zhúyuán Bīnguǎn (Bamboo Garden Hotel)

Street and Bus Stop Names

北三环中路	Běi Sān Huán Zhōng Lù (north third ring middle)
德胜门内、外大街	Déshèng Mén Nèi/Wài Dàjiē
地安门外大街	Dì'ān Mén Wài Dàjiē
地安门东、西大街	Dì'ān Mén Xī/Dōng Dàjiē
鼓楼	Gǔlóu
鼓楼西大街	Gǔlóu Xī Dàjiē
鼓楼外大街	Gǔlóu Wài Dàjiē
后海	Hòu Hǎi (Back Lake)
后海北、南沿	Hòu Hǎi Běi/Nán Yán
护国寺街	Hùguó Sì Jiē
旧鼓楼（外）大街	Jiùgǔlóu (Wài) Dàjiē
旧鼓楼路	Jiùgǔlóu Lù
柳荫街	Liǔyīn Jiē
平安大道	Píng'ān Dàdào
平安里	Píng'ān Lǐ
前海	Qián Hǎi (Front Lake)
前海西街	Qián Hǎi Xī Jiē
小石桥胡同	Xiǎoshí Qiáo Hútòng
西海	Xī Hǎi (West Lake)
新街口	Xīnjiēkǒu
新街口北、南大街	Xīnjiēkǒu Běi/Nán Dàjiē
西直门内大街	Xī Zhí Mén Nèi Dàjiē
羊房胡同	Yáng Fáng Hútòng

The mass beautification of Běijīng for 1999 reached the lakes, which were dredged of silt, and hemmed with new paved walkways, benches, grassy areas, and fences. 'Beautiful,' said one retired resident gloomily, 'but I suppose they'll start charging us to go in soon.' There's lots of new traditionalism with boats in 'ancient style', a recreated market area which promises to have performances of various kinds, and signs that other former temples and mansions may re-emerge, re-built, presently.

It's easy to put together walking routes around the *hútòng*, or you may choose just to get lost, using the tops of the Drum and Bell Towers for orientation. This is the area chosen by the made-for-Gold-Card-holders *hútòng* tours, their Cadillac-style rickshaws with gilded mudguards and fringed awnings waiting in the road outside Guō Mòruò's house on the way to Prince Gōng's Mansion.

Former Residence of Guō Mòruò (Guō Mòruò Gù Jū) 郭沫若故居

Open 9–4, closed Mon; adm ¥5.

See map p.172, no.5. The residence is in Qián Hǎi Xī Jiē, which runs north from Píng'ān Dàdào just west of the north entrance to Běi Hǎi park. Bus 13 comes here from Bái Tǎ Sì and from Yōnghé Gōng (Lama Temple), stop name Běi Hǎi Hòu Mén.

Three attempts made to see this sight over a period of four years all met with failure due either to cadres' meetings or, twice, restoration work. One of several 'former residences' or 'memorial halls' in this area, the scale of its gate suggests there'll be a fine mansion inside, although descriptions are hard to find elsewhere either.

Guō, 1892–1978, was a poet, novelist, playwright, literary critic and historian whose quickness to jump on the communist bandwagon despite a wealthy background has spared him from objective criticism. Historian Frances Wood describes him in her *Blue Guide China*, with memorable tartness, as 'a tireless apologist for whatever seemed safest to defend'. He was sufficiently flexible to end up holding several token offices, even escaping the effects of the Cultural Revolution, which spared few capable of holding a pen.

Prince Gōng's Mansion (Gōng Wáng Fǔ) 恭王府

Open 9–4,30; adm ¥5.

See map p.172, no.12. *See* directions for Guō Mòruò Gù Jū, *above*. Walk further on and turn left (still Qián Hǎi Xī Jiē), crossing the next *hútòng* and then turning right into Liǔyìn Jiē ('shaded by willows street'). The entrance is a short walk up on the right, often surrounded by tour buses.

You get a lot for your ¥5: green and leafy gardens, pools and pavilions, rockeries, winding pathways, and an assortment of fairly well-kept halls often connected by winding passageways—smaller versions of the Summer Palace's Long Corridor, and similarly decorated. The mansion is thought to have provided inspiration for some of the settings in the classic *A Dream of Red Mansions* (*see also* 'Grand View Garden, p.170). Some of the gardens are designed to be landscapes in miniature (including a rocky recreation of the pass at Shānhǎiguān), others simply have frilly bamboo or roses, and gardeners wander around with long-necked watering cans. Loitering under the grape vines is pleasant on a hot Běijīng summer's day. If travelling independently go in the morning as tour groups seem more concentrated in the afternoons, and the tour guides wield megaphones. If you are with such a group you'll probably be served tea in the three-storey 'Grand Opera House', its interior brightly painted with patterns of wisteria, and shown opera excerpts and acrobatics.

The halls are set on three axes, but wandering paths through moon gates, around piled rocks and through gardens, make the whole site seem rather larger and more complicated. The elegant Hall of Tranquility and Goodness has a board with Kāngxī's calligraphy but is now a jewellery shop. Exciting as it sounds in English, The Peak of Self-Enjoyment is merely a 5m-high rock garden which can be climbed by several winding routes. One pavilion in the middle of a small lake is reached by an ingenious bridge of boats, and a group of halls at the rear of the site have their columns bizarrely painted in imitation of bamboo.

The palace was once the home of a notorious Manchu officer-cum-official called Heshen, who prospered from 1775 towards the end of the Qiánlóng emperor's reign. At 25 he was showered with an extraordinary combination of promotions and titles for one so young, and gossip had it that he was the 65-year-old emperor's catamite. He used his ever-increasing number of revenue-generating offices to amass millions by charging for services and by fiddling the accounts of military costs on the various rebel-suppressing campaigns that became necessary due to poor local government, religious problems and corruption at lower levels. Once Qiánlóng nominally retired in 1796 to avoid out-reigning his famous grandfather Kāngxī, Heshen's power grew as Qiánlóng effectively continued to reign using him as the instrument of his will.

Heshen was often ill, and having been failed by Chinese medicine took the highly unusual step of summoning the Scottish Dr Gillan, who accompanied the Macartney embassy of 1793. Gillan diagnosed rheumatism and a hernia, and fitted him with a truss. When Qiánlóng died in 1796, his son, the Jiāqìng emperor, finally took control and forced Heshen to commit suicide.

In 1851 the Xiánfēng emperor granted the palace to Prince Gōng, his younger brother, who was later to sign the 1860 Conventions of Peking on his behalf, which reconfirmed the rights of foreign powers to station permanent ambassadors in Běijīng, already granted in 1858, and additionally ceding Kowloon to the British, permitting Chinese emigration (hitherto illegal) on British ships, opening Tiānjīn for foreign trade, and granting yet further indemnities. Gōng was later a founder of the first Qīng Foreign Office and was well known to the inhabitants of the Legation Quarter.

Turning left out of the entrance you'll soon pass the new premises of the Sìchuān Restaurant (*see* p.265), and turning left (east) around the top of the palace compound and continuing east and north where necessary you'll soon reach the Hòu Hǎi. To your right there's a small arched bridge between two lakes and across it there's both cheap eating and a long-established and over-priced roast meat restaurant. Going straight on, left at the T, and first right will bring you out at the Drum and Bell Towers.

Drum Tower and Bell Tower (Gǔlóu, Zhōnglóu)

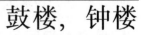

Open 9–4.30; adm ¥6 each or ¥10 for both, annual ticket accepted.

See map p.172, no.4. The towers are on Běijīng's main axis and to the north, directly in line with the main halls of the Forbidden City, the Zhèngyáng Mén, and other long vanished gates.

Walk south for 10–15 minutes from ⓜ Gǔlóu Dàjiē on the north side of the circle line, or take bus 58 to the stop Gǔlóu. Bus 5 runs from Qián Mén up the east side of Tiān'ān Mén Square, and the west side of the Forbidden City and Jǐng Shān Park.

The two towers are quite different in style. The original Drum Tower was built in 1272 as the 'orderly administration tower' and stood a little further to the west in the centre of the Mongol city of Dàdū. When the Míng emperor Yǒnglè remodelled the city in the 15th century a portion of the northern end fell outside his new wall, thus placing the Imperial Palace at the centre. The original of the modern Drum Tower was built partly from materials taken from the Mongol one, and has a wooden superstructure topped by imperial yellow tiles and standing on a brick plinth. It's a substantial, squat, three-storeyed structure in red with complex roof brackets and its exterior painted with dragons in blue and green. Destroyed and rebuilt on at least five occasions, the tower originally contained 24 drums, the destruction of 23 of which has been blamed on the allied forces in 1900.

It's a stiff climb up to the interior, where one drum remains, and the rest of the space is used for 'exhibitions', but everything (carved tree roots and assorted souvenirs) is for sale. The ground floor now has its own 'Curio City' but is of limited interest compared to other antique and curio markets.

The Bell Tower to the north of the Drum has a similar history, although it was reconstructed in stone in 1745, and is also easily distinguished from the Drum Tower by its black tiles. It's on a very high crenellated brick plinth with a marble walkway inside, and then a paler brick pavilion with a plain two-tiered green and gold roof. The bell, a 42-ton bronze monster, was cast sometime between 1403 and 1424, and it and the drums were sounded together to mark the changes of the morning and evening watches. Time was kept using a clepsydra (water clock). Legend has it that the foundry, after several unsuccessful attempts to make a perfect casting, was facing the emperor's possibly lethal displeasure. At the next attempt the daughter of the foundry's head threw herself into the molten bronze hoping to placate whatever force was interfering and thus to save her father. A servant tried to save her, but was left holding merely a shoe. A perfect cast was made, but when the bell was struck it was said that in the reverberations could be heard a cry of '*Xié*!', the Mandarin word for 'shoe'. This is a popular story, however, and is sometimes told of the slightly larger bell at the Great Bell Temple, and also of bells in other parts of China.

The time-keeping functions of the two towers were abolished in 1924, and during the Republic the Nationalist Party established a propaganda office in the Drum Tower, while the Bell Tower became an unlikely cinema.

There are excellent views across Běijīng from both towers and you can take your bearings before setting off into some of the best-preserved *hútòng* in the city.

There's a small street food market between the two towers, and more *jiǎozi* restaurants in the neigbouring *hútòng* as well as more comfortable places in Dì'ān mén Wài Dàjiē, which runs south towards the rear of Jǐng Shān Park. A 24-hour quick noodle place on the west side of the street has Chinese fast food with an English menu and fair prices, including dumplinfs (*sic*); buy your ticket from the cashier first, then sit down and give it to the waitress.

Former Residence of Soong Ching Ling
(Sòng Qìnglíng Gùjū)

宋庆龄故居

Open 9–4, closed Mon; adm ¥8.

See map p.172, no.6. The residence, in Hòu Hǎi Běi Yán on the northeast side of the Hòu Hǎi, can be reached on foot from Prince Gōng's Mansion, from Ⓜ Gǔlóu Dàjiē, the Drum and Bell Towers, or Déshèng Mén. Bus 5 comes from Qián Mén and passes the Drum Tower on its way to Déshèng Mén.

Soong Ching Ling, 1893–1981, was the daughter of a wealthy Shanghainese who had converted to Methodism. Her elder sister married a rich banker, and her younger sister married Chiang Kai-shek, the Nationalist leader who succeeded Sun Yat-sen and ultimately lost control of the Chinese mainland to the communists. Her brother held various ministerial posts in the Chiang government and was at one time premier. She herself married Sun Yat-sen, the supposed 'Father of the Republic' who wasn't even in China when the revolution got going and was as surprised by it as anyone (the organizers claimed not to have heard much of him either). Sun, who was 30 years her senior, predeceased her by 56 years, but she continued to play a role in the Nationalist Party (Guómíndàng), being more sympathetic to the left wing and narrowly escaping death during a mass slaughter of communist sympathisers in 1927. After a period of living in Russia, where she converted to communism, she returned to hold largely nominal posts as a walking, talking propaganda victory for the Communist Party of China—someone who was from an oppressor class but now on the side of the angels—although she only joined the Party on her deathbed.

The house is modern, but something remains of the grounds of the mansion of Prince Chun, which stood here. Chun was Pǔyí's father, a rather ineffectual regent for the Qīng's last few years in power and the man who signed the instrument of abdication. According to some accounts Pǔyí was born here. The pavilions and corridors of the garden have been heavily renovated, but there are geese on the ponds and the grounds are pleasantly quiet.

Inside the house, peeling paint and a general sense of decay accompany an exhibition in which Soong's life has been airbrushed to perfection, and nothing is left to the imagination. There's some interest in the style of the furnishings in rooms which have been kept as they were at the time of her death, and in period clothing, but just about everything she ever touched is deemed worth of display, and there are long sequences of photographs of her meeting dignitaries of various kinds.

A little further south there are signs of the reconstruction of an ancient temple, possibly the Yuán dynasty **Guǎnghuà Sì**, which houses offices of the Buddhist Association, not open to the public, or at least not yet. If you continue northwest around the lake shore and across the street to the final lake, the Xī Hǎi, you'll find a Yuán dynasty astronomer and hydrologist, **Guō Shǒujìng**, responsible for much of the canel network which feeds Běijīng its water from the northwest, given a similar hagiographic treatment in a small former temple on top of an artificial rockery at the north end of the lake (*open 8.30–4.30; adm ¥0.50, annual ticket accepted*). Lovers sit on the paths leading up, and an area of reeds at the base is full of loud frogs sounding like typewriters.

The **Déshèng Mén** Ancient Coin Exhibition Hall is nearby, Ⓜ Jīshuǐtán is just to the east, or you can walk west and south to the memorial hall to the painter **Xú Bēihóng** (*see* below).

Déshèng Mén Jiànlóu and Ancient Coin Exhibition Hall (Gǔdài Qiánbì Zhǎnlǎn Guǎn)

德胜门箭楼，古代钱币展览馆

Open 9–4, closed Mon; adm ¥0.50, annual ticket accepted.

See map p.172, no.3. The tower is on the northwest side of the second ring road at Déshèng Mén, 10mins walk east of Ⓜ Jīshuǐtán, or a little further west of Ⓜ Gǔlóu Dàjiē. Bus 5 comes here from Qián Mén and the west side of the Forbidden City.

The tower still standing is the Déshèng Mén Jiànlóu, the outer, embrasured tower (or 'arrow tower') of the pair which once stood here, used by emperors when they left to lead military expeditions themselves. Many possible translations of its name include 'Gate of the Victory of Morality'. The main tower was the first of Běijīng's towers to be pulled down and not replaced, on the grounds that it was no longer safe, in 1921.

There are stalls selling coins, notes, phone cards, and other collectibles around the base of the tower which stands in the centre of a traffic island. Halls at the base and on top of the tower itself have an exhibition of ancient coins and how they were made, from the variety pre-Qín shapes and sizes to the circular 'copper cash' with their central square holes, which were kept on strings, and the shoe-shaped silver ingots of post-Qín standardization.

Buses to Bā Dá Lǐng (*see* p.303), Shísān Líng (*see* p.309) and beyond leave from the northeast side of the tower, so it can be seen on the way. The Back Lakes lie just to the south (*see* above).

Xú Bēihóng Jìniànguǎn (Xú Bēihóng Memorial Hall)

徐悲鸿纪念馆

Open 9–11.30 and 1–4, closed Mon; adm ¥5, annual ticket accepted.

See map p.172, no.13. Ⓜ Jīshuǐtán at the circle line's northwest corner and walk south down Xīnjiēkǒu Běi Dàjiē. Bus 22 comes from Qián Mén via Xī Dān to stop Xīnjiēkǒu. Walk north and the hall is on the west side.

To the casual visitor this is probably the most interesting of all the memorial halls, except for those with traditional architecture interesting in its own right. Xú Bēihóng, 1885–1953, who studied in Paris and travelled around Europe and Japan, put Chinese ink-and-brush technique into his Western oils, and brought Western techniques to introduce a new liveliness to the rigid forms of Chinese painting. The official line, perpetually unwilling to give foreigners credit for anything, is that he 'absorbed Western techniques into his Chinese painting' and that he thus espoused Máo's policy of 'making ancient things service the present and making foreign things serve China'. He held several of the top arts jobs which should tell you, even before you see some of his canvasses, that he was a good Party member, too. However little interest you have in art, you will still almost certainly find his paintings of horses familiar, not only because copies are on sale at almost every souvenir stall in China, but also because of their popularity in the West, particularly in the 1950s.

It's tempting to say as you view the rest of the work that he wouldn't have won so many prizes if he hadn't been a good communist. But the oils are worth seeing for their distinctly Parisian influences with hints of Degas and Corot, and a Cézanne-like style applied to Chinese landscapes, some labelled to elucidate a communist moral. There are portraits of Máo Zédōng, including one which makes him look startlingly jolly. Upstairs there's a hagiographic account of Xú's career and items preserved from his study. The shops sells books of his paintings.

Those who travelled in China 10 years ago may get a sense of nostalgia from the obvious suspicion of visitors shown by the *fúwùyuán*, who shout to tell each other to keep an eye on you, and the opening hours designed to suit their convenience rather than yours. It's said that the museum is run by Xú's wife, one of his students.

Walking south from here past the next major junction (a McDonald's on the corner), the *hútòng* to the left (east) are quiet and contain the remains of the **Hùguó Sì**, whose temple fair was, until about 50 years ago, second only to that of Lóngfú Sì (*see 'Hútòng* Walking', p.78). Some shops in the neighbouring *hútòng* claimed to trace their origins to the Míng dynasty, specializing in flowers, shrubs and trees, kept in hothouses and forced to bloom at Chinese New Year by an ingenious system of flues and steam heating. The temple itself was formerly the residence of a Mongol prince, later banished on suspicion of treason, rehabilitated after his death, and his mansion turned into two temples, one of which still stood in the '30s. Of the other, the shops and markets, and of several other princely mansions in the vicinity, all that remains is a single hall—delapidated, walled in, and completely inaccessible, which inexplicably continues to appear on Chinese maps. The *sìhéyuàn* home of **Méi Lánfāng** can be reached by a further walk south and east along Hùguó Sì Jiē, which runs east from the south side of the remaining hall (*see* below).

Méi Lánfāng Jìniànguǎn (Méi Lánfāng Memorial Hall)   梅兰芳纪念馆

Open mid-April–mid-Nov, 9–4, closed Mon; adm ¥2, annual ticket accepted.

See map p.172, no.11. The house is at Hùguó Sì Jiē 9. Take bus 22 from Qián Mén or Xī Dān to stop Píng'ān Lǐ. Walk north and turn right into Hùguó Sì Jiē.

> *We walked slowly, knowing we should be only a little over two hours late for the performance. To have arrived sooner would have been tedious, because great actors like Mei Lan-Fang seldom condescended to appear on the stage until two thirds of the way through the opera in which they were performing. Their understudies were good enough to satisfy those undiscriminating ticket-holders who, to get their money's worth, sat through six acts from the beginning. Such people were usually countrymen or visitors from distant provinces.*

> John Blofeld, *City of Lingering Splendour,* 1961

Blofeld saw Méi Lánfāng (1894–1961) perform in the '30s, when the actor, who was to perform overseas many times in his career, meeting Berthold Brecht amongst other Western theatrical luminaries, was probably at the peak of his powers. As is still the case with *kabuki* in Japan, there were no mixed troupes, and the most famous actors were those who could impersonate to perfection the idealized delicacy and grace of a young girl. Méi was the most famous of his day. In the opera performances of today you'll now see women play women's roles, and the nearest living equivalent of Méi is probably *kabuki*'s Bando Tamasaburo.

Méi's *sìhéyuán* (courtyard house) is a little more luxurious than that of Lǎo Shě, for instance (*see* p.180), the side rooms now containing a small museum (photographs, theatre programmes, costumes, props, etc.), and the rear living room, study, and bedroom preserved as they were at the time of Méi's death, with a mixture of Victorian and Qīng furniture, some inlaid with mother-of-pearl.

For details of Chinese opera performances, *see* 'Běijīng opera', p.274.

The Lama Temple, North and East of the Imperial City

The area covered in this section, stretching from the Imperial City walls out to the third ring road to the north and east, is the modern-day entertainment district for foreign residents and visitors alike, containing most of the better hotels, both the diplomatic quarters, and clusters of bars and restaurants designed to service those who stay, live and work at these places.

But it also houses galleries, a 24-hour food street (*see* p.267), and some of Běijīng's more spectacular temples, and in particular the Lama Temple (*see* p.187), which should be your choice if you plan to see only one temple during your stay.

Lǎo Shě Jìniànguǎn
(Lǎo Shě Memorial Hall)

老舍纪念馆

Open 9–4, closed Mon; adm ¥5, annual ticket accepted.

See map pp.182–3, no.48. The hall is just inside Fēngfù Hútòng, which runs north off Dēngshìkǒu Xī Jiē, which is off Wángfǔjǐng. For now you can also buy a special memorial souvenir ticket set for ¥30 ('only 10,000 printed').

1999 was the centenary of novelist and playwright Lǎo Shě's birth, and after substantial renovation this small *sìhéyuán*, where he lived from 1950 until his death in 1966 (a Cultural Revolution-assisted suicide), was opened to the public in spring that year.

The exhibition begins in the right-hand hall of this traditional small courtyard house with details of the boyhood and student days of Lǎo Shě, photographs of the various places in which he lived (including four in London; there's a photograph of what looks remarkably like Holland Park (although the sign has it as Délán Gōngyuán—'Germany Park'), and the library at London's School of Oriental and African Studies, where he taught for a while. There are stills from films of his work and copies of texts translated into various languages, some of which were published in English under an Anglicized version of his name—Lau Shaw. The rear hall has rooms in which (presumably) everything is preserved as at the time of his death, including his working desk, a Míng-era bed, and a sofa shrouded in plastic. Either he was enjoying a game of patience at the time of his death, or that's just the friendly *fúwùyuán* killing time not spent tending to the hostas in the courtyard. Lǎo Shě is more genuinely loved than the communist-picked icons, and even before the house was open many Chinese came to try and see round it.

Lǎo Shě's play, *Teahouse*, which was filmed some years ago, is still staged regularly, and is enough of a classic now to be appearing in adapted versions. His best known novel, *Rickshaw Boy* (sometimes known as *Camel Xiángzi*), is a bitterly comic story of the life of a hard-working, good-hearted, but simple-minded rickshaw puller called Happy Boy, set in Běijīng shortly after the downfall of the Qīng, with the city itself as a central character, and a cast of extras including looting soldiers, political conspirators, idealistic students, and girls sold into prostitution as an escape from poverty.

Modern Happy Boys, although they pedal rather than run, are to be found not too far away in cheap noodle restaurants just south of the Imperial Archive, for instance. Here they sit talking in just the same manner as London cabbies—'I had a foreigner in the back the other day'. But although easy-going Happy Boy hated haggling and often told his passengers to pay on arrival, his non-fiction counterparts tell each other stories of just how much they've overcharged foreigners. One rickshaw man spoken to owns his own vehicle (the aim of Happy Boy) and claims to earn about ¥100 ($12.50) a day—about three to four times the salary of a skilled factory worker, more than double a teacher and nearly as much as an interpreter starting work with a foreign joint-venture company. No charity is necessary here. On the other hand he works 12-hour days and commutes by bus from 30km outside Běijīng (far enough for his accent to be noticeably different).

Dōng Sì Qīngzhēnsì (Dōng Sì Mosque)

Open daylight hours, but avoid Fridays; adm ¥10.

东四清真寺

See map pp.182–3, no.32. The mosque is at the northern continuation of Dōng Dān, at Dōng Sì Nán Dàjiē 13. It's a 15min walk west of Ⓜ Cháoyáng Mén, or bus 101. Bus 106 runs up from the Nán Zhàn, up the west and across the north side of Tiān Tán, then straight north up Dōng Dān. The bus stop name is Dōng Sì. Dōng Dān or 'east single' is named for a widow-honouring *páilou* that once stood over the street, and Dōng Sì, its northern continuation, for where, until the middle of the last century, four of them stood, one over each arm of the crossroads.

There are Islamic communities in most of China's major cities made up of Huí, Chinese descendants of Arab traders, now largely indistinguishable from other Chinese except in diet, and of Uighurs from the Xīnjiāng region and of Turki stock. Like other Běijīng mosques the Dōng Sì has neither dome, minaret nor muezzin, and its brick-arched first courtyard looks disappointingly a little like a Victorian country railway station. Its second courtyard is a pleasant refuge from the clangour of one of the city's busiest districts, with a restful garden of roses and hostas, and aerobatic performances from multiple swallows. Its red walls and brightly decorated beams at first give little indication that this is not a Buddhist temple, but the rearmost hall has decorative Koranic scriptures in gold, clockfaces showing times for prayer, and the white hats favoured by Chinese Muslims, a little like those of chefs, hanging to dry. The staff claim imperial patronage for the mosque and are immensely proud of its antiquity and almost continuous operation since its original construction in 1356, save an inevitable hiatus during the 1966–76 Cultural Revolution. A restoration of 1447 is commemorated on a stele in both Chinese and Arabic.

The mosque's few foreign visitors are allowed in free if Muslims, but must be prepared for cross-questioning in Chinese to prove their knowledge of the faith. An office labelled the Department of Islamic Souvenirs and Handicrafts (in other words 'shop') is staffed by a genial man who says that his few foreign visitors love to buy gaudy ceramic jars decorated with Arabic script, although whether that's the visiting devout or just those in search of an unusual souvenir isn't clear.

Běijīng's largest mosque is Niú Jiē Qīngzhēn Sì. *See* p.168 for this and 'Islam in China'.

Wángfǔjǐng is a short walk to the west, the daoist temple of Dōng Yuè Miào about 20–25 mins to the east, back past the subway station (*see* p.197). The Yōnghé Gōng lamasery is straight north, about 15–20mins on foot.

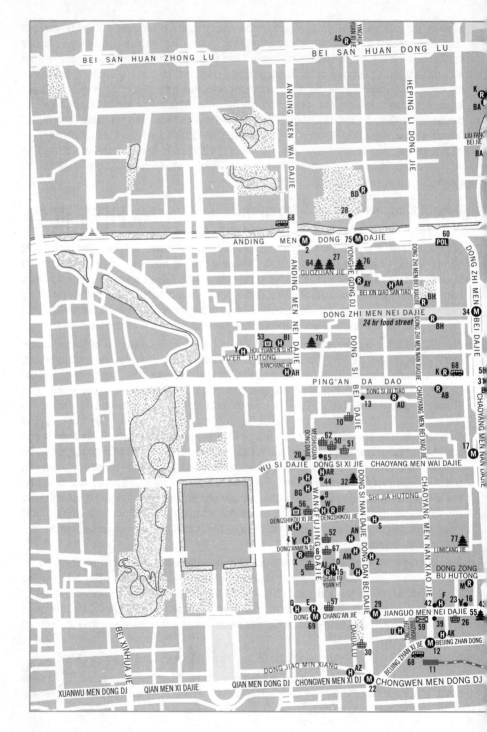

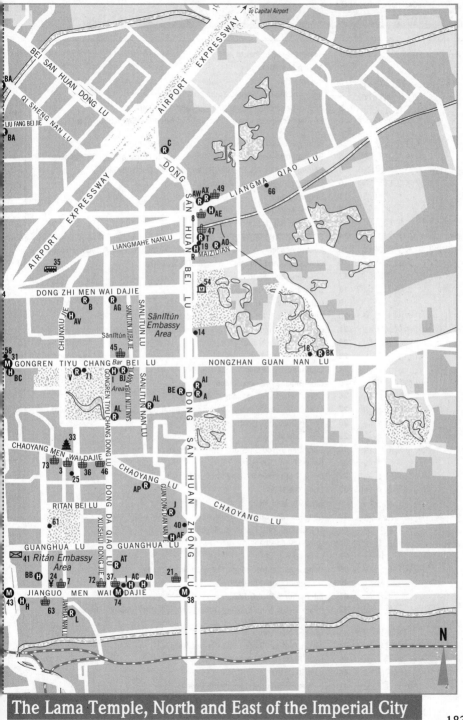

To Capital Airport

BEI SAN HUAN DONG LU

QI SHENG NAN LU

AIRPORT EXPRESSWAY

BA

LIU FANG BEI JIE

BA

DONG SAN HUAN BEI LU

C

LIANGMA QIAO LU

AX AW
49
R R
66

8
AE

47
T
19 R AO
R
MAIZIDIAN

35

54
M

DONG ZHI MEN WAI DAJIE

B
R
AG
R

SANLITUN LU

SANLITUN JUBA LU

CHUNXIU JIE

H
AV

Sānlǐtún
Embassy
Area

Sānlǐtún

45

14

18
R BK

58
31
M
H
BC

GONGREN TIYU CHANG BEI LU

NONGZHAN GUAN NAN LU

V
R
71

GONGREN TIYU CHANG DONG LU

Bar
Area

SANLITUN NAN LU

BJ

AL
R

AL
R

BE
R

AI
R
R
A

33

CHAOYANG MEN WAI DAJIE

73

3
36
46

25

DONG DA QIAO LU

CHAOYANG LU

GUAN DONG DIAN NAN LU

CHAOYANG LU

DONG SAN HUAN ZHONG LU

AP
R

J
R

RITAN BEI LU

61

XIUSHUI DONG JIE

40
AF
H

GUANGHUA LU

GUANGHUA LU

41 Ritan Embassy
Area

AT
R

BB
H

24
7

72
37
1 AC AD

21

JIANGUO MEN WAI DAJIE

M
43
H
H

JIANHUA NAN LU

63
R
L

74

38
M

N

The Lama Temple, North and East of the Imperial City

	1	Airtrans Service Co. Ltd
安定门	2	Ānding Mén Metro
百脑会	3	Bǎi Nǎo Huì
中国银行	4	Bank of China (Zhōngguó Yínháng)
北京百货大楼	5	Běijīng Department Store (Běijīng Bǎihuò Dà Lóu)
北京外文图书大楼	6	Běijīng Foreign Languages Publications Building (Běijīng Shì Wàiwén Túshū Dàlóu)
北京友谊商店	7	Běijīng Friendship Store (Běijīng Yǒuyí Shāngdiàn)
燕莎友谊商城	8	Běijīng Lufthansa Centre Yǒuyí Shopping City (Yānshā Yǒuyí Shāngchéng)
北京人民艺术剧院	9	Běijīng People's Art Theatre (Běijīng Rénmín Yìshù Jùyuàn)
北京永久自行车	10	Běijīng Yǒngjiǔ Zìxíngchē (bicycle shop)
北京站	11	Běijīng Zhàn
北京站	12	Běijīng Zhàn Metro
忙蜂酒吧	13	Busy Bee Bar (Máng Fēng Jiǔbā)
CD 咖啡屋	14	CD Café (CD Kāfēi Wū)
中央美术学院画廊	15	Central Academy of Fine Arts Gallery (Zhōngyāng Měishù Xuéyuàn Huàláng)
长安大戏院	16	Cháng'ān Grand Theatre (Cháng'ān Dà Xìyuàn)
朝阳门	17	Cháoyáng Mén Metro
朝阳公园	18	Cháoyáng Gōngyuán (south gate)
	19	China Air International Travel Service
中国美术馆	20	China National Art Gallery (Zhōngguó Měishùguǎn)
中国国际贸易中心	21	China World Trade Centre (Zhōngguó Guójì Màoyì Zhōngxīn)
崇文门	22	Chóngwén Mén Metro
	23	Citibank ATM
	24	Citic Industrial Bank
巴那那俱乐部	25	Club Banana (Bānànà Jùlèbù)
中粮广场	26	COFCO Plaza (Zhōng Liáng Guǎngchǎng)
孔庙，首都博物馆	27	Confucius Temple (Kǒng Miào) and Shǒudū Bówùguǎn (Capital Museum)
地坛公园	28	Dì Tán Gōngyuán (south gate)
东单	29	Dōng Dān Metro
东单集邮市场	30	Dōng Dān Jí Yóu Shìchǎng (stamp market)
东四十条	31	Dōng Sì Shí Tiáo Metro
东四清真寺	32	Dōng Sì Qīngzhēnsì (Dōng Sì Mosque)
东岳庙	33	Dōng Yuè Miào
东直门	34	Dōng Zhí Mén Metro
东直门长途汽车站	35	Dōng Zhí Mén Chángtú Qìchēzhàn
丰联广场	36	Full Link Plaza (Fēnglián Guǎngchǎng)
贵友商场	37	Guìyǒu Shāngchǎng
国贸	38	Guómào Metro
恒基中心商场	39	Henderson Centre (Héngjī Zhōngxīn Shāngchǎng)
热点	40	Hot Spot Disco (Rè Diǎn)
邮电局	41	International Post Office
国际总社票务中心	42	International Train Booking Office (Guójì Zǒngshè Piào Wù Zhōngxīn) in International Hotel
建国门	43	Jiànguó Mén Metro
金帆乐厅	44	Jīnfàn Yuètīng (Golden Sail Concert Hall)
麒麟大厦	45	Kylin Plaza (Qílín Dàshà)
蓝岛大厦	46	Lándǎo Dàshà
亮马河大厦	47	Landmark Building (Liàngmǎhé Dàshà)

Hotels and Restaurants

好园宾馆	S	Hǎoyuán Bīnguǎn (Hǎoyuán Guesthouse)
	T	Hard Rock Café
华美伦酒店	U	Harmony Hotel (Huáměilún Jiǔdiàn)
哈瓦那咖啡	V	Havana Café (Hāwànà Kāfēi)
国际艺苑皇冠饭店	W	Holiday Inn Crowne Plaza (Guójì Yìyuàn Huángguān Fàndiàn)
香港美食城	X	Hong Kong Food City (Xiānggǎng Měi Shí Chéng)
华凯宾馆	Y	Huákǎi Bīnguǎn
华龙饭店	Z	Huálóng Fàndiàn
华侨饭店	AA	Huáqiáo Fàndiàn
沪江香满楼	AB	Hùjiāng Xiāng Mǎn Lóu
建国饭店	AC	Jiànguó Fàndiàn (Jiànguó Hotel)
京伦饭店	AD	Jīnglún Fàndiàn (Hotel Běijīng-Toronto)
北京燕莎中心凯宾斯基饭店	AE	Kempinski Hotel Běijīng Lufthansa Centre (Běijīng Yànshā Zhōngxīn Kǎibīn Sījī Fàndiàn)
嘉里中心饭店	AF	Kerry Centre Hotel (Jiālǐ Zhōngxīn Fàndiàn)
老巴刹	AG	Lau Pa Sak (Lǎo Bā Shà)
侣松园宾馆	AH	Lǚsōng Yuán Bīnguǎn
松子	AI	Matsuko (Sōngzi)
	AJ	Mexican Wave
宝辰饭店	AK	Paragon Hotel (Bǎochén Fàndiàn)
巴拉地	AL	Parati Restaurant (Bālādì)
王府饭店	AM	The Palace Hotel (Wángfǔ Fàndiàn)
和平饭店	AN	Peace Hotel (Hépíng Fàndiàn)
	AO	Peter Pan
京港泰式美食	AP	Phrik Thai (Jīng Gǎng Tài Shì Měi Shí)
华侨大厦	AR	Prime Hotel (Huáqiáo Dàshà)
七省办大厦	AS	Qī Shěng Bàn Dàshà
全聚德烤鸭店	AT	Quánjùdé Kǎoyādiàn
	AU	Red Capital Club
瑞秀宾馆	AV	Red House (Ruìxiù Bīnguǎn)
	AW	Ristorante Pizzeria Café Adria
西乐酒屋	AX	Schiller's (Xīlè Jiǔwū)
韶山毛家菜馆	AY	Sháo Shān Máo Jiā Càiguǎn
社科宾馆	AZ	Shèkē Bīnguǎn (Academy of Social Sciences Guesthouse)
水煮鱼	BA	Shuǐ Zhǔ Yú
北京国际俱乐部饭店	BB	St Regis Beijing (still ask for Běijīng Guójì Jùlèbù Fàndiàn)
港澳中心瑞士酒店	BC	Swissôtel Běijīng (Gǎng Ào Zhōngxīn Ruìshì Jiǔdiàn)
坛根院	BD	Tán Gēn Yuàn
	BE	TGI Friday's
天食	BF	Tiān Shí
王府井大饭店	BG	Wángfǔjǐng Grand Hotel (Wángfǔjǐng Dàfàndiàn)
小洞天麻辣烫	BH	Xiǎo Dòng Tiān Má Là Tàng
友好宾馆	BI	Yǒuhǎo Bīnguǎn
	BJ	1001 Nights
	BK	The Big Easy

Street and Bus Stop Names

安定门东大街	Āndìng Mén Dōng Dàjiē	北三环东路	Běi Sān Huán Dōng Lù (north third ring east)
安定门内、外大街	Āndìng Mén Nèi/Wài Dàjiē		
板厂胡同	Bǎnchǎng Hútòng	北新桥三条	Běi Xīn Qiáo Sān Tiáo
北京站西、东街	Běijīng Zhàn Xī/Dōng Jiē	朝阳路	Cháoyáng Lù

186

Street and Bus Stop Names

朝阳门南大街	Cháoyáng Mén Nán Dàjiē	建国门北大街	Jiànguó Mén Běi Dàjiē
朝阳门北、南小街	Cháoyáng Mén Běi/Nán Xiǎo Jiē	建国门内、外大街	Jiànguó Mén Nèi/Wài Dàjiē
朝阳门内、外大街	Cháoyáng Mén Nèi/Wài Dàjiē	建华南路	Jiànhuá Nán Lù
崇文门东大街	Chóngwén Mén Dōng Dàjiē	金鱼胡同	Jīnyú Hútòng
春秀街	Chūnxiù Jiē	宽街	Kuān Jiē
大北窑	Dà Běi Yáo	亮马河南路	Liàngmǎhé Nánlù
大佛寺	Dà Fó Sì Dōng Jiē	亮马桥	Liàngmǎ Qiáo
大华路	Dàhuá Lù	亮马桥路	Liàngmǎ Qiáo Lù
灯市口（东）街	Dēngshìkǒu (Dōng) Jiē	柳芳北里	Liǔ Fāng Běi Jiē
东安门大街	Dōng'ān Mén Dàjiē	禄米仓街	Lùmǐcāng Jiē
东长安街	Dōng Cháng'ān Jiē	麦子店	Màizidiàn
东单北大街	Dōng Dān Běi Dàjiē	美术馆东街	Měishùguǎn Dōng Dàjiē
东大桥路	Dōng Dà Qiáo Lù	农展馆南路	Nóngzhǎn Guǎn Nán Lù
东交民巷	Dōng Jiāo Mín Xiàng	平安大道	Píng'ān Dà Dào
东四	Dōng Sì	七圣南路	Qī Shèng Nán Lù
东三环北、中路	Dōng Sān Huán Běi/Zhōng Lù (east third ring north/middle)	日坛北路	Rìtán Běi Lù
		日坛使馆区	Rìtán Embassy Area (Rìtán Shǐguǎnqū)
东四北、南大街	Dōng Sì Běi/Nán Dàjiē		
东四西街	Dōng Sì Xī Jiē	日坛路	Rìtán Lù
东四九条	Dōng Sì Jiǔ Tiáo	三里屯	Sānlǐtún
	Dōng Zhī Mén Běi Dàjiē	三里屯使馆区	Sānlǐtún Embassy Area (Sānlǐtún Shǐguǎnqū)
东直门北、南小街	Dōng Zhī Mén Běi/Nán Xiǎojiē		
东直门内大街	Dōng Zhī Mén Nèi Dàjiē (24 hour food street)	三里屯酒吧街、南街	Sānlǐtún Jiǔbā Jiē/Nán Jiē
		三里屯南路	Sānlǐtún (Nán) Lù
东直门外大街	Dōng Zhī Mén Wài Dàjiē	史家胡同	Shǐ Jiā Hútòng
东总布胡同	Dōng Zǒng Bù Hútòng	帅府园胡同	Shuài Fǔ Yuán Hútòng
丰富胡同	Fēngfù Hútòng	苏州胡同	Sūzhōu Hútòng
工人体育场北路	Gōngrén Tǐyù Cháng Běi Lù	团结湖	Tuánjié Hú
工人体育场东路	Gōngrén Tǐyù Cháng Dōng Lù	王府井大街	Wángfǔjǐng Dàjiē
关东店南街	Guān Dōng Diàn Nán Jiē	五四大街	Wǔ Sì Dàjiē
光华路	Guānghuá Lù	秀水东街	Xiùshuǐ Dōng Jiē
国子监街	Guózǐ Jiàn Jiē	樱花园西街	Yīnghuā Yuán Xī Jiē
和平里东街	Hépíng Lǐ Dōng Jiē	雍和宫	Yōnghé Gōng
和平里火车站	Hépíng Lǐ Huǒchē Zhàn	雍和宫大街	Yōnghé Gōng Dàjiē
后圆恩寺胡同	Hòu Yuán'ēn Sì Hútòng	雨儿胡同	Yǔ'ér Hútòng

Yōnghé Gōng (Lama Temple)

雍和宫

Open 9–4.30; adm ¥15.

See map pp.182–3, no.75. The 116 bus runs straight north from the northeast corner of Tiāntán Gōngyuán through Chóngwén Mén. Get off at the stop called Yōnghé Gōng in Yōnghé Gōng Dàjiē. It's better if possible to take the metro to Yōnghé Gōng. Leave by the south exit and turn left, then immediately left, and the entrance is about 200m further. Bus 13 runs from Xī Sì Dàjiē, north of Xī Dān. Get off at stop no.21.

Although usually known as the Lama Temple, Yōnghé Gōng means 'The Palace of Peace and Harmony', and was built during the reign of the Qīng emperor Kāngxī in 1694 as the residence of his fourth son, who later became the third Qīng emperor to rule from Běijīng (Yōngzhèng—reigned 1723–35). The palace was converted to a lamasery during the reign of Qiánlóng in 1744. It now functions partly as a genuine place of worship and teaching for around 80 monks and innumerable visitors, and partly as a vehicle for Chinese propaganda concerning Tibet.

Their former role as an imperial residence has left the main halls of the Lama Temple with the same yellow roofs as the Imperial Palace, and with the same figures on the eaves. Running south to north, these increase in size and importance, ending with the towering and impressive Wànfú Gé (Pavilion of Ten Thousand Fortunes), with its aerial passages to side halls. Reflecting the Tibetan and Mongolian roots of Lamaist Buddhism, and the Manchurian origins of the dynasty that set up the temple, signs and stelae within the temple are carved with Tibetan, Mongolian and Manchu, as well as Chinese scripts.

Passing throught the first courtyard with its drum tower, bell tower and stele pavilions, you reach the **Tiānwáng Diàn** (Hall of the Heavenly Kings) with the four statues found at all Chinese Buddhist and Lamaist temples. The next courtyard is bordered with halls for teaching various disciplines such as mathematics, plus halls for exoteric (public) doctrines, originally coming from an inner circle of adepts. As elsewhere esoteric Buddhism is represented by statues of larger males figures enjoying sexual pleasure with smaller female ones, although due to official prudery these are usually draped. The courtyard contains a substantial and ornate incense burner, dating from 1747, and a pavilion housing a single four-language stele carved with Qiánlóng's views on Buddhism, its Chinese characters in his handwriting.

Ahead is the **Yōnghé Gōng** after which the whole temple is now known, with bronze and gold statues of the past, present (Sakyamuni, in the middle), and future Buddhas, along with two of Sakyamuni's favourite students and the 18 *luóhàn* (saints).

Beyond is the **Yǒngyòu Diàn** (Hall of Eternal Blessing) with further figures, and through that the main hall of the complex, the **Fǎlún Diàn** (Hall of the Wheel of Law). Despite the constant chatter of visitors, this cross-shaped hall is gloomily atmospheric, lined with racks of cloth-wrapped religious texts and dominated by a 6m-high bronze of Tsongkhapa (Zōngkābā), the founder of the 'Yellow Hat' sect of reformed lamaism to which this temple belongs, and of which the Dalai Lama is the leader. Closer examination of the walls reveals their covering of painted scenes, while rows of kneeling places lit by Ikea-style desk lamps shows the hall's continuing purpose as a place of teaching. At the rear behind Tsongkhapa is an elaborate carving, 'The Mountain of the 500 Arhats'.

The smaller halls to the left and right of the Yǒngyòu Diàn are entered from the rear, and contain exhibitions which require a separate ticket (¥3 for the two). The left (west) side hall contains Qiánlóng's court dress and crown, and, perhaps inappropriately for a Buddhist temple, the gun and sword he used when out hunting. Other Buddhist ceremonial items include masks used in religious dances, and an enormous rosary with beads the size of cricket balls or softballs. The hall on the east side is named after the Panchen Lama, the most senior reincarnation after the Dalai Lama, and whose last adult version resided in Běijīng and did much as he was told, although he showed signs of rebellion towards the end of his life. The hall contains an exhibition about Tibetan Buddhism, whose aim is to show, falsely, that Tibet has always been subservient to China, and suggesting that Běijīng always authorized the appointment of the new Dalai Lama and other important reincarnations. There are paintings and photographs of all of the Dalai and Panchen lamas and of other important monasteries, as well as gold and bronze statuary and other valuable and beautiful religious items.

The rearmost hall accessible to the public is the three-storey **Wànfú Gé** (Pavilion of Ten Thousand Fortunes) with flying buttress-like foot passages forming connections to two side halls. It contains a serene 26m-high Maitreya (future) Buddha statue carved from a single white sandalwood trunk and transported all the way from Tibet as a gift to Qiánlóng from the 7th Dalai Lama. Its copper-coloured bulk is hung with scarves of respect, and enclosed by three storeys of galleries with many more statues. For once in China fact replaces hyperbole— there is an incongruous testament to the statue's uniqueness in a brass reproduction of a *Guinness Book of Records* certificate displayed outside.

Buddhism and Lamaism

 Buddhism was an alien import to China which was at times denounced as a barbarian religion and banned. Arriving via the Silk Routes from Gandhara, it gradually spread from oasis to oasis around the Tarim basin, and by CE 166 could count a Hàn emperor amongst its devotees. The religion gained ground in the 4th century when it attracted the attention of the upper strata of Chinese society through the activities of scholar-gentleman monks, familiar with both secular and religious literature, and by the 5th century was widespread. The speculation in China that daoist founder Lǎozi was the originator of Buddhism partially sprang from the use of existing daoist vocabulary to translate Buddhist terms, which gave a false sense of similarity between the two systems. More rigorous translations were produced and an acceptance of Buddhism on its own terms began towards the end of the 4th century.

The Buddhist begins by recognizing that life is impermanent, without real essence, and characterized by suffering. His or her concern is to escape from the cycle of successive lives in which the form of each depends upon behaviour in the one before, and to arrive at *nirvana* (literally 'extinction'), a transcendent state without further pain, death or rebirth. This can be achieved by discipline, moral behaviour, wisdom and meditation, leading to the denial of all desires and cravings. The key text of Buddhism is the three-part *Tripitaka* ('three baskets'), containing accounts of the origins of the Buddhist community and rules for the behaviour of monks and nuns, discourses attributed to the Buddha and his immediate disciples, and various philosophical and psychological texts. Laying stress on individual texts over others and interpreting them in different ways has led to the creation of numerous different schools of Buddhism, some of them native to China.

The historical Buddha ('awakened one') and founder of Buddhism, Sakyamuni, was born the son of a prince in what is now Nepal in 563 BCE. In general a Buddha is a being who has achieved full enlightenment, and thus *nirvana*, and during his final passage through life can be identified by numerous signs. According to Buddhist doctrine Sakyamuni had been preceded by numerous Buddhas and will be followed by many others. These are usually symbolized at Chinese Buddhist sites by the statues of the 'Buddhas of the three times'—Dipamkara (past ages), Sakyamuni (present age) and Maitreya (future ages).

The peak of Buddhist strength in China was during the Suí (589–618) and Táng (618–906), when the main Chinese schools were developed and the monasteries became numerous, rich and powerful. Although Buddhism had been persecuted before, in 845 it received a blow from which it never completely recovered as the Chinese state ordered the dismantling of the monasteries and the return of monks and nuns to everyday life. Subsequent centuries saw a fusing of the various schools into one, but the arrival of the Manchu Qīng in 1644 brought the Lamaist version of Buddhism to the fore.

Lamaism, or Tibetan Buddhism, evolved both from the indigenous shamanism of *Bon* and a particular Indian form of Buddhism. Khubilai Khan appointed the Tibetan Grand Lama as his religious advisor in the 13th century, and by the 17th it had become the dominant creed of the Mongols. The Manchus had been converted to Lamaism before conquering China in 1644, and supported Lamaism to keep the Dalai Lamas happy and to pacify Tibet and Mongolia. 'Lama' is a term now often applied indiscriminately to Buddhist monks, but which more exactly is applied only to the most senior and enlightened who have passed rigorous qualifications. The key lamas of Tibetan Buddhism are each seen as a reincarnation of their previous selves, and the two most senior, the Dalai Lama and Panchen Lama, have each come to hold political as well as spiritual authority. Following the death of one of them, the other leads a search committee which investigates children with the right physical characteristics and subjects them to tests of recognition of items owned by previous incarnations. The 14th Dalai Lama was born in 1935 and now lives in enforced exile in India, still regarded by Tibetans and Mongolians as their spiritual leader. The late Panchen Lama became largely a creature of the Běijīng government and mostly resided in the Chinese capital.

The Panchen Lama's current reincarnation, Gedhun Choekyi Nyima, an infant recognized by the Dalai Lama in 1995, was promptly arrested by government, hasn't been seen since, and is often described as the world's youngest political prisoner. Meanwhile the officially atheist government announced (despite often trumpeting its belief solely in Marxism and dialectical materialism) that it had identified the 'true' Panchen Lama, another very young boy, Gyaincain Norbu. This version was also largely kept out of sight until June 1999 when he was taken for his first appearance at Tashilumpo monastery in Tibet, but kept separated from his supposedly devoted followers (who aren't quite so easily gulled) by tight security. The Panchen Lama plays an important role in helping to identify the reincarnation of the Dalai Lama, and so control over him is crucial for the future of China's control over Tibetans. In early 2000, a 14-year-old boy recognized in infancy both by Tibetans and by the Communist Party as the 17th reincarntion of the Karmapa, the spiritual leader of the black hat sect of Tibetan Buddhism and the third most important reincarnating lama, walked away from more than a decade of political indoctrination and over the high passes to Dharamsala, the north Indian seat of the Dalai Lama's government in exile, throwing the communists into confusion. 'He's not left—he's in the monastery praying,' said one official. 'He's just gone shopping for black hats, and left a note saying he loves China and he'll be back,' said another at the same time. The Indian government received warnings not to give him refugee status.

Within days Běijīng announced, coincidentally, that it had identified a two-year-old boy, Soinam Puncog, as the 7th Reting Lama, and promptly enthroned him in a ceremony at Lhasa's Jokang Temple, giving him a certificate of authenticity, a little like Donald Duck giving a sainthood authenticity certificate to the Pope, and hardly likely to gain him much credit with Tibetans since the Dalai Lama does not recognize the appointment. The 5th Reting led the party searching for the reincarnation who subsequently became the current (14th) Dalai Lama, and he ran Tibet as regent between 1933 and 1940, becoming the Dalai Lama's senior tutor before being imprisoned in 1947 for collaboration with the Chinese and dying shortly afterwards. His next reincarnation, the 6th Reting, was also a communist sympathiser, and the Party expects the new reincarnation to be no different: 'Child Tibetan Lama to Love Communist Party,' announced the government-controlled press. The Dalai Lama's own candidate can be expected to play an important role in the search for the Dalai Lama's next incarnation, when the time comes.

Buddhists are usually vegetarians, but most Tibetans and Mongols are not. The inappropriateness of both the mountainous regions occupied by the one and the nomadic lifestyle in the grasslands of the other made intensive vegetable farming impractical, and even then unlikely to provide the calorific needs of life in a harsh environment. But the matter of the occupation of the body of an animal by the soul of another being remains a concern:

> I learned that by the Mongol way of thinking it is not right to fire at antelope, nor at wild asses, when they are in big herds. It may be that the soul of a saint or a Buddha has passed into the body of a wild animal, whose holiness gathers the others about it in great numbers. A Mongol will spend a great deal of time first breaking up a herd and then going after two or three evidently profane animals which have separated, rather than run the risk of shooting a 'magic' creature.
>
> Owen Lattimore, *The Desert Road to Turkestan*, 1929

Since the communist victory of 1949 a nominal freedom of religious belief has not included the right to believe anything that deviated from the Party line. Land reforms of 1950–2 stripped the monasteries of their lands, and left the monks with no alternative but to return to conventional life. The Cultural Revolution of 1966–76 caused the mass destruction of Buddhist buildings and relics. Since then there has been partial restoration of a few monasteries, and a limited amount of teaching is permitted.

Despite the destruction there are vast numbers of Buddhist temples, pagodas and cave sites, often richly furnished with statuary and paintings. Constantly repeated images include those of the 'Buddhas of the three times', the four celestial kings (guardian figures), Bodhisattvas (beings on the road to enlightenment willing to share their spiritual credit with others), Arhats (beings about to attain *nirvana*), and the eight auspicious symbols (parasol, two fish, conch shell, lotus blossom, vase of sacred water, wheel of teaching, knot of eternity, banner of victory.)

Confucius Temple (Kǒng Miào) and Capital Museum (Shǒudū Bówùguǎn) 孔庙，首都博物馆

Open 8–5; adm ¥20 ($1.25).

As a former Assistant Imperial Tutor put it:

> 'Emperors have gone. Republican Generals come and go, but our Chinese people rise and fall according to how far we continue to live by the good sense and reasoned behaviour taught by the Sage. Now, as you, Hsienshêng [Xiānshēng—Sir], can see, we are falling headlong into plain barbarity. When you reach his temple you will probably find only herons for company.'

John Blofeld, *City of Lingering Splendor*, 1961

The herons are gone although jays and other birds inhabit the ancient trees, but it's true that visitors to the Confucius Temple number only a small fraction of those to the nearby Lama Temple.

See map pp.184–5, no.27. The temple is about 60m down Guózǐjiān Jiē (Imperial College Street), a turning off Yōnghé Gōng Dàjiē almost opposite the entrance to the Lama Temple. This street contains three of the handful of Běijīng's surviving *páilou* (arches commemorating individuals who demonstrated Confucian values—children who sacrificed themselves for their parents or widows who refused to remarry, for example).

Confucius having until recently been one of the Communist Party's *bêtes noires*, the Kǒng Miào (Temple of Confucius) is still more usually known as the Capital Museum, a fine collection of locally discovered artefacts being housed in buildings on the right-hand (east) side.

Around the first courtyard stand 198 stelae bearing the names of all those who passed the highest level triennial civil service exam. Altogether the stelae carry 51,624 names, places of origin and position numbers, from the Yuán, Míng and Qīng dynasties. The Yuán, like the later Qīng, learned that to conquer China on horseback was one thing, but it could not be governed without adopting Chinese ways and using Chinese administrative skills. It was a Mongol emperor who in 1307 conferred on Confucius the title 'Sage of Great Accomplishment', the highest title he was ever awarded (although Confucius—551–479 BCE—had been dead for nearly 1,800 years). It was the Mongols, too, who built the original temple in the 13th century, but the stelae listing the graduates of their day were removed and buried by the Míng, who probably considered that examinations held under barbarian rulers did not count. These were rediscovered and re-erected in the time of the Qīng emperor Kāngxī, who also restored the buildings in 1689. Another restoration was carried out under Qiánlōng, who replaced the roofs with imperial yellow tiles. Having the results written in stone has not saved the candidates' names from oblivion, many of the stelae being heavily weathered or otherwise damaged. The last graduates, of 1905, had to pay for the stelae themselves. Signs next to individual stelae tell the stories of some of the individuals named there, including one who took the examination at the age of 98.

Civil Service Examinations

The Chinese are generally credited with the invention of a meritocratic civil service with entrance based on examination. Lists of successful candidates have survived from as early as 165 BCE, and the Chinese model is thought to have led to the introduction of civil service exams in Britain in the 19th century, where senior civil servants are still labelled 'Mandarins', and later in the USA. The examination system would collapse when the country did, but revived under the Táng it ran almost continuously in different forms until abolished by decree in 1905. At its best it allowed candidates from families without *guānxi* (connections or influence) to compete fairly with those more powerful, but for much of the time candidates' names were left on their papers, and patronage was as important as examination success. Given the years or even decades of study necessary, access remained open only to those families who could afford to pay to support a candidate's studies. By the Míng and Qīng the requirements of the examinations were driving the entire education system. Success guaranteed social advancement, employment as an official, and the resulting opportunities for enrichment through means both legitimate and corrupt.

It was first necessary to pass an examination at district level, graduates of which were exempt from corvée labour (work on public projects, such as containing the Yellow River, required as a form of tax) and corporal punishment. They also qualified to take the triennial examinations at the provincial capital. Success here led to the triennial metropolitan examination in Běijīng, the results of which were confirmed by an examination in the Imperial Palace itself. In later years other intermediate qualifying examinations were added, as well as separate tests for military candidates.

Papers involved writing commentaries on the Confucian classics, literary composition and the drafting of memorials in favour of a particular policy, supported by quotations from the classics. In later times handwriting was also taken into account, and to write a single character incorrectly could be fatal to a candidate's chances. They were put into cells at special locked examination halls for up to three days at a time, and it was widely believed that their past misdeeds would come back to haunt them, often in the form of the ghosts of those they had harmed. The stress was sometimes too much, and candidates would run mad, or be found hanging in their cells. The Běijīng examination halls were erected, as much of the rest of the capital, by the Yǒnglè emperor of the Míng, and stood just to the north of the Ancient Observatory (*see* p.200). Although the examinations were abandoned at the beginning of the century when Cíxī finally and reluctantly put into operation some of the reforms she had suppressed 20 years before, the halls survived until the 1930s, when, already ruinous, they were pulled down to create a rubbish dump. If they still stood, the candidate's deliberations would be disturbed by the roar of traffic on the second ring road.

Much as the British civil service was criticized in the 20th century for valuing knowledge of Homer and Thucydides above real administrative skills or knowledge of the second law of thermodynamics (in C.P. Snow's famous example), so the emphasis on philosophy and ancient history in the Chinese examinations little prepared candidates to deal with pressures from the outside world, and played their part in the Qīng policy failures which led to the end of imperial rule. One punishment forced on the Qīng by the allied powers after the Boxer Rebellion was the suspension of the examinations for five years, a blow aimed shrewdly straight at the anti-trade, anti-foreign Confucian literati, and a few years later the Qīng themselves abolished them for good.

In a continuing backwards march from the anti-intellectual, anti-specialist stance of the Máo years, the government has announced that all civil servants will once again be recruited by examination, although it's probably fair to say that a knowledge of Confucius is less likely to be of assistance than a willingness to toe the Party line. New graduates will probably be more concerned to see their names written on pay cheques than on stelae.

Eleven Qīng-era double-eaved stele pavilions in the second courtyard are in a poor state of repair and roughly bricked up, their roofs more heavily overgrown with grasses than most other temples. In some you can see detritus leaning against the giant stones; others you can enter to pat the heads of the massive *bìxì*, already polished by earlier visitors. The stelae texts contain accounts of repairs to the temple, edicts related to Confucian teachings and stories of various Qīng military campaigns during the reigns of four emperors. Statues of Confucius and his principle commentators stand around, with cypress trees of considerable antiquity, one nearly 700 years old.

Much of the site was formerly connected directly to the Imperial College to the west (*see* below), where the emperor would come annually to expound the classics to the scholars. His representatives would come several times a year to the temple for ceremonies in honour of Confucius, especially on the sage's birthday. The main hall of the temple, the **Dàchéng Diàn** (Hall of Great Perfection) stands on a broad terrace and contains a central shrine to Confucius, surrounded by a think tank of tributes to 60 top scholars. The hall also contains a number of Chinese classical musical instruments (and often someone playing them), as well as incense burners and other artefacts.

A passage at the rear left-hand corner of the compound gives access to the **Qiánlóng Stone Scriptures**, with the stones arranged in five long rows in a shed to which they bring a certain library-like quality. These are the classics produced by Confucius and his students during the Spring and Autumn period (770–475 BCE) and other texts which were the subjects of the imperial examinations. The stones originate from the desire of one man to produce a perfect copy of these classics, amounting to some 630,000 characters, which he undertook between 1726 and 1738. His finished version was presented to Qiánlóng, who later had them thoroughly proofread and caused them to be carved on stelae in around 1790. 189 stelae contain the text and the 190th is a copy of the emperor's order that the work be undertaken. The stones were relocated from the neighbouring Imperial College and restored in 1988. Tucked amongst them are two late-Qīng fire engines, one clearly meant to be carried by bearers and one on metal wheels, with brass, hand-operated pumps decorated with dragons and covered in dust. Just to the north a smaller hall has the **Dàxué Shí**, a large stone incribed with a classic text on developing moral character.

The buildings on the east of the main hall house the **Capital Museum**, an exhibition of the history of Běijīng from Paleolithic times onwards, well lit and presented, and with English introductions. Běijīng may not have become China's capital until the time of the Mongols, but many earlier dynasties left their mark in the form of funerary objects, coin and seals, Buddhist devotional objects, and ceramics. The exhibition ends with copies of ancient maps, a picture of influential Jesuit Matteo Ricci and modern aerial photographs of the city.

Confucianism

 Part philosophy, part social theory, and only part religion, Confucianism is based on writings attributed to Confucius (Kǒng Fūzi, 'Venerable Master Kǒng', 551–479 BCE), and those of followers who developed his ideas, such as Mencius (Mèngzi, c. 372–289 BCE) and Xúnzi (c. 313–238 BCE). The ideas in these writings provided the framework in which the majority of Chinese philosophical thinking took place until modern times. A key text is the *Analects* (*Lúnyǔ*), a compilation of Confucius's conversations and pronouncements, made by his followers. This, with the book of Mencius and two other Confucian-interpreted classics, eventually came to be studied in schools, and became the canon upon which candidates for administrative posts were tested. Although Confucianism at times lost its place as the orthodox ideology, it was only at the termination of the imperial examination system in 1905 that its influence on government began to wane. A key idea was that the hierarchy of society reflected a natural moral order; patriarch as head of family, prince as head of state. State ceremonial and more domestic ritual demonstrated the subservience of inferiors to superiors, and observance of these rituals helped to ensure the harmonious operation of society. The prince, so long as he behaved morally, held the 'mandate of heaven', the source of his legitimacy. Like other moral beings, his behaviour would demonstrate *rén*, a benevolent mixture of filial piety, loyalty, friendship, courtesy, reliability and a general 'do-as-you-would-be-done-by' reciprocal altruism. In the elaboration of Confucian thought by Mencius, human nature was held to be fundamentally good, but creating the conditions for its nurture was the responsibility of the individual and above all of the ruler. Later interpretations, often known as neo-Confucianism, saw daoist and Buddhist ideas (such as that of the 'way') replace some of the original more mechanistic ideas.

In the centuries following Confucius's death, in which states contended for the overall mastery of China, it was argued by Confucians that only a Confucian ruler would succeed in unifying the country, but China's first unification took place under the anti-Confucian Qín (221–206 BCE). However, Confucianism was adopted as the orthodox state ideology under the following Hàn dynasty. The Táng (618–907 CE) began to build temples to Confucius, which were used to display tablets commemorating the principal men of letters after their deaths.

There's long been a tendency to take from Confucius what appeals and ignore the rest. The Jesuits, who were responsible for Latinizing Confucius's name and introducing him to the West, liked his paternalistic family values. Some authoritarian Asian leaders have made Confucius the core of the 'Asian values' which were supposed to have driven the region's now rather battered economic success, in an attempt to legitimize their own undemocratic positions. But Confucius regarded it as a moral duty to tell rulers the truth, and it's doubtful whether he himself would have been a Confucian as the word is understood by touchy modern autocrats. Excoriated by the communists, he's been quietly rehabilitated in recent years, and in 1999 they organized celebrations of the 2,550th anniversary of his birth. As their haphazard progress toward capitalism ('socialism with Chinese characteristics') produces an increasing amount of unrest amongst those missing out on the benefits, any support for authoritarian government is welcome, although the chances of the Communist Party allowing any independent criticism of the kind of which Confucius would have approved are slim indeed.

Shǒudū Túshūguǎn (Capital Library) and Guózǐ Jiàn (Imperial College) 首都图书馆，国子监

Open 8.30–7, Sat and Sun 8.30–5.30, closed Mon; adm free.

See map pp.182–3, no.27. The Imperial College was once directly connected to the Confucius Temple next door. The highest national academy from the Mongol Yuán dynasty onwards, it was first built in 1306, and rebuilt during the Míng and later. A magnificent glazed archway in the Qīng dates from around 1784 and Qiánlóng's calligraphy front and back encourages students to study hard.

The main sight is a wonderful central hall called the Bìyōng Gōng or Hall of Classics, rebuilt in the Qīng, a square, yellow-tiled two-storey pavilion with finely carved and perforated wooden screens and a deep verandah, which is now used for occasional exhibitions (*open 9–4, adm ¥6*). It's reached by bridges over a circular moat at each of the four compass points. Here the emperors would come in the second month of each year to expound the classics to the students.

The site as a whole is now a functioning library, and the quiet courtyards are dotted with reading students.

The rear building is the Hall of Sacrifice for Ethics, and was a stack room during the Yuán dynasty, rebuilt in the Míng. There was a special seat here for the emperor before the Hall of Classics was built. The stones carved with the Confucian canon are now next door in the Confucius Temple.

Dì Tán Gōngyuán 地坛公园

Adm 6–9; adm ¥1, ¥5 for the cultural relics and altar.

See map pp.182–3, no.28. Just north of Ⓜ Yōnghé Gōng.

The main altar to see is that at Tiān Tán (*see* p.161), none of the others being as large or spectacular and none having as many surrounding buildings, or ones as intact. Dì Tán, the Altar of Earth, was, however, the second most important for imperial ceremonies. Occupied by foreign troops in 1860, it was also the first to become a public park, in 1925.

The Hall of Cultural Relics, entered from its north side, and the altar were originally built in the Míng around 1530, and reconstructed by the Qiánlóng emperor in 1749. When the grounds became a park, the hall became a library, only reverted to its current state in 1986, and now houses models of a ceremony taking place. Other halls, open unpredictably (one of which held a wax museum which has disappeared elsewhere), have labels in amusing English, such as 'Deity Warehouse'.

The altar itself, following the same symbolism found at Tiān Tán, is square to symbolize the earth. Sacrifices here were buried rather than burned. It's a double-layered terrace surrounded by twin yellow eaved walls.

The grounds are now divided into gardens of no particular interest except that, as evidence of the changes in society and the growth of a secondary market for property, individuals and agencies selling and renting apartments can be found under the trees to the north of the altar.

A temple fair has now been revived and is held here in the spring. A hall just outside the east gate holds the lively Tán Gēn Yuàn Běijīng-style restaurant (see p.262).

For details of other altars, see Tiān Tán, p.163.

Dōng Yuè Miào　东岳庙

Open 9–4.30, closed Mon; adm ¥10, annual ticket accepted.

See map pp.182–3, no.33. This daoist temple (for a brief account of daoism, see p.217) is a short walk east of Ⓜ Cháoyáng Mén. Cháoyáng Mén Wài Dàjiē passes right through the grounds. After a long period as a school for the Public Security Bureau, and the expenditure of around $3 million in repairs, what was regarded as one of Běijīng's most important sites in the 1930s reopened to the public in February 1999 (although parts are still used as a police station). The main entrance *páilou*, a slendid green and yellow tiled affair, now stands separately on the south side of the road, between the Full Link and the (closed) Sea Sky department stores. Two neighbouring wooden *páilou* have disappeared.

The temple's drum and bell towers are now outside what is the main gate, and the left-hand one is the ticket office.

Dates given for the original construction of the temple are as early as 1317, but the first hall is dated 1322 and has threatening images of General Dragon and General Tiger, otherwise known as 'Hēng!' and 'Hā!' (you can tell from their facial expressions who is who) performing the protective role taken by the Four Heavenly Kings at Buddhist temples (although daoism has versions of these too), and 10 further guardian statues. A raised causeway lined with shrubs and potted plants crosses a large courtyard with two stele pavilions and assorted stelae standing about, most recording renovations to the temple funded by trade societies. The biggest stele of all, in the northeast corner and in a glass case, has an account in very fine calligraphy of the construction of the temple and of the daoist masters involved in it. Inevitably the Kāngxī emperor gets in on another stele dating from 1704, recording the rebuilding of the temple in 1689 following a fire, and a Qiánlóng stele records further renovations in 1761. There are two statues, one the 'White Jade Horse', and the other the 'Bronze Wonder Donkey'—an assembled creature like a Père David's deer (see p.343) with the head of a horse, body of a donkey, tail of a mule and the split hooves of a bull (there are further examples in the animal line-up at the Míng Tombs, see p.309). Touching the first is supposed to give you 'safe movements and business fulfilment' and touching the second is supposed to cure diseases.

But the main point of interest is the surrounding buildings, divided into 72 little cubicles with a significant numbers of daoism's more than 10,000 gods represented in garish statuary, and with good English explanations as to why they are here and what they are up to. All are presided over by the deity of Tài Shān, a holy mountain in Shāndōng Province thought to be the home of dead souls, after whom the temple is named. This is all about settling accounts, about being weighed and found wanting, and indeed the now disappeared entrance gate once had a giant abacus mounted on the wall to warn those who entered that they would be judged. The Chinese themselves could learn a great deal from what's written here now, and it almost seems that those who commissioned and installed what is entirely new statuary had both the moral and the environmental state of modern China in mind.

Gods are divided into departments with various jobs, such as The Department for Controlling Bullying and Cheating and The Department of Pity and Sympathy, suggesting that rulers should exercise benevolence over their subjects and that inhabitants of the same neighbourhood should take care of each other. One could hope for a more global consciousness, but it's a start. There are departments for judging you in hell, departments for escorting you to heaven, and various departments busy with deciding whether you should be reborn as bird, fish or mammal. Daoists can be rewarded or punished for their intentions, whether or not they carried them out (rather as it's said that in the days of the emperors you could be beaten just for thinking about entering the Forbidden City).

Not all the departments yet have figures and of those that do certain ones clearly gain a lot more attention from Chinese visitors than others, as indicated by the numbers of tassled and belled wooden plaques hung at particular shrines. Sadly this doesn't seem to be the more human ones, but those such as the Department of Accumulating Justifiable Wealth, and the Department for Increasing Wealth and Longevity, although some attention seems to be paid to the Department for Upholding Loyalty and Filial Piety, the numerous plaques coming perhaps from those with unreliable business partners, or whose children haven't been to see them for a long time. There's a nasty hint of nationalism in some of the Chinese captions which isn't always translated into the English. The Door God department is perhaps the most popular, the Door God's job being to keep out devils and bad influences, and to refute hearsay and other attacks on family security.

Empty departments include, appropriately, that for Wandering Ghosts. Bits of ecology, like a department encouraging the care of birds and another the setting free of animals, and one for keeping an eye on corrupt officials, suggest that a wholesale return to daoism would probably do China a lot of good, in lieu of democracy.

1930s resident John Blofeld knew a priest here, and once asked him why there was all the crudeness of the outer courtyards when the rest of daoism advocated harmony. 'You must make a peasant believe he is at death's door before he'll call a doctor,' said the priest.

> *People like it that way. Tell them that they are holy and beautiful, that every one of them is a living embodiment of the sacred Tao, and they will think you are a stupid fellow, or smell your breath to see if you are drunk. But tell them they are worse than devils or hungry ghosts and only fit for hell, then they will respect your powers of perception and ask you privately to reveal the special tastes of hell's judges so they will know how to bribe them.*

John Blofeld, *City of Lingering Splendour*, 1961

Some of the cubicles are the ancestral halls of figures who played a part in the temple's founding. The Department of Official Morality, which sets standards of behaviour for rulers, demanding impartiality and fairness in the enforcement of laws and rules and resistance to corruption, seems to receive a lot of attention. Wooden plaques hanging here suggest a few officials have been snitched on perhaps.

The main hall at the rear, also from 1322, burned down in 1698, was reconstructed in 1700, and repaired for reopening in 1999. It is a shrine to the God Dōngyuè, who lives on Tài Shān, in charge of all human beings, and in charge of the 76 departments and the 18 layers of hell.

Behind the main hall is a covered causeway to Dōngyuè's bedchamber where his two wives were separately housed.

At the very rear there's a two-storey gallery whose rooms contain an exhibition on the history of the temple, daoist artefacts and photographs of other daoist temples. The main daoist temple in Běijīng is the Báiyún Guàn (see p.215).

Rì Tán Gōngyuán 日坛公园
Open 6.30am–10pm; adm ¥0.20

See map pp.182–3, no.61. The park is in the heart of the Rìtán embassy quarter. Walk east from Ⓜ Jiànguó Mén and turn north up Rìtán Lù.

Here is yet another altar, this time to the Sun, far smaller in scale than either Tiān Tán (*see* p.161) or even Dì Tán (*see* p.196). There are entrances on all four sides, but a particularly magnificent *páilou* on the west side, and a small altar in a central enclosure of red wall topped with green tiles. Otherwise this is an identikit Chinese park with benches under its pines, often occupied by sleeping people with their heads wrapped in newspaper. People fly kites and play tennis with a ball on a bit of elastic, and Chinese chess. There's a children's playground with trampolines and bumper cars on the southeast side, together with a curious aerial monorail whose vehicles need to be pedalled around the line.

The streets around the park afford a number of restaurants catering for embassy staff, and the Xiùshuǐ Silk Market and Friendship Stores (with further foreign food) are 10 minutes' walk east and south.

Zhìhuà Sì and Běijīng Culture Exchange Museum (Běijīng Wénbó Jiāoliúguǎn) 智化寺，北京文博交流馆
Open 9–4, closed Mon; adm ¥4, annual ticket accepted.

See map pp.182–3, no.77. The temple is in a maze of *hútòng* at Lùmǐcāng Jiē 5. From Ⓜ Jiànguó Mén walk north on the west side of the second ring road and enjoy getting a little lost, or take bus 24 from Běijīng Zhàn to stop Lùmǐcāng.

Only reopened in 1997, this quiet temple has few visitors and is pleasantly quiet, the presence of a basketball court marked in the courtyard suggesting the temple, now a museum of sorts, spent a period as dormitory accommodation, and the *fúwùyuán*'s washing still hangs about. They seem quite pleased to see visitors.

It was constructed in 1443 as the family temple of a rich Míng eunuch whose statue stood here until removed by a disapproving Qīng official in 1742. The *fúwùyuán* say that it was on the orders of the Qiánlóng emperor himself, but that a small stele inside the rear main hall on the left carries his image. According to some accounts the eunuch was executed only a few years after completing the temple, although there were repairs to it on several occasions later in the Míng and much rebuilding during the Qīng. The sweep of the roofs with their deep blue tiles is still said to retain something of a Míng flavour.

There are three courtyards altogether. The first hall, entered from the rear, has a collection of calligraphy boards, and the left hall a heavily carved rotating octagonal rack for storing scriptures which sits on a carved marble base. The temple's original owner bought a complete copy of the Buddhist *Tripitaka*, which was perhaps stored here in the device's gridwork.

Other halls display Běijīng opera pictures, early scripture, Buddhist sculpture and photographs showing the temple in a state of total disrepair which the ceilings still have—although still panelled and beautifully painted in places.

The rearmost hall, the Rúlái Diàn, has a 9m coppery seated Maitreya Buddha of the future, after whom the hall is named, with two attendants, all under a thick layer of dust. It's also known as the Ten Thousand Buddha Hall, and the walls are lined with hundreds of small Buddhas in small carved niches (the staff, perversely, claim there are 9,999), and further sutra slots. The ceiling here has been recently painted, but that's probably because it's of recent date—the monks took down the original in the 1930s which is now in The Nelson-Atkins Museum of Art in Kansas City, Missouri, <*http://www.nelson-atkins.org/>*.

You can climb up a dusty and rickety staircase to the rear on the right to find more miniature figures and three further substantial carved seated Buddhas, as well as views down into the courtyard and across the roofs of neighbouring *hútòng*. Modern gates to one side of the courtyard suggest that this was used as a storage yard at some point for trucks to drive through, as do the lean-tos against various walls.

Old Observatory (Gǔ Guānxiàngtái) 古观象台

Open 9–11.30 and 1–4.30, no lunch break, May–Oct; adm ¥10, annual ticket accepted.

See map pp.182–3, no.55. Adjacent to the southwest exit of Ⓜ Jiànguó Mén, at the junction of the second ring road and Jiànguó Mén Nèi Dàjiē.

Chinese observations of the heavens go back as far as 1300 BCE, and recordings of supernovae and the passage of Halley's Comet are still being used in astronomical research today. Accurate clocks, essential for proper astronomical and calendrical calculation, were also invented in China, the escapement mechanism being known from at least the 8th century CE. The method of giving co-ordinates to stars universally used today is one invented by the Chinese, which superseded in the West a different technique invented by the ancient Greeks. Nevertheless, by the end of the Míng the Chinese were still unable accurately to reconcile the 29½ day lunar month, and the 365.25 day solar year. The calendar was a mess, and help was needed from more accurate Western instruments and more advanced mathematics.

The observatory can claim to be one of the oldest in the world, having been established around 1279–96 during the Mongol Yuán dynasty using instruments brought to the city during the Jīn dynasty (1115–1234), nearly 300 years before Europe was to have a similar institution. When the Míng established their capital in Nánjīng in 1368 the instruments went there, but when the Yǒnglè emperor returned the capital to Běijīng he thought it would be disrespectful to the first emperor, buried in Nánjīng, to bring the instruments back. He therefore had copies of some of them made in wood, which then served as the models for new bronze versions. The current observatory is of approximately the same size and scale as a building erected on the same or nearly the same site during the Míng, probably around 1522.

Matteo Ricci (1552–1610) was the first Jesuit to receive permission to reside in Běijīng. Sympathetic to Chinese civilization, he acquired a detailed knowledge of classical and spoken Chinese, and impressed the emperor and Chinese intellectuals with his prodigious memory and scientific skills. He won imperial favour through his map-making and clock-regulating, and imported Western clocks and other high-tech items to use as gifts and to get him past hostile eunuchs. Adam Schall von Bell, who took over from Ricci in 1622, correctly predicted the 1629 solar eclipse and was appointed to the Board for Calendar Regulation. Although the Qīng replaced the Míng in 1644, Schall remained in favour, and was appointed president of the Board by the first Qīng emperor to reign from Běijīng.

Kāngxī, his successor (reigned 1661–1722), having been taught by Schall, appointed another Jesuit, Ferdinand Verbiest, to assist in reforming the calendar. According to some accounts, when the matter was debated before the emperor by ministers and princes, the Manchus were in favour of Verbiest, while the Chinese officials would rather have had a faulty calendar than one tainted by foreigners (an argument which must have needed tactful phrasing to present to the foreign Manchus). To correct the calendar, Verbiest had to cut out a month, which provoked widespread anti-foreign feeling at its supposed theft.

Verbiest was in charge of the Imperial Astronomical Bureau from 1662 to 1722, and supervised the construction of a collection of Western measuring instruments, which remained with their Chinese counterparts at the observatory until after the Boxer Rebellion of 1900. Following the occupation of Běijīng by foreign powers, the French suddenly remembered that some of the instruments had been given to China by Louis XIV and proposed to take them away as spoils of war. The Germans objected, since the observatory was in the 'German sector', and insisted that the instruments belonged to them. In fact Louis had donated one, an altazimuth, but in the end five went to the French Legation until the French were shamed into returning them in 1902, and six went for display in Potsdam, half-scale copies having been made and left in their place. One minor benefit to China of the Treaty of Versailles, which marked the end of the First World War, was the instruments' return in 1921. Half of them were to make yet another journey when they were removed to Nánjīng by the Nationalists in 1933 to prevent them from falling into the hands of the Japanese. Although Nánjīng itself was later overrun, they are still on display there.

The remaining instruments stand on a 17m-high plinth once reachable by a link from the now-vanished Tartar City wall. The building is now entered at ground level, and a right turn brings you to a courtyard with reproductions of early instruments. The first hall on the right has a well-displayed exhibition of early Chinese astronomical observation with English explanations. The instrument platform is reached by a brick staircase opposite the courtyard. Eight of the massive bronze instruments remain, up to 2m in diameter, including an ecliptic armilla, altazimuth, quadrant, azimuth theodolite, sextant and equatorial armilla. Each has an explanation of its purpose in English, and all are impressive due both to their size and decoration, supporting struts often cast as writhing dragons.

Wén Tiānxiáng Cí (Ancestral Temple of Wén Tiānxiáng)

Open 9–5; adm ¥1, annual ticket accepted.

See map pp.182–3, no.70. This small shrine, more reminiscent of *sìhéyuàn* than temple, is in Fǔxué Hútòng, off Jiāodàokǒu Nán Dàjiē, a long walk north of the National Art Gallery across Píng'ān Dàdào. Take bus 2 from Tiān Qiáo, Qián Mén, or Tiān'ān Mén past the National Art Gallery to the last stop, Kuān Jiē.

This is an ancient counterpart to the hagiographic museums of communism's saints. Versions vary, but Wén Tiānxiáng was a general faithful to the 960–1279 Sòng dynasty, which was crushed by the Mongols who founded the 1279–1368 Yuán dynasty. Wén was executed for refusing to swear loyalty to the new regime, and this shrine was later erected in his honour.

The first courtyard has a small stele with a picture of Wén, 1236–83, the shrine being built later to commemorate him. The first hall has a brief biography in Chinese, pictures of the area he was from, a bust, and a map showing his movements in various campaigns.

The hall at the rear of the second courtyard has more photographs, route maps, pictures of other monuments to his achievements, and two unusual Táng dynasty circular stelae on the right, of dubious relevance since they pre-date him by several hundred years.

A jujube tree (a small date), supposedly planted by the man himself, faces south to show his fidelity to the Sòng, whose two Northern and Southern dynasty capitals both lay a long distance in that direction. The jujubes glow a pleasant deep red in the autumn, and look just like small lanterns. This tiny site is very quiet unless you're unlucky enough to encounter a bedlam of schoolchildren undergoing indoctrination in nationalism at the shrine of another resister of foreigners.

It's a short walk to the Former Residence of Máo Dùn from here. Return to Jiāodàokǒu Nán Dàjiē and walk north, taking approximately the fourth *hútòng* on the left, Hòu Yuánsī Sì Hútòng.

Máo Dùn Gù Jū (Former Residence of Máo Dùn)   茅盾故居

Open 9–4, Tues, Thurs and Sat; adm ¥2.

See map pp.182–3, no.53. The house is at Hòu Yuánsī Sì Hútòng 13. Take bus 2 from Tiān Qiáo, Qián Mén, or Tiān'ān Mén past the National Art Gallery to the last stop, Kuān Jiē. Walk north until you find the *hútòng* on the left.

Another small but homely museum for collectors of courtyard houses (*sìhéyuàn*), this one is much less luxurious than that of Méi Lánfāng the opera star (*see* p.179), as befits a good communist. Part of the intended effect of this display is to show a wholesome frugality, with very ordinary and unimpressive possessions on display. Máo Dùn, 1896–1981, is best known for the novel *Midnight* of 1932 which depicted the corruption and exploitation of the Shànghǎi of the time. It followed the prevailing Stalinist line that art should clearly portray the different classes, the struggle between them, and the clear and inevitable direction of socialism. Máo (no relation) returned from exile in Hong Kong in 1949 to become Minister of Culture in Máo Zédōng's government, and to make sure everyone else's thinking was 'correct' too.

Museum of Agriculture (Zhōngguó Nóngyè Bówùguǎn)   中国农业博物馆

Open 9–4, closed Mon; adm ¥6, annual ticket accepted.

See map pp.182–3, no.70. The museum is set well back behind the Agriculture Exhibition Hall, south of the Great Wall Sheraton Hotel on the northeast third ring road, east of the Sānlǐtún diplomatic enclave. Ⓜ Dōng Zhí Mén and a long walk east, or get to the third ring and take bus 300 to Liàngmǎ Qiáo.

The museum was once a marvel by Běijīng standards, but like the Natural History Museum (*see* p.165) has been left far behind by the high-tech aquariums and other shows. There are three halls. The first is educational, with stuffed exotica such as a panda, tiger, deer and ostrich, plus domestica such as a sheep and chickens. There are stuffed monkeys in plastic trees with plastic apples. The central hall has fish tanks and a slightly alarming trickle of water across the floor; the collection includes gold fish and edible fish, as well as the tropical fish beloved of collectors, mostly in empty tanks. The right hall has a bizarre presentation of deep sea habitat with stuffed fish and sea-going mammals, suspended in mid-air as if swimming underwater, and there's an indescribable smell of fishy decay.

West of the Imperial City

Two sets of sights on this side of the city are laid out in convenient strings, with a mixture of shrines to communism and the crumbling remnants or heavily restored duplicates of old China. The broad and windy Cháng'ān boulevard which bisects Běijīng, passing in front of the Tiān'ān Mén, here becomes Fùxīng Mén Dàjiē, and crossing the west side's version of the Wángfǔjǐng shopping street, Xī Dān Běi Dàjiē, it passes first fashionable Sino-American architect I. M. Pei's Bank of China building and then a row of Běijīng's most modern blocks, some anonymously international, some absurd International-Style-with-Chinese-characteristics (of which the worst example is Běijīng Xī Zhàn, further to the south) and some works of genuine imagination.

On this route, which runs along the westbound metro line, the Minorities Culture Palace, National Treasure Museum and Army Museum can be seen, while a parallel route further north links the most spectacular of the ancient sites on this side, the White Dagoba Temple, with the museum for the writer Lǔ Xùn, passing the remains of several other ancient temples, either closed to foreigners or converted to other purposes. One of these is the Guangji Sì, a fine temple only open on special occasions, although monks seem quite tolerant of idle wanderers, and housing the Buddhist Association.

Not far east of the Bǎi Tǎ Sì there's a substantial Míng dynasty temple formerly known as Temple to Successive Generations of Emperors, which once housed tablets representing the spirits of almost all the emperors of China from the Liáo onwards, with the omission of one or two Míng emperors considered too debauched to qualify. By the 1930s it had become the headquarters of a short-lived version of the Red Cross and, like some other temples around Běijīng, has now become a middle school.

Fùchéng Mén Nèi Dàjiē is also home to China's first sex shop, although these are now commonplace in many cities, and rather more so than in the West. The Běijīng Adam and Eve Health Centre at no.133 even has its own web site, <*http://www.adameve-bj.com/*>, and seems to attract many curious people but few shoppers. Sex as recreation is an idea to which the government is firmly opposed, and in fact it barely acknowledges the existence of sex at all, other than trying to suppress it where possible, and the ignorance in which the population as a whole is kept has only led to unjustified fear of intimacy of any kind ('But if you kiss me won't I get pregnant?'), and the more rapid spread of sexually transmitted diseases.

Most of the products on sale here are Chinese, are often based on herbal remedies which have never been scientifically tested, and are more likely to lighten your wallet than heighten your desire. Viagra has been a big hit in China, and for a while became the number one 'gift' for

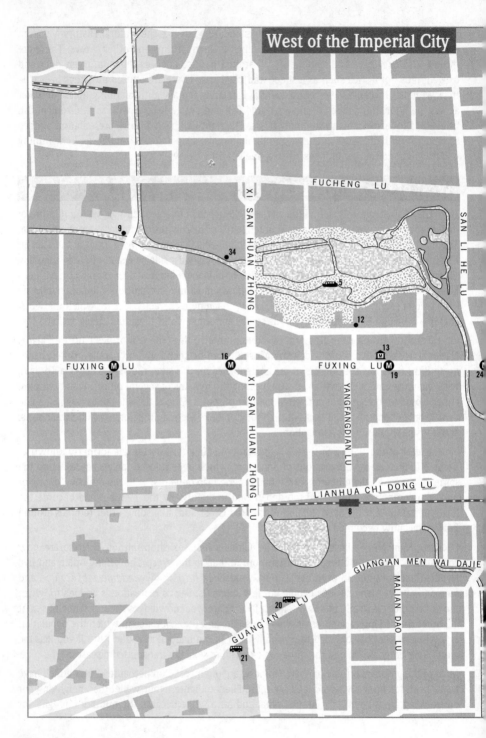

FUCHENG LU

XI SAN HUAN ZHONG LU

SAN LI HE LU

9

34

5

12

13

16

FUXING LU
31

FUXING LU
19

24

YANGFANGDIAN LU

LIANHUA CHI DONG LU

8

XI SAN HUAN ZHONG LU

GUANG'AN MEN WAI DAJIE

MALIAN DAO LU

20 LU

GUANG'AN

21

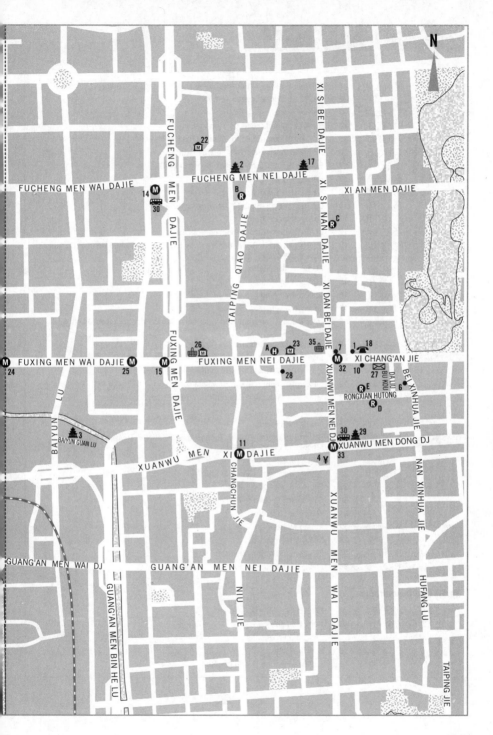

N

FUCHENG MEN DAJIE

22
M

2

17

FUCHENG MEN NEI DAJIE

FUCHENG MEN WAI DAJIE

XI SI BEI DAJIE

XI AN MEN DAJIE

14
M
30

B
R

C
R

XI SI NAN DAJIE

TAIPING QIAO DAJIE

XI DAN BEI DAJIE

26
M

A
H

23
M

35

7
1 18

M

FUXING MEN WAI DAJIE

FUXING MEN NEI DAJIE

XI CHANG'AN JIE

M
24

M
25

M
15

28

32

10

27
DA LIU
BU KOU

6

BEI XINHUA JIE

FUXING MEN DAJIE

XUANWU MEN NEI DJ

E
R
RONGXIAN HUTONG
R
D

3
BAIYUN GUAN LU

BAIYUN LU

11

30
29

M

XUANWU MEN DONG DJ

XUANWU MEN XI DAJIE
M

4 ¥
33

NAN XINHUA JIE

CHANGCHUN JIE

XUANWU MEN WAI DAJIE

GUANG'AN MEN WAI DJ

GUANG'AN MEN NEI DAJIE

NIU JIE

GUANG'AN MEN BIN HE LU

HUFANG LU

TAIPING JIE

民航大楼	1	Aviation Building (Mínháng Dàlóu)
白塔寺	2	Bái Tǎ Sì (White Dagoba Temple)
白云观	3	Báiyún Guàn
中国银行	4	Bank of China (Zhōngguó Yínháng)
八一湖码头	5	Bāyī Hú Mǎtou (Boats to Summer Palace)
北京音乐厅	6	Běijīng Concert Hall (Běijīng Yīnyuètīng)
北京图书大厦	7	Běijīng Túshū Dàshà (Běijīng Books Centre)
北京西站	8	Běijīng Xī Zhàn (west)
滨角园码头	9	Bīnjiǎo Yuán Mǎtou
首都电影院	10	Capital Cinema (Shǒudū Diànyǐng Yuàn)
长春街	11	Chángchūn Jiē Metro
中华世纪坛	12	China Century Altar (Zhōnghuá Shìjì Tán)
中国人民革命军事博物馆	13	Chinese People's Revolutionary Army Museum (Zhōngguó Rénmín Gémìng Jūnshì Bówùguǎn)
阜城门	14	Fùchéng Mén Metro
复兴门	15	Fùxīng Mén Metro
公主坟	16	Gōngzhǔfén Metro
广济寺	17	Guǎngjì Sì
电报电话公业厅	18	International Telegraph and Telephone Service Hall (Diànbào Diànhuà Gōngyètīng)
军事博物馆	19	Jūnshì Bówùguǎn Metro
莲花池长途汽车站	20	Liánhuā Chí Chángtú Qìchē Zhàn
六里桥长途客运站	21	Liù Lǐ Qiáo Chángtú Kèyùn Zhàn
鲁迅博物馆	22	Lǔ Xùn Museum (Lǔ Xùn Bówùguǎn)
民族文化宫	23	Mínzú Wénhuà Gōng (Minorities Culture Palace)
木樨地	24	Mùxīdì Metro
南礼士路	25	Nánlǐshì Lù Metro
百盛购物中心, 中国工艺术馆	26	Parkson (Bǎishèng Gòuwù Zhōngxīn) and National Treasure Museum (Zhōngguó Gōngyìshùguǎn)
邮局	27	Post Office
三味书屋	28	Sānwèi Bookstore (Sān Wèi Shū Wū)
南堂	29	South Church (Nán Táng)
	30	Tour buses to outside Běijīng
万寿路	31	Wànshòu Lù Metro
西单	32	Xī Dān Metro
宣武门	33	Xuānwǔ Mén Metro
中央电视塔码头	34	Zhōngyāng Diànshì Tǎ Mǎtou
中友百货	35	Zhōngyǒu Bǎihuò

Hotels and Restaurants

民族饭店	A	Minzu Hotel (Mínzú Fàndiàn)
能仁居	B	Néng Rén Jū
砂锅居饭庄	C	Shāguōjū Fànzhuāng
三峡酒楼	D	Sānxiá Jiǔlóu
四川楼	E	Sìchuān Pavilion (Sìchuān Lóu)

Street and Bus Stop Names

白云观路	Báiyún Guàn Lù	六里桥南里	Liùlǐ Qiáo Nán Lǐ
白云路	Báiyún Lù	绒线胡同	Róngxiàn Hútòng
北新华街	Běi Xīnhuá Jiē	三里河路	Sān Lǐ Hé Lù
百塔寺	Bǎi Tǎ Sì	太平桥大街	Tàipíng Qiáo Dàjiē
大六部口	Dà Liù Bù Kǒu	西安门大街	Xī Ān Mén Dàjiē
阜成路	Fùchéng Lù	西长安街	Xī Cháng'ān Jiē
阜成门（内、外）大街	Fùchéng Mén (Nèi/Wài) Dàjiē	西单北大街	Xī Dān Běi Dàjiē
阜成路	Fùxīng Lù	西三环中路	Xī Sān Huán Zhōng Lù (third ring)
复兴门（内、外）大街	Fùxīng Mén (Nèi/Wài) Dàjiē	西四北南大街	Xī Sì Běi/Nàn Dàjiē
缸瓦市	Gāngwǎ Shì	宣武门西、东大街	Xuānwǔ Mén Xī/Dōng Dàjiē
工会大楼	Gōnghuì Dàlóu	宣武门内大街	Xuānwǔ Mén Nèi Dàjiē
莲花池东路	Liánhuā Chí Dōng Lù	羊坊店路	Yángfángdiàn Lù

increasing your *guānxi* and improving your chance of closing a business deal or getting official approval for it. Also needless to say, Chinese medicines claiming to have the same effect appeared thick and fast, one of them pirating Viagra's Chinese name. Clearly the imposter company's *guānxi* wasn't enough, however, since its ardour for market share was dampened by court action. That still leaves many items with entertaining names, such as Sea Dog Pills and All Night Capsules. The shop has two entrances, the one for men on the left and the one for women on the right. Guess which side has the biggest condom selection.

Bái Tǎ Sì (White Dagoba Temple) 百塔寺

Open 9–4.30, closed Mon; adm ¥10, annual ticket accepted.

See map pp.204–5, no.2. The temple is in Fùchéng Mén Nèi Dàjiē west of Běi Hǎi Park. Bus 103 and 103kuài both come up Wángfǔjǐng and turn left past the National Art Galley and pass Jǐng Shān Gōngyuán. The 101 coming from the east passes the National Art Gallery and Xī Sì, and the 13 passes Yōnghé Gōng (the Lama Temple). The stop is named Bǎi Tǎ Sì.

More correctly known as the Miàoyīng Sì, or Temple of the Miraculous Response, it's a white Tibetan-style dagoba at the rear, the shape of an inverted goblet, which gives the temple its more common name. Both bigger and earlier than the dagoba in Běi Hǎi Park, both were known as 'peppermint bottles' by the foreign residents of the 1930s.

The 51m dagoba was originally constructed by a Nepali architect on the site of a Liáo dynasty temple during the reign of Khubilai Khan and completed in 1279, as the main centre for the Yuán dynasty's Buddhist observances. The dagoba was renovated or rebuilt a number of times, including in 1753 by the Qiánlōng emperor, who placed many cultural relics here. An earthquake in 1976 revealed miniature copper stupas inside the dagoba, and repairs in 1978 turned up Hàn to Qīng dynasty coins and some scriptures. For years access was restricted to one hall and to the dagoba itself, but the front half of the temple had been put to more practical uses until it re-opened to the public after a rebuild in early 1999 which was still continuing in 2000. During this restoration a tiny solid gold Buddha encrusted with 43 rubies was discovered in the top of the dagoba.

The layout is conventional, although the Hall of the Deva Kings is *sans* kings, but full of sutras in cases, black and white photos of past temple fairs and other Buddhist bits and pieces, with English explanations.

The first major hall is the Dàjué Diàn, 'Hall of the Great Enlightened Ones', where the major statues would once have been but which is now used for an exhibition of Tibetan Buddhist artefacts, including a large and impressive collection of Buddha statues, showing the development of style over the centuries, from the very slender high-cheekboned Indian to the plumper rounder shapes of later Sinicized figures. From plain, calm, seated images to threatening multi-armed eleven-faced ones, it seems as if almost the entire Buddhist pantheon is here, many of them labelled, and providing an introduction to which hand positions indicate which figure.

Behind this is the Hall of the Seven Buddhas, which holds three, two attendants and 18 *luóhàn*. These are said to be Yuán dynasty and made of long-enduring nanmu cedar wood. At the rear there's a fine multi-armed Guānyīn, Goddess of Mercy.

The Hall of the Buddhas of the Three Periods (past, present and future) is unrestored, and contains dusty Yuán and Míng Buddhas, the obligatory Qiánlóng calligraphy board, and some Qīng *thangka* (hangings with Buddha images). At the rear of the site, the very substantial flask-shaped dagoba on a stepped base towers over its raised brick plinth and is topped with a copper 'umbrella'.

It's short walk west to the Lǔ Xùn Museum (*see* below).

Stupa, Dagoba, Chorten or Pagoda?

 The original purpose of a stupa (the Sanskrit name) was to house the mortal remains of the historical Buddha, and later of other key Buddhist saints; they also served the purpose of commemorating key events in his life, being built at the place of his birth, death, first sermon, etc. Later still they were also used to house sacred texts and images, or simply existed as symbols or reminders, becoming sacred in their own right as supporting objects for meditation. Originally a hemisphere topped by an umbrellaed spire, the stupa eventually developed different shapes in different cultures, including the flask shapes you can see at Tibetan monasteries, and at the White Dagoba Temple in Běijīng—'dagoba' is Sinhala for stupa, and the Tibetan word is 'chorten'. By this stage of development, each part of the stupa, from the multiple levels of its now square plinth to the increased number of umbrellas or ridges on its spire, capped by a solar disk and crescent moon, has detailed symbolism. All Buddhist processions proceed in the direction of the sun, and reverence is shown to a stupa or its contents by processing around it in a clockwise manner (the way you should also proceed around Buddhist temples).

In China, Japan and Korea the stupa developed into the pagoda, a four- or eight-cornered tower of wood or brick, still often with a spire or ridged roof of similar symbolism and doing the same job of housing relics or texts. Additionally the pagoda was thought to have some kind of beneficial geomantic influence on its surroundings. Pagodas usually have an internal staircase, which makes you go clockwise as you climb, thus showing veneration as you ascend. The central pillar represents the Buddha and his position at the centre of the universe, and the passages or windows pointing towards the four points of the compass are associated with other individual Buddhas, and function as an aid to meditation. The multiple stories represent different worlds on the path to enlightenment, and the octagonal plan pagodas additionally suggest the eight spokes of the wheel of *dharma*, a key principle of Buddhism that what you do in one life affects what you are in the next.

Lǔ Xùn Museum (Lǔ Xùn Bówùguǎn) 鲁迅博物馆
Open 9–3.30, closed Mon; adm ¥5.

See map pp.204–5, no.22. The museum is north up a *hútòng* from Fùchéng Mén Dàjiē, west of the more easily visible Bǎi Tǎ Sì and served by the same buses; stop Fùchéng Mén. There's a vertical red sign at the corner of the *hútòng* with Lǔ Xùn Museum in small English print at the bottom. At the top of the *hútòng* you can see a concrete arch with a hall behind it and a white statue. Small and simple noodle restaurants line the *hútòng* leading to the museum.

Lǔ Xùn (1881–1936) is a contender for the title of China's greatest writer, remaining almost as popular with educated young people today as the new wave of 'hard-boiled' writers dealing with the underside of city life, such as Wáng Shuò. Part of the 'May Fourth' group of writers who looked to wake up China following the demonstrations for reform in 1919, his sympathy for communism grew as he realized how the revolution had made little difference to the lives of ordinary people, but he avoided dancing to the Stalinist tune and representing nothing but class struggle. Much of his work contains scathing criticism of the Chinese character, and puts the blame for the failures of the revolution squarely on the Chinese themselves. To the foreign reader, Lǔ Xùn's work, and especially his powerful short stories, at first seem simply Kafka-esque, but his heroes, often incomprehending victims of their circumstances, stand for the state of the nation as a whole. In perhaps his best known work, 'The Story of Ah Q', the hapless Q is merely a symbol of China's peasant population, and makes the point repeated in other works, that the 1911 revolution merely saw the exchange of one set of scoundrels for another. Lǔ Xùn was perhaps fortunate to die with his sympathy for the communist cause intact, and before he would be forced to say the same thing about 1949.

The museum has no English introductions or labels, but hold prints of illustrations from his books, photographs, copies of his notes, calligraphic work, copies of works in various translations, and diverse artefacts connected with his life displayed in date order. His bedroom study in Shànghǎi is recreated in one corner, and there's a model of the *hútòng* in this area at the time of the Jiāqìng emperor, as well as models of various houses where he lived including his home in Běijīng from 1912 to 1926. This still stands to the left of the new building housing the exhibition. It's a single courtyard house, its tables and chairs draped in plastic, and a small well is behind it.

Appropriately there's a literary bookshop to the left of the museum entrance which can be entered without going into the museum, and where Lǔ Xùn's works are on sale in English translation, but stickered up at five times the publisher's price.

Mínzú Wénhuà Gōng
(Minorities Culture Palace)

民族文化宫

Open 9–4; adm ¥3, annual card accepted.

See map pp.204–5, no.23. The palace is in Fùxīng Mén Nèi Dàjiē, west of Ⓜ Xī Dān, or east or Ⓜ Fùxīng Mén.

This is the physical expression of the constant PR campaign to demonstrate that China's more than 50 recognized minority groups are happy, love the Communist Party and are possibly even greater pro-China nationalists than the Hàn themselves. The building, one of several Stalinist exhibition halls around Běijīng, does house a programme of exhibitions of minority arts and crafts which are often worth seeing. There are also shops selling minority crafts which offer the best selection in Běijīng, certainly at lower prices than hotel souvenir shops, but not at low as at the Pān Jiā Yuán market (Pān Jiā Yuán Jiù Huò Shìchǎng—*see* 'Markets and traditional shopping streets', p.236).

There's more shopping back east in Xī Dān, or west past a parade of Běijīng's most modern buildings (some interesting, most anonymously international) to the Parkson Department Store where there's convenient fast food and the National Treasure Museum.

National Treasure Museum
(Zhōngguó Gōngyìshùguǎn)

中国工艺术馆

Open 9–4.30, closed Mon; adm ¥5, annual ticket accepted.

See map pp.204–5, no.26. The museum is on the 5th floor of the Parkson Department Store (Bǎishèng Gòuwù Zhōngxīn), Ⓜ Fùxīng Mén.

Despite its discouraging location, this small crafts museum, mainly featuring superbly carved stone, has well-lit and displayed objects with English labels.

Many of the pieces are in such grotesquely poor taste, so monumentally ghastly that the exhibition might realistically be renamed the National Kitsch Museum. But the painstaking skill and delicacy of the carvers' work and their long drawn out dedication to bringing raw stone to such a high degree of finish can only be admired. Items on display include a basket of flowers carved from a block of jadeite and with several interlocking chain links carved from the raw stone—the overall dimensions of the finished item larger than the original block. This is essentially, as are many of the other pieces, an advertisement for the Běijīng Jadeware Factory where it was made, as are other equally clever pieces for other giftware producers. One designer, four carvers and four instructors get credit.

If you've failed to do your homework before leaving home, this exhibition might be the place to get an understanding of what real jade looks like, although unfortunately you can't touch it. For those considering climbing one of China's holy mountains, Tài Shān is modelled here in jade, but climbing it is not nearly as hair-raising as the model seems to suggest. Political consciousness is here, too in carvings such as one representing the Red Army on the Long March. Other items are carved from coral, jade, bone, stone, lapis and other materials, and there's a variety of gaudy ceramics, lacquerware and an assortment of teapots—all contemporary work and produced by specialist factories around the country as evidence of their skills.

There's cheap Chinese fast food lunch with views on the top floor of this building, and you can continue west from here, three stops to the Army Museum at Ⓜ Jūnshì Bówùguǎn (*see* below).

Chinese People's Revolutionary Army Museum (Zhōngguó Rénmín Gémìng Jūnshì Bówùguǎn)

中国人民革命军事博物馆

Open 8.30–4.30; adm ¥5, annual ticket accepted.

See map pp.204–5, no.13. Directly outside the north exit of ⓜ Jūnshì Bówùguǎn metro station.

The forecourt has a coastguard vessel, a missile, and what looks like a Chinese copy of a Russian copy of a Trident jet, boardable for an extra ¥5.

The relative antiquity of the museum should be obvious, since the classic materials of communist self-promotion, are all here—marble, gilt and gloom—together with a large statue of Máo, and portraits of Marx, Lenin and even Stalin. Depressingly, the Chinese can be found photographing their small sons and daughters in front of field artillery and dusty tanks. The weapons range from the First World War era (although in use rather later in China) to relatively modern rocket launchers, although China's military is still thought to be technologically about 30 years behind the West. There are four storeys of pistols, machine guns, torpedoes, shells, swords, grenades and rockets.

Behind the museum is the new **Altar to the Century**, built at vast expense by the government to celebrate the 'new millennium'—meaningless to a culture which does not share the Christian reference point and which only began to use the Western calendar after 1949. But when everyone else was wasting millions, and despite constant insistance on the glory, longevity, and general superiority of its own culture, China didn't have the nerve not to join in.

Also behind the museum is Bāyì Hú (lake), where you can board boat services to the Summer Palace (*see* p.290).

South Church (Nán Táng)

南堂

Open Sundays for religious services.

See map pp.204–5, no.29. ⓜ Xuānwǔ Mén, northeast side, in Xuānwǔ Mén Dōng Dàjiē, west of Tiān'ān Mén. You'll see the church if you come here to take one-day bus trips out of Běijīng.

The South Church, St Mary's, stands on the site of Italian Jesuit Matteo Ricci's Běijīng residence (*see* 'Christianity in China' below), and its architecture is Italianate, although its history is far more interesting than its physical form. It has slightly dismal gardens at the front, with shops called 'Holy Things Handicraft Department' and a Chinese-style rockery with a ceramic Virgin Mary surrounded by flowers.

The cathedral is serviced by a dozen priests, all members of the government-approved patriotic church which has no links with the Vatican and claims a congregation of 20,000 followers. In 1999 the government spent ¥1.3 million (about $160,000) on repairs.

The first church on the site was begun by Adam Schall in 1650 with a donation from the Kāngxī emperor, and completed in 1703. It burned down in 1775. The Qiánlóng emperor offered to help with repairs but the Jesuits had lost the rites accommodation battle and been temporarily suppressed by Pope Clement XIV in 1773, while hard times fell on all missionaries of whatever order who were not prepared to sign an agreement to allow Chinese Christians to continue ancestor worship and rites for Confucius, directly contradictory to the Vatican's demands.

The building (whatever there was at the time) was occupied by Portuguese Lazarists for a while in the 19th century. In 1861 the Treaty of Tiānjīn and the Conventions of Peking, which opened further treaty ports to foreigners and forced the Qīng to accept permanent foreign representatives in the capital, also returned all church property to foreign ownership. French Lazarists had the church rebuilt by 1862, but it was destroyed again in the Boxer Rebellion of 1900, which saw the deliberate targeting and execution of thousands of Chinese Christians as ersatz foreigners ('lesser hairy ones') and the destruction of foreign religious premises right across China.

In 1999 the government tried to ban a Chinese phrase for the new millennium which had Christian overtones (although certainly very few Chinese indeed realized that), announcing, 'As a Communist Party member one should only believe in Marxism and dialectic materialism and not use terms like "thousand happiness year" with a religious connotation'. A few days later the atheistic government ignored protests from the Vatican and appointed several bishops, then took upon itself the authority to enthrone a child as a reincarnated lama of Tibetan Buddhism (*see* p.189). The aetheist Communist Party may be the world's most ecumenical organization.

There are Catholic services here, and at several other churches around Běijīng but—except at the Běi Táng (the North Church), a grey-blue and white neo-Gothic wedding cake of a place in Xī Shíkù Dàjiē—these are almost all in Chinese or Korean. If it's Chinese atmosphere you're after you might find the East Church (St. Joseph's) in Wángfǔjǐng (enter from the rear—the front gates are always locked), or **St Michael's** (Dōng Jiāo Mín Xiàng Tiānzhǔ Táng) in the old Legation Quarter (*see* p.135) more convenient. If it's reliable access to Christian worship whether Catholic or Protestant you require, call the German Embassy, ℂ 6532 1241, for details of services of both varieties for residents and visitors. Services for foreign passport holders only are also held by the Congregation of the Good Shepherd; call ℂ 6438 6536 for details of locations and times.

Christianity in China

The Nestorian Christians were the first to reach China, and the most ancient Christian artefact yet found in the country is the Nestorian Tablet in Xī'ān's Forest of Stelae, rediscovered by the Jesuits in 1623, and thought (perhaps hoped) to be a fake, until Nestorian documents were found in the Library Cave at Dūnhuáng (along with daoist, Confucian, Manichaean and Buddhist papers). It records a Nestorian mission to the Táng capital Cháng'ān (now Xī'ān) in 635 CE.

Named after Nestorius, Bishop of Constantinople in the 5th century, the Nestorians' view that Christ had two separate human and divine personalities was banned as heretical (the modern Chinese regime would probably call them 'splittist'). Nevertheless, the church flourished in Persia and spread eastwards to India and China from the 6th to the 10th century. Envoys from Europe to the Mongol court at Karakorum in Mongolia, such as the Franciscan John of Plano Carpini (Giovanni da Pian del Carpine) in 1246, Dominican André de Longjumeau in 1250, and another Franciscan, William of Rubruck (Guillaume Rubruquis), in 1253, found themselves reliant on the Nestorians for communication with the Mongol Khans.

After their first (and quite possibly only) meeting with Khubilai Khan, at Karakorum in around 1260, the Polo family were given a message to the Pope for 100 teachers to spread the Catholic word. But they were unable to obtain more than two for the return journey, and even these dropped out (*see* 'Was Polo Here', p.337). However, the Franciscan John of Monte Corvino (Giovanni da Montecorvino) reached Khanbalik (Běijīng) in 1294 and was sent seven bishops, three of whom survived the journey to arrive in 1308 and consecrate him first Archbishop of the Catholic Church in China. There were subsequent missions, but Catholics came under attack during revolts against Mongol rule and the last Western bishop was expelled in 1369, the year after the restoration of Chinese rule over China by the Míng.

The next major achievement by Christianity was the permission given to the Jesuit Matteo Ricci to live in Běijīng from 1602. Ricci had entered China from Portuguese controlled Macao in 1583, and decided on an approach different from that of his fellow missionaries, dressing as a scholar rather than as a member of the priestly class. He devoted himself to gaining a thorough understanding of the classics needed to pass the imperial examinations, the route to advancement in Chinese society, and taught the sons of the influential not only the content of the classics but memory techniques known to Jesuits and thought of as a branch of ethics. It was thus that he gained the support necessary to reach Běijīng, a move strongly resisted by the inward-looking Míng and the eunuchs who held power at the court.

Once there, Ricci won respect by his demonstrations of technical skill with clocks and maps. He adapted Catholic rites to make them more understandable for Chinese converts, and did not forbid the continuance of traditional ancestor-worship or displays of respect for Confucius. By 1610, the year of Ricci's death, the Chinese claimed 2,000 converts, but most of these were sick infants baptized only shortly before they died (a policy continued with sick, unwanted and abandoned children—usually girls—right up to the time of the Boxers, contributing to Chinese suspicions that the children were used for alchemical and deviant sexual purposes). They had, however, established the residence of a total of eight priests and eight friars to live in China.

Their influence at court became substantial. The Jesuits demonstrated the inadequacies of the Chinese calendar by accurately forecasting the time and duration of solar eclipses in 1610 and 1629. Johann Adam Schall von Bell was appointed to the Board of Calendar Regulation in 1634.

Their erudition kept the Jesuits at court through the transfer from the Míng to the Manchu Qīng in 1644, despite the Manchus' adherence to Tibetan Buddhism, although there was a reaction against them following the death of the Shùnzhì emperor in 1661, and during the subsequent minority of the Kāngxī emperor. Nevertheless, a Belgian, Ferdinand Verbiest, demonstrated to Kāngxī that errors had once again crept into the calendar and the Jesuits once again took control. Verbiest became science tutor to Kāngxī, cast cannon for him, and other Jesuits acted as interpreters and translators, helping to negotiate and draw up the first agreement between China and a foreign power, the border-fixing Treaty of Nerchinsk with Russia of 1689. Later Jesuits worked as cartographers, completing a map of the whole of China for Kāngxī by 1717. By 1700 the Jesuits were claiming more than 300,000 converts to Catholicism.

Kāngxī issued an edict of tolerance to the Christian religion in 1692, but this increased the numbers other missionary sects to join the Jesuits, not all of whom agreed with

Ricci's accommodation of ancestor worship, homage to Confucius and other traditions. Debate over this issue had begun in 1632, quickly developing into a fierce campaign of letter-writing and denunciation by orders envious of the Jesuits' successes. While the struggle to 'save souls' took place in China, infighting at the Vatican led to Ricci's position being at first confirmed and then rejected. A legate sent by Pope Clement XI had meetings with Kāngxī in 1705 and 1706, then ordered all missionaries under pain of excommunication to forbid converts to practise these rites. Kāngxī despised this intolerance, and ordered the expulsion from China of all those who failed to sign a certificate accepting his position, beginning with the legate himself. Most Jesuits signed, but Franciscans and Dominicans didn't. It was the Christians' own squabbling that lost them their influence in China.

The Yōngzhèng emperor removed the protection of the state in 1724, leading to the expulsion of many missionaries. The Qiánlōng emperor hand-picked those who pleased him, and most of those who remained at court were artists, such as painters Jean Attiret and Guiseppe Castiglione who painted several portraits of Qiánlōng, and Michel Benoit, who with Castiglione designed the Western-style buildings at the Yuánmíng Yuán, the 'Old' Summer Palace. The Jesuit order was itself dissolved by Pope Clement XIV in 1773, although it took two more years for news to reach China.

If Matteo Ricci was a marketing expert par excellence, who observed the needs of the powerful and earned their support through assisting them, the Christians who followed down the centuries seemed to have lacked the touch, right up to modern times. The treaties forced on China by foreign powers in the mid-19th century allowed a flood of missionaries from all over the world into the country, many of whom combined intolerance with poor education. Many other foreign residents expressed antipathy towards them and a lack of surprise that they should be the first target of the Boxer Rebellion. (*See* 'The Boxer Rebellion', p.66.)

In a repeat of 17th-century problems, different sects fought amongst themselves and deliberately confused issues by choosing different translations for Christian terms, including 'God'. Many observers commented that Chinese converts were 'rice Christians', whose Christianity lasted only as long as the free hand-outs of food some well-funded missionaries were able to provide. The novelist Pearl S. Buck, daughter of two Presbyterian missionaries to China who lived much of her life here, thought that they had no more effect than 'a finger drawn through water'.

Some ideas did indeed stick, however. The Tàipíng Rebellion, which between 1845 and 1864 gained control of large areas of China including Nánjīng, was led by a man who claimed to be Jesus Christ's younger brother. Two of his lieutenants claimed to speak with the voices of God and Jesus. Missionaries were excited about this new religious community, at least until some broke through Qīng lines and found the Tàipíng ideas deviant and heretical. Cynical communist historical orthodoxy claims the Tàipíng as revolutionaries.

Modern-day missionaries, especially from North American sects, still view China as a massive opportunity. Largely prevented by Chinese government policies from carrying on missionary work, some sneak in through the porous Indo-Chinese borders, while others arrive on tourist visas with no Mandarin and little comprehension of the mammoth task they face. Many undergraduate language students find themselves getting a large dose of dogma along with a diet of vocabulary, as evangelical fervour creeps into China under the cloak of teaching experience.

The first official visit by representatives of the World Council of Churches in 1996 was given the official view of religious tolerance in China. Afterwards there were comments that while it was exhilarating to preach to congregations many times larger than those they would reach in the West, the church in China was a *Chinese* church practising Chinese Christianity, with little interest in membership of a wider organization or a wider faith. The Chinese government, taking upon itself the task of appointing bishops for the reported four million members of the Patriotic Church in early 2000, would be very happy with that conclusion, less happy with the fact that several of their appointees turned them down, and that the Vatican, neither recognizing nor being recognized by the Běijīng government, claims twice as many Chinese are Catholics loyal to the Pope.

Báiyún Guàn

Open 8.30–4.30, 4pm Oct–April; adm ¥8.

白云观

See map pp.204–5, no.3. This daoist temple is in the narrow Báiyún Guàn Lù, east off Báiyún Lù, reached by bus 48 to stop Báiyún Lù. Walk north and turn right or bus 1 along Cháng'ān past Wángfǔjǐng, Tiān'ān Mén, Xī Dān, to stop Gōnghuì Dàlóu and walk south.

There are many English explanations in this temple, often differing wildly from the accompanying Chinese ones, but at ¥8 this is a bargain given the amount and variety of things to see. It's a large complex with a complicated layout, and with halls to many of the thousands of daoist deities with different duties and belonging to different sects, such as the 'All Truth Dragon Sect'. A white marble statue of Lǎozi himself, the founder of daoism, China's only native religion (*see* below), is said to have been given to the temple by a Táng emperor in CE 739, and the site is said to be Táng, although much was built in the Yuán (1279–1368), destroyed and reconstructed in the Míng in the 14th century. Daoist priests can easily be spotted by their Míng-style top knots, both wandering around the temple and eating in nearby restaurants.

The carved arch of the first gate has a stone monkey which you are supposed to touch for luck, and there's further superstition just beyond, at the Wind Containing Bridge, an arched marble affair reminiscent of those to be found in front of Tiān'ān Mén and popular at daoist temples or at Buddhist ones where entrepreneurs think there's profit in it. The original was 17th-century but this is a modern copy from 1989, supposed to contain a wind that was terrorizing Běijīng at the time, and beneath it hang two giant copper coins with the square central holes common to old Chinese 'copper cash' which was kept on strings, in each of which hangs a bell. 50 coin-like discs to throw can be bought from a neighbouring kiosk for ¥10, and if you hit a bell you'll have luck—perfect entertainment because it makes a noise. The *fúwùyuán* climb down a knotted rope at night to collect all the coins.

The Shrine Hall for the Tutulary God of 1456, renovated in 1662, has statues of four marshalls which are the daoist equivalent of the Deva or Heavenly Kings, and who are supposed to have distinguished themselves in Chinese military history. The main statue is bug-eyed and with real hair for a beard.

On the left the Hall for the God of Wealth, with three gods inside, formerly well-known civil officials and military officers at different periods, are popular with those who wish to get rich soon, says the sign, which must make them wildly popular in China. Appropriately gilded, cloaked in the fortunate colour red, and with beards of real hair, their hall is decorated with detailed murals showing their exploits. On the right another hall houses the officials of heaven, earth and water, some of the oldest daoist deities—seated wild-eyed figures, also with murals showing their exploits.

At the rear of this compound (built in 1438, rebuilt in 1662, renovated in 1788) is a hall for the Jade Emperor, the celestial counterpart of the emperor on earth. This sits on a raised terrace, which is connected by a raised walkway at the rear to the next hall, The Shrine Hall for Seven Perfected Beings. On the left is the Hall for the Medical King who protects the sick, a relatively modern deity only recognised in 1103, with two very smiley attendant statues. On the right there's the Shrine Hall for the Saviour Worthy, chief officer of the daoist version of Hell and not smiley at all; the murals inside depict suitably bloody scenes of pain and suffering. Note on the right in the second mural people wearing cangues (*see* p.150). The statue has a sword and a cup, and his attendants have scrolls containing the names of those who need to be dealt with. A mural to the left illustrates the daoist theory of reincarnation which has people being reborn as insects, animals or humans again, depending on their behaviour during their lives.

Built in 1228 and rebuilt in 1456, the hall for the Seven Perfected Beings has a terrace for ordinations; behind this the site broadens and there are turnings to left and right to smaller courtyards. On the left a small bronze donkey is supposed to have the same medicinal powers as the one at Dōngyuè Miào (*see* p.197). Whisper to it the nature of your problem, then touch the part of the donkey corresponding to the location of your pain (presumably particularly effective if it lies in the ears). Further to the left the Shrine of the Eight Immortals, from 1808 (English version says 1807), has small painted wooden statues, identifiable as particular deities according to what they are carrying. At the rear on the left there's the Shrine Hall of the Patriarch Lù, 1887, the most popular of the eight immortals. A daoist monk taps a bronze bowl with a wooden beater as people bow to the relevant image, which gives a mellow ring.

Going back south there's the Goddess Shrine Hall, plain, but with pretty hangings, dedicated to the daughter of another god and an assortment of other daughter goddesses who look after the important business of giving women baby boys and good eyesight. In front of the hall to the north there's a splendid bronze of 1443, with a rather shiny tummy which suggests that there's luck to be had by rubbing him there. A small undecorated hall with several large bronze figures is the Hall for the Lord Wen San, protector of scholars, where people came to pray for success in the Confucian examinations (*see* p.192).

A courtyard towards the rear has the signs of the Chinese zodiac carved in marble, and another 24 images showing examples of filial piety. Further back is the Shrine Hall for 60 Protectors, with 60 small wooden statues, looking prosperously tubby. There's a barrier in front of the zodiac, but of course everyone clambers under it to touch their own particular sign and those of their relatives, lighting incense sticks and putting them on the backs of the animals along with gifts of money.

The Cloud Gathering Garden stretches across the rear of the site, with rock gardens and walkways for daoist meditation and, according to the sounds from one hall, daoist mahjong too. Daoism is known for being a very relaxed religion with a generally good-humoured outlook.

Returning south on the main central axis from the ordination terrace, the two-storey building is the Shrine Hall for the Four Celestial Emperors (rulers of Heaven, Earth, the North and the South), with the Three Pure Gods Pavilion, possibly built in 1428, and the upstairs section in 1662. Climb up by entering a door on the right and descend on the left. Side halls are administrative and also house exhibitions of daoist paintings and religious artefacts, texts, rubbings and ceremonial costume, some beautifully embroidered.

The Shrine Hall for Patriarch Qiū honours a man put in charge of daoist affairs during the Yuán, supposedly buried underneath, and contains a large alms-collecting bowl, made from knotted tree roots, a present from the Qiánlóng emperor, on a carved stone plinth.

Daoism

 The *dào*, or 'way', of daoism (often rendered *taoism*) is the invisible reality underlying appearances. If Confucianism stresses humanity and rejects mysticism, daoism sees humanity as getting in the way of perception of the indescribable and imperceptible 'way' with which all daoists strive to unite. This unity cannot be achieved through the fussy intellectual emphasis of Confucianism, but only by achieving an awareness of inner simplicity and emptiness. The key sage of daoism was Lǎozi, a contemporary of Confucius sometimes given credit for writing the central daoist text *Dàodéjīng*, 'The Way and Power Classic', but who probably lived well before that book was written. The complete daoist canon amounts to around 1,400 texts from a variety of sources, many of them 'revealed' to later disciples, together with texts on the alchemical achievement of immortality.

The difficulty in identifying Lǎozi with a concrete historical figure allowed his biography to expand with increasingly superhuman legend as time went by. His reputed disappearance to the West, riding an ox, not long before the arrival of Buddhism allowed daoists to claim that the Buddha was either Lǎozi himself in disguise or an Indian disciple who, as a barbarian, had only received a weakened version of Lǎozi's doctrines. The contest between daoists and Buddhists was only brought to an end by Kubilai Khan, who ordered the destruction of all literature containing the story. Despite daoism's connections with organized rebellion during the Hàn dynasty, it nevertheless received state support, particularly during the Táng dynasty, whose emperors considered themselves descended from Lǎozi. There were various other important sages, but no others received his deification. One 2nd-century figure, Zhāng Dàolíng, led a daoist 'Way of the Celestial Masters' movement, which survived conflict with the Hàn emperors to be claimed as an antecedent by every organized daoist group since, up to and including that of the current Celestial Master, who lives in Tāiwān and is the 64th in a line of what Westerners in 19th-century China called the 'daoist Popes'.

Members of the daoist pantheon (around 72,000 deities, depending on the school) sometimes share space with Buddhist and Confucian images, and, like Buddhism, daoism has its holy mountains, such as Tài Shān.

The northwest is the home of the Zhōng Guān Cūn high-tech high-investment area, intended to be China's silicon valley, and offering incentives to encourage more than the usual handful of students to return from overseas and set up businesses.

The district also contains the most important of the capital's more than 50 higher education institutions, including Běi Dà, China's most prestigious university, the self-styled 'Harvard of China'. The student area does have a sprinkling of lively bars, particularly around the west and south gates of Běi Dà, the east and south gates of the Language and Culture University, and in the nearby Wǔ Dào Kǒu area.

The Zoo is of interest mainly as a major transport interchange in the northwest corner of the city, reached by several bus routes, and with suburban buses departing to several major sites to the northwest. There are some quiet temples and gardens amongst green hills, relatively free of the city's pollution.

From the Xī Zhí Mén, which would once have stood at the northwest corner of the city walls and is now merely a name on the map, you can follow westwards the route of the imperial families of the Qīng period to the Summer Palace, passing a succession of gardens and temples they favoured, some of which are highly unusual and contain good museums. If you don't wish to stop you can also in summer do this by boat, as they did.

Educating Emigrants

 Although very high examination scores are required to enter Běijīng University (Běi Dà), its infrastructure is very poor, its attitude to its students one of ensuring that they know it's run for the administration's benefit and not for theirs, and care is taken to keep the curriculum as unimaginative and uncontroversial as possible.

Foreign exchange students may find themselves dragooned into teaching courses in subjects they are still struggling to master themselves, and for no pay. Neither failing to turn up to a course at all, nor turning in weak exam papers, prevents students from getting a degree, and foreign teachers who mark poor students down just find their marks adjusted upwards—only political activism of the wrong kind fails students. Those who have a serious interest in an education must seek out the truly qualified teachers from amongst the politically acceptable time-servers, and demonstrate enough devotion to the subjects they teach to gain attention. Inevitably it's those with the drive and intelligence to achieve this who go abroad for postgraduate studies and form part of the 82% or more who never return. The Communist Party, only recently (following the Cultural Revolution's complete destruction of the education system) reconverted to the idea that you can't stick any old peasant in a cadre's job and expect results, has nevertheless created a system in which only the brightest and most determined get anything other than brainwashed and are then driven overseas.

Běi Dà is traditionally the principle home of student activism, including some of the leaders of the bloodily suppressed demonstrations of 1989, (although the starting point is thought to have been the People's University, 'Rén Dà'). One of the origins of the university, originally located at a site called the 'red house' to the north of the Forbidden City, was a college for interpreters, set up by Sir Robert Hart at the end of the 19th century when he was in charge of the Imperial Customs. The Imperial University which absorbed the college was where the strange adventurer and diary forger Edmund Backhouse taught for a while (*see* p.144) and one of the few results of the Guǎngxù emperor's 'hundred days' of reforms to last. Later it moved out to its current location, taking over the site of a university already set up by American missionaries in an area well beyond the city walls, dotted with temples, and which had become popular with eunuchs grown fat on squeeze (corruption) to build estates for their retirement. The grounds of one, and those of another estate originally belonging to Qiánlóng's favourite, Heshen, became the university campus.

In 1999 the university celebrated its centennial, and newspaper articles made great play of its important role in the development of communism in China. One of the founders of the Communist Party had been librarian there, and a major influence on Máo Zédōng, who also worked in the university library. Its revolutionary credentials included the 4 May demonstrations, when students took to the streets (and Tiān'ān Mén Square) to protest at the results of the Versailles conference, which handed over Chinese territory formerly occupied by Germany to the Japanese, rather than returning it to Chinese control. The demonstration was against the spinelessness of the Nationalist government then in Nánjīng, but also in favour of proper democratic reform, which the Communist Party has never supplied. Nevertheless, in a bid to make 4 May a pro-communism anniversary, the Party has anachronistically designated this Běi Dà's birthday, although the demonstrations didn't occur until 1919, 20 years after the university's founding. The articles lauding student activism must have made bitter reading to those who demonstrated in favour of democracy in 1989, and who faced the tanks on the night of 4 June.

All intending students have to do some military training but, in an effort to crush the independent-mindedness of Běi Dà, students who want to go here require not only the highest test scores, but also a *year* in the army. Until recently, visitors to Běi Dà needed an invitation from a student or member of staff, and had to sign in at the gate, but strolling past the guards in an unconcerned manner usually avoided this problem. Such regulations are reinstituted at politically tricky times, such as around Liù Sì, the 4 June anniversary of the Tiān'ān Mén massacre. Now tours to the campus are promoted in conjunction with a visit to the 'Old Summer Palace' not far away (*see* p.293). However, the Qīng-era pagoda on campus which looks so impressive from a distance is actually a 1924 water tower, and there's little else to see, although the Sackler Museum of Art and Archaeology (*open 9–4.30*), originally only open by appointment, can now be seen by casual visitors but is open irregularly. You might also enjoy the irony of seeing that the campus has a road called Mínzhǔ Lù, Democracy Road.

According to UNESCO, China's record in education spending continues to be abysmal, even compared to considerably poorer countries. It ranks 145th out of 153 countries in terms of per capita spending, and 101st out of 120 in terms of the number of university graduates—a mere two per cent of the population.

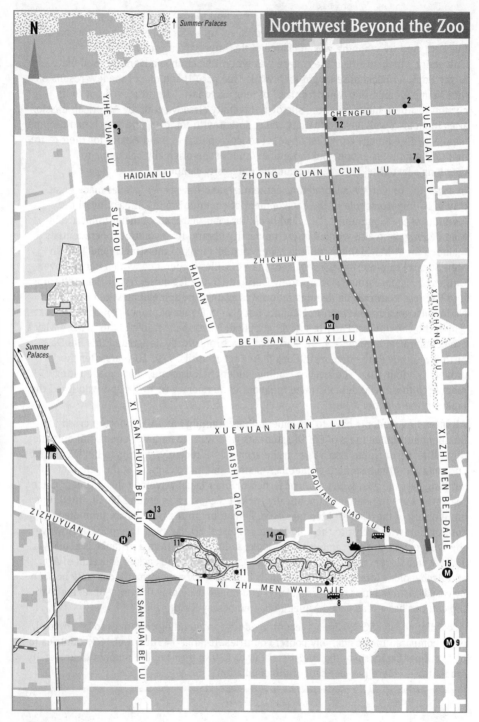

N

↑ Summer Palaces

Northwest Beyond the Zoo

YIHE YUAN LU

●3

SUZHOU LU

HAIDIAN LU

HAIDIAN LU

CHENGFU LU ●2

●12

XUEYUAN LU

7 ●

ZHONG GUAN CUN LU

ZHICHUN LU

XITUCHANG LU

10
Ⓜ

BEI SAN HUAN XI LU

Summer
Palaces

XI SAN HUAN BEI LU

XUEYUAN NAN LU

BAISHI QIAO LU

GAOLIANG QIAO LU

16

XI ZHI MEN BEI DAJIE

6

ZIZHUYUAN LU

13
Ⓜ

Ⓗ A

11 ●

11 ●

11

14 Ⓜ

5

1

15
Ⓜ

XI ZHI MEN WAI DAJIE

8

XI SAN HUAN BEI LU

Ⓜ 9

北京北站	1	Běijīng Běi Zhàn (north, also known as Xī Zhí Mén Zhàn)
北语	2	Běijīng Language and Culture University (usually known as Běi Yǔ) south gate
北大	3	Běijīng University (Běi Dà) west gate
北京动物园	4	Běijīng Zoo (Běijīng Dòngwùyuán)
北展后湖码头	5	Běi Zhǎn Hòu Hú Mǎtou (Boats to Summer Palace)
长河湾码头	6	Cháng Hé Wān Mǎtou (dock)
公共汽车酒巴	7	Bus Bar (Gōnggòng Qìchē Jiǔbā)
	8	Buses to Summer Palace, Old Summer Palace, etc.
车公庄	9	Chēgōngzhuāng Metro
大钟寺	10	Dà Zhōng Sì (Great Bell Temple)
紫竹院公园	11	Purple Bamboo Park (Zǐzhúyuàn Gōngyuán)
五道口	12	Scream Club and Wǔdàokǒu bar area
万寿寺，北京艺术博物馆	13	Wànshòu Sì and Běijīng Yìshù Bówùguǎn (Běijīng Art Museum)
五塔寺，北京石刻艺术博物馆	14	Wǔ Tǎ Sì (Five Padoga Temple) and Běijīng Shíkè Yìshù Bówùguǎn (Museum of Carved Stone Art)
西直门	15	Xī Zhí Mén Metro
西直门长途汽车客运站	16	Xī Zhí Mén Chángtú Qìchē Kèyùn Zhàn

Hotels and Restaurants

香格里拉饭店	A	Beijing Shangri-La (Xiānggélǐlā Fàndiàn)

Street and Bus Stop Names

白石桥	Báishí Qiáo	西三环北路	Xī Sān Huán Běi Lù (West Third Ring North)
白石桥路	Báishí Qiáo Lù		
北京大学	Běijīng Dàxué	西土城路	Xītǔchéng Lù
北三环西路	Běi Sān Huán Xī Lù (North Third Ring West)	西直门北大街	Xī Zhí Mén Běi Dàjiē
		学院路	Xuéyuàn Lù
成府路	Chéngfǔ Lù	学院南路	Xuéyuàn Nán Lù
大钟寺	Dà Zhōng Sì	西直门外大街	Xī Zhí Mén Wài Dàjiē
高梁桥路	Gāoliang Qiáo Lù	颐和园路	Yíhé Yuán Lù
海淀路	Hǎidiàn Lù	中关村路	Zhōng Guān Cūn Lù
苏州路	Sūzhōu Lù	知春路	Zhīchūn Lù
万寿寺	Wànshòu Sì	紫竹院	Zǐzhúyuàn
五道口商场	Wǔdàokǒu Shāngchǎng	紫竹院路	Zǐzhúyuàn Lù

Běijīng Zoo (Běijīng Dòngwùyuán)

北京动物园

Open 9–5; adm ¥7.

See map p.220, no.4. Ⓜ Xī Zhí Mén, northwest exit and walk west past the Soviet-style exhibition hall, refurbished in 1999, and containing a highly indifferent Russian restaurant—the kind with too long a history. Buses include the 7, which comes here from Ⓜ Hépíng Mén, bus 15 from Xī Dān, and bus 45 from Tiān Qiáo, near Tiān Tán, which passes Hépíng Mén and Xuānwǔ Mén. Trolley bus 102 comes all the way from Běijīng Nán Zhàn (south station), and the 103 and 103*kuài* (quick) routes come from Běijīng Zhàn, passing the National Art Gallery at the top of Wángfǔjǐng.

The ¥7 ticket lets you see the whole zoo including the pandas, although there's a ticket for ¥5 which will let you see everything but. There's also a ticket which includes access to the new aquarium for ¥120.

The use of the space as a park dates back to the reign of the Shùnzhì emperor (1644–1661) and the area received extensive development by the Qiánlóng emperor. But a menagerie only appeared here after the Empress Dowager Cíxī took an interest in the largely abandoned site as she passed it on her way to the Summer Palace and, when a Manchu Prince returned from a 17-country overseas tour in 1903, he brought with him a selection of animals and birds bought in Germany as a present for Cíxī, which were installed here. The site was renamed the Wàn Shēng Yuán or 'Garden of Ten Thousand Animals', 'ten thousand' really meaning, as it does in the name of the Great Wall, 'rather a lot'. By the 1930s the numbers were down to less than 100, including an elephant kept in a cage scarcely large enough for a baboon, and all severely malnourished. The remainder had been stuffed, 'the only time that this term could be applied to them after their arrival', commented guidebook authors Arlington and Lewisohn, acidly.

Attitudes haven't changed much. Go here only if you fear you'll never have another opportunity to see pandas in your lifetime. Although some areas have improved, the zoo will probably upset those who hate to see animals ill-cared for, and the casual cruelty of some Chinese visitors can also be very distasteful. The new aquarium is one of several competing multi-million-*yuán* operations which opened at more or less the same time in the late '90s. Another is the Blue Zoo (Fùguó Hǎidǐ Shìjiè) at the south gate of the Worker's Stadium.

Recently the zoo has picked up on an idea popular elsewhere in the world, of allowing companies and individuals to adopt animals. One company paid ¥66,000 ($8250) to adopt a four-month-old panda and will use it as a mascot. Donating money to Chinese organizations is always a risky proposition, but if this scheme appeals call ✆ 6831 4411, ext. 206, for more details.

Zoos all over China have been desperate to attract some of urban China's new discretionary spending, which is mainly going on education for children and other more up-to-date pleasures. In the late '90s several zoos and wildlife parks took to putting on shows in which live domestic animals were put in with hungry but often incompetent lions and tigers. This was widely reported in the Western media in 1999 and subsequently banned (which means that it probably can still be seen in various places).

For a well-run albeit panda-less wildlife reserve, which really does have the right idea about animal care and environmental issues, visit the Mílù Yuàn, the home of reintroduced Père David's Deer and other endangered and rare quadrupeds (*see* p.343).

Several buses to outlying temples and parks leave from the street outside the zoo, or the bus station opposite, including routes to the 'old' and 'new' Summer Palaces. One of the boat routes to the Summer Palace leaves from northeast of the Zoo (*see* 'Summer Palace', p.290, for details).

Wǔ Tǎ Sì (Five Padoga Temple) and 五塔寺，北京石刻艺术博物馆
Běijīng Shíkè Yìshù Bówùguǎn (Museum of Carved Stone Art)

Open 8.30–4; adm ¥3.

See map p.220, no.14. The Wǔ Tǎ Sì is to the north of the zoo and best reached from the west side, although there's an alternative route from north of Xī Zhí Mén bus station which at times looks so unlikely there's a tendency to give up. From the zoo main entrance walk west and turn north up Báishí Qiáo Lù and turn right down a lane immediately after crossing the bridge, a good 20mins' walk. Bus 808 from Qián Mén, Fùchéng Mén and Xī Dān, bus 332 from the Zoo (which continues to the Summer Palace), and the double-decker tè4 from Qián Mén, Hépíng Mén and Xuānwǔ Mén all stop here at Báishí Qiáo. The entrance to the temple is opposite a newly constructed white stone bridge over the river a further 10mins down the lane.

This is a museum where the grumpy and unreasonable staff will shut up shop and kick you out as soon as they can. Go no later than 3pm.

The single remaining ancient building at what is properly the Zhēnjué Sì (Temple of True Enlightenment) gives the site its modern name, and is refreshingly different from other temples in Beijing, with the exception of Bìyún Sì (Temple of the Azure Clouds—see p.331), which is a partly Sinified copy built more than three centuries later.

Completed just after the Míng Yǒnglè reign (1403–24), the Wǔ Tǎ Sì is a stone cube carved in relief with rows of Buddha figures, wheels of life, various animals, Sanskrit characters, lotuses, etc., topped with five stepped and carved spires of an obviously Indian flavour, and a small pavilion with a circular yellow roof. The whole is said to be based on a small model of the Diamond Temple at Bodhgaya in the Indian state of Bihar, a town sacred to Buddhists as the place the historical Buddha gained enlightenment. The model was brought to Yǒnglè by an Indian monk, perhaps returning the call made by the Chinese monk Xuánzàng, who had visited Bodhgaya in the 7th century. The tiered pagodas on the roof are carved with further rows of Buddhas and other images of elephants and other beasts. The central one has a life-size relief of the soles of a pair of feet, traditionally a representation of those of the Buddha himself. Climbing the interior of the pagoda to the roof to see all this costs an extra ¥5, although it's free to those with an annual ticket. Since the building is not made of wood, it's one of the few in Běijīng which can be said to be authentic.

Some authorities put the disappearance of the remainder of the temple down to retributive action of foreign troops in both 1860 and 1900, but if so the Chinese are surprisingly quiet about it. The remainder of the site is a kind of hostel for orphaned carved stonework of all kinds. The inevitable stelae are complemented by a large collection of Tibetan images, Buddha figures, animals and life size figures from rows of tomb guardians, all perhaps the final remains of the dozens of now destroyed temples and tombs around the city. Other oddities include a memorial to Sūn Zhōngshān (Sun Yat-sen), and a tomb in the shape of a pavilion complete with fake doors, pillars and roof with the brackets carved in the stone.

Walking back west and slightly south at the main road it's possible to walk through Purple Bamboo Park to the Wànshòu Sì or Longevity Temple, see below, or to continue by bus 320 and other passing minibuses to the Summer Palace (although you'll probably have to stand).

Purple Bamboo Park (Zǐzhúyuàn Gōngyuán)

Open 6–9; adm ¥5.

See map p.220, no.11. Reached by bus from ❶ Xī Zhí Mén or nearby, nos. 105, 107, and 111.

Worth mentioning because it's a pleasant way to walk to or from the Wànshòu Sì (*see* below), although otherwise little different from many other parks in Běijīng. Yuán dynasty in origin, the purpose of its lakes was to control the flow of water to Běijīng's moats, and the park was used as a resting place for members of the imperial entourage on their way to and from the Summer Palace.

Now it's a place of magpies, discreetly affectionate couples, motorized rides for children, fishing areas, cafés, snack stalls, the odd duck and lots of bamboo.

Wànshòu Sì and Běijīng Yìshù Bówùguǎn (Běijīng Art Museum) 万寿寺，北京艺术博物馆

Open 9–4, closed Mon; adm ¥10, annual ticket accepted.

See map p.220, no.13. The temple is north of the Shangri-La Hotel on the west third ring road, or reachable by following the Cháng Hé (river) west from the rear of Purple Bamboo Park on foot. It's easily reachable by bus 300 for those in southern budget accommodation or anywhere near the third ring road which it circles. The stop is Wànshòu Sì, or Zǐzhùyuàn (walk north). Take bus 332 from the Zoo or 320 from Běijīng Xī Zhàn (West Station) to stop Báishí Qiáo and walk through the Purple Bamboo Park.

The Longevity Temple was built in 1577 during the reign of the Míng Wànlì emperor by a rich eunuch, who shortly afterwards became a victim of court intrigues and was stripped of his powers for his arrogance. The temple was restored by Qiánlōng and part of it was used as a 'temporary palace' on trips to and from the Summer Palace when a change of boat was necessary at a sluice nearby. The temple was a favourite with the Empress Dowager Cíxī, whose generous donations kept it in good order until modern times; one two-storey building at the rear whose upper floor is reached by a sloping corridor is referred to as her 'dressing tower'. She was said to have sat and admired the view, which until less than 30 years ago would still have been largely of green fields.

The temple complex has a long sequence of courtyards, and would today give Cíxī views of the third ring road. The giant bell from the Great Bell Temple (*see* p.225) once hung here, but today the temple is one of those which is attractive for doubling as a small museum with an excellent collection of antiquities.

The ceiling of the gate as you enter is painted with an image of 100 red bats in a blue sky, which forms a visual pun. The expression *hóng fú mǎn tiān*, meaning 'the sky is full of red bats', sounds the same as 'day full of great luck'.

The Hall of the Heavenly (or Deva) Kings contains not the usual Maitreya Buddha and his four guardians, but a small exhibition of carved seals of different kinds, many carved from jade and ivory with a delicacy reminiscent of Japanese *netsuke*. Look particularly for an ivory one carved in the shape of a *bìxì*, the primitive dragon often incorrectly called a turtle in whose back more important stelae are set, and looking particularly lively in comparison to its giant brethren. Note also nearby the more pictorial copper seals from the Mongol Yuán dynasty, which had no written forms and eventually learned the script of the Turkic Uighur people of the northwest (although the Uighurs, as they became more Muslim, went on to use Arabic). A Míng set of six cuboid seals fit one inside the other, all of them having five usable faces, except the sixth and smallest which has six.

The halls of the next courtyard have exquisite statues in gold plated bronze of Buddhist entities including exoteric ones in mid-coitus (*see also* Lama Temple, p.187), and a Qīng statue of Tsongkhapa, the founder of the currently predominant Yellow Hat sect of Tibetan Buddhism.

The main Mahavira Hall's statuary includes the Medicine Buddha (pray here for a pain-free death), surrounded by expressionless but delicately executed arhats (*luóhàn*), and there's a Guānyīn, Goddess of Mercy. Dust lies in the folds of their drapery, and the interior is dim. Two tablets inscribed with a couplet by Qiánlōng are immediately to right and left as you enter.

Further in, a hall on the right has a modern interior full of carved ivory (including a complex knotted dragon) and buffalo and rhinoceros horn figurines, lacquerware, carved jade and agate seals, and other exquisite things, labelled in English.

On the west side are ceramics from Neolithic to Táng, early iron and copperware, some gold plate including a gold plated silver mask from the Liáo dynasty, and Qīng embroidery.

At the slightly modernized rear there's a modern seating area and formal garden, a big meditation hall, undergoing renovation, and a large rock garden behind, reportedly beloved of Cíxī, which represents famous Buddhist mountains including Wŭtái Shān. Three halls on top represent famous places where Buddhist preaching took place, reached by stone bridges across gullies in the rock. An octagonal pavilion behind the rock garden houses a Qiánlōng stele from 1761 detailing repairs to the temple. The Hall of the Buddha of Infinite Life, a Qīng extension, once housed a statue of brass lacquered in gold 5m high, but now there's an ornate Míng pagoda for storing scriptures made of gold alloy, and a few pieces of ancient furniture.

The bizarre rearmost courtyard is built in mixed Sino-Western style, influenced by the work of the Jesuits at the 'Old Summer Palace' for Qiánlōng—not in any way the Jesuits would recognize, yet as un-Chinese as you can get.

From here you can return east via Purple Bamboo Park, or use the third ring road to get to the Great Bell Temple on bus 300 or 323 (*see* below), or on the 300 around the city to other destinations.

Dà Zhōng Sì (Great Bell Temple)　大钟寺

Open 9–4.30, closed Mon; adm ¥10, annual ticket accepted.

See map p.220, no.10. The temple is on the west side of the north third ring road. Bus 300 runs around the third ring road to stop Dà Zhōng Sì. The temple is described in Juliet Bredon's *Peking* of 1931: 'This temple lying amongst quiet farms is an easy and pleasant walk of two miles from the Hsi Chih Mên [Xī Zhí Mén] or an excellent ride of four or five from the An Ting Mên across the plain, passing through the old Tartar mud wall, once the northern boundary of Kublai Khan's capital.'

The temple, at its founding in 1733 called the Juéshēng Sì, which expresses in a very compressed manner the idea of awakening to the Buddhist idea of the cycle of birth and rebirth, is also known as the Gŭ Zhōng Bówùguǎn (Museum of Ancient Bells). It's this that's the point of interest, rather than the largely conventional layout of the restored temple, with the exception of the unusual bell tower at the rear.

In general Chinese bells lack clappers, but are struck from outside. If large, this is done with a log mounted on chains which can be swung end-on into the bell. The main exhibition is the 'forest of bells' in a long hall on the left, a collection of bells of all sizes from all over China, many topped with double-ended dragons, and all of which Chinese visitors tap or stroke. A separate hall has many bells cast with elaborate texts on their surfaces, and some English explanations of their meaning. Other halls contain exhibitions on bell-casting methods, and one exhibition on famous foreign bells includes a still from the original black and white Hollywood movie of *The Hunchback of Notre Dame*. A courtyard on the eastern side has further bells hanging outside.

The champion bell, described as one of China's 'five consummate things' claims, dubiously, to be the largest in the world, although the bell in the Bell Tower—*see* p.175—is claimed to be the largest in China. The 46,500kg monster, 3.3m in diameter and 6.7m tall, hangs in an elegant square pavilion with a round upper storey. It is said to have been cast in the Yǒnglè reign (1403–24) and originally hung at the Wànshòu Sì, which is a little difficult to understand since that temple wasn't erected until six emperors later. It arrived at the Dà Zhōng Sì in 1743, being moved either on hardwood rollers, or slid on ice along a specially dug channel, depending on whose account you read. The interior and exterior surfaces of the bell are covered in a mixture of Sanskrit and Chinese amounting to over 230,000 tiny characters. There's an extra ¥2 charge to climb and view the bell from above.

The battle of the bells has now been won by a new 50-ton, 6.8m 'China Century Bell', the 'largest copper bell in China' made at Běijīng's major polluter, the Capital Iron and Steel Works. It hangs at the Altar of the Century and was rung to welcome the year 2000 by the Western calendar in a tone stressing Chinese nationalism. Rather than Sanskrit sutras, however, this one has illustrations of 'major historical events' and the Chinese national anthem.

Shopping

Běijīng's shopping now ranges from tiny *hútòng* markets to glossy multi-storey department stores with glass-fronted elevators. Neither contain much the visitor wants to buy, but the *hútòng* markets are lively and photogenic, the bright fruit sold from the back of tricycles livening up the grey streets, pedestrian bridges and subways. The department stores have travel necessities, and Western snacks for those in need of a change. If you really want top-notch Western brands from Armani to Ermenegildo Zegna visit the basement of The Palace Hotel, but as for all imported foreign products expect to pay more than you do at home.

Most of Běijīng's street markets are now under cover, and the city government has ordained that the rest will be as soon as possible. But those selling live fish and birds, for instance, are very colourful, and those selling antiques and curios the best sources of souvenirs for the cautious haggler, as well as in some cases offering a chance to meet minority people from remoter corners of China. Whether you want to shop or not, visiting one or two markets ought to rank in importance with visiting Běijīng's major historic sites.

Xīdān Běi Jiē, Wángfǔjǐng Dàjiē, Dōng Dān (also nicknamed 'Silver Street'), Jiànguó Mén, and the Qián Mén Dàjiē are the main shopping streets, with multiple department stores and speciality stores. These are the places to look for practical items, and to some degree souvenirs, since although prices are high there's a wide range of choice.

Opening hours vary from twelve hours a day for the newest shopping complexes, to rather limited hours for older shops which survived the Cultural Revolution and other upheavals, but which have retained their insouciant attitudes to service.

Look below first for some discussion of what there is to buy in Běijīng, and for the names of individual shops as well as malls and markets specializing in each kind of item, and then below that for detailed addresses and descriptions of malls and markets worth browsing, or which should be visited just for their atmosphere.

Beware of cheats (*piànzi*) everywhere, and avoid buying jewellery or precious or semi-precious stones, especially jade, unless you really know what you are doing. Even official outlets are unreliable. Recently commemorative solid silver coins manufactured by two Chinese companies and sold through post offices (there could hardly be a more official outlet) turned out to weigh only around half the weight inscribed upon them.

antiques

Approach all curios, and most dealers, with caution. A thief may be considered innocent till he is proved guilty, but a first-class K'ang Hsi vase (according to the merchant) should be held guilty of fraud till it is proved to be above suspicion by some one who knows and is disinterested... Whenever a Chinese offers to let a good piece go at a sacrifice, be sure that the sacrifice is on the side of the buyer and the victim is the customer, not the shopkeeper.

Juliet Bredon, *Peking*, 1919

Nearly a century later Bredon's advice is still sound. The Chinese have a long history of manufacturing fake antiques, and unless you are particularly expert you will find that you have paid a high price for something of no value. Bredon had the advantage of knowing what a good Kāngxī vase should cost, but you probably don't even have that. Unless you are a specialist your chances of success here are not good, so stick to modestly priced items which appeal to you whatever their authenticity may be. And more than in any other area of shopping, realise that you may be asked 10 to 15 times more than Chinese for fake and real goods alike. That chipped Sòng dynasty bowl with its luminous celadon glaze was quite likely manufactured last month, deliberately distressed, and buried for a week or two. Its price is not ¥400, but ¥40 or less. The same is equally true for Cultural Revolution items with cracked glazes over transfers of Máo Zédōng and Lín Biāo, which, because of their rarity and therefore high value, have recently been appearing in rather large numbers.

Pān Jiā Yuán Jiù Huò Shìchǎng is the most colourful place to look, but more for curios and bric-à-brac than antiques. Neighbouring **Curio City** (Gǔwán Chéng) is for more serious buyers. The **Hóng Qiáo Market** (Hóng Qiáo Jímào Shìchǎng) top floor is similar, as is **Liúlichǎng**, which is much more attractive to wander around. In all cases beware JCB and Amex card signs—a guarantee that you'll pay even more over the odds than usual. The market at **Bàoguó Sì**, inside the former temple, is more for bric-à-brac but is little known by foreigners. Serious buyers should also consider a day trip to **Tiānjīn** for the vast antique market there (*see* p.345). Numismatists should head for the markets mentioned under philately below, and for the coin and note market at Déshèng Mén (*see* p.178).

artists' and calligraphic materials, and stationery

Shops around the **National Art Gallery** (*see* p.279) at the top of Wángfǔjǐng have framing services, paper, canvas, graphics materials, Western artists' materials, oils, watercolours, inks, brushes, pencils, etc. **Liúlichǎng** has the most famous shop of this kind in Běijīng, the long-standing Róngbǎozhāi, but its prices are more oriented to tourists, although its selection is wider.

books

The new **Běijīng Túshū Dàshà** (Běijīng Books Centre), Xī Cháng'ān Jiē 17, at Ⓜ Xī Dān (*open 9–8.30*), is the biggest book store, and has an good selection of city maps and provincial road atlases. **Běijīng Foreign Languages Publications Building** (Běijīng Shì Wàiwén Túshū Dàlóu), Wángfǔjǐng Dàjiē 235, has also recently been modernized, and comes in second place. There are some English titles on the ground floor, typically 19th-century English novels and dubious translations of Chinese classics, and a few in other European languages, too, and possibly the best selection of imported English novels in Běijīng up on the fourth floor. Just north of Wángfǔjǐng Grand Hotel, two private bookshops have a good selection of art books. There are further art books on sale inside the National Art Gallery at the top of the street, and beyond that, on the right, the **Sānlián Tāofèn Túshū Zhōngxīn**, Měishūguǎn Dōng Jiē 22, also has stocks of art and architecture titles in a modern setting. The best place of all for art and architecture books are the shops in **Liúlichǎng** where you'll pay proper publishers' prices for books the museums love to mark up. Particularly try the two shops on the south side of the western half of the street, and on the north side at the entrance to the eastern half. Tucked away behind the calligraphic materials store just to the right of that is a second-hand bookshop with a mixture of books abandoned in hotel rooms and the out-of-date reference collections of Běijīng embassies, still with their bookplates. There's an occasional find here. There are branches of the official state store **Xīnhuá Shūdiàn** everywere, some of which have a few English titles, and small, private bookshops are cropping up, some of which have second-hand English books which they seem to think they can sell for the cover price; see the small shop halfway along the south side of **Lóngfú Shìchǎng**, for instance.

bicycles

Serious long-distance cyclists should bring their own bikes with them. The Flying Pigeon company, makers of one of China's many sit-up-and-beg gearless models, has moved on from 'any colour you like so long as it's black', to pink. The Chinese have now started making imitation mountain and touring bikes, but the mountain bikes might well be named for their weight rather than their use, and have a tendency to fall to pieces under stress. For travel around Běijīng most hotels have some kind of bike rental service, from ¥10 per day for decrepit, unmaintained, single gear boneshakers, to ¥100 ($12.50) per day for newer, unmaintained, single gear boneshakers if your residence has five stars. However, given the low prices of simple bikes, those staying a few weeks might like to consider a purchase, and to see Běijīng the way most Běijīng people still see it.

The **Dàzhàlán Zìxíngchē Shāngdiàn**, Dàzhàlán Jiē 44, ✆ 6303 5303 (*open 9–8.30*) has bikes for rent for ¥10 for one day from around 8–8, and which are relatively new and in condition, with ¥1–200 deposit depending on the bike. They also have a wide selection of relatively modern Chinese bikes for sale. **Běijīng Yǒngjiǔ Zìxíngchē** at Dōngsì Běi Dàjiē 303 (*open 8.30–7*), has everything from minibikes to the kind of tricycles which do duty for everything from heavy haulage to mobile shop. The bicycle shop just to the west of Dōngyuè Sì in Cháoyáng Mén Wài has mountain bikes for as little as ¥400 ($50).

cameras and optical equipment

Not the high-tech kind—these are cheaper at home—but a chance to experiment with expensive formats at a low price. Ancient Chinese full-plate cameras of *Seagull* brand can be bargained down to ¥100 ($12.50), or try a Russian *Horizon* brand swing-lens camera which uses standard 35mm film to make 120° panoramic images without the distortion of a panoramic lens or the cropping necessary to produce the same effect with the APS format. (*See* <http://silvestricamera.com/horizon/> or <http://www.al.nl/phomepag/markerink/> for a fuller explanation.) Both types of camera are clockwork and should be checked over thoroughly before purchase, although the Russian cameras are far better made than the Chinese brands. Shopkeepers like to tell you that the swing-lens cameras cost $500 at home (they certainly do not), but if you can find them they certainly cost more than the under $200 for which you should be able to buy them in Běijīng.

The Russian cameras pop up all over the place—try the shop with suits of armour and other bric-à-brac just south of the Huáqiáo Dàshà (Prime Hotel) in Wángfǔjǐng, shops in Dōng Sì around the entrance to the Lama Temple, and inside any department store or market away from the centre. If you have a beloved ancient Western camera, finding old bodies to cannibalize for spare parts or long unavailable accessories presents few problems. For this and for Chinese cameras try the ground floor of Hóng Qiáo Market.

carpets

There are several carpet shops which promote themselves heavily to foreign visitors, some based inside the joint-venture hotels where they should be approached with caution. You'll do better at shops such as the **Línxià Flying Horse Carpet Co. Ltd**, (Gānsù Línxià Fēimǎ Máofǎng Dìtǎn Zhuānyíngdiàn), Zhūshìkǒu Xī Jiē 66, © 6302 2029, where prices vary from a few hundred to several thousand RMB for carpets hand made from wool and silk in Gānsù Province, which they claim to come directly from a factory under Uighur minority management.

Also look in the furniture markets (*see* Furniture below), at the rear of the Xiùshuǐ Silk Market, in the nearby Friendship Store (bargain hard here, too, and *not* just for the token 10%), in carpet shops at Liúlichǎng, and the **Yuánlōng Sīchóu Gǔfèn Yǒuxiànsī** (Yuánlōng Silk Corporation Ltd—*see* 'Silk', below).

CDs, VCDs, DVDs and CD-ROMs

'Seedy!' they shout at you, which often describes them quite well. Then 'CD-ROM, CD-music' which makes things clearer.

Street vendors selling pirate copies of disks are everywhere there are foreigners, all claiming to have 'new' stock, which often includes Fleetwood Mac and Eagles discs from the 1970s. Despite the government's limits on the numbers of Western films which may be seen on the big screens each year (about 10 a year getting approval) anyone with a VCD player can be watching almost any major and many very minor Western movies of the last 50 years on demand. Pirated VCDs of 1999's *Star Wars* movie were on the streets in Běijīng in just over a week, for ¥15 ($2).

Many of the movie VCDs are made by erecting a video camera at the back of a movie auditorium, and occasionally figures pass in front of the lens on their way for more popcorn. The picture and sound quality are both, not surprisingly, rather murky. Software problems or inept copying may make both these and direct copies of legal disks impossible to play.

China Daily continues to carry stories about copyright and trademark protection, and about the smashing up of pirate CD manufacturers and distributors. This is complete window-dressing as five minutes in a Běijīng market will tell you, and there's a good chance that even if you shop in what looks like a reputable department store that the discs will be fakes, laser-hologram-stickered security packaging or no. At the classical music end, Deutsche Grammophon seems to be a particularly popular target for pirating, their cover booklets reproduced by poor colour photocopying. There's also a Chinese brand which copies the DG packaging right down to having (meaningless) German words on the cover, but the main title in Chinese. These pirated discs are ¥10–15.

In stores legitimate (if you're lucky) local CDs are around ¥40 ($5) and imports around ¥80 ($10). There are also smuggled imports for around ¥30 (¥15 in Tiānjīn).

computer products

Computer hardware and software is widely on sale in an area called Zhōngguāncūn near the university campuses in the northwest of the city. This area is receiving substantial financial incentives from the government, which wishes to develop it further as China's 'Silicon Valley'. Tax relief and free office rent is being offered to Chinese scholars who return home from overseas to start companies here, in the hope of turning the trickle of those who return into a flood. Apple, IBM, Microsoft, Compaq, HP, Mitsubishi and Fujitsu already have sales and distribution offices, along with more than 4,000 other high-tech companies. Take bus 332 from the Zoo.

Home computers have become much desired by parents anxious for their children to compete educationally, but government investigators discovered that in only 30% of cases did machines do what the advertisers claimed. Although you may pick up Chinese versions of software programs, don't expect after-sales service or refunds for non-performance in the case of hardware or software. Better than 90% of all the software in use in China is thought to be pirated, with government departments and large enterprises leading the way.

The latest edition of *Microsoft Office* will be on sale complete with imitation packaging and registration number (usually added in a read me file on the first disc) within days of being officially issued. Major and usually very expensive graphics programmes are available at a fraction of the usual price, but when you get them home you may find a missing or duplicated disc, that one of them won't load, that the registration number is missing, or that there are Chinese quirks incompatible with your particular operating system. Or you may not.

Within much easier reach of most visitors is the three-storey store of kiosks selling computers and accessories in Cháoyáng Mén Wài, just west of Lán Dǎo Dàshà, called **Bǎi Nǎo Huì** (*open 9–9*). Chinese slang for computer is *diàn nǎo*—'electric brain', *Bǎi Nǎo Huì* is '100 brains collected together', but sounds so like 'Buy Now' it's probably a bilingual pun.

furniture

Huáyì Classical Furniture (Huáyì Gǔdiǎn Jiāju) at Curio City, and with its own exhibition space off the airport highway, © 6432 9807, <*infor@cyjj.com*>, <*http://www.cyjj.com/*>, has a good reputation. It sells old and restored furniture, and things made with old wood in old styles, from around ¥2,000 ($250), and will obtain customs clearance and organize shipping.

Liàngmǎ Qiáo Furniture Market, opposite the north side of the Lufthansa Centre, has some fine things deeper in if you know what to look for, but prices are pushed upwards by its nearness to several five-star hotels and diplomatic housing.

Guānfù Classical Furniture Gallery (which also runs the private furniture museum in Liúlichǎng, *see* p.239) is at Liúlichǎng Xī Jiē 22. The main showroom is in a remote location off the southeast third ring road. Talk to the museum people or contact © 6767 2309, ✆ 6317 7930, <*guanfu@public.east.cn.net*>, <*http://www.antique-art-china.com/*>.

kites

Although these are made of modern materials they are still very attractive, often in the shape of animals and birds. The Hóng Qiáo market and Lufthansa Centre have a selection, as do stalls at the Yùtíng Flower and Bird Market. However, if you approach kite flyers at Tiān'ān Mén Square or on bridges over the second ring road you'll often find they are also selling kites, for around ¥30 (or at least that's all you should pay).

models

Small *hútòng* shops often have a surprising range of die-cast models and plastic model kits long discontinued in the West and for far lower prices. There's a shop just south of the Xú Bēihóng Museum (*see* p.178) on the east side of the road just north of the Xīn Jiē Kǒu Fàndiàn (hotel), another in Dà Liù Bù Kǒu, a *hútòng* running south of Xī Cháng'ān Jiē near the Telecommunications Office and another in Huángchéng Gēn Nán Jiē, a *hútòng* running parallel with Běi Hé Yán Dàjiē west of Wángfǔjǐng and many others, mostly with TAMIYA signs outside. Stalls outside the Aviation Museum (*see* p.342) have a good selection of aircraft and spacecraft models.

philately

Stamp collecting and dealing is very popular in China, not least since one Běijīng resident famously turned himself into a millionaire by judicious collecting. Shops and markets dealing with stamps nearly always have baseball cards, telephone cards and other small collectibles. Taking items from home to trade can make you very popular.

The street parallel to Dàzhàlán Jiē on the north side has **Qián Mén Yóu Pǐn Shìchǎng** with several stalls selling stamps, and major post offices such at that in Jiànguó Mén Nèi have special philately departments with first day covers, mint sets and more. The enthusiastic collector will enjoy **Dōngdān Jí Yóu Shìchǎng**, a market of stamp kiosks (*see* below). Lots of envelopes with foreign stamps have been filched from the waste bins of hotel rooms by staff ever creative in making an extra bit of money, and you can even find envelopes here from letters written to ambassadors.

practical necessities and travel needs

Many *hútòng* have small groceries and convenience stores open long hours, and familiar Western snacks useful for travelling can be found in the branches of Hong Kong supermarkets in the basements of many of the glitzier department stores, such as Park 'n' Shop in Cofco, Watson's in Full Link Plaza and Wellcome in the China World Trade Centre. Here there are also stocks of familiar simple proprietary medicines, cosmetics and feminine hygiene products, condoms, toothpaste, shampoo, etc. Sleeping bags, camping equipment, greatcoats and anything need for an invasion of Táiwān except the weapons can be bought from the **PLA** shop on the west side of Dōng Sān Huán Běi Lù just south of Cháoyáng Lù, ✆ 6585 9312.

silk

The ancient **Běijīng Silk Store** (Běijīng Sīchóu Shāngdiàn), Zhūbǎo Shì 5, in the narrow alley parallel to Qián Mén Dàjiē immediately south of Qián Mén, ✆ 6301 6658 (*open 8.30–8*), has a large collection of silk fabric at low prices and is packed with Chinese, which is a guarantee that the prices must be better than those in the tourist-oriented destinations.

With its large rooftop signs saying 'Chinese Silk', the **Yuánlóng Sīchóu Gǔfèn Yǒuxiànsī** (Yuánlóng Silk Corporation Ltd), Yǒngdìng Mén Nèi Dōng Jiē 15, ✆ 6702 4059, can hardly be missed, and indeed is a stop on some organized tours. Nevertheless its clearly marked prices are competitive, and it has two floors of silk fabric in a wide variety of weights and styles, at between ¥58 ($7) and ¥150 ($19) per metre. There are also some made-up goods, mostly in Chinese traditional styles, as well as silk carpets and other items.

Made-up goods are cheaper at the **Xiùshǔi Silk Market** if you haggle hard, but this is now so well-touristed that getting the 'right' price is almost impossible, and the emphasis here has switched to fake labels in any material, rather than just silk. But both traditional Chinese clothes and Western styles are available.

tea

Yúnnán girls in blue neo-traditional blouses sell loose tea straight from the bamboo pole-borne canister on the street. Special tea shops such as Tiānfú (signs with 'Ten Fu', 'TEA' and the Chinese word for tea, *chá*, in big letters), which can be found on almost every street in Běijīng it seems, say that the quality of the girls' tea is not as good as theirs, but there seems no particular reason to believe this is true, and many reasons to believe the girls need the money more than the shops. The shops carry a good selection of tea ware, too, but if it's the famous earthen Yíxīng ware teapots you're after (or at least lookalikes), many in humorous designs, you'd better go to **Pān Jiā Yuán** market, where they are no more than ¥15 each.

Department Stores and Shopping Malls

These mostly stock items unlikely to be of interest to the casual visitor to China, such as clothing, shoes and appliances. The most upmarket are the Shì Dū (One World) in Wángfǔjǐng and Parkson (a Hong Kong chain) in Fùchéng Mén. A notch down are Sogo (from Japan), south of Ⓜ Xuānwǔ Mén, and the Sun Dong An (Xīn Dōng'ān). Oriental Plaza, the vast new complex on the corner of Wángfǔjǐng and Dōng

Cháng'ān Jiē, will probably be fairly upmarket, although who will shop there is not clear, as existing department stores are full of window-shopping peasants and precious few shoppers as it is. At least two have shut down in recent times, and one which decided to cut its staff by a third suffered a sit-down occupation and had to close for a week. Here's a selection of survivors in alphabetical order:

Běijīng Department Store (Běijīng Bǎihuò Dà Lóu). Once just about the only department store in Beijing. Look for the bust of the diligent employee at the front. Bus 103 stops outside.

Běijīng Friendship Store (Běijīng Yǒuyí Shāngdiàn), originally one of several and now the only one of significance, mainly because of its position on the edge of the Jiànguó Mén embassy area and near several upmarket hotels. Friendship stores were once the only ones to stock decent goods in the whole city, and were only open to those with foreign currency or the parallel currency which could only be bought with foreign exchange. The store was opened in 1964 and has recently had a major overhaul, but it is still more expensive for almost anything you can buy elsewhere, and is losing money. The small supermarket on the ground floor used to be a mecca for foreigners, but now its selection is matched or exceeded in the basements of other stores around town. Starbucks, Baskin Robbins, Rotary Sushi, Hong Kong fast food and Pizza Hut at the entrance. Silk and silk goods upstairs, as well as cashmere and a variety of souvenirs. Bookshop on the ground floor with English imported magazines.

The **Běijīng Lufthansa Centre Yǒuyí Shopping City** (Yānshā Yǒuyí Shāngchéng) has imported foods and goods with a duty-free feel such as perfume, lighters and luggage, as well as Italian, German, French and Korean restaurants. There's a basement supermarket with imported foods, but it's probably the most expensive in the whole of Běijīng. It does have a good selection of imported wines, a modest deli counter and a branch of Délifrance. This is on the northeast third ring, reached by bus 300 around the ring or the tè3 double decker from Yǒngdìng Mén. *Open 9am–9.40pm.*

China World Trade Centre (Zhōngguó Guójì Màoyì Zhōngxīn), usually just known as Guómào, at ⓜ Guómào, on Jiànguó Mén Wài Dàjiē. This has a basement food court, an Internet café, delicatessen, airline offices, American Express, and so on. Basement shopping is of the more upmarket international brands, mostly fashions, although there's also a supermarket.

COFCO Plaza (Zhōng Liáng Guǎngchǎng), just north of ⓜ Běijīng Zhàn, in Jiànguó Mén Nèi Dàjiē. Mostly clothes with a few restaurants. The ground floor has an Italian delicatessen, and there's a Park 'n' Shop in the basement. DHL, Starbucks, Baskin Robbins and McDonald's are all here.

Full Link Plaza (Fēnglián Guǎngchǎng), Cháoyáng Mén Wài 18, ⓜ Cháoyáng Mén, is very upmarket, with mostly expensive clothing, but also a Watson's, Air France, Starbucks, and a cyber café and Park 'n' Shop in the basement.

Henderson Centre (Héngjī Zhōngxīn Shāngchǎng) mostly has clothing stores with some international brands, and a supermarket in the basement along with The Universal Studios Experience (apparently universally ignored by the Chinese, *open 10–9*, adults ¥35, children ¥25, family ticket ¥85), and food court with four outlets, plus A&W, Viva Curry and a Korean restaurant. At the rear there's Irish Pub P. J.

O'Reilly's with lunch specials for ¥35 and Be There or Be Square, a 24-hour Hong Kong food operation. 'High class fair price superlife in Henderson', say the adverts. You decide. *Open 9–10.*

The **Kylin Plaza** (Qílín Dàshà), in Gōngrén Tǐyù Běi Lù near the north gate of the Workers' Stadium, is of little consequence, but there's a selection of silk on the fourth floor and decent tailoring services. *Open 9–9.*

Lóngfú Dàshà, just to the east of the top of Wángfǔjǐng, has general Chinese goods, a ground-floor Chinese supermarket, and an imitation temple on the roof to remind you of the one on whose site it stands, once famous for its temple fairs.

Lǚwū Bǎihuò, in Wángfǔjǐng just north of Sun Dong An (*open 9–9*), has various travel snacks, fruit (check marked prices and buy more cheaply on the street), sushi, bakery, noodle stalls, coffee, and teriyaki. Upstairs lots of imported Korean products of all kinds. There's also a ticket agency for the Běijīng Concert Hall near the main entrance.

One World (Shì Dū Bǎihuò), Wángfǔjǐng (*open 10–10*). So expensive that even expats don't shop there much; it's for *nouveaux riche* Chinese to show off. Mostly clothes and cosmetics, and you're greeted at the entrance by people selling apartments. The basement supermarket is particularly good for imported goods, with everything from baby formula and feminine hygiene products to *Jules Destrooper* biscuits from Belgium.

Parkson (Bǎishèng Gòuwù Zhōngxīn) Ⓜ Fùxīng Mén (*open 9–10*). Young people's fashions, fairly expensive for Běijīng, with good supermarket in the basement, and a good food court on the top floor. Also houses the Crafts Museum (*see* p.210).

SCITECH (Sàitè Gòuwù Zhōngxīn), Jiànguó Mén Wài Dàjiē 22 (*open 9–9.30*). An unreasonably expensive general department store—aims at foreigners. Watch-mending here and some jewellery.

Sogo (Zhuāngshèng Chóngguāng Bǎihuò), 5 mins' walk south of Ⓜ Xuānwǔ Mén. This Japanese department store is at first indistinguishable from other stores but stocks French, Italian, Hong Kong and American designers, as well as Wedgwood and Royal Doulton, all of which you'll find more cheaply at home. There's a food court in the basement, and Japanese (UCC) coffee shops on the 2nd and 6th floors.

Sun Dong An (Hong Kong funded and named in Cantonese—in Mandarin Xīn Dōng'ān). Immense shopping mall on about seven levels, with music and book stores in the basement, some reproduction old tea and traditional medicine shops, several restaurants (including the ancient hot pot restaurant Dōngláishùn), food street on the top floor, Délifrance, Pizza Hut, McDonalds and Starbucks. Big fashion names include Burberry. There's a **market** at the rear also approachable from Jīnyú Hútòng (*open 9.30–8*) which is the cheapest place in the centre of town to buy cheap bags and suitcases. These can cost up to five times as much for the same item in the store itself, and up to three times as much at the Silk Market. They are not fake brand names, nor aesthetically pleasing, but the cheapest option for those who discover that their shopping has overflowed their available packing space.

The Station (Lǎo Chē Zhàn Shāngchǎng). The 100-year-old British-built first station within Běijīng's city walls, recently rescued from a patina of advertising and later additions, and restored as a shopping mall. Italian ice cream, mediocre Chinese clothes, good food court in basement.

The basement of **Xīn Shìjiè Bǎihuò (New World Department Store)**, just south of Ⓜ Chóngwén Mén, includes a fake version of Kenny Rogers' Roasters and a bakery and supermarket. The rest is mostly clothes.

Wángfǔjǐng and Other Modern Shopping Streets

Wángfǔjǐng Dàjiē

Entering the well-lighted Wang Fu Ching Street, our rickshaws set us down at the Tung An Market. There was no room for vehicles amongst those acres of alleyways lined with stalls, small shops, restaurants and tea houses. Good-natured crowds of shoppers and loiterers allowed us to push our way through them until, pausing only to buy a handful of toffeed grapes speared on sticks to eat after dinner, we reached a dingy doorway overhung by a black-lacquered board inscribed with three Chinese characters in gold.

John Blofeld, *City of Lingering Splendor*, 1961

There's nothing dingy about **Wángfǔjǐng** anymore—the great clean-up of 1999 having been responsible for that with the refurbishment of existing stores to match the colossal new emporia. The shopping complexes are largely indistinguishable from those of suburban North America, although Oriental Plaza, built on a block-long 1,000-square-metre site at the Dōng Cháng'ān Jiē, is the largest building complex in Asia and hardly provincial. Once the home of the Australian journalist and *Times* correspondent Morrison, the foreign residents of the Legation Quarter renamed Wángfǔjǐng Dàjiē 'Morrison Street', and it sprouted Chinese shops catering to their needs or selling imported goods to the Chinese. These were amongst the first targets of the Boxers in 1900, but if these rebels returned now they would need to set fire to almost the entire street.

A few of the shops that Blofeld might have seen still exist, selling traditional Chinese goods, but the broad semi-pedestrianized boulevard is dominated by the big department stores, foreign brand names and fast food outlets. Out-of-town Chinese gather to gawp at the newly installed dancing fountains outside the Běijīng Department Store, and have their photos taken with statues of period shoppers, hawkers and rickshawmen. In another nod to tourism, the well referred to in the street's name, which means 'Well of the Prince's Palace', has supposedly been rediscovered and is now marked. For the visitor there are several five-star hotels, a foreign language bookshop, ATM machines at several locations (*see* p.115), souvenir shops selling ceramics, cloisonné and handicrafts, and some reasonable budget accommodation on or just off the street. It makes for a pleasant stroll, and a chance to see the image of China the government wants to present to the world—one, which for all its anti-foreign rhetoric, appears to be almost entirely Western, and is certainly entirely superficial. Take almost any side turning to find yourself immediately back in the kind of decay which truly still characterizes Běijīng.

A vast development plan for Wángfǔjǐng began in 1991 and will continue until 2010. Believe it or not, Wángfǔjǐng is twinned with Paris' Champs Elysées—some people will clearly sell their souls to boost trade.

Parallel to Wángfǔjǐng a block to the east **Dōng Dān** (East Single) and its northern extension **Dōng Sì** (East Four), Ⓜ Dōng Dān, named for the wooden *páilou* or memorial arches which once stood here, is rather more hectic since it's a major north–south traffic artery with narrow pavements and long rows of smaller shops selling everything from household goods (anything in the pot, pan, knife and brush line marked 'made in China' when you buy it at home can be bought more cheaply here) to toys, bicycles and food, and services such as wedding preparation (see bridesmaids receiving industrial make-up jobs and grooms uncomfortable in ill-fitting tails).

Xī Dān, Ⓜ Xī Dān, named on the same principle, would like to be the western counterpart of eastern Wángfǔjǐng, but is half that and half the bustle of Dōng Dān with equally practical shopping, although the vast spaces and large buildings of the southern end seem to promise more. A brand new department store opened in late 1999 at the southern end, called Zhōngyǒu Bǎihuò, which by the middle of 2000 was having almost continuous sales in order to stay open.

Jiànguó Mén Nèi and **Jiànguó Mén Wài Dàjiē** have immense palaces to commerce, with long windy walks between them, and there's a similar collection in **Cháoyáng Mén Wài Dàjiē**, which are rather closer together (although one has closed).

Qián Mén Dàjiē, running south from Ⓜ Qián Mén, is rather more interesting since it's on a smaller scale, with fewer Western fashions, several long-standing famous restaurants and lots of bustle, both in the main street and in a parallel alley at the northern end, as well as in neighbouring *hútòng* particularly on the western side, and in the traditional shopping street of Dàzhàlán Jiē (*see* below).

Markets and Traditional Shopping Streets

Many of these should be treated as attractions, even if you don't want to shop. Look out, too, for the recently revived temple fairs, a major feature of the Běijīng year before communism, although many of the venues have disappeared too, and the fairs are now spread throughout the spring.

Street markets have coalesced round certain backstreets and spare pieces of land over the last few years but where they have been allowed to flourish and latterly actively encouraged, that encouragement has taken the form of moving them to new, less successful locations, and or roofing them over, or both, with a consequent rise in prices. Several have gone through the process of being only for foreign residents 'in the know', to known by just about everyone, to appearing in guide books. Ask your hotel reception staff, no doubt as canny as the next Chinese, for recommendations of the newest 'in the know' thing.

Dà Zhàlán (Dàshílanr)

Dàzhàlán (in Běijīng dialect Dàshílanr) means 'big gates', and refers to those that once stood at the end of the street to bottle up the pleasure quarter (*see* p.154). It runs west from Qián Mén Dàjiē a short walk south of Ⓜ Qián Mén, and contains a mixture of well-preserved Qīng-era shops, badly preserved ones (one shop front stands forlorn, just a façade with a car park behind it), and modern cinemas and video parlours which have replaced the theatres for which the district was also famous. (Theatres were not permitted within the Tartar City, but only here in the Chinese or Southern City.) The street spent much of 1998 being reconstructed, and was the first in Běijīng to be pedestrianized, with 13 historic shops being restored or rebuilt.

Amongst long-standing institutions here, the Chinese traditional medicine shop **Tóngréntáng** is one of the best known, with several branches in Běijīng, a factory near one entrance to the underground city, and branches and imitators as far flung as Hanoi. The Dàzhàlán branch claims to have been open on this site since 1669, on the south side. Just east of this is the **Zhāngyìyuán Cházhuāng** tea shop, more than 90 years old, which has a good selection of tea. Opposite on the northern side the **Ruìfúxiáng Chóubù Diàn**, more than 105 years old, has detailed friezes of flowers and birds, contains Chinese-style clothing and some silk, and specializes in *qípáo*, the traditional high-collared dress with a slit skirt now most often seen on waitresses and restaurant greeters. Just to the east another old store, now a shoe shop, has a marvellous wrought-iron frontage. Further west there's a good bicycle hire service at the **Dàzhàlán Zìxíngchē Shāngdiàn**, and shops selling arts, crafts and minority costume, including Made in Paradise specializing in Tibetan goods. In amongst all this there's a small bookshop, video parlours with deafening loudspeakers, and many other shops with gift items for tourists.

In 1999 the Dàshílanr Street Supervising Committee and the district government organized five inauthentic reproductions of the kind of rickshaw common on Běijīng's streets until 40 years earlier, and shops on the street costumed the rickshaw boys appropriately in yellow vest and blue trousers. This gimmick didn't last very long.

Further west beyond the pedestrianized section in Dàzhàlan Xī Jiē on the north side, there's a new little tea house called **Tiānhǎi**, which shows the video of Lǎo Shě's *Tea House*, birds in cages hanging on the front, and there are a few other late Qīng shop frontages—look upwards for clues rather than at the obscured or altered ground level. Turning at random to north or south will take you into a labyrinth of *hútòng* full of surprises, some of them visual, some olfactory.

Běijīng Shì Yuánlín Huāhuì Shìchǎng

A market just inside the wall of Tiāntán at the northeast corner and entered from there is mostly for gardening needs, but has a spectacular display of giant ceramics, including a vast choice of teapots, bowls, jars, vases, dishes and plates, from the miniature to the bigger than you.

Chángchún Jiē and Bàoguó Sì

This is a small bird market completely unknown to foreigners but excellent for photography. From ⓜ Chángchūn Jiē walk south and take the third turning to the west (right). The street here is lined with caged smaller birds, including love birds, finches and larks, with some *bā gē* and *liáo gē* (mynahs). Busiest on Thursdays, Saturdays and Sundays.

Walk on and turn left at the entrance to a park, then right when the path makes you, and then first left and carry on south. At the T turn right, then left at the next T and the temple buildings of Bàoguó Sì are on your right—enter from the south side. *Open*

7–4.30, busier at the weekends. The front half of this temple is a brand new reconstruction, showing that the old skills have not been lost, occasionally special 'exhibitions' which really mean opportunities to buy—for instance, Pakistani products. One hall has an exhibition of early bone implements and ceramics, not for sale. The markets are in the halls and in stalls set out in the courtyards, or just on blankets on the floor. The selection of antiques and bric-à-brac is not as great as that of Pān Jiā Yuán, but the number of visiting foreigners is very low, and the prices accordingly so, but still bargain very hard. There are stamp, coin and card exchanges here, too, and second-hand books, but mostly in Chinese.

Curio City (Gǔwán Chéng)

This multi-storey market is on the east third ring south (Dōng Sān Nán Huán Lù), just south of the Pān Jiā Yuán *open 9.30–5.30.* Confusingly it has expensive modern items in the windows and the odd duty-free sign (don't believe it) attached to a store on part of the ground floor, but inside has three storeys of antique shops, and a top floor of upmarket imported electronics. Some shops here specialize in Tibetan, Mongolian and other regions' art, and others in carpets and furniture.

Dōngdān Jí Yóu Shìchǎng

This market for postage stamps, phone cards, basketball cards, banknotes, etc. is at the south end of Dōng Dān Gōngyuán, just south of Ⓜ Dōng Dān (*open 9–5.30*), busiest on Saturday and Sunday. Stamp catalogues and price lists are on sale but are often out of date, and there are many fakes here—buying the complete envelope and franked stamp in position is thought to be the more reliable way. Bring some of your own stamps and cards for sale or exchange.

Politics also plays a role here: a serious set of Máo stamps from the Cultural Revolution is ¥1,000 ($125), but if you buy them individually the ones with Máo alone are ¥100 ($12.50), and the ones with both Máo and Lín Biāo are ¥400 ($50). But at these prices all may be fakes.

Hóng Qiáo Jímào Shìchǎng

The Hóngqiáo Market of antiques and curios used to be huddled against the northeast wall of Tiān Tán, but has now moved to the top floor of a modern building opposite to the east (*open 9-6.30*). Take bus 106 south from Dōng Sì or Dōng Dān.

On the way up to the antiques you pass stalls of smuggled electronics (CD, MD), Chinese cameras and personal stereos, fake watches, clothing, shoes and bags, and freshwater pearls, for which the market is also famous. Popular items here include the Cultural Revolution clocks, featuring red-cheeked Red Guards, one of whom waves her arm with a little red book while the second hand sports a soaring aeroplane. The antiques market has become perhaps a little too popular with tourists, as evidenced by the sprouting of credit card stickers everywhere, and even Bill Clinton shopped here on his 1998 visit. Antiques are no more likely to be real than anywhere else, however.

Liàngmǎ Qiáo Jiājù Shìchǎng

This antique furniture market, opposite the north side of the Lufthansa Centre, has some fine things deeper in if you know what to look for, but prices are pushed upwards by its nearness to several five-star hotels and diplomatic housing.

Liúlichǎng

Perhaps the most attractive area for shopping is Liúlichǎng (named after a tile factory that once existed in the area), a few minutes' walk south of ⑩ Hépíng Mén, where old buildings have been restored and rebuilt to house antiques and art materials shops. This makes for a pleasant two-hour browse, even if you don't shop. *Caveat emptor:* almost every shop window sports credit card signs, and there's an unhealthy understanding of the depth of foreign pockets. Some antiques are freshly manufactured. Nevertheless, there's a large selection of cloisonné, lacquerware, ceramics and painting, as well as theatre puppets, old clocks and watches, and vast amounts of bric-à-brac. The **Běijīng Fine Arts Publishing House** at no.4 on the west side has guides and art books at the proper cover price rather than the tourist mark-up. Further up the ancient books bookshop (**Gǔjí Shūdiàn**) has sets of out-of-print books. Opposite, an artists' materials shop has an inkstone the size of a double bed for ¥1.3 million (plus considerable excess baggage charges should you choose to fly it home). More portable goods include blank fans for painting on, oil paints, pastels and other media, pestles and mortars, etc. The eastern half of the street also has the **Cathay Bookshop** on the corner of Nán Xīnhuá Jiē, with a neighbouring stationery/art equipment shop, through which is a **second-hand bookshop** with many foreign language books rescued from the libraries of embassies and private collections. There's also a flea market here, with Běijīng attempts to cash in on the peasant art so wildly successful in Xī'ān, Cultural Revolution memorabilia (Máo watches, little red books), and much else. Similarly, on the west side, there's the **Róngxīng Jiù Huò Shìchǎng** with lines of stalls. Other shops specialize in old carpets, old furniture (*see* also the 'Guānfù Classic Art Museum', p.167), porcelain, and general bric-à-brac. Smaller *hútòng* turnings to north and south have 'Hello, lookee-lookee' people beckoning your wallet in, and shops to the north and south of the Liúlichǎng turnings specialize in both modern and traditional musical instruments.

Lóngfú Shìchǎng

This runs east from opposite the east side of the National Art Gallery at the top of Wángfǔjǐng past the front of the Lóngfú Dàshà deparment store to Dōng Sì, and is of interest mostly for viewing Běijīng teenagers and trophy mistresses in a frenzy of clothes shopping, although the clothes are neither expensive nor in particularly good taste. There are also several cinemas here, fast food outlets both Chinese and Western, and some more fashionable Hong Kong clothing chains. The western end has stalls with T-shirts and snacks.

Pān Jiā Yuán Jiù Huò Shìchǎng

Open 7–5 Sat and Sun officially but in fact gets going from dawn, and runs on a smaller scale during the week. Some of the neighbouring antique shops are *open Sat and Sun 9–6, Mon–Fri 7–11 and 2–7.* Now covered over, the market still retains some of the atmosphere which gave it the nickname 'dirt market', although Amex card signs have started to appear, and there are signs in English indicating (inaccurately) what each aisle holds. This includes Buddha statues, Buddha heads, jade, 'jade', Yíxīng teapots galore, giant calligraphy brushes, metal dragons, metal Buddhas, metal Dèng Xiǎopíngs, ornate door knockers and handles for drawers, hinges, walking sticks, carved tortoiseshell, decorative tassels, furniture, saddles, shadow puppets, old newspapers, Chinese 78s and minority crafts. Foreign visitors are still few enough that starting prices are significantly lower than at other places, and only three to five times what they should be, but this won't last. Minority people from the far south and Tibet used to be numerous here, but are now getting squeezed out by the majority Hàn Chinese. Still very colourful.

Sānlǐtún Market

This is a row of stalls (*open all day*) opposite the expat-haunted bars of Sānlǐtún Jiǔbā Jiē (*see* 'Entertainment, Culture and Nightlife, p.280), catering to their needs for luggage, table linen, and T-shirts, as well as providing a similar if more limited selection of brand name fakes as Xiùshuǐ (*see* below).

Xiùshuǐ Silk Market (Xiùshuǐsīchóu Shìchǎng)

The market is a narrow and shady awning-hung alley just east of the Jiànguó Mén Friendship Store and Jiànguó Hotel, running north from Jiànguó Mén Wài Dàjiē immediately west of the junction with Dōngdàqiáo Lù. However, the market is now misnamed, and is the haunt of Chinese nymphettes shopping for fake Hermès, Lauren, Chanel, Givenchy and DKNY, and foreigners shopping for fake Prada, Burberry and North Face, and real T-shirts. Watch out for pickpockets. There are silk and wool carpets on sale in shops at the rear, but you should have a good look at those in the Friendship Store (take an absolute minimum of 10% off marked prices) and have some knowledge of prices at home before starting to bargain. The river of trade here is soon to be canalized and forced under cover too.

Yǎbǎo Lù

This is the place for fishing tackle and other odd practical items hard to find in Russia or cheaper to buy here, and clothing catering to Russian tastes: dyed leather and gangster's moll furs. The market is no longer in the street of the same name, but in **Yǎbǎo Dàshà**, on the south side of Cháoyáng Mén Wài Dàjiē, just outside the 2nd Ring Road, Ⓜ Cháoyáng Mén. The interest here is more in the atmosphere than the contents of the market, where Russians and Eastern Europeans shop in bulk for items when, despite the state of their economies and the banditry of the customs officials, it still seems worthwhile making frequent return trips on the modern answer to the Silk Route, the Trans-Siberian railway. Chinese stall holders here are likely to speak to you first in Russian, there are signs everywhere in Cyrillic, and Russian food is available. Other goods and services less publicly on offer at the market include pirate CD-Roms (some duff), VCDs (some duff) and black market money-changing (deception guaranteed).

Yùtíng Huā Niǎo Shìchǎng

The Yùtíng Flower and Bird Market, just outside the southeast corner of Tiān Tán on the south side of the canal (*open 7–sunset*), has kittens (including *Bōsī māo*, 'Persian cats', white but not so fluffy, and with each eye a different colour from the other— very popular), Pekinese, rabbits, parakeets, pigeons, finches, turtles, newts, terrapins, tropical fish, flowering cactus, video games, plumbing, tea, tobacco in its natural state, bicycle bells, handicrafts and groceries, and kites in the forms of fish, dragons and birds, or at least painted with their images. The market is shaken by passing trains on their way to Běijīng Zhàn. At its western end the market is big enough that various sections are labelled with the names of various kinds of bird stocked, and in particular two kinds of similar mynah, the *bā gē* (which makes a surprising range of ear-splitting noises) and the *liáo gē* (which can be taught to talk). Insatiable demand for these birds has been denuding the forests of southwestern China and Nepal. Even small birds of prey can be found here as well as peacocks (fed *jiǎozi*), and there are lots of things to feed your bird with, some of which are still crawling around. You may see chicks being carefully hand-fed using chopsticks.

Běijīng ① (010) *Where to Stay*

There are said to be more than 400 hotels scattered around the city, many of these inconveniently far out from the centre, but still charging the same prices as more central accommodation, although in general distance from Tiān'ān Mén does affect rates. Conference delegates are often displeased to find themselves well beyond the third or even fourth ring roads. Most of these hotels are ignored as being irrelevant for visitors.

Běijīng's early morning and mid-afternoon to early evening traffic jams make getting around to see two or three sights in a day very difficult. Being central is therefore very important, and being on a subway line—the best way to accomplish as much of your journey as possible—is very helpful. Even budget travellers should consider spending a little more to be the centre and save perhaps 45mins each way each day in trundling in from the third ring road backpacker ghettos. There's plenty of central accommodation which works out only slightly more expensive than a third ring road dormitory if two or more are sharing.

Those listed below are chosen as follows:

The best **upmarket joint-ventures** and familiar names, which are those which come closest to providing what would be considered four or five star levels of service in the West (for full information on star ratings, joint-ventures, etc. *see* 'Where to Stay', p.59, and *below*)

Some **Chinese hotels** with significant numbers of foreigners with hotel management experience in senior positions

Higher quality Chinese-run **hotels with something extra**, such as particularly large rooms or location in an old mansion or *sìhéyuàn* (courtyard house), that makes them worth considering

Mid-price hotels which are central or close to metro stations for those who'd like a private bath but few other frills

Cheap hotels which are central or close to metro stations—backpackers and budget travellers should consider spending a little more in Běijīng for the convenience of these

Rock-bottom hotels where price is the sole criterion and distance no object.

finding a hotel and paying the right price

Don't be afraid to haggle pleasantly, but hard, even with the five- or four-stars, and even those with fearsome foreign names. For most of the year, most of them are suffering, very few having occupancy rates of more than 75%, and very many considerably less. Despite published rack rates, only one hotel (the St. Regis, formerly Běijīng International

Club) averages significantly above $100 per night, one just scrapes over it (The Grand Hotel), a handful are in the $90 range (mostly those clustered around the China World Trade Centre), but more then 75% have averages well under $60, squeezed by the tour operators who only pass on enough discount to you so that you are impressed by the difference with the rack rate, which almost nobody actually pays. When empty rooms are taken into account the average yield per room in five- and four-star hotels on a typical night, when there's no special conference or convention in town, is around $40. You may even be able to negotiate a four- or five-star hotel for yourself for between $50 and $60, although you may well not get your first choice. Rates quoted below are rack rates—published prices—and should only be regarded as a starting point.

Those seeking relatively luxurious accommodation should always choose joint-venture hotels (those run in partnership with a foreign company) or the usual recognized international chains, however bland and 'un-Chinese' they may be. Those staying in self-designated five-star Chinese hotels in Běijīng can find themselves in a room whose corners seem not to have been vacuumed or swept since the place was built, and with a decaying bathroom. This is almost to be expected in a long-established Chinese three-star, but is unacceptable in notionally $200 per night hotels. At all levels, hotels are *hǔ tóu shí wěi* ('tiger's head, snake's tail')—opening with fanfares and promises of spotless accommodation and impeccable service, and immediately starting to slither downhill as enthusiasm switches to making money, and no further investment is made in staff training, repairs or redecoration. Senior foreign managers in the better hotels helps to slow down this process and keep standards up, although it's a continuous fight.

At the time of writing there were officially 16 five-star hotels in Beijing, but several others part-way through the four-year waiting period for classification, including some of the best. New hotels under Western supervision will open soon, such as in the Oriental Plaza complex at Cháng'ān and Wángfǔjǐng. Five- and four-stars, whether joint-ventures or entirely Chinese, almost all have executive floors, a Presidential suite or two, swimming pools, health centres, hairdressers, massage services, multiple restaurants and cafés, bakery, business centre, souvenir shop, and satellite TV channels usually including CNN, CNBC, HBO and other US-oriented sports and entertainment channels, and, in the case of the St. Regis, Great Wall and Palace, BBC too. Many Chinese hotels of four stars and up have bowling alleys, although there rarely seems to be anyone using them except the staff. These hotels often quote their rates in US dollars, but payment can also be made in ¥RMB.

The old terminal at Běijīng's Capital Airport had desks for the upmarket hotels, but the new one has only agents whose advice is highly unreliable and who should only be consulted in order to get benchmark prices you can beat yourself, and to check availability. Even then you cannot necessarily believe what they tell you, and they offer Chinese lower prices than they will offer you. They do not know about, or deny the existence of hotels which do not use their services, and ignore lower priced hotels, so budget travellers in particular need not waste their time here. The counters marked 'tourist information' are equally merely hotel booking agents with no free information.

Remember, for most of the year there's an oversupply even of the best quality accommodation, so view the rates quoted as a starting point for bargaining.

four- and five-stars: Jiànguó Mén and Wángfǔjǐng

The hotels listed below are mostly on the two major roads running east from Tiān'ān Mén Square, or in and around the Wángfǔjǐng shopping street, and are thus mostly fairly central (some in walking distance of the square in fact), close to Běijīng Zhàn (railway station) and mostly well-served by the recent extension to Běijīng's metro system.

For now the best hotel in Běijīng is the five-star Sheraton-managed **St Regis Beijing** (formerly the Beijing International Club Hotel and still known to taxi drivers as the Běijīng Guójì Jùlèbù Fàndiàn), Jiànguó Mén Wài Dàjiē 21, ✆ 6460 6688, ☏ 6460 3299, <*http://www.luxurycollection.com/*>, and should be the first choice of those for whom price is a secondary consideration to comfort. Rooms from $225–255, suites from $285–3,800 (the Presidential), all plus 15% and $1 tax. The hotel's white marble foyer with full scale palms is easily the most elegant in Běijīng and the attention to detail in both furnishings and service can make you almost forget you are in China; it's often the choice of visiting dignitaries. Excellent restaurants, priced to match, include Danieli's (Italian) and the Celestial Court (Cantonese), and the hotel has the best breakfast buffet in Běijīng. Toll-free booking from the UK ✆ 0800 973 119, USA and Canada ✆ 1-800 325 3589, Hong Kong ✆ 800 96 6812. The St Regis will be challenged by the opening of the luxurious although not so centrally located Radisson Plaza State Guest Hotel, <*http://www.radisson.com/*>, and by the high-tech Harbour Plaza Hotel in Wángfǔjǐng's Oriental Plaza.

The Palace Hotel (Wángfu Fàndiàn), Jīnyú Hútòng 8, between Wángfǔjǐng and Dōng Dān, ✆ 6512 6192, ☏ 6512 7118, <*tph@peninsula.com*>, <*http://www.peninsula.com/hotels/beijing/beijing.html*>, is partly owned and entirely managed by The Peninsula Group, and basks in the reflected glory of the Peninsula Hong Kong. It lacks quite that level of luxury or the spaciousness, but is certainly very well-appointed. Rack rates begin at $300 for a double, plus 15% and $1 city tax, but you'll be able to improve on that. Two levels of basement shopping contain the best names in Běijīng, and amongst several restaurants are extremely good Italian and Cantonese. One of the more truly five-star hotels.

The **Jiànguó Fàndiàn** (Jiànguó Hotel), Jiànguó Mén Wài Dàjiē 5, well-positioned between the second and third ring roads and right next to Ⓜ Yǒng'ān Lǐ, ✆ 6500 2233, ☏ 6500 2871, <*res@hoteljianguo.com*>, <*http://www.hoteljianguo.com/*>, was the first joint-venture hotel in Běijīng but unlike most long-standing hotels has kept up with modernization and refurbishment, and remains very popular with expats, visiting businessmen and diplomats. Many of the rooms look into enclosed gardens and goldfish-stocked ponds and are pleasantly calming after a day rushing around the city. The large lobby is always lively, with evening string quartets and a Sunday morning string orchestra. A large selection of restaurants includes Justine's with possibly Běijīng's best French food. Four stars, but better than many of the supposed five-star hotels. Rack rates begin at $190, plus 15% and ¥6 per person, but published off-season special rates are often around $100 including breakfast.

The four-star **Peace Hotel** (Hépíng Fàndiàn) is almost opposite the glittering and considerably more upmarket Palace Hotel, at Jīnyú Hútòng 3, between Wángfǔjǐng and Dōng Dàn, ✆ 6512 7150 (reservations), ☏ 6512 6863. The hotel has some Hong

Kong management and the lobby is impressive. The hotel's east wing is more expensive than the west one. Doubles in the east are from $150, and in the west from $110, prices which are far too high for the standard of accommodation, but reductions of around 40% to ¥880 and ¥500 are often available, all plus 15% and ¥6 per person.

The 487-room **Kerry Centre Hotel** (Jiālǐ Zhōngxīn Fàndiàn), Guānghuá Lù 1, ✆ 6561 8833, ✆ 6561 2626, <*hbkc@shangri-la.com*>, <*http://www.shangri-la.com/*>, is one of the newest hotels, having only opened in late 1999, under Shangri-La management, between the second and third ring road and just north of Jiànguó Mén. The hotel is part of an apartment, office and shopping complex, and the high-ceilinged rooms have a fresh, modern design unique in Běijīng. The bathrooms have separate glass-walled shower cubicles. Teething troubles at the time of opening should by now have been cured, but rates should be competitive for a while yet, although first asking prices are from $210.

Shangri-La, in addition to having their own flagship property in the northwest, also manages the popular upmarket **Trader's Hotel**, ✆ 6505 2277, from $140, and **China World Hotel**, ✆ 6505 2266, from $185, both at the China World Trade Centre nearby. Details at the Shangri-La website, given above.

Holiday Inn Crowne Plaza (Guójì Yìyuàn Huángguān Fàndiàn), Wángfǔjǐng Dàjiē 48, ✆ 6513 3388, ✆ toll-free in China 010 800 650 8288, <*hicpb@public3.bta.net.cn*>, <*http://www.crowneplaza.com/hotels/pegwf*>. Good location, and the model used for other Chinese-run hotels in the street, which ask the same prices without providing the same service. Double rooms $220–280, suites $300–800, all plus 15% and ¥6. The hotel has leanings towards the arty, with a gallery and a small number of larger 'Art Studio' rooms with large windows into the central atrium ($250).

There are two other Holiday Inns, the vast **Holiday Inn Lido** (Lìdū Jiàrì Fàndiàn), ✆ 6437 6688, ✆ 6437 6237, halfway out to the airport, with its own constellation of neighbouring expat-oriented services, and **Holiday Inn Downtown**, at Ⓜ Fuchengmen, northwest exit.

The **Chángfùgōng Fàndiàn** (Hotel New Otani), Jiànguó Mén Wài Dàjiē 26, Ⓜ Jiànguó Mén, ✆ 6512 5555, ✆ 6513 9810, USA and Canada toll-free ✆ (800) 421 8795, UK ✆ 0171 584 6666, has a beautiful internal garden and is popular with Japanese tour groups and Japanese major travel agents. Lots of bowing in the foyer (always a good sign) indicates the Japanese success with bringing staff round to their way of thinking. Well-appointed and with every possible facility, the hotel is east of the observatory on the south side of the road. Single rooms are from ¥1530 ($190), doubles from ¥1700 ($212), plus ¥6 tax and 15% service.

The **Wángfǔjǐng Grand Hotel** (Wángfǔjǐng Dàfàndiàn), Wángfǔjǐng Dàjiē 57, ✆ 6522 1188, ✆ 6522 3816, is a three-year-old Chinese-run hotel, perhaps due four stars, originally a Singapore joint-venture, now losing its sheen, but still glossier than most Chinese-run hotels. Doubles are a highly negotiable $180–200, and suites $300–1800, all plus 15% (dropped upon request) and ¥6 per person tax.

The older 400-room **Prime Hotel** (Huáqiáo Dàshà), Wángfǔjǐng Dàjiē 2, ✆ 6513 6666, ✆ 6513 4248, toll-free in China ✆ 800 810 3456, USA and Canada toll-free

☎ 1-800 223 5652, UK ☎ (800) 7779 6753, <*rsvn@phb.com.cn*>, <*http://www. primehotel.com/*>, is nevertheless better value than the neighbouring Wángfŭjĭng Grand. Originally a Swedish joint-venture, it's a very solid building and notable for having the largest standard twins and doubles in Bĕijĭng (42 sqm)—choose one facing outwards. It will deserve its five stars when it's had a redecoration, but for now remains good value for money since its rates, particularly off-season, can be bargained down to well below five-star norms. Doubles/twins from $180, suites from $300, plus 15% and $1 tax.

One Chinese-run hotel also worth considering if only for its location is the **Bĕijĭng Guójì Fàndiàn** (Bĕijĭng International Hotel), Jiànguŏ Mén Nèi Dàjiē 9, ☎ 6512 6688, ✉ 6512 9972, a 29-storey tower topped by a revolving restaurant just north of Bĕijĭng Station. Standard single rooms are $100, and doubles $165, with suites from $260 to $1,400, plus tax of ¥6 per person per night. Discounts of 15% are not hard to obtain. Multiple restaurants include one for vegetarians.

The Japanese often seem to lead in getting the best out of their local staff. The **Jĭnglún Fàndiàn** (Hotel Bĕijĭng-Toronto), Jiànguŏ Mén Wài Dàjiē 3, ☎ 6500 2266, ✉ 6500 2022, <*jinglun@public3.bta.net.cn*>, is a Japanese (Nikko) joint-venture hotel, just east of the better known Jiànguó Hotel, with good service and full facilities, including excellent Japanese and Continental restaurants. Doubles are from ¥1,530 ($190, but often available at ¥748), and suites from ¥1,955 ($245), all plus 15% service charge. Breakfast is included. Toll-free in North America ☎ 1-800 645 5687, UK ☎ 0800 282502.

Once the best address before the upstart joint-venture hotels arrived, but still popular and the most centrally located of the large relatively upmarket hotels, the nominally five-star **Bĕijĭng Fàndiàn** (Bĕijĭng Hotel), 33 Dōng Cháng'ān Jiē, ☎ 6513 7766, ✉ 6513 7703, is a Soviet-influenced central mansion connected to other more (but not much more) modern buildings of different dates. It stands on the site of the second Hôtel de Pékin, built after the Boxer Rebellion had severely damaged the first, run by an enterprising Swiss who with his American wife took an active part in the fighting. When the first block of the modern building went up in 1974, it was discovered that a sniper would be able to fire from the top storey across the Forbidden City into the Zhōngnán Hăi compound of the party leaders. An ugly office block was built overlooking the city from the compound so as to block the view of would-be assassins. A Friendship Store-style operation stretches the entire width of the ground floor of the central building. Twins are from $160, doubles from $170 and suites from $300, all plus 15% service charge. If central location is important this hotel is hard to beat, but in terms of value for money you're much better off in one of the international chains or other joint-venture hotels. A thorough refurbishment of the interior still underway at the time of writing may have made this better value for money, although expect service to remain indifferent at best.

However, the western-most block has been hived off as a separate five-star venture good enough to be worth taking more seriously, the **Grand Hotel Bĕijĭng**, Dōng Cháng'ān Dàjiē 35, ☎ 6513 7788, ✉ 6513 0049, <*sales@mail.grandhotelbeijing. com.cn*>, <*http://www.grandhotelbeijing.com.cn/*>. This 10-storey, 218-room hotel would like to be the Mandarin Oriental in Hong Kong in terms of opulence, but would need some refurbishment for that. For those who want to be sure they're in China and not somewhere anonymously international, the rooms are furnished with adapted traditional Chinese furniture. It's unwilling to reduce its rates, so you'd be much better off staying at the St Regis or Palace for these prices. Standard rooms are $275, but a view towards the Forbidden City will cost at least $300, plus 15% service. Suites are $400 and up, the three largest having no fixed price, but the Presidential was said to have commanded $3,000 per night around the 1 October 1999 celebrations, due to its views of Tiān'ān Mén Square. The rooftop café-bar is open to non-residents and makes a pleasant spot for a cold drink at ten times the price at street level.

four- and five-stars: northeast third ring road

There's a cluster of five-star hotels at this northeast corner of Běijīng near where the airport expressway leaves the third ring road, and therefore fairly easy to get to, and with fairly quick journeys around the rim of Beijing possible outside of the late afternoon and early evening rushes. The area has sprouted numerous restaurants and shops catering to expats and the tastes of Western visitors in general, and is not too far from either the Sānlǐtún bar area or the nascent Cháoyáng Mén Park bar area. Two of the best hotels are:

The **Great Wall Sheraton** (Chángchéng Fàndiàn), Dōng Sān Huán Běi Lù 10, ✆ 6590 5566, ✉ 6590 5398, <*http://www.sheraton.com/*>, is a three-winged 1,007-room glass palace more cosy inside than it looks, with a Chinese-style garden at its base, used for 'Dragon Nights' outdoor food and entertainment in the summer. One of the longer-established and more smoothly running joint-venture hotels, its rooftop Sìchuān restaurant and ground-floor French bistrôt are both highly popular, and the breakfast buffet is excellent. Many of the well-appointed rooms have recently received top-notch refurbishment. Toll-free booking from the UK ✆ 0800 973 119, USA and Canada ✆ 1-800 325 3589, Hong Kong ✆ 800 96 6812.

The **Kempinski Hotel Běijīng Lufthansa Center** (Běijīng Yànshā Zhōngxīn Kǎibīn Sījī Fàndiàn), Liàngmǎ Qiáo Lù 50, ✆ 6465 3388, ✉ 6465 3366, <*khbsales@public.east.cn.net*>, is a Korean-German-Chinese joint-venture, part of a shopping mall and apartment complex, and largely oriented towards upmarket business dealings. Doubles are from $270, and suites from $400 to $2,400, all plus 15%. Bookings can be made to toll-free numbers in North America, ✆ 1-800 426 3135, and the UK ✆ 0800 868588.

four- and five-stars: other locations

Another older joint-venture hotel well worth considering despite its apparently isolated location is the **Beijing Shangri-La** (Xiānggélǐlā Fàndiàn), Zǐzhùyuàn Lù 29, on the third ring road just west of Purple Bamboo Park, ✆ 6841 2211, ✉ 6841 8002/3, <*slb@shangri-la.com*>, <*http://www.shangri-la.com/*>. The quiet, well-appointed hotel stands in its own Chinese-style garden, close to parks and the boat routes to the Summer Palace, and gives reasonably easy access around Běijīng via the third ring, and to the other parks and temples to the west and northwest. Double/twins from $120, executive floor from $144, plus 15%.

The **Zǐjīn Bīnguǎn**, Chóngwén Mén Xī Dàjiē 9, ✆ 6513 6016, 📠 6524 9215, is in the grounds of the former Belgian legation between busy Chóngwén Mén and quiet Dōng Jiǎo Mín Xiàng close to Tiān'ān Mén Square, and after 1949 the buildings here were reserved for state guests. But now building no.7, newly-built to match the style of the adjacent 1901 Belgian building, has an impressively retrofitted interior, but bizarrely with a bowling alley in the basement. Surprisingly comfortable rooms have excellent bathrooms and proper shower cubicles. It's a reddish building with green steep roofs and if you come from Chóngwén Mén it's in the far right-hand corner. Or come in from Dōng Jiāo Mín Xiàng and turn left past the original very Belgian building, and you'll see it. Have a look inside the old building where rooms are also sometimes available and which retains its original panelling, frosted glass, and French windows. ¥600 ($75) for a standard room, suites ¥1,000–2,500. Bargaining for up to 20% off is possible.

Swissôtel Běijīng (Gǎng Ào Zhōngxīn Ruìshì Jiǔdiàn), conveniently on the east second ring road right outside the southeast exit of Ⓜ Dōng Sìshí Tiáo, ✆ 6501 2288, 📠 6501 2501, *<swisshotel@chinamail.com>*, *<http://www.swissotel.com/>*, is an unremarkable five-star hotel but with good-sized rooms from $220, sometimes available for $145, plus 15% and ¥6 per person.

Mínzú Hotel (Mínzú Fàndiàn), Fùxīng Mén Nèi Dàjiē 51, 10mins west of Ⓜ Xī Dān, ✆ 6601 1579, 📠 6601 4849. A reasonable Chinese four-star whose facilities include a Turkish restaurant, mostly doing tour group business, and reluctant to lower its rack rates to individuals, even when half-empty. Standard rooms from $85, suites from $144, all plus 10% and ¥12 per room.

City Hotel (Chéngshì Bīnguǎn), Gōngtǐ Dōng Lù 4 on the east side of the Workers' Stadium, ✆ 6500 7799, 📠 6500 7668, and close to the Sānlǐtún bar area, is a mixture of apartments and rooms, starting with singles at ¥680 ($85), twins at ¥860 ($108), and suites from ¥1,280 ($160), all plus 15%. Unexceptional, and for these prices you can be much better located.

The **Qián Mén Hotel** (Qián Mén Fàndiàn), Yǒng'ān Lù 175, ✆ 6301 6688, 📠 6301 3883, is best known to visitors as the most popular venue for Běijīng opera performances (although there are better choices), *see* p.274.

three-stars and moderately priced hotels

The **Paragon Hotel** (Bǎochén Fàndiàn), Jiànguó Mèn Wài Dàjiē 18A (but directly opposite Běijīng Station), ✆ 6526 6688, 📠 6527 4060, *<baochen@public.phent. cn.net>*, is a 10-storey, 277-room three-star hotel as good if not better than most older four-stars, opened in 1998. Twins and singles are from $80, and suites from $110. Rooms look in all directions as well as inwards to an atrium, but outward-facing north rooms are the quietest. A 20% discount can be obtained, with a little effort, by those planning to stay a few days, and 40% by long-staying business customers. Two floors are sublet to a Mongolian couple who specialize in helping expats and Mongols from Ulaan Baatar who shop for business essentials as yet unobtainable there, and may charge less than the main hotel. Ask for them at reception. The staff wear straw hats for no obvious reason.

Harmony Hotel (Huáměilún Jiǔdiàn), well-located close to Běijīng Zhàn at Sūzhōu Hútòng 59, just off Jiànguó Mén Nèi opposite the China Women's Activity Centre, ✆ 6528 5566, 📠 6559 8993, is a new three-star, seven-storey, 122-room hotel, with comfortable clean rooms. ¥488 ($61) for a single or twin with bath, ¥588 ($73.50) for a big double, all plus 10%. At least 10% discount available. A very good choice at this price range.

The **Zhúyuán Bīnguǎn** (Bamboo Garden Hotel), Xiǎoshí Qiáo Hútòng 24, off Jiùgǔlóu Lù, ✆ 6403 2229, 📠 6401 2633, has considerably more style than most hotels in China. A mixture of old and discreetly modern buildings set around a pretty garden that once belonged to a Qīng eunuch and subsequently to a Qīng Minister of Posts, the hotel has several rooms furnished in an interpretation of Míng style. That it was later the home of the architect of China's spy system, Kāng Yǒuwéi, a posthumously disgraced supporter of Máo, is oddly not mentioned in the hotel's publicity material. Despite the emphasis on tradition, there are modern facilities such as IDD telephone and satellite TV. Single rooms are ¥300 ($37.50), doubles are from ¥380 ($47.50) to ¥580 ($72.50) depending upon garden view and size, and there are also suites, all plus ¥6 per person city tax.

Newly opened on Wángfǔjǐng, the **Fù Háo Bīnguǎn**, Wángfǔjǐng Dàjiē 45, ✆ 6523 1188, 📠 6513 1188, is (for now) a spotless three-star hotel with highly negotiable prices. A slight drawback is the nightclub/karaoke operation whose brocaded hostesses take over the bell captain's desk at night time, but having a room on a higher floor (there are only six) and away from the elevator shaft should make this no problem. ¥480 ($60) plus ¥12 per room for a comfy twin is unreasonable, but a 35% discount is easily negotiated, and makes this good value for the location.

Cuìmíng Zhuāng Bīnguǎn (Cuìmíng Manor), Nán Hé Yán Dàjiē 1, ✆ 6559 7453, 📠 6513 6622. This is an important historic site to aficionados of communist orthodoxy. First built in the 1930s, in 1946–7 it became the office of the Communist Party of China delegation of the Executive Department of the Běipíng Military Mediation Section which was responsible for maintaining the ceasefire between the Communists and the Nationalists (KMT or Guómín Dǎng) during the combined effort to repel the Japanese. Restored to its old look (but with rather a better foyer) in 1998 and opened as a good, clean mid-price hotel, it has an excellent location just east of the Forbidden City's east gate and is close to Wángfǔjǐng. The 'single' rooms here have a double bed and a large sitting room, for ¥328 ($41) and a large variety of other rooms, with a negotiable 20% off.

Overseas Chinese Hotel (Huáqiáo Fàndiàn—not be confused with the Huáqiáo Dàshà, the Prime Hotel), Běi Xīn Qiáo Sān Tiáo 5, ✆ 6401 6688, 📠 6401 2386. A 10-minute walk southeast of Ⓜ Yōnghé Gōng, this is a standard three-star in a quiet location. Singles ¥332 ($41.50), doubles from ¥415 ($52), and suites from ¥715 ($89), all plus 10% service and ¥6 per person. These slightly high prices can easily be negotiated down by 30% to something more reasonable.

Dōngfāng Fàndiàn is situated at Wànmíng Lù 11, a south turning off Zhūshìkǒu Xī Dàjiē west of Qián Mén Dàjiē, ✆ 6301 4466, 📠 6304 4801. Within an easy walk of the Tiāntán (Temple of Heaven) north entrance, and a short ride south of Tiān'ān Mén

Square, this relatively plush tower has views from the upper floors towards the park. Standard doubles with in-room IDD are ¥630 ($76), and good-size suites ¥750 ($92) rising to ¥2688 ($324) for those who want space to do business. There's also ¥6 per person per day city tax.

The **Fēngzé Yuán Fàndiàn**, Zhūshìkǒu Xī Dàjiē 83, just west of Qián Mén Dàjiē, ☎ 6318 6688, 🖷 6308 4271, is a piece of pink post-modernism without Chinese touches except in the marble-lined foyer water garden, and reachable by any south-bound bus down Qián Mén Dàjiē. The hotel is only a short walk from Tiāntán Gōngyuán, and has a labyrinth of *hútòng* leading to the Dàzhàlán area at its rear. Standard twins are ¥480 ($60), singles ¥380 ($47.50), all plus ¥6 per person and 10% service. Only worth considering if they'll reduce these rates.

The main benefit of staying at the slightly glum three-star **Yuèxiù Dàjiǔdiàn**, Xuānwǔ Mén Dōng Dàjiē 24, ☎ 6301 4499, 🖷 6301 4609, is that it's right at ⓜ Xuānwǔ Mén. Its twins start from ¥380 ($47.50), and suites from ¥600 ($75), all plus 10% and ¥12 per room.

The **Fēiyīng Bīnguǎn**, Hòu Hé Yán 6, is just east of ⓜ Chángchūn Jiē and just south of Xuānwǔ Mén Xī Dàjiē, ☎ 6317 1116, 🖷 6302 1278. The hotel will immediately knock ¥100 off its rack rates of ¥380 ($47.50) for twins, ¥480 ($60) for triples, and ¥580 ($72.50) for suites, all-inclusive. In need of a redecoration, but then so are almost all the others at this price. There's a lively street market adjacent.

The **Yuǎn Dōng Fàndiàn** (Far East Hotel), Tiěshù Xiéjiē 90, ☎ 6301 8811, 🖷 6301 8233, is amongst the small *hútòng* west of Qián Mén and east of Hépíng Mén, within 10–15mins' walk of ⓜ Hépíng Mén and ⓜ Qián Mén, Tiān'ān Mén Square and Tiāntán, enabling several of Běijīng's major sights to be seen on foot, and offering easy access to many others via the metro. The reception staff leave something to be desired, but the floor staff are friendly and work hard to keep the rooms clean, although most are in need of redecoration. ¥298 ($37) for a standard twin or double, ¥398 ($50) for a superior one, all plus ¥12 city tax, and including Chinese breakfast. Going south from ⓜ Hépíngmen about 10mins on foot you will see a sign to the left, or continuing west from Dàzhàlán Jiē keep on the left when the road forks.

The **Gélányún Tiān Dàjiǔdiàn** (Grand Skylight Hotel), Běi Xīnhuá Jiē 45, ☎ 6607 1166, 🖷 6605 3705, just north of ⓜ Hépíng Mén and diagonally opposite the Hépíng Mén Quánjùdé Kǎoyādiàn roast duck restaurant, walkable from Tiān'ān Mén Square. This is a relatively new 200-room hotel with singles ¥380 ($47.50), twins/doubles from ¥400 ($50) to ¥480 ($60), and suites from ¥700 ($87) plus 10% and ¥6 tax, but a discount of 30% is easily obtainable. There's Internet access here for ¥15 per hour.

Close by on the south side of Xuānwǔ Mén Dōng Dàjiē, the slightly overpriced **Wénxuān Bīnguǎn**, Nán Xīnhuá Jiē 1, opposite the south entrance to ⓜ Hépíng Mén, ☎ 6301 9832, 🖷 6318 8182, is much the same but more expensive: ¥458 ($57) to ¥498 ($62) for doubles, ¥888 ($111) to ¥1380 ($173) for suites, all plus 15%.

Běijīng Níngbō Bīnguǎn, Xīzhōng Hútòng 25, ☎ 6605 2226, 🖷 6607 7320; walk north from ⓜ Hépíng Mén Hépíng and turn left. Small (45 rooms), clean and bright with good bathrooms, in a quiet *hútòng* close to both Tiān'ān Mén and a metro station, and with very few foreign visitors. Two stars, but as good as an older three-star. Single rooms ¥280 ($35), twins ¥360 ($45) all with bath, and all plus 10% service and ¥6 per person tax. 10% discount can be negotiated with a little persis-tance, effectively the removal of the service charge, and a free breakfast. There's a Zhéjiāng restaurant in the basement, clean and reasonably priced.

Hǎoyuán Bīnguǎn (Hǎoyuán Guesthouse), Shǐ Jiā Hútòng 53, ☎ 6512 5557, ∰ 6525 3179. A minute's walk west of Dōng Sì Nán Dàjiē, its entrance marked by two red lanterns at a metal gate that you'll need to push open, this hotel is a converted *sìhéyuàn* or traditional courtyard house with only eight rooms, most of the others having been block booked by the British embassy and others. The rooms have new plumbing and good showers with period furniture. ¥300 ($37.50) single, ¥380 ($47.50) double, all-inclusive.

Huáfēng Bīnguǎn, Qián Mén Dōng Dàjiē 5, ☎ 6524 7311 ext. 8402. Gloomy and overpriced but well-positioned within walking distance of ⓜ Qián Mén on the corner of Zhèngyì Lù. Stands on the site of the former Legation Quarter's Grand Hôtel des Wagons-Lits within walking distance of both Běijīng Station and Tiān'ān Mén. Standard twins are from ¥418 ($52), and triples ¥748 ($93.50).

The **Qomolangma Hotel** (Zhūmùlǎngmǎ Bīnguǎn) is next to the representative office of Tibet (in the grounds of a largely vanished Daoist temple, the Guānyuè Miào) at Gǔlóu Xī Dàjiē 149, ☎ 6404 3672, ∰ 6401 1330. Uninteresting but toler-able doubles for ¥300 ($37.50). There's said to be some rooms in an ancient building here, too, but they could not be seen at the time of writing. There's a Tibetan restau-rant inside the hotel.

The **Yǒuhǎo Bīnguǎn**, Hòu Yuán'ēn Sì Hútòng 7, ☎ 6403 1114, ∰ 6401 4603, is an odd collection of buildings belonging to the Chinese People's Association for Friendship with Foreign Countries. The main administration building ahead as you enter was once occupied by Chiang Kai-shek (Jiǎng Jièshí), and there's a brick building to the right which accurately preserves the era of armchairs, antimacassars and worn red carpets, once the standard decorations for all places where senior cadres gathered. The point of interest is a courtyard of ancient buildings to the left, refurbished as guest rooms, ¥296 ($37) single, ¥392 ($49) twin, and ¥800 ($100) for a two-room suite, all-inclusive, and a 10% discount with a little haggling, although these rooms are often booked up.

Chóngwén Mén Hotel (Chóngwén Fàndiàn), Chóngwén Mén Xī Dàjiē 2, ⓜ Chóngwén Mén, ☎ 6512 2211, ∰ 6521 2122. Dull, but well-located right on the metro circle line and close to Běijīng Station. Standard twin ¥480 ($60); suites ¥550 ($69) and ¥650 ($81), all plus 10%. Overpriced and not necessarily willing to bargain.

Opposite the Chóngwén Mén is the vast **Hademen Hotel** (Hǎdé Mén Fàndiàn), Chóngwén Mén Wài Dàjiē 2, ☎ 6711 2244, ∰ 6711 6865, named for the gate which once stood here, well known to occupants of the Legation Quarter (the name survives in the Wade-Giles spelling *Hatamen* as a popular brand of cigarettes). Uninteresting three-star with a recent refit, and tour groups are quite often put here. Excellently located at ⓜ Chóngwén Mén. Singles ¥360 ($45), twins ¥450 ($56) and up, suites from ¥580 ($72.50). 20% discount on request.

Grand View Garden Hotel (Běijīng Dà Guān Yuán Jiǔdiàn), Nán Cài Yuán Jiē 88, ℡ 6353 8899, ℻ 6353 9189, <htl-bc@gvghotel.com>, <http://www.gvghotel.com/>. Not ideally located, but quiet, with some rooms overlooking the Grand View Garden itself (see p.170) and a twice daily shuttle bus service to the Jiànguó Mén Friendship Store and Wángfǔjǐng. A four-storey building with white tiled exterior topped with blue tiled traditional roofs, under four-star Chinese management. Opened 1992 but still in fairly good condition. Overpriced double rooms ¥1,090–1,260 or $130–150, but discounts of up to 60% available, and often offers rooms at ¥430 ($54). All prices include service.

cheap and central

Each listing here has at least some beds for ¥100 ($12.50) or less if a twin is shared, and are either very central and convenient for transport, or quite central and with some other charm over the southern dormitory and other budget accommodation are listed under *rock bottom*, below (where there are beds for ¥50 or less).

Běijīng Yùdū Bīnguǎn, Dōng Ān Mén Dàjiē 37, ℡ 6527 5533, ℻ 6513 7544. Only recently opened and so far in good condition, this 50-room hotel is just off Wángfǔjǐng to the west and a short walk from the Forbidden City. Singles ¥180 ($22.50), but doubles for only ¥220 ($27.50), ¥280 ($35), and ¥320 ($40), triples ¥360 ($45) with bath. In demand in high season, but bargain for a 20% discount at other times.

Běijīng Běifāng Fàndiàn (North Hotel), Dōng Dān Běi Dàjiē 45, ℡ 6525 4406, ℻ 6525 2831, 10mins walk north of Ⓜ Dōng Sì. Worn, dark and basic, but with common bath twins at ¥150 ($19), twins with bath at ¥260 ($32.50) and ¥400 ($50), the cheaper rooms certainly good value for the location. Cheap restaurant.

The **Shèkē Bīnguǎn** (Academy of Social Sciences Guesthouse), Dōng Jiāo Mín Xiàng 4 , ℡ 6522 1155 ext. 3155, ℻ 6512 9521, is reached from a passage which runs from Dōng Jiāo Mín Xiàng to Qián Mén Dōng Dàjiē just west of the northwest exit of Ⓜ Chóngwén Mén. Spotless when first opened, it's taken a bit of a beating, but is still far cleaner and more comfortable than most others in this price range. There are no room rates posted, and they have an annoying habit of asking foreigners to pay ¥50 more per room than Chinese, although this is usually quickly withdrawn when challenged. The rooms mostly have showers rather than baths, and are ¥230 ($29) for a small single, ¥270 ($34) for a double, and ¥290 ($36) for a twin, including free Chinese breakfast.

Fāng Yuán Bīnguǎn, Dēngshìkǒu Xī Jiē 36, ℡ 6525 7047. Grubby two-star long overdue for a refurbishment and with an unwillingness to discount, but a central location and reasonably friendly staff. Double upstairs ¥267 ($34), downstairs ¥217 ($27), mini-double ¥177 ($22), singles for ¥126 ($16, rarely free because there are only two) plus ¥6 per bed city tax. The downstairs rooms have little natural light. Reasonably priced restaurant upstairs. Rates include simple Chinese and an attempt at Western breakfast (fried eggs and bread) served until 8.30am. If the hotel is full (say at National Day), you may be sent around the corner to the nearby **Běijīng Gōngshāng Bīnguǎn** at Běihéyán Dàjiē 95, ℡ 6524 8825, ℻ 6527 7528, with common bath triples for ¥300 ($37.50), not really worth considering unless you can haggle the price down.

Lǔsōng Yuán Bīnguǎn, Bǎnchǎng Hútòng 22, ✆ 6404 0436, 📠 6403 0418, <lsyhotel@263.net>, offers another opportunity to stay in modernized courtyard buildings down a quiet *hútòng*, this time four interconnected ones, some having their own doors into interior semi-private green spaces. While the common areas need a refit and some of the bathrooms could be better, a few rooms have been given a very thorough upgrade and fitted with double beds. A common bath single is ¥150 ($19), and there are beds for ¥100 ($12.50) in common bath triples. Standard singles are from ¥258 ($32), twins/doubles from ¥410 ($51) to ¥600 ($75), and suites ¥700 ($87.50). A 10% discount is available if you plan to stay a few nights. Proceeding north from Wángfǔjǐng past the National Art Gallery, the hotel is well hidden down the second *hútòng* on the left after crossing the new, broad Píng'ān Dà Dào. Walk south from ⓜ Āndìng Mén or take any southbound bus; or take any version of bus 104 from Běijīng Zhàn (west side) to stop Kuān Jiē.

The **Huákǎi Bīnguǎn**, Yǔ'ér Hútòng 15 (one block west of the Lǔsōng Yuán above), ✆ 6407 0268 ext. 100, is an odd 24-room, five-storey block probably owned by the neighbouring factory, of which half the rooms have no windows but are larger than usual for a hotel of this quality, and the others have views across the uneven roofs of the *hútòng* towards the White Dagoba Temple. The staff seem fresh from the country-side, and obscurity is the hotel's main attraction, with doubles for ¥230 ($29), plus (bizarrely when the tax is ¥6) ¥2 per person. But the real price is ¥180 ($22.50), bargainable down to ¥150 ($19), at which rate it's good value, well inside the third ring amongst the labyrinth of *hútòng* southeast of the Drum and Bell Towers.

Bāfāng Lái Kè Bīnguǎn (which means 'guests come from the eight points of the compass hotel'), just south of ⓜ Chángchūn Jiē, ✆ 6316 4477, a blue glass frontage set back on the east side of Chángchūn Jiē. Small and simple, with twins at ¥190 ($24) and ¥280 ($35), and triples also at ¥280, all-inclusive. Hot water 7–8 and 8–11.

Qiánxīn Bīnguǎn, Lángfáng Tóu Tiáo 45, ✆ 6303 2331. A near-perfect location in a *hútòng* parallel with Dàzhàlán Jiē just south of Qián Mén and new enough (1999) still to be in good condition. Given the location, particularly good value for money—as little as ¥30 per bed to stay within 10mins of Tiān'ān Mén Square. Singles ¥140 ($17.50), twins ¥160 ($20) all with bath, and common bath triples ¥90 ($11), quads ¥120 ($15).

Huálóng Fàndiàn, Dōng Dān Běi Dàjiē 30, ✆ 6524 0131 ext. 2005, 📠 6513 8649, almost opposite the east side of the five-star Palace Hotel on the corner of Hóngxīng Hútòng. Basic but cleaner than many of this type, with an excellent location. A standard twin with bath is ¥288 ($36) including all taxes, service and a Chinese breakfast. There are triples for ¥300 ($37.50), and suites for ¥400 ($50). These prices are amenable to a little gentle haggling.

rock bottom, distance no object

The common bath triples for ¥150 ($20) plus ¥18 at the **Yuǎn Dōng Fàndiàn** (*see* above) are worth considering for the *hútòng* atmosphere if you are three, although the common bath is decrepit, and there's a disco and karaoke bar on the same floor. For ¥10 per person more, you can do much better elsewhere.

The **Qiánxīn Bīnguǎn**, also above, has common bath triples and quads for only ¥30 per bed, and could scarcely be more central, so try this too before heading south. You are more likely to succeed if in a group of three or four, or you may be asked to pay for all the beds, since Chinese and foreigners are usually not allowed to share rooms and your presence in one bed may make the others unsaleable.

Central Academy of Fine Arts (Zhōngyāng Měishù Xuéyuàn), ☎ 6528 2122. Walk north up Wángfǔjǐng and turn right into Shuài Fǔ Yuán Hútòng past the Wángfǔjǐng Quánjùdé Roast Duck and carry on to the junction (the Arts Academy is on your left). Turn left and go in the first entrance to your left and turn left to walk to the back of the Arts Academy block. The elevators are slightly to your left at the rear of the building. Go to the eighth floor to find reception, from where the *fúwùyuán* will walk you down to the 7th (don't ask why) and past the rooms of full-time arts students, their desks with forests of brushes in pots, to show you a neat, clean, bright, simple double for ¥120 ($15). The common showers are adequate and there's hot water from 6am to midnight. A reasonable bargain, given the location, if you are two, and possibly with a chance to meet some students without a long trek to the university district.

The **Jīnghuá Fàndiàn** (Jīnghuá Youth Hostel in English on top of bulding) in Yǒngdìng Mén Wài on the south side of the third ring road (Nán Sān Huán Xīlù), ☎ 6722 2211, 🖷 6721 1455, is the cornerstone of a rapidly growing empire of three hotels, the others being, in descending order of merit, the Lìhuá and Hǎixīng *below*.

The management here does seem to have been investing some of its gains back into the building, having refitted quite a number of the rooms and remodelled the foyer to look more like a three-star hotel. There are also signs that they are hedging their bets with the Chinese market, having built a Chinese-style karaoke-nightclub on the side.

Cheapness is the most attractive aspect of the Jīnghuá, beds being crammed into the dorms, many of which are in the basement. Inspect before choosing between the ¥25 ($3), ¥30 ($3.75) (larger dorms and in basement) or ¥35 or ¥50 (quads, triples) all with common showers. Double rooms with tiled floors and bath range from ¥140 ($17.50) to ¥192 ($24). Profits are increased by overcharging for just about everything else, including Great Wall, opera and acrobat tours: ¥80 ($10) for a trip to Sīmǎtāi, for instance (and if the trip is cancelled you only get half your money back), and an outrageous ¥50 commission for train or plane tickets. Internet access is an expensive ¥30 per hour. There's cheap food both in a restaurant outside the hotel and in neighbouring streets. The hotel is a 10-minute walk west of the terminus of bus 2, which runs down Wángfǔjǐng Dàjiē then down Qián Mén Dàjiē; or from Ⓜ Hépíng Mén take the 14 south down Nán Xīnhuá Jiē to the stop called Yáng Qiáo, and walk five minutes east.

Lìhuá Fàndiàn, Mǎ Jiā Bǎo Dōng Lù, Yǒngdìng Mén Wài, ☎ 6721 1144, 🖷 6721 1367. Take bus 14 from near Ⓜ Hépíng Mén to just south of Yáng Qiáo, and walk a little further south. Similar to the Jīnghuá Fàndiàn but less popular, and not in as good condition. ¥30 ($3.75) or ¥56 ($7) for a bed in a common bath quad or triple, but ¥132 ($16.50) for a common bath twin or ¥198 ($25) for a twin with bath, all-inclusive, is not particularly good value. Internet access for ¥30 an hour.

Hǎixīng Dàjiǔdiàn (Sea Star Hotel), Nán Yuàn Lù, ☎ 6721 8855, 🖷 6723 8675, much closer to the bus 2 terminus than the Jīnghuá, opposite the west side of the

Mùxī Yuán long-distance bus station. It's a grimy cream-tiled building with hints of chalet, set back from the road, and also with basement dorms from ¥26 per bed ($3.25, eight beds) to ¥35 ($4.50, four beds), and twins with bath from ¥262 ($33), bargainable to ¥170 ($21).

The **Jǐngtài Bīnguǎn**, Ānlèlín Lù, ✆ 6722 4675, is also to the south of the centre, but not so far. Basic doubles with common bath are ¥90 ($11), with bath and a/c ¥162 ($20), and larger two-room suites are ¥208 ($26), all-inclusive. Bus 43 passes just west of Běijīng Zhàn, running down Chóngwén Mén Wài Dàjiē, and down the east side of Tiāntán. Get off one stop after the bus turns into Ānlèlín Lù at the junction with Jǐngtài Lù. Continue walking west on the south side of the road, and the hotel is down an alley with a small branch of the Construction Bank of China on the corner (MC and Visa signs). Bus 45 runs from ⓜ Hépíng Mén and along Ānlèlín Lù. Get off at the stop called Liúlíjǐng half way along. The 39 runs from Běijīng Zhàn past the east end of Ānlèlín Lù. Get off at the stop called Púhuángyú. Ānlèlín Lù has street food and a lively market.

During 1999 the hotel closed because of a legal dispute, although this didn't seem likely to eject the rather unhelpful staff. It should be open again by now, but during the dispute guests were forwarded to the rather more friendly **Kǎihuá Bīnguǎn**, just east at Ānlèlín Lù 10, ✆ 6723 6814, 🖷 6723 6801, reached by crossing a bus yard— look for a sign saying 'Welcome friends' and the entrance is on the left under a sign with red characters on a white background. A double with bath is ¥232 ($29), which can be bargained down to ¥162 ($20), triples and quads are ¥362 ($45), which can be got down to ¥262 ($33). Not too clean, but acceptable.

The **Qiáoyuán Fàndiàn,** in Yòu'ān Mén Dōng Bīn Hé Lù, a short walk north and west of Běijīng South Railway Station, ✆ 6303 8861, 🖷 6303 0119, was once the main budget residence of Běijīng until it decided to close for rebuilding, and the back-packers followed travel agents John and Su to the Jīnghuá (*see* above). Following some kind of dispute, John ended up at the Fènglóng (*see* below) and began to attract dissenting backpackers with the same set of convenient services, but still at prices you could beat yourself if you tried. The cheaper block still existed at the Qiáoyuán—¥30 ($3.75) per bed in a 10-bed room, ¥40 ($5) in a quad or triple, or ¥50 in a twin ($6.25), all with common shower, and ¥60 ($7.50) per bed in a twin with decrepit bathroom)—but was forgotten until John (real name Zhāng) moved back there in mid-2000, naming it **Mr John's Budget Hotel** and bringing down the prices to as little as ¥25 per bed. He offers the same ticket booking services, tourist info, bike rental, laundry, and tours to the Wall, acrobatics, opera, etc., is generally helpful, and speaks good English. Book beds in this block on ✆ 139 0112 3938 (a mobile phone) or by email <*jian_min@hotmail.com*>, <*http://www.channel21.com/asia/fenglong*>. As backpackers come back to what is a much better located hotel than the Jīnghuá, expect a cluster of supplementary surrounding services to reopen.

The more modern block has twins from ¥372 ($46.50). All prices are bargainable. The reception is right inside the interior courtyard of what is still a large complex, with a Western restaurant which claims to do English, French, Russian and Italian, but not necessarily in ways you'll recognize. This hotel has an eager GM, but staff who still obviously think their lives would be easier without guests, much as they did years ago.

Take bus 122 from Běijīng Zhàn to Nán Zhàn (South Station)., bus 20 or 54 from Běijīng Zhàn via Tiān'ān Mén and Qián Mén, or the tè5 from Běijīng Xī Zhàn (West Station). From the south station terminus walk back to the main road (which is the second ring) and walk two minutes west (left).

The **Fènglóng Bīnguǎn** ('Youth Hostel'), Yòu'ān Mén Dōng Jiē 5, ✆ 6354 5836, ✆ 6353 6452, <*jian_min@hotmail.com*>, <*http://www.channel21.com/asia/fenglong/*>, has quads with private bath for as little as ¥40 ($5) per person (inc. city tax), but these are grim and windowless and not up to the standard of the Jīnghuá, although they seem to be attracting a number of dissenting backpackers. There are more upmarket quads for ¥240–280 ($30–35) per room, triples from ¥270–330 ($34–41), twins from ¥180–280 ($22.50–35—but for this you can stay far more centrally and in much better conditions), and single rooms ¥120–180 ($15–22.50). The hotel has Sìchuān and Roast Duck restaurants, and due to its relatively convenient location opposite the entrance road to the South Station and Yǒngdìng Mén long-distance bus stations is also popular with Chinese.

airport accommodation

There are two hotels close to the airport for those leaving or arriving at unpleasantly early times of the morning. When flying in you'll probably have to book these at the accommodation desks in the arrivals hall, in which case the hotel will pick you up, as no taxi, having waited in the rank, will be willing to take you such a short distance. The hotels have shuttle buses to town or you can use the airport shuttle, ¥16.

The **Běijīng Jīngdū Hotel** (Jīngdū Yúlè Zhōngxīn), ✆ 6456 6555, ✆ 6456 2423, has twins for ¥150 ($19), and the newer and more upmarket **Airport Garden Hotel** (Kōnggǎng Huāyuán Jiǔdiàn), ✆ 6456 3388, ✆ 6456 2991 has them from ¥380 (¥47.50—with a little bargaining).

self-catering

Red House (Ruìxiù Bīnguǎn) 'B&B service for touring guests', Dōng Zhí Mén Wài in turning opp. Pizza Hut, ✆ 6416 7500, ✆ 6416 7600, <*redhouse@ht.rol.cn.net*>, <*http://www.redhouse.com.cn/*>. A red building about 10 mins' walk from ⓜ Dōng Zhí Mén at Chūnxiù Jiē 10, the Red House has individual a/c suites complete with cooking facilities, washing machine, fridge, sitting room with satellite TV, bedroom (twins and doubles available), good bathroom with shower cubicle, direct line to room, IDD out, and breakfast included. The corridors could do with carpeting but have some pieces of period furniture standing around—it's moderate China four-star quality. Those staying for a year get cleaning service once a week, over shorter periods it's daily like hotel service. There are some English-speaking staff. Rent includes management expenses, gas, electricity, water and central heating: from ¥12,000 ($1,500) per month (negotiable down to ¥9,000 or ¥10,000), ¥10,000 ($1,250) for stays of one year or more (equally negotiable). Probably open to negotiation for stays of a week or two. The daily rate (must book in advance) is ¥95 ($12) for a single bed in a seven-bed dorm. All rates include a substantial Western breakfast, and may include the odd inducement such as free ironing.

apartments

Not really an option for visitors unless you house-sit for a friend. But look in *City Weekend* <http://www.beijing-cityedition.com/>, the email newsletter *Xiànzài Běijīng* and other expat publications (*see* p.115). Sample prices can also be found at <http://www.roofinder.com/>.

Běijīng © (010)   *Eating Out*

As might be expected, Běijīng offers not only its own specialities, but also samples of regional cuisine from all over China, and if there was no Forbidden City or other sights, it would still be interesting to come here just to eat.

The listings below begin with foods special to Běijīng or which it has made its own, and go on to deal with some of the myriad regional possibilities, especially from areas not reached by this book. The kind of general Chinese restaurant whose menu consists of the greatest hits of the main Chinese cooking schools (like most in the West) are largely ignored. But food away from the main tourist areas and in the *hútòng* is unbelievably cheap and plentiful, and the difficulty is not in finding a restaurant but more in avoiding them. There are notes of general guidance in the main text on where to look, and many options for the budget traveller are given below. For those in need of a change, Běijīng also has a great number of foreign restaurants of varying degrees of authenticity and price, and a brief selection of those is also given.

For much of the period of communist power, private enterprise was forbidden altogether, and at times almost all restaurants were shut down. Those that you have heard of are probably amongst those very few which survived the disasters of the second half of the 20th century, but which in some cases have also managed to preserve their uninterest in service intact, too. These tend to be open only fairly briefly for lunch—it's all over by 1.30pm, and close by 9pm in the evening. Many of them have long outlived reputations which is some cases were anyway merely based on the fact that they existed when little else did, and have been omitted here. A clue to the antiquity of many of these restaurants is their use of the word Fànzhuāng—'food village'—in their names.

On the other hand brand new ventures are opening all the time, many achieving great success in a short time due to some novelty such as odd ingredients, reviving cuisines of times past, or having some historical or political angle. Gaining popularity (with foreigners in particular) is often the immediate cause of a rise in prices and fall in quality of food and service, and success fades rapidly. Meanwhile new joint-venture foreign restaurants are immediately packed by expats desperate for something fresh, but even the most successful can close within a few months, typically because once the money starts rolling in the Chinese partner attempts to dump the foreign one, or refuses to honour terms promised to the foreign chef. The food and service quality immediately drop, and the expats who make up the majority of the clientele head for the next big thing. If in doubt use the telephone numbers given to check the restaurants listed below still exist; many will not. Consult *City Weekend* and other free papers to find out what's new.

Some of the best food of all kinds is inevitably to be found in the major joint-venture hotels, together with reasonable service, at capital city prices which may exceed those you pay at home. It would be a shame not to venture out into real China, and into the restaurants both old and new that the Chinese visit, especially for the local dishes. Restaurants are so numerous and food in general so good, that only a small selection of the possibilities can be listed below, and you should not fear trying to find places for yourself.

Local Specialities

Běijīng duck

Peking duck, as prepared in Peking, must be allowed to stand first amongst the culinary miracles of the world. The dish which goes by that name in Hong Kong, Bangkok and elsewhere is, at best, but a pale reflection of its august prototype; for even a duck maestro imported from Peking is as powerless to display his art in other cities as a concert pianist performing on the tinkling piano in some village hall.

John Blofeld, *City of Lingering Splendour,* 1961

Běijīng's **roast duck** (Běijīng Kǎoyā) is available as everything from polystyrene box take-away to multiple-course banquet, especially concentrated in the Qián Mén area but spread throughout Běijīng. Běijīng duck is roasted in a manner which largely separates the skin from the meat and makes it remarkably crispy. A dish of carved meat and skin is served or the bird is carved for you at the table. You are also provided with sliced onions, plum sauce, and a pile of small pancakes. Smear the pancake with a little sauce and place a few greens near one edge (or dip the greens in the sauce and use them for smearing). Put pieces of duck on top of the greens and roll the whole thing up. The meal is usually followed by duck soup, and can be accompanied if you wish by extra dishes involving every other part of the duck except the feathers.

The sign of a large concrete duck in a chef's hat is an indication of the ever-expanding **Quánjùdé** chain, of which some branches are better than others. The first Quánjùdé opened in 1864, famed for its traditional hanging stove slow-roasting method. As with other long-established restaurants which survived the upheavals of the second half of the 20th century, service is indifferent (although 10% is charged) and the restaurants are mostly closed by 9pm. The Quánjùdé ovens are fired with the stumps of apple, jujube (a small date), pear and persimmon trees. Water is injected between the skin and the meat of the duck, and then it's roasted at high temperature, crisping the skin and bringing the meat to a tender softness.

The staff are quite keen that you should order the ¥168 ($21) 'lucky' duck on the menu's first page (¥84 for a half duck), which you are taken to select for yourself and upon which you may write your name (or something else). This then takes 50mins to roast and bring to the table, where it is carved for you, the carcass being taken away to make the soup which will follow. While waiting you can sample just about every other part of the duck if you wish, from roast duck hearts to duck webs in mustard sauce at a wide range of prices. On the second page of the menu in Chinese only you will find roast duck for ¥108 ($13.50) or ¥54 for half. This is exactly the same meal, except that it comes more quickly and ready-sliced. In either case you pay a further ¥2 for plum sauce and sliced spring onions, and ¥2 for a fairly liberal supply of pancakes.

Beer is overpriced and warm, but there seems to be no objection to your taking your own cooler beer if you have it. Originally these restaurants often had three rooms serving much the same food but with different decor and different prices. Now they are all the same, apparently demonstrating that the 'socialist market economy' is more egalitarian than the purely communist one was.

The best-known branch is in Qián Mén Dàjiē, one of the most famous restaurants in Běijīng until private restaurants began to dominate almost every street, and there's another just west in Qián Mén Xīdàjiē. Better than either is the branch a little further west still, outside ⓜ Hépíng Mén on the corner of Nán Xīnhuá Jiē. At the Wángfǔjǐng branch, in Shuài Fǔ Yuán Hútòng, ✆ 6525 3310, just east of Wángfǔjǐng Dàjiē, additional dishes include duck wings in red jelly, duck liver in shape of a flower basket, deep fried duck hearts, golden fish shaped duck webs (the webs decorated to make them look like little fish with eyes), fried duck liver and gizzards, duck heartstring, duck tongues with mushrooms, stir-fried duck hearts with a spicy and hot taste, and stir-fried duck intestines with pepper.

Biànyifǎng Kǎoyādiàn The first two characters for this restaurant will probably be read by most as 'cheap' (*piányi*), but when pronounced *biànyi* mean 'convenient'. The prices at the restaurant's two locations are a little cheaper than at Quánjùdé, and the method of preparing the duck a little different. Whereas the Quánjùdé bird is traditionally roasted over pear wood, here the method involves millet stalks. A whole duck costs ¥138 ($17), a half ¥67, which includes soup, pancakes, sauce and onions. Ordinary half duck ¥44, plus ¥6 for soup, ¥2 for pancakes, and ¥1 each for sauce and onions, all plus 5%. The restaurant claims even greater antiquity than Quánjùdé, but not the current building just south of ⓜ Chóngwén Mén, ✆ 6712 0505, or another lesser branch at the southeast corner of Tiān Tán. Have a look around at your fellow diners—many are out-of-town middle-ranking cadres (officials) eating at the work unit's expense.

Lìqún Kǎoyādiàn, Běi Xiáng Fēng 11, ✆ 6702 5681, a duck restaurant tucked away in a decrepit *sìhéyuàn* in a labyrinth of *hútòng* off the southern end of Zhèngyì Lù, is usually full of expats revelling in the 'Old China Hand' credibility merely finding the place has given them in the eyes of the visitors they've brought here. From ⓜ Qián Mén walk east on the south side of Qián Mén Dōng Dàjiē and turn first right into Zhèngyì Lù. At the end turn right and then left following the English sign towards the Lìjùn Roast Duck restaurant, reached by a further left turn, and it's on the left. Various rooms around the courtyard are now used for dining and the courtyard itself has a makeshift screen over it. Whether you view this as a grotty dump or a chance to see, in a sense, 'real' Běijīng life is up to you. The restaurant opts for the Quánjùdé method of roasting, using fruit tree wood outside the oven (as opposed to millet stalks inside), and you are invited to go to the kitchen to see your duck sliced. The duck and supplementary dishes are excellent, however, and significantly cheaper than those of the famous names. A whole duck is ¥80 ($10).

In ordinary 'undiscovered' restaurants in the *hútòng* south of Qián Mén you can eat Běijīng duck for only about ¥30 ($4), or order the cooked meat by weight.

Another famous meal that Běijīng has made its own is **Mongolian Hotpot** (*huǒguō*). Prices vary widely from very cheap in the *hútòng*, to self-evidently more expensive in the glossier main street restaurants, also depending what you choose to put in the pot or eat as side dishes. Restaurants are easy to spot, showing the characters *huǒ guō* 火锅 ('fire pot') or a picture of the pot itself.

The pot itself is a large chimney-like device with a charcoal fire in the base, ringed by a channel containing soup which can be divided into two compartments, for spicy and milder flavours. The menu consists of a variety of foods which arrive cut into thin slices. The essential ingredient is lamb in marbled rolled up slices, to which you can add various vegetables, a close relative of black pudding, lamb tripe, bean curd, noodles and many other items. Take whatever you want to eat and put it in the bubbling soup, retrieving it when cooked, which only takes a few moments, especially as the soup gets hotter and hotter as the meal progresses. Cooked items can be dipped into a creamy sauce made from sesame paste, fragrant garlic and fermented bean curd, to which you can add pepper oil and fresh coriander if you wish. Other specialities with a Mongolian flavour include cold stewed donkey slices with vinegar to dip them in, various brittle versions of cheese and 'milk skin' (*bā sì nǎi pí*)—balls of a relative of cottage cheese in hot sugar, which you dip in cold water to harden before eating.

When you've finished cooking, spoon the hot liquid from the pot into the bowl containing the remains of the dipping sauce, add any remaining vegetables, and treat as a soup.

> *Like most good Chinese restaurants the Tung Lai Shun offered a choice of not less than 200 dishes, but most of its experienced customers seldom bothered to call for the menu. Like their fathers, grandfathers and great-grandfathers before them, as soon as they had sat down and wiped their faces with the hot scented towels brought to them at a run, they would give one brief order*—Suan Yang Rou.

John Blofeld, *City of Lingering Splendor*, 1961

Dōngláishùn Fànzhuāng was supposed to have three particular ingredients for its success. One was the fineness with which it sliced the lamb, another was that it bred its own sheep to a particular balance of meat and fat, and the third the customer's own skill in mixing his sauce. The restaurant no longer has 200 dishes, and the speed of the staff would be better described as an amble, but it still exists on the 5th floor of the Sun Dōng'ān Plaza in Wángfǔjǐng, ✆ 6525 3562, its original site long built over, and it still serves *shuàn yáng ròu* 涮羊肉 'quick boiled lamb'. There's a fee for the pot, and then separate charges for ingredients. About ¥100 ($12.50) for two.

Another famous hot pot restaurant with a long history is **Néng Rén Jū** near Bái Tǎ Sì, ✆ 6601 2560.

political eating

A considerably less well-known Běijīng dish might be called the Cultural Revolution's leftovers. The Cultural Revolution (1966–76), inspired by Máo Zédōng's struggles to re-establish himself in the face of criticism from his colleagues for the failure of the

Great Leap Forward and other campaigns, brought the education system in China to a standstill following the disgrace and sometimes murder of intellectuals and teachers, and saw millions of people sent to the countryside to be 're-educated' by the peasants. After Máo's death, many found it impossible to return home without the connections to find jobs and accommodation for them. Others, their education having been totally disrupted, found it hard to compete in a China that was beginning to put a value on brains again, and which wished to forget the horrors and turmoil of that decade. Those who have reached retirement have found life bitter. Living on pensions of only ¥260 ($32) a month, they have been forgotten by officialdom. In the 1990s several younger returnees found ways to express themselves by opening restaurants which celebrated this period in an ironic way, serving the minimalist peasant dishes of the bleak northeastern plains where many of them had been sent. The restaurants were decorated sarcastically with shrines to Máo and copies of now rare Cultural Revolution posters idolising him, but taken at face value were immune to attack by the authorities. These restaurants have now largely disappeared, an indication of just how quickly fashions come and go and how quickly novelty wears off, but new examples may open, so ask around to find out whether there are any new versions of Hěi Tǔdì Dàjiǔdiàn (Black Earth Restaurant—a reference to the soil of the northeast), or Yì Kǔ Sī Tián Dàzáyuàn ('Compare Past Misery with Present Happiness' Restaurant—a Cultural Revolution slogan).

At the same time there was a burst of nostalgia for Máo and his times, partly reflected in the creation of a restaurant serving solely the peasant dishes of his home town in Húnán Province, which spawned hundreds of imitators almost instantly. The original **Sháo Shān Máo Jiā Càiguǎn** has closed, but the same operation is now at Yōnghé Gōng Dàjiē 30, ✆ 6401 4969, immediately south of the main entrance to the Lama Temple. There's an attempt to create a village-like atmosphere with bamboo hut-like alcoves along one wall, decorated with plastic grapes and plastic bamboo, a large white bust of Máo and black and white photographs around the wall in various scenes, including Máo at Běidàihé. Main dishes are around ¥30, mostly served in small round clay dishes, and you get a free Máo badge.

Máo's favourite dish, according to the staff (although there are other opinions), was *dòu chǐ chǎo là ròu* 豆豉炒腊肉 , stir-fried bacon and fermented soya, authentically simple and not particularly hot. Surprisingly, the restaurant has learned from foreigners the use of the chilli symbol to indicate hot food, although two chillies (medium), is still bland, perhaps weakened in deference to local tastes. Stir-fried shark stomach with bamboo shoots can't be an everyday dish in an ordinary Húnán village, especially since the province is land-locked, but it's on the menu at ¥60 ($7.50), the most expensive item on the menu and hardly a proletarian dish. The result is rubbery but, despite coming from the wrong part of the shark, has a little more bite. The pork with chestnuts is as fatty as the Chairman was said to have liked his meat, but simple and filling.

Paying high prices in Běijīng never guarantees you good service and the **Red Capital Club** at Dōng Sì Jiǔ Tiáo 66, ✆ 6402 7150 (reservation required), ✆ 8401 8886 (nights, weekends), which celebrates Dèng Xiǎopíng's partial liberation of the economy, also apparently preserves the incompetence of 'service' in all eras up to the present. A couple of good English speakers may appear long after desperation has set in. The restaurant is in a tastefully restored mansion formerly belonging to a Manchu bannerman and claims to serve the cuisine of Zhōng Nán Hǎi (the parkland neighbouring the Forbidden City, former playground of emperors and now the high security home of the current aparatus of government) from a menu like a long conceited novel. The courses are named for step by step progress into this 'new Forbidden City'— Entering the Front Gate, Entering the Moon Gate, Front Courtyard, etc. Each dish has a pretentious name explained at length ('Dream of Red Chamber', 'Dowager Empress's Choice', etc.), but difficult to read in the low levels of light, before you finally get down to the price which tends to be at least ¥70 ($9) per dish and can be considerably higher. There are set meals (the 'Chairman's Recommendations') which are ¥198 ($25) or ¥250 ($31) per person depending on the courses chosen. The presentation of the food is, however, spectacular and includes items such as a dragon's head carved in magnificent detail from cucumber, and the place settings, right down to the fine chopstick rests, are in keeping with the general late Qīng style. The extended joke goes on with furniture collected from the Cultural Revolution Reparations Committee (presumably not returned to its owners due to their deaths), and you can just go for a coffee and sit on a couch used by members of the politburo in the '50s.

Imperial dishes

Fǎng Shàn Fànzhuāng (Fǎng Shàn Restaurant) in Běi Hǎi Park, ✆ 6401 1889, was opened in 1925 and mainly serves large banquets based on an idea of the Forbidden City's menus, although short of the dozens of dishes said to have been prepared for Cíxī each meal time. Prices range from ¥100 to ¥500 ($12.50 to $62.50) per person, going up in price as camel paw, walnut gruel, sharks fin, steamed venison, turtle meat, bird's nest and egg white soup, deer tendon with brown sauce and other exotica are added. Enter via the east gate in the evening to avoid paying the park entrance ticket. There's a lesser-known, cheaper version which also serves individual dishes at the eastern end of Dōng Zǒng Bù Hútòng 12, ✆ 6523 3555, which runs between Cháoyáng Mén Nán Xiǎo Jiē and the east second ring road. The courtyard of a sihéyuàn has been roofed to make the main dining area, but the atmosphere is not as luxurious as that at the main branch.

The **Běijīng Hotel** (Běijīng Fàndiàn) has a restaurant on the ground floor, which in 1999 began serving an imitation of the banquet served in the evening of the 1 October 1949 announcement by Máo of the founding of the People's Republic. Imitators were starting up as this book went to press, so a new temporary fashion might have started. All the communist big names were at the original feast, including those now airbrushed out of official histories. You are warned that China was poor then and this banquet is not as extravagant as most nowadays. You might think this item belongs under 'political eating' rather than 'imperial dishes', or you might say that this was the occasion when a new emperor mounted the dragon throne.

The **Shāguōjū Fànzhuāng** is more than 250 years old and possibly the oldest restaurant in Běijīng, although the current building is modern. The restaurant's origins are said to lie in giving a more useful afterlife to pigs slaughtered in ceremonies by the emperors. It does for pigs what the duck restaurants do for ducks, giving you every part of them except the grunts, these being provided by your fellow diners. The restaurant is now best known for a variety of meat and vegetarian dishes baked in clay pots (*shā guō*) of which the best known dish is *shāguōbáiròu* 砂锅白肉 , layers of pork slices baked with ginger and silk noodles. The pot is brought directly from oven to table, together with a bowl of dipping sauce made from *dòufu* (tofu), chives, and pepper oil, which give it a creamy, red colour (¥30—$3.75—plus ¥2 for the sauce). The restaurant is on the east side of Xīsì Nándàjiē 60, ✆ 6602 1126, a northern continuation of Xīdān Běi Dàjiē, and reached by the 22 bus from Qián Mén to the stop called Gāngwǎ Shì.

The **Lì Jiā Cài** (Lì Family Restaurant), Yáng Fáng Hútòng 11, which runs east from Déshèng Mén Nèi Dàjiē, ✆ 6618 0107, is still fashionable with expats who want to impress guests. The recipes are said to have been handed down from the imperial kitchens and to be much more authentic than those of the Fǎng Shàn. The restaurant came to public notice when a daughter of the family won a cooking competition, but she is said now to be in Australia, and smug overcharging of foreigners for food of modest quality to be the norm. The dining room is in an unimposing private house with seating for a very few, so booking a few days in advance is essential. What you are given depends on what you are prepared to pay—from around ¥500 ($62) or so per person.

Běijīng style

Although the foods are northern, the main elements of Běijīng style are noisy staff and noisy customers, sat on traditional high-backed wooden chairs at square wooden tables, perhaps with a background of Běijīng opera singing. The experience is lively and enjoyable, but these restaurants are certainly not the place for a quiet tête-à-tête.

Tán Gēn Yuàn, at the east gate of Dì Tán, a few minutes' walk north of Ⓜ Yōnghé Gōng, ✆ 6428 3358, is bedlam. The interior is painted to look like the very traditional exterior (although the building is not ancient). A long corridor runs down one side, and the washrooms at the rear are constructed to look like *hútòng* houses. The corridor and some of the private rooms inside it are lined with ancient photographs of Běijīng, and there are some tables outside in a courtyard which is bordered on one side by the park's ancient wall. There are optional rickshaws to convey you from the car park, although this is quite a short distance—so it's all about atmosphere. Traditional Běijīng dishes include an interestingly sour paste made of beans (*chǎo má dòufu* 炒麻豆腐), beef and potatoes (*tǔdòu dùn niúròu* 土豆炖牛肉), 'Běijīng flavour' braised aubergine (eggplant) with pork (*Jīng wèi shāo qiézi* 京味烧茄子), pork placed between two slices of lotus root and deep fried, which you dip into a mixture of salt and pepper (*zhá ǒu hé* 炸藕合), a slightly sweet snack made from sweet red bean paste, rolled up and steamed, then dusted with dry bean powder (*lǘ dǎ gǔnr* 驴打滚儿) and pancakes (*jiā cháng bǐng* 家常饼)—all excellent.

Dào Jiā Cháng is far less well-known, in Qī Shèng Nán Lù not far from one branch of Shuǐ Zhǔ Yú (*see* Sìchuān, below), ✆ 6422 1078. One dish is a bowl of thick noodles with an assortment of optional additions in separate side dishes, each of which is added to the noodles in a manner which clashes the dishes together, called 'Clanging Dish Noodles' (*zhá jiàng miàn* 炸酱面). The additions are cucumber, radish, yellow beans, chopped spring onion, bean sprouts, and a plum sauce to mix it all up with.

Other specialities include a sweetish cold dish made from solidified beans (*wāndòuhuáng* 豌豆黄), cabbage in a mustard sauce (*jièmodūnr* 芥末墩儿), pig's intestine with garlic and sliced peppers (*jiān jiāo féi cháng* 尖椒肥肠), and beef in a chafing dish with Chinese wolfberries (*guō zǎi luóbo niúnán* 锅仔萝卜牛腩). All the waiters are men dressed in the loose clothes of a century ago, loudly announcing each dish on arrival as if the whole restaurant wants to know about it, and shouting orders to each other. This is a tea house on steroids. A *bā gē* or hill mynah sits in a cage hanging outside. There's another newly opened branch at the east end of Píng'ān Dàdào.

Dūyīchù Shāomàiguǎn is a very long-standing Běijīng institution serving wheaty steamed dumplings (*shāomài*) for ¥20 per *lóng* (steamer), which gives you about two dozen with mixed fillings, and jugs of cold beer for ¥5. Tasty and filling. There's a wider Shāndōng menu available upstairs. The restaurant is on the east side of Qián Mén Dàjiē, almost opposite the turning to Dàzhàlán Jiē.

Cuisine from Other Regions of China

The governments of China's provinces and autonomous regions all maintain offices in Běijīng, and these often contain restaurants offering the local cuisine, of varying standards and usually (but not always) open to the public. The building with the Ānhuī restaurant mentioned immediately below, the Qī Shěng Bàn Dàshà, has seven provincial offices and several restaurants. It's at the junction of Běi Sān Huán Dōng Lù (northeast third ring road) and Yīnghuā Yuán Xī Jiē. The Běijīng Níngbō Bīnguǎn, at Xīzhōng Hútòng 25, ℭ 6605 2226, has a Zhéjiāng restaurant in the basement.

Ānhuī

The **Héféi Cāntīng** is downstairs in the Qī Shěng Bàn Dàshà building, ℭ 6443 3161. The staff seem unclear about what Ānhuī food is, but what they do bring is pleasant enough: an Ānhuī-style dofu called *Bā Gōng Shān dòufu* 八公山豆腐, *hóng shāo yú zhōng duàn* 红烧鱼中段, 'red cooked' fish mid-section, a typically Shāndōng dish, and *háoyóu shēng cài* 蚝油生菜, green cabbage in oyster sauce—a Chinese staple. Cheap.

Cháozhōu

Shāo'érzǎi (which means 'roast young goose') is at Dōng Huá Mén Dàjiē 16, just east of the Forbidden City's east gate, ℭ 6513 6559, and other branches. It has roast goose from around ¥38 ($5), and specials of the day listed on a red board near where all the goose bits are displayed. You select the dishes you want to eat from chilled shelves and these are added to a trolley with a basket and taken away to be cooked. The dining hall is a large red pillared room with green ginghamed tablecloths, napkins in little bowls shaped like geese, a concrete goose outside, and all the staff are wearing minority costume and paper hats with a picture of a goose on them. The restaurant is open bizarre hours—8.30pm–5am—and thus useful for late-night dining. The roast goose, cooked in a style found mainly in Guǎngdōng and Hong Kong, is excellent. Other specialities include *dòufu* sliced up with a sauce made from vinegar and garlic (*lǔ dòufu*), and yolks of salted eggs put into rings of non-sweet melon and then steamed in a sauce made partly from the whites and dusted with crab eggs (*xián dàn wáng ràng guā huán* 咸蛋王让瓜环). There's a live pianist from mid-evening and as an odd and not entirely successful technical addition there's a button on the table to summon staff.

Guǎngdōng (Cantonese)

Hong Kong Food City (Xiānggǎng Měi Shí Chéng), Dōng'ān Mén Dàjiē 18, ✆ 6525 7349. Reasonable food but overpriced, once popular with Běijīng's *nouveaux riches* for demonstrating their buying power, but they've now moved on to pricier things. The dishes are those most familiar to foreigners, and a dinner for two will cost about ¥150 ($19), unless you venture to order shark fin soup.

The **Fortune Garden** in Wángfǔjǐng's Palace Hotel, ✆ 6559 2888, ext. 7900, is probably the best Cantonese restaurant in Běijīng, with prices to match the luxurious interior. But an excellent set dim sum lunch costs only ¥99 ($12.50).

Hong Kong

Be There or Be Square Café (Bú Jiàn Bú Sàn Chá Cāntīng), ✆ 6518 6515. Hong Kong 24-hour fast food, with a modern orange and blue interior with industrial trimmings, efficient staff who find you a table in the bedlam, and a menu of typical Hong Kong rice and noodle plates familiar from your local takeaway, mixed with British specials such as toast and butter, Horlicks, and milk tea strong enough to allow the spoon to stand up by itself. Buns and snacks are around ¥8, rice and noodle plates are around ¥18 ($2). The restaurant is named after a hit comedy film from 1998, which followed the fortunes of two Chinese living in the USA, and the film's director has an investment. If you happen to hear the words 'Be There or Be Square' emerging from the Mandarin of some restaurant PA system, that's the highly popular theme tune, although the Mandarin translates as 'not see, not scatter'—I won't leave until I see you. The restaurant is reached by walking south through the Henderson Centre to where the service road crosses it.

Kèjiā (Hakka)

The Kèjiā are the Hakka or 'guest people' who are mostly in the south and are significantly represented in Hong Kong, Malaysia and some other overseas Chinese communities. **Bāozǎi Wáng** is in the east third ring road north near the junction with the airport expressway, ✆ 6463 8632. Look for a restaurant with a picture of a pig, and go upstairs to the right. The interior is villagey with bamboo chairs and fittings. Try *dòu chǐ líng yú chǎo mài cài* 豆豉凌鱼炒麦菜 —black beans, salted fish, and a special southern green vegetable stir-fried together. *Ràng dòufu bǎo* 让豆腐煲 is peppery meat balls steamed in *dòufu* and topped with chopped onions, and *jiāng zǎi mèn jī* 姜仔焖鸡 is a delicious combination of jugged chicken and ginger. *Xián yú zhēng ròu bǐng* 咸鱼蒸肉饼 is pork flattened by hammering and steamed with salted fish. As this book went to press the restaurant announced a change of approach, but promised to keep the main Kèjiā dishes.

Shànghǎi

There are dozens of Shànghǎi restaurants in Běijīng. One of the most lively is **Hùjiāng Xiāng Mǎn Lóu**, on the south side of Píng'ān Dà Dào, a few minutes' walk west of Ⓜ Dōng Sìshì Tiáo, a noisy, bustling, but bright and clean restaurant with a mixture of waitress service and, convenient for foreigners, counters with point-to-order Shànghǎi snacks. A big meal for two people is about ¥100 ($12.50), but much more economical if only snacks at ¥5–10 are ordered. Try *Shànghǎi shàn hú* 上海鳝糊 (sliced eels in soya oil, lightly dusted with white pepper), *xián ròu dōngguā máodòu* 咸肉冬瓜毛豆 (salty pork with winter melon and young soya beans), *tángcù xiǎo pái* 糖醋小排 (pork spare rib in sweet soya sauce), or snacks such as *shēng jiān bāozi* (shallow fried pork dumplings), *yóu dūnzi* 油墩子 (deep fried cakes of daikon radish topped with shrimp) and *zhá chòu gān* 炸臭干 (deep fried stinky dofu).

Sìchuān

The best-known Sìchuān restaurant was the **Sìchuān Fàndiàn** on the north side of Róngxiàn Hútòng at no.51, which runs between Xuānwǔ Mén Nèi Dàjiē and Běi Xīnhuá Jiē to the south of and parallel to Xī Cháng'ān Jiē. This restaurant in an ancient courtyard mansion is said to once have been the residence of Yuán Shìkǎi, the first president of the Republic of China, before he moved to Zhōngnán Hǎi where the paramount leaders still live, and decided to declare himself emperor. This has now reopened as the **China Club**, redecorated in the style kept by Yuán Shìkǎi himself. Opened by a Hong Kong tycoon, it imitates both the private clubs of Hong Kong and those of the treaty port-era Shànghǎi—an echo of an echo. $10,000 to join. The **Sìchuān Pavilion** (Sìchuān Lóu), ✆ 6603 8855, open to the public to the left of the main entrance, is not the original restaurant but does Sìchuān food in the same way a flame thrower does flame. The interior is dark and woody with attractive deep green place settings. The prices are surprisingly affordable, with set meals including Sìchuān staples such as *gōng bǎo jī dīng* 宫保鸡丁 (spicy chicken with peppers and peanuts) and *yú xiāng ròu sī* 鱼香肉丝 (shredded pork cooked in the sauce used for fish—a garlicky one) for ¥158 for two–three people, and ¥360 for four–six—as little as ¥60 ($7.50) per person.

The famous original operation, established on the orders of then Premier Zhōu Ēnlái at a time when restaurants were exceedingly few, has reopened in attractive, traditionally furnished lantern-hung premises on the west side of Prince Gōng's Mansion not far beyond the main entrance, as the **Gōng Wáng Fǔ Sìchuān Fàndiàn**, Liǔyīn Jiē 14, ✆ 6615 6924. Sìchuān banquets, and main courses at around ¥30–40 ($3.75–5).

A little to the east of the Sìchuān Pavilion on the south side of the same *hútòng* at no.76 is the **Sānxiá Jiǔlóu** (named for the Three Gorges on the Yangtze River), ✆ 6601 4612, another good Sìchuān restaurant, unused to dealing with foreigners, but friendly and with standard low prices. Imitating its more prestigious former neighbour, it has waiters in traditional costume who refill your tea cup from an ornate, long-spouted, copper tea pot. Not all Sìchuān food is spicily hot. Try the subtly flavoured smoked duck (*zhāng chá quán yā*, a bit more expensive), and pork on a sizzling crispy rice base (*guō bā ròu piàn*).

Shuǐ Zhǔ Yú 水煮鱼 is both the name of a restaurant and of its most famous Sìchuān speciality—a bowl of hot, oily, red liquid, covered in floating chillies which the waiter scoops away to reveal sliced fish with beansprouts and thick with black peppercorns. The initial burn is followed by the warmth of the meaty fish. There are two locations, differentiated from neighbouring imitators by the bark porches over their doors: Liǔ Fāng Běi Jiē not far inside the northeast third ring road (take bus 116 which runs along Cháng'ān Jiē and up Xī Dān to the terminus, Hépíng Lǐ Huǒchē Zhàn), and the older branch a little to the northwest in Qī Shèng Nán Lù, next to the Chóngqìng Fàndiàn, popular with models, film directors, and other members of Běijīng's nascent glitterati. The interiors are plain, woody and unpretentious, but the food excellent. Also try *gān biān biǎn dòu* 干煸扁豆, spicy hyacinth beans, stir-fried then stewed, and *jiāng bào cù ròu* 姜爆醋肉, large slices of quick-fried vinegary pork. Fish and side dishes around ¥120 ($15) for two.

Xiǎo Dòng Tiān Má Là Tàng is in the 24-hour food street at Dōng Zhí Mén Nèi Dàjiē Yī (south side) 258, ✆ 6404 5746, and both it and a neighbouring branch serves another kind of Sìchuān hotpot very popular with Běijīng people, whose name translates roughly as 'numb spicy hot', but it isn't exceptionally so. You order by ticking the ingredients you want on a form, and will probably pay around ¥60 ($7.50) a person and be the only foreigner there. This is also the place to try *láo zāo* 醪糟, a smooth, slightly oily liquor made from rice.

Another good Sìchuān restaurant is the surprisingly cheap rooftop **Yuen Tai** (Yúntái) at the Sheraton Great Wall Hotel, which only charges ¥18 ($2) per dish at weekend lunch times (*open 11–2*). Over 100 Sìchuān specialities; ✆ 6590 5566 ext 2295.

Singapore

Singapore is not (yet) a region of Greater China, but is run by ethnic Chinese. **Lau Pa Sak** (Lǎo Bā Shà), Dōng Zhí Mén Wài Dàjiē 18, ✆ 6415 7598, has authentic Singapore street hawkers' food but not at hawkers' prices, including chicken curry with rice ¥45 ($6), fried fish balls in oyster sauce ¥35 ($4), Hǎinán Chicken Rice ¥45 and Lau Pa Sak fried beef noodle ¥35.

Xīnjiāng

China's northwestern region, re-conquered by the Qīng and named 'new territories' in the mid-19th century, is about as Chinese as the Anatolian Plateau, and so is its food. Until mid-1999 there were two areas of northwestern Běijīng with groups of Uighur minority restaurants which the authorities decided to bulldoze at short notice and without compensation to the owners, viewing them as hotbeds of the independence movement. These may regroup, but for now the obvious survivors of the cheap and filling roast lamb restaurants are the rather less affordable expat versions.

One example is **Almuhan (Ālāmùhàn)**, Dōng Zhí Mén Wài Dàjiē 26, 10 mins' walk west of Ⓜ Dōng Zhí Mén on the south side of the road, ✆ 6417 4888, which serves toasted nan bread with mutton for ¥48 ($6), and lamb kidneys in an iron pan for ¥42 ($5). Other unexpected items include roasted hare, Uighur pop videos on suspended screens and live Uighur pop later in the evening. Also try the rather wild **Afunti**, with live entertainment, Xīnjiāng folk music and table dancing, in a *hútòng* off Cháoyáng Mén Nèi Dàjiē, ✆ 6525 1071.

Yúnnán

Dǎi Jiā Cūn Dà Jiǔ Diàn, Guǎngdōng Diàn Nán Jiē, ✆ 6594 2455. The Dǎi are one of the principle minorities of the far southwestern province of Yúnnán, and, like all minorities in the minds of the Hàn majority, are famous for singing and dancing. So, in the centre of a bamboo-lined hall pretending to be a traditional Dǎi stilt house delicate dances are performed, although you may be distracted by the mobile phones of businesswomen, or the sight of a live snake being cut open and its blood added to diners' drinks.

Beware the pretty girl who ties a red thread to you for good luck as this will later lead to enforced participation in the dancing culminating in a conga-like exit to the outside world where you will be splashed with water—the Dǎi have a taste for practical jokes.

The menu has scorpion, ants and queen bee embryos, as well as snake, but there's lots to tempt those looking for a good meal rather than cheap thrills. Try *xiǎn liū niú gān jǔn* 鲜溜牛肝菌 , a dish of special Yúnnán mushrooms, *zhú tǒng yě tù* 竹筒野兔 , hare baked with spices in a half section of bamboo, *cǎi dié pū quán* 彩蝶扑泉 , literally 'colourful butterflies flap to the spring'—fish slices cooked by adding red hot stones to the broth in which they sit, and *lìzi cài xīn* 栗子菜心 , fried cabbage heart with chestnuts. There's a second branch of this restaurant at Tǐyùguǎn Lù 13, east of the Temple of Heaven's northeast corner, ✆ 6714 0145.

General Chinese

Most restaurants in China offer their own local specialties, plus the greatest hits of all the other regions, and Běijīng has hundreds of these. The **Royal Park Restaurant** (Ōuměi Shí Fǔ), Nán Hé Yán 111, ✆ 6522 3237, inside the Western Returned Scholars Association building opposite the west side of the Grand Hotel, is notable because it allows you to eat outside in the courtyard of a former temple, or inside the main, sadly modernized, hall. The service is appalling, however.

Chinese fast food, street food, snacks, and budget eating

Many *hútòng*, particularly at junctions with more major arteries, have cheap and grubby fast food places. Typical would be the alley running north where Měishùguǎn Dōng Dàjiē turns left, Dà Fó Sì Dōng Jiē (named for a vanished temple) with steaming bowls of noodles and as much *jiǎozi* you can cope with for ¥3–5, as well as smarter fast food places with plastic chairs and uniformed waitresses.

Mǎlán, a ¥5 fast beef noodles specialist with a Western fast food style interior although not quite as clean, has branches all over Běijīng, including Běi Hé Yán on the west side just north of the Dōng Huá Mén crossroads, by Běijīng North Station and Dōng Zhí Mén bus station.

Běijīng has several food streets such as Dōng'ān Mén, which fills with stalls at night time, and the **24-hour food street** Dōng Zhí Mén Nèi Dàjiē, which the Chinese call Ghost Street, Guǐ Jiē (Ⓜ Dōng Zhí Mén), lined with almost permanently open cheap restaurants, some intensely specialized such as the one just doing spinal marrow dishes, but a lot more with conventional food. Even the big hotels sometimes come down to modest levels of pricing with the Jīnglún's fourth floor food street offering Běijīng snack dishes for ¥10–20, ✆ 8500 2266, ext 8111.

food courts

Almost all of Běijīng's glitzy new department stores have food courts in the basement or on the top floor, usually with a central seating area surrounded by counters serving food of different types, regions of China or countries. These combine a relatively hygienic environment with very modest prices, often the same price or very little more than eating on the street.

Basement of **The Railway Station** at Qián Mén (*open 9–9.30*), has an a/c food court with different counters for regional foods from all over China, with clear signs and displays and clearly marked prices. Eat for ¥10 or less. There are early photographs of the former station and the surrounding area on the walls.

Sogo (*open 9.30–9.30*), the Japanese department store in effect indistinguishable in China from other stores, has a food court in the basement.

The 6th floor of **Parkson Department Store** (*open 9–10*) has a bustling cheap bright and loud food court with various regional Chinese foods and Western snacks, and a slightly more comfortable Táiwān section with views over Běijīng.

Lǜwū Bǎihuò (*open 9–9*) has various travel snacks and fruit (check marked prices and buy more cheaply on the street), as well as sushi, a bakery, noodle stalls, coffee shop, and teriyaki (Táiwān style).

The **China World Trade Centre** has a food court in the basement with Japanese, juices, curries and a fast food Chinese called Quickly. There's also a deli with cheap muffins and good bread beyond Starbucks on the ground floor.

Foreign Food

fast food

Foreign fast food has standard Western prices, but seems expensive compared to the tasty and usually more nutritious Chinese food you can get for the same money. However, the choice for those who are craving a change is extensive.

Bìsàkè (Pizza Hut) can be found in several locations including Zhūshìkǒu Xī Dàjiē, the Jiànguó Mén Friendship Store and Xīn (Sun) Dōng Ān Plaza in Wángfǔjǐng Dàjiē. On the south side of Qián Mén Xījiē a clutch of fast food restaurants include **KFC** (Kěndé Jī), McDonald's (Màidānglǎo) and Délifrance (Dàmòfáng). The Qián Mén branch of KFC was the first foreign fast food outlet, opened in 1987 and, in a radical change from the policy of maintaining an international corporate image at all costs, has refitted its interior in something approaching a Chinese style and exhibits Chinese art on its third floor. Ordinary Chinese regard **McDonald's** as *haute cuisine*, and there are now more than 55 branches in Běijīng, including three in or near Wángfǔjǐng. These are sometimes called McDěng-yí-hǔir (McWait-a-Moment), since it's rare for them to be able to complete your order and they are perennially out of fries. **Délifrance**, also in the Sun Dong An Plaza, the Lufthansa Shopping City and many other locations, has passable croissants, pastries and bread. **Domino's Pizza** (Dàměilè) has a few locations, including one near Dōng Zhí Mén long-distance bus station. There are decent bakeries in most hotels, such as those at the Kempinski (half price after 8pm), Jiànguó (small discount 7–8pm), and another one with good bread on the ground floor of the World Trade Centre past **Starbucks** (*see* 'Bars, Pubs and Cafés').

Dunkin' Donuts (Dāngkěn) is in Wángfǔjǐng and at the Jiànguó Mén Friendship Store. Even **A&W** (Aì Dé Xióng) has a few locations, including opposite the Lufthansa Centre. Ice cream giant **Baskin Robbins** is in Xīdān, at the Jiànguó Mén Wài Friendship Store, at the east end of the Lóngfú Market at Dōng Dān. Vastly superior but considerably more expensive, **Häagen-Dazs** (Hāgēndásī) has premises next to the Běijīng International Club Hotel.

Eurasian

'Eurasian' is the café-bar-restaurant **Bar Code**'s (Bā Kòu) description of its menu of Italian, French, Chinese and Japanese light meals, all done well and served in a bright modern interior in the mall of the Kerry Centre Hotel (Jiālǐ Zhōngxīn Fàndiàn) in Guānghuá Lù, ✆ 8529 9405. Two courses and a drink about ¥80 ($10), but there are various satisfying dishes for ¥30 or less. 'All you can read' international magazine rack.

French

French restaurants seem to come and go with particular speed, but **The French Bistro**, inside the Great Wall Sheraton, has a business lunch for ¥119 ($15) and lunchtime specials at ¥120–140, with very un-nouvelle portions of excellent bistro food; ✆ 6590 5566 ext 2119.

The longest established French restaurant is the excellent **Justine's** in the Jiànguó Hotel, which, while being one of the most expensive restaurants in Běijīng, still delivers value for money and has an excellent value Sunday lunchtime buffet for ¥199. ✆ 6500 2233, ext.8039 for details.

Outside the big hotels, the champion is the excellent **Café Flo** (Fú Lóu) in the Rainbow Plaza, Dōng Sān Běi Lù 16, ✆ 6595 5139. About ¥500 ($62) for two.

fusion

The **Courtyard Restaurant and Gallery**, Dōng Huá Mén Dàjiē 95, ✆ 6526 8883, is in an adapted beyond recognition *sìhéyuàn* on the moat outside the Forbidden City's eastern gate. Currently one of the most popular locations for serious social dining. Around ¥250 ($31) per person.

German

Paulauner Brauhaus inside the Kempinski Hotel has beers brewed on site, but at up to ¥80 ($10) a litre. The centrepiece of the restaurant is giant coppery vessels where the beer is made, and the food is solid meaty German fare, about ¥105 ($13) for main courses.

Schiller's (Xīlè Jiǔwǔ) opposite the north side of the Kempinski Hotel, ✆ 6461 9276, serves populist meaty German fare, but with a few dishes for vegetarians. Beers include a rather fine Chinese-made wheat beer. There are two other branches on the same side of town, including one at the west gate of Cháoyáng Park.

Indian

The Taj Pavilion, in the west wing of the China World Trade Centre, ✆ 6505 5866, <ahuranet@public2.bta.net.cn>, is excellent, but costs more than you would pay at home. A less expensive snack branch is promised for Sānlǐtún. The cheaper **Asian Star Spicy** (Yàzhōu Zhī Xīng Xīnmǎyìn Cāntīng) on the east third ring road north almost opposite TGI Friday's, ✆ 6591 6716, has a mixed menu of Indian, Malaysian and Chinese food, of moderate quality.

Italian

Ristorante Pizzeria Café Adria, Liàngmǎ Qiáo opposite the north side of the Kempinksi Hotel, ✆ 6460 0896, has convincing pizzas at ¥60–80 ($7.50–10), and pasta at ¥45–50 ($5.50–$6). The **Angel Western Food and Bar** (Ānjí'ěr Yìdàlì Xīcān

Jiŭbā) in Sānlĭtún Jiŭbā Jiē, ✆ 6415 7384, has a vast Italian menu, and good pizza, around ¥100 ($12.50) per head. **Annie's,** at Cháoyáng Park's West gate, ✆ 6591 1931, as credible pizza and pasta from around ¥40 per person, and staff trying very hard to please.

In the search for the finest upmarket Italian restaurant the winner is the Běijīng International Club's excellent **Danieli's,** ✆ 6460 6688, although the Palace Hotel's Italian restaurant comes a very close second. Danieli's features dishes from southern Italy and is a cosy restaurant full of Italian details, with an inventive and comprehensive menu, one of Běijīng's largest wine lists, and some of the best restaurant service in the city. Well worth the approximately ¥380 ($22.50) for three courses, and a modest imported wine at ¥500 ($62) per bottle, plus 15%.

Japanese

Matsuko (Sōngzi) has a branch just to the north of Asian Star Spicy (*see* Indian, above), ✆ 6582 5208, and has a wide variety of sashimi for about ¥60 ($7.50) per portion, tempura ¥23, assorted sushi ¥100 ($12.50), and katsudon or pork rice set for ¥30 ($3.75). A good deal. There's also the **Fúzhù Rotary Sushi Restaurant** at the Jiànguó Mén Friendship Store, ✆ 6501 7798, where you pay according to the colour code of the dishes you take from the moving belt. Other good Japanese can be found mainly inside the hotels catering to Japanese visitors, such as the Jīnglún.

Korean

Korean food is also popular with Chinese, so there are numerous, although not particularly cheap, Korean restaurants. Try **Korea Restaurant** in Basement 2 of the Henderson Centre, ✆ 6518 2324, or in the Landmark Building next to the Great Wall Sheraton, but there are numerous back street options too. Those up in the university district will find cheap versions on university campuses.

Latin

Mexican Wave Bar and Café in Dōng Dà Qiáo Lù not far north of Jiànguó Mén Wài Dàjiē on the east side, ✆ 6506 3961, has a business lunch for ¥45 ($5.50) which includes the usual burgers, pizza and other Western baby food as well as Mexican items.

Havana Café (Hāwànà Kāfēi), north gate of the Workers' Stadium, ✆ 6586 6166, <*http://www.afunti.com.cn*>. Tango music (loud at weekends), bar and café with some seats outside in the summer, and a mixed menu of Central and South American dishes from ¥45 ($5.50).

El Gaucho Churrasqueria-Rodizio (Gāo'ěrqiáo Bāxī Kǎoròu Diàn), Jiànhuá Nán Lù 12, which runs south just opposite the Jiànguó Mén Friendship Store, ✆ 6502 2851/2198. Vaguely Spanish colonial décor and Brazilian food, with a buffet and all-you-can-eat meatiness brought to your table. Not quite as good as **Parati Restaurant**, 120 Sānlĭtún Nán Lù, ✆ 6595 8039. ¥90 for all-you-can-eat freshly barbecued meats brought to your table non-stop, with a good salad bar and choice of deserts thrown in. Recommended.

Salsa Cabana inside the Lufthansa Centre, ✆ 6465 3388, features a serious seven-piece Columbian band, space to dance, and a comprehensive South American menu (even *ceviche*). ¥100 plus per person.

Middle Eastern

1001 Nights, one branch east of the north gate of the Workers' Stadium, ✆ 6507 6325, and other just east of Sānlǐtún, ✆ 6532 4050. Broad Middle Eastern menu, lamb kebabs for ¥30–40 ($3.75–5), lots of good chewy starters including pitta bread and dips, steaks, chicken at around ¥35 per main course.

North American

American and Americanized food is widely available in familiar formats at American prices. **TGI Friday's** is on the third ring road in the northeast at Dōng Sān Huán Běilù 19, and just north the **Mother Earth Café,** ✆ 6503 1099, <motherearth@ yeah.net>, with a menu of global Americanized food and chairs in the shape of animals. The **Hard Rock Café,** just south of the Běijīng Lufthansa Centre, ✆ 6590 6688 (open 11.30–10 daily), has the usual menu of burgers for around ¥68–82 (($8–10) plus 15%, plus the odd local dish such as Hunanese chicken. As crass as anywhere else, with live rock music until 2 or 3am at the weekends. Much better than these is **The Big Easy** at the south gate of Cháoyáng Park, ✆ 6508 6776, which serves cajun dishes in a balconied New Orleans-style building with live jazz most evenings. About ¥100 ($12.50) per person.

Thai

Thai Garden (Chāng Tài Yuàn) Fāngzhuāng Lù 8, ✆ 6760 1900-2, <techj@public. bta.net.cn>, is slightly remote from most foreign haunts in the southeast of the city, but worth the trip. One of the three owners is Táiwānese pop star Gāo Míngjùn, once big in Běijīng. The dishes are authentic and fiery, and the interior decor highly unusual. About ¥200 ($25) for two.

Phrik Thai (Jīng Gǎng Tài Shì Měi Shí), just off the south side of Cháoyáng Lù west of the third ring road, ✆ 6586 9726, is small and popular. Around ¥100 for two.

vegetarian

Gōngdélín Fànzhuāng, Qián Mén Dàjiē 158, ✆ 6511 2542 / 6702 0867 (open 10.30–8.30). This is a very long-standing restaurant with correspondingly casual service, dingy surroundings and early closing times of older restaurants, but justly famous for its ability to produce almost any dish whatsoever from vegetable protein and convince you that it's really meat, fish, or anything else. The **Tiān Shí** restaurant, Dēngshìkǒu Dōng Jiē 57, ✆ 6524 2476, is a modern, private version of the same thing, with fake everything including tripe and lobster. Dishes from ¥40 ($5) upwards.

Běijīng ✆ (010)   *Entertainment, Culture and Nightlife*

> *In fact, my uncle's choosing me to be your guide shows how much he disapproves of me. As he is convinced that all foreigners indulge in disreputable pleasures, his sense of hospitality required him to find you a disreputable guide.*
>
> John Blofeld, *City of Lingering Splendor,* 1961

Venues for all kinds of entertainment fall into three kinds: those specifically aimed at foreign visitors and residents working in Běijīng, those serving mainly Chinese and foreign students, and those that have nothing to do with foreigners at all.

The first are found inside the big hotels and neighbouring streets, and in and around the diplomatic quarters and main business areas. Here prices are completely out-of-synch with anything except New York or London standards and have nothing to do with the local economy. The ¥20–30 bottle of beer has become the norm in the Sānlǐtún bar district, for instance (a foreigner ghetto), ¥3–5 elsewhere. The Chinese you'll meet here are the employees of joint-venture businesses, who are exposed daily to foreigners and whose salaries can reach to these prices; the nouveaux riche *dà kuǎn* (big money) guy wanting to show off to his *xiǎo mì* (little honey) but not knowing what most of the drinks are; and Chinese who come to nurse a beer and stare at foreigners doing glamorous foreign things.

In student areas bars and clubs often inspired by foreigners or foreign ideas (and sometimes run by foreign former students) can be quirky and inventive, and while considerably less luxurious are also considerably cheaper. These include cafés, tea houses, bars and venues for live bands, mostly up in the northwest. Like venues in the expat bar areas these, too, come and go with startling rapidity.

Finally there are the innocuous places for Chinese such as ordinary cinemas, and less innocuous ones which only the long-term resident and fluent Mandarin speaker is ever likely to discover except by accident, and in some cases would not want to find. These include small karaoke bars with small private rooms where pretty girls sit very close and sing very badly, delivered and collected by icy-visaged madames, who interrupt the deafening jollity to encourage the pink-faced customers to buy more and more small cans of imported beers at astonishingly high prices. Well-lit frontages with lines of glamorous greeters in metallic brocade full-length dresses can be equally dangerous to ears and pocket alike.

For more reputable pleasures read the email newsletter *Xiànzài Běijīng* (*see* p.38), or the free English-language newspapers *City Weekend*, *Běijīng Scene* or *Metro* for full details of what's on, as well as *Běijīng Weekend*, a free supplement to *China Daily*. All are available free at major hotels or wherever expats can be found in significant numbers, such as the Sānlǐtún and Cháoyáng Gōngyuán bar areas, or branches of Starbucks. Only publications coming out at least once a month can possibly keep up, since venues come and go so quickly.

Traditional Chinese cultural activity such as opera, acrobatics and 'tea house art' has been going through a revival, although that's mostly because profit can be made from selling it to foreign visitors and few local Chinese, who are at home watching VCDs or out 'singing' karaoke, are ever seen there. Meanwhile news of foreign pleasures, especially of the musical kind, have finally reached the ears of younger Chinese and inspired them to imitation, particularly in the fields of heavy metal and punk, and to a certain extent in jazz.

'*Tiān tiān kàn miào. Wǎnshàng shuìjiào*' used to be the Chinese view of travelling in their own country—'During the day see temples. In the evening go to sleep.' Although it's not worth travelling to Běijīng just for its bars or live entertainment, there are now enough choices to keep you awake until the small hours. Those with limited time should see Běijīng opera once, while those with more might like to discover why no Chinese band will be entering Western charts in the near future. Samples of all options are reviewed below.

Traditional Chinese Entertainment

tea houses

The **Lǎo Shě Cháguǎn**, in the Dà Wǎn Chá building, Qián Mén Xī Jiē 3 on the south side, ✆ 6304 6334/6303 6830, claims to recreate 'what life was like in a Běijīng tea house of the bygone days'—apparently a combination of extracts from Chinese opera, acrobatics, magic shows and ballad singing. Performances begin at 7.40pm and finish at 9.20pm daily, and tickets are between ¥40 ($5) and ¥130 ($16), depending on proximity to the stage. Patrons are seated eight to a table, and tickets include tea and pastries. George Bush, Henry Kissinger and Lǐ Péng have all preceded you here. The 'tea house' is two floors up, and opposite its theatre has a smaller room which serves a variety of China's more famous teas with live music for ¥10 in the afternoons Mon–Fri, and reasonable roast duck in the evenings.

Other tea houses have been opening in imitation of the profitable Lǎo Shě including the **Tiānqiáo Happy Teahouse** (Tiānqiáo Lè Cháguǎn), Tiānqiáo Nándàjiē 113 (on the west side of Tiāntán), ✆ 6304 0617, which has a similar combination of martial arts, acrobatics and Běijīng opera, but in a rather older building and for substantially higher prices—this venue is popular with Japanese tour groups and often booked out, so it's advisable to call ahead. Dinner and show from 6.30–9, ¥330 ($41), or come at 8pm and pay ¥180 ($22) to watch the show if there are vacant seats. Get a Mandarin speaker to call ahead. Advertising cards with a 10% discount offer can be found in the foyers of major hotels.

Not all tea houses feature live entertainment, however, and some merely have tea in a pleasant atmosphere. **Purple Vine Teahouse** (Zǐténg Lú), Nán Cháng Jiē 2, on the corner of Xī Huá Mén (the road leading to the western entrance to the Forbidden City), ✆ 6606 6614 (*open 12noon–2am*). Marquetry screens separate individual small rooms seating four or five, with period furniture and a pleasant woody smell. Your feet go into a small well beneath the table, and you select from a long list of teas written on a fan, and which are kept refrigerated until needed. You'll pay ¥40–60 ($5–7.50) per person for a pot, but do it for the atmosphere and the peace and quiet. For ¥180–248 ($25–31) for two to four people you can receive a demonstration of the Chinese version of the tea ceremony (taken to a rather higher level in Japan). All prices plus a 10% charge for rather sweet and pleasant service.

Tiān Hǎi Měi Shí Tīng at Dàzhàlán Xī Jiē 38, ✆ 6304 4065, is a small and casual tea house with a good selection of teas for around ¥20 per pot, and which shows a video of the classic film of Lǎo Shě's *Tea House*. Also has a reasonably priced standard Chinese menu.

Other possibilities include: Běijīng Teahouse at Liúlichǎng Xī Lù 76, the western half of Liúlichǎng, which has story-telling and *xiàngsheng*, the comic dialogue form which consists of two smart alecs (or one and a straight man) yelling at each other—often played over the speakers on long train journeys and likely to drive all but the most fluent Mandarin speakers to murder. The east side of Liúlichǎng has Bófú Cháyìguǎn at Liúlichǎng Dōng Dàjiē 71, the Wǔfú Cháyìguǎn is at Qián Mén Dàjiē 104, and outside Běijīng there's the Mínghuì Cháyìguǎn at Dàjué Sì (*see* p.333). Also try the informal but pleasant tea house over the Sanwei Bookstore, *see* 'Traditional Chinese Music', *below*.

Foreigners when visiting Peking should on no account miss going to see a Chinese play of some kind, if they wish to understand Old China. For it is only at the theatres that the costumes worn by the various classes of men and women in any particular dynasty, or in ancient times generally, can still be seen, as well as the curious weapons, queer headdresses and armour, and the other paraphernalia of court and camp, to say nothing of many strange ceremonials and customs.

Arlington and Lewisohn, *In Search of Old Peking*, 1935

American David Kidd met his Chinese wife at the opera in 1948:

I indulged myself in the usual opera fan's pastime of cracking salted watermelon seeds and drinking cup after cup of tea from the pot, replenished from time to time by the waiters, on my table...Tonight Hsiao Ts'-ui-hua, an impersonator of coquettish girls, would end the program. He was one of the last actors in China who could still perform in toe shoes, the better to emulate the bound feet and swaying gait of a high-caste woman.

David Kidd, *Peking Story*, 1996

These days women play the women's parts and to see the tradition of old men impersonating young girls preserved, you'd need to go to Japan to see *kabuki*. The audiences, too, are not so raucous at Běijīng venues, which are too splendid and too expensive for most ordinary Chinese, although some allow the older people who remain enthusiasts to fill up seats not bought by foreigners, and chattering and melon seeds remain part of the pleasure for them.

Kidd was given a glimpse backstage.

We found the actor in his dressing room before a mirror, removing his make-up with cold cream. Meanwhile attendants were busy, first removing the rows of flittering colored stones from his black wig, next the wig and its many separate pieces, and last the bands of starched white cotton placed at the hairline, which Aimee explained to me, when applied wet, tightened the actor's face, creating the illusion of youth I had seen on stage. Seated before me now, his makeup, jewels, and starched bands removed, Mr Hsiao was an old and ordinary looking man.

David Kidd, *Peking Story*, 1996

To have a chance of capturing the same atmosphere today as Mr Kidd did in the late 1940s, you need to see a performance at the Míng-era Zhèngyìcí Theatre, the Qīng-era Húguǎng Guildhall, or a smaller venue attended by Chinese, rather then the presentations in the modern theatres. Few now show whole operas, performances of which might take a whole afternoon and evening, and generally offer a selection of extracts designed to show a range of typical opera characters and ranging from the comic to the tragic.

Visitors on tours usually end up at the modern **Líyuán Theatre** (Líyuán Jùcháng) in the Qián Mén Hotel, Yǒng'ān Lù 175, ✆ 6301 6688 ext 8860. Tickets ¥30–150 ($3.75–18), 7.30pm. The venue also has most Chinese concierges and travel agents in its pocket, and you'll be told that this is the only place to go. It isn't, and shouldn't be your first choice.

This should be the **Zhèngyǐcí Theatre** (Zhèngyǐcí Jùchǎng), Qián Mén Xī Hé Yán Jiē 220, walk south from Ⓜ Hépíng Mén and turn left (east) immediately south of the Hépíngmén Roast Duck Restaurant, ✆ 6303 3104. More than 340 years old, this was originally a temple in the Míng (1368–1644), subsequently converted into a theatre by some of the founding artists of Běijīng Opera (a relatively modern hybrid of other forms), before ending up after the revolution as a dormitory for teachers. A restaurateur took control of the theatre to prevent it from being pulled down in 1995, and it re-opened in 1996 before he disappeared (allegedly leaving many bills unpaid) in 1998, having never managed to persuade (bribe) the travel agencies into bringing groups here and having failed to spend a *fēn* on advertising. Performances still take place at 7.15pm, but not every day, so phone ahead, or drop in during the daytime, when you may be allowed to treat the place as a tea house or view the magnificent red, galleried interior for a charge of ¥5. Tickets are ¥150 ($18), and there are no subtitles for foreigners, but occasional hand-outs which explain the plots, although there's a digital display for any Chinese—the tones of the Mandarin are exaggerated to perfect clarity, but the vocabulary is archaic.

The interior has been beautifully restored, with gleaming red pillars supporting its galleries and the roof of the lantern-hung interior, the walls hung with traditional opera masks and calligraphy-covered banners. The audience sits on hardwood chairs at square tables, while deferential staff pass topping up teapots during the breaks. The music is heavily percussive, a variety of bowed string and blown double-reed instruments playing all the same line. The wood blocks and cymbals may be trying to those with hangovers from the previous evening, as may the brilliance of the costumes. The performances are very disciplined, a combination of stylized movement and expression, equally stylized fights, acrobatics and high-pitched nasal singing.

Something resembling modern opera probably dates from the Míng (1368–1644), and flourished in the Qīng (1644–1911), although the Běijīng style, which became the most popular, is a relatively modern fusion of different forms, about 200 years old. Visiting companies with different styles also appear in Běijīng, or their performers can be heard singing at 'Běijīng style' restaurants such as Tán Gēn Yuàn (*see* p.262). Since this is an indigenous art form, the government is keen to claim the population's total devotion to its 'distinctive national characteristics', but in urban areas all but older people stay away in droves. If they want opera, there's one television channel which seems almost entirely devoted to it. Nevertheless, in 1997, the government claimed there were 113 Běijīng opera troupes with 10,854 performers.

Another old theatre, which had become a storehouse for a pharmacy, recently re-opened with nightly performances and a small museum of opera memoribilia. This is the **Húguǎng Guild Hall** (Húguáng Huìguǎn Gǔ Xìlóu—*see* p.166 for museum details and directions south from Ⓜ Hépíng Mén), Hǔfāng Lù 3, ✆ 6351 8284/6352

2110. This has a fine late-Qīng interior dating from 1807. For performances, the ticket office is on the north side. Performances at 7.15pm most nights, tickets ¥60–¥150 ($7.50–19). It also has Shāndōng restaurant which can be entered from the north. Performers are from the Drama Institute. For more opera history visit the Méi Lánfāng Jìniànguǎn (Méi Lánfāng Memorial Hall—see p.178), the old sìhéyuàn home of the 20th-century's greatest opera performer.

Prince Gong's Peking Opera is held in the splendid Prince Gong's Mansion (Gōng Wáng Fǔ—see p.174) on demand from tour groups. Performances run 7.30pm–8.50pm and cost ¥80–¥120 ($10–15). Call ✆ 6618 6628 to get yourself attached to a package.

The **Cháng'ān Grand Theatre** is another modern venue, sometimes offering full-length operas at weekends, at Jiànguó Mén Nèi Dàjiē 7, just east of the Běijīng International Hotel, north of Ⓜ Běijīng Zhàn, ✆ 6510 1309. Evening performances at 7.15pm.

Opera productions in both Běijīng and regional styles are also sometimes performed at Běijīng Workers' Club at Hǔfāng Lù 7 (just south of the Húguǎng Guild Hall), ✆ 6352 9574/6353 5390 at 7.15pm; the People's Theatre (Rénmín Jùchǎng), Hùguó Sì Jiē, ✆ 6618 4979; and the Dà Guān Yuán Theatre inside Grand View Garden (see p.170), 7.45pm, ¥50–120 ($6.25–15), ✆ 6351 9025/6303 7979.

acrobatics

While acrobatics is more usually connected with Shànghǎi and parts of Shāndōng and Shānxī Provinces, inevitably the capital must have its show, and it's an art at which the Chinese truly excel, winning many prizes at international circus festivals overseas. It's all here: oscillating and revolving umbrellas, chairs, plates, jars, poles and hoops, and people carrying dozens of these while wire walking, riding unicycles, or building themselves into small mountains.

The best place to see acrobats (zájì) is the **Wàn Shèng Theatre** (Wànshèng Jùchǎng) at Tiān Qiáo; take bus 17, 2 or 20 from the west side of Qián Mén—stop Tiān Qiáo—and walk south then west down Běi Wěi Lù to an oddly Victorian-looking building which 10 years ago was a cinema immediately west of the Tiān Qiáo Happy Tea House, ✆ 6303 7449. A sign on the front says 'Welcome to acrobatic show', and the booking office is on the right. Shows are at 7.15pm and last 90mins, ¥120–150 ($15–19). In the early days of China travel these people could be found at the acrobatic rehearsal hall in Dàzhàlán Jiē, now converted to other uses, then in Cháoyáng, and eight years ago moved down here. The performers are mostly from the Běijīng area, but their acrobatic school also draws people from elsewhere and in particular Shāndōng.

There are occasional performances by visiting and local companies at the Poly Plaza International Theatre (Bǎolì Dàshà Guójì Jùyuàn), right outside Ⓜ Dōng Sì Shí Tiáo, northeast side, ✆ 6504 5520, ¥80–¥500 ($10–63), as well as at the Cháoyáng Theatre (Cháoyáng Jùchǎng), Dōng Sān Huán Běilù 36, ✆ 6507 2421 (7.15pm nightly, ¥60/$7.50).

Chinese traditional and Western classical music

The **Běijīng Concert Hall** (Běijīng Yīnyuètīng), Běi Xīnhuá Jiē 1, a south turning a short walk east of Ⓜ Xī Dān, ✆ 6605 5812, claims to have the only pipe organ in

China, and hosts a variety of performances of both Western and Chinese classical music. Tickets range in price from ¥20 ($2.50) to ¥200 ($24), depending on the event, most of which begin at 7.30pm. Large scale concerts of visiting foreign orchestras and those of 'Three Tenors' scale are also given in **The Great Hall of the People** (*see* p.130), ✆ 6605 6847.

Also try the newly restored Jīnfàn Yuètīng (Golden Sail Concert Hall, Wángfǔjǐng Dàjiē 24, ✆ 6525 0614; the Yīnyuè Táng concert hall in Zhōng Shān Park; Mínzú Concert Hall (Mínzú Wénhuà Gōng), Xiǎoyíng Lù 15, ✆ 6491 9081; the Century Theatre (Shìjì Jùyuàn) inside the Sino-Japanese Youth Centre (Zhōng-Rì Qīngnián Jiāoliú Zhōngxīn), Liàngmǎ Qiáo Lù 40, ✆ 6466 3311; or the Central Conservatory of Music (Zhōngyāng Yīnyuè Xuéyuàn), Bào Jiā Jiē 43, ✆ 6605 3531. Traditional Chinese music can also be heard in the tea house above the **Sanwei Bookstore** (Sān Wèi Shū Wū), Fùxīng Mén Nèi Dàjiē 60, ✆ 6601 3204, for ¥30 ($4) cover charge on Saturday evenings at 7pm, (and there's jazz on Fridays).

Western and Modern Entertainment

theatre

There's not much straight drama in Běijīng, and very little of that is in English outside expat amateur dramatics. Consult *City Weekend*, *Běijīng Scene* or *Běijīng Weekend* for performance information. Live performances need special licences from the government, which may vacillate and cancel shows which turn out to be worryingly popular for what might be political reasons, or to have elements of *jīngshén wūrǎn* (spiritual pollution). There's not much adventure here.

Běijīng has never had a National Theatre building, although now construction of a vast four-auditorium venue has begun in Cháng'ān Xī Jiē just west of the Great Hall of the People. To everyone's surprise, the international competition was won not by a Chinese but by Frenchman Paul Andreu, whose design will be the first modern construction in Běijīng not either hideously unimaginative or simply hideous. A glass and titanium UFO of a building to be surrounded by a lake and entered through a tunnel, it is forecast to cost $420 million and will be completed in 2003. Several hundred families have been forced out of a large area of ancient *hútòng*, which have been razed to make room for the new building.

The big Japanese musical and revue companies are increasingly popular in Běijīng, including Keita Asari's Gekidan Shiki, which has mounted co-productions with part-Chinese part-Japanese casts, such as 1999's production of the Disney-owned 'Beauty and the Beast', and the all-female Takarazuka Revue Company. These large-scale productions are usually found in the **Century Theatre** (Shìjì Jùyuàn), inside the Sino-Japanese Youth Centre, Liàngmǎ Qiáo Lù, ✆ 6466 3311, and the **Běizhàn Jùyuàn**, Xī Zhí Mén Wài Dàjiē 135, ✆ 6835 1383 / 6608 6147 / 8528 2168.

Check schedules for the Central Academy of Drama Theatre (Zhōngyāng Xìjù Xuéyuàn Shíyàn Jùchǎng), Dōng Miánhuà Hútòng 39; Central Experimental Drama Theatre (Zhōngyāng Shíyàn Xìjù Jùchǎng), Māo'ěr Hútòng 45, off Dì'ān Mén Wài Dàjiē, ✆ 6403 1099, and Cháoyáng Theatre (Cháoyáng Jùchǎng), Dōng Sān Huán Běilù 36, ✆ 6507 2421.

The dark and arty **Busy Bee Bar** (Máng Fēng Jiǔbā), upstairs at Dōng Sì Běi Dàjiē 208, ✆ 6605 7574, occasionally has small experimental productions which are not announced in advance—probably because they don't bother to ask for a licence. At weekend nights it has rock music. Also ask about nightclub **Vogue** in Sānlǐtún, whose performance art events can occasionally be stomach-churning.

Try also the Cháng'ān Grand Theatre (Cháng'ān Dà Xìyuàn), Jiànguó Mén Nèi Dàjiē 7, next to the International Hotel, ✆ 6510 1309; the recently renovated Běijīng People's Art Theatre (Běijīng Rénmín Yìshù Jùyuàn), Wángfǔjǐng Dàjiē 22, ✆ 6305 4992, 6505 0123, just south of the Huáqiáo Dàshà; and the Běijīng Theatre (Běijīng Jùyuàn), A Qū 10, Ānhuì Běilǐ (Asian Games Village), ✆ 6491 0516 / 6491 1228.

rock, pop, jazz

Again, look for details in *City Weekend*, etc. Travelling to China for its rock music would be like travelling to London for its sunshine. Nevertheless, in the expat bar areas something pretending to be rock or similar is almost impossible to avoid, some of it in the form of spectacularly appalling Western bands with expat members. Much more interesting in general are Chinese attempts at heavy metal, punk, etc., whether or not you usually listen to this kind of thing. Cover charges or entrance fees vary between around ¥10 and ¥30.

For those desperate to escape from China, there are local bands every night except Sunday at the Hard Rock Café just south of the Lufthansa Centre on the northeast third ring road, and in a large number of restaurants and bars in Sānlǐtún (*see* Bars, *below*) and other expat-oriented venues. Try Jazz Ya, ✆ 6415 1227, in Sānlǐtún Jiǔbā Jiē; and Minder Café, ✆ 6500, Rider's Club and Bar, ✆ 6508 9439, Durty Nellie's Irish Pub, ✆ 6501 2808, and Jam House, ✆ 6506 3845, all in Sānlǐtún Nán Jiǔbā Jiē; the third branch of Schillers Bar at the west gate of Cháoyáng Gōngyuán, ✆ 6593-1078; and Keep in Touch, opposite the Lufthansa Centre, ✆ 6462 5280. There are dozens more. Also try the more studenty Busy Bee Bar in Xī Sì (*see* 'Theatre', *above*). For directions to Sānlǐtún, *see* 'Bars', *below*.

Try also the Wǔdàokǒu area, a grotty collection of clubs and bars with a mainly student clientele, but home to, amongst others, the **Scream Club**, ✆ 6234 7755, a small space with raw brick walls that feels like it should be a basement, where especially on Fridays Běijīng's thriving punk scene recreates with astonishing accuracy the 1977 it never knew, with sweaty, muscled guitarists screaming incomprehensible (even if you do speak Mandarin) over-amplified lyrics, and an equally sweaty pincushion-faced pogo-ing audience. Unlikely as it may seem, several of the bands which play here have issued CDs. Pick up a copy of a Xīn Kùzi (New Pants) album, at the more melodic end of punk, with song titles like 'Wǒ shì yí ge fúwùyuán' ('I'm a shop assistant'), and lyrics about not having a girlfriend. Quite brilliant. Take bus 375 from Xī Zhí Mén to stop Wǔdàokǒu Shāngchǎng and navigate south towards the noise. Also try Solutions Bar amongst a cluster opposite the west gate of Běijīng Dàxué, ✆ 6255 8877.

The restaurant-style nightclubs of the big hotels have Philippine you-name-it-we-can-play-it bands with easy listening repertoires, and they can also be found in some restaurants and bars with a (slightly) harder edged sound.

CD Café (CD Kāfēi Wū) on the east side of the east third ring north, a short walk south of the Agricultural Exhibition Centre, ℭ 6501 8877 ext 3032, is a small oblong room set back from the road behind a pedestrian bridge, with a yellow sign. Friday and Saturday night there's live jazz from what's claimed to be the best jazz band in Běijīng, although this is fairly trad in style. ¥20 admission at weekends; other nights when there's no music entrance is free. Cuī Jiàn, a trumpeter in a Běijīng orchestra whose switch to the guitar and a gravel-voiced repertoire of carefully worded protest songs made him China's first rock star and truly something of a hero, also sometimes plays here—he's not allowed to play anywhere much bigger. Open until 2am at weekends.

Internationally famous jazz bands appear at the Běijīng Concert Hall. Smaller, local outfits, some with expat members, and some foreign bands well-known to jazz enthusiasts appear at the **Big Easy** restaurant at the south gate of Cháoyáng Gōngyuán, ℭ 6508 6776, and in the China World Trade Centre branch of **Starbucks**, ℭ 6505 2288 ext 8122. The tea house above the Sanwei Bookstore has jazz every Friday night, *see* 'Chinese Traditional Music', above.

Larger concerts by the rare Western band or, more often, by Asian superstars such as Táiwān's Ā Mèi (locals say Ā Méi) or Běijīng's own Wáng Fēi (Faye Wong in HK where she records) take place in the Worker's Stadium. Corruption is rampant, and tickets change hands for as much as ¥1,000 ($125) each.

Exhibitions and Galleries

China National Art Gallery, east of Jǐng Shān Gōngyuán at the top of Wángfǔjǐng Dàjiē (*open 9–4, closed Mon, adm ¥4, annual ticket accepted*), has programmes of everything from book illustration and calligraphy to architecture and visiting exhibitions from abroad, on two storeys, in a building of mammoth ugliness. Details of exhibitions can be found in the English-language media, or by calling ℭ 6401 2252. **Gallery of the Central Academy of Fine Arts** (Zhōngyāng Měishù Xuéyuàn Huàláng), in Shuài Fǔ Yuán Hútòng just east of Wángfǔjǐng north of Oriental Plaza (*open 9.30–4, closed Mon; adm ¥2*), has exhibitions of work by its own students and visiting exhibitions, including those organized by the cultural promotion agencies of foreign countries. This gallery may move during the next few years.

The **Wan Fung Art Gallery** (Yúnfēng Huàyuàn) is a Hong Kong operation housed in the side halls of the Imperial Archive (*see* p.151) at Nán Chízi 136, (*open 9–5 inc. public holidays*), ℭ 6532 3320, *<http://www.wanfung.com.cn/>*. There are some exhibitions of foreign painters, but the gallery is mainly a medium for selling work created by Chinese to appeal to foreigners, rather than anything authentically Chinese—*hútòng* under snow, very literal portraits of ethnic minorities, a Chinese ballet dancer with the name Lǐ Xīxī ('Li hopes for the West'), for example. Prices are often in excess of $1,000. The **Hanmo Gallery** (Chūnxià Hànmò Huàláng) on the north side of Curio City on the east third ring, ℭ 6774 7711, is slightly more adventurous and less concerned with pleasing foreigners, but still often features an uneasy marriage of Western techniques and self-consciously Chinese subjects. **The Courtyard Gallery** (Sìhéyuán Huàláng) beneath the Courtyard Restaurant at Dōng Huá Mén Dàjiē 95, ℭ 6526 8882, is more cutting edge still, but still there's little that doesn't seem derivative of Western movements. There's a gallery called the **International Art Palace** with a varied programme inside the Holiday Inn Crowne Plaza in Wángfǔjǐng, and various commercial galleries with works for sale aimed mostly at the expat market, such as the Red Gate Gallery inside the China World Hotel, ✆ 6505 2266, and the Creation Gallery in the Rìtán diplomatic enclave at Rì Tán Dōng Yī Jiē.

Cinema

The box office record for China is held not by some soft focus account of heroism during the Long March, some politically correct propaganda on the moulding of the new post-Liberation society or even the latest sumptuously photographed Zhāng Yìmóu historical epic, but by *Titanic*. Two years after its release the theme tune was still being played repeatedly in shops, bars and restaurants. If you'd seen it in Běijīng, however, you would most likely have found it to be dubbed, as are most prints of the handful of foreign films permitted to reach the big screen each year, which range in style from *Saving Private Ryan* to *Notting Hill* (quite a big hit in its own right).

Cherry Lane shows Chinese films with English subtitles on alternate Fridays at the Sino-Japanese Youth Exchange Centre (Zhōng-Rì Qīngnián Jiāoliú Zhōngxīn), Liàngmǎ Qiáo Lù 40, ✆ 6466 3311.

If you want to experience a night at the cinema with a Běijīng crowd, easily accessible cinemas include the Capital Cinema (Shǒudū Diànyǐng Yuàn), Xī Cháng'ān Jiē 46, Ⓜ Xī Dān, ✆ 6605 7574; the Dìzhì Diànyǐng Yuàn, Yángròu Hútòng 30, Xī Sì, ✆ 6616 8376; and those in Lóngfú Shìchǎng just east of the top of Wángfǔjǐng. There's also an IMAX screen at the China Science and Technology Museum (call ✆ 6237 1177 for directions and details), French films at the Salle De Cinéma, Sānlǐtún Dōngsì Jiē 13, part of the French Embassy, ✆ 6532 1422, usually at 6.30pm.

Bars, Pubs, Cafés

The **Sānlǐtún** bar area, to the north and south of Gōngrén Tǐyù Běi Lù east of the Workers' Stadium, is the most notorious of the foreigner hangout areas. There's rarely trouble, but if anti-foreigner feeling is running high then the trouble will take place here, and occasionally male Chinese who come to gawp rather than just to enjoy the long string of bars find the sight of their womenfolk enjoying the company of foreign men too much to take. Sānlǐtún Nán Jiē, the northerly of the two main streets, has a long string of bars and cafés up its eastern side and a street market catering to foreign tastes up its western one. This street is always just about to close, but hasn't yet. One story is that the retired widows of senior cadres live in the area and object to the noise and all the foreignness. They are used to getting what they want, but the bar owners have what the officials now in power want—money, acquired from outrageous beer prices willingly paid by expats trying to forget for a while that they are in China.

Most bars sport tables and chairs outside, and the latest state of play between the bar owners and officials can be judged by whether these are actually out or have been banned (again). Rumour constantly has it that Sānlǐtún will be packed up, imported keg beers, uniformed short-skirted cigarette and beer promotion girls, plastic garden chairs and all to Cháoyáng Park (Gōngyuán), and dates are often set for the final move. A few institutions have moved, but new ones have opened to take their place, and the chances are you'll find both Sānlǐtún in full swing *and* fairly lively activity at Cháoyáng Park's south and west entrances when you arrive in Běijīng.

Sānlǐtún Jiǔbā Jiē and parallel alleys have a constant parade of slow moving taxis looking for fares, whereas the more labyrinthine area to the south, around Sānlǐtún Nán Jiǔbā Jiē, is a little quieter, although with larger interior spaces and more live music. Several of the bar-restaurant-pubs in this area are mentioned under 'Rock, pop, jazz' above. Simply walk up and down until you find one whose atmosphere appeals. The choice of imported beer and other drinks varies slightly, but the overpricing is fairly consistent from bar to bar.

Sānlǐtún is reached by a 20–25min walk east of ⓂDōng Sì Shí Tiáo, or by bus 113 from stop Dà Běi Yáo east of the China World Trade Centre to stop Sānlǐtún (the bar streets are just west of the stop). Cháoyáng Mén Gōngyuán is further east across the third ring road on Nóngzhǎn Guǎn Nán Lù and really needs a taxi, although the terminus of bus 43, stop Tuánjié Hú, is a short walk west of the park's south entrance.

Not surprisingly all the four- and five-star hotels have bars catering to the foreign palate and budget. The Paulauner Brauhaus inside the Kempinski Hotel brews excellent beers on site but at up to ¥80 ($10) a litre, plus 15%.

The foreign student and teacher population in the university quarter has spawned many strange bars, none more bizarre than **Bus Bar**, occasionally referred to as Gōnggòng Qìchē Jiǔbā, mostly open at weekends, 200m west of the Xuéyuàn Lù and fourth ring road junction in the northwest, ℰ 6207 1631, made from three sawn-up buses. Inside the dim interior painted fish tanks fluoresce in ultra-violet, and the music is early King Crimson and Black Sabbath, although whether this is calculatedly retro or a failure to catch up isn't clear. The lavatory is in the driving compartment of one bus, where a sign says 'no driving while shitting'. Take bus 902 from just outside ⓂXī Zhí Mén to stop Xuéyuàn Lù and walk east on the south side of the road. A little further north from that stop and west along Chéngfǔ Lù around the south entrance of the Language and Culture University (usually known as Běi Yǔ) there's another clutch of odd bars, cafés and small restaurants including Japanese and Korean ones, and even more interesting groups around the west and south gates of Běijīng University (Běi Dà). Bus 332 from the Zoo will take you to stop Běijīng Dàxué.

Starbucks Coffee (the Seattle-based mega-chain) opened its first store in Běijīng in early 1999 and has been expanding rapidly, with branches in China World Trade Centre (which has jazz some evenings), COFCO, Cháoyáng Mén Wài, Xī Dān, Kerry Centre, Sun Dong An and the Jiànguó Mén Friendship Store. Furnishings are identical to those in the West, but 'tall hazelnut latte to go and hold the whip' comes out interestingly mangled if that's all the English someone has. Prices are also Western—a small house coffee ¥9, expresso drinks more than double that, and muffins ¥18.

Nightclubs and Discos

Since the revolution, the Lambeth walk and the conga had become the two most popular Western dances in Peking, the non-Communist

population and foreigners hoping that they looked like the kind of
healthy, mass-participation dances of which the Communists would be
apt to approve.

David Kidd, *Peking Story,* 1996

The Communist Party didn't only interfere with dancing. As part of its propaganda drive to the peasants during its fight for control of China, the communist armies took the traditional folk tunes of the areas through which they passed, fitted them with new pro-communist lyrics and encouraged group singing, which it claimed once in power to be the authentic voice of modern China. The authentic voice of 21st century China is a solo one, over-amplified, often drunken and certainly out of tune, and it emerges from any building, bar or restaurant bearing the letters 'KTV' or 'OK' amongst the Chinese characters on its sign.

Many of Běijīng's hotels have nightclubs and discos featuring Filipino bands, or karaoke, or expensive hostesses, or all of these, and most of them are bland and avoidable if you are looking to experience China rather than an unidentifiable international atmosphere.

The real nightlife is beyond that, but very variable, and in a period of economic retrenchment sometimes deserted, even on a Saturday night. If after about 11pm there's not a long line of taxis waiting for emerging clients then you've hit a ghost night. Don't expect cutting edge music, or, if you get it, expect it to be mixed with last year's granny-friendly Benidorm hit, or a Chinese sound-alike.

D.D.'s, Dàhuá Lù A-2, Dōngdān, ✆ 6528 5989. Directly south of the centre of Oriental Plaza. Buried in the basement along a red corridor, this club has struggled to find a niche for itself, mixing comfortable seating and pool tables with loud music and occasional live bands. Sometimes packed, sometimes empty. ¥30 upwards to non-members.

Club Banana (Bānànà Jùlèbù), 5th floor, Seasky Shopping Centre (Hǎilányúntiān Gòuwù Shāngchéng), Cháoyáng Mén Wài Dàjiē 12, ✆ 6599 3351. Amusingly not a translation of *xiāngjiāo*, which is Mandarin for 'banana', but nonsense. Gimmicks vary, but recently the waitresses were all dressed in white dresses and wearing blonde wigs. Free for foreigners on Friday and Saturday nights, otherwise ¥80 ($10). The coolest club in Běijīng until something else opens, which it will have done by the time you get there.

The Loft (Zàng Kù), Gōngrén Tǐyù Cháng Běi Lù 4 (look for signs on south side of street), ✆ 6501 7501, is a large but convincingly Western restaurant-cum-club with a high-tech interior and heavy-duty dancing at weekends, sometimes with imported European DJs. Dull food, watery drinks (stick to beer and wine) but impressive atmosphere.

Look in the local papers to see if NASA Disco and Nightman are still functioning. Avoid the disco at the Táiwān Hotel in Jīnyú Hútòng—¥100 up to enter, and always someone to take home, for a price. There are lively night clubs at the Sheraton Great Wall and Holiday Inn Lido, but some pick-up activities here too. If you really prefer to mix with local people, Hot Spot Disco on the east third ring just south of Cháoyáng Lù is almost entirely Chinese.

Around Běijīng

Day Trips and Overnight Stays

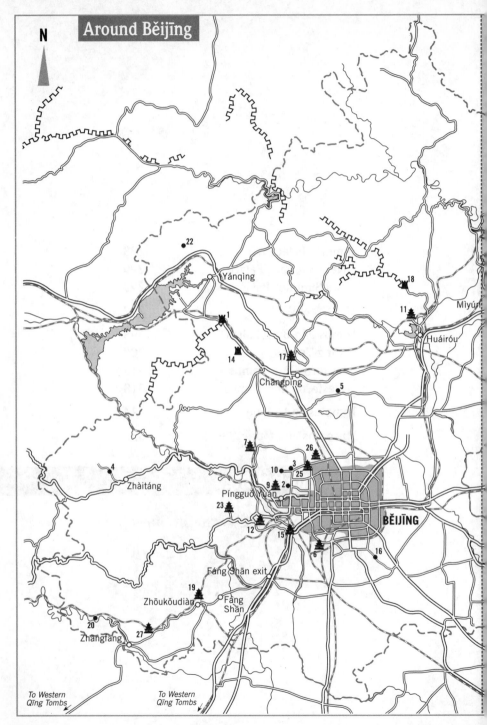

Around Běijīng

N

22

Yánqìng

18

11

Mìyún

1

Huáiróu

14

17

Chángpíng

5

7

26

4

10   3

25

Zhàitáng

9   2

Píngguǒ Yuán

23

12

15

BĚIJĪNG

6

16

Fáng Shān exit

19

Zhōukǒudiàn

Fáng
Shān

20

Zhāngfāng   27

To Western
Qīng Tombs

To Western
Qīng Tombs

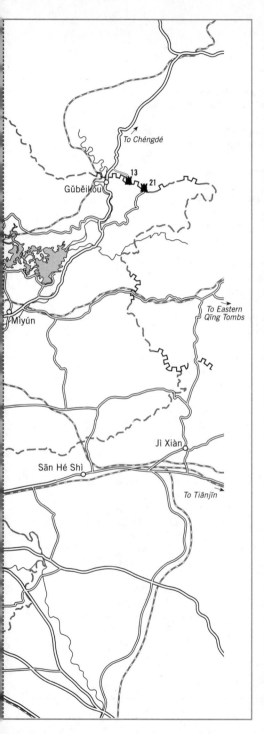

To Chéngdé

Gǔběikǒu 13 21

Mìyún

To Eastern
Qīng Tombs

Jì Xiàn

Sān Hé Shì

To Tiānjīn

Until only a few years ago, almost the only viable day trip from Běijīng was a circular route taken by almost everyone, including visiting heads of state, to the Great Wall at Bā Dá Lǐng, and on to the Shísān Líng, or Míng Tombs, and that was slow and uncomfortable. A day's travel by bus in any other direction would have got you almost nowhere, and there seemed to be nowhere else to go anyway. The Chinese themselves had neither the interest nor the resources nor the permission to go on trips out of their own towns, and the expression 'spring travel' referred to a single day out of the immediate neighbourhood arranged especially for high school and university students.

The recent construction of freeways from Běijīng to other parts of the country and of decent highways to urban areas has caused a rapid opening of tourist facilities in the region around Běijīng. Many new sections of the Great Wall have become suddenly accessible to the casual visitor, and almost forgotten temples have smartened themselves up for a surge of arrivals on cheap and convenient bus tours with departure points all over Běijīng.

But the countryside has also been blighted by the construction of garish funfairs and theme parks (*lè yuán*) designed to draw Beijingers and some of their new-found discretionary spending power. To your right as you speed up the Bā Dá Lǐng Freeway, for instance, you'll see a partly built castle, a Chinese version of a confectionary Disneyland construction, shockingly out of place and destined never to be completed. It's just one example of a rash of several hundred theme parks thrown up in the late '90s, almost all of

八达岭	1	Bā Dá Lǐng
八大处	2	Bā Dà Chù (The Eight Great Sites)
北京植物园	3	Běijīng Botanical Gardens (Běijīng Zhíwù Yuán)
川底下	4	Chuán Dǐxià
中国航空博物馆	5	China Aviation Museum (Zhōngguó Hángkōng Bówùguǎn)
大葆台汉墓	6	Dàbǎotái Hàn Mù (Western Hàn Tomb)
大觉寺	7	Dà Jué Sì
清东陵	8	Eastern Qīng Tombs (Qīng Dōng Líng)
法海寺	9	Fǎ Hǎi Sì
香山公园	10	Fragrant Hills (Xiāng Shān Gōngyuán)
红螺寺	11	Hóngluó Sì
戒台寺	12	Jiètái Sì (Ordination Terrace Temple)
金山岭	13	Jīn Shān Lǐng
居庸关	14	Jūyōng Guān
卢沟桥，宛平城	15	Marco Polo Bridge (Lúgōu Qiáo), Wǎnpíng Chéng
麋鹿苑	16	Mílù Yuàn (Mílù Deer Park)
十三陵	17	Míng Tombs (Shísān Líng)
慕田峪	18	Mùtiányù
北京猿人遗址	19	Peking Man Site (Běijīng Yuánrén Yízhǐ)
十渡	20	Shí Dù (Ten Crossings)
司马台	21	Sīmǎtái
松山古崖居	22	Sōng Shān Ancient Cave Dwellings (Sōng Shān Gǔ Yá Jū)
潭柘寺	23	Tánzhè Sì (Temple of the Pool and Mulberries)
清西陵	24	Western Qing Tombs (Qīng Xī Líng)
颐和园	25	Yíhé Yuán ('New Summer Palace')
圆明园	26	Yuánmíng Yuán ('Old Summer Palace')
云居寺	27	Yúnjū Sì

Extra Navigational Help

昌平	Chāngpíng	堡子店	Pǔzidiàn
房山	Fáng Shān	三河市	Sān Hé Shì
高碑店	Gāo Bēi Diàn	世界公园	Shìjiè Gōngyuán
古北口	Gǔběikǒu	四合古宅客栈	Sìhé Gǔzhái Kèzhàn
怀柔	Huáiróu	卧佛寺	Wòfú Sì
黄草梁	Huáng Cǎo Liáng	兴隆	Xīnglōng
京爨饭店	Jīng Cuàn Fàndiàn	延庆	Yánqìng
九坟	Jiǔfén	易县	Yìxiàn
旧宫	Jiùgōng	斋堂	Zhàitáng
蓟县	Jì Xiàn	张坊	Zhāngfāng
卢沟桥史料阵列馆	Lúgōu Qiáo Shǐliào Zhèn Liè Guǎn	詹天佑纪念馆	Zhān Tiānyòu Jìniànguǎn
马兰峪	Mǎlányù	周家乡	Zhōujiāxiāng
密云	Mìyún	周口店	Zhōukǒudiàn
模式口	Móshì Kǒu	遵化	Zūnhuà
苹果园	Píngguǒ Yuán		

which failed either before or shortly after opening due to unrealistic expectation of public demand being met by vast public indifference. Meanwhile many of the highway projects suffered from similarly poor planning. The same Bā Dá Lǐng Freeway, opened in 1996, has to pay off ¥4 billion (roughly $0.5 billion) within 30 years, but during its first few years of operation was only collecting about ¥150 million per annum in tolls, not even enough to keep up with the interest charges on the loan. Its response was to cut the numbers of discount passes available to the newly created commuting class, who responded with loud protests and by avoiding the freeway altogether, clogging the side roads and reducing toll income yet further.

The rise in the numbers of privately owned cars and in the numbers of cadres borrowing the work unit's vehicles for the weekend has produced a Friday evening rush on the roads out of Běijīng, and similar congestion on the way back on Sundays. As keen to avoid the crowds as everyone else, they head for undisturbed scenic spots not on the bus tour routes and disturb them by discarding mineral water bottles, film canisters and plastic sausage skins. But no area attracting day- or weekend-trippers is left unenclosed for long, and soon a ticket booth appears, followed by mineral water sellers, food and souvenir stalls, and a funfair.

Destinations promoted simply for their scenery are largely ignored in this guide since from the point of view of outsiders these have been despoiled—see the details of Shí Dù, p.334, for example, an area of gorges now full of firework throwers and bungee jumpers. Those wanting peaceful scenery are best simply to set off on foot from one of the Great Wall sites, or from temples in leafy locations, such as the Tánzhè Sì, Jiétài Sì, or Dàjué Sì.

Long-distance, surburban, and tour buses are increasingly comfortable, and many of the destinations mentioned below are served by no-frills Chinese tours which are well within reach of budget travellers. Even cheaper public bus alternatives are also given where possible.

If chartering a taxi for the day, the final price should be considerably less than the number of kilometres times the kilometre rate. There are too many taxis, and most spend much of the day driving round with no one in them. A day trip out of Běijīng is a treat for the driver, and will represent a substantial increase in takings over his normal day. When taking taxis around town, if you discover a driver who seems safe and agreeable, take a business card from the pocket on the grille separating him from the front passenger and try asking for a quote for a one-day hire if you have a Mandarin speaker to hand, or think ahead and have the characters for your chosen destinations written down to show him. Do this with taxis you've flagged down in the street, and not with those that cluster outside the big hotels.

If not, then find a helpful receptionist or student and begin negotiations by phone for a day in the future. While some taxi drivers are owner-operators, others rent their vehicles and the owners may have the final say on out-of-town trips. Also remember to deal with *all* the fine print at the time of negotiation. The first priority of any driver, once you are on the road, will be to begin re-negotiations on the grounds of some supposed slight difference from what he expected. You should be clear on: pick-up point and time of collection (and be prompt yourself), on destinations and the order in which they are to be visited, and on drop-off point. If you are unsure of the number of kilometres or the distance, do not under any circumstances be specific as the slightest deviation will be the basis for renegotiation. Unless the destination chosen is particularly popular it's very unlikely that the driver will have been there before and, given the vagueness of Chinese road signs, there's a good chance you'll have to double back once or twice. Be clear who is to pay road tolls (usually about ¥10 to ¥20 each time, and few trips are without about four tolls to pay). Eating on time and eating properly matter a lot to the Chinese, and an offer to pay for lunch is a good bargaining tool, especially right at the end to clinch negotiations.

Summer Palaces

The suburbs of Peking are very extensive. We were fifteen minutes from our entering the east suburb to the east gate. We were above two hours in our progress through the city, fifteen minutes from the west gate to the end of the west suburb and two hours from thence to Yuan-ming Yuan. The house at this last place alloted for our habitation consists of several small courts and separate pavilions, and is situated in a little park or garden, laid out in the Chinese manner with serpentine walks, a narrow winding river forming an island with a summer-house in the middle of it, a grove of various trees interspersed with a few patches of grassy ground diversified with inequalities and roughed with rocks, the whole surrounded with a high wall and guarded by a detachment of troops at the gate. Some of the apartments are large, handsome, and not ill-contrived, but the whole building is so much out of repair that I already see it will be impossible to reside in it comfortably during the winter. It appears, indeed, to be only calculated for a summer dwelling, though I understand it is the best of the hotels at this place destined (as several more are) for the reception of foreign ambassadors.

Lord Macartney, *An Embassy to China,*
J. L. Cranmer-Byng [Ed.], 1962

Macartney was particularly proud of the sprung carriages in which his party rode from Běijīng to Chéngdé) during his 1793–4 embassy to the Qiánlóng emperor and imagined that they would be widely copied when left behind, but foreign residents in the 1940s were still complaining about the bone-shattering effects of the springless Peking cart. The invention of the internal combustion engine having also led to the the creation of traffic jams, it can still take an hour to get out to the site of the pavilions Macartney describes.

There are now two summer palaces to the northwest of Běijīng, about 10km from the centre, one of which is usually known as the New Summer Palace, and the other as the Old Summer

Palace, neither to be confused with the Summer Resort at Chéngdé, considerably further out to the northeast (*see* p.373). The 'new' palace is visited by almost everyone who reaches Běijīng, and the 'old' by very few.

The 'new' Summer Palace had its foundation during the pre-Mongol Jīn dynasty as a stopping place for travelling emperors around 1153. During the Yuán dynasty (1279–1368), the efforts of the hydrologist Guō Shǒujìng (*see* p.177) to bring water supplies to Běijīng included improving the lake, and the area was prettily cultivated during the Míng (1368–1644) with further imperial palaces established, then considerably redeveloped and expanded by the Kāngxī emperor (1749–64) in celebration of his mother's 60th birthday (as were parts of Chéngdé), and renamed **Yíhé Yuán**, or Garden of the Preservation of Harmony. It was one park in a large area of parks and gardens belonging to Qīng princes, and considerably predated the 'old' Summer Palace of **Yuánmíng Yuán**, the Garden of the Perfect Brightness. This general name is given to a group of three Qīng gardens built from 1709, the Yuánmíng Yuán eventually absorbing the other two, the Qǐ Chūn Yuán (Garden of Gorgeous Spring) and Cháng Chūn Yuán (Garden of Eternal Spring). By the time of the Qiánlóng emperor, this was one of the most extensive areas of palaces and parklands in the world, and was compared to Versailles, although as Macartney pointed out, already fading in grandeur. His accommodation was not suitable for winter because the court had decided even before his embassy arrived to reject its requests, and in particular not to permit the embassy to leave a permanent representative in the capital.

Modern misconceptions of the differing antiquity of the two park areas, and their relative importance, is due to the rather substantial drop in grandeur brought about by Anglo-French military forces during their occupation of Běijīng in 1860. They looted most of the treasures, set fire to what would burn and pulled down what wouldn't. And that, as far as the Chinese authorities are concerned, is all you or visitors to the two sites need to know, and signs constantly bring it to your attention.

There is, of course, more to the story. Whether appropriate or not, the troops' destruction of the Summer Palace on the orders of Lord Elgin was intended to punish the dynasty for the execution and imprisonment of foreign envoys who had been sent to Běijīng to complete the implementation of the Treaty of Tiānjīn, forced on China at the end of the Arrow War in 1858.

It was China as a whole that suffered as the Empress Dowager Cíxī spent vast amounts of her country's limited funds to rebuild the southwestern section where destruction had been less complete, now the 'new' Summer Palace, including money that should have been spent on a modern navy, and this suborning of the national interest to her own personal tastes is regarded as a major betrayal, while providing a handy face-saving excuse for China's defeat at the hands of the upstart Japanese in the Sino-Japanese war of 1895. She was sensitive enough, perhaps, to write an edict in the name of the Guǎngxù emperor saying that he was undertaking the repairs out of gratitude to her, and have him sign it, but no one was fooled. Popular opinion in subsequent years had it that even if the navy had been built it would certainly have been sunk on its first engagement.

Further punishment was inflicted on the Qīng following the relief of the Siege of the Legations, and Cíxī's investment in rebuilding was once again lost to the flames. Finding, probably to her astonishment, that the Qīng were to be left in control of the country, she set about rebuilding the same section again once she returned to Běijīng from exile in Xī'ān, completing its reconstruction in 1902. Meanwhile the Yuánmíng Yuán, the 'old' Summer Palace, was abandoned, and much of it went back under the plough, while peasants carted away useful portions of the remains for their own building purposes. The 'new' Summer Palace is new because it's been twice rebuilt, and the 'old' one is old because it hasn't.

Yíhé Yuán (New Summer Palace)

Open 8.30–4.45, adm ¥25 ($3).

颐和园 The ¥25 ticket is a *tào piào*, which includes access to the Tower of the Fragrance of Buddha (the main tower dominating the site), Sūzhōu Street (where the imperial family and eunuchs would play at shopping and shopkeepers, recreated for the purposes of modern commerce), and the Garden of Virtue and Harmony (Cíxī's theatre), and the opening hours above refer to these. The site itself can also be entered with a cheaper *mén piào* and stays open until dusk.

There are three Palace Gates: the main one in the east, the 'new' gate a little way south, and the north gate. Most buses arrive and depart at the main east gate, most usefully the 332 from outside the Zoo and the 375 from outside Ⓜ Xī Zhí Mén, ¥3 or less. The 375 passes the 'Old Summer Palace' en route.

For a change of pace, rather greater comfort and an escape from Běijīng's crawling traffic, a better alternative (albeit considerably more expensive) is now to travel **by boat** up the extensively refurbished canal system, a method often chosen by the emperors and Cíxī herself. She would have left from the dock now called Běi Zhǎn Hòu Hú Mǎtou, off Gāoliang Qiáo Lù after the bridge (traditionally a popular suicide spot) and behind the Zoo. There are two departures from there (route B) and seven a day from Bāyī Hú (route A), a broadening of the Yǒngdìng River in Yùyuān Tán Park behind the Chinese People's Revolutionary Army Museum (*see* p.211). Boats run from mid-March to mid-November (in between the waterways may be frozen) and on either route in either direction the cost is ¥50 one-way, ¥90 return (you must say on which boat you plan to come back). You are given two tickets, one of which has a map of your route and the other your seat number, although these are widely ignored. Boats arrive at a dock at the far southeastern corner of the Summer Palace within sight of an elegant camel-backed bridge.

The number of sailings per day will no doubt increase, and additional embarkation points en route are under construction, including at Zhōngyāng Diànshì Tǎ (south of the TV tower on Xī Sān Huán Zhōng Lù), Bīnjiǎo Yuán (a park, and junction with another west-flowing waterway) and Cháng Hé Wān (at the junction of the two routes). There will probably soon be cheaper commuter services as well as boats with beverages, snacks and karaoke; and as work continues on refurbishing the canals, rivers and former moats elsewhere in the city, perhaps extensive boat travel will eventually be possible.

This collection of halls, pavilions and temples beside the large Kūnmíng Hú (lake), overlooked by Wànshòu Shān (Longevity Hill), was a favourite haunt of the Dowager Empress Cíxī, who preferred it to the Forbidden City, and named it Yíhé Yuán (roughly 'Garden of Health and Harmony'), following its reconstruction in 1888. Earlier Qīng emperors had favoured Chéngdé for the summer, or ruled from the far more extensive Yuánmíng Yuán, but Cíxī conducted affairs of state in the name of the hapless Guāngxù emperor from here for most of the year.

The densest group of buildings is around the east gate, many of them relatively simple single-storey structures and considerably less grand than the halls of the Forbidden City. There are several impressive bronzes in their forecourts, but their contents can often only be seen by peering through smeared glass at gloomy interiors. The **Hall of Happiness and Longevity** was Cíxǐ's residence, first built in 1750 and rebuilt in 1887. You can peer through the doors from a distance to see dark, late-Qīng furniture, in theory left as Cíxǐ had it when the Summer Palace was closed up after her death. Behind, the **Hall of Jade Billows** was the imperial accommodation and, after the coup against the Guāngxù emperor, was his prison whenever the court moved to the Summer Palace. The **Garden of Virtue and Harmony** (adm ¥5 if you don't have the *tào piào*) is a splendid three-storey theatre building echoing the Forbidden City's Pavilion of Pleasant Sounds and where Cíxǐ indulged her love of Běijīng opera in the summer, reportedly maintaining a troupe of 300 performers. The surrounding galleries are now used for exhibiting a variety of articles in everyday use during the Qīng, elaborate gowns and shoes, and photographs of Cíxǐ wearing similar items. Even the *fúwùyuán* are dressed in mock-Qīng style, too, though they look fairly mournful about it. On the way to the stage you pass through a room with a superb old car, horsedrawn vehicles and other bric-à-brac, and the western verandah has an exhibition of particularly vile glassware, similar to that on display at the mountain resort at Chéngdé (*see* p.373).

Preceding west you enter the aptly named **Long Corridor** of 1750, rebuilt 1885, which zig-zags along the northern shore for 728m, its course occasionally broken up by pavilions. Being able to walk the entire length is rare since every beam is painted with a landscape or other scene, said to number 8,000 in all. As soon as touching up the artwork is completed it needs to be started again. The passage will bring you to what is perhaps Cíxǐ's most lasting monument. Having spent the naval funds on her repairs, perhaps what little conscience she had led her to open a token school for naval officers, and perhaps a taste for irony led her to create the **Boat of Purity and Ease** (or Boat for Pure Banquets according to one Chinese guide). The hull-shaped base had already been carved from an offshore rock, and Cíxǐ added the ornate two-storey marble superstructure. The neighbouring **Pavilion for Listening to Orioles** is fine, and the café is good for snacks during the day, but its lacklustre dining room is one of those open-too-long and overrated restaurants, now mainly visited by tour groups.

On your way to the boat you pass the **Cloud Dispelling Hall**, at the base of **Longevity Hill**, which was artificially raised in height at the time of the Qiánlóng emperor's improvements to the site. Here was the throne room, and while the regency was in place Cíxǐ sat behind a screen, but after she had deposed the Guāngxù emperor she sat on the yellow silk-covered throne herself.

A steep climb brings you to the terrace in front of the fat octagonal four-storey, red-pillared, yellow- and green-tiled **Tower of Buddhist Fragrance** (¥10 without the *tào piào*), its beams a riot of blue gold and green and the whole thing topped with a giant yellow knob. The views from the terrace over the sweeping yellow roofs below recall in miniature those from Jǐng Shān Gōngyuán over the Forbidden City. Across the lake the Seventeen-Arch Bridge looks particularly elegant, and distant pagodas still top hillside spurs. Inside the pagoda there are ceramic Buddhas in niches and a single large seated figure in front of which the devout leave money and peaches. Other buildings of interest at this level include the **Bronze Pavilion** similar to that at Wǔtái Shān, which copies those of wooden construction in minute detail but entirely in metal. Dating from 1750, it is one of the few parts of the palace to survive the Anglo-French destruction, although there was an attempt by the Japanese to export it in 1945. The magnificent brick, stone and tile **Cloud Dispelling Hall**, above, is also largely original, although the statuary inside isn't, and the hundreds of green- and yellow-tiled Buddhas which stud its surface are in many cases headless, the Anglo-French forces having used them for target practice. There's a view down on the north side to the north gate and the garish McDonald's just outside it, as well as to **Sūzhōu Jiē**, a recently reconstructed series of shops around the edge of the slender Back Lake, where the illusion of being normal people would be created for members of the Imperial family, the eunuchs performing as shopkeepers and pickpockets (and being punished if caught). Visitors are now supposed to be able to sample the life of the emperors by paying to visit the street, and paying again for overpriced souvenirs from men and women in period costume.

Gate of Good Luck

 Although the north was usually viewed as the direction of ill-omen, according to some traditional accounts, Běijīng's good luck flows in from the Western Hills through the north gate of the palace, and then out through the main gate on its way to the city. When the Manchus fell, the north gate was shut and Běijīng went into decline, losing its capital status to Nánjīng. In 1948 the palace administration opened the gate again, which was timely for the communists, who took the city early in 1949, then announced the formation of the People's Republic and the re-establishment of Běijīng as the national capital.

In exchange for giving English lessons to the Palace's director, the American David Kidd was given rooms over the dilapidated north gate, formerly a haunt of the Qiánlóng emperor's mother, and as part of the process of refurbishment the gate was unsealed from 40 years of disuse and reopened to the public. Members of the Chinese family into which Kidd had married suspected he had therefore allowed the good luck to flow to the communists. 'The fate of Peking determined by a foreigner!' cried one in horror. 'The fate of all China ordained by my nephew-in-law!'

Most visitors take a ferry from the marble boat across to near the Seventeen-Arch Bridge, but following the rim of the lake past the old boathouse and along the west dyke which bisects it takes you on a peaceful walk past various pavilions and over several bridges to the southeast corner, and you can then walk up the eastern shore to the bridge. To view the whole site and take this long promenade will take a good half day.

The graceful **Seventeen-Arch Bridge** crosses to a small island housing the temple of the Dragon King, a water-controlling deity. Like the Marco Polo Bridge (*see* p.336), the carved lions on the balustrades are all supposed to be individual. At the eastern end of the bridge is an octagonal pavilion housing stelae with Qiánlóng's poetry, and just to the north is a **bronze ox** dating from Qiánlóng's expansion of the site, there to suppress river dragons. At the urging of their parents, urchins clamber over the railing there to protect the life-size beast and sit on its shiny back for photographs. Between here and the main entrance there was once a maelstrom of pedalos and other leisure craft, ice-cream stalls, electronic rifle ranges and other amusements, which were mercifully suppressed before the UNESCO inspectors came and the site was added to the World Heritage list in 1998. On your way back to the main gate you also pass the tomb of a descendant of the Khitan Mongol Liào dynasty, who was an adviser on Chinese matters to Genghis Khan.

Construction and Corruption

In 1913 Yuán Shìkǎi, then President of the Republic, already secretly planning the attempt to enthrone himself as emperor which was to come two years later, suggested the court should move itself permanently to the Summer Palace. The court resisted on the grounds that the perimeter wall was too low for security, and Yuán offered to have it raised by about three feet, but at the expense of the imperial household rather than the state purse. The real source of resistance to the move was in fact the Imperial Household Department, which would lose most of its source of squeeze once the maintenance of the numerous palaces of the Forbidden City slipped from its grasp.

However, it also saw the profit to be made by increasing the height of the wall, and set about doing so at immense cost to the imperial coffers and immense benefit to itself. It accepted bids for expensive materials and workmanship but oversaw the use of the shoddiest materials and cheapest methods in a direct parallel to practices which continue with bridge, dam, public building and road construction to this day. Once referred to by Premier Zhū Róngjī as 'tofu' or 'tofu dregs' projects, Communist Party cadres siphon public funds to build houses for themselves and buy cars for their own enjoyment while the use of poor materials leads to collapses which kill the people the cadres are supposed to serve. When this happens, whether or not the Party cadres are punished rather depends on their connections.

Yuán Shìkǎi, fearing that some of his own supporters nevertheless expected him to honour the Republic's promise to protect the imperial household, eventually relented, and the move never took place.

The imperial tutor Reginald Johnston encouraged the start of reforms of the Imperial Household Department in 1923, and advocated that the court should take the initiative to move to the Summer Palace so that its continued occupation of the Forbidden City could not be used as an excuse by radicals for the abrogation of the agreement between the imperial family and the Republic. He found himself appointed Warden of the Summer Palace and discovered that the additional construction ordered earlier had often done considerable damage, and that sections of the perimeter collapsed whenever it rained. Commissioning fresh repair work, he was directed to two contractors in a neighbouring village who always handled work at the Palace. Their tenders received approval from the rest of the staff, but when Johnston obtained sealed bids from contractors in Běijīng he was able to get the work done for one seventh of the cost.

Yuánmíng Yuán (Old Summer Palace)

Open 8.30–5; adm ¥15 ($2).

The palace can be reached by the 810 a/c bus from the north gate of the Forbidden City (¥6), or by bus 375 from Ⓜ Xī Zhí Mén or the Yíhé Yuán.

This place is truly an Imperial residence; the park is said to to be eighteen miles round, and laid out in all the taste, variety, and magnificence which distinguish the rural scenery of Chinese gardening. There is no one very extensive contiguous bulding but several hundreds of pavilions scattered through the grounds and all connected together by close arbors, by passages apparently cut through stupendous rocks, or by fairy land galleries, emerging or receding in the perspective, and so contrived as to conceal the real design of communication and yet contribute to the general purpose and effect intended to arise from the whole. The various beauties of the spot, its lakes and river, together with its superb edifices, which I saw (and yet I saw but a very small part), so strongly impresssed my mind at this moment that I feel incapable of describing them.

Lord Macartney, *An Embassy to China,*
J. L. Cranmer-Byng [Ed.], 1962

Of palaces and pavilions, of formal and landscape gardens, nothing remains now but a dust-heap, in which the small children of neighbouring farmers play, throwing large stones at the few plumed helmets that remain, and battering at the balusters of a marble bridge—as I saw them doing during my first visit to the site—for the sheer joy of the thing, with a ram they had made of wood.

Osbert Sitwell, *Escape with Me!*, 1939

Although both the Yuánmíng Yuán and the Yíhé Yuán palaces were destroyed by British and French troops during the occupation of Běijīng in 1860, the 'old' palace went swiftly back under the plough, and there are now only a few remains of what George Kates called 'Européenerie'—neo-Baroque buildings of stone and Chinese glazed tile, built by the Jesuits at the request of Qiánlóng, but which make the otherwise rather sad site well worth visiting.

The Jesuit painter Attiret said that the Kāngxī emperor, on seeing plans of European houses of several storeys, remarked, 'Europe must be a very small country, and very wretched, if there is not enough land to extend the city and people have to live in the air.' His grandson clearly had a more modern outlook, for in addition to the vast area of Chinese gardens and pavilions already constructed by Kāngxī he employed two Jesuits, Benoist and Castiglione (another painter), to design and supervise the construction of buildings for him in the north of the Cháng Chūn Yuán (Garden of Eternal Spring), which occupies the northeast corner of the site.

The main entrance, where buses drop you, is on the south side of the Qǐ Chūn Yuán (Garden of Gorgeous Spring), which is itself the southernmost extant part of the site. To reach the ruins you pass an 'animal world,' 'world primitive totem galacy' (*sic*), lakes fouled with algae and refuse, others with animal-headed rowing boats, optimistic anglers with primitive equipment, electronic rifle ranges, dodgems, a go kart track (what for?—just drive in the street) and build-ings which you mistake for temples but which turn out to be souvenir shops, restaurants or snack bars. The route is a complicated meander but made possible by frequent path-side maps, and not as far as it appears.

The extensive ruins are unlike anything else in China—pieces for life-sized models of Sinicized Italian Baroque buildings lying in heaps like a 3D jigsaw puzzle freshly emptied from the box, waiting to be assembled into a reduced-scale oriental Versailles, to which the Jesuits compared their work. Benoist (despite swearing to his lack of ability) was asked to design complicated series of fountains which played amongst several palaces, pavilions, kiosks, music rooms, a theatre, an orangery, an aviary and a maze. One of the fountains had statues of the 12 Chinese zodiac signs each in turn spouting a jet of water for two hours, so that it also functioned as a clock. The bronze heads of a monkey, ox and tiger from the fountain turned up in auctions at Sotheby's and Christie's in April and May 2000. When threats from the Chinese government failed to halt the sale, a company with connections to the PLA paid $4.01 million to acquire the pieces, which will eventually by put on display in Běijīng.

The larger ruins have adjacent models showing quite how extravagant they were. The decorative style of mid 18th-century Europe was executed by Chinese craftsmen who knew nothing of it at all and introduced mutations of style and proportion; there was considerable use of the glazed tile beloved of Chinese on top of European classical detail.

According to the signs at the site, one building was a mosque, supposedly built for Qiánlóng's concubine, the Xiāng Fēi or 'Fragrant Concubine', traditionally his favourite (and buried with him at the Eastern Qīng Tombs, see p.313). This was supposed to soothe the homesick woman (for whom Qiánlóng supposedly built several follies around Běijīng, including one only pulled down in modern times at the Zhōng Nán Hǎi). Had she been from Paris this might have worked, but she was of the Turki Uighur people from Xīnjiāng in the far northwest of the Qīng empire. In the unlikely event the Jesuits actually built a mosque they failed to record it, and this was probably the theatre in which animated scenery reproduced (according to one source) the landscape around Aksu in Xīnjiāng, although her home is mostly given as being Kashgar (which also claims to have her tomb).

The boxwood maze, all the rage in Europe at the time, has been reconstructed in stone (so its Chinese name, Maze of Myriad Flowers, now seems odd) with walls about four feet high, so cheating is easy. Nevertheless it's full of Chinese shouting to each other from different parts of the maze and saying 'Where's your mother got to?' At the mid-autumn festival the emperor sat in the pavilion at the centre, and the princesses ran around trying to reach him carrying lotus lanterns made of yellow silk, the winner receiving a reward. Presumably the maze was harder in the dark.

In the site's museum there are prints of the illustrations of the work the Jesuits made at the time, and it's possible to see from early photographs that even after the troops had done their work in 1860 the buildings were substantially more intact than they are now. There's a large relief map of the whole site, and some charred beams on display, perhaps from the original conflagration.

Architecture and Xenophobia

In a letter dated 25 November 1861 (of which there's a copy in the site museum) Victor Hugo compared the Summer Palace *en orient* to the Parthenon, the pyramids, the Coliseum and Nôtre-Dame de Paris. 'Cette merveille,' he put it simply, 'a disparu.' According to him two bandits were responsible, one called England and one called France. This tune is played again and again by the signage at both Summer Palaces, and particularly loudly at the Yuánmíng Yuán, which is maintained, as one guide chillingly puts it, as a 'site for the education of patriotism for youngsters', but which might just as well be called a 'site for the encouragement of xenophobia'.

The rabble-rousing begins at the entrance, with the national anthem displayed (in Western musical notation) and the signs full of '*wǒ guó*'—our country's—this, that and the other, continues with constant reminders of who destroyed the place originally ('Do not forget the humiliation'), and climaxes with a bronze urn set up near the ruins of the 'foreign' buildings to celebrate the return of Hong Kong to Chinese rule, seen as wiping out 'a century of humiliation'. Foreign visitors have occasionally been accosted by angry Chinese asking, 'Which country are you from? Well, are you happy with what you did?' as if anyone of European origin could be held responsible for actions committed by a tiny number of Europeans more than 100 years before they were born.

There have been suggestions from members of the Běijīng Communist Party and Chinese historians of the Qīng that the site should be restored as an education in China's 18th-century greatness, countered by others that the country should not be allowed to forget that it was once so weak that foreigners could set fire to the imperial palaces. Chinese logic in these matters is completely unidirectional, and Chinese memory singularly selective.

It seems from Macartney's account that even in Qiánlóng's time the palaces weren't being looked after, and the Chinese actively contributed to the continuing destruction of the site after 1860, didn't even open the remainder to the public until the late 1980s, and they certainly don't look after the place now either. During 1999 more than a thousand people living illegally on the site were ejected as part of the pre-1 October clean-up of Běijīng.

No mention is made of the reason why the foreign troops were in Běijīng—to gain the release of some of their envoys and avenge the murder of others—and given that the Chinese response to the deaths of their own envoys in Yugoslavia was to smash up the US, British and Albanian embassies, it seems that what they condemn others doing in 1860 is still perfectly valid for them to do in 1999. While there were no deaths, the events echoed eerily those of 1900 when Chinese boxers and Qīng troops jointly attacked the Legation Quarter with the aim of murdering every foreigner and foreign sympathiser in Běijīng—events which themselves led to the second firing of the Yíhé Yuán, not that that's ever mentioned at the site either. In neither 1860 nor 1900 did the Chinese sit idly by after foreign forces entered the city, but joined in the looting with gusto. In the case of the Yuánmíng Yuán they stripped and sold the lead from the fountains, chopped down the trees for firewood, smashed up the marble columns to get at the iron clamps inside, and carried off stone, brick and tile for their own building purposes.

While the Chinese-style buildings at the Yuánmíng Yuán were far more extensive than those built by the Jesuits, the Chinese choose to forget that all were built on the instruction of foreigners—the Manchu Qīng who had taken control of China in 1644, and who forced all male Chinese to shave their foreheads and wear their hair in a long pigtail as a perpetual reminder of their subjugation. The greatness they want to celebrate was actually that of the foreign rulers of the Great Qīng Empire as the territory was referred to rather than 'China'. When the foreigners attacked it was during a 350-year period in which the Chinese were merely onlookers in their own affairs. If they insist on talking about humiliation, surely having their country under the complete subjugation of foreigners right into modern times would be something to lament, rather than one particular instance of vandalism. They might also note that while the foreign ships were on their way round the coast to Tiānjīn, Chinese residents of coastal ports were happy to sell them supplies.

And on cultural vandalism the Chinese memory is also very selective. At the time of the Boxer Rebellion they set fire themselves to the greatest library in Asia, and in living memory the Great Leap Forward and Cultural Revolution campaigns have aimed at the complete smashing of 'old things', and immeasurable quantities of priceless art were destroyed, along with temples, city walls and monuments galore (not to mention tens of thousands of lives). Indeed, foreigners have often seemed far more concerned to preserve Chinese culture than the Chinese. But they are quick to excuse themselves: 'We had to build a ring road, so the city wall had to go.' And on the 1966–76 Cultural Revolution, 'It was ten years of madness. I was against it. I didn't do anything. I wasn't there.' Well, in 1860 during what was comparatively speaking an infinitesimally small act of vandalism—but still, we admit, regrettable—neither were we.

The Great Wall (Wánlǐ Cháng Chéng)

He expressed a particular enthusiasm with respect to visiting the wall of China. I catched it for the moment, and said I really believed I should go and see the wall of China had I not children, of whom it was my duty to take care. 'Sir,' (said he), 'by doing so, you would do what would be of importance in raising your children to eminence. There would be a lustre reflected upon them from your spirit and curiosity. They would be at all times regarded as the children of a man who had gone to view the wall of China. I am serious, Sir.'

Boswell, *Life of Samuel Johnson*, entry for 10 April 1778

万里长城 China's long and toothy Great Wall, once a not particularly effective device for keeping out foreigners, has in modern times proved remarkably useful for bringing them in. Now arriving by bus and car rather than on horseback, and armed with fat wallets rather than bows and arrows, they swarm over watchtowers and embrasures, taking souvenirs as hostages, and add to the local economy rather than pillage it.

Sections of the Wall go in and out of fashion with foreign visitors and 'belong' to different groups. These days the section at Bā Dá Lǐng, most easily accessible from Běijīng, and once the only official choice, is sneered at by some independent travellers on the grounds that it's full of foreign tour groups and local tourists (which must make visiting many other Běijīng sights rather difficult too). Good enough for US President Nixon and Queen Elizabeth II, and good enough to be listed by UNESCO as a World Heritage Site, it's not good enough for those who head for other harder-to-reach sections, only to find that each of these has its chairlift and souvenir vendors too, some clinging more persistently to foreign visitors than lichen does to the Wall itself.

China is relatively unfenced, and the Wall can be walked up to and climbed almost anywhere it is spotted. But county and township governments are desperate for permission to open sections 'officially', and in some cases paths up to the wall have been prepared or repaired, alternative routes blocked and ticket booths are ready, only waiting for enough strings to be pulled for permission to start business. They open usually with lower entrance fees than the better known areas, and the first arrivals are often cadres with the work unit's car and expats with their own transport, who, finding themselves alone, then fret about whether they should tell anyone else of their discovery (but can't resist). The souvenir sellers are never far behind. News then trickles down by word of mouth to visiting relatives and friends, and finally to a website or two, a column in *City Edition* or *Běijīng Scene*, and then the budget hotel organizers of Wall trips for their crowds of 'I'm-a-traveller-not-a-tourist' guests get going. At this point the destination becomes officially hip, the 'too-cool-even-to-call-myself-a-traveller' crowd start to sneer, as do the expats who want to avoid travellers and tourists alike, and somewhere else becomes the next big thing.

Those who want to go independently to unpopulated sections of Wall should buy William Lindesay's *Hiking on History, Exploring Beijing's Great Wall on Foot* (Oxford), a guide to walks on the Wall around Běijīng away from tourist sites, with detailed maps and public transport information.

The Great Wall began life in the Warring States period (475–221 BCE) as a series of earthworks erected by individual kingdoms as a defence against each other as well as from invasions from the north. The Qín (221–207 BCE) unified some of these into a more coordinated system at the time of a particularly dangerous confederation of Xiōngnú (Hun) tribes. Some Chinese histories claim that a fifth of the population, one million people, were involuntarily involved in its construction. The success of defensive walls depended upon large quantities of manpower, which was not always available either under the Qín or succeeding dynasties. The wall was extended under the Hàn (206 BCE–220 CE), and was extensively repaired under the Suí (589–618 CE). The sections of familiar, stone-clad, crenellated wall date only from the Míng (1368–1644) whose extensive repairs and reinforcements also involved a partial rerouting. It was perhaps the physical expression of the dynasty's desire from the 1400s to shut itself off from outside influences, and its extensive construction of fresh walls on new routes are mostly those which survive today.

The Míng wall has an average height of 8m and an average width of 6m, is made of rubble and earth clad with stone, and topped with brick, broken up by brick watchtowers, about 12m square and 12m high. Its construction varied according to the terrain, the general in charge of building a particular section, the materials available, the time of construction, and the perceived level of threat. At some particularly high points it narrows to a single strand of brick and the watchtowers become infrequent, but most of it is wide enough for three or four horses to be ridden abreast. It aims always for the highest and most inaccessible parts of the terrain, and even those sections officially open to the public all have parts so steep that hands as well as feet are needed for the climb, and handrails have been installed. Often on these sections, interior walls with their own embrasures looking down the slope suggest plans for retreat to higher points should the invaders successfully mount the wall. On the northern side the terrain is often studded with flat-topped earthen pyramids, the remains of beacon towers with their own garrisons, a more economical way of defending territory and of giving advance warning of raiders.

Those visiting more than one Wall site will detect differences of detail, such as in the carvings around embrasures, and those venturing beyond the reconstructed sections will marvel at the difference between the decayed and the new. Peasants carting off the stone, poor drainage, plant life and the politically-inspired destruction of modern times have all done their work. Most of the Wall is completely dilapidated with little more than the core remaining.

It was already falling to pieces by the time the Macartney embassy passed through the important pass of Gŭbĕikŏu in 1793–4, and the Chinese themselves showed little interest in it:

> *It was not without a little management that we contrived to examine this wall so much at our leisure, for some of our conductors appeared rather uneasy and impatient at the length of our stay upon it. They were astonished at our curiosity, and almost began to suspect us, I believe, of dangerous designs. Wang and Chou, though they had passed it twenty times before, had never visited it but once, and few of the other attending Mandarins had ever visited it at all.*

Lord Macartney, *An Embassy to China*,
J. L. Cranmer-Byng [Ed.], 1962

Wall Stories

 If the wall is big, the myths are bigger, but the idea of a single, continuous, extremely long, picture-perfect crenellated wall which kept out marauding barbarian hordes has a grip on the imagination of the travelling public the Chinese have no intention at all of correcting. As Macartney put it more than 200 years ago, 'all their writings agree that this wall was built above two hundred years before the Christian era,' and no Chinese publication is going to disabuse you today.

The length of the Great Wall is, however, almost impossible to calculate. Figures from 2,400km to 5,000km are quoted for the Míng wall alone, which runs from Shānhǎiguān in the east to Jiāyùguān in the west, crossing the Yellow River several times. The higher estimate is perhaps due to an overly literal translation of *Wànlǐ*, '10,000 *lǐ*', where a *lǐ* is about ½km, although *wàn* is often just a Chinese way of saying 'rather a lot'. In some areas there are two or three overlapping walls, in other areas gaps. Long defensive spurs spread out from the main route, and many sections lie separate and disconnected often at some considerable distance. One Great Wall ticket has a claim of 6,000km, others put the figure at more than 7,500km, but even some aerial survey charts mark sections of wall as sections of road, and vice versa.

One story about the Wall that is endlessly repeated is that it is the only human construction visible from the moon. This is even perpetuated on some Great Wall tickets, although the wall has been demoted to one of two (the other is not listed). As the wall is only 6m wide, this would be similar to seeing a thread lying in the street from the top of the Empire State Building, and might lead you to wonder why considerably wider and electrically lit highways could not be seen, too. Not surprisingly, none of the lunar astronauts commented on it.

Before the mid-to-late Míng the majority of the many defensive walls were simply made of rammed earth, and required continuous maintenance lest natural erosion make them insignificant within two or three generations, or make them vanish altogether. Those who argue that Marco Polo never visited China, but merely passed on hearsay to his ghost writer, Rustichello, point out that although Polo's journeys both to and around China must many times have taken him past or across sections of the Great Wall, he never mentions it once. One reason may be that there had been little defensive wall building during the few hundred years before his arrival, and there was simply no Great Wall to see. Many others travelling before and after Polo—papal emissaries, missionaries, and traders—fail to mention it either, and in Chinese historical documents there are only references to 'long walls', some of only a few tens of kilometres, rather than a single long or great wall. Most of what you'll see today was built in the reigns of the Jiājìng (reigned 1522–1566), Lóngqìng (1567–1572) and particularly Wànlì emperors (1573–1620), so much so that some thought the wall—in Chinese the *Wánlì* Cháng Chéng—was named for him, despite the difference in tones. The officially open parts on which you walk were substantially rebuilt no more than 50 years ago, and may be a complete reconstruction as little as five years old.

It's not clear that the Chinese ever quite thought of the Wall the way that Westerners do, and the modern presentation of it may, as with the idea of the 'Silk Road', be merely the Chinese selling back to foreigners an idea of their own coining, for fun, profit and national prestige.

Nor was it even effective at its job. According to one theory, nomadism becomes dependent on settled societies for the products it cannot easily produce for itself, such as metal stirrups, and needs to trade the meat, dairy products, leather and raw materials and textiles it can produce. Shut out of settled society, nomads have little choice but to attack, and the Chinese desire to view all societies other than their own as subsidiary, barbarian and supplicant to the glory of Chinese culture forced them into an arms race which, for all their resources, they could only lose. For brief periods, and particularly for part of the more outward-looking Táng dynasty (618–907), a cultural high point, the Chinese traded with mounted forces to their north (although they professed, as always, to regard it as an exchange of tribute and gifts), and the peace was thus kept very cheaply.

The Míng Empire's decision to close itself off from outsiders altogether was, by contrast, extremely expensive. The overlapping layers of Wall constructed in this period were often effective in tactics and successfully repulsed individual attacks, but were hopeless strategically since the highly mobile nomads just went around the end of stretches of wall, or found holes where it had not been properly maintained, or outflanked the garrisons at key points. The Chinese needed constantly to upgrade and to man an increasingly long frontier, while the Mongols needed merely to use their existing equipment, their horses, to move to another point of attack. As one tactician put it, 'If there is one weak point and then one hundred strong points, the whole is weak.'

And so it proved. The Mongols wanted trade, and the Míng spent vast sums attempting to deny it to them. Even one of the major advocates of wall-building admitted in the 16th century that permitting trade was the only long-term solution, but intrigues in the insular court made sure that any attempt to do so was short-lived. In 1549 the Mongols fired a message-bearing arrow into a Chinese general's camp saying that if no trade relations were forthcoming then they would attack Běijīng. So ineffective was the Wall, that despite this advance announcement they duly made their way up to the Āndìng Mén itself in 1550, from which Chinese nobles could no doubt watch columns of smoke rising from their estates.

Small wonder, perhaps, that the Chinese viewed the antics of the Western Ocean barbarians and their requests for trade in the same way several hundred years later. Failing, as ever, to learn from their experience, and secure in the sense of their own superiority, trade was once again forced on them by military might.

Nevertheless, the myth of the Wall's impregnability had a grip on the Chinese imagination which lasted well into the 20th century. David Kidd was told by his wife's aunt:

> *'I bought that radio in 1937 to hear the hour-by-hour news of the Japanese invasion,' she might say, indicating a cabinet against the wall, 'and I haven't turned it on since. When the Japanese came south from Manchuria, they entered China through the gate in the Great Wall at Shanhaikwan... If we had closed that gate, the Japanese could never have got into China.'*

David Kidd, *Peking Story*, London 1996

Which Wall?

There's not only a wide choice of sites within reasonable access of Běijīng, but also a number of different ways of experiencing the Wall, from the tour which allows you a quick hour and a half photostop (more than enough for many people), through participating in a full-day litter clean-up campaign to a weekend of organized trekking on overgrown sections not officially open to the public.

Bā Dá Lǐng is the most popular, and thus least fashionable section. However, for those who would like a full day on the Wall it's far and away the easiest and quickest to reach by public bus, zig-zags manically from high point to high point, and it doesn't take long for the (reasonably) fit to leave the crowds behind and reach unrestored sections. A trip can easily be combined with a visit to **Jūyōng Guān** nearby, the most recently reconstructed section and still relatively quiet, if a little artificial, but with a greater assortment of supplementary towers and temples than other sites. **Mùtiányù** was the 'secret' alternative to Bā Dá Lǐng about 10 years ago, and is in a pleasant very green location, but is now nearly as busy. It can easily be reached by Chinese tour bus, however. **Sīmǎtái**, considerably further away, is just on the verge of losing its status as the destination for those too cool to mingle with everyone else, not least because it's well known for being precisely that and because there's no regulation of the souvenir sellers, who attach themselves to tourists like limpets for the whole of their visit. The Wall is particularly high and difficult to scale here, and all the more spectacular as a result, but access is less easy even than at **Jīnshānlǐng**, slightly further away, which is really still very little visited and from which you can walk to Sīmǎtái along high ridges with the Wall stretching away into the distance in two directions. This can be reached by public bus, but an early start is needed in order to have a decent amount of time at the Wall.

Long-time Běijīng resident William Lindesay, who has walked along the walls from Jiāyùguān in the west to Shānhǎiguān in the east, has been leading efforts to clean up the Wall in which dozens of foreigners and Chinese troop off at weekends to **pick up litter** two to four times a year. He's also arranged anti-littering signs at various sights, and the installation of bins on and around the Wall itself, laudably sponsored by the Sheraton Great Wall Hotel and Norsk Hydro.

He's also involved with the Sheraton Great Wall **Hiking Club**, open to all, which organizes walking trips at lesser known spots with Lindesay as guide, and which includes transport, lunch and drinks. For further information on both options, call ✆ 6590 5455.

Almost every hotel in Běijīng offers tours to one Great Wall destination or another, although this often only means finding a taxi for you and adding a large mark-up; or at some you may be in a minibus with other hotel guests, have an English-speaking guide and be given lunch. Prices vary wildly, but will amount to at least ¥400 ($50) per person to the nearest site at Bā Dá Lǐng, less as numbers increase.

You can charter a *Xiàlì* for ¥3-400 to Bā Dá Lǐng and the Míng Tombs (the drivers like to claim that the 'proper' price is ¥450), but, again, be careful with negotiation. You can take a Volvo a/c bus organized by **Ati Jarrah Pour**, ✆ 138 0100 4866, 9089 3026, for $20 (payable in $US or RMB) including drinks and snacks, and the company of the amiable Ati, who has climbed the Wall hundreds of times. The bus picks up at the Hard Rock, and mostly serves regular business visitors to Běijīng such as air crew. It usually runs on Tuesdays and Fridays, but more often if there's demand, and varies its choice of destination between Sīmǎtāi, Jīnshānlǐng and Mùtiányù.

On the Wall there is little protection from sun or wind, so dress appropriately and take suntan lotion and drinking water.

Staying At or Near the Wall

 There are guest houses at or near most sites now, with charges typically of ¥50 ($6) per bed. More adventurous people camp out overnight in towers, but this is undoubtedly illegal, the meaning of which is that if you're caught there's an excuse for a big fine. There are also occasional stories of banditry, so some caution is needed.

William Lindesay maintains a cottage at the tiny village of Xīzhàzi in Huairou County beyond Mùtiányù and has rooms available all year round, but most in demand March–May and September–early November. Weekend hiking trips cost $150 per person sharing and last from Friday afternoon to Sun afternoon, including two dinners, two lunches, two breakfasts and assorted drinks. The accommodation is simple but comfortable. Return transportation by car is available for $35 per person (steep, but advisable since you'll have difficulty instructing the driver to find it yourself). Trips usually leave from the Hilton Hotel, but other arrangements can be made. There's an optional early rise to see dawn on the Wall, and up to three walks a day on the Wall or in the countryside nearby (there's about a week's worth of walking in the neighbouring valleys). Lindesay, who is a source of information on everything from the Wall's construction to its destruction, leads walks along the Wall in sections which often involve pushing back or ducking under substantial shrubs growing out of the Wall itself, and sometimes holding it together. Book in advance on ✆ 6849 8888 ext. 62833, <*wildwall@public.netchina.cn*>, <*http://www.wildwall.com/*>.

Bā Dá Lǐng 八达岭长城

Open 9–4.30; adm ¥25 ($3) or ¥30 ($3.50).

The ¥30 ticket has a plastic souvenir coin embedded in it. Either ticket also gains you admission to the Great Wall Museum and a 360° 'circle vision' film in a separate building. There's free entrance to the museum for holders of the annual ticket for Běijīng museums, but that's of little use unless you plan to visit Bā Dá Lǐng but not mount the Wall.

Access is easy. Take bus 919 from Déshèng Mén (walk east from ⓴ Jīshuǐtán), a ¥10 a/c high speed non-stop to Bā Dá Lǐng, taking just under an hour. The ordinary version of the same route is cheaper, but takes about 20 stops to get there. There are also tour buses all year round from various locations around Běijīng (see 'Special Tourist Bus Routes', p.105).

It's a 10-minute walk up to the wall passing a cable car to your right and the **Zhān Tiānyòu Museum** (Zhān Tiānyòu Jìniànguǎn) to your left (open 8.30–4.30; adm ¥5, annual ticket accepted). This museum honours the man who built this railway line, the first ever completed with Chinese funds (1909), through particularly difficult terrrain here, and which burrows under the Wall. Zhān (1861–1919) studied in the USA, and he solved the problems here by having trains reverse direction to deal with the gradient at a point where there was no room for a loop. There are large table models of the junction he designed, of alternative routes the railway could have taken and of local sections of the Great Wall under which the railway passes, as well as general information about early railway building in China, almost all of which was done by foreigners and initially with great resistance from the Chinese. The French built the first railway line in China in Shànghǎi. It was then bought by the Chinese who tore it up. Nevertheless, in 1896–1905 foreign powers built 10,076km, including 2,790km by Russia, and 2,860km by the UK, forming the backbone of the modern system, to which China, admirably, is still making substantial additions annually. There are photographs of railway construction around Běijīng, models of railway engines and other paraphernalia of interest to railway buffs but not greatly enlightening to anyone else, with no English explanations. Neighbouring Qīnglóngqiáo Dōng Zhàn (one of two stations where the trains reverse) has a statue of Zhān.

Further up the **Great Wall Museum** (Zhōngguó Cháng Chéng Bówùguǎn), one of several around the country including at Shānhǎiguān (see p.364) and Jiāyùguān at the Western end of the Míng wall, has nine halls altogether (including one called the 'Let Us Love Our Motherland and Restore Our Great Wall Hall'). There's a giant wall-mounted aerial view of the Wall in this location, maps and photographs of sections from different periods, a sketch map of its construction dynasty by dynasty, and plentiful English explanations. There are also samples of construction tools and of weapons, photographs of sections of wall from all over China, some of which make clear how Polo might have missed it (see 'Was Polo Really Here?' p.336, and 'Wall Stories' above), and introductions to overlapping walls, different defence techniques, walls with ditches in between them, and walls along the edge of marshes, using very good models, including one of the recently completed Jūyōng Guān (see below), and one of the Tiānxià Dìyī Guān in Shānhǎiguān (see p.365). Towards the end the museum loses its way with Silk Route material and 'friendship of the nationalities' political orthodoxy. 'Love our China and renovate our Great Wall,' said Deng Xiaoping in 1984, since when its destruction has often continued unabated.

Once everyone was very enthusiastic about Bā Dá Lǐng, but now there are other sections open it has fallen out of fashion at least with independent travellers, although the site's natural beauty and the Wall's acrobatic behaviour remain the same. Wherever possible it runs through mountainous or hilly areas and, as here, never fails to climb the steepest slopes to the highest points, even if that means doubling and redoubling back on itself. At Bā Dá Lǐng it is possible to stand on the Wall, turn through 180 degrees with some part of it at varying distances in view through every degree. Admittedly the area around Bā Dá Lǐng might well be renamed the Great Wall Shopping Experience, heaving as it is with T-shirt sellers, but once on the Wall itself, climbs to left and right soon thin out the crowds and, in either direction, 30 minutes' effort will bring you to unrepaired sections with very few people about, although a little caution is needed as there have been reports of muggings by peasants here.

Jūyōng Guān   居庸关长城

Open 8–5; adm ¥25, optional ¥1 insurance.

Easily reached by travelling back from Bā Dá Lǐng on the stopping version of the 919 in 20 mins for ¥2. Or ¥5 on the stopping version of the 919 from Déshèng Mén, and some tour routes (*see* 'Special tourist bus routes', p.105).

It would be worth pausing here to view the genuinely ancient and highly unusual Yún Tái 'Cloud Platform' built in 1342, the stone base of three now-vanished stupas from the end of the Yuán, replaced in the early Míng with a Buddhist temple, now also vanished. The two longer sides and a passage through the centre are all very beautifully carved with Buddha figures, elephants, dragons, snakes, the four heavenly kings and inscriptions in Mongolian, Uighur, Tibetan, Sanskrit, Xī Xià and Chinese.

So close to Běijīng, this was a vital pass, and there may have been wall building here as early as the Northern Wèi (386–535), although there was no Běijīng at that time. The tower, wall and other defensive works copied here date right from around 1368, the very beginning of the Míng; they were repeatedly improved, and were perhaps intended to prevent the rapid return of the Mongol Yuán the new dynasty had just driven out. The wild scenery was much approved of by the Qiánlóng emperor, who added the pass to his list of eight great scenic spots, and left his calligraphy carved into a stele, 'Spreading greenery on the hills around Jūyōng Pass' (*see also* the Marco Polo Bridge and Běi Hǎi Park).

The most recent enhancements to the fortifications were 1993–7, when more than four kilometres of wall, including 28 towers and 30 other temples (to the horses used in battle, the town god, and the god of war), governmental and military structures were rebuilt from the ground up, at a cost of ¥100 million (roughly $12.5 million). The two-storey triple-eaved gate here is marked *tiānxià dìyī xióng guān*, 'the first impregnable pass under heaven', and from it the Wall climbs steeply up in two directions, with handrails to assist, past a gaggle of other buildings which take quite some time to explore. Almost nothing seems to have been spent on publicity, and so several years after opening it seems unlikely that the local government is getting much of a return on its investment, as the site, especially in the afternoon, is usually quiet.

Mùtiányù   慕田峪长城

Open 8–5; adm ¥20.

Buses run to Huáiróu Xiàn (county) from both Dōng Zhí Mén and Xī Zhí Mén stations (Xī Zhí Mén is more convenient), from where there are local buses to Mùtiányù, but the best route is on the tourist bus from Xuānwǔ Mén (*see* p.106) which takes about about 1½ hours, allows a decent period of time at the wall, but then takes you briefly to the dull Hóngluó Sì (Red Snail Temple) 20 mins away, *see* p.336, and a regrettable lakeside amusement park where it stops for 1½ hours.

At Mùtiányù a short walk uphill from the car park past various stalls brings you first to an office which will sell you a ticket for ¥55 to go up by chairlift and down by 'speed chute' on a wheeled plastic sled. Buy your Wall entrance ticket when you get off the chairlift. Walking up further there are two offices selling entrance tickets to the Wall and the path up continues beyond them, passing the ticket office for a cable car which will take you up to a higher point further to the left for ¥25 one-way, ¥50 return.

If you take the path or the chairlift, once on the Wall turn right to face a steep climb, after which there's a chance to view a section of the Wall which is relatively intact but overgrown, forming a Y-shape as it sends off a defensive spur to one side. The site is green and pleasant, a comfortable distance from Běijīng and, although it's become quite popular, the vendors are reasonably well-controlled.

Sīmǎtāi

司马台长城

Open 24 hrs; adm ¥25 ($3).

There's a weekend tourist bus to this site from Xuānwǔ Mén and elsewhere (route 12, *see* p.106), but during the week there is public transport from Xī Zhí Mén or Dōng Zhí Mén bus stations (just northeast of Ⓜ Dōng Zhí Mén). Catch a very early morning bus to Mìyún, for ¥10, 48½km. A clamour of taxi and minibus drivers will surround you, and careful negotiations are necessary. The taxis are too unreliable to be worth considering. A seat in a minibus can be had for about ¥20, but make sure that you are being taken to the *entrance to the Wall*, and not just to a nearby village. To return to Běijīng will involve hitching a ride with a returning tour group, or similar minibus negotiations, but with far less choice, so begin early. You must be back at Mìyún before 4pm if you hope to catch a bus back to Běijīng, although you may be able to flag down buses coming from Chéngdé for a while after that. The Jīnghuá Fàndiàn runs minibus tours on demand for ¥80 ($10) per person return. You can also catch services to Chéngdé. There are comfortable Iveco minibuses at 7.30 and 8.30 from Dōng Zhí Mén for ¥40, and ordinary minibuses later in the day for ¥23. There are more frequent comfortable departures from Xī Zhí Mén from 7.30–4.30, but an early start is recommended. Get off at the turning for Sīmǎtāi which is well signposted at the 113km marker on highway 101, after about 2hrs. From there it's a question of hitching a ride on passing transport or a 10km walk, forking left a little after the 5km marker.

At 120km northwest of Běijīng and alarmingly described on the ticket as being 'the most dangerous part of the Great Wall', this section is less visited than most, although it seems to be preparing for mainstream tourism, with the reconstruction of long sections and the installation of a cable car. The 'danger' is in the ease of access to sections both unrestored and very steep and narrow, where outer stones have disappeared to leave a barrierless raised walkway. The towers are partially ruined and heavily weathered, and are entered by balancing on wobbly piles of stones. There's a 15min walk from the ticket office to the Wall, where it plunges down both sides of a steep valley to be cut by a stream, and can be climbed. The stream having now been dammed, it's possible to travel part of the way by boat when there's enough water, and a chain bridge has been constructed to connect the two banks, which, if you plan to walk to Jīnshānlǐng (west, left) you'll need to cross (¥5, *see* below), or take a long detour back to nearly the ticket office and then up the other bank.

The Wall on the left-hand side of the valley is in a better state of repair, but the right-hand (eastern) 'dangerous' side is the choice of most visitors, and has about 15 watchtowers rising up to 986m about sea level, reached by a section called the Tiān Qiáo or 'Heaven Bridge', about 100m long. Here the spininess of the ridge became too much even for the Míng artesans, and the Wall becomes merely a wall, a single course in width. This section is also of fairly early date, being constructed during the reign of the Hóngwǔ emperor, first Míng emperor, from 1368.

As at Bā Dá Lǐng and Mùtiányù the less limber can take a cable car up.

Jīnshānlǐng
金山岭

Open 24hrs; adm ¥30 ($3).

In theory there are Chinese tour buses out here from Xuānwǔ Mén at weekends, but in fact they only ever seem to get enough passengers at the end of the summer when there's a burst of domestic travel before the winter sets in. *See* directions to Sīmǎtái, above, except that buses from Mìyún to Gǔběikǒu are less fuss, and it's a further 15mins on the Chéngdé buses to the well-signposted turning. The route along the edge of the Mìyún reservoir is pleasant, with plentiful blossom in spring, and in the autumn people selling walnuts, russet apples and neon persimmons at the roadside. Boats dragged up from the reservoir are filled with water and used to sell live fish. The Wall comes right down to the road at Gǔběikǒu, where the Macartney embassy came through the pass on their way to visit Qiánlóng at Chéngdé and stopped to make a minute examination of the Wall:

> *These mountains, gradually approaching, almost close the passage, leaving only a narrow defile or ravine through which there is barely room for the road, and a small rivulet that runs in the bottom. Across the road is built a tower of eighteen feet wide (with the gate in the centre) and forty-five feet long. This pass had been formerly quite closed by the side walls of the tower continuing up the hills both on the east and west, but on the latter it was now open, for both the arch through which room had been left for the stream to flow and the wall raised upon the arch have been destroyed and there now appears a complete disruption of the whole from top to bottom. Through the lower gate we proceeded on for a considerable way, I suppose near 1,000 yards, through a large extent of ground with several houses built upon it enclosed by high walls connected with the great one, till we came to another gate and from thence to the town of Ku-pei-k'ou which is very populous and strongly enclosed by two or three rows of walls, which at a few miles distance converge together and unite with the main one. After breakfast we set out from Ku-pei-k'ou in order to visit this celebrated wall which we had heard such wonders of, and after our passing through the outermost gate of the Tartar side, we began our peregrination on foot, there being no other method of approach. In less than half an hour, after travelling over very rough ground, we at last arrived at a breach in the wall, by which we ascended to the top of it...*

> Lord Macartney, *An Embassy to China,*
> J. L. Cranmer-Byng [Ed.], 1962

You can do the same at this point, either before or after the tunnel through which the road passes. Beyond this point you are in Tartary, or Manchuria, an area the Chinese were prevented from entering for most of the Qīng dynasty, and which, while part of the Qīng empire, only became de facto Chinese territory after the 1912 abdication. It was the Manchu homeland to which the emperor might reasonably have been expected to return to rule as his own.

The turning to Jīnshānlǐng is only a few minutes further on. Peasants here are very keen to carry you in a variety of vehicles for ¥5 or so, or you can walk through villages with goats, pigs, goats, chickens, cows, and cultivation for about 45 mins to the Wall, perhaps 6km. Beyond the pay booth there's a 10min walk up to Wall itself past a go-kart racing track and various shops, although Jīnshānlǐng's relative inaccessibility means that there are precious few visitors. There's a choice of left turns which will cut out a section if you plan to walk all the way to Sīmǎtái.

The Wall here is of fairly solid brick construction, the base intact but the upper portion rebuilt. Get on and turn left to find a left fork to a lookout point and note the two unusual circular free-standing towers. Fork right and there's a steep climb up past internal defensive walls and from the top spectacular views in both directions for several kilometres, the older brick seeming yellowy and the newer more grey, and the Wall looping gracefully higher for extended sections along high ridges. There are plenty of litter bins, precious little litter by Chinese standards and very few visitors; the loudest sound is birdsong. Unrestored sections, reached fairly quickly, are perfect—just dilapidated enough to appeal to those with a taste for the Gothic, but not overgrown or dangerous enough to be impassable. Some unreconstructed towers have piles of neatly stacked bricks in them, which suggest that like so many building projects in Běijīng this is in suspension.

The Chinese still call a broad, well-surfaced road a *mǎlù*, or 'horse road', and this is also applied to broad sections of the Wall. Continuing towards Sīmǎtái, there are about 25 towers to pass through, depending on exactly where you mounted the Wall. After about 20 mins or so there's a section where the inner part of the wall has fallen away revealing how the interior was filled merely with earth and rubble, and you have to walk part way along this tightrope-like section. Further on there's a section where the exterior has fallen away, but is still easily passable. The remainder is ruinous but still easily walkable, and inside towers there are red arrows painted to point you in the right direction. There are various obvious short cuts to avoid some steep climbs where both hands and feet will be needed, but these often involve standing on wobbly piles of stones in order to remount the Wall. It's altogether three hours to Sīmǎtái going fairly gently and including pauses for photography and snacks. You know when you are reaching Sīmǎtái because the pestilential peasant souvenir-selling women will appear and dog you until you buy something, after which they will dog you all the more and start asking for fees for being guides. The Wall suddenly becomes well-repaired and as broad as an autobahn again, and a little later there's a sign which tells you that you are entering Sīmǎtái scenic area and reminds you to 'please pay consciously', an indication that they'll take a second entrance fee off you if they can. The last section of walk is along the interior face of the Wall—look for narrow paths to your right to avoid paying ¥5 to cross the chain bridge unless you plan to continue eastwards, or cross it anyway for a final steep climb up to the path to the Sīmǎtái entrance.

Tombs and Burial Sites

The construction of vast mausolea ensured that the Míng and Qīng emperors had nearly as luxurious accommodation in death as in life, the main halls, especially those of Yǒnglè at the Míng Tombs, echoing central palaces of the Forbidden City, but often made of even finer materials. Probably most visitors will be satisfied with a visit to just one of the three main sites: the Míng dynasty Shísān Líng ('Thirteen Tombs'), the Qīng Xī Líng (Western Qīng Tombs) or the Qīng Dōng Líng (Eastern Qīng Tombs). Each has a group of tombs in a valley or at the base of hills, and each tomb consists of a series of halls in much the same layout. They stand in sites, originally walled, into which agriculture has long ago encroached.

The scale of each tomb varies according to the fortunes of the dynasty at the time, and no two are quite alike. An initial *páilou* or gate-like arch may be followed by a gate building or tower containing stelae, large character-inscribed stones often topped with carved dragons and set into the backs of *bìxì*—large primitive dragons often referred to as tortoises or turtles, even by Chinese guides, but no conventional shelled creature ever had teeth or claws. The stelae pavilion may be flanked by two to four *huábiǎo* (*see* Tiān'ān Mén, p.125) and beyond it, possibly through another *páilou* or gate, the 'spirit way'. The most magnificent of these is at the Míng Tombs with rows of alternate standing and seated statues of mythical and real animals, civil and military officials, to either side of the path, in a protective role. At some tombs these are preceded by *wàngzhù*, tall, decorated stone columns with knobbed tops, which in earlier times marked the entrance to a tomb site, but whose function was replaced by stone *páilou*, making a purely ornamental beginning to the lines of guardian figures.

At the end of the spirit way, a further *páilou* may precede three or five arched marble bridges over a stream which loops around the front of the main tomb site in the same manner as that beyond the main entrance to the Forbidden City, and beyond that a further stelae pavilion. A collection of halls to the right behind their own wall were where the animals were slaughtered and prepared for sacrifice rituals, but are not usually now open; they are hung with washing, have modern interiors fitted and are used as residences by the *fúwùyuán*. Ahead, the main gate leads to the first courtyard, with tiled offering burners to the left and right, looking like miniature temples in their own right, and used for burning offerings of silk. Beyond these halls on either side are where prayers were said and preparations for ceremonies made, but now often house small exhibitions of items recovered from the tomb or otherwise related to it. These were held on traditional days for honouring the dead, and on anniversaries of the death. The main hall, ahead, usually called the *Léng'ēn Diàn* or Hall of Eminent Favour, is where the ceremonies took place, and often now contains some kind of display relevant to the life of the emperor in question, or waxworks of a ceremony honouring him, including a collection of mournful animals themselves about to go to the great farmyard in the sky. The terrace in front, similar in style to those at the Forbidden City and often with a pavement carved with dragons running up between the stairs in the middle, often features bronzes of cranes and deer, symbols of peace and prosperity.

The tombs for emperors, empresses and senior consorts have yellow roofs; those for concubines, where not buried with the emperor in question, are usually on a significantly smaller scale and have green roofs.

At those tombs where you are allowed to proceed further, behind the main hall you'll find a further gate in the enclosing wall which leads to a sloping path up to the tomb itself. There's usually an elaborately carved marble altar, complete with carved offering vessels on top, and a further ornate *páilou*, before a steep slope up to the 'soul tower'. In most cases this has ridges rather than steps, said to be so that the climber is forced constantly to look down as if bowing reverentially.

The tomb itself, with some exceptions, is a mound with a circular wall around it. If the tomb chamber itself has been excavated and is open to the public, a ramp down beneath the soul tower takes you to it, sometimes through a series of smaller rooms each with its own ponderous doors of solid stone. Through the soul tower, stairs to right and left lead to a walkway atop the wall, allowing you to circumnavigate the overgrown mound and gain views across the site as a whole. The upper portion of the soul tower contains a final stele.

Which Tombs?

The **Míng Tombs** are the easiest to reach, but are the most commercialized and busy, being on several tourist bus routes and included in almost all tourist itineraries, usually combined with a visit to the Great Wall at Bā Dá Lǐng. The independent traveller can easily take public buses, or charter a taxi for the day, and visit not only the three tombs open to the public, but also walk to those parts of the site which are merely a blur from the tourist bus windows, including the impressive 'spirit way' leading to the site, and the overgrown and atmospheric closed tombs. The only open chamber is that at the Dìng Líng—large, but vaguely disappointing.

The **Eastern Qīng Tombs** have fascinating open tomb chambers including those of the Dowager Empress Cíxǐ, and the magnificently carved chamber of the Qiánlōng emperor. There is only a fraction of the visitors here, but while the site can be reached by bus to do this as a day trip requires an early start, and it is not possible to see much of the tombs and get back in the same day unless you have a taxi. It would be possible to stay in the town of Zūnhuà, however, not far away, and there is one hotel at the site itself (asking around ¥300/$37).

The **Western Qīng Tombs** are easier to reach by car, thanks to the Jīngshí Freeway, but the least visited of all. The tombs are spread out and it's helpful although not essential to have a vehicle to get around, but for now this is the most overgrown, least visited, and most atmospheric of all the tomb complexes. An overnight stay is recommended.

For a well-preserved early prototype of later luxury, visit the **Dàbǎotái Hàn Mù**, from the Western Hàn dynasty, just south of Běijīng and reachable by public transport.

Míng Tombs (Shísān Líng)

十三陵 The first emperor of the Míng, the Hóngwǔ emperor, was buried near his capital of Nánjīng, and the location of the tomb of the second, Hóngwǔ's grandson, deposed after a bitter civil war by his uncle, the Yǒnglè emperor, is unknown. The Jīngtài emperor, who usurped the throne after his brother the Zhèngtǒng emperor had been captured by the Mongols, is not buried here, but near the Summer Palace, and little remains. After his restoration, the Zhèngtǒng emperor adopted the new reign name, Tiānshùn, so the Yù Líng has two names for one tomb.

Yǒnglè	1403–24	Cháng Líng	open
Hóngxī	1425	Xiàn Líng	
Xuāndé	1426–35	Jīng Líng	
Zhèngtǒng	1436–49	Yù Líng	
Tiānshùn	1457–64		
Chénghuà	1465–87	Mào Líng	
Hóngzhì	1488–1505	Tài Líng	
Zhèngdé	1506–21	Kāng Líng	
Jiājìng	1522–66	Yǒng Líng	
Lōngqìng	1567–72	Zhāo Líng	open
Wànlì	1573–1620	Dìng Líng	open
Tàichāng	1620	Qìng Líng	
Tiānqǐ	1621–27	Dé Líng	
Chóngzhēn	1628–44	Sī Líng	

The Chóngzhēn emperor, the last of the Míng, hanged himself in Jǐng Shān as peasant armies entered the city, only to be displaced shortly afterwards by the arrival of the Manchus. The same peasants also caused considerable destruction at the tombs, but the Qīng made repairs and converted the tomb of an imperial concubine to make the Sì Líng for the Chóngzhēn emperor. While they campaigned long to overthrow the Míng and replace the Chinese Great Míng Empire with what would turn out to be the even greater Manchu Great Qīng Empire, the Manchus had no interest in seeing the institution of imperial rule, which they had adopted from the Chinese, fall into disrepute.

Organized tours to Bā Dá Lǐng Great Wall almost always include a visit to the 'Thirteen Tombs', built to house the corpses of all but three of the Míng emperors and their empresses. Often only one tomb is visited (although three are open). This takes 45mins by tour bus from Bā Dá Lǐng. There are multiple Chinese tour bus routes out here (*see* 'Special Tourist Bus Routes' p.105).

There are also several public bus possibilities, of which the most convenient is the 845 with large a/c buses from Xī Zhí Mén to the terminus at Chāngpíng Běi Zhàn, ¥8.5, with a change to the 314 to reach the tombs. The stopping versions of the 919 from Déshèng Mén and the 912 from Ⓜ Āndìng Mén will drop you on the western side of Chāngpíng (both ¥3) and minibuses running the same route on the Bā Dá Lǐng Freeway, and thus rather more quickly, will drop you at the same point for ¥6. From there you can wait for a 345 or walk into town and catch one at a later stop. Only a few 345s go all the way into and out of Běijīng, and a local version of the service in town is far more frequent. This may take you to a different terminus, Chāngpíng Gōngyuán or Chāngpíng Dōngguán, but the 314 starts from here. Just cross the road. If you've missed breakfast, various street stalls here have yoghurt, *bāozi*, and roast sweet potatoes on sale. Stop 11 is for Dà Gōng Mén—the Great Palace Gate, but also written on some signs as Dà *Hóng* Mén—the Great Red Gate, approx. 15 mins and ¥1.5, easily spotted as you see a large red gate in front of you. Staying on until stop 16 will bring you to the Dìng Líng, and stop 17 the Chāng Líng. There are also intermittent minibuses to and from the tombs for ¥2.5.

Spirit Way

神通

The Chinese, *shén dào*, is charmingly translated on the ticket as *God Street.*

The modern road access to the tombs runs either side of the original route. The bus forks right, you cross and walk up the middle. On the way, before you get off the bus, you pass a highly avoidable waxworks palace, and perhaps a collection of stelae by a magnificent quintuple arch stone *páilou*. The entrance is a red-painted, yellow-roofed, three-arched plain building which looks as though it's been borrowed from the Forbidden City, and in the autumn contasts nicely with the yellow of the corn cobs laid out to dry on the road that passes through, and with the green of the pines that line the route. The two-tiered Great Gate, actually both red and palatial, is straight ahead, 5mins on foot, and has stalls selling various knick-knacks to the right. The ticket office is about 20m to the right (*open 8–dusk; adm ¥12*).

According to some, the spirit way was originally conceived for the first tomb, the Chāng Líng, built for the Yǒnglè emperor around 1409 at the same time he was remodelling Běijīng as a whole, but in the end served the whole site. None of the remaining 12 tombs have their own guardians, although the tombs of the Qīng dynasty, otherwise generally less magnificent than those of the Míng, do. But construction of the spirit way and the stelae pavilion which heads it, was not begun until 1435, 11 years after the Yǒnglè emperor's death. The pavilion holds a stele on the front of which his successor, the Hóngxī emperor (1378–1425), who died within a year of taking the throne, records Yǒnglè's merits. On the back there are poems by that inveterate scribbler the Qīng Qiánlóng emperor and his successor the Jiāqìng emperor.

Photographs from the 1930s show the path ahead abandoned and overgrown, but it's now a pleasant willow-lined walk. The fenced-in statues to either side are of a mixture of mythical and legendary beasts, a standing and recumbant version on each side, supposedly operating a shift system to give 24hr security. The literature sold at the site and the introductory signs disagree on what some of these animals are, but look for lions, bearded camels of the two-hump variety which until the '30s used to come in trains to the gates of Běijīng, horses and anatomically incorrect elephants whose front knees bend the wrong way. This is surprising given that the emperors owned elephants which they once stabled about where the History Museum now stands, yet seated elephants are almost always shown this way.

The confusion is with the *qílín*, a mythical composite beast with a wolf-like face on a cone-like head apparently made of flames, and twin horns, despite which it is known as the 'Chinese unicorn'. Its body is scaly, it has a lizard-like ridge down its back, leading to a brush on the end of its tail and horse's hooves. In another version it does have a fleshy single horn (if male), the body of a musk deer, the tail of an ox, and may still be wreathed in flames or clouds. But this might be another beast—the Chinese aren't very clear. It has entered the English language as *kylin*, and Japanese as *kirin*, and in both Japan and China can be found amongst the figures on the eaves of important buildings pursuing the chicken-mounted prince. It is said to be the noblest animal of all, unwarlike, and a thoroughly Confucian beast of good omen. It is discriminating in matters of morality—so much so that it hasn't been seen in China since the birth of Confucius (nor seems likely to appear in the foreseeable future). A necklet with an image of a boy riding on a kylin is a traditional gift to babies after their first 100 days of life.

The row of figures ends with those of civil and military officials carrying maces and swords, and the triple-doored Dragon and Phoenix Gate (Lóng Fēng Mén).

From the north of the tomb figures it's 4km straight on to the Cháng Líng, or you can pick up the 314 at a stop on the right just before the crossroads ahead as you exit, which will pass the left turn to Zhāo Líng and Dìng Líng on the way. It's a pleasant walk through apple and persimmon orchards, especially where parallel paths allow you to get down from the road. The roofs of various tombs, open and closed to the public, are visible to the left, and the modern entertainment areas around the reservoir to your left.

Chāng Líng

昌棱

Open 8.30–4.50; adm ¥20.

This is the most magnificent tomb of all, although not necessarily the most interesting. At the entrance the original stele of 1542 was left blank, but the three keenest Qīng scribblers, the Kāngxī, Yōngzhèng and Qiánlóng emperors, later left their opinions here. Three halls of ever greater size exactly match the Forbidden City in style; the last, the Hall of Eminent Favour, built 1409–16, is only slightly smaller than the Hall of Supreme Harmony, and with the same triple terraces, but built of *better* materials. Beautiful solid plain columns stand inside a largely unpainted and dignified interior, with the internal structure of the fine *dǒugǒng* (roof brackets) clearly visible. The hall contains small displays of period artefacts, costume and weaponry,.and there's a modern statue of Yǒnglè. Behind, through a *hòu*-topped *páilou*, up a ramp and through the tunnel beneath the soul tower, the circular walkway around the substantial tree-covered tomb mound can be reached. Concubines are buried to either side of the main tomb palace.

Take the 314 again (usually a bit of a scrum) to the Dìng Líng, or walk back and take sign-posted first right, after about 2km, about 20mins' brisk walk. Just before reaching the Dìng Líng you pass the left turn to the Zhao Líng.

Dìng Líng

定陵

Open 8.30–6; ¥26.

The Dìng Líng (Tomb of Security) was built for the 13th Míng emperor Wànlì, who died in 1620, aged 57. The tomb was begun when the emperor was only 22, taking six years and eight million taels of silver to construct. Wànlì had two wives, only the second of which bore him a son and who predeceased him by several years. Not an empress, she could not be buried in the Dìng Líng, and was buried in a nearby tomb for imperial concubines. Wànlì's son, Tàichāng, died less than a month after taking the throne in 1620, and was succeeded by his own son, Tiānqǐ (reigned 1621–7), who moved his grandmother into the Díng Líng. The buildings above ground were damaged in the peasant uprising which helped to bring down the Míng in 1644, but were restored by the Qīng emperor Qiánlóng. They burnt down again in the early 20th century, and the tomb itself was excavated in 1956–58. There is a pleasing path behind the tower which makes a complete circuit around the cypress-topped mound.

The tomb is entered from the rear down a deep staircase to seven largely empty interlocking chambers, with an atmosphere reminiscent of Victorian railway stations, although one contains marble thrones. A slightly shorter climb up at the end brings you back to the original blue-tiled entrance gate beneath the soul tower, which houses a large red stele. Small exhibitions in side halls are little more than excuses for souvenir shops.

Zhāo Líng

Open 9–5.30; adm ¥20.

Turn left just in sight of the Dīng Líng entrance. A sign with three large red characters suggests that it's 500m, but in reality a good 30mins' walk.

The Zhāo Líng is the tomb of the 9th Míng emperor, Lōngqíng (reigned 1567–72), and the much damaged halls above ground have been repaired with the donation of 144 Douglas fir and hemlock trees from the USA.

The tomb follows the usual plan and has several halls and gates behind one another on rising ground, not as impressive as those of Chāng Líng and heavy-handedly repainted. But the path around the tomb mound is open and very quiet and makes for a good stroll, with views of pine-covered hills and persimmon orchards as well as the tomb and mound of the Dìng Líng. Unpaved tracks snake intriguingly into the hills, and other more distant tombs can be seen. The stele in the soul tower, smashed up by the peasant uprising of 1644, and the damaged tower itself, were restored by the Qīng in their own style rather than reconstructed.

Eastern Qīng Tombs (Qīng Dōng Líng)

Open 8.30–4.30; adm ¥55.

清东陵   The tombs are 125km east of Běijīng in Héběi Province, and can be reached by public bus from the Mǎjuàn bus station (*see* p.104), with departures at 7, 7.30, and 8.30am, taking about four hours to reach Zūnhuà for ¥20. From there it's necessary to take a minibus to the site itself. It's also possible to jump off at Pǔzidiàn, and get a local bus to the village of Mǎlányù directly east of the main group of tombs. Although there's accommodation in Zūnhuà, it's best to take a taxi for the day, and make a very early start.

A *Xiàlì* or equivalent can be hired for ¥300 ($37) for the day with a bit of persistence. Expect to pay most or all of the road tolls on top of that (about ¥80 round trip). Head east from Jiànguó Mén Wài along highway 102 through Sānhé Shì, and follow signs to fork left to Jì Xiàn and then north towards Xīnglōng, looking for signs to the right to Qīng Dōng Líng or Mǎlányù. Xīnglōng can also be reached by travelling east from Mìyún (*see* Sīmǎtāi, p.305).

The ¥55 is for a 'set ticket' (*tào piào*) which admits you to a total of 10 tombs, temples and exhibitions, not all of which are worth visiting, and not all of which can easily be visited in a single day without scurrying and without extensive use of a vehicle to get about the site. An assortment of three wheelers will offer their services, however, with a first asking price of ¥10. This claims to be the largest and most complete group of imperial tombs in China, including five for emperors, four for empresses, five for concubines and one for a princess, containing altogether five emperors, 15 empresses, 136 concubines, three princes and two princesses. There's a sketch map of the site on the back of the ticket. The first to be buried was the Shùnzhì emperor, the first Qīng emperor to sit on the throne in Běijīng, in 1663, and last was an imperial concubine as late as 1935. The five emperors here are:

Shùnzhì	1644–61	Xiào Líng	open
Kāngxī	1662–1722	Jǐng Líng	open
Qiánlōng	1736–95	Yù Líng	open
Xiánfēng	1851–61	Dìng Líng	open
Tóngzhì	1862–74	Huì Líng	

The tombs of the Dowager Empress Cīxī and Empress Cí'ān in the twin Dìng Dōng Líng are also open, as are those of the Qiánlōng emperor's concubines.

The Eastern Qīng tombs have been open for 20 years but are still little visited due to their relative inaccessibility, and the tombs, lapped by orchards and rows of cabbages, have both more atmosphere and a far more rural feel than those of the Míng. There are also now small villages within the grounds of the original vast enclosure, but the site has applied for UNESCO World Heritage listing anyway. The main spirit way, built on the long north-south approach road to the Xiào Líng, is now a dead end, and you arrive from the west, halfway up it. Several of the other imperial tombs have smaller collections of guardian figures close to their own entrances although the Qīng animals don't tend to be as well-carved as the Míng ones. The Xiào Líng is both the oldest and the largest tomb, and was the model for the construction of most of the others, but the most interesting are the Dìng Dōng Líng, and the Yù Líng, both of whose tomb chambers can be entered. The most obvious place to park, and also where minibuses from Zūnhuà arrive, is at a collection of poor and overpriced tourist restaurants almost directly outside the Dìng Dōng Líng, the twin tombs of the Dowager Empress Cīxī and Empress Cí'ān; it's a good place to start.

Dìng Dōng Líng

定东陵

The nursery-rhyme flavour of the name of this tomb often brings an involuntary smile to the face of the English speaker, but means quite soberly that as often the case the empresses were buried to the east (*dōng*) of their emperor's tomb—in this case the Xiánfēng emperor's Dìng Líng, or tomb of calmness or stability.

Cīxī, in the right-hand of the twin complexes, was a concubine of the Xiánfēng emperor who rose to higher favour after bearing the emperor a son, which the Empress Cí'ān, buried in the left-hand (or western) of the two tombs, and whom Cīxī may have poisoned, had failed to do. *See* 'The End of the Emperors', p.141.

The two tombs are identical in scale and with nearly identical exteriors, although Cīxī had hers rebuilt in 1895 on the pretext that it had fallen into disrepair, long after Cí'ān's death in 1881, using far more expensive materials. She died in 1908, but didn't occupy it until an auspicious date almost two years later.

Cīxī's tomb is approached over an arched bridge, and everywhere there are reminders of the Forbidden City, such as the water-loving dragons (*chī*) acting as spouts at the corners of the terraces. However, the courtyards (as at every other tomb on the site) are pitted and uneven—how the imperial palace would look if it hadn't received at least some maintenance.

The layout is standard, the left-hand halls being intended for annual praying sessions for Cīxī, the painted beams here magnificent in 1895 but not much touched up since then. Unlike the gaudiness of most other palaces and tombs, the halls of Cīxī's tomb have their motifs strikingly painted in gold on the dark wood, recalling the atmosphere of the buildings in the northeast of the Forbidden City where she spent her last years.

The main hall (as usual, named the Hall of Eminent Favour) is on a single plinth with a phoenix-dragon pavement between the stairs up, said to be unique in that the phoenix takes the superior position—an indication that Cīxī, and no emperor, was the true ruler of China, although the same can be found even at Cí'ān's tomb next door. The walls are made entirely of carved and gilded bricks, and gilt bronze dragons curl spectacularly all the way round and down the columns said to be of rosewood instead of the usual cedar. The dragons may be modern replacements for those ripped down by warlord Sūn (see below), but are impressive nevertheless. The beams are painted with further golden dragons and are said to be of pear wood. The ceiling is high so most of the internal beam structure of the hall is visible, and it contains display cases with models of the various ceremonies performed here, assorted burial paraphernalia and waxworks of Cíxī herself with attendants. She's shown here as she often liked to appear, dressed as the Goddess of Mercy, Guānyīn, and came to believe herself a reincarnation of the goddess, although a less merciful person would be hard to imagine. Eight carved brick screens carry patterns of Buddhist peace symbols, and further evidence of Cíxī's interest in bats (see 'Wànshòu Sì', p.224), the word for 'bat' being homophonous with that for 'good fortune'.

The remainder of the tomb has the usual arrangement, but in the soul tower at the rear a passage leads down to the tomb chamber itself, through sets of vast solid marble doors with carved lion head door knockers, to a plain chamber with a single decaying shipping-container-like coffin. An alternative wooden walkway gives access to the rear, from where stairs lead up to the soul tower's balcony, and a circular crenellated raised walkway around the tomb mound itself. The stele inside the tower has inscriptions in both Manchu and Chinese, and there are views across the site to neighbouring towers which enable you to get your bearings.

Cíxī is said to have been buried with three jewel-encrusted gold thread quilts and hundreds of other treasures, all looted by a minor warlord called Sūn in 1928 who scattered her bones around the site for good measure. He also broke into Qiánlóng's tomb, which may account for why the tomb chambers of these two are open to the public today and the others are not. Under article four of the abdication agreement of 1912, the Republic guaranteed to guard the Qīng mausolea and continue the rites performed regularly there. Its apparent complete indifference to Sūn's pillaging of the tombs is said to have helped to drive a distressed Pǔyí into accepting the position of puppet emperor of Manchuria from the much-hated Japanese forces in China.

There is an exhibition centre at the southeast corner of the site, included in the ticket, used for a regrettably nationalistic exhibition which can be avoided.

A neighbouring bridge leads to Cí'ān's tomb and the layout is the same. The left-hand hall in the courtyard has a display of ceramics. The tomb is not as magnificent as its neighbour, and more conventionally painted (all the tombs seem gaudy after Cíxī's), the courtyard more broken up still, and the carved pavement again has the phoenix on top which is supposed to be a unique indication of Cíxī's political control, but perhaps refers to Cí'ān's period 'behind the curtain' until she was unwise enough to cross Cíxī. There are signs of recent repair to the main hall's painted interior with red pillars, which contains more ceramics on display, a large collection of rúyì (ornamental sceptres), comb sets made from ivory, saddles, cloisonné and costume. In the right-hand hall there's fine lacquerware, embroidery, necklaces and fans. There's no access to the soul tower or tomb chamber.

Dìng Líng   定陵

The Dìng Líng is a short walk west (to the right as you exit the Dìng Dōng Líng, alongside a watercourse lined with stone. As in most cases at the Eastern Qīng Tombs, the water has been diverted for agriculture, and most of the watercourse is dry, small dams being used to keep some stagnant water in the channels immediately in front of the tombs. You pass the entrance to a green-roofed lesser concubine's tomb, the Dìngfēi Yuán Qǐn, which isn't open, its entrance blocked by large piles of neatly stacked yellow roof tiles and its entrance path ending abruptly amongst orchards. The path passes fruit vendors and goat herds perhaps, and chickens peck at the crevices between the slabs of the marble bridges.

The tomb belongs to the Xiánfēng emperor, the 7th of the Qīng to reign from Běijīng, and is the westernmost one at this site. The long approach to the Dìng Líng from the south has a small group of standing guardian animals, and as with other tombs the complex at the southeast corner which was the slaughterhouse (referred to in Chinese guides as the 'offerings kitchen') is now used as residences for the staff and offices.

In the main courtyard the hall on the left side has disappeared altogether, and the right contains a contains an extra exhibition of the very small naked corpse of a Míng dynasty woman, married to an official who was buried with her, and found in very good condition on a nearby farm in 1957 (¥10 entrance may be asked; pay ¥3). She's a little shrunken, her teeth still visible, and her burial clothes removed and taken to a museum. The corpse does provide an opportunity to view the results of foot-binding, her feet gruesomely elongated, pointed and folded, with a blocky heel like that of a court shoe.

The large two-storey green and blue hall, slightly unusual in its lack of a porch or of surrounding balustrades on three sides, contains a waxwork of a ceremony taking place to honour the emperor. The rear part of the tomb is not open.

Yù Fēi Yuán Qǐn

裕妃园寝

Concubines' tombs were sometimes called literally 'gardens of sleep'. Returning past Cíxǐ's tomb, take a little path down some steps which then swings around in front of the green-roofed tomb, just to the northeast.

The Qiánlóng emperor was clearly an active man. In addition to various successful military expeditions and several major tours around the country he ruled for more than 50 years, the tomb for his consorts and concubines contains no fewer than 37 of them, and there are five more in his own tomb. The partly restored tomb has its right-hand hall missing, and the main hall contains portraits of various concubines. The tomb chamber contains one favoured consort, and the coffin of an empress whom Qiánlóng grew to dislike and to whom he delivered the ultimate snub by burying her with his concubines rather than with himself. From the walkway behind the soul tower you can look down on 35 mossy circular tumuli containing the remains of other concubines.

The Legend of the Xiāng Fēi

There are several versions of the Xiāngfēi's story, but in all she is a beloved concubine of the Qiánlóng emperor, a member of the Turki Uighur people, named Iparhan in her own language, from Kashgar in what the Qīng were later to name Xīnjiāng, 'New Territories'. More mystical Hàn versions of her story have her naturally emitting a pleasant fragrance, and more prosaic Uighur ones describe her as fond of wearing a sprig of oleaster in her hair. Born in 1734, she was chosen to be an imperial consort at the age of 22, but was only sent to the court on certain conditions, including that her remains be returned to Kashgar for burial after she died. Alternatively, she was the wife of a rebellious Kashgar chieftain and part of the spoils carried off for the emperor by his general Zhàohuì after the bloody quelling of a Muslim uprising in 1759. Or yet again her elder brother helped in the quelling of the rebellion, and being summoned to the Qīng court to be created Duke, he took his younger sister with him. She was talent-spotted while there, subsequently rising rapidly up the hierarchy of concubinage from Distinguished Lady, through Junior Imperial Consort, to Imperial Consort.

All accounts have Qiánlōng heartbroken at her death, despite her supposed iciness towards him. She either committed suicide rather than sleep with the emperor, or committed it at the age of 29 on the instruction of the emperor's mother, or died naturally of old age at 55. 120 guards are supposed to have accompanied her remains back to Kashgar for burial in the Hoja family tomb, as a sign there claims, but it seems she was buried here. Her coffin was found to contain papers with Arabic script and strands of fair hair. A few grey ones reportedly found amongst them suggest she survived to old age, but modern communist myth-makers would require that she did, since she's promoted by them as making a major contribution to the 'unity of the nationalities', whereas back in Kashgar they prefer to believe that she stood up to the rulers of China in the same way that Chinese overlordship of Xīnjiāng is resisted by modern Uighurs.

See also Yuánmíng Yuán, p.290.

Yù Líng

The Yù Líng can be reached on foot, walking to the southeast, but if you have a vehicle you may care to drive to the parking space on the east side of the tomb's spirit way, and then on to the courtyard of the Xiào Líng, which is 15mins' walk further north.

The highlight of the Qiánlōng emperor's own tomb is over the three particularly beautiful marble bridges behind his main Hall of Eminent Favour, which contains various imperial portraits, and down the ramp beneath the soul tower to a series of chambers separated by finely carved vast solid marble doors. Every square inch of the walls and of the high arched ceilings is engraved with an assortment of Buddhist figures, and with more than 30,000 words of Tibetan scripture. The first chamber has in relief the four heavenly kings, or Deva kings, found as guardians at the entrance of most Buddhist temples. The doors are also carved with figures of Bodhisattvas (beings on the road to enlightenment willing to share their spiritual credit with others), the last pair off their hinges, having been broken down by tomb robbers, probably Sūn and his confederates, who also destroyed three of the original six coffins. The underground chambers with their three-ton solid marble doors are by far the most magnificent of any imperial tomb yet excavated, and would, by themselves, be worth coming all this way to see.

Xiào Líng

To reach the Xiào Líng walk back to the car park and then east to reach the tomb's spirit way (the guardian figures are a fair distance to the south), and turn north—a route which can also be taken by vehicles and which parallels the spirit way, passing the low rise of a very elegant five-arch bridge on the way. If you walk you'll find yourself dodging peasant tractors. This can also be a starting and finishing point for some minibuses, and a variety of three-wheelers wait to take you around the site.

The Shùnzhì emperor's tomb was the first on the site, and a model for others at both the Western and Eastern Qīng Tombs, although the others are mostly a little less elaborate. By now the pattern is familiar, although the attendants allow their children to play badminton in the courtyard. The left hall has what appear to be modern restorations of paintings detailing scenes from the Shùnzhì emperor's life, but suspiciously include those modern politics would like you to see, for example the 1652 visit of the 5th Dalai Lama to Shùnzhì, at a place where some construction is taking place in the countryside (perhaps the tomb site itself?). Note the stelae pavilion swathed in scaffolding, the carver at work on a stone lion, and the pillars for a large hall going past on carts.

In front of the Hall of Eminent Favour the bronzes of deer and cranes are joined by ones of two goats and a cow, representing sacrificial animals. The rear of the tomb is not open.

Jǐng Líng, Shuāng Fēi Yuán Qǐn, Èrláng Miào   景陵，双妃园寝，二郎

For those with remaining energy, the *tào piào* also admits you to three more sites, and there are many tombs not open to the public whose exteriors can be viewed, although some of these are at quite a distance from the main group.

The Jǐng Líng is the tomb of Kāngxī and surprisingly modest given that he oversaw a period of stability and prosperity, and was possibly the greatest emperor the Chinese ever had. The tomb is to the south and east of the Xiào Líng and best reached by road, perhaps using one of the available three wheelers. The spirit way has another elegant five arch bridge, and the *wàngzhù* and guardian figures are placed on an unusual curve in the way, quite close to the tomb itself, and more decorated than those at earlier tombs. The Shuāng Fēi ('pair of concubines') tomb is just to the southeast (but not the nearest tomb) and houses two particularly honoured by Kāngxī, since rather than being housed in simple circular tumuli, they rated a complex similar to those for empresses, although with green rather than yellow roofs. The Èrláng Miào is a heavily restored Daoist temple dedicated to Lǚ Dòngbīn, one of the Daoist Eight Immortals, and others, east of the concubines' tomb.

Western Qīng Tombs (Qīng Xī Líng)

Open 8–5; adm ¥50 for tōng piào.

清西陵 The *tōng piào* is a 'through ticket', but has the same function as *tào piào*, admitting you to nine locations, although one of these is only a stelae pavilion, albeit a rather big one. The ticket can be used on two consecutive days to see all parts of the site.

After the construction of the foreign railway line the Dowager Empress used to visit the Western Tombs by train. It's not possible to go from Běijīng directly to Yìxiàn, the nearest town to the site, but you can go to nearby Gāo Bēi Diàn, and take a minibus from there. Few trains heading *towards* Běijīng stop at Gāo Bēi Diàn, however, so for a day trip, return should be by bus. You can also continue by this route by bus or train to Shíjiāzhuāng and Tàiyuán.

For a day trip start early with the 435 from Běijīng Zhàn at 05.10, arriving 06.19. All the other trains go from Běijīng Xī Zhàn (West Station): the K211 at 07.30, arr. 08.24 (¥15–20), the 505 at 13.33, arr. 14.40 (¥7), and the 185 at 17.40, arr. 18.41 (¥9). Returning there are only morning trains: the 508 to Běijīng Xī Zhàn at 08.28, and the 436 to Běijīng Zhàn at 09.46, so you'd need to come back by bus if attempting to do this as a day trip.

The site is 130km southwest of Běijīng and there are buses from Lízé Qiáo and Liù Lǐ Qiáo long-distance bus stations. From Lízé Qiáo take bus 73 at 10am, bus 45 at 10.30, or bus 3 at 2.40pm to Yìxiàn, ¥15, a little over two hours, and then a further ¥4 minibus to get to the tombs themselves. The last bus from Yìxiàn leaves at 4pm, and since the site is quite spread out, some rapid movement will be needed if you are not to be restricted to seeing merely a small part of it.

By taxi road access is much more convenient than for the Eastern tombs, by taking the Jīngshí Freeway from the southwest third ring road to the turning for Gāo Bēi Diàn to the west, and on westward to Yìxiàn. After a toll gate on the main road look for slip roads down to the old road on the right from which an assortment of signposted roads lead to the tombs themselves. You can get between most of them using a road which runs east-west a short distance from the main tombs, but it seems to be necessary to return to the main road again to reach a turning for the westernmost tomb, the Tài Líng, despite suggestions otherwise on the map on the back of the ticket and that on the leaflet you can buy at the site. If you visit the Peking Man exhibition first (see below) there's an excellent country road through small villages and a military exercise area (you may encounter tanks) which crosses into Héběi at Zhāngfāng and comes down to Yìxiàn from the north.

The tombs are more spread out than those of the Eastern tombs, so while a central group can be seen on foot, to see all of them a vehicle is almost essential (although returning a three km or so to the main road which passes the sites and flagging down a passing bus for a short ride to the next turning would also be possible, if inconvenient). Hiring a vehicle for the day from Yìxiàn would be better, as there are, as yet, none hanging around the site waiting for custom. There's a parking fee of ¥5–10 at every single site, and even if you park on the road away from the site, if the staff see your car they'll pester you to pay. Agriculture is pleasantly intrusive, with the odd cow to be encountered on a spirit way perhaps lined with orchards.

This is certainly a much better trip with an overnight stay. There's a modest hotel which pushes itself heavily in advertisements at entrances to all the tombs, the Qīng Xī Líng Bīnguǎn, ✆ (0312) 471 0038, ✉ 471 0012. It's a little overpriced, but open to bargaining if you demonstrate that you know there are plenty of other choices in Yìxiàn. However, this is better than most of those, and the cheapest bed you'll find in town, with part-time hot water, will be about ¥50 with hard bargaining. The hotel is at the eastern end of the site, and marked on maps at the tombs themselves.

The site has only opened relatively recently, but is being groomed for stardom, with an application for listing by UNESCO, the installation of fire prevention facilities in the buildings, and the claimed mass mobilization of the peasantry in eight local villages to take more care of the tomb area. For now this is the most overgrown, least visited and most atmospheric of all the tomb complexes.

Despite the existence of the Eastern tombs, the Yōngzhèng emperor ordered his tomb to be constructed here, breaking with the Míng tradition that sons were always buried near their fathers. The Qiánlóng emperor decided to be buried near his admired grandfather the Kāngxī emperor and ordained that burials should afterwards alternate between the two sites. This rule was not followed consistently, however. The Dàoguāng emperor, having buried his first empress at the Eastern Tombs, then discovered there was a leak, whereupon he had her moved to the Western Tombs and had himself buried here in the Mù Líng. The next two emperors were then buried at the Eastern Tombs, after which the last to complete his reign on the throne, the Guǎngxù emperor, was buried here. Qiánlōng's rule was broken one more time with the final addition of the ashes of Guǎngxù's successor, Pǔyí, the last of his line, in 1998.

The emperors buried here are:

Yōngzhèng	1723–35	Tài Líng	open
Jiāqìng	1796–1820	Chāng Líng	open
Dàoguāng	1821–50	Mù Líng	
Guāngxù	1874–1908	Chóng Líng	open

The Xuāntǒng emperor (Pǔyí) and two companions have been added to a collection of four emperors, four empresses, four princes, two princesses and 57 concubines.

The ticket includes access to the four tombs listed above, to the Chāng Xī Líng with the extraordinary sonic effects of its Huí Yīn Bì—'return sounds wall' or echo wall, the Chóng Fēi Líng and the Yǒngfú Sì (temple). The best place to start may be at the Dàbéilóu—the giant stelae pavilion on the approach to the site's first tomb, the Tài Líng, roughly in the middle of the site, and within sight of various other tombs.

Dàbēilóu

Perhaps the Qiánlōng emperor, who left records of his opinions everywhere else, felt that it would be either too soon or too unfilial to write an assessment of his father's reign, so the two massive stelae inside this large stelae pavilion are still blank. Four large *huábiǎo* stand one at each corner, following which the approach to the Tài Líng has lions, elephants, horses and standing military and civil officials. Like the Jǐng Líng, the spirit way has a kink in it. Attendants say the walk to the tomb is five *huálǐ*, 'Chinese miles', or about 4½km, but it's a pleasant, quiet stroll of under 2km, although the whole length of the way from the initial gate is said to be 2½km. It can also be reached by car, going a little further east and swinging north, but attracting, inevitably, another parking fee.

Tài Líng

The Tài Líng, the first tomb at the site, sets the tone for the rest—the separate enclosure on the right where the sacrificial animals were slaughtered now full of *fúwùyuán* and hung with their washing, the tomb complex approached over a dry watercourse crossed by three low bridges, some or all of the three halls containing exhibitions or waxworks, the climb at the rear to the soul tower, and through that the climb to the circular walkway around the mound, often, unlike the Míng tombs, bricked over.

The Tài Líng was begun in 1730 but not completed until two years after the Yōngzhèng emperor's death, and contains the remains of the emperor, one empress and a concubine. The Tài Dōng Líng to the east contains the Qiánlōng emperor's mother, who, although only a concubine when Yōngzhèng fathered Qiánlōng, was posthumously made an empress after Qiánlōng's accession. The remainder of Yōngzhèng's 21 concubines are in another tomb yet further to the east, the Tài Fēi Líng.

In the main courtyard the left-hand hall where the lamas chanted on ceremonial occasions now houses a display of images of various Qīng emperors, mostly taken from well-known paintings by Jesuits and others, and there are figurine models of various ceremonies.

On the circular walk behind the tomb, the crenels lean alarmingly inward, suggesting repair work will be necessary before long.

Chāng Líng

The Chāng Líng, the next tomb to the west, is so uncannily similar to the Tài Líng from the outside that if you drive to it you may believe you've gone round in a loop and arrived back where you started.

It was built in 1796–1803 for the Jiāqìng emperor, the fifth Manchu emperor to reign from Běijīng, who died in 1820 at Chéngdé (one of two emperors struck by lightning there, so tradition has it), and was buried here in 1821. The courtyard is overgrown; the main hall, which signs here like to call the Hall of Enormous Grace, rather than 'Eminent Favour' at other tomb sites, is gaudy and peeling; and the rear part of the tomb is not open.

To stress the rural nature of the site, on the spirit way to this tomb you find nets stretched across the path, used to catch rabbits which are then clubbed to death.

Chāng Xī Líng

This tomb for Jiāqìng's empress is a short distance down a track to the west, past a smaller, closed tomb for his concubines, the Chāng Fēi Líng. The scale of the tomb is considerably smaller than that of the emperor's and the interest lies at the rear. The modest, drum-shaped tomb mound, encased in brick topped with imperial yellow tiles, stands in front of the rear wall of the compound, which describes a perfect semi-circle at this point. This is where you can perform the sonic feats promised by the circular wall at the Temple of Heaven, but made impossible by the Chinese themselves (see p.163). Quite likely you'll meet none at all at this tomb, so a whisper at one side of the enclosure can clearly be heard on the other side, and a single hand clap produces multiple echoes. Indeed, the reverberation effect is so great that speaking while standing almost anywhere in the enclosure is like being a sound technician testing equipment before a rock concert. It's slightly eerie.

It may be possible to cut across country on foot to the westernmost tomb on the site, the Mù Líng, a walk of perhaps 5km, but with a vehicle it seems necessary to return south to the main road, and then drive west, looking for a signed turning to the tomb.

Mù Líng

The Dàoguāng emperor's second tomb, after his first effort at the Eastern tombs sprang a leak, was built in 1831–5, and he was buried here with three empresses in 1852, with one empress and 16 concubines in the Mù Dōng Líng just to the east.

The tomb is on a smaller scale, and misses many of the elements common to grander tombs, including a stelae pavilion or row of guardian animals on its spirit way. Its interior also remains largely unpainted, although the fragrant cedar of its beams is nicely carved with dragons and phoenixes. The tomb itself is a modest brick-walled drum in shape, with projecting water spouts.

Chóng Líng

崇陵

In the far northeastern corner of the site, this tomb for the Guǎngxù emperor and his empress was finished three years after the 1912 abdication of his successor using Qīng family money, although the 'Articles Relating to the Favourable Treatment of the Ta Ch'ing Emperor after his Abdication' guaranteed that the Republic would complete construction of the tomb. It's also on a more modest scale than those of earlier emperors, but built with more modern methods and materials, including supposedly 'copper beams and iron columns', and its stone carvings are unique. The tomb chamber was excavated in 1980 and later opened to the public.

The Guǎngxù emperor was Cíxī's nephew and manoeuvred onto the throne in violation of the Qīng house law of succession, since he was of the same generation as the previous emperor (Tóngzhì), his cousin. He became emperor when only four, and languished under house arrest after Cíxī squashed his modernizing 'self-strengthening movement'; he died under suspicious circumstances aged only 38, one day before his aunt. The tomb is said to be modelled on that of the Tóngzhì emperor, his predecessor, at the Eastern Tombs, but as that's not open to the public you cannot decide for yourself. Despite its relatively recent date, the tomb is not noticeably in better condition than the rest.

The **Chóng Fēi Líng** is the tomb of the Guǎngxù emperor's concubine, with green roofs and considerably scaled down. Even its main hall cannot be entered, and its low-key spirit way has long disappeared under the plough. Slightly back down the approach road to the two Chóng tombs, the **Yǒngfú Sì** is a fairly heavily restored and conventional temple.

Sleeping with an Emperor

 The Xuāntǒng emperor, Aisin Gioro Henry Pǔyí (1906–67), was cremated and his ashes stored at the Bā Bǎo Shān mausoleum with those of common people, then moved by Dèng Xiǎopíng to be with those of various heroes of the revolution on the grounds that in the last few years of his life he'd worked to be a model citizen and 'served the people'. But in 1998 he was transferred to be with his ancestors in a small plot at the eastern end of the Western Qīng Tombs.

At the entrance to the site new triple bridges have been constructed in imitation of the approach to the other tombs, although clumsily carved, behind which, in 1999, a vast *páilou* was erected at enormous cost. His grave, on the hillside behind, is a toy version of the other Qīng tombs, little more elaborate than the armchair graves that stud the hillside of any rural area, but with a shoddily carved miniature *huábiǎo* and balustrade, and a small concrete mound, two smaller stones to either side marking the graves of two consorts.

All this is said to have been funded by a Hong Kong businessman, and is run as a private cemetery within the perimeter wall of the Qīng enclosure. The official policy in China is that everyone should be cremated, saving valuable land. But those with enough funds can, as usual, buy their way out of this, and even get themselves a plot near the emperor for a modest one-off fee of ¥266,000 (about $33,250), plus ¥14,600 ($1,825) for the first 20 years. There's even a web site: *<http://china.cfanc.com/>*.

Poor Pǔyí; exploited even in death.

Dàbǎotái Hàn Mù (Dàbǎotái Hàn Tomb)

Open 9–4; adm ¥10; annual ticket accepted.

大葆台汉墓 The tomb is just beyond the third ring south-southwest of the city. Take bus tè7 from Qián Mén which goes west to the third ring and then south round to the site via Liù Lǐ Qiáo. There are minibus alternatives which go to the World Park just west of the tomb from outside the China Numismatic Museum in the southeast corner of Tiān'ān Mén Square. You can also take the 937 from Liù Lǐ Qiáo, 5 mins walk east of World Park. There's a direct bus to the World Park (Shìjiè Gōngyuán—a vile theme park which wants to be Florida's Epcot Centre) from outside Běijīng Zhàn. Dragon Bus (*see* 'one day tours', p.107) runs a tour here on Sundays which also includes the Marco Polo Bridge (*see* p.336) for ¥230 ($29).

A museum building stands over the site of the Western Hàn dynasty (206 BCE–25 CE) tomb of king Liú Jiàn (73–45 BCE), discovered in 1974. Inside is a hall with a well-displayed exhibition of artefacts from the main tomb, although it had been robbed long before its rediscovery, and from a second tomb for Liú Jiàn's wife, which was destroyed in a fire. The exhibits include the bones of animals buried with the king for food, bronzes, some exquisite jade and agate ornaments, and terracotta figurines.

A ramp leads down to a gallery around the pit, past the remains of three utilitarian single shaft chariots with red and black lacquered wheels which are still partly buried in the tomb passage, the first of their kind to be discovered in China. They were buried along with 11 horses, whose fossilized skeletons can also partly be seen.

Each layer of the tomb's construction has been partly removed so that the view from the gallery is as if at a cut-away drawing of a series of coffins within coffins and chambers within chambers. The substantial walls were made by stacking square-cut logs of yellow cypress wood and using mortice and tenon joints, suggesting a fairly advanced level of tool-making.

There are good explanations in English of the tomb's original construction methods, and of those used in excavation and subsequently in preservation. If you pay a higher entrance fee of ¥30 you can dress up as a Hàn prince for a photo-op, play at being an archaeologist, and see a photographic exhibition of the tombs of different dynasties, together with a reconstruction of one of the chariots from the Terracotta Warriors tomb in Xī'ān, none of which you can see using the annual ticket.

Peking Man Site (Běijīng Yuánrén Yízhǐ)

Open 8.30–4.30; adm ¥20 & ¥5.

北京猿人遗址 The tomb is 48km southwest of Běijīng at Zhōukǒudiàn, about 18km west of the Fáng Shān turning (14A) off the Jīngshí Freeway. Buses run here from Tiān Qiáo and Liù Lǐ Qiáo long distance bus stations.

Homo erectus Pekinensis took shelter in the caves here more than half a million years ago and occupied them intermittently until about 230,000 years ago. Large numbers of human and animal fossils and artefacts have been found with evidence of the use of fire, 'evidence for the theory of evolution', and evidence 'demonstrating the theory of labour-creating mankind' say the signs, along with more than 20 other Palaeolithic sites in the vicinity. The limestone caves gradually filled up with layers of sand, shale and mud after Peking Man left; they were excavated in 1927 following the discovery of a wisdom tooth in 1921. In 1929 a half million year-old skull was discovered, and later five more. There's little to see now, and unless you are an archaeologist the site is remarkably dull, despite being another UNESCO World Heritage site.

On the left as you enter there are two exhibitions in small halls, the first a small display of dinosaur bits and pieces, the second, requiring the extra ¥5 ticket, of two late Míng/early Qīng corpses. These are preserved (if that turns out to be the right word) in the most low-tech way imaginable, using sticky tape to seal up the glass case in which they are contained. The male is said to have been 70 at death and the female 20, supposedly killed to be buried with him and keep him company. Her vilely distorted tapering feet are evidence that they were bound from an early age. Quite startling are the remains of her eyes and the way her tongue protrudes, as if she had been strangled.

The main cave is straight ahead and signposted to the left, while straight on there's a museum building, also included in your ticket. This has a recreation of a cave dwelling, photographs of the excavation team, a display of their tools, maps of the site, English chronology, various fossils and a model of the skull of Peking Man to compare with an assortment of other ape and humanoid skeletons. What the museum doesn't have is any of the original crania, which in 1941 were sent to the USA to keep them out of the hands of invading Japanese forces, and disappeared mysteriously on the way.

The Chinese government has been happy to seize upon the discoveries as further evidence of the long presence of Chinese civilization in the area, its general longevity and implied superiority to other cultures. In an expensive and meaningless ceremony, as 1999 turned into 2000 by a foreign calendar only adopted by the Chinese after 1949, a torch bearer arrived from Zhōukǒudiàn to light a flame at the 'China Century Altar'.

Temples and Scenery

To the west and northwest of the capital lie large green and hilly areas which make the perfect escape on hot summer days, and which house some of Běijīng's more interesting temples. On spring and autumn days when the humidity has dropped and the winds have blown away some of the pollution, these hills can sometimes be seen from the upper floors of the central five-star hotels.

Key starting points for local buses are Ⓜ Píngguǒ Yuán, the Yíhé Yuán and Yuánmíng Yuán summer palaces (see above). If there's only time for one trip, then the individuality and closeness of the Tánzhè Sì and Jiétài Sì to each other and the particularly lush locations of these temples make them an obvious choice, but there are several more obscure temples with quite individual characteristics which can be reached on short trundles by public bus through the countryside, where you are unlikely to bump into any other visitors, even, in some cases, Chinese ones.

Tánzhè Sì (Temple of the Pool and Mulberries)   潭柘寺
Open 8–6; adm ¥20.

From Ⓜ Píngguǒ Yuán turn right and walk to the 931 stop. There are alternate routes so ask when boarding—you want the plain 931 not the 931 *zhīxiàn*. First bus 7am, last 5.35pm, ¥3. Tour bus 7 also comes here, *see* p.106 for details.

There's an unpleasant start, passing the Capital Iron and Steel Works and accompanying chemical plants and other heavy industry, this area being the single biggest cause of atmospheric pollution in Běijīng, at least until threats to break it up and move it elsewhere are finally carried out. But after a while the bus begins to climb up into hills on a pleasant, very green and winding route, passing the turning to Jiètái Sì (which can be seen before or afterwards—*see* below) after about an hour, and arriving at Tánzhè Sì, the terminus, about 20 minutes later. On the way you also pass several new and rebuilt temples funded in part by overseas Chinese, as well as small villages with herringbone pattern dry walling, and from spring roadside beekeepers with their hives.

Just to the west of the entrance to the car park, the Tǎ Lín ('Forest of Towers', *open 8.30–4.30, 4 in winter; adm ¥3*) is a huddle of stupas in a leafy setting and in a variety of sizes and shapes. They hold the remains of monks or function as grave markers, dating back as far as the Jīn dynasty (1115–1234). It is claimed that the temple is older than Běijīng itself, although given the capital's relative youth that's a modest achievement, and its foundation is sometimes said to have been as early as 400 CE, although probably Sòng dynasty (960–1279). It was favoured by one of the daughters of Khubilai Khan, who became a devout Buddhist and is said to be buried here. The temple once housed a flagstone which had mystically taken the impression of her footprints, but this has long disappeared.

Walk uphill to the temple from the rear of the carpark along a roughly stone-flagged path through a cordon of trinket sellers. This is a splendid, sprawling temple, with three main axes, courtyards with large ginkgoes and ancient pines, and a series of halls rising ever more steeply up the hillside, surrounded by lush green slopes covered with scholar trees, which flower prettily in the spring. There are some mulberry trees at the entrance.

The ticket office is on the right, and after crossing a bridge the first hall through the entrance gate contains the four heavenly kings, and the first main Mahavira Hall contains statues of Sakyamuni and the 18 *luóhàn*. A large hall has disappeared from the main courtyard behind, but this has trees of considerable antiquity including a vast ginkgo and a nearly recumbent pine, held up by scaffolding and marked aptly as 'resembling a reclining dragon'. Some effort has been made to create colourful displays of flowers in small marble-walled enclosures around the site, and there are potted plants, rose and peony gardens. Side halls hold an exhibition about the expeditionary scholar-monk Xuánzàng (*see* 'Yùnjú Sì', below), although opening hours are unpredictable.

The pavilion at the rear of the main courtyard has five golden statues hung with brilliant fabrics, and paths behind give splendid views down over the site. The western axis has a small ordination terrace and the northwest a hall containing the Guānyīn Goddess of Mercy with 'thousands of hands and eyes' for which she needs lots of heads.

Further to the west you can pay a further ¥3 to see the West Guānyīn Cave, which amounts to no more than a small niche with a statue, and a path which leads to a cave with a modern statue of a tiger, which tradition had it used to live in the cave and frighten the monks.

On the eastern side the Watercup Pavilion has a reminder that the Qiánlóng emperor used the temple as a 'travelling palace' or stopping place on his trips west. As at the Flower Garden of the Palace of Peaceful Old Age in the Forbidden City, to which he supposedly retired, water flows from a gargoyle-like spout into a winding channel on which you may float little paper boats for ¥1, or a cup of beer for ¥5. A little further east there's a possible walk to the Dragon Pool after which the temple is partly named (closed during the summer due to a fire risk with the surrounding vegetation), or over a dry watercourse to the Eastern Guānyīn Hall which includes a passage down to an electrically lit grotto with a handful of small statues (a further ¥3).

On the east side near the entrance to the temple a giant cooking pot set into the ground was traditionally used to prepare meals for the monks.

You can return to the turning to Jiètái Sì on the 931 bus. *See* below.

Itinerant Beekeepers

 The beekeepers from Huáng Shān in Ānhuī Province and elsewhere arrive in Běijīng's leafy west from the late spring when the scholar trees that cover the hillsides start to flower, and you may well see them sitting at the side of the road outside drab tents surrounded by 30 or 40 blue-painted hives. Patterns of movement for these migrant apiarists vary, some taking long tours through Inner Mongolia for instance, but for an Ānhuī farmer a typical year might begin with the bees feeding on cabbage flowers before a move to Shāndōng Province in the early spring, well south of Běijīng where the trees flower earlier, then north to Běijīng after about two months, returning to Ānhuī in July, honey production dropping as the flowers disappear and the bees requiring a supplementary diet of sugar. In some Huáng Shān villages many people keep bees, and a light industry is formed around them with specialist carpenters making the hives, although these look far from sophisticated. Local workers are hired to look after the farms while the bees are taken on tour.

The reason to come to Běijīng is for the sophoras or scholar trees, which give a particularly transparent honey with a premium price, although still very cheap if you're buying almost straight from the hive. Those who go to Inner Mongolia, for instance, feed their bees on sunflowers and the flowers of a type of grain, and the resulting honey, black in colour, costs only a few *máo* a half-kilo. The apiarists live simply—husband and wife in an ex-army tent, sleeping on a trestle bed surrounded by oil drums used to store the honey, and cooking on a single gas ring which doubles as a heater. They keep moves to a minimum; the trucks they hire to transport the hives cost ¥3 per kilometre, and roadside officials pop up with unexpected 'taxes'.

The hives themselves are made of two boxes stacked one on top of the other, and the beekeepers are often willing to take off the roof, and slide out one of the vertically mounted honeycombs to show you the bees hard at work, entering and leaving the hive by small holes at the top and bottom, clustered round these entrances in furry lumps. Rarely wearing veils, the beekeepers fearlessly pick up individual insects and identify for you worker and drone. In hot weather bees can be seen collecting water from dishes put out for them and carrying it back to the hive. The queens, which the Chinese call *fēngwáng*—'bee kings', are moved from hive to hive several times a year to improve the honey, but they are otherwise kept in place by plastic barriers.

If you want to buy some honey, you'll need to take your own container. A mineral water bottle will do. This is attached to a (long illegal) stick balance and the price calculated by weight, unlikely to be more than ¥10. Or there are flasks of royal jelly, for ¥80 or ¥70—much cheaper than in Běijīng's shops, and a fraction of the cost at home.

Either honey or jelly make an unusual souvenir of the continuance of at least one ancient rural tradition in China.

See the characters for 'bee' and 'honey' in 'How Chinese Works', p.82, and the Apiary Museum in the Botanical Gardens, p.330.

Jiètái Sì (Ordination Terrace Temple)

戒台寺

Open 7.30–5; adm ¥20.

For access to Jiètái Sì see Tánzhè Sì above. Walk uphill for less than 1km and then turn left across a car park (where you may encounter a flock of sheep) to stairs you'll see on the opposite side. You may be greeted by the cries of peacocks, although these seem to keep themselves invisible. The last bus back to Píngguǒ Yuán passes at about 5.50pm and there may also be *miándì* (the little yellow minivans now driven out of central Běijīng) at the road junction, charging ¥5 for each person they can squeeze in.

This is another very pleasant temple built up a leafy hillside but on an east-west axis, with views across a variety of different scenery, and the best collection in Běijīng of ancient, twisted and gnarled pine trees with individual personalities. There may have been a temple on this site as early as the Suí dynasty (581–618), and the monastery buildings were added in the Liáo dynasty (907–1125).

The temple's main interest is the white marble triple-layered ordination terrace, one of the three largest in China, housed in an unusual large and square hall, topped with a gilded Buddha seated on a lotus, and set with chairs for the three masters and seven witnesses necessary to the ordination ceremony, in which ordinands were raised to higher grades in the Buddhist hierarchy. Signs suggest special permission was required from the emperor to perform the ceremony, but that may just be modern politics which likes to suggest that all the religions in China have always regarded the government of the day as their highest authority, and thus the current government can interfere with the practice of religion as much as it wants to now.

The complex bracketing of the roof is visible in the interior, and the ceiling is gaudily painted and with a gilded section over the statue. The terrace itself is carved with niches housing 113 statues (the lower ones of which have a resemblance to Batman), and the stone between them is extensively carved with flying dragon and cloud motifs. The attendants for once actually seem to be involved with the temple's function, standing around and discussing 'what the Master said'.

Other points of interest include the fine statues in the first gate of Hēng (can blow out a white cloud from his nostrils) and Hā (can blow out a yellow cloud from his mouth), thus also known as the White and Yellow Generals, the Mahavira Hall containing three Míng bronzes, and on the east side of the temple a small hall with a remarkable altarpiece completely covered in dragons worked in both high and low relief, ranging from 0.4 to 3.3m in length. This would be worth coming to see in its own right. A broad terrace running across the site gives views across the valley and looks down on two Liáo dynasty brick relic pagodas standing in a pleasant garden, holding the remains, clothing and alms bowls of two monks, and between which are shady benches where you can rest before the trip back to town.

The pines here come in a wide range of types, some with mottled and curling bark. The Embracing Pagoda Pine is in danger of pushing over one of the pagodas, and the Nine Dragon Pine, resembling 'nine dancing dragons in the sky', is supposedly 1,000 years old. The particularly knotted Sleeping Dragon Pine projects impressively from the terrace. There's also a lilac which is claimed to be 2–300 years old, and a 1,000-year-old sophora.

Oddly, Prince Gong's (*see* p.174) red sandlewood furniture with its traditional cooling stone inlays sits abandoned in a hall at the rear (which cannot be entered).

Shall We have Dinner on the Terrace?

 The foreigners resident in Běijīng in the first part of the last century took full advantage of the willingness of temples to rent out large sections to them and an invitation to 'pop down to my temple for the weekend' was commonplace. According to visitors such as Somerset Maugham and Osbert Sitwell, and residents who took an interest in Chinese culture such as George Kates and John Blofeld, the atmosphere amongst the diplomats and businessmen was almost anti-intellectual, their time taken up by cocktail parties, love affairs, weekends in the country, and racing 'griffins', their name for the stocky Mongolian ponies. The temples were used as country cottages, nothing more. (In 2000 the temple again started to receive paying guests: around ¥300/$37 for a twin, ✆ 6086 2780.)

No one depicted this world in more detail than the novelist Ann Bridge, the wife of a British diplomat, whose first novel *Peking Picnic* made her an instant success, praised even by fastidious critics such as L. P. Hartley, her strong-minded central female character in particular capturing the imagination of male and female readers alike. Both *Peking Picnic* and a second novel set in Běijīng, *The Ginger Griffin*, show the constant battle of wills with servants, the inanity of diplomatic life, the desperation to create a familiar world away from home, a profound reluctance to engage with the Chinese themselves in anything other than a master–servant relationship and, as Bridge's more intellectual central characters complain, a complete lack of interest in the world of ideas. Not all of these traits are entirely absent from expat life today.

The central events of *Peking Picnic* take place on a weekend trip to Jiétài Sì involving strings of donkeys carrying beds, halls converted into temporary residences, and servants in charge of food supplies that would shame Běijīng restaurants today. Chilled wines, gin and cigarettes are served at dining tables set out on the broad terrace, flirtatious exchanges take place near the Sleeping Dragon Pine, and there are romantic moonlight strolls, while the normal ceremonial of the then still fully functioning temple carries on, observed but undisturbed. One visitor with a fine voice sings a variety of traditional English songs for the others. The throb of the monks' chanting is in the background.

All goes wrong when part of the party decides to make a side trip to Tánzhè Sì, and is captured by bandits, but rescued at the last minute. Several lives are changed—a philanderer is persuaded to marry, a new love affair begins, and another ends with a death, caused not by the bandits but by over-exposure to the sun. Bring a hat.

Běijīng Botanical Gardens (Běijīng Zhíwù Yuán)   北京植物园

Open 6–8; adm ¥10.

Take bus 333 from just beyond the main entrance to the Yuánmíng Yuán ('Old Summer Palace') to stop Wòfú Sì, 30 mins, 12 stops, ¥1.5, about 7km (and 5 more to Xiāng Shān). Or from ⓂPíngguǒ Yuán take bus 318, or from the Zoo bus 360.

The large, slightly scruffy 72-hectare site was begun in 1956 and is home to 2,000 species of trees and shrubs, 200 species of herbaceous plants, the largest rose garden in China—7 hectares with 100,000 Chinese roses of 500 species (the Chinese rose is the city flower of Běijīng)— Běijīng's largest peony garden with several hundred types of peony, 22 species of lilac, and so on.

A miniature railway runs around the site from the main (south) gate to the Wòfú Sì ('Sleeping Buddha Temple') and beyond, ¥5. It's vastly overstaffed with *fúwùyuán* who sit round chatting and ignoring the customers. Trains wait until there are enough people to start—not a problem in the spring or autumn, when the gardens are very popular with Běijīng people, but you could be in for a wait in the summer.

Běijīng's revamp for the celebration of 50 years of communist rule reached as far out as this suburb, and manifested itself in the construction of a very impressive multiple-environment giant glass and steel observatory, which opened in January 2000 at a cost of ¥200 million (roughly $27.5 million). The areas inside have been designed by experts who studied at London's Kew Gardens, and include a tropical environment to house plants from the far south's Yùnnán Province, as well as a desert area and displays of imported species. Entry is a further ¥30.

Buildings on the southeast side have an exhibition of documents connected with Cáo Xuěqín, the author of the Chinese classic 'Dream of Red Mansion' also known as 'Story of the Stone'. Chinese sources contradict each other on whether this is a 'former residence' or just a 'memorial hall' as its name in Chinese suggests.

Directly north of the main entrance, a lengthy walk, are the Wòfú Sì (*see* below) and, to its left, the small Apiary Museum. From the gardens it's easy to continue by bus 333 a short way west to the Xiāng Shān, or Fragrant Hills, or straight south down the road opposite the entrance by bus 318 to ⓜ Píngguǒ Yuán. The bus goes within about 30mins' walk of Bā Dà Chù (*see* p.332) but it would be better to flag down passing minibuses from the Zoo on their way there.

'Sleeping Buddha Temple' (Wòfú Sì)　　　　卧佛寺

Open 8–4.45, less in winter; adm ¥2.

The temple is inside the Botanical Garden, *see* above.

The temple is said to be of Táng origin (618–907), and renovated in the Yuán (1279–1368) although clearly much is of considerably later date. There's a substantial tiled *páilou* archway at the entrance, followed by halls with Generals Hēng and Hā, the four Heavenly or Deva Kings, and three Buddhas with attendant *luóhàn*. One of the *luóhàn* here, quite lively in style but modern, is said to be an image of the Qiánlóng emperor.

'Sleeping' Buddhas may be lying down, but they are dying and about to attain *nirvana* (extinction), not just having a nap. Around China some are even referred to as 'sleeping' Buddhas when their eyes are open, although those of this 5.3m-long coppery image are closed. A more accurate translation of *wò* here (a character which should be familiar to travellers from their train tickets) would be *recumbent*.

It's claimed that this Sakyamuni ('awakened one'—the historical Buddha) was cast in 1321, but is much more likely to be a modern copy, and weighs 250,000kg. Twelve delicate and pale attendant clay figures are supposedly receiving final instruction from their dying master. The statue is robed except for its feet and, rather charmingly, glass cases around the figure contain giant pairs of shoes left as offerings.

Apicultural Museum of China (Zhōngguó Mìfēng Bówùguǎn)

中国蜜蜂博物院

Open 8.30–5; ¥2, annual ticket accepted.

About 15mins' walk into the Botanical Gardens (*see* above), straight north from the south gate heading towards the Sleeping Buddha Temple, fork left when you see an English sign and follow the path around, ahead and up a slope to the gate of The Bee Research Institute. Inside, straight on and slightly to the left, the museum is a bamboo-shrouded hall to your right where you see some hives, which may have veiled collectors picking up specimens with their fingers.

The museum is small and tatty, but erudite, and has some explanations in English. Its displays include fossilized bees, a time line chart of bee development and of the character for bee, photographic images of apiculture from around the world, the role of the lost wax process in casting, bees in art, ethnic minority bee keeping, a translation of a poem from the early Qīng which draws Confucian morals from bee behaviour, bee kites, giant wild honeycombs in glass cases, lots of dried bees in boxes pinned like butterflies, samples of plants and trees that bees like (including sophora), images of bees in art from around the world (including Lucas Cranach), and photographs of various species. There are also lots of bee products, tools used in beekeeping and honey production, and an explanation of bee life-cycles.

Fragrant Hills (Xiāng Shān Gōngyuán)

香山公园

Open 6am–7pm; adm ¥5.

Take bus 333 from just beyond the main entrance to the Yuánmíng Yuán ('Old Summer Palace') to the terminus, about 30 mins, 13 stops, ¥2, or take bus 360 from Beijing Zoo, or 318 from Ⓜ Píngguǒ Yuán. Buses drop you in the car park leaving you with a 10-minute walk uphill to the main gate.

The parkland here, a playground since 1168 during the Jīn dynasty, was also renovated by the Yuán, Míng and Qīng, and in 1745 the Qiánlóng emperor made further improvements. More than 20km from Běijīng, the modern park covers 160 hectares and the highest peak on the hilly site is 557m, and is supposed to look like an incense-burner. A chair lift to the top costs ¥30 one way, ¥50 return. There are officially 28 scenic spots, amongst them multiple pools, pavilions, temples, villas and ancient trees, but your opinion may differ. Several ancient buildings in the park were damaged by British and French troops in 1860, and again by the eight allied powers in 1900. In 1949 Máo Zédōng stayed here while commanding the battle of crossing the Yangtze River (Cháng Jiāng) which clinched victory over the Nationalist forces. Needless to say, the building where he stayed is maintained as a shrine.

The tree-shaded paths have a welcoming coolness in the summer, and there are park benches near puttering sprinklers. But early November is the best time to visit as the trees turn red and yellow. Stalls sell deep red laminated maple leaves.

Bìyún Sì (Temple of the Azure Clouds)

Open 8.30–5; adm ¥10.

After your ticket is torn at the park's main gate, turn right following signs for the cable car and beyond that, through a gate, turning left to find the entrance to the temple—less than 10mins' walk. This and the other sights are signposted.

This temple is pleasantly different in several ways, being a succession of halls ever higher up the hillside connected by flights of steps passing through a number of glazed tile and marble *páilou*, and gate buildings with plain, red-painted brick exteriors and calligraphy boards in Tibetan, Mongolian, Manchu and Chinese. The climb through bamboo-filled courtyards ends at the large stone pagoda-topped cube of the Diamond Throne, a more substantial version of that at the Five Pagoda Temple behind the Zoo (*see* p.222), and like it supposedly a copy of a temple at Bodhgaya in India. Chinese guides like to say that the temple is 'conspicuously Chinese', a remark of such obvious redundancy if true that it alerts you before you even arrive to expect the opposite.

The Mountain Gate Hall has good Hēng and Hā statues leaning forward in a particularly threatening way with bulging eyes, weapons in raised fists. Further up beyond the drum and bell towers, the Míng dynasty Maitreya Buddha Hall has a particularly podgy and substantial Maitreya. Further up are two octagonal carved stupas with dragons writhing up their corners and halls with a collection of lively statuary. Unexpectedly in these surroundings, there's then the Memorial Hall for Sun Yat-sen (1866–1925), whose body was stored in the pagoda until 1929 when it was taken with great pomp to the railway station at Qián Mén and put on a train to Nánjīng for burial there, but his hat and clothes are still sealed up in the pagoda. This is odd, given that Sun was supposedly a Methodist. The hall contains a statue, and photographs and small displays about his life in English and Chinese (don't examine the historical detail too closely), which state that his last words were: 'Peace...struggle...to save China'.

In the same courtyard is the very recently restored Luóhàn Hall containing an astonishing 500 1½m Qīng dynasty painted clay statues of *luóhàn*, seven gods, and a small figure carved into a roof beam. Behind, up yet more stairs, and through a very fine stone three-arch *páilou* carved in direct imitation of a wood and tile one, right down to the detailed bracketing, dragons and eave-top animals, stands the Diamond Throne Pagoda of 1748. Climb the stone base to enter the main body which is covered with animal and human figures on the outside. It's a short climb through the interior to the roof, where there are several stupas both flask-shaped and square, with 13 sets of miniature eaves, topped with metal umbrellas and with finely carved surfaces. There are views across hills dotted with pagodas and pylons.

Jiànxīn Zhāi

见心斋

Open 8.30–4.30; adm ¥5 including a packet of fish food.

Return to the park and turn right after crossing Spectacles Lake, easily recognizable as two circular pools. The Pavilion of Introspection was built during the reign of the Míng Jiājìng emperor (1522–66) and enlarged in 1796. An irregularly shaped corridor encloses a pool of thick greenness in which the vague soft orange shapes of Nautilus class goldfish move murkily. Your efforts with the fish food will cause a piscine riot and turn the pool golden-red.

The passage climbs to the upper floor of the two-storey pavilion and gives access to further halls with a motley collection of exhibitions, including a stone-carved star chart, portraits of Chinese emperors, and one of butterflies.

Zhāo Miào

昭庙

The remains of this temple lie beyond the Jiànxīn Zhāi, beginning with a spectacular three-arched yellow-topped *páilou* with Tibetan influences, and indeed the temple itself, initially impressive, is modelled after Tashilumpo in Tibet and was built to house the 6th Panchen Lama on his way to visit the Qiánlōng emperor in 1780. It was severely damaged in 1860 and 1900, and the rest of the ruining has been done by the Chinese, as there are ugly modern additions to the top of the remaining building and the blank-windowed mock-Tibetan buildings behind are in a desperate state of repair.

Bā Dà Chù (The Eight Great Sites)　　　　八大处

Open 5.30–7; adm ¥10.

The 347 comes in bus and minibus forms and leaves from a lane beyond the bus station opposite the Zoo. The terminus is Bā Dà Chù, about 45mins, ¥2.5.

There are several military camps in the area which until quite recently was off limits to foreigners altogether, so you may share the bus out with military personnel.

This would more accurately be called the 'Eight Sites of only Moderate Interest', and those looking for a leafy break from Běijīng would do far better to visit Tánzhè Sì and Jiétài Sì (*see* above) or even the Fragrant Hills—much less of the fairground atmosphere. Although once an important site with a total of eight temples of varying antiquity, a thorough job of destruction in 1900 means most of what you can see now is rebuilt, and done without a great deal of enthusiasm. One large pagoda at the base of the hilly site was built in 1957 to house a Buddha tooth revealed by the destruction of one temple.

Any remaining atmosphere is driven away by an broadcast rock music, souvenir stalls, chair lift, rope way and chute rides, 'snack city', and pestilential men with horses who will pursue you all the way up the hill, as will hectoring voices from tree-mounted PA systems. You'll find mostly small temples, the earliest founded in the 10th century, but most from the 15th, and all clumsily restored or rebuilt, and modern attractions with further entrance tickets such as the 'Animal Happy Garden'.

The climb is perhaps more worthwhile for the views, and in the autumn the thickly wooded hillsides change colour prettily, making the cable car ride down particularly attractive, 15mins, ¥20. It takes an hour to walk to the top if you dither at the sights. It's ¥40 to take the option of riding down on the sled, and ¥55 to go up on the chairlift and down on the sled.

Fǎ Hǎi Sì　　　　法海寺

Open 9–4; adm ¥10.

Amazingly, this temple still has a sign announcing that 'foreign guests' must pay ¥20. The government has instructed museums to charge everyone the same price, and demands for double the entrance price can confidently be ignored.

The temple is four stops from Bā Dà Chù (*see* above) on bus 311, ¥1 (first walk back 10mins to the main road). There are lots of schools in the area and from mid-afternoon you are likely to share the bus with plenty of curious children. Get off at Móshì Kǒu, carry on in the direction of the bus and almost immediately turn right. After a little more than five minutes you'll see a sign with green characters pointing you to the right (on a pole raised up on the left-hand side of the street). The road climbs and narrows a little. At the T-junction turn right, and you almost immediately arrive at the temple steps. Coming from Běijīng directly, take the metro to Ⓜ Píngguǒ Yuán and catch bus 311 for two stops, also ¥1.

The point of visiting this temple, other than its rather pleasant quiet obscurity, is that the temple, completed in 1443 and despite having lost some of its halls, has original unretouched murals covering the inside walls of its main Mahavira Hall. These murals, heavily influenced by the Táng whose Buddhist images were often strongly Central Asian in style, show various Buddhas, bodhisattvas, and apsaras (flying, angelic creatures). There's evidence of the work of 15 different hands, and the 550-year-old murals are still clear, even in the dim light of the hall. The substantial stone figures occupying the hall, wrapped in yellow shawls, have eyes which glow eerily in the dark.

A small hall to the left side has photographs of ancient religious inscriptions on rocks around China, and the four heavenly kings in the entrance gate are notable for being painted rather than statues, and are also said to be Míng. Small octagonal stupas in the courtyard have columns of Chinese and Tibetan in parallel, and there's a large bronze bell covered in Chinese and Tibetan.

The temple has the forlorn, slightly abandoned air of somewhere that doesn't generate enough revenue to make anyone care, although a few specialist Japanese and Korean tour groups, interested in the passage of Buddhism to their own countries through the filter of China, come out here.

Dà Jué Sì 大觉寺

Open 8–5; adm ¥10, annual ticket accepted.

From the main gate of the Summer Palace take bus 346 to the 18th stop, Zhōujiāxiāng, or minibuses on the same route for ¥2 (might ask for ¥3), which go when they are full. The buses are round to the right as you are leave the palace. The trip takes about 45mins. After getting off carry on up the main road, ignoring a right fork a little further on (which is where the minibus will drop you). The 23rd stop of route 903 (which doesn't come from anywhere useful) is at a right turn about 10mins' walk away. Take that and walk for 1km uphill through orchards, crossing the railway line at Dà Jué Sì station.

There's the possible pleasant alternative of taking the train. The *jiāoyóu*5 starts at 06.30 from Běijīng Běi Zhàn and gets to Jiǔfén at 07.28 and will in the future stop here at Dàjué Sì. Trains continue in a loop to Píngguǒ Yuán Zhàn, opposite Ⓜ Píngguǒ Yuán, and you can also start from there on the *jiāoyóu* 211 08.36 or the *jiāoyóu* 213 at 11.03, arriving at Jiǔfén about 36mins later. Return trains include the *jiāoyóu* 214 from Jiǔfén to Píngguǒ Yuán at 14.56, or to Běijīng Běi Zhàn at 16.53. Until Dàjué Sì's station opens, the walk to Jiǔfén, along the track, takes about 25mins.

The temple is pleasant and quiet and, although attempting to double as a conference centre with occasional obtrusive strings of electric lights over its courtyards, makes a pleasant day trip or even an overnight stay. It was founded during the Liáo dynasty in 1068 (as recorded on an ancient stele which needs a brick frame to support it), rebuilt in the Míng in 1446, with later Qīng additions, and, unusually, oriented from east to west. Several curious trees include a rattan growing around a cypress, a gingko which is claimed to be 1,000 years old, and entwined magnolia, plum and cypress trees. There's a small spring above the temple whose waters are channelled round the site and emerge from a stone dragon's mouth to fall into the Lotus Pool near the entrance.

The Hall of the Deva Kings no longer has its four occupants and has become a shop, but the main Mahavira Hall, of Míng date, retains a fine caisson ceiling with a carved dragon peering down on the dusty three seated Buddhas below, flanked by 20 figures seated in their own gallery with its own pillars, the roof supported by complex brackets.

Renovation continues at the hall behind, with its Qiánlōng calligraphy boards, Buddha and two boddhisattvas, but to a better standard than the rearmost hall, it is to be hoped, with its appalling strip-lighted interior, where a *fúwùyuán* listens to the radio next to an exhibition of the temple's history.

Behind this is a white flask-shaped stupa topped with umbrellas and with a lotus flower base, seated on an octagonal plinth carved with flower motifs and dragons, and reached by uneven stone steps to the left. The stupa is named for a cypress and pine which form a rather elegant natural canopy over it.

A hall in the northwest corner of the site turns out to be a guest house which has an ultra-modern interior, three duplex rooms with attached jacuzzi downstairs, ¥580 ($72.50), as well as three standard doubles in a separate bulding for ¥280 ($35). The operation also runs a mid-priced restaurant, and the Mínghuì Cháguǎn tea house, making a weekend stay within the quiet temple grounds a possibility.

Shí Dù (Ten Crossings)
十渡

Open daylight hours; adm ¥20 for Wǔ Dù, ¥30 for Shí Dù.

Most easily reached on weekend tourist bus *yóu*10, ¥43, 8.30am from Xuānwǔ Mén, Fùchéng Mén or Āndìng Mén, of which Xuānwǔ Mén is more likely to have enough passengers to make a departure possible. By car take the Jīngshí Freeway southwest from the third ring, and leave at exit 18, and follow signs to Yúnjū Sì (*see* below), and then Shí Dù. It's also possible to take an inconvenient train from Běijīng Nán Zhàn, or bus 917 from Tiān Qiáo to Fāng Shān, and take local transport from there, or minibuses from Liù Lǐ Qiáo or Liánhuā Chí (¥20). Local transport between Fāng Shān station and Shí Dù has a first asking price of ¥15, dropping straight down to ¥10; the correct price is ¥2–3.

The road from the Jīngshí Freeway passes the gleaming but unattractive villas of the new rich, then through new boating areas, mock forts, and man-made waterfalls, all trying to make something off the increasing popularity of Shí Dù, further on. The bus eventually begins to run along a narrow, winding, and poorly surfaced road along a cliff (sections of it have fallen away) then descends to run alongside a river running between pointy low peaks. The 'ten crossings' were across this river and may originally have been ferries, although they are now bridges. At Wǔ Dù, the fifth crossing, about 1hr 50mins after departure, tour buses make a two-hour stop.

A path runs along a narrow defile carrying a tributary to the main river, although this is dry for most of the year. There are horses for hire (first asking price ¥30 but goes down rapidly), however you don't ride yourself, but are led. Goats can be seen nimbly leaping about on sheer cliff faces, and there's an occasional loud bang from detonating fireworks. These are banned in Běijīng itself and, since they sound particularly loud in the narrow confines of the gorge, are popular here (¥15 for something that looks like a Second World War German grenade, and will probably take your fingers off). Various paths lead up to higher points, and the scenery is pleasant, although not spectacular, and the bleats of goats and the birdsong are sometimes lost amongst the yells of Chinese who have just discovered you can make an echo without using the reverb switch on a karaoke amp. The gorge is prettier in the wet period of June and July, but also impassable then.

A further half hour by road brings you to Shí Dù, the Tenth Crossing, with another two-hour stop if you are on a bus tour. The attraction here is boating in bamboo punts, bumper cars and other amusement rides, and a chairlift to the top of a hill (¥20 one way, ¥30 return), from where you can walk along a ridge looking across the hills in two directions, paying a further ¥5 if you wish to reach the highest point. There are multiple echoes from a huge curve of cliff on the opposite side, which also seems to offer good trekking. In the haze the rows of hills seem like theatrical gauzes or scenery layers, one behind the other. You can also see other attractions in neighbouring valleys such as tethered balloon rides, and rides in military semi-amphibious half-tracks. A few years ago the area was probably delightful.

The main attraction to the Chinese is the introduction of bungee jumping—¥180 ($22) or ¥150 ($19) per jump depending on the height of the tower chosen. The word 'bungee' has been very successfully assimilated into Mandarin as *bèng jí*, which sounds very similar and means 'extreme jump'.

Tour buses stop at Yúnjū Sì on their way back to Běijīng.

Yúnjū Sì

Open 8–5.30; adm ¥30.

云居寺

If you've come on the tourist bus, you may be given a ¥2 discount voucher off the entrance price, and there's a one-hour stop here. Buses run irregularly to the temple, about 120km southwest of Běijīng from Liánhuā Chí.

This temple is extremely ancient, having originally been built in 631 CE, but was almost completely destroyed by Japanese forces, although for the most part they respected China's ancient buildings rather better than they did the Chinese people, and rather more than the Chinese have since. Until recently the site was a highly picturesque ruin, with merely ten brick and stone stupas dating as far back as the Liáo dynasty (907–1125). Now there's a brand new temple pretending to be the old one.

From the entrance a path to your left through a bamboo grove leads you on a recommended route around the site, beginning with the main reason to come here: the thousands of stone sutras of the Suì, Táng, Liáo and Jīn dynasties. As with the Confucian classics (*see* Confucius Temple, p.192), Buddhist scriptures were carved onto stone slabs to produce a definitive version, and one from which authoritative copies could be made. The sutras were discovered in 1957, carved into more than 10,000 slabs walled up in caves in the neighbouring mountains. Some of the texts had been lost for centuries, and forgotten. Several hundred sutras were the translations of the expeditionary scholar-monk Xuánzàng, who left the Táng capital of Cháng'ān (modern day Xī'ān) in 629 CE on a mission to India to collect scriptures. His travels were mythologized in the classic of Chinese literature, *Journey to the West* or *Monkey*, the source of plots for everything from Chinese opera to television cartoon series. The sound of tamping reveals that authoritative copies of his work are still being made by the process of wetting the stone, laying on a sheet of fine paper which then adheres to it, and using a cloth-wrapped wooden disk to tamp on colour, with a result which resembles a brass rubbing.

Various of the brand new halls contain minor exhibitions, often with a further entrance fee attached, although the rearmost does contain a single tall slender multi-armed figure of some antiquity which can be seen for free. The stupas on the east side, one 30m high, are worth seeing, although a number have been glued back together with concrete.

Red Snail Temple (Hóngluó Sì)　　　红螺寺

Open 7–6.30; adm ¥15.

50km and 1½hrs to the north of Běijīng, this temple is usually only seen when taking the tourist bus which visits Sīmǎtái Great Wall (*see* p.305), and not worth a special visit in itself. On tours it's followed by a visit to a lakeside amusement park 15mins away. There is, however, a lively temple fair at the end of April and beginning of May each year.

After your ticket is torn, turn right through a bamboo grove to reach what's really a giant tourist trap spun round the story of two immortal princesses who came to earth disguised as red snails, and reproduced in concrete. The layout of the temple is otherwise conventional, and most of the paintwork and statuary of recent date.

Museums and Other Sites

All the sights in this apparently throwaway category are worth serious consideration. Even those catering for specialist tastes, such as the Aviation Museum, have some bizarre quality likely to appeal to those who haven't just come to find some relic China of nothing but endless Walls and temples, but a real life country with a turbulent modern history, and which is still trying to find its place in the world. They include caves for hiding in and not just for Buddhist relics, a village of ancient houses, their walls still daubed with the rhetoric of the Cultural Revolution, and a wildlife park where the meaning of conservation is properly understood.

Marco Polo Bridge (Lúgōu Qiáo), Wǎnpíng Chéng　　　卢沟桥，宛平城

Open 6.30–7; adm ¥6 (bridge), ¥5 (city walls).

The bridge is reached by taking bus 6, which passes the north gate of Tiāntán, and proceeds west from the junction of Zhūshìkǒu Xī Dàjiē and Nán Xīnhuá Jiē. Get off at the terminus (Liùlǐ Qiáo Nánlǐ) and catch the 339 suburban bus which takes you back roads parallel to the Jīngshí Freeway. Tell the conductor 'Lúgōu Qiáo' and the bus will drop you just before the new road bridge (Lúgōu Xīn Qiáo, 30mins, ¥1.50). Continue walking in the same direction as the bus and then turn right along the river bank to reach the bridge, about a 5min walk. The 339 or 309 will take you back to Běijīng.

Dragon Bus (*see* 'one day tours', p.107) runs a tour here on Sundays which also includes the Dàbǎotái Han Tomb (*see* p.323) for ¥230.

Lúgōu Qiáo means 'Reed Ditch Bridge', and the bridge has gained its English name through being mentioned in Polo's *The Travels*. It was originally built between 1189 and 1194, and thoroughly restored after being partially washed away in 1698. Two imperial stelae under stone canopies carved with dragons stand at either end of the bridge, accompanied by two *hòu*-topped *huábiǎo* (*see* p.125). One stele celebrates the rebuilding, and the other, in the calligraphy of the Qīng emperor Qiánlōng (reigned 1736–96), celebrates the bridge's beauty with the characters *Lúgōu xiǎo yuè*—'moon at dawn over Lúgōu'—one of a traditional list of the eight most scenic spots of the region, all of which were graced with Qiánlóng stelae. The 11-arched white marble bridge has balustrades down either side, each upright topped with lions which appear to be individual. Local tradition has it that attempting to count the lions will drive you mad. Polo has 1,200 (but he has them at the base of the uprights as well as at the top), and modern guide books give numbers varying between 140 and 501, although there seem to be 120, so perhaps the tradition is right (in which case 120 is wrong, and this writer is a lunatic, too). One of the pleasures of the bridge is that since it is constructed from stone, although it has been restored (most recently in 1986–7), it is far more the genuine article than most of the frequently incinerated wooden structures that make up the majority of China's historic sites. Although the paving slabs of the now pedestrianized bridge have been replaced, a strip of the original surface down the middle has the same rounded surfaces as the steps to the crypt of a medieval cathedral.

At the near end of the bridge, on the far side, a small museum called the Lúgōu Qiáo Shǐliào Zhèn Liè Guǎn (*open 8.30–5.30; adm ¥2, annual ticket accepted*) principally has photographs of things you can see for yourself, although with some good close-ups of less easy to see carved animals on the sides of the bridge. At the far end there's a souvenir market.

The little town of **Wǎnpíng**, built under another name in 1644, opposite the near end of the bridge, has now outgrown its city walls, but they remain largely intact. Their layout is not typical of small towns, having no north or south gate and no central drum or bell tower.

Passing under the double west gate to enter the town, turn left to find the ticket office and stairs up to the top (*open 7–6; adm ¥3*). A pleasant 30mins' walk will give you roofscapes of the older interior *hútòng* and more modern exterior ones, and bring you back the same point having made a complete circuit. Stone bases indicate that there were once other towers at the corners and north and south sides. You will very likely see no other foreigners. Noodle restaurants in the town can restore you before you return to Běijīng.

The town also contains the Anti-Japanese War Museum, *see* below.

Was Polo Here?

 Polo's description of the bridge is typical of most of his descriptions of China—as much wrong as right. He gives the number of arches as 24, not 11, and makes other mistakes in describing a bridge generally agreed to have survived largely unchanged since its construction.

Following the publication of Frances Wood's entertaining book, *Did Marco Polo go to China?*, or rather since the companion television documentary was broadcast, popular imagination has finally caught up with what some academics have being saying for years: probably not.

Wills and other legal documents convince that he existed, and the mention in one of them of a Mongol *laissez-passer* seems to suggest that there was some contact between the family and the Mongols. According to *The Travels*, in around 1260 two Venetian merchants, Niccolò and Maffeo Polo set off for the Crimea looking for new markets. They then adventurously proceeded to the Volga where the lord of the Western Tartars (a sub-division of the Mongol empire) had his capital. A civil war which broke out between this khan and one of his neighbours prevented the Polos from returning to the Crimea, so they sought refuge at the court of a third Khan in Bokhara. They were given the opportunity to join a mission to the Great Khan, Khubilai, and ventured to his pre-Běijīng capital of Karakorum in Mongolia. He sent them to the Pope asking for 100 teachers who could speak convincingly about Christianity, and provided a safe-conduct in the form of a gold tablet. The Polos got back in 1269, to find Christendom Pope-less due to the death of Clement IV the previous year. In 1271, no new Pope having been elected, the Polos returned to Acre and enlisted the support of the papal legate there, who gave them letters explaining why they had been unable to fulfill their mission. They had not long set off when they were recalled. The new Pope turned out to be none other than the same legate, now Gregory X, who gave them full diplomatic credentials, but at such short notice could only find two missionaries rather than 100, and even these dropped out. Undeterred, the Polos set off again, and it was only on this second occasion and at the age of 17 that Marco joined his father and uncle on a trip that was to last 20 years.

The Polos left China in 1292 by a sea route through the Malay Straits, arriving back in Venice in 1295. Fighting on behalf of Venice against Genoa in the sea battle of Cursola in 1298, Marco was taken prisoner and probably not released until the following year. While in captivity he had little to do but talk about his travels. One of his companions in what was probably fairly comfortable house arrest was a well-known romance writer called Rustichello who set down what Polo had to say. Rustichello was not the greatest of writers, and those sections that did not fall into his usual experience come across as little more than a merchant's shopping list. Very little of the book comes vividly to life, and where Rustichello's florid pen takes over from the laconic Polo, he has no scruples about lifting passages from his earlier work and dropping them wholesale into *The Travels*, although these insertions become fewer as the narrative proceeds to less well-known territory.

The success of *The Travels* probably lay in its coverage of such a large part of the world at a time when there was a great eagerness to know more. Although there were many other published accounts of travel to the Far East, the Polos went further, and took some routes of which no other European was to leave records for nearly 600 years. There are more than 80 Polo manuscripts extant, in a variety of languages, and scholars still argue about the original language used by Rustichello, although most now think that it was an Italianized form of French. Former correspondent G. E. Morrison at his death left a copy of what *The Times* referred to as 'the first edition of 1496 in Italian', as well as first editions of versions in English, French and German. Few of the manuscripts are entirely alike, various hands having perhaps added some passages, or deleted others.

The evidence against Polo is substantial, although the jury is still out. While in China Marco is supposed to have undertaken various offices for the khan, yet he fails to appear in any Chinese records, although other foreign travellers do. These travellers also appear in each other's notes, while the Polos do not. The narrative begins with a description of a route and a sequence of places visited, but by the time China is reached this has largely descended into confusion, and many an incautious commentator claims Marco's presence in a town where a more careful reading of the text would suggest that a hearsay description is being offered. There is far too little material in the book to cover the whole period of time supposedly spent away, and much of the historical material is contradicted by other sources. Major omissions include the Great Wall, tea (unknown in Europe at the time), the bound feet of all but the poorest of Chinese women, and the Chinese script, so different from the phonetic systems familar to Europeans.

It is perfectly possible that Polo only went as far as the Middle East, where his family had business, or only as far as the courts of the nearest Mongol khans, and the rest is all hearsay. That a fictional work could be convincing is demonstrated by Sir John Mandeville's *Travels*, slightly later than Polo, immensely popular in its day, which was later discovered to be entirely concocted from imagination and snippets of others' work. A contemporary of the Polos, a banker called Pegelotti, compiled a guide to trading in the Far East entirely and openly derived from the accounts of others, published in 1342.

It will take a long time for the idea of Polo to fade or change, as so much hyperbole has been expended on him over the centuries, and he serves as a symbol of adventurous travel and east-west contacts. In 1999 the dry-as-dust business information service Bloomberg named Marco Polo as one of the most influential businessmen of the millennium. Chinese guide books claim Polo caused Chinese noodles and *jiǎozi* to appear in Italy as spaghetti and ravioli. (Some Italians claim the transmission was in the opposite direction.) The truth is probably that pasta was Middle Eastern in origin and travelled to both west and east.

The Museum of the Chinese People's Anti-Japanese War 中国人民革命军事博物馆
(Zhōngguó Rénmín Kàng Rì Zhànzhēng Jìniànguǎn)

Open 8–4; ¥12, annual ticket accepted.

The Marco Polo Bridge's significance to modern history is as the site for what might be described as the opening battle of the Second World War. The peace protocol at the end of the Boxer Rebellion entitled the Japanese to station 1,350 troops in the area of Běijīng and Tiānjīn to ensure that the route to the sea, which had been blocked during the Rebellion, was kept open. By July 1937 Japan had more than five times the permitted number of soldiers in the area, was conducting manoeuvres beyond the agreed territorial limits, and looking for an excuse to take control of the lines issuing from the Fēngtái railway junction, one of which almost touches the northeast corner of Wǎnpíng's walls. On 7 July the Japanese used the excuse of a missing soldier to bombard Wǎnpíng, and on 9 July attacked it, but without success. The Nationalist government sent troops north from Nánjīng, the Japanese sent reinforcements, and by the end of July had occupied both Běijīng and Tiānjīn. The Marco Polo Bridge Incident marked the beginning of the war known in China as the Anti-Japanese War of 1937–45.

Head straight east from the city gate nearest the Lúgōu Qiáo and the museum is a long grey frontage set back from the north side of the road.

As at that other site commemorating foreign invasion, the Yuánmíng Yuán (*see* p.293), the music of the Chinese national anthem is written out for you in gold. This is not, as is often imagined, 'The East is Red', but the theme tune from a popular 1935 film called 'The March of the Volunteers'. The film was about people who volunteered to fight against the Japanese invasion in the 1930s, and the anthem is like the *Marseillaise* but less bloody.

The collection at the museum is imposing, but at usual nothing is labelled in English, although (highly unusually) exhibits *are* labelled in Japanese. Almost all Chinese museums have a political message to deliver, and this one gives a view of the Japanese occupation of China to Chinese who are growing up, and to Japanese who've already grown up with history books distinctly light on details of this period. The presentation has a powerful single-mindedness, some of its contents are gory.

The first exhibition hall is on the left, and a succession of rooms contain maps and charts of troop movements, period photographs of Wănpíng and Lúgōu Qiáo, dioramas of the battlefield, copies of propaganda magazines, some video footage and maps with dates of Japan's steady expansion into China following the end of the First World War, when the Treaty of Versailles handed it control of much of the territory in China formerly controlled by Germany.

There's a copy of the later agreement between Roosevelt, Chiang Kai-shek and Churchill, dated November 1943, on reclaiming from Japan all territory occupied since 1914, and a copy of the Japanese instrument of surrender dated nearly two years later.

One hall has bombs hanging from the ceiling and nothing else but photographs and projected slides of Chinese deaths at Japanese hands. These include images of some of the hundreds of thousands of executions, beheadings, sessions of torture and scientific experiments carried out on Chinese, with a background of tragic music and the sounds of bombing noises.

There's also a reproduction of the village entrance to a series of underground tunnels which the Chinese built to hide in and from which to attack, and you can enter through an old house, descend to a small labyrinth and walk around.

The exhibition is one-sided insofar as the hundreds of thousands killed by the Japanese represent only a fraction of what the current regime has achieved since 1949, and which stands accused of still condoning torture and arbitrary imprisonment. You can be quite sure the Japanese didn't eat the Chinese, whereas they've been driven to eat each other either from starvation caused by their own government's policies, or in revenge during political campaigns. Although such events have been widely documented, there is, sadly, no museum marking the demonic behaviour of the Chinese towards each other, and those who try to research such matters are likely to find themselves imprisoned for revealing state secrets. Equally sadly, no lessons learned from this period seemed to enable the Chinese to empathize with the murders of thousands of Kosovo Albanians, but only with the sad side-effect of the deaths of a handful of their own people in the bombing of the Chinese embassy in Belgrade. Despite the repulsiveness of the behaviour of the Japanese military in the '30s and '40s, museums like this need to be viewed with caution. Their message is in no way humanitarian. It's simply pro-Chinese.

Chuān Dǐxià

川底下

Open 24hrs; adm ¥10.

From ⓜ Píngguǒ Yuán turn right out of the metro station and go the furthest of the 929 bus stops, the one for the 929*zhīxiàn* (alternative route—*see* characters p.401). The first bus is at 7am, the last at 5pm. Either alight at Zhàitáng and take a *miándì* taxi to Chuān Dǐxià for ¥10, or continue for four further stops to Chuān Dǐxià Lù, just after the 84km marker, ¥8.2, and walk up to the village from there, about 5km. The last bus back leaves at 5pm. The turning is altogether about 100km west from the centre of Běijīng, along the rather scenic route 109, which winds pleasantly through hilly territory. Parking just outside the village is ¥5.

The village was originally called Cuàn Dǐxià, meaning 'under the earthenware stove', a name which still appears on some signs and on the tickets, and was probably renamed to simplify writing it—a character requiring more than 30 strokes was replaced with one requiring only three, and it now means 'under the river'. The village contains a number of fairly well-preserved Míng and Qīng dynasty *sìhéyuàn* courtyard houses, not kept as museums but as functioning family houses, in which, in some cases, you can stay.

After the ticket office the road swings round to the left and the village is immediately to your right as well as above you on the hillside. Initial turnings to the right end up at blank cliff, which with further scrutiny seems to have steps cut in it, but further up on the left there's a fully functioning well and a stone-flagged path up to the higher sections to the right. Not only the drum stones and carved beams at the entrances have been well preserved, but the slogans of the 1966-76 Cultural Revolution remain on the walls as if freshly daubed (*Yòng Máo Zédōng sìxiang wǔzhuāng wǒmén de tóunǎo!*—Use Máo Zédōng thought to arm our minds!). In season there are brilliant camellias and other flowers in tubs, the roofs are made bright yellow with corn set out to dry, and the eaves are bristly with hanging bunches of red peppers.

There are said to be about 70 *sìhéyuàn* here, but only about 40 of them are occupied as younger people have all left for the cities. You may encounter the last of the 'lily-footed' ancients, their feet bound from childhood, now white-haired, walnut-faced, watery-eyed and nearly toothless.

Several of the houses have signs indicating they sell honey, and there are one or two shops and the odd English sign, but there's little to buy except a fine hard-back picture book of the village in Chinese (¥100–110), and you are mostly left alone. The odd satellite dish suggests that tourism, although still sporadic, may be reviving the village slightly, but beneath it you may see someone washing clothes with a scrubbing board under a tap.

You can stay in the village for as little as ¥12 in a clean, if primitive, dormitory, and eat cheaply depending on what's cooked. For ¥35 you can order an immense feast, but a bowl of what the family's having will cost a lot less than that. You may have to share the bathroom with honking geese. Is there hot water? 'Oh yes.' Pause. 'Not in winter of course.' Have a look at the Jīng Cuàn Fàndiàn, ✆ 6981 8096, or the Sìhé Gǔzhái Kèzhàn, ✆ 6981 8087, both in the lower part of the village (and both willing just to serve lunch if that's what you want).

5.5km further on the now unmade road there's another village, where it will generally be assumed you want to climb the 1733m Huáng Cǎo Liáng ('Yellow Grass Bridge') for the views, and you'll be pointed in the right direction, roughly another 6km or so. The villagers also say that after two hours' walking you can reach yet another bit of the Great Wall.

Sōng Shān Ancient Cave Dwellings (Sōng Shān Gǔ Yá Jū) 松山古崖居

Open 24 hours; ¥30, optional ¥1 insurance. Maps for ¥2.

Take the 919 (*not* the 919*zhīxiàn*) to its terminus station at Yánqìng, 1hr 20mins, ¥10. Then catch the 920, which comes in several variations, but you want the one with the characters for Sōng Shān on the front, which will drop you at the turning to the caves. Minibuses run the same route for ¥2. If you take a *miándì* taxi make it clear you want Sōng Shān *Gǔ Yá Jū*, not the Sōng Shān scenic area. Haggle hard. It's only 15km to the turning, and a further 3km to the entrance to the caves. Farm vehicles at the turning can be hired for ¥5 (although the first asking price can be five times that). The road runs through fields of maize and small orchards.

Chinese sources are spectacularly vague on the history of the caves, but for once at least frank about it. The caves may be Wèi, Táng or Yuán, and may have been hiding places for bandits, an army camp, or simply developed by canny villagers as a place of refuge during military invasion, and they certainly served the last purpose during the Japanese occupation. They number more than 130, and may have originally been cut by an ethnic minority called the Xī.

A path leading away from the ticket office climbs gently round in a curve giving you your first view of the caves, which have been carefully cut to be invisible from outside the range of low hills in which they are found. You pass stairs roughly hewn in the soft rock to your right. Don't take these, because you'll need to perform a tricky scramble over a barrier at the top, but if you do you'll see the rock is like Swiss cheese, pitted with numerous small caves of different sizes. The three main groups are very formal and angular, however, as if produced by a building developer, many having several rooms with different purposes, and some arranged one above the other with narrow stairs cut in the rock to make them accessible.

The most densely packed and interesting group of caves are the Hòu Shan, which you come to first. The upper storeys can be reached only by a vertical scramble for the most agile, and that's probably why there's a ¥1 insurance fee at the entrance.

This gives to several galleries of square caves carved in soft pebbly rock which crumbles easily and suggests that the caves might not have taken too long to cut; they now require buttressing in places. The interiors are often elaborately moulded into sleeping and washing areas. A side track takes you down to the Western King's Palace, the most spectacular cave—a two-storeyed affair with wings.

This unusual site makes a pleasant day trip. The climbing isn't too strenuous, although the more intrepid can scale the Hòu Shān for higher level walking. The areas buzzes with red-winged crickets and has a lot of butterfly-attracting buddleia bushes.

There's a basic hotel at the entrance asking ¥100 for a twin room.

China Aviation Museum (Zhōngguó Hángkōng Bówùguǎn) 中国航空博物馆

Open 8–5.30; adm ¥30, plus optional ¥5 to enter one plane.

Take bus 912 from Ⓜ Āndìng Mén, to the stop named after the museum, about 1hr 15mins, ¥3. The bus trundles up what looks like a runway and drops you at the gate.

Rusting Mig fighter planes and all kinds of troop transport, Chinese copies of Russian helicopters, missiles, field artillery, flying boats, early jets, VC10 lookalikes, AWACs planes and Second World War vintage mobile radar trucks fill the large apron of what was once a military air base. An extra ¥5 allows you to board a 1950s Russian troop and truck transport, and you can go into the cockpit. Further on you can be photographed sitting inside a Mig, ¥5 a time.

The aircraft, not all of which are whole, intermittently have signs explaining what they are all about. One Convair 240 now missing its engines flew from Běijīng to HK in 1949 for the

China National Aid Corporation and has 'Běijīng' in Máo's calligraphy on the side. There's also the first plane to fly onto the Tibetan plateau, and a British Vickers Viscount which was hijacked while carrying a foreign military delegation in 1982, but the crew subdued the hijackers and saved the day. A nice row of bombs are lined up on their tips against one wall.

A small tunnel curves into the mountain now set out as if it's the interior of a plane, sometimes with *fúwùyuán* asleep in the seats, and leading to what were probably originally the administration offices, and now contain exhibitions of aviation paraphernalia, including airborne surveillance equipment, aircraft machine guns, flying suits and other flying bric-à-brac.

But the main interest is in a vast curved underground hanger tunnel, like a miniature NORAD, which passes right through the mountain, inside which there's a strangely chilly and misty atmosphere. Smaller aircraft line both sides. The display begins with copies of early planes of political significance, including those which defected to China during the civil war, and goes on up to modern Hind helicopters and helicopter gunships. At the entrance souvenir shops sell model kits and die-cast models of stealth bombers.

Mílù Yuàn (Milu Ecological Research Centre)

Open 8am–6pm; adm ¥10, annual ticket accepted.

Take bus 352 from Guāngmíng Lóu, in Guāngmíng Lù, east of Tiān Tán, 13 stops to Jiùgōng, ¥1.5, about 50mins. Or take the 377 from Yǒngdìng Mén, southeast corner of the junction between Yǒngdìng Mén Wài Dàjiē and the second ring road for ¥2, about 30mins. Three-wheeled devices will carry you in discomfort from bus to park, ask ¥5 but ¥4 or maybe ¥3 possible, or you can walk. Get off the bus, and go back the way it's just come, crossing the road at the junction and heading south past a collection of grubby but cheap snack restaurants, ignoring the main willow-lined left turn and carrying on south past the Volkswagen Audi offices. It's about 2½km to a left turn marked 'Mílù', and then a further ½km to the building which is on your right at the end of the lane.

The centre, usually just known as the Milu Deer Park, is located in the remains of the Nán Hǎizi Imperial Hunting Park, in Dà Xīng County, directly south of Běijīng, where the Yuán, Míng and Qīng emperors would all come to hunt. In modern times it has become the best place in Běijīng to see animals in captivity.

The park is a breeding ground for the Père David's deer, or Mílù, sometimes known to the Chinese as the *sì bú xiàng* or 'four dissimilarities'. The park itself has at least four dissimilarities to most other open air animal sites in China—it doesn't have shooting galleries or other irrelevant noisy entertainments, people are actively discouraged from poking the animals with sticks, there are no crowds, and no one shouts '*lǎo wài*' (foreigner) at you.

After buying your ticket swing to the left and there's a map in a grassy area with peacocks, and a few mottos on signs which China could do with taking to heart, 'Care for nature today and nature will care for you tomorrow,' and 'Produce trees not children' (although presumably not by the same method). A few supposedly pettable deer wander around rather nervously, as if wary from previous encounters, but can be encouraged with a little patience. A little further on the right an enclosed area contains little Sika deer, roe deer and the rare Prezwalski's horse looking plump, healthy and far from endangered, as well as tame and curious to meet visitors. There are bird recognition charts everywhere: owls, crows, kingfishers, cuckoos and more.

The main large enclosure, dotted with lakes, is at the rear, and contains a few emus grazing beneath the willows as well as a large flock of these strange and slightly ungainly deer. The Chinese say it has 'the horns of a deer but it's not a deer; face of a horse but it's not a horse; hooves of a cow but it's not a cow; tail of a donkey but it's not a donkey.' It was identified by Père Armand David, a French Lazarist missionary, in 1865, and he sent some skins to France, but the deer was extinct in China by 1900, and only a few specimens survived in European zoos. The Duke of Bedford collected 18 remaining animals at his Woburn Abbey estate, and in 1985 a group from that herd was brought back from Britain, and has now grown to more than 800 head. The enclosure is large enough to allow the flock to wander off to quite a distance occasionally, but there are small grey brick viewing platforms to give you a good view. But in case you feel inclined to go any further there's a sign: 'The mīlù says, "Inside here is mine. Don't come inside if you're not a deer."'

The site also features a stone with (inevitably) the Qiánlóng emperor's calligraphy, a picnic area with proper tables and litter baskets, and signs with questions for schoolchildren to answer such as 'Why do we protect birds?' ('No, Xiǎoměi. The answer isn't, "So we can eat them."') Those who've been in China for a while may begin to feel strangely disoriented, and it really comes as no surprise to find that the park's director, an energetic man seen wielding a shovel to plant a new sign, worked in Dublin and studied in Germany.

Other pleasures include a jokingly named Mílù Yuán, the characters in this case not referring to the deer at all, but meaning 'lose one's way garden', and a startlingly effective installation designed to demonstrate the peril of endangered species, the World Extinct Wildlife Cemetery.

Large crosses are erected to the extinct animals of the five continents, and murals behind have images of those now gone. Rows of toppling slabs lined up like dominoes mark the disappearance of individual species from 1,500 onwards. On each is marked the name of the species, the date of its disappearance, and two stark Chinese characters miè jué, meaning 'extinct'. Those slabs nearer the vertical name endangered species, and those towards the end are still upright, but with the clear message that the disappearance of other species will eventually lead to the disappearance of humans, too, although they are expected to be outlasted by rats, mice and insects.

The park is a little scruffy and clearly in need of an increase in funding, but it's quiet enough for you to enjoy the birdsong, only disturbed by the chug of the occasional military transport plane from some nearby airfield. But this place is striving in an imaginative way to raise ecological consciousness in China—a little like trying to convert the Hindu population of India to the taste of beef—and the staff deserve your support.

Tiānjīn

天津

Tianjin holds little attraction for the Occidental sightseer, and compara-
tively few tourists stop in Tientsin on the journey between Shanghai
and Peiping. Its foreign settlements are modern with well-paved streets,
handsome buildings and efficient administrations, but in these features
there is nothing that cannot be seen elsewhere. The business man and
student of industrial development, however, will find much of interest.

Carl Crow, *Handbook for China*, 1933

The general managers of Tiānjīn's present-day Sheraton and Hyatt hotels still lament that they do little business with leisure travellers, much as the manager of the venerable Astor Hotel probably did 70 years ago, partly thanks to Crow's influential guide. Tiānjīn, amongst the biggest cities in China, has long been a metal bashing town, producing everything from Flying Pigeon bicycles to the *miándì* vans and *Xiàlí* saloon cars which form the majority of China's taxi fleet. The latest model can be found on an illuminated rotating plinth outside the main railway station. The city was the capital of Héběi Province until under the communist regime it became one of a handful of cities reporting directly to Běijīng, and the provincial capital moved to Shíjiāzhuāng. 60 per cent of north and northwest China's maritime exports pass through the port here, and there's an international ferry service to South Korea.

But the reasons Crow gave to regard Tiānjīn as of little interest are those which do attract visitors now, if only on day trips from Běijīng—the splendid mansions that were once the consulates, banks and clubs in a city which boasted more foreign concessions than any other in China. Tiānjīn can be seen as a preliminary study for a trip to Shànghǎi, and its atmosphere is quite different from that of Běijīng.

But there's more still to see in a place which was one of the first in China to become industrialized, has surprisingly active places of worship, and has atmospheric back alleys to match Běijīng's. When seen on foot Tiānjīn has a lot for those who love to get away from the main sights and who relish the obscure, and merits more than a day trip for those who have time to spare.

The lower prices of the department stores and of an electonics market in the seaport at Tánggū are what draw Běijīng residents here, and for souvenir-hunting foreign visitors there's a long, narrow street of antique stalls famously cheaper than anything in the capital (*see* 'Antiques Market' below). Regular walk-on double decker trains with no advance ticket purchase necessary make it an easy trip.

The city's original prosperity was founded in its role as Běijīng's port although, since China conducted little maritime trade with foreign countries during its long periods of self-imposed isolation, most traffic was inland from the south up the Grand Canal, which passed through Tiānjīn on its way to Běijīng. The city was originally about 90km from the sea by winding Hǎi Hé (river), but canal building subsequently reduced that distance substantially. The Macartney embassy to the Qiánlóng emperor came by ship to Tiānjīn in 1793, and then travelled up to

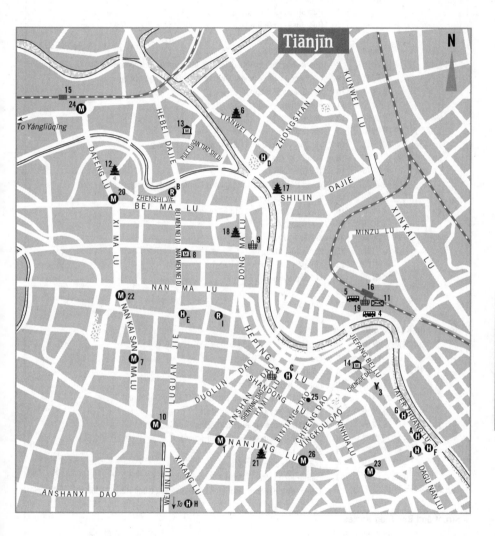

Tiānjīn

N

To Yángliǔqīng

347

Key: Tiānjīn

鞍山道	1	Ān Shān Dào Metro
沈阳道旧货市场	2	Antiques Market (Shěnyáng Dào Jiùhuò Shìchǎng)
中国银行	3	Bank of China (Zhōngguó Yínháng)
	4	Bus Buses to Tánggū
	5	Bus Buses to Běijīng
大悲院	6	Dàbēi Yuàn Metro
二纬路	7	Èr Wěi Lù Metro
广东会馆，戏剧博物馆	8	Guǎngdōng Guildhall and Theatre Museum (Guǎngdōng Huìguǎn, Xìjù Bówùguǎn)
古文化街，天后宫	9	Gǔ Wénhuà Jiē (Ancient Culture Street), Tiānhòu Gōng
海光寺	10	Hǎi Guāng Sì Metro
邮局	11	Post Office
清真寺	12	Qīngzhēn Sì
三条石历史博物馆	13	Sān Tiáo Shí Lìshǐ Bówùguǎn
天津文物馆藏	14	Tiānjīn Art Museum (Tiānjīn Wénwùguǎn Zàng)
天津西站	15	Tiānjīn Xī Zhàn
天津站	16	Tiānjīn Zhàn
望海楼教堂	17	Wàng Hǎi Lóu Jiào Táng (Notre Dǎme des Victoires)
文庙	18	Wén Miào (Confucius Temple)
永安百货	19	Wing On Department Store (Yǒng'ān Bǎihuò)
西北角	20	Xīběi Jiǎo Metro
西开教堂	21	Xī Kāi Jiǎo Táng
新华路	22	Xīnán Jiǎo Metro
新华路	23	Xīnhuá Lù Metro
西站	24	Xī Zhàn Metro
新华书店	25	Xīnhuá Shūdiàn
营口道	26	Yíngkǒu Dào

Hotels and Restaurants

利顺德大酒店	A	Astor Hotel (Lì Shùndé Dàjiǔdiàn)
耳朵眼炸糕店	B	Ěrdǔoyǎn Zhágāo Diàn
狗不理包子铺	C	Gǒubùlǐ Bāozi Pù
假日饭店	D	Holiday Inn (Jiǎrì Fàndiàn)
华富宫大酒店	E	The Huafu Palace Grand Hotel (Huáfùgōng Dàjiǔdiàn)
凯悦饭店	F	Hyatt Regency (Kǎiyuè Fàndiàn)
皇宫饭店	G	Imperial Palace Hotel (Huánggōng Fàndiàn)
喜来登大酒店	H	Sheraton Tiānjīn (Xǐláidēng Dàjiǔdiàn)
狮林大街	I	Shípǐn Jiē
唐达饭店		Tángdá Fàndiàn (in Tánggū)
天津第一饭店	J	Tianjin First Hotel (Tiānjīn Dìyī Fàndiàn)
新港国际海员俱乐部		Tiānjīn International Seamen's Club (Xīngǎng Guójì Hǎiyuán Jùlèbù – in Tánggū)

Street and Bus Stop Names

百货大楼	Bǎihuò Dàlóu	大寺前	Dà Sì Qián
北门内大街	Běi Mén Nèi Dàjiē	东、南、西、北马路	Dōng/Nán/Xī/Běi Mǎ Lù
滨江道	Bīnjiāng Dào	哈密道	Hāmì Dào
承锝道	Chéngdé Dào	和平路	Hépíng Lù
赤峰道	Chìfēng Dào	解放北路	Jiěfàng Běi Lù
大丰路	Dàfēng Lù	金钢桥	Jīngāng Qiáo

348 *Tiānjīn*

Běijīng on barges with banners describing its members as tribute bearers from the King of England. Foreign ships were again seen here during the Opium Wars, and between then and 1900 attacked the forts at the river's mouth four times, forcing agreement to the Treaty of Tiānjīn and the subsequent Conventions of Peking, whose provisions opened up Tiānjīn to foreign trade, allowing the creation of individual areas built, run and policed by foreign countries entirely according to their own laws.

The original Chinese city, its walls built in 1403, quickly became a tiny island almost surrounded by foreign concessions, which sprouted tall brick and stone buildings in an assortment of national styles, lining broad paved streets. Foreign forces had to fight their way ashore again in 1900 during the Boxer Rebellion, in order to relieve a 27-day siege of the concessions and proceed to Běijīng to relieve the siege of the Legation Quarter there. Foreigners took complete control of Tiānjīn 1900–02, dismantled the forts at Tánggū and pulled down the walls of the Chinese city to prevent it from being used as a base for future attacks. Its position on the city map is still quite clear although it's dwarfed by the modern metropolis, its street names referring to gates which even if they still stood would be many kilometres from the edge of the city.

The disastrous 1976 earthquake which flattened the town of Tángshān not far to the north also severely damaged Tiānjīn, which was only slowly rebuilt, news of the disaster being kept from the people of China for some time, and foreigners excluded.

Tiānjīn feels a little more relaxed than Běijīng, not having to be the public face of China, and not so closely scrutinized by the central government. In the evenings pavements around the station and in many other locations are taken over by vendors with their wares spread out on mats, selling everything from the commonplace to the bizarre, such as model aircraft made entirely out of cartridge casings. The history of foreign involvement seems to be viewed by the mayor as a source of potential tourism revenue, rather than humiliation, and he's working to get foreign governments involved in the rehabilitation and conservation of the areas they once controlled.

Despite the small resident community of experts of various nationalities working in manufacturing joint-ventures, foreign visitors are a tiny fraction of those in Běijīng and if this is your first trip out of the capital you may be a little taken aback by the catcalling you get just for being foreign. All a foreigner has to do is to stand still for a minute to become a magnet for every Chinese who knows the word 'hello' and nothing else (but wants to try it out), every taxi driver and pedicab rider ('Hello taxi?), and every lame-brained gawping cockaninny for hundreds of metres. This, however, is the experience of travel in most of China, so you'll just have to deal with it.

Getting to and from Tiānjīn
by air

Tiānjīn has an unexpected list of international connections: Samara Airlines weekly to Samara and Irkutsk, Japan Airlines twice weekly to Nagoya, Siberia Airlines twice weekly to Novosibirsk, ANA twice weekly to Osaka, and Korean Airlines four times a week to Seoul. Air China flies to Hong Kong daily and to Nagoya three times a week, and a collection of Chinese airlines serve 28 domestic destinations. Hong Kong's Dragonair also flies to Tiānjīn at times of economic growth, but had suspended its service at the time of writing.

Several airlines and useful ticket agents for both domestic and foreign flights are in the International Building on Nánjīng Lù right next to ⓂXīnhuá Lù, and buses run from here to Běijīng airport every 30 mins. A little further down the street, nearer to Ⓜ Yíngkǒu Dào, the Air China Building has domestic and international tickets on Chinese flights. Buses run from here to Tiānjīn airport, about 15km out of town.

Airlines: Aeroflot ✆ 2300 0993, Korean Air ✆ 2339 9257, ANA ✆ 2330 4318, JAL ✆ 2313 9766.

by sea

Ships leave for Inchon (Rén Chuān) in South Korea every four or five days from the passenger terminal (kèyùn zhàn) at the port at Tánggū. This can be reached by bus directly from Běijīng's Zhàogōng Kǒu long-distance bus station, or by a new rail service from Běijīng Nán Zhàn (South Station), although at rather inconvenient times: 02.06 or 04.11, taking about two hours. Buses to Tánggū leave from outside Tiānjīn's main railway station, although not all go to the port. Change at Tánggū railway station to bus 102 whose terminus is at the passenger terminal. The ships take about 24hrs to reach Inchon, and the cost for a berth ranges between ¥1,020 ($127) and ¥1,900 ($237). For schedules and bookings get a Mandarin speaker to call ✆ 2579 5694. The number of coastal services in China is falling off, but there are still services to Dàlián in the northeast at the time of writing.

by train

There are several convenient double decker trains a day from Běijīng to Tiānjīn and back, and there's no need to buy tickets in advance. Go into Běijīng Zhàn, up the escalator and straight ahead, and buy your ticket on the way to the gate. You can buy and board up to a few minutes before departure. Prices vary according to time of day, but the cheapest (perfectly comfortable) hard seat is ¥25, and the most expensive soft seat ¥40. At **Tiānjīn Zhàn** roving railway staff shouting 'Běijīng! Běijīng!' sell hard seat tickets outside the main entrance and just inside it. The platform entrance is at ground floor level to the far right as you enter, and there's a counter here for buying soft seat tickets if you prefer those. The journey takes 1hr 19 minutes. Coming from Běijīng don't get off at Tiānjīn Běi Zhàn (north station) but stay on to the main station, Tiānjīn Zhàn (sometimes called the Dōng Zhàn, or east station). The schedule is bound to change, but will be something like this:

From Běijīng: the K261 at 07.50, K231 at 09.02, K233 at 11.00, K235 at 13.00, K251 at 14.06, K237 at 15.10, K253 at 16.50, K239 at 17.51, K241 at 19.09, and K243 at 19.40.

From Tiānjīn: the K232 at 06.00, K234 at 07.00, K252 at 09.00, K254 at 10.00, K236 at 11.00, K262 at 13.20, K238 at 15.00, K240 at 16.03, K242 at 16.56, and K244 at 17.50.

Other destinations: At Tiānjīn Zhàn the main ticket office is to the left of the station as you face it, but there's one for foreigners upstairs inside the main building, so no particular need to face the push and shove here. If you ordered your ticket by phone (✆ 9922 9999) they'll tell you where to pick up the ticket at the time of ordering. Windows 4–17 are for ticket buying, and no.18 to return tickets (20% fee charged). There's a left luggage office immediately to the left of the main entrance as you face the station, costing between ¥2 and ¥6 depending on the size of the bag. **Tiānjīn Xī Zhàn**, an old German building, is almost worth going to see in its own right. Climbing the grand staircase is rather like entering a mansion, and you find a bizarre neoclassical interior with tacky carriage lamps on the walls and traditional Chinese furniture. This is the waiting room for soft sleeper passengers, and the main business is in the newer building to the left. Trains from here go further afield, especially south to Shànghǎi, and there are discouraging numbers of ticket touts around, although some trains in this direction also start from Tiānjīn Zhàn, which is easier for foreigners. Enquiries and platform tickets at window 1, ticket sales at no. 2, and 4–10, open almost 24hrs. Tiānjīn Xī Zhàn publishes its own small and relatively easy-to-read timetable booklet, ¥1.5. The left luggage office is below the main entrance.

Trains to other places mentioned in this book include the 612 at 21.47 to Chéngdé arr 04.37, and several trains a day to Běidàihé (¥19), Qínhuángdǎo (¥20), and Shānhǎiguān (¥22). There are also irregular trains to Tánggū, but these are not as convenient as the minibuses from outside the station.

There are plentiful food and snack outlets around the main station, and Mǎlán fast food noodle restaurant underneath the west station.

by bus

For those in the southern budget accommodation in Běijīng, the bus services from Běijīng's Zhàogōng Kǒu bus station may be more convenient than the train, and they drop you outside Tiānjīn Zhàn. The first bus is at 06.50, then roughly every 10mins, and takes 90mins to get there. The last service is at 19.25. A/c buses ¥31, regular buses ¥21. All Tiānjīn buses go to the main railway station, and the following continue to Tánggū for ¥41: the 501 at 07.00, 502 at 09.00, 507 at 11.00, 503 at 12.00, 504 at 13.30, 508 at 17.00, and 506 at 19.00.

The main long-distance buses back to Běijīng start from outside the station just to the left of the main entrance, but even for the budget traveller the fractional saving hardly makes them worth the relative discomfort compared to the train, unless a return to the south of Běijīng is needed.

In Tiānjīn the *miándī* **taxi**, now banished from Běijīng, still thrives, partly because it, like the *Xiàlī*, is built in Tiānjīn. These little yellow vans will take you almost anywhere for a flagfall of ¥10, which includes 10km, after which it's ¥1 per km. However, if the driver pushes a little button on the meter, after 10km the rate will jump to ¥1.5 per km. This is only for when he's taking a one-way trip out of town, so if you're going around town for more than 10km, or going out and coming back with the same driver, insist that the meter is reset and the button not pushed. It's assumed in Tiānjīn that all trips are ¥10 and you often have to ask for the meter to be started, and if it's not clearly agree ¥10, or you may be asked for a lot more on arrival. *Xiàlī* are either ¥1.2 including 4km, or ¥1.4 including 6km, flagfall in both also being ¥10. There are also Santana (¥1.6) and Nissan Cedrics hanging around outside the better hotels. Tiānjīn also has a rather grotty **metro** system, although its short route reeks of a vanity project, and it's quite often deserted. Flat fare ¥1. There are four trains an hour from around 5.30am to 10.30pm, but rather fewer around lunch time and in the early evening when the operators have their dinner. A total of seven stations begin with the Xī Zhàn in the north, and end at Xīnhuá Lù in the centre of town. There's no underground connection between platforms at some stations, so you have to cross the road to get to the right entrance.

Several useful routes start from the **bus** station to the left as you leave Tiānjīn Station, or to the left of the main entrance as you face it. The 8 will take you through the former French and British concessions down Jiěfàng Běi Lù, the 24 along the major shopping street of Hépíng Lù and past the antiques market, up the east and along the north side of the Chinese city, the northeast corner being a good starting point for a walk round a collection of Tiānjīn sights.

Tiānjīn ✆ (022)   *Tourist Information*

The *Tiānjīn Telegraph*, an amateur monthly free sheet available in expat cafés, has a list of what's on (which isn't much) and observations such as 'The longer you spend here, the more abundantly clear it becomes to you that you really don't understand much about these people,' which discourages you from believing it might tell you much else about Tiānjīn. There are **ATM machines** which accept foreign cards in the Bank of China's branch at Jiěfàng Běi Lù 80 (which is also the main place for changing travellers' cheques), the Astor Hotel, the Sheraton and the Holiday Inn, all accepting Cirrus, Mastercard, Visa, JCB and Amex. **Travellers' cheques** can be exchanged in the Bank of China entrance just to the left (*open 9–12 and 1.30–5, closed Sat and Sun*), at windows 18 and 19. Go into both just to see the chandeliered glass banking halls, dating back to the days of the concessions. Eager money-changing touts outside, masters of the quick switch, are best avoided. There are **post offices** next to the main railway station, in Jiěfàng Běi Lù, in Hépíng Lù, Chìfēng Dào (*open 9–5.30*) near the junction of Xīnhuá Lù. For long-distance telephone calls there are plenty of IC telephone card phones in the street. **Internet** access is available at branches of Sparkice one floor up in the Wing On Department Store next to the main railway station and in the ground floor café of the Imperial Hotel (only *2pm–10pm*) for ¥20 per hour. There are free minimalist but English-language tourist **maps** available at the bigger hotels, and detailed Chinese-only maps from bookshops such as the Xīnhuá Shūdiàn in Bīnjiāng Dào and street vendors for ¥3, but even these miss the smaller streets. For those with a deeper interest and a command of Mandarin, there's a street atlas, the *Tiānjīn Shēnghuó Dìtúcé*, for ¥14. **Visa extensions** are available from the ground floor of a new office in an alley off the north side of Mínzú Lù (no sense of humour, coy about its opening hours, closed for lunch). If you have any **complaints** about services in general, you could try the Supervisory Office of Tourism Quality of Tiānjīn Municipality (*open 8.30–5.30 and 6.30–8.30*), ✆ 2835 8814, ✉ 2835 2324, <*http://www.online.tj.cn/*>, at Yǒuyi Lù 18. If you feel inclined to report a taxi problem, call ✆ 2336 0004.

Foreign Concessions on Foot

The British and the French, having forced the Qīng empire into submission and occupied Běijīng, were on hand to build the first concessions in the newly opened-up Tiānjīn. The layout of the British concession was drawn up by General 'Chinese' Gordon, who had earlier led Qīng forces to victory over the dynasty-threatening Tàipíng Rebellion of pseudo-Christian rebels. A Japanese concession was added in 1895, and after 1900 the existing areas were expanded (the British had three), and Russian, German, Austro-Hungarian, Italian and Belgian concessions added, although the Belgians never did anything with theirs and it was handed back in 1930. The German and Austrian concessions were taken back by China after it finally entered the First World War on the side of the Allies in 1917.

The obvious starting point for a brief view of worthy civic grandeur, sometimes in self-conciously national styles, is Jiěfàng Běi Lù, which can be reached on foot from the main station. If coming straight from the train, turn left around the building to get to the main front entrance, then head directly away from it toward the river, and you'll see an iron bridge to your right, built a hundred years ago by foreign engineers, but now called Jiěfàng Qiáo, 'Liberation Bridge'. On the other side what's now 'Liberation Road North' was the Rue de France of the French Concession, and then as it crosses Yíngkǒu Dào (formerly Bristow Road) it enters the former British Concession, where it was formerly known as Victoria Road. Art Deco and neoclassical mansions line the street, formerly banks, stores, clubs and government offices. Look, for instance, for two buildings influenced by the Art Deco movement (note the doors) diagonally opposite each other at the junction with Bīnjiāng Dào, one looking like it is or has been a cinema. There's a fine building on your left after the Chìfēng Dào crossroads which had become the Tiānjīn Art Museum, although that's now moved round the corner to the right into an even finer porticoed building which was a French administrative office in Chéngdé Dào (*see* below).

Beyond Yíngkǒu Dào (Bristow Road) the first two buildings on the right were and still are banks, now the Bank of China, but both banking halls can be entered to view their period ceilings, glass and lamps. On the right further on, the battlemented fortress-like building, looking very out of place amongst the foreign buildings let alone the context of China, was the headquarters of the British administration, and just beyond that on the left is the venerable Astor Hotel whose ground floor passages are lined with photographs from the beginning of the last century, mainly of the many warlords, stars and starlets, who stayed there. The deposed emperor Pǔyí came regularly with a wife and a concubine to dance the tango during his stay in Tiānjīn from 1925 to 1931.

Perhaps the finest collection lies around the circular Central Park (Zhōngxīn Gōngyuán). Walk down Yíngkǒu Dào, and after crossing the major shopping street of Hépíng Lù look for a right turn into a short road at the top of which the park can clearly be seen. The circular green space, with its benches and monuments to modern communist heroes, is surrounded by a variety of extraordinary and extravagant European mansions, transplanted from Surrey and the best Parisian *arrondissements*.

For the keen student of decaying foreign architecture in China there are few streets in central Tiānjīn without something to please or surprise. The Italian concession on the same side of the river as the main station, and spread out to its west, is worth a stroll, as is the German concession, to the south of the main British one across Mǎcháng Dào (Racecourse Road). Some of China's most impressive remaining churches are to be found in Tiānjīn, turned to other uses since the revolution, but reopened in a limited way in recent times. The triple white domes of the Xī Kāi Jiào Táng at the junction of Nánjīng Lù and Bīnjiāng Dào are quite impressive, although visitors are more usually directed to the relatively anonymous Wàng Hǎi Lóu Jiào Táng (Nôtre-Dame des Victoires, although its Chinese name means 'Sea Watching Tower Catholic Church') across the river from the northeast corner of the old Chinese City. This was the site of a notorious massacre of missionaries in the 1860s when it was burned down, as it was again during the siege of Tiānjīn in 1900; the current building dates from 1904.

Tiānjīn Art Museum (Tiānjīn Wénwùguǎn Zàng)　天津文物馆藏

Open 8.30–12 and 1.30–5, closed Mon; adm ¥5.

In 1997 the museum moved to Chéngdé Dào 12, just off Jiěfàng Lù, in the former offices of the French concession administration, a splendid colonnaded stone mansion with large lanterns outside, and hints of Art Deco in the interior lighting and the shape of the windows. The exhibitions are up the broad carpeted dusty stairs from the foyer.

The museum is not large, but its collection is substantial and is presented on a rotating basis. At the top of the stairs to the right (past the original lavatories with frosted glass in the windows) there's a changing selection of contemporary art and calligraphy, hanging in small, panelled, interconnecting rooms which still reek of office. One floor up, archaeological and other artefacts include bronzes, tiles, carved seals, inkstones and other essentials of the study, printing blocks and samples of impressions taken from them, very early carved jade, fine wall hangings and scrolls, all contrasted oddly with areas of Art Deco glass-panelled ceiling. If you are fortunate you may see one very fine pair of scrolls showing the route of the Cháng Jiāng, usually known to foreigners as the Yangtze River, unrolled in long glass cases. Walking past the length of the scroll you follow the course of the river: look for small villages and pagodas on high promontories, people fishing from a variety of boats, walled towns, and at the end the seals of previous owners.

A small shop on the ground floor has lots of *nírén*, 'mud men', for sale—the clay figures which are a local speciality, and you may see a street vendor with calligraphy brushes for sale at the front door, looking to exploit the many art students who visit the museum.

Dàbēi Yuàn (Temple of Great Compassion)

Open 9–4.30, closed Mon; adm ¥4.

Take bus 1 from the north side of Zhōngxīn Gōngyuán, which runs up Hépíng Lù and Dōng Mǎ Lù, the east side of the old Chinese city, then turns right along Shílín Dàjiē. Get off at stop Jīngāng Qiáo, just after crossing back over the river. Walk on and take the left turn just after the Holiday Inn into Tiānwěi Lù.

The street is thick with hawkers for snacks, books, carved seals and beepers. As you continue the merchandise becomes increasingly religious—gaudy miniature shrines, and wrapped fruit and incense sticks for offerings. The number of beggars increases and stalls compete to deafen you with tapes of Buddhist chanting.

The monastery was first built in 1669, and is now a large and active Buddhist temple, although little remains of two of its three original axes and an accompanying pagoda. Some parts only date from this century, and there was major reconstruction in the 1980s to replace buildings destroyed or damaged in the 1966–76 Cultural Revolution. The hubbub diminishes as you enter its solid red gates and the commercial pressure is replaced with a hushed and genuine piety. Even sophisticated metropolitan misses of the kind more often seen in the temples of commerce than religion make the long descent from their platform shoes to their knees before a gleaming, grinning Maitreya or Buddha of the future, of prosperous tubbiness.

The red-pillared halls have the clutter of a functioning place of worship more reminiscent of the temples of Hong Kong than more spectacular, better preserved but relatively sterile tourist temples of much of China. Smoke drifts from the spidery sticks in ornate incense burners and further in, if your timing is good, you may hear the live chanting of rows of robed women in one hall and shaven headed monks in another, with onlookers a mixture of the serious-visaged faithful (who nevertheless still have to pay the ¥4 entrance fee) and gawping onlookers. Photography is not always welcome, so do ask permission.

It's possible to continue on foot to a small industrial museum hidden away in a back street or *hútòng. See* below.

Sān Tiáo Shí Lìshǐ Bówùguǎn   三条石历史博物馆

Open 9–4.30; ¥1.

Turning left out of the Dàbēi Yuàn and first right brings you to one of Tiānjīn's several rivers. Join the crowds wheeling heavily laden bicycles over the pedestrian bridge and you then enter a warren of *hútòng* more tangled than those of Běijīng, filled with the hum of light industry. Long before the arrival of the foreigners and their new technologies this area was one of the cradles of Chinese industry, and even in the 18th century was a metal-bashing district, producing water carts, oil presses and simple machines for making yet more simple machines. Go straight ahead and turn right into Sān Tiáo Shí Dàjiē (which is anything but the avenue its name implies), then after a few minutes right into the short Sān Tiáo Shí Xiǎo Mǎ Lù ('little horse road'), and the museum is on your left, opposite an English sign for a worm gearing factory.

This may be a museum of industry, but it is not itself industrious, and even mid-morning a heavy pounding on the door recessed under a low brick arch may be needed to bring out a sleepy attendant to turn on the lights and sell you a ticket.

The museum deals with the history of the Sān Tiáo Shí area, and opens with a passage of ancient photographs and even older maps, but at the rear there are two halls of ancient machinery, the first bright and clean, the second an atmospheric indoor graveyard for lathes, presses and stamping machines, its ceiling hung with pulleys and wires, all covered in dust. On 'tomb-sweeping day', when the Chinese traditionally tidy graves to show respect for their ancestors, this is where the machines in Tiānjīn's throbbing car factories ought to come.

You can continue on foot to a hidden back street mosque in Tiānjīn's Muslim quarter—*see* below.

Qīngzhēn Sì (Mosque) 清真寺

Open on request; adm free.

Turn right out of the Sān Tiáo Shí History Museum, and then left along Sān Tiao Shí Dàjiē and almost immediately right into the narrow, washing-hung Pǔlè Dàjiē and follow that for a few minutes to a T-junction. Turn right to bring you to the bigger shopping street of Héběi Dàjiē. Cross over and turn left. Just after crossing another of Tiānjīn's rivers, you'll find on your right the *Ěrduǒyǎn Zhágāo Diàn*, a restaurant selling this Tiānjīn Muslim speciality to eat in or take away. Amongst Tiānjīn's best-known exports are the meat-filled dumplings called *gǒubùlǐ*, or 'dogs won't touch them'—far more appetizing than their name suggests. But the deep fried rice snacks called *ěrduǒyǎn* are less well-known and more tasty—hot, oily, crunchy and filled with sweet bean paste—perfect for fuelling the rest of your walk (¥0.8 each).

Just past the restaurant a right turn into Zhēnshì Jiē, its name—'Needle Market Street'—another hint of Tiānjīn's early light industry, takes you into the heart of the Muslim quarter. Its inhabitants are easily recognizable by their white hats, which make them look a little like chefs, and you may find, for instance, one selling the skins of stoats and martens, which dangle from the back of his bicycle.

A right turn into a claustrophobically narrow dog-leg *hútòng* called Dà Sì Qián, immediately after a large three-storey building also on the right (the 'Minorities Cultural Palace'), leads past malodorous public toilets, from which emerge the echoing conversations of its squatting occupants, and almost immediately into a sunny square, with what appear to be churchyard railings opposite but with Buddhist swastikas in their ironwork. This is again a functioning place of worship and not formally open to visitors, but a polite request to the ancient gate-keeper will let you through beneath an arch of carved brick to the first courtyard, although not into the prayer hall itself unless you are also a Muslim. Originally early 18th century, the renovated exterior is a particularly fire engine red, and you can peer inside to see the beams decorated with verses from the Koran in golden Arabic script. The gatekeeper is inscrutable on the size of the congregation. 'There's days when there's lots and days when there's only a few.' Oh. You may want to avoid the prayer hours of 5.50am, 1.30pm, 4.30pm, 5.30pm and 7.40pm.

There's a map of the square not far from where you entered. Facing that, turn to your right and walk down to the main road, Dàfēng Lù, and you can continue on foot to the Guǎngdōng Guildhall (*see* below), or the 37 bus from across the road will take you along the east and south sides of the Chinese City and down Hépíng Lù to the central park, Zhōngxīn Gōngyuán. Or turning left on the same side of the road you quickly reach ❿ Xīběi Jiǎo.

Guǎngdōng Guildhall and Theatre Museum (Guǎngdōng Huìguǎn, Xìjù Bówùguǎn)   广东会馆，戏剧博物馆

Open 10–4.30, closed Mon; adm ¥4.

Walking south down Dàfēng Lù from near the mosque brings you into what in the days of the sprawling concessions was the Chinese quarter. Turn left along Běi Mǎ Lù and right down Běi Mén Nèi Dàjiē to the central crossroads of the old city. A little further along on the left is the Guildhall, reached by dodging soccer players in the grounds of the Sūn Zhōngshān (Sun Yatsen) Middle School.

The Guildhall's late-Qīng exterior rivals that of the more famous foreign buildings with a stone version of a wooden frontage, carved stone pillars, and large, foreign-looking brass lanterns, and would have been just one of numerous guildhalls serving as meeting places for merchants from other provinces, in this case the southern province often known in English as Canton, from where elements of the building's style and decoration are taken. (*See also* Běijīng's Huǔguáng Guildhall, p.166.)

Just inside the entrance murals painted on the walls show people performing opera in various locations in front of happy crowds. Exhibitions in the three halls of the first courtyard have materials on various opera companies and performers, mostly in the form of old photographs and programmes, *nírén* (clay figurines) of various performers, old tickets and chipped 78s of opera. The left hall has early woodblock prints, rubbings from a stele, early photographs and maps of Tiānjīn showing its drum and bell towers in place along with many other old guildhalls and tea houses.

These are the prelude to a magnificent and beautifully preserved century-old theatre which smells of wax like a church hall. Beams of hazy sunlight through the frosted glass at the rear of the galleries reveal a large thrust stage with an ornate wooden canopy and a carved and painted screen at the rear, surrounded by traditional dark wood square tables, and little stools with inset stone panels to cool the audience in the heat of a northern summer. Only the modern footlights suggest that performances still occasionally take place and that the theatre has not been locked up for a hundred years.

If you've followed the route described on foot from the Dàbēi Yuàn to here, walking south from the Guildhall will bring you to the vast open spaces more typical of modern Chinese cities, and close to lunch. Turn left into a vast modern edifice with a Chinese pavilion topping, which is Lǚguǎn Jiē, 'Hotel Street', and through that you reach a similar building with a large assortment of restaurants at Shípǐn Jiē, 'Food Street'. *See* 'Eating out', below.

Wén Miào (Confucius Temple)   文庙

Open daylight hours; adm ¥4.

The temple is in the northeast corner of the Chinese City, entered from Dōng Mǎ Lù.

On the axis you can visit, imperial favour is indicated by the yellow roofs, but there's a matching set of buildings on a parallel axis to the west with dark roofs, now a warehouse and not open to the public. To left and right as you enter, beyond the first triple-arched *páilou*, halls have small exhibitions on the life of Confucius, so little visited and so little cared for that people have left long messages scrawled in the dust on the cases. Further on are other small displays with models of various ceremonies and wax figures wearing scholar clothes. The seven-bay hall at the rear sits on a single-storey terrace with a small dragon pavement, and has a statue of Confucius and some traditional musical instruments inside.

Gǔ Wénhuà Jiē (Ancient Culture Street), Tiānhóu Gōng 古文化街，天后宫

The Ancient Culture Street, parallel to Dōng Mǎ Lù on the east side of the Chinese City, is a modern attempt to create a version of Běijīng's Liúlichǎng for Tiānjīn, but with the emphasis on souvenir selling and traditional crafts rather than antiques (for those see the excellent Antiques Market, below). Still, the pedestrianized street is colourful enough, and makes a pleasant stroll, and for those searching for typical Chinese souvenir items there's a wide range of choice from kites and cloisonné, to 'jade' and pirate VCDs, at lower prices than Běijīng.

Halfway up on the west side is the Tiānhóu Gōng, or 'Palace for the Heavenly Empress' (*open 8.30–4.30; adm ¥3*). This deity is a protector of seafarers and very popular on the Chinese coast, particularly round to the south, where she becomes Tin Hau, and A Ma, often with multiple shrines in her honour, sometimes appearing as an incarnartion of the Buddhist Guānyīn Goddess of Mercy and sometimes as a figure of folk religion. The temple itself, said to be early 14th century and around which signs claim great antiquity for various halls, is in fact an almost complete rebuild from the 1980s, and doubles as a rather neglected folk museum, with displays of *nírén* and other local crafts.

Antiques Market (Shěnyáng Dào Jiùhuò Shìchǎng) 沈阳道旧货市场

The market is busiest at weekends, but busy enough in the week to make it worth visiting whether you want to shop or not. It runs down Shěnyáng Dào, a narrow street omitted from most maps which runs off Xīnhuá Lù between Hāmì Dào and Ān Shān Dào. Take bus 24 from the main station and get off at stop Hāmì Dào, or walk west from Zhōngxīn Gōngyuán (park) up Hépíng Lù, turn left into Hāmì Dào and take any of the right-hand turns into which the market also spreads.

This market is halfway between the formality of Běijīng's Liúlichǎng and the spread-it-out-on-the-floor business of Pān Jiā Yuán, being made up mostly of lock-ups and stalls rather than formal shops. These are packed with a very wide selection from furniture to Máo memorabilia, mostly at lower prices than anywhere in Běijīng. If you plan to buy a large item or a few smaller ones you can easily recoup the rail or bus fare from Běijīng, and the change of pace and atmosphere is thrown in for free.

Around Tiānjīn

Shí Jiā Dàyuàn 石家大院
Open 9–11.30 and 1.30–4.30; adm ¥8.

Bus 153 from Ⓜ Xī Zhàn goes to the town of Yángliǔqīng, now a suburb of Tiānjīn, and stops near the *hútòng* leading to the mansion. Everyone will know where you want to go. By taxi head west out of town along the Xī Qīng Dào. About 16km from the centre the main road turns right into an industrial area but you continue straight on, and shortly afterwards turn left into Guāngmíng Lù. The narrow *hútòng* leading to the mansion is on the right after about 1km. Use the characters above to ask.

For those not planning a visit to the better-known mansions of central Shānxī, this is an expedition well worth making. It is a three-axis mansion of about 12 courtyards which claims to have a total of 278 rooms—a miniature Forbidden City for the family of a well-to-do provincial merchant called Shí. Like the Shānxī mansions it has also featured in the films of fifth generation film director Zhāng Yìmóu (in this case in *Huózhe*, 'To Live').

At the beginning of the mansion's left (west) axis you'll find a model of the entire mansion. Some rooms are furnished in a late-Qīng style to match the period of the mansion itself (particularly fine are the bedrooms on the east side), others now replicate ancient shops from the town, and some hold displays of traditional local products, and in particular the colourful New Year Pictures which once constituted an important local industry, and brick carving for which Tiānjīn was famous. The local *nírén* figurines are used to show the printmaking and brick carving process.

Ornate gates featuring brick carved with scenes of mythical events, people, birds and flowers connect courtyards of halls with grey roofs, black pillars and red window frames. A long corridor down one side is hung with lanterns whose panes are painted with images of beauties and which passes a two-storey theatre, its interior hung with bright red papercuts and orange lanterns.

Shopping

Bīnjiāng Dào, 'a walk street' as the sign says, meaning it's pedestrianized, is the home of Tiānjīn's larger department stores and more fashionable shops, a mix of new glass and chrome frontages and old buildings. For once in China it is a pedestrianized street that's genuinely free of vehicles. However, the main interest to visitors lies in the Antiques Street and 'Old Culture Street', detailed above.

Tiānjīn ℂ (022)   *Where to Stay*

Tiānjīn hotels recognize that the tourist market is as yet tiny, and concentrate their efforts on attracting and serving businessmen, and particularly long-staying expats. The contraction in the Chinese economy in the late '90s reduced the expat community to about a third of its former size, and until it recovers all published room rates for better accommodation, including those given below, are merely wishful thinking—it's a buyer's market. On the other hand there's little choice for the budget traveller, although there are some decent beds for as little as ¥45.

expensive

While the Chinese hotel industry has several nominally four-star offerings, at this level stick with the Sheraton (the only five-star) or Hyatt Regency (four). There's also a Holiday Inn (four). Add 15% service at all of these, and sometimes ¥5 City Development Fee.

The **Sheraton Tianjin** (Xǐláidēng Dàjiǔdiàn), ✆ 2335 3388, 🖷 2335 8740, <*sheraton@mail.zlnet.com.cn*>, <*http://www.sheraton.com/*>, is in a quiet spot on the edge of a park to the south of the centre, and recently thoroughly refurbished. Facilities include a brand new fitness centre and an excellent Cantonese restaurant— possibly the only one in northern China where they know without being told to bring the rice at the same time as the other dishes. Room rates begin at $220, suites at $350, and there are substantial discounts for advance bookings of two weeks or more.

The **Hyatt Regency** (Kǎiyuè Fàndiàn), is a comfortable tower conveniently placed at the south end of Jiěfàng Běi Lù, ✆ 2331 8888, 🖷 2331 1234, with good views over the old concessions, and in walking distance of several sights. Amongst its restaurants the Japanese one is particularly good. Rooms begin at $128, and executive floor from $168, although there are a variety of special offers for the asking.

The **Holiday Inn (Jiǎrì Fàndiàn)** is in Zhōngshān Lù beyond the northeast corner of the old Chinese City, ✆ 2628 8888, 🖷 2628 6666. Rooms are from ¥1079 ($135).

The century-old **Astor Hotel**'s previous guests have included first President of the Republic of China Yuán Shìkǎi, Máo Zédōng (who had a meeting here with the Dalai and Panchen Lamas in 1954), and Méi Lánfāng the opera star, many pictured in a display in the old lobby on the west side of the hotel, entered from Jiěfàng Běi Lù. Audrey Hepburn is also pictured, although it's not explicitly said that she stayed here. The original Astor was advanced for its day, installing the first electricity generator and telephone switchboard, and still has in place the oldest lift in China, installed in 1924 by the American Otis company, which now once again has offices and a factory in Tiānjīn. It's not used now but merely available for observation, and bolted, so you are safe. A modern tower has been added to the rear so that the hotel's main entrance is now on Tāi'er Zhuāng Lù, ✆ 2331 1688, 🖷 2331 6282, <*astorbc@mail.zlnet. com.cn*>, but at the rates quoted (from $130) you'd be better off in the Hyatt nearby. The only reason to stay would be to capture something of the old colonial flavour of the original high ceilinged and spacious rooms on the Jiěfàng Lù side, although the country house atmosphere of these is rather spoilt by carpet choices unlikely to have been considered by the original management, some of which require the wearing of sunglasses indoors. Something of the hotel's atmosphere can be sampled by visiting the moderately priced *jiǎozi* (think ravioli) restaurant on the ground floor on the Jiěfàng Běi Lù side.

moderate

A little further north, the slightly younger **Imperial Palace Hotel** of 1923 (Huánggōng Fàndiàn), ✆ 2319 0888, 🖷 2319 0222, <*imphotel@shell.tjvan.net.cn*>, is another partial remnant from treaty port days, now a Sino-Singapore joint-venture. Interior redesign has removed much of the period feel although it can still be detected in the angularity of some room interiors. Single rooms are ¥581 or $70, twins from ¥664 or $80, but the hotel rapidly and realistically offers rooms at half price, and throws in breakfast, taxes and the 10% service charge, which makes it worth considering as a mid-range hotel.

On the east side of the south end of Jiěfàng Lù, opposite the Hyatt, the 1922 **Tianjin First Hotel** (Tiānjīn Dìyī Fàndiàn), ✆ 2330 9988, ✆ 2312 3000, has recently refitted its big, high-ceilinged rooms and their large bathrooms and done so more in keeping with the originals than the other two—a good choice. Prices start at ¥664 ($83), but a 40% discount is easily obtained. Single rooms can be as low as ¥300 ($37).

inexpensive

The **Huafu Palace Grand Hotel** (Huáfùgōng Dàjiǔdiàn), ✆ 2735 0066, ✆ 2734 7370, a modern block with Chinese topping, dominates Nánshì Lǚguǎn Jiē, the 'hotel street' just west of the 'food street' to the south of the old Chinese City (take bus 24 from the station to stop Bǎihuò Dàlóu in Hépíng Lù, and fork left into Qīnghé Dàjiē at the next junction). The large range of rooms in several blocks includes twins for ¥150 ($19), singles for ¥120 ($15), and triples for ¥240, in which individual beds are ¥80 ($10). All these rooms have private baths. Bathless twins are ¥135, and triples ¥45 per bed. These rates all include Chinese breakfast, and there's a reluctance to discount further.

Tánggū accommodation

Those who arrive or depart by ferry from Tánggū might need to spend a night there. The accommodation opposite the passenger ferry terminal is not pleasant, but all right for one night. The **Tiānjīn International Seamen's Club** (Xīngǎng Guójì Hǎiyuán Jùlèbù), ✆ 2579 3204, has twins from ¥160 to ¥242; glum, decaying and unappealing. Its more basic neighbour, the **Tángdá Fàndiàn**, ✆ 2579 5941, has decrepit and dirty twins for ¥144 with 24hr hot water, and common bath doubles for only ¥56, with hot water from 6pm.

Eating Out

Tiānjīn wants to be Běijīng, and a variety of wannabe-foreign bars and restaurants has opened up around the city serving bad versions of foreign food, often with the accompaniment of live Filipino bands of only modest talent. However, these places tend to be cheaper than their equivalents in Běijīng. A typical example would be the **Cozy Café** beneath the bridge next to the Hyatt at the bottom of Jiěfàng Běi Lù (fish and chips ¥38). In some sense these are the inheritors of the traditions of Kiessling's and Bader's tea rooms, which still exist, although not in their original locations, and have menus which reveal the influence of the White Russian refugees who haunted all the treaty ports with items such as Beef Stroganoff—fairly exotic and adventurous in its day—as well as pastries which don't seem to have seen an egg. These places were exciting before the arrival of joint-venture pizza houses, private bakeries, KFC and McDonald's, all of which infest Tiānjīn.

Tiānjīn's most famous dish is *gǒubùlǐ*, or 'dogs won't touch them', steamed dumplings. Restaurants all over town serve these and there are nearly as many stories as to the origin of the name, some involving the ugliness of the original inventor, some their suitability only as a cheap snack for poor people, although they are in fact tasty enough, if nothing special. The most famous place to eat them is the **Gǒubùlǐ Bāozi Pù** in Shāndōng Lù just off the pedestrianized shopping street of Bīnjiāng Dào and very close to the antiques market. The restaurant itself is undistinguished, and there's an atmosphere of reluctance common to long-established restaurants in China. You can buy a take-away package at the entrance for ¥6, or a *lóng* (bamboo steamer) of 10 in the restaurant upstairs for ¥10.

The city's other noted speciality is the deep-fried rice cake called *ěrduǒyǎn*. *See* 'Qīngzhēn Sì', above.

Shípǐn Jiē, 'Food Street', is a cross-shaped arched-roofed market with restaurants on two levels serving various regional and ethnic minority cuisines, including more *gǒubùlǐ*, and stalls selling the fried dough twists which are another Tiānjīn speciality. There are about 30 or 40 restaurants altogether, some of which close at 8pm.

There's plenty of travel food and snacks available around the main railway station, including several *gǒubùlǐ* specialists, and the Hong Kong Wing On Department Store (Yǒng'ān Bǎihuò) has a bakery which includes a decent Battenberg cake in its repertoire.

Shānhǎiguān

山海

Shānhǎiguān, an ancient fortified town of mostly late-Míng date built into the Great Wall, whose eastern end plunges into the sea at this point, is the northernmost part of a ribbon of coastal development which extends south through industrial Qínhuángdǎo to the faded beach resort of Běidàihé, created by early 20th century expats resident in Tiānjīn as the oriental alternative to Brighton, although with better weather and better beaches. *See* 'Around Shānhǎiguān', below.

Shānhǎiguān is three hours away from Běijīng by air-conditioned express train. There's not only the sight of the Wall springing athletically up sheer hillsides as it does elsewhere, but the dramatic bonus of seeing one of its many ends, as it runs out of land to defend, and at a point known as 'the old dragon's head' drops to the sea.

The Wall sweeps down from the mountain called Jiǎo Shān to form the east side of a square around the town, before continuing across the plain to the sea. Shānhǎiguān's role was to prevent northern invaders from slipping around the end of the mountains and a long board on its tower-topped east gate magnificently announces it as Tiānxià Dìyī Guǎn—the first pass under heaven. The streets within the square of the city wall remain narrow and claustrophic, the usual boulevardization which has transformed almost all Chinese cities largely restricted to beyond the walls.

The Qīng dynasty was formed by mounted Manchu nomads who had replaced the Xiōngnú and the later Mongols as providers of mounted irritation from the north. In spite of whatever walls may then have been standing, the Mongols had successfully invaded China in the 13th century to form the Yuán dynasty, the Míng's predecessors. Despite the Míng's huge investment in civil engineering, the Wall failed to save them either. It was through the First Pass that the Manchu forces entered China to set up a foreign dynasty which lasted from 1644 until the last Qīng emperor abdicated in 1912.

But it was events in Běijīng which destroyed the Míng, not weak defences in Shānhǎiguān. Imperial incompetence had led to empty coffers, and the decision to extract high taxes from an already starving populace had them banding together in armies, one of which, led by a Shǎnxī peasant, entered Běijīng on 25 April 1644. The last Míng emperor, Chóngzhēn, fled to the hill behind the Forbidden City and hanged himself. It's perhaps not surprising that the defenders of Shānhǎiguān were distracted and allowed the Manchu forces into China. Some accounts excoriate the general concerned for betraying the Hàn (majority Chinese), others suggest that his intention was only to save the Míng. However, as a result the Chinese were to spend more than 250 years under foreign rule. To add insult to injury perhaps, troops for the march on Běijīng by the Eight Allied Powers were landed here in 1900 and occupied the city.

Getting to and from Shānhǎiguān

by air

There's an airport between Shānhǎiguān and Qínhuángdǎo, a short taxi ride from either, with occasional flights to seven Chinese cities including Shànghǎi and Nánjīng.

by train

Shānhǎiguān, Qínhuángdǎo and Běidàihé all have stations and a wide variety of services which call at one or two of the three, the vast majority departing from Běijīng Zhàn. The trains in each direction are a mixture of local services and long-distance trains heading to and from the northeast. At the Běijīng end book two or three days in advance, and if you plan to stay a couple of nights in Shānhǎiguān, which is enough, book your return ticket as soon as you arrive. Usually it's quite feasible to go to Shānhǎiguān, by bus or minibus from there to see Běidàihé (not particularly recommended) and then back by train from there. Tickets on an a/c K express are typically about ¥42 for soft sleeper.

by bus

The Xī Zhí Mén and Mǎjuàn bus stations in Běijīng both have buses to Qínhuángdǎo, the Mǎjuàn ones early in the morning, and the Xī Zhí Mén ones at 10.00 and 11.40, passing through Běidàihé on the way.

Getting Around

An assortment of transport infests Shānhǎiguān and will never fail to pester you as soon as you appear. There's a variety of meterless taxis, *sānmǎchē* (powered three-wheelers), *sānlúnchē* (pedicabs), minibuses and public buses. Tourist bus routes connect several of the main sights four times a day, but only in summer. The Nán Mén or south gate, the nearest to the railway station, is the transport hub, although there's a bus station of sorts further east along Xīnkāi Dōng Lù, although buses actually seem to depart from a yard opposite it. *Xiàlì* taxis are 1.2 per km, with a flagfall of ¥5 which includes 2km. The walled area of the town is small enough to walk around, but buses or taxis are needed to see the sights outside.

Bus 3 runs between Shānhǎiguān and Qínhuángdǎo for ¥1, bus 6 between Qínhuángdǎo and Běidàihé for ¥2, and bus 5 runs from Běidàihé station to Běidàihé Middle Beach for ¥0.5.

Shānhǎiguān ℃ (0335) · **Tourist Information**

The Bank of China main branch is within the southeast corner of the city walls on Dìyī Guǎn Lù (*open 8–6, 5.30 in winter*), but only expect money changing facilities Mon to Fri. The main post office, which also has long-distance telephone facilities, is outside the west gate (*open 8–6 for mail, 8–9 for telephone*). Vendors on the street and a variety of small kiosks have Mandarin-only maps for ¥2, and there are ¥1 versions available at the Xīnhuá Shūdiàn in Nánguān Dàjiē (*open 8.30–6*). The bigger department stores with anything you might need for travelling are just outside the south gate.

Tiān Xià Dìyī Guān (The First Pass Under Heaven and City Walls)

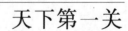

天下第一关

Open 7.30–6, longer in summer; adm ¥20, or ¥25 with a video camera.

The ticket includes the cost of visiting the Great Wall Museum.

A sloping ramp, broad enough for four horsemen to ride abreast, leads up from within the city to the south of the gate, and the freshly renovated wall stretches to north and south,

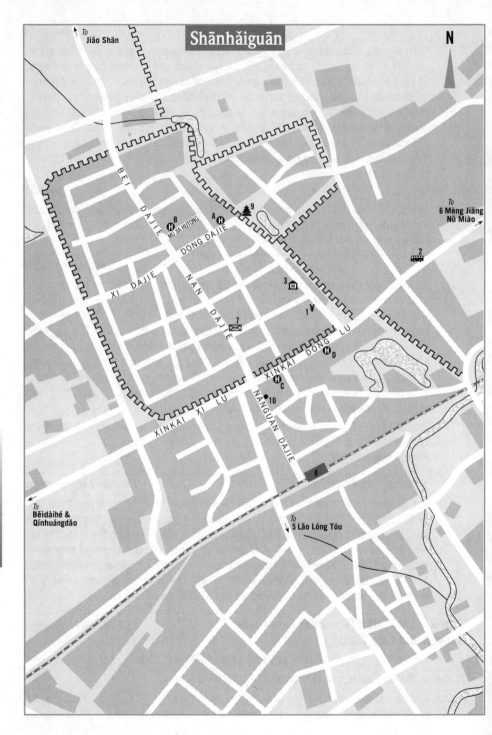

Shānhǎiguān

N

To Jiǎo Shān

To 6 Mèng Jiāng Nǚ Miào

BEI DAJIE

DONG DAJIE

B
MU JIA HUTONG

A

9

XI DAJIE

NAN DAJIE

3
M

1 ¥

2

7

XINKAI DONG LU

D

XINKAI XI LU

C

NANGUAN DAJIE

10

8

To Běidàihé & Qínhuángdǎo

To 5 Lǎo Lóng Tóu

中国银行	1	Bank of China (Zhōngguó Yínháng)
汽车站	2	Bus station
长城博物馆	3	Great Wall Museum (Cháng Chéng Bówùguǎn)
角山	4	Jiǎo Shān
长城博	5	Lǎo Lóng Tóu (Old Dragon's Head)
孟姜女庙	6	Mèng Jiāng Nǚ Miào
邮局	7	Post Office
火车站	8	Railway station
天下第一关	9	Tiānxià Dìyī Guān
新华书店	10	Xīnhuá Shūdiàn (bookshop)

Hotels

京山宾馆	A	Jīngshān Bīnguǎn
北街招待所	B	North Street Hotel (Běi Jiē Zhāodàisuǒ)
山海关大酒店	C	Shānhǎiguān Dàjiǔdiàn
友谊宾馆	D	Yǒuyì Bīnguǎn

Street and Bus Stop Names

北大街	Běi Dàjiē	南关大街	Nánguān Dàjiē
北戴河	Běidàihé	秦皇岛	Qínhuángdǎo
东大街	Dōng Dàjiē	西大街	Xī Dàjiē
穆家胡同	Mù Jiā Hútòng	新开西、东路	Xīnkāi Xī/Dōng Lù
南大街	Nán Dàjiē		

punctuated by further towers. A short walk to the north, past an old brass cannon of 1643 cast with fading inscriptions on a modern concrete mount, one tower contains samples of early Míng bricks although, like most of the construction here, it originally dates from 1584. Behind the first pass itself, a small enceinte—a semi-circular loop of wall—would have made attacking the city very difficult. The only entrance is from the south, requiring a sharp left turn to attack the gates while being subject to bombardment from all sides across what is now a small park filled with pines, but then would have bare of any such protection. The tower itself has rows of small square windows with vermilion shutters, clearly intended to house archers, but it is now put to more gentle use with a display of Qīng costume.

South of the First Pass the city wall has been fitted with street lighting, souvenir stalls, and rows of garish plaster statues of mythical and historical figures, some amusingly graffitied, but the more interesting views are down to the ramshackle interior of the city, a mini-Běijīng of narrow criss-crossing *hútòng*—a Mongol word for lanes absorbed by Mandarin. Many of the tiled roofs are so overgrown as to appear to be gardens. The southeast corner of the city wall has old cannon and another tower, full of the kind of pottery figures you can buy at the Terracotta Warriors in Xī'ān. The tower's history is like that of so much in China: built 1381, rebuilt 1781, damaged in 1933 by the Japanese and rebuilt in 1985.

At this corner, the Great Wall, now similarly overgrown, detaches itself and heads crumbling and unrestored both south towards the sea. It's easy to find places to scramble up on either that on the city wall on the southern side, following paths made by the locals, and free in both cases.

On the inner side of the south city wall, the brick facing has long since disappeared, much of it doubtless recycled into housing. Trees grow out of its exterior, and in parts the earthen interior has largely worn away, too, leaving only the uneven metre-wide top of the outer casing to act as a path for those with the nerve to use it. You may meet a goatherd indulging his charges with some elevated grazing. As with other unrestored walls, and despite the heavy traffic along the road below and the tendency of some local people to use it as a rather exposed public toilet, the melancholy atmosphere seems more authentic than any careful restoration could possibly make it.

Great Wall Museum (Cháng Chéng Bówùguǎn)   老龙头

Open 8.30 to 5, longer in summer; adm ¥5.

If you visit the 'First Pass' first, admission to the museum is included.

This does not match the Great Wall Museum at Bā Dá Lǐng outside Běijīng, but it does have photographs of various sections of the wall in date order, as well as sample of implements used in construction, and models.

Lǎo Lóng Tóu (Old Dragon's Head)   长城博物馆

Open daylight hours; adm ¥30.

Take bus 13 from the Nán Mén to stop Lǎo Lóng Tóu, less than 10mins, ¥0.5, or ¥1 in a minibus. The route runs through countryside with ribbons of greenhouses, mud walls on three sides and bamboo hoops supporting shiny plastic sheets. Three-wheeled taxis ask ¥5 for this trip, but quickly drop to ¥3. When the tourist route bus is running it leaves the south gate at 8, 8.30, 10.30, 2, 2.30 and 4.

Once past the row of identical restaurants with garish signs and the heckling of the souvenir sellers, the site begins disappointingly with numerous rebuilt pavilions, supposedly a reconstruction of a 1620 barracks. The original, or one of its earlier reconstructions, was destroyed by foreign forces in 1900 on their way to prevent the massacre of foreign diplomats and others under siege by the combined forces of the Boxer Rebels and imperial troops in the Legation Quarter of Beijing. Rebuilt 92 years later, it looks like a film set and is stocked with a movie prop boat and siege engine.

The real interest is behind, beyond a two-storey pavilion adorned with boards bearing the calligraphy of the Qīng dynasty's Qiánlóng emperor. A smooth highway of beach stretches to the right, where local visitors paddle in the shallows looking for shells, some still in their shoes. Fishing boats bob on the waves, and large tankers further out await their turn at the port to the left. Beyond the pavilion the Wall forms a short promontory with a final mini-watchtower, before finally expiring. Steps help you over one section of rammed earth, far more ancient than the surrounding stone and brickwork and protectively cased in glass. An imposing stele, more than 2½m high in its dragon-carved brick surround, undated but probably Táng (618–907), reads poetically but puzzlingly, 'Sky separates sea and mountains.' Ten years ago beyond this point there was nothing left to see.

Steps down lead down to beach level, the view disfigured by a hideous red, green and yellow fast food restaurant, connected to the wall by a no doubt equally historic staircase. Chinese squat at the shoreline looking for shells of the kind on sale at stalls lining the path.

Temple of the Sea God (Hǎishén Miào)

海神庙

Your ticket also admits you to the Temple of the Sea God along the beach to the right, originally Qīng but rebuilt in 1989, whose arches with a slight point and windows carved from stone are reminiscent of many of Běijīng's temples. Generals Hēng and Hā occupy the entrance and the main halls have garish statues of the God of the Sea and his attendants, and behind that his wife, and various gods and goddesses of different weather states of particular interest to seamen. A bell tower to the left of the entrance allows you to strike the bell three times for ¥1 (for luck).

Jiǎo Shān

角山

Open at least 7–6; adm ¥10.

If Lǎo Lóng Tóu is Shānhǎiguān's most picturesque sight, the Jiǎo Shān section of the Great Wall is its most impressive, three km from the north side of town. It was until recently possible to walk along a decayed section of Wall from the city to the refurbished section. Despite Dèng Xiǎopíng's 'Love the Great Wall, Love China' instruction (possibly no other language in the world is as fond of using the verb to love in the imperative mood) a section here was pulled in down in 1998 to facilitate the expansion of a vegetable warehouse, and officials looked the other way, thus demonstrating that laws on conserving the Wall are more honoured in the breach than the observance. Tourist bus 25 comes here from the Nán Mén, but you can easily haggle wth a variety of private transport for a price to take you, wait, and bring you back if you wish. For most of the year there are more of them than of you.

Three kilometres to the north by bus or taxi, the wall rushes down from the mountains as if it itself is on the attack. Appropriately for a place so concerned with defence, there's a firing range here, and your walk along a path lined with forsythia is punctuated with the sound of gunfire and the equally staccato shouts of 'Hello!' from souvenir vendors. As with more popular sections of the wall near Běijīng, there's a cable car for the less sprightly (¥15), its lower building in vaguely Míng style.

This section of the wall was restored in 1961 and stretches away broad and smooth, but most of all *up*. Your first target is clearly a two-storey watchtower above, but you'll need hands as well as feet to get there. Railings have been inserted to help, and when you finally reach the tower itself, you can skirt it on a gunmetal-grey staircase, or scale it on a metal stepladder, hooped to prevent you plummeting all the way back down to the entrance. The climb is worth it for the views across to the town, now clearly connected by a ribbon of earth you might have missed on the way here and which represents the true state of the Wall for most of its various lengths. Other than tourism Shānhǎiguān survives on the petroleum industry, brewing and other manufacturing, the plants visible across the river to the west.

Beacon towers of the kind you can see scattered around the surrounding hills sometimes replaced the Wall altogether, making it a dotted rather than a continuous line. Beyond the watchtower it continues to climb steeply, but parapets disappear, as do other visitors, and those with enough energy will find themselves alone amongst grand decay more quickly than at the better known sites nearer Běijīng, and on a clear day will have a view of the sea. Before this it's possible to take steps down to ground level, and a concrete path leads around the chairlift's upper winch room to a distant made-for-tourists temple, not worth the walk in itself, although you may wish to follow the path just for the views, including a pretty lake in the distance (which is in fact a noisy amusement area when seen close up).

Mèng Jiāng Nǚ Miào 孟姜女庙

Open 8.30–5; adm ¥15.

Bus 23 from the Nán Mén, or a *Xiàlì* taxi for ¥20 there and back, including 30mins waiting time.

Shānhǎiguān has a monument to the human cost of the wall at its Mèng Jiāng Nǚ Temple, about 8km to the east of town. Here a steep staircase leads to halls honouring a Qín dynasty (221–206 BCE) woman, who came searching for her husband, conscripted to help with construction under a system in which labour was donated in place of taxation (corvée labour).

Behind the temple is the oddly shaped look-out point, 'Looking for Husband Rock', whose flat areas are supposed to represent her bed and dressing table. She supposedly left her footprints there, a distinctly Buddhist mark of divinity, but the Qiánlóng emperor definitely caused his own remarks to be carved in it, and other worthies left calligraphy boards, too. A small pavilion beyond was supposed to be her dressing pavilion, but is now occupied by telescopes and binoculars for hire, looking down on a modern theme park.

Their enthusiasm is for her fidelity. Just as parts of the wall have frequently been recycled into housing, so her story has been recycled from city wall construction elsewhere in China, and comes in many versions. But in all she finds her husband dead, and at her tears the wall crumbles from pity and reveals his bones—clearly construction quality in China was no better then than it is now. Her devotion to her spouse has made her the subject of many Chinese operas and plays, as well as giving her supernatural status, not least because in some versions she subsequently turns down the emperor's invitation to join his harem, and throws herself into the sea instead.

The rather distressed halls here have roofs as overgrown as those of the town's *hútòng*, but one of them sports a famous antithetical couplet on two calligraphy boards, which delights more literary-minded Chinese. The boards are easy to spot, since each contains a character repeated several times, but which can be pronounced in two different ways. and whose fun is based on the long string of repeated characters each half contains:

Hǎi shuǐ *cháo, zhāo zhāo cháo, zhāo cháo zhāo* luò,

Fú yún *zhěng, cháng cháng zhěng, cháng zhěng cháng* xiāo.

Remarkably resistant to casual translation, the first cleverly describes the ebbing and flowing of the morning tide, and the second the increasing coverage of the floating clouds, and their final disappearance. Both hint perhaps at Mèng Jiāng Nǚ's suicide.

Around Shānhǎiguān

Běidàihé and Qínhuángdǎo 北戴河，秦皇岛

For access details *see* 'Getting Around', above. Qínhuángdǎo is a place to pass through on the way to Běidàihé from Shānhǎiguān but there is no reason to stop, unless it's to catch a bus or train to Běijīng. A former treaty port (one where foreigners were permitted to reside and trade), its principal business is still shipping.

Běidàihé was developed as a beach resort with the first foreign cottages appearing around 1895, only to be burned to the ground in 1900. Nevertheless, the attractiveness of the beaches made it very popular from May to October, and after it was incorporated in the treaty port area of Qínhuángdǎo, and thus under more foreign control, and linked by rail to the main line to the northeast in 1917, the number of foreign buildings grew rapidly. Ann Bridge (another of whose novels, *Four-part Setting*, was set in Běidàihé) wrote:

> *At Pei-t'ai-ho, by the sea, she rode, walked, played tennis, swam four times a day ... ate enormous meals, relished the rain when it rained, revelled in the sun when it came out again. She learned the correct seat on a donkey, well over the tail, and so mounted hooshed along the narrow field paths between the tall maize and kaoliang, or down the sandy donkey-track that runs throughout its entire length beside the one long road which links together the three miles of villas of the pleasant straggling wooded resort. She also learned never to put on anything but a bathing-suit or a wrapper till 5 P.M. and became quite accustomed, on that same road, to ride about in a ricksha with a bathing dress and a painted paper parasol as her only costume on her way to bathing-parties... Like everyone else, she consumed quantities of ginger biscuits and cherry brandy on the beach at these parties, before riding back, damp but warm, the way she had come.*

Ann Bridge, *The Ginger Griffin*, London 1934

Long after the foreigners had all been ejected Běidàihé the resort remained a dream destination for Běijīng people, and the extensive bungalows and houses of the foreigners were quickly appropriated by party cadres for their own use. Máo bathed here, to the consternation of his doctor and others worried about sharks, and senior Party figures still hold an annual conference here. In a sense Běidàihé never changed. Still only the privileged come here, and the governments of various less clement provinces built sanatoria for the relaxation of senior cadres tired from 'serving the people' (helping themselves), and for model workers.

Travel restrictions having been lifted, the common man, model or not, now comes here en masse. Expats, feeling the need to see the sea, or for some bracing sea air as a change from smoggy Beijing, also show up in the summer. They find it soothing, but not that soothing.

Badly constructed restaurants and hotels have replaced most of the bungalows whose architecture was once admired. Rows of seafood restaurants line their frontages with red plastic bowls in which the creatures are kept alive by hoses and pumps. Souvenir stalls sell anything you like as long as it can be made from shells, and dried fish. Commercial bathing beaches alternate with commercial fishing beaches, both lined with forlorn villas and nasty tiled buildings. It costs ¥5 to enter middle beach and watch PSB officers in full uniform careering about the shallows in pedalos. The best beach is supposedly Nándàihé, further south, but the atmosphere is the same.

If this sounds appealing, enthusiastic touts will drag you to an assortment of the plentiful and often cheap accommodation, especially on weekdays and out of season.

Few hotels in Shānhǎiguān accept foreigners.

The **Jīngshān Bīnguǎn** on Dōng Dàjiē right next to the Dìyī Guǎn, ✆ 505 1130, 📠 505 1897, is a dismal reproduction of Qīng architecture with unfriendly staff and grubby rooms. Breakfast is included unless you have the temerity to haggle the room price down with the staff. You'll be disturbed by karaoke and the hooting of steam engines (of which the second are more melodious) until well past midnight. Some of the corner room doubles (e.g. 105) have bathrooms with windows and two windows in the main room. Standard twins are ¥160, and superior ones on the upper floor ¥260. There are also triples for ¥240. A second building on the south side of the road, and only open in the summer, has twins from ¥120 and triples from ¥150.

The **North Street Hotel** (Běi Jiē Zhāodàisuǒ) in Mù Jiā Hútòng a little to the north-west of the Jīngshān, ✆ 505 1680, has several washing-hung courtyards and doubles with bath for ¥100. There are also ¥20 beds in common bath six-bed dormitories. The bathrooms are decrepit but with large tubs, and hot water is only available 8pm–10pm.

The Shāngyè Bīnguǎn has a tempting location by the Nán Mén, but a far better choice is the newer two-star **Shānhǎiguān Dàjiǔdiàn**, a little further east at Xīn Kāi Dōng Lù 107, 506 4488 ext. 3600, with twins for ¥288 and triples for ¥430.

Further east still the **Yǒuyì Bīnguǎn**, ✆ 404 1613, has doubles from ¥260 (¥150 off-season), triples ¥280 and quads from ¥320, all with fairly simple facilities and, in a throwback to the Chinese hotels of a few years ago, no towels, toilet paper or phone.

Eating Out

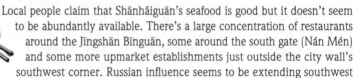 Local people claim that Shānhǎiguān's seafood is good but it doesn't seem to be abundantly available. There's a large concentration of restaurants around the Jīngshān Bīnguǎn, some around the south gate (Nán Mén) and some more upmarket establishments just outside the city wall's southwest corner. Russian influence seems to be extending southwest from its concentrations in Harbin, and surprisingly there's a Russian restaurant on the south side of Xīn Kāi Xī Lù beyond the western wall, and a tiny Korean place on the east side of Nán Dàjiē not far inside the wall.

Chéngdé

'Sons of heaven' and so deities in their own right, China's emperors were still only human and, as spring wore into early summer, they tired of the increasingly oven-like breath of the winds from the Gobi, and retreated from their Běijīng palaces northeast into the mountains beyond the Great Wall, and back to their geographical and cultural roots.

At the cool mountain resort of Chéngdé, then called Rèhé or 'warm river' (Jehol, in a common earlier style of transliteration), they built a lavish pleasure-dome of palaces, temples, lakes, pagodas, parks and hunting grounds where during the summer months they could rule their empire while hunting, camping and play-acting at the mounted military skills that originally won them China.

They also indulged themselves in diplomacy by architecture. Some palaces were built in a plain style to suggest the emperor's indifference to wealth and fame, and that he remained at heart a Manchu. Others, including copies of the most extravagant buildings of China's south, an imitation of Lhasa's Potala Palace and temples with Islamic overtones, were intended both to overawe envoys from unruly border peoples and to seduce them with demonstrations of the emperor's respect for their religions.

They still impress today. Begun by the Kāngxī emperor in 1703, the complex was substantially expanded by his grandson, the Qiánlóng emperor, and like the Manchu monarchs you can retreat from Běijīng's heat to stroll in leafy parkland and see Chinese architecture at its most ingenious and extravagant. 1930s guidebooks speak of the necessity of obtaining permits, the difficulties of the 144-mile-long road and the need for a reliable interpreter, but now you can relax in air-conditioned comfort while the train winds into the mountains and arrives in Chéngdé a mere four and a half hours later. The emperors themselves never had it so good.

Foreigners weren't always as welcome at Chéngdé as they are today. An early visitor was Britain's Lord Macartney, an envoy from King George III, who arrived in 1793 with the aim of increasing trade and installing a permanent British representative in Běijīng. Quite used to admitting barbarians to his summer stronghold, that being part of its purpose, the Qiánlóng emperor found the new arrivals less supplicant than his other guests—Macartney was prepared to make the same obeisance he would make to his own monarch, but would not knock his forehead on the floor in the traditional kow-tow (*kòu tóu*—'knock the head') and perhaps treated them accordingly. Failing to impress the emperor even with the most ingenious products of Western technology, Macartney took home a tart warning to George III to 'tremble and obey'. (*See* 'A Missed Opportunity', below.)

Nevertheless in 1860 the living quarters at the rear of the palace saw the Xiánfēng emperor signing treaties which allowed foreign ambassadors to reside in Beijing, ceded Hong Kong's Kowloon district to the British in perpetuity and reaffirmed agreement to a list of previous concessions. Signs in English and Chinese now condemn the emperor for his betrayal but, with Anglo-French troops occupying Běijīng and his Summer Palace there already in smouldering ruins, he had little choice.

Chéngdé has more than just architectural and scenic pleasures. Steam engines are still used to haul coal down a branch line and there's a level crossing in the middle of town through which the hissing monsters regularly pass. Wherever you stay in the centre of town you are likely to hear the ringing of the level crossing gate bell and the wail of the trains, which will have you reaching for your hound dog and steel guitar. The gates are shut at the last moment, and simply rammed into any pedestrians who happen to be in the way, so be careful. At night a crowded market takes over Chéngdé's main street, with clothing, bric-à-brac and open air eating, and restaurants around town have the most comprehensive menus north of Guăngdōng (Canton).

Hunting may no longer be on the agenda for visitors (although CITS does offer a tour to a firing range), but the tradition of eating wild meats lives on in Chéngdé's restaurants. The park was once stocked with quantities of game, including Père David's deer, the curious animals known to Chinese as the 'four dissimilarities' for being neither reindeer, horse, donkey or cow, but having some attributes of each. After the Jiāqìng emperor died here in 1820, and the Xiánfēng emperor in 1861, the Qīng viewed the site as unlucky and abandoned it. Xiánfēng's concubine, Cíxī, always preferred the Yíhé Yuán and Yuánmíng Yuán outside Běijīng. By 1900 the deer had disappeared into the stomachs of local people (but reintroduced stock can be seen in the Mílù Deer Park, a remnant of large imperial hunting grounds just south of Běijīng—see p.343).

Chéngdé claims about three million visitors per annum, including around 75,000 foreigners. Touts are at their worst and hotel prices highest in June, July and August.

The Last and First Emperor

Imagine a chain of huge, brightly coloured forts, set dispersedly in a waste of jagged and spectacular hills. They are deserted save by a shy handful of monks, who can less justly be called caretakers than the impotent spectators of decay. In their dark halls the gods gesticulate in silence: a thin filament of smoke, rising from a bowl full of the grey dust of joss-sticks, is their only certificate against complete oblivion.

Peter Fleming, *One's Company*, 1934

When you venture to Chéngdé you venture beyond the Great Wall and beyond traditional China into an area where no Chinese was permitted to go until modern times—the Qīng homeland of Manchuria. During Fleming's visit this was occupied by the Japanese although, as Fleming reported for *The Times*, they were having difficulties with bandits and warlords (often the same thing).

As the Qīng empire weakened and foreigners encroached more and more on Qīng territory, much of Manchuria had fallen under the control of the Russians. In giving up the throne of China there was no reason for the Qīng also to give up the throne of their Manchurian homeland, but control was taken by the Japanese, who converted it into the highly imaginary state of Manchukuo. Its first emperor was the last of the Qīng—Pǔyí.

Fleming interviewed Pǔyí, and left a memorable sketch of him: 'He is a tall young man of twenty-nine, much better-loooking and more alert than you would suppose from his photographs, which invariably credit him with a dazed and rather tortoise-like appearance. He has very fine hands and a charming smile. He was wearing spats.'

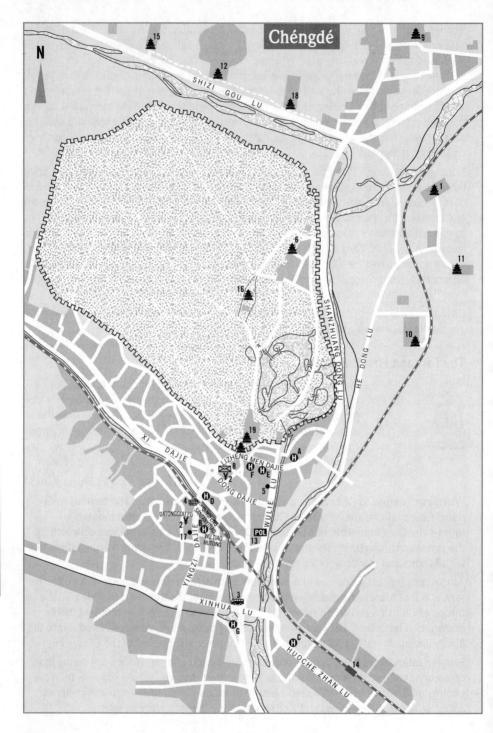

Chéngdé

SHIZI GOU LU

SHANZHUANG DONG LU

HE DONG LU

XI DAJIE

LIZHENG MEN DAJIE

DONG DAJIE

WULIE LU

DATONGGOU LU

SHANGYING

YINGZI DAJIE

WU TIAO HUTONG

POL
13

XINHUA LU

HUOCHE ZHAN LU

Key

安远庙	1	Ānyuán Miào (Temple of Distant Peace)
中国银行	2	Bank of China (Zhōngguó Yínháng)
汽车站	3	Bus station
承德商厦	4	Chéngdé Shāngshà
中国旅行社	5	CITS (Zhōngguó Lǚxíngshè)
六和塔	6	Liù Hé Tǎ
避暑山庄	7	The Mountain Resort for Escaping the Heat (Bìshǔ Shān Zhuāng) main entrance
邮局	8	Post Office
普宁寺	9	Pǔníng Sì (Temple of Universal Peace)
溥仁寺	10	Pǔrén Sì (Temple of Universal Love)
普乐寺	11	Pǔlè Sì (Temple of Universal Joy)
普陀宗乘之庙	12	Pǔtuózōngchéng Zhī Miào ('Potala Temple')
公安局	13	PSB Aliens Entry-Exit Bureau (Gōng'ān Jú)
火车站	14	Railway station
殊像寺	15	Shūxiàng Sì
文津阁	16	Wénjīn Gé
新华书店	17	Xīnhuá Shūdiàn (bookshop)
须弥福寿命庙	18	Xūmífúshòu Miào (Temple of Happiness and Longevity at Mount Sumeru)
正宫	19	Zhèng Gōng

Hotels

德汇宾馆	A	Déhuì Bīnguǎn
红鑫宾馆	B	Hóngxīn Bīnguǎn
会龙大厦	C	Huìlóng Dàshà
劳动大厦	D	Láodòng Dàshà
明珠大酒店	E	Míngzhū Dàjiǔdiàn
山庄宾馆	F	Mountain Villa Hotel (Shān Zhuāng Bīnguǎn)
云山饭店	G	Yún Shān Fàndiàn

Street and Bus Stop Names

北兴隆街	Běi Xīnglōng Jiē	山庄东路	Shānzhuāng Dōng Lù
大佛寺	Dà Fó Sì	狮子沟路	Shīzi Gōu Lù
大佟沟路	Dàtónggōu Lù	武列路	Wǔliè Lù
东大街	Dōng Dàjiē	五条胡同	Wǔ Tiáo Hútòng
河东路	Hé Dōng Lù	西大街	Xī Dàjiē
火车站路	Huǒchē Zhàn Lù	新华路	Xīnhuá Lù
丽正门大街	Lízhèng Mén Dàjiē	营子大街	Yíngzi Dàjiē
清风三饭一条路	Qīngfēng Sānfànyītiáo Lù		

Getting to and from Chéngdé

The common road from Peking to Jehol is, in general, pretty good for the two first days, but I must observe that there is another road parallel to it, which is laid off for the sole use of the Sovereign, no other person being permitted to travel upon it, a circumstance of Imperial appropriation which I don't recollect even in Muscovy or Austria. As the Emperor is expected to return to Peking in the latter end of this month the repair of this road is already begun, and we calculated that in the hundred and thirty-six miles from Peking to Jehol above twenty-three thousand troops were employed upon it.

Lord Macartney, *An Embassy to China,*
J. L. Cranmer-Byng [Ed.], 1962

by train

From Běijīng the best train is the relatively upmarket Y225 at 07.25, arriving 11.23, with perfectly comfortable and well-padded hard seats at ¥41, and soft seats (same as hard but two across rather than three) for ¥61. The *fúwùyuán* supplement their incomes by the rather over-enthusiastic peddling of assorted souvenirs and act as touts for Chéngdé hotels (don't book with them). There's a slower early morning train, the 855 at 06.52 arriving 14.20, for less than half the price and in considerably less comfort, as well as the 613 at 23.40, which arrives at the absurd hour of 04.37. Returning to Běijīng, the best choice is the Y226 at 14.20, arriving 18.39. There's also a direct train to Tiānjīn, the 614 at 22.29, arriving 05.59.

To buy tickets from Chéngdé go up the main steps at the front of the station and turn right along the frontage to find the ticket office. Windows four and five are of the most use and are open 24hrs except for short breaks. Windows five and six sell tickets only to Shíjiāzhuāng between 7.10pm and 8pm.

The left luggage office is inside the main building on the right, and the soft sleeper waiting room is to the left.

by bus

There are services every 30mins or so all day from Xī Zhí Mén, and less frequently from Dōng Zhí Mén. The Xī Zhí Mén services are principally comfortable and rapid Iveco buses, ¥41—don't be fobbed off with a Chinese substitute—as are some of the Dōng Zhí Mén ones. Ordinary minibuses are ¥31. Dōng Zhí Mén's are a little cheaper still. The journey time is under four hours from Dōng Zhí Mén, and from Xī Zhí Mén about the same as the train, depending on the state of traffic on the third ring road. For those in the southern budget accommodation there are more convenient departures from Zhàogōngkǒu: bus 705 at 05.35, or 706 at 16.00, both ¥30. There are also minibuses from outside Běijīng Zhàn, which leave when they are full, for ¥45. All these buses pass Gǔběikǒu and the turnings to the Sīmǎtái and Jīnshānlǐng Great Wall sites.

Leaving Chéngdé there are buses back to Běijīng between 06.00 and 16.40, as well as buses direct to Qínhuángdǎo at 06.30 and 07.30, 413km, ¥46.60, 8hrs.

Taxis are mostly *Xiàlì* at ¥1.4 per km, flagfall ¥5 including 2km, and add 50% after 8km if a button on the meter is pushed, applicable to one-way trips out of town—so if you plan to take the same taxi back do not allow this. Alternatively agree ¥10 one way to any temple outside the town. Other pestering three-wheelers will take you around for ¥2–3. Buses serve almost everywhere you want to go for a flat fare of ¥1 in a slot at the front (no change given), and there are frequent private minibus services on most routes, also for ¥1. Route 7 leaves from the right as you exit the railway station, running past the long-distance bus station and several of the hotels and up the main central street of Yíngzi Dàjiē. Many minibuses run the same route. The 66 and 6 buses run up the same street and up the eastern side of the resort to the outer temples.

Chéngdé © (0314)   *Tourist Information*

Even CITS says there's little point in using their services, although they do offer one- or two-day **tours** for ¥300 ($37) per day including accommodation, guide and car with driver. Their office is in the city government compound on the second floor of a building through an arch on the far right, © 226827. Almost every branch of the **Bank of China** changes **money** and travellers' cheques. For withdrawal on credit cards, go to the branch on Dōng Dàjiē (*open 8–12 and 2–5.30*), window no. 5. There are no ATMs in Chéngdé accepting foreign cards. The main **post office** is on the traffic island at the junction of Dōng Dàjiē and Yíngzi Dàjiē (*open 8–6.30, 6 in winter*). You are unlikely to get very far without being offered inaccurate **maps** of the Mountain Resort and Chéngdé town for ¥4, starting on the train itself, which is lucky because the unhelpful and lazy **Xīnhuá Shūdiàn** on Yíngzi Dàjiē has none, although it has a few 19th-century English novels on the upper floor. Read the maps with care: almost all have a map of the Mountain Resort and surrounding temples on their reverse, and show quite detailed plans of the many pavilions, temples and hall that dot the landscape. Some forget to note that many of these have long disappeared. **Visa extensions** are available from the Aliens Entry-Exit Bureau on the right of the main entrance to the city PSB on Wǔliè Lù (*open daily 8.30–5*, they claim, but don't depend on weekends or lunch hours).

The Mountain Resort for Escaping the Heat (Bìshǔ Shān Zhuāng)

避暑山庄

Open 5.30am–6pm; adm ¥50.

Constructed between 1703 and 1792, quite a number of the buildings in the main enclosure with its 10-kilometre wall have remained intact since Macartney saw them in 1794 and are still surrounded by temple-studded hills. The upheavals of 20th-century China left the site dilapidated from neglect rather than actively destroyed, and there's been much fairly tactful restoration of what is still the second greatest surviving complex of ancient buildings in China.

The main enclosure is a few minutes north of the town's compact centre, and can be entered through the palace which housed the main living quarters of the emperors, the **Zhèng Gōng** (Main Palace), once accompanied by the East Palace, which has now disappeared.

While the remaining groups of buildings in and around the park are a riot of gilded tile and garishly painted beams, where golden dragons and phoenixes chase each other across fields of green and blue, this palace of low-rise halls arranged around several courtyards is deceptively plain. The throne room was called the 'Hall of Frugality and Sincerity', but there was little true economy either about the beams of cedar, brought at vast expense from the remote west of China, or the red sandalwood platform and fantastically carved screen behind the throne. The emperors would sit here to watch Manchu nobles practising their archery skills in the large courtyard with its many ancient and gnarled pines. The trips to Chéngdé marked a return to Manchu home territory, beyond the Great Wall which had failed to keep them out, and the archery practice and hunting trips in the surrounding hills were a reminder of their mounted warrior past.

Even in Qiánlóng's day, at the time of Macartney's visit, such skills had been made irrelevant by technological advances elsewhere, but such traditions perpetuated themselves until the early 20th century, by which time aristocratic Manchus were effete pension-takers of little use to anyone, more Chinese than the Chinese themselves. As one of John Blofeld's students told him in the 1930s:

> My father grew up in an atmosphere where the only accomplishments expected of him were expert horsemanship, skill in archery—this at a time when our enemies had iron battleships—a cultivated taste in dress, manners and deportment and a connoisseurship of such seductive trifles as chrysanthemums or goldfish or the jade thumb-rings used in archery.

John Blofeld, *City of Lingering Splendour*, 1961

Side halls now display samples of Qīng military equipment including ornate swords and colourful uniforms, conches used as battle horns, and matchlock guns with barrels almost two metres in length.

The numerous tranquil and pleasing little courtyards of the residential quarters, with their hostas and roses, bamboo in tubs, and delicate names such as the Hall of Refreshing Mists and Waves, hardly seem an appropriate site for international *realpolitik*—this was where the Xiánfēng emperor is said to have signed the Conventions of Běijīng, which reaffirmed permanent foreign presence in the capital.

Peer through windows like a tardy eavesdropper to see the period furniture, clocks, ceramics, and examples of imperial calligraphy, now occupying the emperor's bedchamber and the connecting rooms of the empress and concubines. Further halls have displays of impressively hideous glassware made specially in Europe for Chinese taste, wall-hung carved wooden and ivory landscapes of extreme delicacy, and intricate tapestries.

Behind, in the park itself, a complex network of paths leads to pavilions hidden amongst groves of trees. They wind around the shores of several interconnected lakes and follow pavilion-topped bridges to islands with further halls and temples. To the northwest, trails snake into pine-covered hills and climb steeply into yet cooler air.

From the rear of the Main Palace, a short walk north along a shady strip of land between two lakes brings you to the **Pavilion of Literary Delight** (Wénjīn Gé), based on a famous library building in the coastal town of Níngbō. The main building is reached through an artificially constructed grotto and rock garden and round the rim of a pool alive with butterflies and dragonflies. According to the attendants, the Qiánlóng emperor had a hankering to see the sun and moon at the same time. He ordered the garden constructed so that sunlight, passing through a cleft, threw a crescent shape onto the waters of the pool beyond. This is only visible from a certain spot on the stone terrace in front of the elegant hall, but the attendants determinedly shuffle you into position.

The building originally stored a vast collection of 36,300 manuscripts, but is now an art shop. The interior beams have been painted with an alternative to the usual dragons or landscape scenes seen almost everywhere else, in a pattern of books. According to local lore, the coolness of the stone plinth and the special three-storey interior inside a two-storey exterior keep the temperature 'half a month behind' to protect the books, although these are long gone to the National Library in Běijīng.

Macartney was given a boat tour of the lakes, which impressed him immensely:

> *I dare say that in the course of our voyage we stopped at forty or fifty different palaces or pavilions. These are all furnished in the richest manner, with pictures of the Emperor's huntings and progresses; with stupendous vases of jasper and agate; with the finest porcelain and japan, and with every kind of European toys and sing-songs; with spheres, orreries, clicks, and musical automatons of such exquisite workmanship, and in such profusion, that our presents must shrink from the comparison and 'hide their diminished heads'.*

> Lord Macartney, *An Embassy to China,* J. L. Cranmer-Byng [Ed.], 1962

These items were rounded up and catalogued at the end of the Qīng dynasty, and under the 'Articles of Favourable Treatment' the imperial family was supposed to receive an agreed purchase price as soon as the state could afford it. No such payment was ever made, and the treasures disappeared along with the Nationalist forces to Táiwān at the end of the civil war. Now, exhibitions include one celebrating the late Dèng Xiǎopíng's visit to the site, but the numerous halls and pavilions make for a pleasant hour or two's stroll.

The most eye-catching building in the park is the nine-storey **Pagoda of the Six Harmonies** (Liù Hé Tǎ), close to the east gate and beyond a yurt (felt tent) hotel presuming to offer you the experience of living like Mongols (if they had access to concrete, of course). The pagoda is all that remains of a once substantial temple where the emperors worshipped their ancestors. Set on a carved stone base, its yellow- and green-tiled eaves are hung with gently chiming bells and each storey carries a board bearing characters in Qiánlóng's calligraphy. Modelled after pagodas in Hángzhōu and Nánjīng, it rises to a gold-topped black knob, visible for miles around. Climbing the claustrophic interior staircase gives ever more impressive views of the surrounding countryside, including the Eight Outer Temples to the north and east of the enclosure. Most of the dozens of small buildings in a vast area of hilly greenness to the northwest of the enclosure have gone, but there's hours of peaceful trekking here.

A Missed Opportunity

Another characteristic that every Chinese I have ever known possesses, bred into his fiber, is his sense of belonging to an order of things loftier, by far, than any introduced to China from the West. I have never observed a single exception to this attitude; it engenders a doctrinaire conviction of superiority as by birth, quite irrespective of whether pertinent facts are in glaring contradiction or not. At its best this gives complete self-respect to one of the large divisions of mankind; at its worst it degenerates into quite unjustifiable conceit.

George N. Kates, *The Years that Were Fat*, 1952

Kates, immensely sympathetic to Chinese culture, might as well have been writing at the end of the 18th century when Lord Macartney (1737–1806), a career diplomat and administrator with experience which included negotiating a trade treaty with Catherine the Great of Russia, travelled to China from England on behalf of George III. His mission was to obtain agreement from the Qiánlóng emperor to the stationing of a permanent trade representative at Běijīng, and the opening up of China to goods of British manufacture. Macartney was, as Dr Johnson said, 'in some degree a literary man', had had his portrait painted by Reynolds, was friends with both Boswell and Johnson, and his notes on the first edition of Boswell's 'Life' were used in the preparation of the second edition. His lively diaries of his trip to China were not published until after his death, although in the decade following the embassy accounts by other members of the party were amongst the bestselling travel books of their day. When Macartney's own account was eventually published, it, too, because a bestseller—little Fanny Price's cousin catches her reading it in the old schoolroom of Jane Austen's *Mansfield Park*. Reaching Běijīng along the grand canal on ships which described him ignominiously as a tribute bearer, he found the emperor had retreated to his summer resort and was forced to follow him up to Chéngdé.

Macartney brought with him a vast quantity of expensive gifts, technical novelties and demonstrations of Western scientific prowess, many completely unknown to the Chinese. Yet he was sent home having achieved none of his aims, and with a message that the Qīng had no need of foreign ingenuity, having everything they needed within their own borders. This was manifestly untrue. Since the time of the Qiánlóng emperor's grandfather foreign mathematical knowledge and technical expertise had been running the calendar accurately. The portraits of the Qiánlóng emperor in which he most delighted had been produced by foreign painters using Western perspective techniques unknown to Chinese painting. The Qīng had also had weapons cast and buildings constructed for them using Western technology, maps produced using Western cartographic knowledge, and Qiánlóng himself had used the Jesuits to produce his own suite of 'Western-style' buildings, fountains and a maze at the Yuánmíng Yuán.

In the way in which he responded, the Manchu Qiánlóng emperor showed himself to have become a master of cultural double-think and to that degree completely Sinicized. Counted as barbarians themselves when they took control of China 150 years before Macartney's arrival, the Kāngxī and Qiánlóng emperors' highly successful reigns have led to them being counted as Chinese emperors when the glory of Chinese culture is being promoted, but their Qīng dynasty as alien rulers brought down by legitimate revolution when modern history is being considered. During their reign comfort could be taken that the Manchus found it necessary to imitate the Chinese so faithfully—one more demonstration that everyone who was not Chinese aspired to acquire superior Chinese culture. The Manchus' assimilation led them to adopt the same arrogance towards all outsiders.

Since the Hàn dynasty, the Chinese had refused to regard trade with foreigners as anything of the kind, but merely as a generous exchange—the foreigners bringing their tribute, drawn to the superior brilliance of Chinese culture, and being given gifts to take home. They managed to maintain this view while often adopting foreign things and taking useful foreign techniques wholesale. By the Táng (a period in which foreign dress, hairstyles and foreign music were all very popular) they were laughing at other Asians for being floor sitters, whereas they, the superior culture, sat on chairs. The idea of the chair had in fact been imported from Central Asia, but that inconvenient fact was conveniently forgotten. Even the invention of gunpowder, with which the Chinese are usually credited, required foreign assistance in the use of saltpetre, which was subsequently imported from Japan.

In late 1999, China's first successful launch of a space vehicle which could return to earth, and its successful retrieval, was trumpeted by the media as being entirely the product of Chinese science, while puzzled foreign experts pointed out that substantial parts of the technology had obviously been purchased from the Russians. Reports in the Chinese press of increases in the popularity of Chinese-made goods which are in direct competition with foreign ones can usually be taken as a sign that the opposite is true. Their smug acceptance of their own superiority doesn't prevent the Chinese from choosing to purchase 90.8 per cent of their mobile phones from foreign suppliers in preference to Chinese ones, to manufacture limitless quantities of fake Western brands to satisfy the insatiable demand for them—even barefoot peasants can be seen in Calvin Klein T-shirts—or packing out McDonald's in preference to even the most Westernized of Chinese fast food outlets.

In fact, Kates might have made his comments at any time in the last 2,000 years and they would have been equally true. But by turning away the Western Ocean barbarians the narrow-minded and short-sighted Qīng missed an opportunity to make China the dominant nation in Asia. Japan, given the opportunity less than 100 years later, seized it and went on to beat the West at its own game, sinking the Russian fleet, taking over large areas of China and establishing much of the manufacturing in the northeast which has led to its remaining a major Chinese manufacturing base ever since. Even when one of Qiánlóng's descendants decided finally to modernize the country, it was in terms of 'study the barbarian techniques to defeat the barbarian'.

Macartney went home assuming that the Chinese would soon be entirely converted to forks and spoons and that, although it would be more difficult than originally expected, trade in China might eventually be channelled to suit the British—a nation which at that time, although the Qīng's closed door policy kept them ignorant of it, was the most powerful in the world.

The Mountain Resort for Escaping the Heat   383

The view that you can't trade with the Chinese if you don't publicly agree with their position on many things is often demonstrated to be false, but still prevails. Traditionally, the failure of Lord Macartney's mission is blamed on his unwillingness to kowtow to the emperor and play the supplicant barbarian. Macartney was himself sensitive to this charge, but his own notes on the success or failure of other foreign trade missions showed that even those who made fools of themselves with the extravagance of their subservience (one envoy's wig fell off) still failed to achieve their aims.

Chris Patten, a contender for the position of foreigner most vilified by the Chinese in the 20th century, who as last Governor of British Hong Kong pursued liberal policies inimical to the communists, and who came under attack from British industry and Foreign Office mandarins alike on the grounds that his actions were damaging trade prospects, was able to demonstrate that not only had British exports to China gone up during his stewardship of Hong Kong, they had gone up faster than those of other countries.

During the 'demonstrations' in Běijīng following the NATO bombing of the Chinese embassy in Belgrade, the bused-in crowds were encouraged to attack the Albanian embassy for supporting the NATO offensive, yet within a few months China was signing a deal to help Albania built a hydro-electric plant. Indeed, within a few months of the severe damage to the British and US embassies caused in complete violation of international norms, President Jiāng Zémín was on a state visit to London, receiving the warmest welcome ever given a Chinese head of state visiting the West (although even that was eclipsed by subsequent treatment at the hands of the French), and President Clinton of the USA had rushed into agreement with China on entry to the WTO.

Only the Chinese can carry the blame for the failure of the Macartney mission. It's been demonstrated that the famous letter refusing his requests was drawn up even before he reached Běijīng, and the first version completed a mere nine days after his arrival in China, before he'd even met the emperor at Chéngdé. This failure to treat the foreigners seriously led them to miss an opportunity for opening, reform and modernization and to a 'century of humiliation' which, in the same spirit of blindness, they blame on everyone except themselves. Only 200 years later are they groping dimly towards opening and reform, but it's they who approach the rest of the world for trade deals, and largely on the foreigners' terms. The Japanese, who adopted Western institutions and Western technology with gusto, have the largest economy in Asia.

The Eight Outer Temples (Wài Bā Miào) 外八庙

There was a god which stood 120 feet high and had eighteen pairs of arms. I climbed musty and untrodden wooden staircases in which, when I went up, one step in three was missing and which I left still further demolished. The face of the image, viewed at disconcertingly short range from a balcony among the roof beams, wore a complacent expression. In another temple there was a blue-tiled roof on which complex golden dragons raced furiously. One is missing and is said to have flown away, an action betraying, in my view, a lack of sagacity. It was a lovely place.

Peter Fleming, *One's Company*, 1934

Despite all the common ugliness of Chinese urban development, all the litter-strewing crass-ness of modern Chinese tourism and the amusements developed for it, and the disappearance of several temples (there were originally 12, built between 1713 and 1780), the remainder are unusual, lavish and spectacular, and there's still beauty in their setting.

The extant temples run in a line along the northern side of the resort, and then are scattered around the northeast and eastern side. Five can easily be reached on bus 6 or 66 from Yíngzi Dàjiē, getting off at the river bridge at the northeast corner of the resort and walking east for four of them, or staying on the bus to the stop called Dà Fó Sì to see the Pǔníng Sì, just to the right. Minibuses also run this route.

Pǔníng Sì (Temple of Universal Peace)　　普宁寺

Open 8.30–5; adm ¥25 (or ¥30 for a pictorial souvenir ticket).

Pǔníng Sì and the other northern temples seem to be on the morning itineraries, and the eastern ones on the afternoon. If not on a tour, you may wish to work the other way round.

The temple was built by the Qiánlōng emperor in 1755 to celebrate his suppression of a Mongol rebellion in the Central Asian region of Ili. Unfortunately his 'universal peace' broke down again four years later. The suppression of *two* rebellions is recorded in Manchu, Tibetan, Mongolian and Chinese on giant pavilioned stelae in the temple's first courtyard. Since the Mongols were Buddhists Qiánlōng ordered the temple to be built in imitation of Tibet's oldest monastery, and although the front half is typically Chinese, the rear contains several Tibetan-style slab-sided buildings and stupas set out in a physical representation of the key stages of Buddhist progress towards *nirvana.*

The central feature is the giant Hall of Mahayana, which houses a 22m-high statue of Guanyin, the Goddess of Mercy—the largest of its kind in the world (and the one mentioned by Fleming, above). Only when nearly climbing on the statue's giant toes is it possible to crane back and look up the immense dusty coppery torso to a blizzard of arms and heads far above. The figure sits in solid, serene, multi-armed grace, hung with strings of jewels, the folds of its clothing carved with a delicate airiness. There are three layers of interior galleries—climb up to the level of Guānyīn's navel for closer inspection (the stairs have now been repaired) and look down at her feet, spotlit by shafts of sunlight which carve their way through the solemn, dust-laden atmosphere.

In 1999 the Buddha was given a 'medicinal bath' by sealing it in a huge plastic bag and fumi-gating it, and it was remeasured and found to be 22.291m tall (according to 'experts' from the Ministry of Construction), standing on a 1.22m stone base. Various parts of the statue were dismantled and soaked in chemicals to deter boring insects.

Each successive hall is higher than the other, reached by steep stone stairways. The temple's Mahavira Hall has plenty of monkish activity and kneelers for the devout, who pay for the plea-sure of having their names added to one of the plastic Buddhas on tawdry electrically-driven rotating towers, or leave money in what are labelled 'virtue boxes'. There's further commercial activity at the site's bell tower, where you can pay ¥5 to strike the bell three times.

You can walk back to the bridge and turn right (west) towards the other northern temples or hop on a bus for one stop. There are pestering three-wheelers to help you get around, but the walking time on a rubbish-strewn footpath to the first temple and to each of the two successive ones is only five to ten minutes. In between, barn-like structures have snacks and hot food stalls, whose owners may attempt almost physically to drag you in. You will pass cabbage patches and a greenhouse with most of its panes missing.

Xūmífúshòu Miào (Temple of Happiness and Longevity at Mount Sumeru) 须弥福寿命庙

Open 8–4.20; adm ¥20.

This temple also shows substantial Tibetan influence, parts of it inspired by Tashilumpo monastery in Tibet and constructed to make the Panchen Lama (number two in the Tibetan Buddhist hierarchy after the Dalai Lama) feel at home on a visit in 1780, although the imitation of the Tibetan style is often quite crude. A central hall was intended to house the Panchen, and surrounding galleries, which now house extensive exhibitions, to house his attendants.

The most striking parts of the complex are a four-storey square tower, on whose roof frolic the dragons mentioned by Fleming (above), and a substantial octagonal tiled pagoda at the rear. Modern restoration has made sure that all eight dragons, four facing upwards to the central point and four with their heads towards the eaves, are there, and these splendidly sinuous creatures can be viewed almost at eye level by climbing upwards towards the rear of the temple. The temple also has one of several fine tiled *páilou* and some of the anatomically inaccurate elephant statues featured in lines of tomb guardians at various tombs.

Pǔtuózōngchéng Zhī Miào ('Potala Temple') 普陀宗乘之庙

Open 8–4.20; adm ¥20.

Five minutes' walk to the west lies the most obviously Tibetan building in Chéngdé, named for its similarity in style to the vast palace complex dominating the centre of Lhasa, and built to please another group of Mongols who came to pay their respects to the Qiánlōng emperor on his 60th birthday. The outer resemblance to the Potala is striking, although the scale is considerably smaller; most of the narrow tapering windows are blind, and the interior contains a triple-galleried courtyard with a highly decorated Chinese central pavilion. Macartney reported 800 resident lamas, and found the temple as richly furnished as St. Paul's in London.

The roofs here are covered with gilded bronze tiles said to have cost 'over 10,000 taels of first class gold'. In the side galleries two nine-storey model pagodas of elaborately carved sandalwood pierce several floors, while neighbouring rooms display a vast range of devotional items from miniature gold temples to vessels made from incised silver fused into the skulls of young girls. Climb to the roof to be rewarded with views of dragon-topped temples, green hills and Club Rock (*see* below).

In Fleming's day the best view of the Potala Temple was from the hills opposite, topped with the palace of a local warlord who, having announced his intention to defend the region to the last man, had fled a few hours before the Japanese entered the town, and later returned on a Japanese salary. His palace was now the local staff headquarters, and climbing up for the view exposed one to the risk of being shot.

Shūxiàng Sì

殊像寺

The name indicates that the temple contains or contained a statue of Manjusri (Buddha of Wisdom). A further 10mins' walk west past a greenhouse missing most of its panes will bring you to this rather more conventional and purely Chinese temple, closed at the time of writing. Perhaps its appeal is that, as locals say, 'nobody comes here to look at this,' and it sits in the middle of a rather scruffy village. Corn is set out in stacks to dry in the space at the front of the temple. Nothing remains of two further temples which once stood to the west.

Ānyuán Miào (Temple of Distant Peace)

安远庙

Open 8–5; adm ¥20.

This quiet temple on the eastern side of the resort is best reached by taxi either from the town centre or along the new link road from the bridge east of the main northern temple group. You may have to go down the right-hand side to a side gate to wake someone up to let you in, and you may find goats grazing in the courtyard.

The temple was erected in 1764 and is another case of diplomacy by architecture, being based on a now-disappeared temple in Ili in the Xīnjiāng region of China's northwest; it was built to please a Mongol tribe from the region resettled here by the Qiánlóng emperor. The main hall is a very substantial 27m high with a square plan, roofed in black glazed tiles, and its galleried interior supported on 60 columns containing a large, green-coloured goddess, dimly lit by shafts of light from tiny windows. There's considerable intricate carving on the ceiling, and the remains of murals on the walls, especially above shoulder height and above the door, where they've been less exposed to the rubbing of passing bodies.

Pǔlè Sì (Temple of Universal Joy)

普乐寺

Open 8–4.20; adm ¥20.

The temple can be reached either by a 15-minute walk south from the Ānyuán Miào or by hanging on to your taxi. On the way you'll pass the chairlift to **Club Rock**, for which no two publications have the same Chinese name, and which is also referred to as Anvil Rock and Sledgehammer Rock. Clearly visible from all over Chéngdé, its plump erectness would inevitably suggest, even to your maiden aunt, something rather more fleshly. The chairlift costs ¥20 one way or ¥30 return.

A Tibetan advisor was also involved in the construction of the Pǔlè Sì, erected for the annual visits of the eventually defeated western Mongols, yet featuring an entrance gate with Islamic overtones, and having as its climax a copy of the circular Hall of Prayer for Good Harvests from Běijīng's Temple of Heaven. The roofs are imperial yellow rather than blue, but the golden ceiling has the same finely carved golden dragon in superb relief which sports an entirely three-dimensional fanged head.

Restoration has yet to be completed here, and swallows still nest in the ceiling, entering and leaving at high speed by the same door as visitors, alarming for bird and human alike.

Pǔrén Sì

溥仁寺

Most of this temple, the Temple of Universal Joy, down an unmarked turning as you return to town down Dōng Hé Lù, still stands. There are signs that it may be restored and opened to the public. It's the only one of the outer temples to date from the reign of the resort's original developer, the Kāngxī emperor (reigned 1662–1722) but, despite being constructed to allow visiting Mongol princes to continue their Tibetan Buddhist practices while visiting Kāngxī to congratulate him on his 60th birthday, the temple appears from the outside to be conventionally Chinese.

Macartney, immensely impressed by both the resort and its magnificent surroundings, nevertheless indulged himself in a little joke at the emperor's expense:

> *The Emperor, it is affirmed, thinks that he is not only descended in a right line from Fo-hi [the Buddha] himself, but, considering the great length and unparalleled prosperity of his reign, entertains of late a strong notion that the soul of Fo-hi is actually transmigrated into his Imperial body... so that the unbounded munificence he has displayed in the erection of these pagodas may be looked on as not quite so disinterested for, according to this hypothesis, there has been nothing spent out of the family.*

Lord Macartney, *An Embassy to China*,
J. L. Cranmer-Byng [Ed.], 1962

Chéngdé ① *(0314)*   **Where to Stay**

On arrival at Chéngdé you can either surrender to the mob of tour guides and hotel agents, or find your own taxi or bus for the short distance to the centre of town and choose from a dozen or so reasonably comfortable hotels. Just remember who really carries the cost of the agents' commission, and that agents are only necessary when there's a glut of rooms, making them unnecessary to you; for most of the year there's plenty of choice. Room rates are highly negotiable outside of the June to August period, and on weekdays. Take 20% off the quoted prices automatically, and work down from there as best you can. Late spring and early autumn weekdays are the best time to visit.

The six restaurant, 340-room **Mountain Villa Hotel** (Shān Zhuāng Bīnguǎn), almost opposite the main entrance to the resort, ① 202 3501, ext. 5500, ✆ 202 2457, has been around more than 30 years and is the first place towards which touts will drag you. This hotel is tired both in its physical structure and its attitudes, but its convenient location may be irresistible and bus 7 will bring you straight here from the station. Twins range from ¥180 ($22) to ¥300 ($37), and budget travellers may like the triples at ¥120 ($15). The hotel is resistant to further haggling.

The **Déhuì Bīnguǎn** is just east of the main entrance to the resort, ① 216 3449, and while still worn and grubby has larger rooms with slightly better bathrooms for ¥200, and triples for ¥150. There are also suites for ¥400 ($80).

A little closer to the resort, but on the opposite side of the road, the **Míngzhū Dàjiǔdiàn**, ☎ 202 1188, is basic but acceptable, with tiled floor rooms. Double rooms are from ¥280 ($35).

The small side street hotel, the **Hóngjīn Bīnguǎn**, in Wǔ Tiáo Hútòng conveniently in the centre of town just off Yíngzi Dàjiē, ☎ 203 5961, 📠 205 0613, is of relatively recent construction but withering under the pressure of tourism and the lack of maintenance. Standard twins with modest bathrooms are easily haggled down to around ¥130 ($16) here, however. Oddly, the lower rooms are in better condition than the higher ones, in this elevator-free four-storey block.

Also right in the centre, the **Láodòng Dàshà**, ☎ 203 2382, is the cheapest option, with common bath four- or five-bed dorms for ¥30 off-season, ¥40 peak. There are also doubles for ¥260/¥380 ($32/$47). This extremely battered hotel was undergoing a major refit at the time of writing, but promised to keep these prices after renewal.

The slightly battered tower of the **Yún Shān Fàndiàn** is close to the long-distance bus station, ☎ 215 6171, 📠 215 4551, and is where foreign tour groups usually end up. Better than most three-stars, its extensive lobby features giant wooden elephants and more usual facilities such as souvenir shops, a Western restaurant (untried), and quite a good Chinese one with an extensive menu of game. Rooms range from standard twins for ¥440 ($55), to a four-person suite for ¥1600 ($200).

Its nearest competition is the **Huìlóng Dàshà**, only one stop from the station, ☎ 208 2423, 📠 208 2404, <*huilong@cd-user.he.cninfo.net*>, another three-star in the same mould as the Yún Shān. Single rooms are ¥320 ($40), and twins ¥380 ($47), up to three-person suites at ¥1280 ($160).

Eating Out

While Chéngdé's streets are as full as those of any other town with conventional Chinese restaurants, its menus are long enough and varied enough to impress even the most omnivorous diner, and few can resist including considerable amounts of game. Dishes on offer include sweet and sour wild boar, sautéed roe deer fillet with brown sauce, venison steak, venison stir-fried with local wild red mushrooms, Mongolian sheep dishes and pheasant, as well as camel, squirrel, sparrow, hare, dog, donkey and 'three ways of eating live snake soup'. More immediately appealing local specialities include *sōngzhēn bāozi* 松针包子 —fennel-stuffed bread steamed over needles from local pines, ideal for breakfast, and often served with a soup of black wheat noodles. Try the basic but specialist Sōngzhēn Bāozi Wáng, in Dàtónggōu Lù. Local snacks include the sticky *mìmāhuā* 密麻花 , deep-fried buns made with cornflour centres and wheatflour exteriors, mixed with honey. *Huājiāo jī* 花椒鸡 is whole chicken cut up and fried in oil with black peppercorns then steamed and served in a vinegary sauce. Fried chicken is particularly popular in Chéngdé and people line up at take-away counters at the Chéngdé Shāngshà department store.

There's a whole street of restaurants which the local authorities seem to think they've created in a Qīng-era style, called Qīngfēng Sānfànyìtiáo Lù, which runs southeast from just by the level crossing in the centre of town. It would be very Qīng if the Qīng had had neon signs and karaoke, and if its pedestrianization didn't still permit passing cars. There are some dubious karaoke parlours here, but also several surprisingly friendly restaurants, given the onslaught of tourism.

For eating at real street level try an unnamed alley on the east of Yíngzi Dàjiē opposite the Dàtónggōu Lù turning, where you can eat a wide variety of steamed and fried snacks, noodle soup and more at open tables. At night Yíngzi Dàjiē becomes a giant street market with many open-air restaurants.

The Emperors once forbade their subjects to teach foreigners Chinese on pain of death. Never shy of considering their jurisdiction to be global, they also forbade foreigners to learn it. James Flint, sent by the East India Company in 1759 to present complaints to the Qīng court about corruption in Canton and restrictions on trade, was subsequently imprisoned for three years, partly for having learned the language. Today the Chinese tourist industry still makes a great deal of its money from foreigners' unwillingness to tackle even Mandarin rudiments by charging them high prices for services that they would be able negotiate directly for themselves at a fraction of the cost.

Although learning English is back in fashion, and many cities have 'English corners', usually in public parks, where enthusiasts gather to practise, visitors will encounter few English speakers away from the travel agents and the police stations of larger cities. In larger international hotels most of the staff speak some English, but in others that accept foreigners there is perhaps one designated English speaker whose reputation amongst her colleagues may last only until she actually has to deal with a foreigner. Most foreigners spend their entire time in China without being able to speak a word, but those who at least master the ability to order food, ask prices and ask for directions have an easier time. While Chinese do sometimes take lost foreigners in hand and try to solve their problems, many consider the gulf of understanding too vast even to try, and most are anyway getting on with sorting out their own problems. Having just a few words can rapidly break these barriers down and greatly add to the enjoyment of the trip.

Learning Mandarin

According to *China Daily* there has recently been a swelling of interest in learning Mandarin around the world. The official view is:

> *Obviously* [which, when used in *China Daily*, always precedes something contentious], *one of the major factors has to be the allure of Chinese culture, its values and long history, and its inaccessibility in previous years. This has been increased by the rise of China as an economic power and an important force working for world peace and stability.*

China Daily, *Study of Chinese becomes global fashion*, 3/8/99

To understand accounts in China's own newspapers of its work for 'world peace and stability' you'll need to know the Mandarin for 'neutron bomb', 'strike hard', and 'invade Táiwān'.

Language

George III's ambassador to the Qiánlóng emperor, Lord Macartney, thought that the difficulty of the language was much exaggerated, on the grounds that, 'I never heard it complained of by the Chinese themselves.' He mistakenly thought the population largely literate, but even today, fully one in five over the age of 14 is thought not to be so. He did, however, accurately describe one particular difficulty with the language:

The Chinese language seems, however, to have on material defect. It is liable to be equivocal, and appers to depend in a great measure upon the tone or pronunciation of the words used by the speakers, for I took notice that in their conversation together they were often subject to mistake one another, and to require frequent explanations. The same word as written having different significations according as it is spoken with a grave or with an acute accent.

Lord Macartney, *An Embassy to China,* J. L. Cranmer-Byng [Ed.], 1962

An account of tones and their use in Mandarin is given with an introduction to Chinese characters and a few basic grammar points in the topic **How Chinese Works**, p.82.

No-one needs to be able to assemble perfectly grammatical sentences in Mandarin to get what they want, anymore than they do in any other language. Learning to pronounce the sounds or near approximations is vital, and to get a grip on the tones is important, although context will often help you out of difficulties. A lot more will be covered in a full phrase book than can be put here. Berlitz *Chinese for Travellers* is sensibly organized, although it sometimes seems to imagine a more orderly China than really exists. The pocket-size *Concise English–Chinese Chinese–English Dictionary* from Oxford University Press can be of major assistance, with *pīnyīn* pronunciation (*see* below) throughout, and you can give it to others to find the characters they mean and show you the English. This dictionary can sometimes be found in branches of the state book shop Xīnhuá Shūdiàn in China itself (¥25).

Pronunciation

Pīnyīn, the official Romanisation of Mandarin, uses the familiar alphabet and leaves the letters with values that most English speakers expect. Differences are:

c   *ts*, as in *bits*

q   *ch*, as in *chin*, but more aggressive

r   no true English equivalent; the *r* in *reed* is close (and you will be
     understood), but the tip of the tongue should be near the top of the mouth
     and the teeth together

x   between the *s* in *seep* and the *sh* in *sheep*

zh   like the *dge* in *judge*

Vowels sounds are simple and consistent:

a   as in *father*

e   as in *err; lěng* ('cold') is exactly like *lung* in English

i   after most consonants is pronounced *ee*, but after c, ch, r, s, sh, z, and zh,
     sounds a little like the *u* in *upon* (and will be understood), but the teeth are
     together and the noise is more a buzz at the front of the mouth

o   as in *song*

u   as in *too*

ū   as the purer French *tu* and German *ü*; a more forward *oo*, with the lips
     pursed. After j, x, q and y, *ū* (annoyingly) is written without the ¯. Since *l*
     and *n* can be followed by either *u* or *ū*, the ¯ is used when necessary.

Two vowels together retain their individual sounds, (e.g. *ai* like 'eye', *ei* as the *ey* in 'hey'), with the exception of *ian*, where the *an* sounds like the *en* in 'engine', and the whole like 'yen'. This is very common: *qián* ('tchee-en') is 'money'. Also watch out for the difference between *ou* as in 'toe', and *uo*, which sounds a little like 'or'. *ui* sounds like 'way'. *i* by itself is written *yi*, and *ian* by itself is *yan*.

To learn these sounds, and in particular to master the tones, there is no substitute for listening to a tape or a native speaker. To get the purest sounds try to find a northern Chinese, and particularly someone from Běijīng. Cantonese speakers who know Mandarin as a second language rarely seem able to shed their southern accent. The student should begin with a sing-song approach, overstressing the tones to get them right. In relaxed everyday speech, Chinese only actually stress the tones of the words necessary to make the meaning of the sentence clear. Note that when two or more third (dipping) tone sounds follow each other, only the final one is clearly sounded, the others becoming second (rising) tones.

The Běijīng dialect has influenced Mandarin, and tends to contract some sounds and add an *r* to them. This is done more frequently the more colloquially it is spoken, but some are now enshrined in official Mandarin. *Năli* (where), becomes *năr*, which rhymes with 'far', with a little more stress on the *r*. *Yĭdiăn*, 'a little', is written *yìdiănr*, but the *n* is not pronouced so that the final sound is also –ar. The final *r* sound is indicated phonetically with a Chinese character which by itself is pronounced *ér*.

Names

It helps if you can arrange a Mandarin name for yourself, otherwise you will be addressed throughout any conversation as *Lăo Wài*, 'Foreigner'. Ideally get an English speaker to make a name that suits you and sounds genuinely Chinese, rather than a phoneticised version. 'Peter', for instance, is often rendered as *Bĭdé*, but this is obviously foreign whereas its translation as Yán ('ee-en', remember, not 'yang' without the *g*) meaning 'rock', as 'Peter' does, is more Chinese. Surnames are not sur- at all—they come first. For foreigners the trick is often to take the first sound of the family name, and look for a similar Mandarin sound which is part of the very limited list of Chinese family name possibilities.

The Chinese often refer to common people, the 'masses', as *lăobăixìng*, 'old hundred names.' There are only 3,100 family names, of which all but 150 are single character names. The number of people called Wáng in China is greater than the total population of many other countries, and the masses show precious little imagination in their choice of given names, either. In the port city of Tiānjīn east of Běijīng, more than 2300 people are call Zhāng Lì, while Shěnyáng in the north-east has 4800 residents all called Liáng Shūzhēn, and several other names have more than 3,000 takers. Notoriously police round up dozens of people who share the name of a suspect they are looking for and then sort out who's who, but even Chinese newspapers have told stories of people crushed in political campaigns and imprisoned for years before it was discovered that the real culprit was walking free. As in other parts of the world, names come and go in fashion, and it's a fairly safe bet that if someone's given name means 'Love Máo' or 'Build Socialism', then they were born between 1966 and 1976 during the now deeply unfashionable Cultural Revolution (and are sometimes embarrassed by their names).

People are usually called by their entire name, rather than by given name alone, but friends may drop the given name and prefix the family name with *Lǎo* ('old') if the friend is older, and *Xiǎo* ('little'), if not.

A Few Structural Notes

Basic Chinese sentences are like English ones: subject, verb, object. 'I want' + noun, or 'I want' + verb (to go, do, buy, etc) + noun will get you a long way. Note, though, that if you are specific as to quantity, instead of the noun you must use number + measure word + noun. Read **How Chinese Works**, p.82, for an introduction to measure words and a few other important points. Where you are likely to be specific about quantity ('I want to buy three tickets' as opposed to 'I want to see temples') and the multi-purpose measure word *ge* won't do, the correct measure word is given below.

Some basic conversational items are dealt with first, followed by a practical travel vocabulary, and then a list of verbs to try out.

Basic Courtesies

I	wǒ	我
you (singular)	nǐ	你
he	tā	他
she	tā	她
it (rarely used)	tā	它

To make any of the above into the plural add mén

We	wǒmén	我们
You plural	nǐmén	你们
They, etc.	tāmén	他们
Hello	Nǐ hǎo?	你好？
How are you?	Nǐ hǎo ma?	你好吗？
Goodbye	Zài jiàn	再见
Excuse me, I'm sorry	Duìbuqǐ	对不起
Please...	Qǐng...	请
Excuse me (I want to ask you a question)	Qǐng wèn,...	请问
Thank you	Xièxie nǐ	谢谢你
Sorry to bother you, thanks for your trouble	Máfan nǐ	麻烦你
You may hear:		
Bú yòng xiè	No need to say 'thanks'	不用谢

Basic Questions and Requests (begin with 'Qǐng wèn' if appropriate)

Where is X?	X zài nǎr? (X is where?)	X 在哪儿？
Where is the station?	Huǒchēzhàn zài nǎr?	火车站在那儿？
Where's the nearest X?	Zuìjìn de X zài nǎr?	最近的X在哪儿？
Who is X?	X shì shéi (X is who?)	X 是谁？
Who are you?	Nǐ shì shéi?	你是谁？

What is X?	X shì shénme? (X is what?)	X 是什么?
What is this/that?	Zhè/nà shì shénme? (This/that is what?)	这、那是什么?
Why?	Wèishénme?	为什么?
Why is there no bus today?	Wèishénme jīntiān méiyǒu chē? (Why today not have bus?)	为什么今天没有车?
When?	Shénme shíhou?	什么时候?
When will the bus leave?	Chē shénme shíhou kāi? (Bus what time start?)	车什么时候开?
What time is it?	Xiànzài jǐ diǎn le? (Now how many hours?)	现在几点了?
How much is X? (price)	X duōshǎo qián?	X 多少钱?
How much and how many? (quantity), expecting a small answer/large answer	Jǐ ge/duōshǎo ge?	几个、多少个?
May I?/Is this OK?	Xíng bu xíng?	行不行?
Do you speak English?	Nǐ huì shuō Yīngyǔ ma?	你会说英语吗?
Please help me	Qǐng bāng wǒ	请帮我
I want...	Wǒ xiǎngyào...	我想要
I'd like...	Wǒ xǐhuān...	我喜欢
Please give me...	Qǐng gěi wǒ...	请给我

Basic Answers (Yours and Theirs)

To say yes or no in Chinese, identify the main verb in the question, and repeat it to agree, or negate it (but *bù* in front unless it's *yǒu*, to have, in which case use *méi*). The closest statements to 'yes' are:

Correct	Duì	对
Good (OK, let's do that)	Hǎo	好

There are more approximations of 'no':

Not correct	bú duì	不对
Is not	bú shì	不是
Not have	méi yǒu	没有
Not acceptable, forbidden	bù xíng	不行
Bad (I can't go along with that)	Bù hǎo	不好

Other general answers:

I'm sorry, I don't understand	Duìbuqǐ, wǒ tīng bù dǒng	对不起，我听不懂
I don't speak Mandarin	Wǒ bú huì shuō pǔtōnghuà	我不会说普通话
I don't know	Wǒ bù zhīdào	我不知道
I'm not sure/not clear	Wǒ bù míngbai	我不明白

General Curiosity

There is a small set of questions which very many Chinese will ask you, given the chance. Some are dealt with below.

What nationality are you?	Nǐ shì nǎ guó rén?	你是哪国人？

The answer is *Wǒ shì* (I am) or *Wǒmen shì* (We are) + country + *rén* (person). Copying the characters for destination countries on to your mail may help to speed it up.

'I am Britain person'	Wǒ shì Yīngguó rén	我是英国人
Australia	Àodàlìyǎ	澳大利亚
Belgium	Bǐlìshí	比利时
Canada	Jiānádà	加拿大
Denmark	Dānmài	丹麦
France	Fǎguó	法国
Germany	Déguó	德国
Holland	Hélán	荷兰
New Zealand	Xīnxīlán	新西兰
Norway	Nuówēi	挪威
Sweden	Ruìdiǎn	瑞典
USA	Měiguó	美国
What is your name? (very polite)	Nín guì xìng?	您贵姓？
My family name is X, and my first name is Y	Wǒ xìng X, míngzi jiào Y	我姓X，名字叫Y
How old are you?	Nǐ jīnnián duōdà suìshu le?	你今年多大岁数了？
I'm X years old	Wǒ X suì le	我X岁了

Practical Needs and Administration

Where's the lavatory/toilet?	Cèsuǒ zài nǎr?	厕所在哪儿？
Signs: men's toilet	nán (man/men)	男
women's toilet	nǚ (woman/women)	女
travel agent	lǚxíngshè	旅行社
Bank of China	Zhōngguó Yínháng	中国银行
post office	yóujú	邮局
poste restante	cún jú hòu lǐng	存局候领
telephone office	diànxīn lóu	电信楼
facsimile (fax)	chuánzhēn	传真
email	diànzǐ yóujiàn	电字邮件
Xīnhuá Book Shop	Xīnhuá Shūdiàn	新华书店
Foreign Languages Book Shop	Wàiwén Shūdiàn	外文书店
city map	chéngshì dìtú	城市地图
English books	Yīngwén shū	英文书
police (Public Security Bureau)	gōng'ān jú	公安局
Foreign Affairs Office	Wàibàn	外办
visa extension	yánshēn qiānzhèng	延伸签证

Numbers, Money, Time, Dates

Note that *yī* ('one') changes its tone according to what follows it, and is only pronounced yī when said by itself or at the end of a word (*shíyī*, eleven). Otherwise it's fourth (falling) tone, but second (rising) tone before other fourth tones. The numbers on banknotes, and sometimes on receipts, tickets, and even on entrance fee signs are written in a fuller form to reduce fraud, and are given in brackets after the everyday forms below. In speech be careful to differentiate between *sì* (four) and *shí* (ten).

zero	líng	0 （零）
one	yī	一 （壹）
two	èr	二 （贰）
three	sān	三 （叁）
four	sì	四 （肆）
five	wǔ	五 （伍）
six	liù	六 （陆）
seven	qī	七 （柒）
eight	bā	八 （捌）
nine	jiǔ	九 （玖）
ten	shí	十 （拾）
eleven	shí yī	十一
twelve	shí èr	十二
thirteen	shí sān	十三
twenty	èr shí	二十
thirty	sān shí	三十
thirty-one	sān shí yī	三十一
thirty-two	sān shí èr	三十二
one hundred	yì bǎi	一百
two hundred	èr bǎi	二百
three hundred	sān bǎi	三百
one thousand	yì qiān	一千
ten thousand	yí wàn	一万
47,986	sì wàn qī qiān jiǔ bǎi bā shí liù ('four ten-thousands, seven thousands, nine hundreds, eight tens, six')	四万七千九百八十六
one million	yì bǎi wàn ('a hundred ten-thousands')	一百万
3.75	sān diǎn qī wǔ ('three point seven five')	三点七五
no.3 (*not* for buses, trains, etc. —*see* 'Getting Around', p.399)	sān hào	三号

To make cardinals into ordinals, use *dì* + number + measure word:

the third one	dìsān ge	第三个

Money

money	qián	钱
yuán (written)	yuán	元
(spoken form)	kuài	快

Kuài is a *measure word* (*see* **How Chinese Works,** p.82, for an explanation) *Yí kuài* means 'a piece of', and the full expression is *yí kuài qián.* Before measure words *èr* (two) becomes *liǎng* (but this is the only number that changes).

jiǎo (one-tenth of a yuán)	jiǎo	角
(spoken form)	máo	毛
fēn (100th of a yuán)	fēn	分

Mandarin assumes any figure given after the units quoted is for the next size unit down, unless otherwise specified.

¥2.40	liǎng kuài sì	两块四

No need to say *liǎng kuài sì máo qián.* But note:

¥2.04	liǎng kuài líng sì fēn	两快零四分
¥20.04	èrshí kuài líng sì fēn	二十块零四分

Similarly in daily speech what's in the brackets is optional:

¥0.24	liǎng máo sì (fēn qián)	两毛四（分钱）
¥240	liǎng bǎi sì (shí kuài qián)	两百四（十块钱）
¥2,400	liǎng qiān sì (bǎi kuài qián)	两千四（百块钱）

But again, drop more than one size of unit and you must make it clear:

¥2,040	liǎng qiān líng sìshí (kuài qián)	两千零四十（块钱）
I want to change money	Wǒ yào huàn qián	我要换钱
a traveller's cheque	yì zhāng lǚxíng zhīpiào	一张旅行支票
a credit card	yì zhāng xìnyòngkǎ	一张信用卡
to give change (also 'to look for')	zhǎo	找
small change	língqián	零钱

Time

one o'clock	yī diǎn zhōng	一点钟
five o'clock in the morning	zǎoshang wǔ diǎn	早上五点
ten o'clock in the morning	shàngwǔ shí diǎn	上午十点
four o'clock in the afternoon	xiàwǔ sì diǎn	下午四点
eight o'clock at night	wǎnshang bā diǎn	晚上八点

Fēn are small units of many different kinds of quantities, in this case minutes.

9.23pm	wǎnshang jiǔ diǎn èrshí sān (fēn zhōng)	晚上九点二十三
a quarter past eleven	shíyī diǎn yí kè	十一点一刻
early morning (before work)	zǎoshang	早上
morning	shàngwǔ	上午

noon	zhōngwǔ	中午
afternoon	xiàwǔ	下午
evening	wǎnshang	晚上
night	yè	夜
day	báitiān	白天

| three hours | sān ge xiǎoshí | 三个小时 |

Days of the week are numbered, Monday being the first. Only Sunday is different.

Monday	Xīngqī yī	星期一
Wednesday	Xīngqī sān	星期三
Sunday	Xīngqī tiān	星期天
the day before yesterday	qiántiān	前天
yesterday	zuótiān	昨天
today	jīntiān	今天
tomorrow	míngtiān	明天
the day after tomorrow	huòtiān	后天
three days	sān tiān	三天

Months are also numbered, beginning with January

January	Yí yuè	一月
February	Èr yuè	二月
March	Sān yuè	三月
December	Shíèr yuè	十二月
23rd August	bā yuè èrshí yī hào	八月二十一号
17th May	wǔ yuè shíqī hào	五月十七号
last month	shàng ge yuè	上个月
this month	zhèi ge yuè	这个月
next month	xià ge yuè	下个月
spring	chūntiān	春天
summer	xiàtiān	夏天
autumn	qiūtiān	秋天
winter	dōngtiān	冬天
2000	èr líng líng líng nián	二零零零年
2004	èr líng líng sì nián	二零零四年
last year	qùnián	去年
this year	jīnnián	今年
next year	míngnián	明年

Getting Around and Directions

East	Dōng	东
South	Nán	南
West	Xī	西
North	Běi	北
to/on the left	dào/zài zǒumiàn	到、在左面

to/on the right	dào/zài yòumiàn	到、在右面
go straight on	yìzhí qù	一直去
alley, lane	hútòng	胡同
alley, lane	xiàng	巷
street, road	jiē	街
road, street	lù	路
avenue, larger street	dàjiē	大街

The above are used in street names. A road in general is:

a road	yì tiáo lú	一条路
crossroads	shízì lù	十字路
end of the road, corner	lù kǒu	路口
aeroplane	fēijī	飞机
train	huǒchē	火车
metro	dìtiě	地铁
public bus	gōnggòngqìchē	公共汽车
branch line, alternative route	zhī xiàn	支线
direct line, limited stop	zhuān xiàn	专线
minibus	miànbāochē	面包车
trolleybus	diànchē	电车
taxi	chūzū qìchē	出租汽车
brand of little red taxi	Xiàlì	夏利
minivan	miàndī	面的
bicycle	zìxíngchē	自行车
boat/ferry	chuán	船
airport	fēijīchǎng	飞机场
ticket office	shòupiàochù	售票处
air ticket office	mínháng shòupiàochù	民航售票处
railway station	huǒchēzhàn	火车站
long distance bus station	chángtú qìchēzhàn	长途汽车站
bus stop/station	qìchēzhàn	汽车站
I want to get off	Wǒ yào xià chē	我要下车
customs	hǎiguān	海关
left-luggage office	xíngli jìcúnchù	行李寄存处
a ticket	yì zhāng piào	一张票
baggage	xíngli	行李
soft sleeper	ruǎn wò	软卧
soft seat	ruǎn zuò	软坐
hard sleeper	yìng wò	硬卧
hard seat	yìng zuò	硬坐
dining car	cān chē	餐车
a seat (e.g on a bus)	yí ge wèizi	一个位子
Are there any seats?	Yǒu méi yǒu wèizi?	有没有位子？

carriage attendant	fúwùyuán	服务员
Is there a plane/train/bus to X?	Yǒu méi yǒu qù X de fēijī/huǒchē/qìchē?	有没有去X的飞机、火车、汽车?
What time does the plane/train/ bus to X depart?	Qù X de fēijī/huǒchē/ qìchē jǐ diǎn kāi?	去X的飞机、火车、汽车几点开?
What time does it reach X?	Shénme shíhou dào X?	什么时候到X?
Two tickets to X, please	Duìbuqǐ, wǒ xiǎng mǎi liǎng zhāng qù X de piào.	对不起，我想买两张去X的票
Is there a bus to the airport/ to the town?	Yǒu méi yǒu qù fēijīzhǎng/ zhōngxīn de gōnggòngqìchē?	有没有去飞机场、中心的公共汽车?
How far is it to X?	X dūoyuǎn?	X多远?
Chinese 'mile' (0.5km)	lǐ	里
kilometre	gōnglǐ	公里
metre	mǐ	米

The following characters may appear before or after bus numbers:

branch line, alternative route	zhī	支
direct line, limited stop	zhuān	专
express (faster bus alternative to trolley route)	kuài	快
special (in Běijīng usually double decker)	tè	特
tourist	yóu	游

Bus and train numbers are often like telephone numbers, spoken as individual digits. Additionally note that yī (one) becomes yāo, and that there are a variety of ways to describe the services of each. Bus no.113 is yāo yāo sān lù.

Which number bus goes to X?	Jǐ lù chē qù X?	几路车去X?
no.197 (train)	yāo jiǔ qī cì	一九七次
service no.636 (for long distance buses and for flights)	liù sān liù bān	六三六班

You'll see cì and bān heading the columns of bus and train numbers on station timetables. Many bus and railway stations display each other's timetables, although it's usually clear which is which.

You'll frequently hear the following on buses and trains:

Kuài yìdiǎnr (repeated)	Hurry up	快一点儿
Mǎi piào (repeated)	Buy a ticket	买票
Dào nǎr?	Where to?	到哪儿?
Jǐ ge?	How many (people need tickets)?	几个?

Sights

caves, grottoes	shíkū	石窟
museum	bówùguǎn	博物馆
screen	bì	壁
temple	sì	寺
temple	miào	庙
temple (lamasery)	zhào	召
mosque	qīngzhēnsì	清真寺
tomb	mù	墓
tomb	líng	陵
public park	gōngyuán	公园
What time does it open?	Jǐ diǎn kāi mén?	几点开门?
What time does it close?	Jǐ diǎn guān mén?	几点关门?
How much is a ticket?	Yì zhāng piào duōshǎo qián?	一张票多少钱?
I'll buy two (of them)	Wǒ mǎi liǎng zhāng	我买两张

Hotels

Terms for hotels are given in very rough order of likely comfort. See 'Where to Stay', p.59.

hotel	bīnguǎn	宾馆
hotel	dàjiǔdiàn	大酒店
hotel	fàndiàn	饭店
hotel	lǚshè	旅社
hotel	lǚguǎn	旅馆
hotel	zhāodàisuǒ	招待所

Use the above to identify what's a hotel from the signs, but if asking for one, say:

Excuse me, where's a hotel?	Qǐng wèn, bīnguǎn zài nǎr?	请问，宾馆在哪儿?
a room	yí ge fángjiān	一个房间
bathroom	wèishēng jiān	卫生间
reception	zǒngtái	总台
attendant (floor lady)	fúwùyuán	服务员
Do you have any rooms?	Yǒu méi yǒu fángjiān	有没有房间?
I would like...	Wǒ xǐhuan...	我喜欢
...a single room	...dān rén jiān	
...a double room	...shuāng rén jiān	
...a triple room	...sān rén jiān	
...a dorm bed	...duō rén jiān	
...a suite	...tào jiān	
I only want to pay for one bed	Wǒ zhǐ xiǎng mǎi yí ge chuángwèi	我只想买一个床位
What time is there hot water (for washing)?	Xǐzǎoshuǐ shénme shíhou lái?	洗澡水什么时候来?
I don't have any boiled water		

(for drinking)	Wǒ méi yǒu kāishuǐ	我没有开水
My sheets aren't clean	Wǒ de chuángdān bù gānjìng	我的床单不干净
The X doesn't work (point at X)	X huài le	X 坏了
I'm checking out	Wǒ tuìfáng	我退房
Please return my deposit	Qǐng tuìgěi wǒ yājīn	请退给我押金
Please give me a receipt	Qǐng gěi wǒ fāpiào	请给我发票

You'll hear:

Jǐ ge rén?	How many people?	几个人？
Hùzhào!	Passport! (needed for check-in)	护照
Méi yǒu	We don't have any	没有

Restaurants

See 'Food and Drink', p.28.

restaurant	fànguǎn	饭馆
restaurant	jiǔjiā	酒家
restaurant	cāntīng	餐厅
bazaar/market	shìchǎng	市场
café	kāfēiguǎn	咖啡馆
tea house	chá guǎn	茶馆
bar	jiǔbā	酒吧
breakfast	zǎofàn	早饭
lunch	wǔfàn	午饭
dinner	wǎnfàn	晚饭
chopsticks	kuàizi	筷子
knife and fork	dāochā	刀叉
spoon	sháozi	勺子

You'll be asked:

Jǐ wèi?	How many people? (polite)	几位？
Chī shénme?	What'll you eat?	吃什么？
Hē shénme?	What'll you drink?	喝什么

You'll say:

Waiter/waitress!	Fúwùyuán!	服务员
Please bring a menu	Qǐng gěi wǒ càidān	请给我菜单
Do you have...	Yǒu méi yǒu...	有没有
Please bring a portion of...	Qǐng lái yí fènr...	请来一份儿
I'd like to pay	Wǒ yào jiézhàng	我要结帐

Single dish meals, snacks, and street food

| snack | xiǎochī | 小吃 |

bread	miànbāo	面包
cake, biscuit (cookie), roll, pitta, etc.	bǐng	饼
noodles	miàntiáo	面条
noodle soup	tāngmiàn	汤面

fried noodles	chǎomiàn	炒面
rice	mǐfàn, báifàn	米饭。白饭
fried rice	chǎofàn	炒饭
steamed/boiled dumplings (like ravioli)	jiǎozi	饺子
steamed dumplings (more bread-like)	bāozi	包子
a steamer of (dumplings)	yì lóng (jiǎozi)	一笼（饺子）
fried dumplings, 'potstickers'	guōtiē	锅贴

kebabs (*shashlyk*)	kǎoròuchuàn	烤肉串
steamed bread roll	mántou	馒头
yoghurt	suānnǎi	酸奶
soup	tāng	汤

Menus usually begin with cold dishes, which it's usually wiser to avoid on hygiene grounds, unless you are in a very upmarket location, and especially if you are on a short trip. The remainder of the dishes usually have four and five character names which in many cases simply describe the contents and the cooking method. What follows are the main cooking verbs, flavour expressions, and some ingredients, followed by some popular dishes you'll find on almost every menu, and the characters versions of local specialities discussed in detail in the main text.

to steam	zhēng	蒸
to boil	zhǔ	煮
to bake, cook, braise	shāo	烧
to stir-fry	chǎo	炒
to quick-fry, sauté	bào	爆
to deep-fry	zhá	炸
to roast (broil)	kǎo	烤
to be hot (spicy)	là	辣
to be sweet	tián	甜
to be sour, vinegary	suān	酸
to be salty	xián	咸
pork	zhū ròu	猪肉

Ròu by itself also means pork, as does:

'big meat'	dà ròu	大肉
chicken	jī	鸡
fish	yú	鱼

| beef | niú ròu | 牛肉 |
| lamb | yáng ròu | 羊肉 |

Lamb is rarely found outside Muslim areas, Mongolia, Tibet, and big city areas.

Chinese cuisine leaves the bone in unless specified. If you want boneless meat look for the following in the name of the dish:

diced, small pieces	dīng	丁
slices, flat thin pieces	piàn	片
shreds, tiny strips	sī	丝

Other Ingredients

aubergine (eggplant)	qiézi	茄子
bean curd/tofu	dòufu	豆腐
bean sprouts	dòuyá	豆芽
bamboo shoots	sǔn	笋
beans	biǎndòu	扁豆
bell pepper, capsicum	làjiāo	辣椒
cabbage	báicài	白菜
carrots	húluóbo	葫萝卜
cucumber	huángguā	黄瓜
eggs	jīdàn	鸡蛋
garlic	suàn	蒜
ginger	jiāng	
(green) vegetables	qǐngcài, shūcài	青菜，疏菜
mushrooms	mógu	蘑菇
onions	cōng	葱
peanuts	huāshēng	花生
peas	wāndòu	豌豆
potatoes	tǔdòu	土豆
tomatoes	xīhóngshì, fānqié	西红柿，蕃茄

The characters for Běijīng and other speciality dishes are given next to the restaurants which do them. Various special dishes described in restaurant reviews are:

Spicy diced chicken with peanuts	gōng bǎo jī dīng	宫保鸡丁
spicy dòufu ('pock-marked old woman's dòufu')	mápó dòufu	麻婆豆腐
sweet and sour pork tenderloin	tángcù lǐji	糖醋里脊
dried cabbage with fatty pork	měi cài kòu ròu	梅菜扣肉
pork shreds in garlic sauce ('fish fragrance pork')	yúxiāng ròusī	鱼香肉丝
'return to pot' pork	huí guō ròu	回锅肉
'mushu' pork	mù xū ròu	木须肉
quick-fried beef and onions	cōng bào niǔ ròu	葱爆牛肉
beef with tomatoes	xīhóngshì chǎo niǔ ròu	西红柿炒牛肉

beef and potato	tǔ dòu dùn niú ròu	土豆炖牛肉
'sizzling' beef	tiě bǎn niú liǔ	铁扳牛柳
braised fish in red sauce	hóng shāo yú	红烧鱼

Not only fish (above) but most meats can be 'red-cooked' in this way.

sweet and sour fish	tángcù yú	糖醋鱼
Běijīng roast duck	Běijīng kǎo yā	北京考鸭
spicy dōufu (pock-marked old woman's dōufu)	mápó dòufu	麻婆豆腐
cabbage with oyster sauce	háo yóu shēng cài	蚝油生菜
vinegar garlic cauliflower	suàn róng xī lán huā	蒜蓉西兰花
vinegary cabbage	cù liū tǔ dòu sī	醋溜土豆丝

Vegetarians: dishes are mostly cooked in vegetable oil. You can ask for any of the vegetables above (or others) cooked together (although you'll be breaking some rules of Chinese cuisine) in the method of your choice. Sometimes you need to make it really clear that you're a vegetarian. The following speech should achieve that (or just show them the characters):

I'm a vegetarian. I don't eat meat.	Wǒ chī sù. Wǒ bù chī ròu.
I don't eat chicken. I don't eat fish.	Wǒ bù chī jī. Wǒ bù chī yú.

我吃素。我不吃肉。我不吃鸡。我不吃鱼。

I'd like some noodle soup	Wǒ yào chī méi yǒu ròu	
without meat in it	de tāngmiàn	我要吃没有肉的汤面
Don't put any meat in	Bié fàng ròu	别放肉
What vegetables do you have?	Yǒu shénme sùcài?	有什么素菜？

If shown to the kitchen point at what you want:

I'd like this one, this one,	
and this one all stir-fried together	Wǒ yào zhèi ge, zhèi ge,
	gēn zhèi ge yìqǐ chǎo 我要这个，这个，跟这个一起炒

Dessert (best stick to fruit you can buy in the market and peel for yourself):

ice cream	bīngqílín	冰淇淋
fruit	shuǐguǒ	水果
apple	píngguǒ	苹果
apricot	xìng	杏
grape	pútao	葡萄
melon	guā	瓜
orange	júzi	橘子
peach	táo	桃
pear	lí	梨
plum	lǐzi	李子

Drinks

boiled water	kāi shuǐ	开水
mineral water	kuàngquán shuǐ	矿泉水
tea	chá	茶

coffee	kāfēi	咖啡
milk	niǔ nǎi	牛奶
fruit juice	shuǐguǒ zhī	水果汁
cola	kělè	可乐
beer	pí jiǔ	啤酒
wine (not recommended)	pútao jiǔ	葡萄酒
spirits	bái jiǔ	白酒
Bottoms up, cheers, etc. ('dry cup')	Gān bēi!	干杯！

Shopping

Quantities

I want to buy...	wǒ xiǎng mǎi...	我想买
Please let me have a look at...	Qǐng gěi wǒ kànyíkàn...	请给我看一看
this one	zhèi ge	这个
that one	nèi ge	那个
a 'catty' or jin (0.5 kilos)	jīn	斤
a kilo	gōngjīn	公斤
one tenth of a jin	liǎng	两
metre	mǐ	米
centimetre	gōngfēn	公分
a bottle of...	yì píng...	一瓶
a can/jar/tin of...	yí guàn...	一罐

Goods:

a book	yì běn shū	一本书
a Chinese chess set	yí fù xiàngqí	一副象棋
a go set	yí fù wéiqí	一副围棋
a mahjong set	yí fù májiàng	一副麻将
a painting	yì fú huà	一幅画
a pair of chopsticks	yì shuāng kuàizi	一双筷子
a writing brush	yì zhī máobǐ	一支毛笔
carpet	dìtǎn	地毯
cloisonné	jǐngtàilán	景泰蓝
jade	yù	玉
seal (chop)	yìnzhāng	印章
silk cloth	sī chóu	丝绸

Description:

big	dà	大
small	xiǎo	小
old	jiù	旧
new	xīn	新

| excellent | fēicháng hǎo | 非常好 |
| beautiful | měilì | 美丽 |

Town and Country

city	shì	市
county	xiàn	县
prefecture	zhōu	州
district, region, area	qū	区
province	shěng	省
autonomous region	zìzhìqū	自治区
town	zhèn	镇
mountain	shān	山
desert	shāmò	沙漠
forest	lín	林
river	hé. jiāng	河。江
lake	hú	湖
sea	hǎi	海

Some Verbs

to speak	shuō	说
to think	xiǎng	想
to eat	chī	吃
to sleep	shuìjiào	睡觉
to drink	hē	喝
to know	zhīdào	知道
to understand	dǒng	懂
to look/see/read	kàn	看
to like/love	ài	爱
to work	gōngzuò	工作
to want	yào	要
to go	qù	去
to come	lái	来

Travel and Memoirs

Marco Polo, *The Travels of Marco Polo*. The complete Yule-Cordier Edition is a splendid read. Originally published by Yule in 1903, revised and updated by Cordier a little later, it was reprinted as two volumes by Dover, 1993. The pleasure lies as much in the illustrations and footnotes as in the original text whose length they exceed. They include contributions by many academics and 20th-century explorers, attempting to make sense of Polo's remarks, identify his place names with real ones, and excuse his mistakes. There's also a translation by Ronald Latham, Penguin, 1958. Either version should be followed up with **Frances Wood**'s thoroughly enjoyable, *Did Marco Polo Go To China?*, Secker and Warburg, 1995.

Lord Macartney, *An Embassy to China*, J. L. Cranmer-Byng [Ed.], Longman, 1962. A portrait of Qīng China and particularly Běijīng and Chéngdé at the end of the 18th century from a perceptive diplomat, which should be compulsory reading for modern businessmen and trade negotiators alike. There's the same economy with the truth on the one side, and the same expectations on the other that the giant market will open and the Chinese will all be using knives and forks before long. Two hundred years on...

Mary Hooker, *Behind the Scenes in Peking*, John Murray, 1910 (reprinted OUP, 1987). Several people rushed out memoirs of their time under siege during the Boxer Rebellion of 1900. From unwilling incarceration in the British legation, to being a reluctant recipient of loot after the lifting of the siege, Hooker's account is one of the few to have lasted.

W. Somerset Maugham, *On a Chinese Screen*, Oxford, 1922 (reprinted OUP, 1985). Dry, sarcastic and vivid vignettes of Chinese life and of foreigners resident in Běijīng, from a master of the form.

Reginald F. Johnston, *Twilight in the Forbidden City*, Gollancz, 1934 (reprinted OUP, 1985). Johnston's long career in China included a period as an administrator of a treaty port, and another as tutor to the last emperor. Johnston, more Confucian than most Chinese, provides not so much a personal memoir of the emperor, but more a comprehensive overview of the events surrounding the Qīng's downfall.

Osbert Sitwell, *Escape with Me!*, Macmillan and Co, 1939 (reprinted by OUP, 1984). A colourful memoir of various oriental travels including a stay of several weeks in Běijīng in 1934, from a member of the famously batty Sitwell family of the Bloomsbury literary mafia.

John Blofeld, *City of Lingering Splendour: A Frank Account of Old Peking's Exotic Pleasures*, Shambala, 1961. The title says it all. Sexually-flexible, opium-addicted singing masters, Běijīng opera performers, and the denizens of the 'lanes of flowers and willows' are all here, along with loquacious daoist monks, English teachers and poets, seen in the 1930s— the last days of traditional China.

George Kates, *The Years That Were Fat*, Harper, 1955 (reprinted OUP, 1988). Kates lived the life of a Chinese gentleman scholar in his own *sìhéyuàn* courtyard house in the 1930s, and

Further Reading

provides a sensitive and appealing portrait of the city, although not without criticism, during what he subsequently came to view as the best years of his life.

David Kidd, *Peking Story,* Eland Press, 1988 (originally published as *All the Emperor's Horses,* John Murray, 1961), is the memoir of an American who studied and taught in Běijīng from 1946 to 1959, 'two years before the Communist revolution and two years after', and saw the handover of power, and the beginnings of the city's destruction.

Tony Scotland, *The Empty Throne,* Penguin, 1993. This is an often silly account of a trip to Běijīng to attempt to discover who the last emperor of China might have nominated as his successor, but with portraits of some of the last emperor's living relatives and unintentional revelations of the pitfalls awaiting the gullible foreigner.

History

Arthur Waldron, *The Great Wall of China: From History to Myth,* Cambridge, 1990. This book charts the history of the Great Wall as an idea in both Chinese and foreign minds, as well as the history of its construction, and its failure to protect China from outside attack.

Peter Fleming, *The Siege at Peking,* Harper, 1959 (reprinted OUP, 1989). Fleming wasn't there, but the former *Times* correspondent's account brings the siege vividly to life.

Hugh Trevor-Roper, *Hermit of Peking,* Eland Press, 1976 (originally published as *A Hidden Life*). A chronicle of the life of Sir Edmund Backhouse, a rather twisted long-time resident of Běijīng who knew everyone in the city at the beginning of the century, deceived them all, and went on to deceive a generation of China scholars as well with the publication of a translation of the diary of a Manchu official during the time of the Boxer Rebellion. This came to be regarded as a primary source for the behaviour of the court at the time. Backhouse faked the original as he faked much of his life, and this history is nearly as thrilling as a detective story as various deceptions are revealed. If you can find it, J. O. P. Bland and E. Backhouse, *China Under the Empress Dowager,* 1921, is still a gripping read, if treated as an historical novel, because of Backhouse's genius in adding convincing but uncheckable detail. Bland was a *Times* correspondent and unwitting collaborator in Backhouse's deception. After his death Backhouse's papers were found to contain claims that he had slept with the Empress Dowager Cíxǐ.

George Black and Robin Munro, *Black Hands of Beijing,* John Wiley, 1993, is the most clear-headed, balanced and accurate book on the Tiān'ān Mén protests of 1989, putting them in the context of other movements for Chinese glasnost.

Jonathan D. Spence, *In Search of Modern China,* Hutchinson, 1990. The best introduction to the forces that have shaped modern China, beginning in the late Míng. Spence has also written excellent books on individual figures in Chinese history, including the Kāngxī emperor.

Chris Elder (Ed.), *Old Peking: City of the Ruler of the World,* OUP, 1997. A compilation of comments on the city from a wide range of sources, sorted by topic.

Jasper Becker, *Hungry Ghosts,* John Murray, 1996. Jasper Becker's columns in the *South China Morning Post* should be required reading for those interested in the realities of modern China. The country's modern history is grim, and Becker's book, which tackles famines, political battles, and their repulsive consequences, is the perfect antidote to the '5,000 years of superior culture' hokum.

Culture

H. Y. Lowe, *The Adventures of Wu*, Peking Chronicle Press, 1940 (reprinted by Princeton, 1983). Out of print but still not too hard to find via the Internet, this chronicles the principal events of the Běijīng year and those in the life of a Běijīng family. A charming guide both to traditions gone forever and those now being revived.

John Gittings, *Real China, From Cannibalism to Karaoke*, Simon and Schuster, 1996. Gittings is a long time China-watcher who chronicles the state of modern China for *The Guardian*, and here uses the theme of a trip through the centre of the country by a semi-secret railway line to link essays on the struggle for existence in the Chinese heartlands.

Tess Johnston and Deke Erh, *Far From Home—Western Architecture in China's Northern Treaty Ports*, Old China Hand Press, 1997, and *Near to Heaven—Western Architecture in China's Old Summer Resorts*, Old China Hand Press, 1995. Beautiful photographs accompany the notes of architecture detective and long time Shànghǎi resident Johnston, and include coverage of Tiānjīn and Běidàihé respectively, although some of the buildings catalogued here have now disappeared.

Novels

Ann Bridge, *Peking Picnic*, Chatto and Windus, 1932 (reprinted by Virago, 1989), and *The Ginger Griffin*, Chatto and Windus, 1934 (reprinted by OUP, 1985). A diplomat's wife who used her husband's postings as source material and was a best-seller in the thirties, set these two novels in the Legation Quarter of Běijīng. Cocktails, horse-racing, love affairs, problems with servants, and (how tiresome!) the occasional spot of diplomatic bother.

Other Guides

Juliet Bredon, *Peking*, Kelly and Walsh, 1931 (reprinted by OUP, 1982). As much a memoir of a rapidly vanishing Běijīng as a guide, from someone brought up there who loved Běijīng and knew it well.

Arlington and Lewisohn, *In Search of Old Peking*, Henri Vetch, 1935 (reprinted OUP, 1987). More journalistic and practical than Bredon, and betraying a note of exasperation that Běijīng is being knocked down as quickly they can write about it.

Index

Lǔ Xùn Museum (Lǔ Xǔn Bówùguàn) 209
Lúgōu Qiáo (Marco Polo Bridge) 336–7

Macao 66
Macartney, Lord 69–70, 145, 289, 296, 374, 382, 384
extracts from writings 70, 288, 294, 299, 306, 378, 381, 388
MacDonald, Sir Claude 67, 68
magazines 115–16
Manchukuo 375
Manchuria 375
Manchus 65–6, 69, 71, 364, 380, 382–3
Máo Dùn 202
Máo Dùn Gù Jū (Former Residence of Máo Dùn) 202
Máo Zédōng 72, 122, 123, 126, 132, 160, 166, 219, 259–60, 330, 371
death 123
mausoleum 65, 122, 126–7
portrait 125
writings 126
Máo Zhǔxí Jìniàntáng (Chairman Máo Memorial Hall) 122, 126–7
maps 22, 114
Marco Polo Bridge (Lúgōu Qiáo) 336–7
markets 236–41, 375
Marxism 76
Maugham, Somerset 133, 328
May Fourth movement 122–3
media 43–4
Méi Lánfāng 80, 179–80
Méi Lánfāng Jìniánguǎn (Méi Lánfāng Memorial Hall) 179–80
Mencius (Mèngzi) 195
Meridian Gate (Wǔ Mén) 140
metro 98, 108–9
Mǐlù Yuàn (Milu Ecological Research Centre) 343–4, 375

Míng dynasty 64–5, 71, 300, 364
emperors 139, 310
Míng Tombs (Shísān Líng) 139, 308, 309–12
minibuses 16
Minorities Culture Palace (Mínzú Wénhuà Gōng) 210
Mínzú Wénhuà Gōng (Minorities Culture Palace) 210
money 7, 44–6, 115
Mongolia, travel to and from 99–100
Mongols 64, 133, 192, 300–1, 364, 385, 386, 387
Monument to the People's Heroes (Rénmín Yīngxióng Jìniànbēi) 122, 123, 125–6
Morrison, G. E. 128, 151, 338
motorbikes 14
Mù Dōng Líng 321
Mù Líng 319, 321
Museum of Agriculture (Zhōngguó Nóngyè Bówùguǎn) 202–3
Museum of Ancient Architecture (Gúdài Jiànzhú Bówùguǎn) 164–5
Museum of Ancient Bells (Gǔ Zhōng Bówùguǎn) 225–6
Museum of Ancient Pottery Civilization (Gǔ Táo Wénmíng Bówùguǎn) 167, 171
Museum of Carved Stone Art (Běijīng Shíkè Yìshù Bówùguǎn) 222–3
Museum of Chinese History 122
Museum of the Chinese People's Anti-Japanese War (Zhōngguó Rénmín Kàng Rì Zhànzhēng Jìniànguǎn) 339–40
Museum of Modern Architecture 132

Museum of the Revolution (Zhōngguó Gémìng Bówùguān) 122, 127, 129–30
museums 47–8, 336–7, 339–40, 342–3
discount tickets 47–8, 112–13
opening hours 48
music 276–7, 278–9
Muslims see Islam
Mùtiányù 301, 304–5

Nán Táng (South Church) 211–12
Nánjīng 292
Nánjīng, Treaty of 65
Nányuàn Jīchǎng 93
National Treasure Museum (Zhōngguó Gōngyìshùguǎn) 210
Nationalist Party 70, 71–2, 381
Natural History Museum (Zìrán Bówùguǎn) 165, 203
Nerchinsk, Treaty of 213
Nestorians 212
New Summer Palace (Yíhé Yuán) 288–9, 290–3
Boat of Purity and Ease 291
Bronze Pavilion 291–2
Cloud Dispelling Hall 291, 292
Garden of Virtue and Harmony 291
Hall of Happiness and Longevity 291
Hall of Jade Billows 291
Long Corridor 291
Longevity Hill 291
Pavilion for Listening to Orioles 291
Seventeen-Arch Bridge 292
Tower of Buddhist Fragrance 291
newspapers 43, 115–16
nightclubs 27, 281–2
Níngshòu Gōng Huáyuán (Flower Garden of the Palace of Peaceful Old Age) 145–6